THE COMPLETE WORKS OF
CHRISTOPHER MARLOWE
VOLUME 2

THE COMPLETE WORKS OF
Christopher Marlowe

EDITED BY
FREDSON BOWERS
LINDEN KENT MEMORIAL PROFESSOR OF ENGLISH LITERATURE
UNIVERSITY OF VIRGINIA

VOLUME II

EDWARD II
DOCTOR FAUSTUS
THE FIRST BOOK OF LUCAN
OVID'S ELEGIES
HERO AND LEANDER
MISCELLANEOUS POEMS

CAMBRIDGE
AT THE UNIVERSITY PRESS
1973

106550

PUBLISHED BY THE SYNDICS OF THE CAMBRIDGE UNIVERSITY PRESS
BENTLEY HOUSE, 200 EUSTON ROAD, LONDON NW1 2DB
AMERICAN BRANCH, 32 EAST 57TH STREET, NEW YORK, N.Y. 10022

LIBRARY OF CONGRESS CATALOGUE CARD NUMBER: 67-10016

ISBN: 0 521 20032 6

PRINTED IN GREAT BRITAIN
AT THE UNIVERSITY PRINTING HOUSE, CAMBRIDGE
(BROOKE CRUTCHLEY, UNIVERSITY PRINTER)

ERRATA

Insert between pages 3 and 4 the evidence were it not that in this manuscript transcript the date in

p. 5, line 9, *for* 1595 *read* 1594

Edward II

I. iv. 76, *for* who me *read* whome
II. ii. 244, *for* If fetcht rom *read* Is fetcht from

p. 125, line 12, *for* Shakespearan *read* Shakespearian

CONTENTS

VOLUME I

VOLUME II

EDWARD II

TEXTUAL INTRODUCTION

Edward II was entered in the Stationers' Register to William Jones on 6 July 1593, the entry containing the same wording for the title itself (without statement of acting) as that on the titlepage of the first known printed edition which was 'Imprinted at London for *William Iones* | dwelling neere Holbourne conduit, at the | *ſigne of the Gunne*. 1594' (Greg, no. 129). This is a 4°-form octavo collating A–M⁴, the text starting on sig. A2 and ending with a colophon on M3ʳ; M3ᵛ and M4ʳ⁻ᵛ (missing) being blank. On the evidence of the initial 'M' on sig. A2 and of the ornaments on A2 and M3 the book appears to have been printed by Robert Robinson.[1]

Whether the 1594 edition is the first or the second is a matter that has been in doubt. The imperfect Dyce copy in the Victoria and Albert Museum of the next edition, in 1598, has had its first two leaves, the title and I.i.0–70, supplied in manuscript written in an early hand.[2] That the transcript was not made from the 1598 quarto is clear from the readings but that any of the variants (which are numerous and sometimes almost inexplicable in their error) reproduce an earlier edition than 1594 is in the nature of the case not to be demonstrated.[3] Indeed, no question of the copy could be raised on

---

[1] Robert Ford Welsh, 'The Printer of the 1594 Octavo of Marlowe's *Edward II*', *Studies in Bibliography*, XVII (1964), 197–8. This corrects Greg, who assigned the book to Richard Bradock who had used the ornaments in his 1598 edition. However, Dr Welsh has located these pieces in various works by Robinson in 1594 and 1596; and since Bradock married Robinson's widow, Dr Welsh plausibly conjectures that his ornament stock had passed to Bradock by 1598.

[2] A photographic reproduction is provided in the Malone Society Reprint of *Edward II* prepared by W. W. Greg (for 1925). The substantive variants alone are recorded in the Historical Collation of the present edition.

[3] In the Introduction to the Methuen edition (1933) the editors Charlton and Waller (pp. 3–5) agree with Tucker Brooke that the manuscript variants *thine*, *dinner*, and *Sylvan* for 1594 *thy*, *dinner time*, and *Sylvian* (I.i.9, 31, 58) are preferable, but this is much a matter of opinion and leans heavily on two manuscript normalizations and one mending of the metre. If these were indeed the readings of a 1593 edition, the rather extraordinary departures from them of a reprint in 1594 are difficult to account for since in the same breath the editors argue for the egregious manuscript errors of *Its* for *As*, *bakt* for *Rakt*, *eate* for *dart*, and *by* for *hard by* (I.i.20, 21, 41, 66), though

the imprint is given as '1593'. This fact, combined with the July 1593 date of entry in the Register, has generally led critics – following Tucker Brooke and Greg – to take with some seriousness the possibility that the known 1594 edition is the second and that an original 1593 edition has been lost.

In the opinion of the present editor the bibliographical evidence is on the whole strongly against the 1594 edition being a reprint. The $4°$-form octavo (for convenience hereafter referred to as a quarto, which was in fact the manner in which the cut double sheets went through the press) was set seriatim starting with sheet B and the seventh page of the text, and was printed by the efficient use of two skeleton-formes, presumably on one press.[1] Compositor X set sheets A–E and Compositor Y set sheets F–M, the division between these coming with the start of II.v heading sig. F1.[1] The same pair

corrected in 1594, as 1593 'mistakes which might easily be made by a printer working hastily from manuscript to catch a public still excited by Marlowe's death', and conclude, 'It will be noticed that the six cases adduced by Tucker Brooke as inferior readings in the manuscript are really stronger evidence for the existence of a 1593 edition than the three in which the manuscript seems preferable; for the latter might be improvements made by the scribe himself, whereas *its*, *bakt*, and *eate* require explanation by some antecedent corruption.' There is difficulty in accepting this view. Superficially of course it is easier to account for the Dyce manuscript corruptions not as scribal errors in transcribing printed copy but as compositorial errors in setting from manuscript. But in the seventy lines of manuscript text plus two lines of stage-direction there are sixteen substantive variants from 1594, and if only three are to be taken as certain 1594 corruptions, then we are left with six clear errors in the Dyce transcript that must be allowed as 1593 mistakes corrected in 1594. To these, however, must be added seven more indifferent substantive variants that in the nature of the case cannot all be 1594 reprint corruptions but must in some part at least be taken as present in any hypothetical 1593 edition. To extrapolate this high proportion of one substantive error for at least every ten lines of 1593 throughout the rest of the text would be a fantastic proposition scarcely to be supported by the evidence of 1594, even given the greater number of errors in the work of Compositor Y.

[1] The presentation of the bibliographical evidence for the order of the running-titles and the distribution of type as indicating the composition and printing of sheet A after sheet M will be found in Robert Ford Welsh, *The Printing of the Early Editions of Marlowe's Plays* (University Microfilms, 1964), pp. 59–72. Dr. Welsh confined himself to this single question without applying it to the problem of a 1593 edition and without distinguishing the work of two compositors in this play. A resumé of Dr Welsh's evidence and its probable interpretation, together with the new evidence drawn from the identification of the two compositors, will be found in Bowers, 'Was There a Lost 1593 Edition of Marlowe's *Edward II*?', *Studies in Bibliography*, xxv (1972), 143–8.

of cases was used by both men.[2] This, with the evidence of the regular use throughout of the same two skeleton-formes imposing respectively the inner and outer formes of every sheet, indicates that the play was set page by page in seriatim order and that Compositor *Y*, therefore, relieved Compositor *X* starting with sheet F, not that the play was set simultaneously in two halves from cast-off copy.

This bibliographical evidence can be applied to the problem whether the 1595 quarto is the first or the second edition. It has long been observed that the printer of a first edition would generally begin with the text and leave the preliminaries for the end in order to accommodate any last-minute additions or alterations in the front-matter but that the printer of a simple reprint, since no changes in the preliminaries would ordinarily be anticipated, was likely in the vast majority of cases to start with the first sheet of the book, without regard for the contents, and to reprint the copy-edition in order. However, from the evidence of identified types it is clear that in the quarto of 1594 sheet A was set from the distributed pages of sheet L and thus in the order of composition was the last sheet to be composed.[3] This evidence joins with that of the peculiar dislocation

---

[1] The clue to the presence of two compositors is the variant system of signing whereby the first three leaves of sheets A–E are signed but only the first two leaves of sheets F–M. Two distinctive spelling habits separate the work of the two men according to this signing division. In sheets A–E the spelling is four times 'France' and twice 'Fraunce'; but of the thirteen occurrences in sheets F–M the spelling is twelve times 'Fraunce' and only once 'France'. In sheets A–E the exclamation 'Ah' occurs six times, and is always spelled 'Ah'. In sheets F–M 'Ah' appears fourteen times, of which no less than nine (starting with sig. F 4^v) are given the rare variant spelling 'A'. (Marlowe's spelling was 'Ah', as we know from the manuscript fragment of *The Massacre at Paris*.)

[2] Actually, because of the low number of only three identifiable types found by Dr Welsh (p. 68) in sheet F – on sigs. F 3^v and F 4^v – from preceding sheet D of Compositor *X*'s stint, there is a slight possibility that Compositor *Y* began with one case of his own and then switched to *X*'s cases after sheet D was distributed. The matter is not certain and has no effect on the line of argument; but it would be a reasonable procedure if *Y* had begun composition from cast-off copy while *X* was still working on sheet E.

[3] Dr Welsh's charts show that distributed types regularly appear in the next sheet but one throughout the quarto. Thus the types of sheet B reappear in sheet D, of sheet C in sheet E, and so on to the end, with distributed L being used to set A. Moreover, as corroborative evidence for the final position of sheet A, Dr Welsh observed no sheet that was set from its distributed types.

of the running-titles in sheet A as a consequence of the imposition of its formes from the skeletons of sheet M and the blank pages M3^v–4^v with removed headlines to indicate not only that sheet A was last composed but that it was last printed. This printing procedure suggests very strongly that the 1594 quarto was a first edition, not a reprint.[1]

The case is not confined to this probability, however, for corroborative evidence is present in the text. Compositor Y was a less expert workman than his fellow X; for example, his share of the text requires a minimum of seventeen necessary substantive emendations to remove error whereas Compositor X requires only eight such emendations to clear errors that can be attributed to him and not to copy. This comparative fidelity to the substantives is parallelled by the relative ease with which X was able to line his copy correctly as compared with Y. Problems of lineation are always present in the setting of dramatic manuscripts, particularly when part lines interrupt the normal pentameter flow.[2] Both compositors had some difficulty with lineation, but X mislined his copy only seven times whereas Y mislined his stint twenty-two times, often in more serious ways. This discrepancy is meaningful in conjecturing that a manuscript and not another printed edition was the copy for the

[1] That Robinson, in dealing with a posthumous play for which he had been furnished no preliminaries save the titlepage, would start his signing with A for the first text gathering is not to be wondered at, for there are parallels to this procedure, notably the 1594 edition of *Dido*. Evidently preliminaries were not anticipated, but nevertheless Robinson left his options open by casting off six pages of text, planned to start on A2, but then beginning his typesetting with the seventh page and sheet B. In this manner he protected himself against any eventuality, for if preliminary matter should unexpectedly arrive during the printing of the book he could readily alter his plans by prefixing, say, an unsigned half-sheet to the A gathering or perhaps no more than a single-leaf titlepage that with luck might be printed as part of his final gathering. If, instead, he had started conventionally with his text on sheet B and if no preliminaries had come in, he might have been forced into uneconomic devices to add the simple title, perhaps by prefixing a half-sheet with an unwanted preliminary blank. As it worked out, he planned his quarto expertly, although a careful casting-off towards the end would have enabled him to print four pages of a half-sheet M instead of five pages on a full sheet, another piece of evidence, perhaps, that 1594 was not a reprint.

[2] For the different ways in which two compositors could treat the lining of difficult copy, see the Textual Introduction to *Cupid's Revenge* in Bowers (ed.) *The Dramatic Works in the Beaumont and Fletcher Canon*, vol. II (1970), pp. 324ff.

1594 quarto. Experience demonstrates that in setting reprints of dramatic quartos the cases are rare indeed in which a compositor takes upon himself to reline printed copy, no matter how faulty; and cases are rarer in which correctly lined printed copy is mislined in a reprint. If the 1594 edition were a reprint, one would need to hypothesize that two compositors had set the 1593 edition in shares almost exactly the same as those assigned the compositors of 1594 and that Compositor *Y* was merely following the errors of his predecessor whereas Compositor *X* enjoyed the superior expertness of the compositor of the earlier sheets of 1593. Although this situation is not theoretically impossible, one would hesitate to hinge an argument on it for a lost 1593 edition.

It would seem that the strictly bibliographical fact that the 1594 quarto was printed in the manner of a first edition with its first sheet last, combined with the textual evidence for the striking difference in the number of errors in mislineation in the quarto in the respective stints of the two 1594 compositors, offers evidence for 1594 as the first edition set from manuscript that is more trustworthy than is the 1593 date on the first leaf of the Dyce transcript as evidence for a lost earlier edition.

After the 1594 quarto come three reprint editions, each set from its immediate predecessor and without authority. The second edition was published in 1598, '*Imprinted at London by* Richard Bradocke, | *for William Iones* dwelling neere Holbourne conduit, | *at the ſigne of the Gunne*. 1598.' This is a quarto with a condensed collation of A–I⁴ K². On 16 December 1611 Jones in the Stationers' Register transferred his right to Roger Barnes, who in 1612 published the third edition, 'Printed at London for Roger Barnes, and are to | be ſould at his ſhop in Chauncerie Lane ouer | againſt the Rolles. 1612.' William Jaggard appears to have been the printer. In turn, Barnes on 17 April 1617 transferred his copy to Henry Bell, but the fourth edition was not published until 1622, 'LONDON, | Printed for *Henry Bell*, and are to be ſold at his | Shop, at the *Lame-Hoſpitall* Gate, neere | *Smithfield*, 1622.' The first state of the titlepage repeats the original statement that the play was acted by the Earl of Pembroke's Servants, but by press-correction the second state alters this to 'As it was publikely Acted by the late Queenes | *Maieſties Seruants at the*

Red Bull | in S. Iohns *ſtreete.*' The collation is slightly expanded to A–K^4 but includes two blank leaves. Greg states that the printer is unknown but that the book may have come from the Eliot's Court Press. On 4 September 1638 Henry and Moses Bell transferred copy to John Haviland and John Wright Senior, but no edition seems to have been published by the new owners.

The copy-text, then, is necessarily drawn from the only authority, the edition of 1594, which up to II.v in the work of Compositor *X* offers a relatively clean text, but thereafter a more faulty typesetting from Compositor *Y*.[1] At the heart of the editorial problem is the question of the manuscript from which the quarto was set. From the time of Dyce editors have recognized the significance of the confusion in nomenclature between Arundel and Matrevis as indicating that the same actor doubled the parts. In II.v.31.1 when Arundel makes his first entrance he is correctly *earle of Arundell* in the stage-direction, has the speech-prefix *Aru.* or *Arun.*, and is addressed in the text (II.v.32, 34, 60) as *Arundell*. Yet at II.v.98.1 when he is among the lords remaining on the stage, he is given in the direction the abbreviation *Mat.*, and in line 104 the speech-prefix *Mat.* Subsequently when he returns to report to Edward, Arundel's stage-directon at III.i.88.1 is *Enter lord Matre*. In line 89 Edward addresses him as 'lord *Matre.*' and as *Matre.* in line 92. His speech-prefixes in this scene are *Mat.* or *Matr.* The opening stage-direction for IV.iii has Arundel once again as *Matr.* and though addressed once in the text in line 7 as *Arundell*, his reply is given the speech-prefix *Matr.* Thereafter Arundel disappears from the play and Matrevis in his proper person plays his part starting with V.ii.45.1. Largely on this evidence, but taking into account some irregularities of identification,[2] Greg conjectures in his Malone Society Reprint

---

[1] Among their other different characteristics one may notice that the words 'Yea' and 'A' (colloquial 'He') do not occur in Compositor *X*'s stint, although present a few times each in the work of Compositor *Y*; but whether this can be attributed to the compositors or to the underlying copy is not to be determined.

[2] Among these Greg lists the stage-directions and speech-prefixes for the Archbishop of Canterburie as *Bishop* in I.ii, iv and presumably in V.iv at the coronation. The unnamed Bishop of V.i appears to be Winchester. The Post from Scotland in II.ii.111.1 is *Poast* in the direction but *Messenger* in speech-prefix. In III.i.150.1 the *Herald* is so named in the direction but in lines 151, 156 is given the prefix *Messenger*. Other messengers are always *Messenger*, but the Post from France in IV.iii.23.1 is

of the play (p. xii), 'it would follow that the piece was printed from a playhouse manuscript, and also apparently that this had undergone some kind of revision for the stage.' This cautious statement has generally been expanded by later critics to the statement that the printer's copy for the play was the promptbook itself, sold by Pembroke's company in the summer of 1593 when they ran into financial difficulties.

In the present editor's opinion the printer's manuscript was Marlowe's fair copy, whether holograph or scribal, that he sold to the company, but given some theatrical annotation in preparation for its transcript into a promptbook. It is most unlikely, although not impossible, that the promptbook itself would copy the numerous descriptive stage-directions characteristic of authorial papers such as '*Enter* Gaveston *reading on a letter that was brought him from the king*' (I.i.0), '*Enter king* Edward *moorning*' (I.v.304.1), '*Enter* Gaveston *moorning, and the earle of* Penbrookes *men*' (II.vi.0), '*Edward kneeles and saith*' (III.i.127.1), '*Enter the* King, Baldock, *and* Spencer *the sonne, flying about the stage*' (IV.v.0), '*Enter the* King, Leicester, *with a Bishop for the crowne*' (V.i.0), '*They hale* Edmund *away, and carie him to be beheaded*' (V.iv.108.1), and '*Then* Gurney *stabs* Lightborne (V.v.117.1). In addition to such as these, the several Latin directions are not characteristic of prompt copy: '*Exit cum servis Pen.*' and '*Exeunt ambo*' at II.v.110.1, 111.1, or '*Manet James cum cæteris.*' (II.vi.17.2), or the speech-prefixes '*Spen. pa.*' and '*Spen. filius*' characteristic of III.i.32, 36, 43, before Spencer the son becomes merely '*Spen.*' or '*Spen. ju.*' and the father '*Spen. fa.*' Difficult to justify as wanting in a professional promptbook are the numerous important stage-directions that not only take persons off stage (for these were sometimes carelessly overlooked in prompt) but bring them on and enable them to perform certain definite and required actions. Frequently, except for a careful marking of the major exits and usually of those characters who

Poaste in prefix at line 25. Greg does not explicitly so state, but his implication is that the identity of speech-prefix for these assorted messengers of different titles may indicate doubling by the same actor, as written in the copy. He also points out the difficulty at V.i.111.1 where the direction calls for Bartley's entrance and line 112 is assigned to him (usually emended to the Bishop) whereas what seems to be his authentic entrance at 127.1 is not noted.

'*manent*' to continue the scene, important action is left without indication. The attendant priest whom the Archbishop of Canterbury sends to the Pope is not mentioned for entrance or exit although clearly addressed (I.ii.32.1–38); in I.iv Kent's entrance is not marked nor is his exit with Gaveston under guard; in II.ii.79–86.1 the wounding of Gaveston and his exit are not described nor, later, is the appearance of the guard who challenges Lancaster and Mortimer (130.1) and, shortly, the entrance of Edward and Kent (138.1).

The most extraordinary case of omitted directions comes in V.ii.22.1–36.1 where the entrance and exit of the Bishop of Winchester are not marked, although he has two speeches; but the Textual Note to this passage discusses the possible disruption in the text here that may account for the absence of the directions. At III.i.220 Edward is given a speech and in the very next line appears a direction for his entrance on return from the battle, which has not been noted. At I.iv.143.1 a direction brings on the Queen in the form, '*Enter Edmund and Queen Isabell*' although Edmund appears to have no part in this scene.[1] Indeed, one may wonder whether his presence with Gaveston in the brief I.iii is not the same sort of error and the scene should not consist merely of a soliloquy, or aside, by Gaveston. Indicative also either of revision, textual disruption, or a simple mistake by an annotator of the manuscript is the entrance of Bartley marked in the quarto at V.i.111.1, with the speech at line 112 given to him instead of (as customarily emended) to the Bishop. Whatever the rights of this scene, and they are obscure,[2] it cannot

[1] Just possibly there is here a compositorial confusion between Edmund and Edward, and the direction should read '*Enter to Edward Queen Isabell*' but this is rather unlikely and the order is not characteristic. Instead, the assignment of an entrance for Edmund may be the same sort of mistake by the annotator that led to the early entrance of Bartley (see below) or else signs of an incompletely worked-out original intention by the author, or else revision not completely erased.

[2] As acted, the usual editorial assignment of the speech at line 112 to the Bishop, and the entrance of Bartley at 127.1 where Edward in line 129 greets him by name, works without difficulty. Moreover, the entrance of Bartley at this point could be rationalized as the mistake of the annotator who mistook the Bishop's speech-prefix at line 112 for Bartley's and felt compelled to mark an entrance for Bartley there to justify the prefix. To bring on Bartley, to have him stand aside in response to Edward's 'out of my sight' and come forward again after the exit of the Bishop with the crown, is not very satisfactory in view of Leicester's 'An other poast, what newes bringes he?' which introduces Bartley at line 128. And Edward's apology at line 114

be acted in its quarto form. In short, the often sketchy and non-existent or even wrong directions can scarcely be taken to be appropriate or workable in a promptbook, whereas they can readily be explained as a combination of authorial carelessness and (like the doubling for Arundel and Matrevis) of partial annotation prior to the preparation of the actual promptbook from the fair copy sold to the company by the author. Hence the text if not set from holograph, which is possible, should have been set from copy at no more than one remove from Marlowe's own papers; and in general its correctness except for error that can be rectified with relative ease confirms this view as to its high authority.

It would seem that the compositors of 1594 faithfully followed the complete lack of notation of act and scene division that must have been a characteristic of the manuscript.

The 1594 quarto has been known in two copies, the one preserved in Switzerland at the Zentralbibliothek, Zurich, and the other in Germany at the Landesbibliothek of Cassel. The latter copy did not survive the Second World War (or to be more precise appears to have been 'liberated' during the Occupation and has not to date been recovered). Fortunately, Sir Walter Greg secured photostats and collated the Cassel copy before the War for his Malone Society Reprint (for 1925) of the play, noting all differences. The present edition has been prepared from photographs of the Zurich copy, with the press-variants in the outer forme of sheet H recorded from Greg's notes. The editions selected for recording in the Historical Collation are as follows: Q2 of 1598 (British Museum C.34.d.28),

is more pertinent addressed to the Bishop (or just possibly to Trussel) if he has ordered the Bishop (or Trussel) away instead of some messenger. Yet the possibility must be recognized that Edward is indeed apologizing to the Bishop for his choleric order to a messenger whom he has refused to hear, and that the speech-prefix for Bartley at line 112 may in fact apply to such a messenger's speech, for only on some such supposition can one explain Leicester's curious remark at line 128 'An other poast, what newes bringes he?' when, as customarily emended, Bartley would have been the first and only messenger. Indeed, if it were not for this 'an other poast' one might conjecture that some of the confusion resulted from an expansion of a scene that originally had progressed from line 111 directly to line 124; even so, perhaps revision is the best explanation for the anomalies of the quarto, a hypothesis that permits an editor to give line 112 to the Bishop, as most appropriate, and not to a first messenger.

Q3 of 1612 (Huntington Library)[1], Q4 of 1622 (British Museum 82.c.22[3]), Dodsley's *Old Plays* (1744), Dodsley's *Old Plays* (1780), *Ancient British Drama* (1810, attributed to Sir Walter Scott), *Edward II* (Sold by J. Chappell Jr, 1818),[2] *Edward II*, ed. William Oxberry (1818), Dodsley's *Old Plays*, ed. J. P. Collier (1825), *Works*, ed. Robinson (1826), *Works*, ed. Dyce (1850, revised 1858), *Works*, ed. Cunningham (1870), *Works*, ed. Bullen (1885), *Works*, ed. Tucker Brooke (1910), *Edward II*, ed. W. D. Briggs (1914), *Edward II*, ed. Charlton and Waller (Methuen, 1933), *Plays*, ed. Kirschbaum (1962), *Plays*, ed. Ribner (1963), *Edward II*, ed. R. Gill (1967).

In *The Elizabethan Stage*, III (1923), 425 Sir E. K. Chambers dates the play in the winter of 1592–3 but in the Methuen edition of 1933 Charlton and Waller discuss at some length the evidence and conclude that composition may go back into 1591 (pp. 6–27). Nothing is known of the theatrical history except for the statement on the title that it was a Pembroke play and had been acted sundry times in the City of London. This might have been in the short season of December 1592 through January 1593 during which time Pembroke's men were called to Court on 26 December 1592 and 6 January 1593. The titlepage of the 1622 edition in its press-corrected form asserts that the play had been acted at the Red Bull by the Queen's Servants. Since this company moved from the Bull to the Cockpit in 1617, presumably the revival mentioned was before that date.

[1] In this edition the duplicated sig. I4ᵛ and K2 in the Huntington copy has been checked against its transfer in corrected British Museum 644.b.68 to sig. K1ᵛ. (see Greg, *Bibliography*, no. 129(c)).

[2] This edition has been included with some reluctance because the large number of its unique variants has swelled the Historical Collation. However, unlike the Chappell edition of *The Jew of Malta*, where the variants become unmanageable, in the present play the recording is still within possibility, and there may be some chance that the rewritten text could represent an early nineteenth-century theatrical tradition. The relation of the Chappell to the Oxberry edition is not entirely demonstrable, but despite some conflicting evidence it would seem that the Chappell preceded Oxberry (as was true for *The Massacre at Paris*) and hence that certain of Oxberry's readings that were to influence later editors originated with the unknown Chappell editor.

[DRAMATIS PERSONÆ

KING EDWARD THE SECOND

PRINCE EDWARD, his son, afterwards KING EDWARD THE THIRD

KENT, brother to KING EDWARD THE SECOND

GAVESTON

ARCHBISHOP OF CANTERBURY

BISHOP OF COVENTRY

BISHOP OF WINCHESTER

WARWICK

LANCASTER

PEMBROKE

ARUNDEL

LEICESTER

BERKELEY (spelled 'Bartley')

MORTIMER the elder

MORTIMER the younger, his nephew

SPENSER the elder

SPENSER the younger, his son

BALDOCK

BEAUMONT

TRUSSEL

GURNEY

MALTRAVERS

LIGHTBORN

SIR JOHN OF HAINAULT

LEVUNE

RICE AP HOWEL

Abbot

Monks

Heralds

Lords, Poor Men, JAMES, Mower, Champion, Messengers, Soldiers, and Attendants

QUEEN ISABELLA, wife to KING EDWARD THE SECOND

Niece to KING EDWARD THE SECOND, daughter to the DUKE OF GLOUCESTER

Ladies]

The troublesome raigne and *lamentable death of* Edward *the* second, king of England: with the *tragicall fall of proud* Mortimer.

Enter Gaveston *reading on a letter that was*   I.i
brought him from the king.

My father is deceast, come Gaveston,
And share the kingdom with thy deerest friend.   *phillips*
Ah words that make me surfet with delight:
What greater blisse can hap to *Gaveston*,
Then live and be the favorit of a king?
Sweete prince I come, these these thy amorous lines,
Might have enforst me to have swum from *France*,
And like *Leander* gaspt upon the sande,
So thou wouldst smile and take me in thy armes.
The sight of *London* to my exiled eyes,   10
Is as *Elizium* to a new come soule.
Not that I love the citie or the men,
But that it harbors him I hold so deare,
The king, upon whose bosome let me die,
And with the world be still at enmitie:
What neede the artick people love star-light,
To whom the sunne shines both by day and night.
Farewell base stooping to the lordly peeres,
My knee shall bowe to none but to the king.
As for the multitude that are but sparkes,   20
Rakt up in embers of their povertie,
Tanti: Ile fawne first on the winde,
That glaunceth at my lips and flieth away:

                                Enter three poore men.

But how now, what are these?
Poore men.   Such as desire your worships service.

22 fawne] Oxberry; fanne Q 1–4

Gaveston.   What canst thou doe?

1. poore man.   I can ride.

Gaveston.   But I have no horses. What art thou?

2. poore man.   A traveller.

Gaveston.   Let me see, thou wouldst do well   30
  To waite at my trencher, and tell me lies at dinner time,
  And as I like your discoursing, ile have you.
  And what art thou?

3. poore man.   A souldier, that hath serv'd against the Scot.

Gaveston.   Why there are hospitals for such as you,
  I have no warre, and therefore sir be gone.

3. poore man.   Farewell, and perish by a souldiers hand,
  That wouldst reward them with an hospitall.   [*Offer to go.*]

Gaveston.   I, I, these wordes of his move me as much,
  As if a Goose should play the Porpintine,   40
  And dart her plumes, thinking to pierce my brest,
  But yet it is no paine to speake men faire,
  Ile flatter these, and make them live in hope:
  You know that I came lately out of *France*,
  And yet I have not viewd my Lord the king,
  If I speed well, ile entertaine you all.

Omnes.   We thanke your worship.

Gaveston.   I have some busines, leave me to my selfe.

Omnes.   We will wait heere about the court.   *Exeunt.*

Gaveston.   Do: these are not men for me,   50
  I must have wanton Poets, pleasant wits,
  Musitians, that with touching of a string
  May draw the pliant king which way I please:
  Musicke and poetrie is his delight,
  Therefore ile have Italian maskes by night,
  Sweete speeches, comedies, and pleasing showes,
  And in the day when he shall walke abroad,
  Like *Sylvian* Nimphes my pages shall be clad,
  My men like Satyres grazing on the lawnes,
  Shall with their Goate feete daunce an antick hay.   60
  Sometime a lovelie boye in *Dians* shape,
  With haire that gilds the water as it glides,

Crownets of pearle about his naked armes,
And in his sportfull hands an Olive tree,
To hide those parts which men delight to see,
Shall bathe him in a spring, and there hard by,
One like *Actæon* peeping through the grove,
Shall by the angrie goddesse be transformde,
And running in the likenes of an Hart,
By yelping hounds puld downe, and seeme to die.　　70
Such things as these best please his majestie,
My lord. Heere comes the king and the nobles
From the parlament, ile stand aside.

Enter the King, Lancaster, Mortimer *senior*, Mortimer *junior*,
　　Edmund *Earle of* Kent, Guie *Earle of* Warwicke, *&c.*

Edward.　Lancaster.
Lancaster.　My Lorde.
Gaveston.　That Earle of *Lancaster* do I abhorre.
Edward.　Will you not graunt me this?——In spight of them [*Aside.*]
Ile have my will, and these two *Mortimers*,
That crosse me thus, shall know I am displeasd.
Mortimer senior.　If you love us my lord, hate *Gaveston*.　　80
Gaveston.　That villaine *Mortimer*, ile be his death.
Mortimer.　Mine unckle heere, this Earle, and I my selfe,
Were sworne to your father at his death,
That he should nere returne into the realme:
And know my lord, ere I will breake my oath,
This sword of mine that should offend your foes,
Shall sleepe within the scabberd at thy neede,
And underneath thy banners march who will,
For *Mortimer* will hang his armor up.
Gaveston.　Mort dieu.　　90
Edward.　Well *Mortimer*, ile make thee rue these words,
Beseemes it thee to contradict thy king?
Frownst thou thereat, aspiring *Lancaster*,
The sworde shall plane the furrowes of thy browes,

71–2 majestie, | My lord.] Tucker Brooke; ~ . | My lord, here Q 1–2;
~ , | My lord, here Q 3–4

And hew these knees that now are growne so stiffe.
I will have *Gaveston*, and you shall know,
What danger tis to stand against your king.
Gaveston.   Well doone, *Ned.*
Lancaster.   My lord, why do you thus incense your peeres,
That naturally would love and honour you,   100
But for that base and obscure *Gaveston*:
Foure Earldomes have I besides *Lancaster*,
Darbie, Salsburie, Lincolne, Leicester,
These will I sell to give my souldiers paye,
Ere *Gaveston* shall stay within the realme.
Therefore if he be come, expell him straight.
Kent.   Barons and Earls, your pride hath made me mute,
But now ile speake, and to the proofe I hope:
I do remember in my fathers dayes,
Lord *Percie* of the North being highly mov'd,   110
Brav'd *Mowberie* in presence of the king,
For which, had not his highnes lov'd him well,
He should have lost his head, but with his looke,
The undaunted spirit of *Percie* was appeasd,
And *Mowberie* and he were reconcild:
Yet dare you brave the king unto his face.
Brother revenge it, and let these their heads,
Preach upon poles for trespasse of their tongues.
Warwicke.   O our heads?
Edward.   I yours, and therefore I would wish you graunt.   120
Warwicke.   Bridle thy anger gentle *Mortimer.*
Mortimer.   I cannot, nor I will not, I must speake.
Cosin, our hands I hope shall fence our heads,
And strike off his that makes you threaten us.
Come unckle, let us leave the brainsick king,
And henceforth parle with our naked swords.
Mortimer senior.   Wilshire hath men enough to save our heads.
Warwicke.   All Warwickshire will love him for my sake.
Lancaster.   And Northward *Gaveston* hath many friends.
Adew my Lord, and either change your minde,   130

107 *Kent.*] Dodsley[1]; *Edw.* Q 1–3; *Ed.* Q 4

Or looke to see the throne where you should sit,
To floate in bloud, and at thy wanton head,
The glozing head of thy base minion throwne.

                                          Exeunt Nobiles.

Edward.   I cannot brooke these hautie menaces:
  Am I a king and must be over rulde?
  Brother displaie my ensignes in the field,
  Ile bandie with the Barons and the Earles,
  And eyther die, or live with *Gaveston.*
Gaveston.   I can no longer keepe me from my lord.
Edward.   What *Gaveston*, welcome: kis not my hand,   140
  Embrace me *Gaveston* as I do thee:
  Why shouldst thou kneele, knowest thou not who I am?
  Thy friend, thy selfe, another *Gaveston.*
  Not *Hilas* was more mourned of *Hercules*,
  Then thou hast beene of me since thy exile.
Gaveston.   And since I went from hence, no soule in hell
  Hath felt more torment then poore *Gaveston.*
Edward.   I know it, brother welcome home my friend.
  Now let the treacherous *Mortimers* conspire,
  And that high minded earle of *Lancaster*,   150
  I have my wish, in that I joy thy sight,
  And sooner shall the sea orewhelme my land,
  Then beare the ship that shall transport thee hence:
  I heere create thee Lord high Chamberlaine,
  Cheefe Secretarie to the state and me,
  Earle of *Cornewall*, king and lord of *Man.*
Gaveston.   My lord, these titles far exceed my worth.
Kent.   Brother, the least of these may well suffice
  For one of greater birth then *Gaveston.*
Edward.   Cease brother, for I cannot brooke these words: 160
  Thy woorth sweet friend is far above my guifts,
  Therefore to equall it receive my hart.
  If for these dignities thou be envied,
  Ile give thee more, for but to honour thee,
  Is *Edward* pleazd with kinglie regiment.
  Fearst thou thy person? thou shalt have a guard:

Wants thou gold? go to my treasurie:
Wouldst thou be lovde and fearde? receive my seale,
Save or condemne, and in our name commaund,
What so thy minde affectes or fancie likes.   170
Gaveston.   It shall suffice me to enjoy your love,
Which whiles I have, I thinke my selfe as great,
As *Cæsar* riding in the Romaine streete,
With captive kings at his triumphant Carre.

Enter the Bishop of Coventrie.

Edward.   Whether goes my Lord of *Coventrie* so fast?
Bishop.   To celebrate your fathers exequies,
But is that wicked *Gaveston* returnd?
Edward.   I priest, and lives to be revengd on thee,
That wert the onely cause of his exile.
Gaveston.   Tis true, and but for reverence of these robes,   180
Thou shouldst not plod one foote beyond this place.
Bishop.   I did no more then I was bound to do,
And *Gaveston* unlesse thou be reclaimd,
As then I did incense the parlement,
So will I now, and thou shalt back to *France.*
Gaveston.   Saving your reverence, you must pardon me.
                                        [*Lays hold on him.*]
Edward.   Throwe of his golden miter, rend his stole,
And in the channell christen him a new.
Kent.   Ah brother, lay not violent hands on him,
For heele complaine unto the sea of *Rome.*   190
Gaveston.   Let him complaine unto the sea of hell,
Ile be revengd on him for my exile.
Edward.   No, spare his life, but seaze upon his goods,
Be thou lord bishop, and receive his rents,
And make him serve thee as thy chaplaine,
I give him thee, here use him as thou wilt.
Gaveston.   He shall to prison, and there die in boults.
Edward.   I, to the tower, the fleete, or where thou wilt.
Bishop.   For this offence be thou accurst of God.
Edward.   Whose there? conveie this priest to the tower.   200

Bishop.   True, true.   [*Exit guarded.*]

Edward.   But in the meane time *Gaveston* away,
  And take possession of his house and goods:
  Come follow me, and thou shalt have my guarde,
  To see it done, and bring thee safe againe.

Gaveston.   What should a priest do with so faire a house?
  A prison may beseeme his holinesse.

                                              [*Exeunt.*]

Enter both the Mortimers, Warwicke, *and* Lancaster.   [I. ii]

Warwicke.   Tis true, the Bishop is in the tower,
  And goods and body given to *Gaveston.*

Lancaster.   What? will they tyrannize upon the Church?
  Ah wicked king, accurssed *Gaveston,*
  This ground which is corrupted with their steps,
  Shall be their timeles sepulcher, or mine.

Mortimer.   Wel, let that peevish Frenchman guard him sure,
  Unlesse his brest be sword proofe he shall die.

Mortimer senior.   How now, why droops the earle of *Lancaster?*

Mortimer.   Wherfore is *Guy* of *Warwicke* discontent?   10

Lancaster.   That villaine *Gaveston* is made an Earle.

Mortimer senior.   An Earle!

Warwicke.   I, and besides, lord Chamberlaine of the realme,
  And secretary to, and lord of *Man.*

Mortimer senior.   We may not, nor we will not suffer this.

Mortimer.   Why post we not from hence to levie men?

Lancaster.   My lord of *Cornewall* now, at every worde,
  And happie is the man, whom he vouchsafes
  For vailing of his bonnet one good looke.
  Thus arme in arme, the king and he dooth marche: 20
  Nay more, the guarde upon his lordship waites:
  And all the court begins to flatter him.

Warwicke.   Thus leaning on the shoulder of the king,
  He nods, and scornes, and smiles at those that passe.

Mortimer senior.   Doth no man take exceptions at the slave?

Lancaster.   All stomack him, but none dare speake a word.

Mortimer.   Ah that bewraies their basenes *Lancaster,*
Were all the Earles and Barons of my minde,
Weele hale him from the bosome of the king,
And at the court gate hang the pessant up,   30
Who swolne with venome of ambitious pride,
Will be the ruine of the realme and us.

       Enter the [*Arch*]*Bishop of* Canterburie [*and attendant*].

Warwicke.   Here comes my lord of *Canterburies* grace.
Lancaster.   His countenance bewraies he is displeasd.
Bishop.   First were his sacred garments rent and torne,
Then laide they violent hands upon him, next
Himselfe imprisoned, and his goods asceasd,
This certifie the Pope, away, take horsse.   [*Exit attendant.*]
Lancaster.   My lord, will you take armes against the king?
Bishop.   What neede I, God himselfe is up in armes,   40
When violence is offered to the church.
Mortimer.   Then wil you joine with us that be his peeres
To banish or behead that *Gaveston?*
Bishop.   What els my lords, for it concernes me neere,
The Bishoprick of *Coventrie* is his.

       Enter the Queene.

Mortimer.   Madam, whether walks your majestie so fast?
Queene.   Unto the forrest gentle *Mortimer,*
To live in greefe and balefull discontent,
For now my lord the king regardes me not,
But dotes upon the love of *Gaveston.*   50
He claps his cheekes, and hanges about his neck,
Smiles in his face, and whispers in his eares,
And when I come, he frownes, as who should say,
Go whether thou wilt seeing I have *Gaveston.*
Mortimer senior.   Is it not straunge, that he is thus bewitcht?
Mortimer.   Madam, returne unto the court againe:
That slie inveigling Frenchman weele exile,
Or lose our lives: and yet ere that day come,

36 him, next⌄] Dodsley¹; ~ ⌄ ~ , Q1–4

The king shall lose his crowne, for we have power,
And courage to, to be revengde at full.   60
Bishop.   But yet lift not your swords against the king.
Lancaster.   No, but weele lift *Gaveston* from hence.
Warwicke.   And war must be the meanes, or heele stay stil.
Queene.   Then let him stay, for rather then my lord
 Shall be opprest by civill mutinies,
 I wil endure a melancholie life,
 And let him frollick with his minion.
Bishop.   My lords, to eaze all this, but heare me speake.
 We and the rest that are his counsellers,
 Will meete, and with a generall consent,   70
 Confirme his banishment with our handes and seales.
Lancaster.   What we confirme the king will frustrate.
Mortimer.   Then may we lawfully revolt from him.
Warwicke.   But say my lord, where shall this meeting bee?
Bishop.   At the new temple.
Mortimer.   Content.
Bishop.   And in the meane time ile intreat you all,
 To crosse to Lambeth, and there stay with me.
Lancaster.   Come then lets away.
Mortimer.   Madam farewell.   80
Queene.   Farewell sweet *Mortimer*, and for my sake,
 Forbeare to levie armes against the king.
Mortimer.   I, if words will serve, if not, I must.

                                      [Exeunt.]

            Enter Gaveston *and the earle of* Kent.   [I.iii]

Gaveston.   *Edmund*, the mightie prince of *Lancaster*
 That hath more earldomes then an asse can beare,
 And both the *Mortimers*, two goodly men,
 With *Guie* of *Warwick* that redoubted knight,
 Are gone towards Lambeth, there let them remaine.

                                Exeunt.

77 *Bishop.*] Dodsley[2]; *omit* Q 1–4

Enter Nobiles [: Lancaster, Warwicke, Penbrooke, Mortimer *senior*,   [I.iv
    Mortimer *junior, the Archbishop of* Canterburie, *attended*].

Lancaster.   Here is the forme of *Gavestons* exile:
  May it please your lordship to subscribe your name.
Bishop.   Give me the paper.
Lancaster.   Quick quick my lorde, I long to write my name.
Warwicke.   But I long more to see him banisht hence.
Mortimer.   The name of *Mortimer* shall fright the king,
  Unlesse he be declinde from that base pesant.

            Enter the King *and* Gaveston [*and* Kent].

Edward.   What? are you mov'd that *Gaveston* sits heere?
  It is our pleasure, we will have it so.
Lancaster.   Your grace doth wel to place him by your side,   10
  For no where else the new earle is so safe.
Mortimer senior.   What man of noble birth can brooke this sight?
  Quam male conveniunt:
  See what a scornfull looke the pesant casts.
Penbrooke.   Can kinglie Lions fawne on creeping Ants?
Warwicke.   Ignoble vassaile that like *Phaeton,*
  Aspir'st unto the guidance of the sunne.
Mortimer.   Their downfall is at hand, their forces downe,
  We will not thus be facst and overpeerd.
Edward.   Lay hands on that traitor *Mortimer.*   20
Mortimer senior.   Lay hands on that traitor *Gaveston.*
                                    [*Seize him.*]
Kent.   Is this the dutie that you owe your king?
Warwicke.   We know our duties, let him know his peeres.
Edward.   Whether will you beare him, stay or ye shall die.
Mortimer senior.   We are no traitors, therefore threaten not.
Gaveston.   No, threaten not my lord, but pay them home.
  Were I a king——
Mortimer.   Thou villaine, wherfore talkes thou of a king,
  That hardly art a gentleman by birth?
Edward.   Were he a peasant, being my minion,   30
  Ile make the prowdest of you stoope to him.

Lancaster.   My lord, you may not thus disparage us,
  Away I say with hatefull *Gaveston.*
Mortimer senior.   And with the earle of *Kent* that favors him.
                    [*Exeunt* Kent *and* Gaveston *guarded.*]
Edward.   Nay, then lay violent hands upon your king,
  Here *Mortimer*, sit thou in *Edwards* throne,
  Warwicke and *Lancaster*, weare you my crowne,
  Was ever king thus over rulde as I?
Lancaster.   Learne then to rule us better and the realme.
Mortimer.   What we have done, our hart bloud shall maintaine.   40
Warwicke.   Think you that we can brooke this upstart pride?
Edward.   Anger and wrathfull furie stops my speech.
Bishop.   Why are you moov'd, be patient my lord,
  And see what we your councellers have done.
Mortimer.   My lords, now let us all be resolute,
  And either have our wils, or lose our lives.
Edward.   Meete you for this, proud overdaring peeres?
  Ere my sweete *Gaveston* shall part from me,
  This Ile shall fleete upon the Ocean,
  And wander to the unfrequented *Inde.*   50
Bishop.   You know that I am legate to the Pope,
  On your allegeance to the sea of *Rome*,
  Subscribe as we have done to his exile.
Mortimer.   Curse him, if he refuse, and then may we
  Depose him and elect an other king.
Edward.   I there it goes, but yet I will not yeeld,
  Curse me, depose me, doe the worst you can.
Lancaster.   Then linger not my lord but do it straight.
Bishop.   Remember how the Bishop was abusde,
  Either banish him that was the cause thereof,   60
  Or I will presentlie discharge these lords,
  Of dutie and allegeance due to thee.
Edward.   It bootes me not to threat, I must speake faire,
  The Legate of the Pope will be obayd:
  My lord, you shalbe Chauncellor of the realme,
  Thou *Lancaster*, high admirall of our fleete,
  Yong *Mortimer* and his unckle shalbe earles,

And you lord *Warwick*, president of the North,
And thou of *Wales*: if this content you not,
Make severall kingdomes of this monarchie,   70
And share it equally amongst you all,
So I may have some nooke or corner left,
To frolike with my deerest *Gaveston*.
Bishop.   Nothing shall alter us, wee are resolv'd.
Lancaster.   Come, come, subscribe.
Mortimer.   Why should you love him, who me the world hates
so?
Edward.   Because he loves me more then all the world:
Ah none but rude and savage minded men,
Would seeke the ruine of my *Gaveston*,
You that be noble borne should pitie him.   80
Warwicke.   You that are princely borne should shake him off,
For shame subscribe, and let the lowne depart.
Mortimer senior.   Urge him, my lord.
Bishop.   Are you content to banish him the realme?
Edward.   I see I must, and therefore am content.
In steede of inke, ile write it with my teares.
Mortimer.   The king is love-sick for his minion.
Edward.   Tis done, and now accursed hand fall off.
Lancaster.   Give it me, ile have it published in the streetes.
Mortimer.   Ile see him presently dispatched away.   90
Bishop.   Now is my heart at ease.
Warwicke.   And so is mine.
Penbrooke.   This will be good newes to the common sort.
Mortimer senior.   Be it or no, he shall not linger here.
                                        Exeunt Nobiles.
Edward.   How fast they run to banish him I love,
They would not stir, were it to do me good:
Why should a king be subject to a priest?
Proud *Rome*, that hatchest such imperiall groomes,
For these thy superstitious taperlights,
Wherewith thy antichristian churches blaze,
Ile fire thy crased buildings, and enforce   100
The papall towers, to kisse the lowlie ground,

With slaughtered priests make *Tibers* channell swell,
And bankes raisd higher with their sepulchers:
As for the peeres that backe the cleargie thus,
If I be king, not one of them shall live.

Enter Gaveston.

Gaveston. My lord I heare it whispered every where,
That I am banishd, and must flie the land.
Edward. Tis true sweete *Gaveston*, oh were it false.
The Legate of the Pope will have it so,
And thou must hence, or I shall be deposd,   110
But I will raigne to be reveng'd of them,
And therefore sweete friend, take it patiently,
Live where thou wilt, ile send thee gould enough,
And long thou shalt not stay, or if thou doost,
Ile come to thee, my love shall neare decline.
Gaveston. Is all my hope turnd to this hell of greefe.
Edward. Rend not my hart with thy too piercing words,
Thou from this land, I from my selfe am banisht.
Gaveston. To go from hence, greeves not poore *Gaveston*,
But to forsake you, in whose gratious lookes   120
The blessednes of *Gaveston* remaines,
For no where else seekes he felicitie.
Edward. And onely this torments my wretched soule,
That whether I will or no thou must depart:
Be governour of *Ireland* in my stead,
And there abide till fortune call thee home.
Here take my picture, and let me weare thine,
O might I keepe thee heere, as I doe this,
Happie were I, but now most miserable.
Gaveston. Tis something to be pitied of a king.   130
Edward. Thou shalt not hence, ile hide thee *Gaveston*.
Gaveston. I shal be found, and then twil greeve me more.
Edward. Kinde wordes, and mutuall talke, makes our greefe
    greater,
Therefore with dum imbracement let us part.

102 make] Dodsley[1]; may Q 1–4

Stay *Gaveston*, I cannot leave thee thus.
Gaveston.   For every looke, my lord, drops downe a teare,
Seeing I must go, do not renew my sorrow.
Edward.   The time is little that thou hast to stay,
And therefore give me leave to looke my fill,
But come sweete friend, ile beare thee on thy way.   140
Gaveston.   The peeres will frowne.
Edward.   I passe not for their anger, come lets go,
O that we might as well returne as goe.

Enter Queen Isabell.

Queene.   Whether goes my lord?
Edward.   Fawne not on me French strumpet, get thee gone.
Queene.   On whom but on my husband should I fawne?
Gaveston.   On *Mortimer*, with whom ungentle Queene——
I say no more, judge you the rest my lord.
Queene.   In saying this, thou wrongst me *Gaveston*,
Ist not enough, that thou corrupts my lord,   150
And art a bawd to his affections,
But thou must call mine honor thus in question?
Gaveston.   I meane not so, your grace must pardon me.
Edward.   Thou art too familiar with that *Mortimer*,
And by thy meanes is *Gaveston* exilde.
But I would wish thee reconcile the lords,
Or thou shalt nere be reconcild to me.
Queene.   Your highnes knowes, it lies not in my power.
Edward.   Away then, touch me not, come *Gaveston*.
Queene.   Villaine, tis thou that robst me of my lord.   160
Gaveston.   Madam, tis you that rob me of my lord.
Edward.   Speake not unto her, let her droope and pine.
Queene.   Wherein my lord, have I deservd these words?
Witnesse the teares that *Isabella* sheds,
Witnesse this hart, that sighing for thee breakes,
How deare my lord is to poore *Isabell*.
Edward.   And witnesse heaven how deere thou art to me.

136 lord,] Oxberry; ~ ∧ Q1–4
143.1 *Queen* Isabell] Chappell; *Edmund and Queen Isabell* Q1–4

28

There weepe, for till my *Gaveston* be repeald,
Assure thy selfe thou comst not in my sight.
                              Exeunt Edward *and* Gaveston.

Queene.   O miserable and distressed Queene!   170
  Would when I left sweet *France* and was imbarkt,
  That charming *Circes* walking on the waves,
  Had chaungd my shape, or at the mariage day
  The cup of *Hymen* had beene full of poyson,
  Or with those armes that twind about my neck,
  I had beene stifled, and not lived to see,
  The king my lord thus to abandon me:
  Like frantick *Juno* will I fill the earth,
  With gastlie murmure of my sighes and cries,
  For never doted *Jove* on *Ganimed*,   180
  So much as he on cursed *Gaveston*.
  But that will more exasperate his wrath,
  I must entreat him, I must speake him faire,
  And be a meanes to call home *Gaveston*:
  And yet heele ever dote on *Gaveston*,
  And so am I for ever miserable.

               Enter the Nobles to the Queene.

Lancaster.   Looke where the sister of the king of *Fraunce*,
  Sits wringing of her hands, and beats her brest.
Warwicke.   The king I feare hath ill intreated her.
Penbrooke.   Hard is the hart, that injures such a saint.   190
Mortimer.   I know tis long of *Gaveston* she weepes.
Mortimer senior.   Why? he is gone.
Mortimer.   Madam, how fares your grace?
Queene.   Ah *Mortimer*! now breaks the kings hate forth,
  And he confesseth that he loves me not.
Mortimer.   Crie quittance Madam then, and love not him.
Queene.   No, rather will I die a thousand deaths,
  And yet I love in vaine, heele nere love me.
Lancaster.   Feare ye not Madam, now his minions gone,
  His wanton humor will be quicklie left.
Queene.   O never *Lancaster*! I am injoynde,   200

To sue unto you all for his repeale:
This wils my lord, and this must I performe,
Or else be banisht from his highnesse presence.
Lancaster.   For his repeale, Madam! he comes not back,
Unlesse the sea cast up his shipwrack body.
Warwicke.   And to behold so sweete a sight as that,
Theres none here, but would run his horse to death.
Mortimer.   But madam, would you have us cal him home?
Queene.   I *Mortimer*, for till he be restorde,
The angrie king hath banished me the court: 210
And therefore as thou lovest and tendrest me,
Be thou my advocate unto these peeres.
Mortimer.   What, would ye have me plead for *Gaveston*?
Mortimer senior.   Plead for him he that will, I am resolvde.
Lancaster.   And so am I my lord, diswade the Queene.
Queene.   O *Lancaster*, let him diswade the king,
For tis against my will he should returne.
Warwicke.   Then speake not for him, let the pesant go.
Queene.   Tis for my selfe I speake, and not for him.
Penbrooke.   No speaking will prevaile, and therefore cease.   220
Mortimer.   Faire Queene forbeare to angle for the fish,
Which being caught, strikes him that takes it dead,
I meane that vile *Torpedo*, *Gaveston*,
That now I hope flotes on the Irish seas.
Queene.   Sweete *Mortimer*, sit downe by me a while,
And I will tell thee reasons of such waighte,
As thou wilt soone subscribe to his repeale.
Mortimer.   It is impossible, but speake your minde.
Queene.   Then thus, but none shal heare it but our selves.
Lancaster.   My Lords, albeit the Queen winne *Mortimer*,   230
Will you be resolute and hold with me?
Mortimer senior.   Not I against my nephew.
Penbrooke.   Feare not, the queens words cannot alter him.
Warwicke.   No? doe but marke how earnestly she pleads.
Lancaster.   And see how coldly his lookes make deniall.
Warwicke.   She smiles, now for my life his mind is changd.

234 No?] Scott; ~, Q 1–4

Lancaster.　　Ile rather loose his friendship I, then graunt.
Mortimer.　　Well of necessitie it must be so.
　My Lords, that I abhorre base *Gaveston*,
　I hope your honors make no question,　　　　　　　　　　　　240
　And therefore though I pleade for his repeall,
　Tis not for his sake, but for our availe:
　Nay, for the realms behoofe and for the kings.
Lancaster.　　Fie *Mortimer*, dishonor not thy selfe,
　Can this be true twas good to banish him,
　And is this true to call him home againe?
　Such reasons make white blacke, and darke night day.
Mortimer.　　My Lord of *Lancaster*, marke the respect.
Lancaster.　　In no respect can contraries be true.
Queene.　　Yet good my lord, heare what he can alledge.　　　　250
Warwicke.　　All that he speakes, is nothing, we are resolv'd.
Mortimer.　　Do you not wish that *Gaveston* were dead?
Penbrooke.　　I would he were.
Mortimer.　　Why then my lord, give me but leave to speak.
Mortimer senior.　　But nephew, do not play the sophister.
Mortimer.　　This which I urge, is of a burning zeale,
　To mend the king, and do our countrie good:
　Know you not *Gaveston* hath store of golde,
　Which may in *Ireland* purchase him such friends,
　As he will front the mightiest of us all,　　　　　　　　　　260
　And whereas he shall live and be belovde,
　Tis hard for us to worke his overthrow.
Warwicke.　　Marke you but that my lord of *Lancaster*.
Mortimer.　　But were he here, detested as he is,
　How easilie might some base slave be subbornd,
　To greet his lordship with a poniard,
　And none so much as blame the murtherer,
　But rather praise him for that brave attempt,
　And in the Chronicle, enrowle his name,
　For purging of the realme of such a plague.　　　　　　　　270
Penbrooke.　　He saith true.
Lancaster.　　I, but how chance this was not done before?
Mortimer.　　Because my lords, it was not thought upon:

Nay more, when he shall know it lies in us,
To banish him, and then to call him home,
Twill make him vaile the topflag of his pride,
And feare to offend the meanest noble man.
Mortimer senior.   But how if he do not Nephew?
Mortimer.   Then may we with some colour rise in armes,
For howsoever we have borne it out,   280
Tis treason to be up against the king.
So shall we have the people of our side,
Which for his fathers sake leane to the king,
But cannot brooke a night growne mushrump,
Such a one as my Lord of *Cornewall* is,
Should beare us downe of the nobilitie,
And when the commons and the nobles joyne,
Tis not the king can buckler *Gaveston*,
Weele pull him from the strongest hould he hath.
My lords, if to performe this I be slack,   290
Thinke me as base a groome as *Gaveston*.
Lancaster.   On that condition *Lancaster* will graunt.
Warwicke.   And so will *Penbrooke* and I.
Mortimer senior.   And I.
Mortimer.   In this I count me highly gratified,
And *Mortimer* will rest at your commaund.
Queene.   And when this favour *Isabell* forgets,
Then let her live abandond and forlorne.
But see in happie time, my lord the king,
Having brought the Earle of *Cornewall* on his way,   300
Is new returnd, this newes will glad him much,
Yet not so much as me. I love him more
Then he can *Gaveston*, would he lov'd me
But halfe so much, then were I treble blest.

Enter king Edward *moorning* [*attended*].

Edward.   Hees gone, and for his absence thus I moorne,
Did never sorrow go so neere my heart,
As dooth the want of my sweete *Gaveston*,
And could my crownes revenew bring him back,

I would freelie give it to his enemies,
And thinke I gaind, having bought so deare a friend.   310
Queene.   Harke how he harpes upon his minion.
Edward.   My heart is as an anvill unto sorrow,   *see Drayton*
Which beates upon it like the Cyclops hammers,
And with the noise turnes up my giddie braine,
And makes me frantick for my *Gaveston*:
Ah had some bloudlesse furie rose from hell,
And with my kinglie scepter stroke me dead,
When I was forst to leave my *Gaveston*.
Lancaster.   *Diablo*, what passions call you these?
Queene.   My gratious lord, I come to bring you newes.   320
Edward.   That you have parled with your *Mortimer*?
Queene.   That *Gaveston*, my Lord, shalbe repeald.
Edward.   Repeald, the newes is too sweet to be true.
Queene.   But will you love me, if you finde it so?
Edward.   If it be so, what will not *Edward* do?
Queene.   For *Gaveston*, but not for *Isabell*.
Edward.   For thee faire Queene, if thou lovest *Gaveston*,
Ile hang a golden tongue about thy neck,
Seeing thou hast pleaded with so good successe.
Queene.   No other jewels hang about my neck   330
Then these my lord, nor let me have more wealth,
Then I may fetch from this ritch treasurie:
O how a kisse revives poore *Isabell*.
Edward.   Once more receive my hand, and let this be,
A second mariage twixt thy selfe and me.
Queene.   And may it proove more happie then the first.
My gentle lord, bespeake these nobles faire,
That waite attendance for a gratious looke,
And on their knees salute your majestie.
Edward.   Couragious *Lancaster*, imbrace thy king,   340
And as grosse vapours perish by the sunne,
Even so let hatred with thy soveraignes smile.
Live thou with me as my companion.
Lancaster.   This salutation overjoyes my heart.

342 soveraignes] Q3 (*i.e.*, soveraign's); soveraigne Q1–2

Edward.   *Warwick* shalbe my chiefest counseller:
These silver haires will more adorne my court,
Then gaudie silkes, or rich imbrotherie.
Chide me sweete *Warwick*, if I go astray.
Warwicke.   Slay me my lord, when I offend your grace.
Edward.   In sollemne triumphes, and in publike showes,   350
Penbrooke shall beare the sword before the king.
Penbrooke.   And with this sword, *Penbrooke* wil fight for you.
Edward.   But wherefore walkes yong *Mortimer* aside?
Be thou commaunder of our royall fleete,
Or if that loftie office like thee not,
I make thee heere lord Marshall of the realme.
Mortimer.   My lord, ile marshall so your enemies,
As *England* shall be quiet, and you safe.
Edward.   And as for you, lord *Mortimer* of *Chirke*,
Whose great atchivements in our forrain warre,   360
Deserves no common place, nor meane reward:
Be you the generall of the levied troopes,
That now are readie to assaile the Scots.
Mortimer senior.   In this your grace hath highly honoured me,
For with my nature warre doth best agree.
Queene.   Now is the king of *England* riche and strong,
Having the love of his renowned peeres.
Edward.   I *Isabell*, nere was my heart so light.
Clarke of the crowne, direct our warrant forth,
For *Gaveston* to *Ireland*: *Beamont* flie,   370
As fast as *Iris*, or *Joves Mercurie*.
Beamont.   It shalbe done my gratious Lord.
                                        [*Exeunt Clarke and* Beamont.]
Edward.   Lord *Mortimer*, we leave you to your charge:
Now let us in, and feast it roiallie:
Against our friend the earle of *Cornewall* comes,
Weele have a generall tilt and turnament,
And then his mariage shalbe solemnized,
For wot you not that I have made him sure,
Unto our cosin, the earle of *Glosters* heire.
Lancaster.   Such newes we heare my lord.   380

34

Edward.   That day, if not for him, yet for my sake,
  Who in the triumphe will be challenger,
  Spare for no cost, we will requite your love.
Warwicke.   In this, or ought, your highnes shall commaund us.
Edward.   Thankes gentle *Warwick*, come lets in and revell.

                              Exeunt. Manent Mortimers.

Mortimer senior.   Nephue, I must to *Scotland*, thou staiest here.
  Leave now to oppose thy selfe against the king,
  Thou seest by nature he is milde and calme,
  And seeing his minde so dotes on *Gaveston*,
  Let him without controulement have his will.   390
  The mightiest kings have had their minions,
  Great *Alexander* lovde *Ephestion*,
  The conquering *Hercules* for *Hilas* wept,
  And for *Patroclus* sterne *Achillis* droopt:
  And not kings onelie, but the wisest men,
  The Romaine *Tullie* loved *Octavius*,
  Grave *Socrates*, wilde *Alcibiades*:
  Then let his grace, whose youth is flexible,
  And promiseth as much as we can wish,
  Freely enjoy that vaine light-headed earle,   400
  For riper yeares will weane him from such toyes.
Mortimer.   Unckle, his wanton humor greeves not me,
  But this I scorne, that one so baselie borne,
  Should by his soveraignes favour grow so pert,
  And riote it with the treasure of the realme,
  While souldiers mutinie for want of paie.
  He weares a lords revenewe on his back,
  And *Midas* like he jets it in the court,
  With base outlandish cullions at his heeles,
  Whose proud fantastick liveries make such show,   410
  As if that *Proteus* god of shapes appearde.
  I have not seene a dapper jack so briske,
  He weares a short Italian hooded cloake,
  Larded with pearle, and in his tuskan cap

393 *Hercules*] Dodsley²; *Hector*   405–6 realme,...paie.] Q3; ~ ,...
    Q1–4   ~ , Q1–2

A jewell of more value then the crowne.
Whiles other walke below, the king and he
From out a window, laugh at such as we,
And floute our traine, and jest at our attire:
Unckle, tis this that makes me impatient.

Mortimer senior.   But nephew, now you see the king is changd.   420

Mortimer.   Then so am I, and live to do him service,
But whiles I have a sword, a hand, a hart,
I will not yeeld to any such upstart.
You know my minde, come unckle lets away.

                                                    Exeunt.

                    Enter Spencer *and* Balduck.   [II.i]

Baldock.   *Spencer,*
Seeing that our Lord th'earle of *Glosters* dead,
Which of the nobles dost thou meane to serve?

Spencer.   Not *Mortimer*, nor any of his side,
Because the king and he are enemies.
Baldock: learne this of me, a factious lord
Shall hardly do himselfe good, much lesse us,
But he that hath the favour of a king,
May with one word, advaunce us while we live:
The liberall earle of *Cornewall* is the man,   10
On whose good fortune *Spencers* hope depends.

Baldock.   What, meane you then to be his follower?

Spencer.   No, his companion, for he loves me well,
And would have once preferd me to the king.

Baldock.   But he is banisht, theres small hope of him.

Spencer.   I for a while, but *Baldock* marke the end,
A friend of mine told me in secrecie,
That hees repeald, and sent for back againe,
And even now, a poast came from the court,
With letters to our ladie from the King,   20
And as she red, she smild, which makes me thinke,
It is about her lover *Gaveston.*

Baldock.   Tis like enough, for since he was exild,

She neither walkes abroad, nor comes in sight:
But I had thought the match had beene broke off,
And that his banishment had changd her minde.
Spencer.   Our Ladies first love is not wavering,
 My life for thine she will have *Gaveston.*
Baldock.   Then hope I by her meanes to be preferd,
 Having read unto her since she was a childe.   30
Spencer.   Then *Balduck*, you must cast the scholler off,
 And learne to court it like a Gentleman,
 Tis not a black coate and a little band,
 A Velvet cap'de cloake, fac'st before with Serge,
 And smelling to a Nosegay all the day,
 Or holding of a napkin in your hand,
 Or saying a long grace at a tables end,
 Or making lowe legs to a noble man,
 Or looking downeward, with your eye lids close,
 And saying, trulie ant may please your honor,   40
 Can get you any favour with great men.
 You must be proud, bold, pleasant, resolute,
 And now and then, stab as occasion serves.
Baldock.   *Spencer*, thou knowest I hate such formall toies,
 And use them but of meere hypocrisie.
 Mine old lord whiles he livde, was so precise,
 That he would take exceptions at my buttons,
 And being like pins heads, blame me for the bignesse,
 Which made me curate-like in mine attire,
 Though inwardly licentious enough,   50
 And apt for any kinde of villanie.
 I am none of these common pedants I,
 That cannot speake without *propterea quod.*
Spencer.   But one of those that saith *quandoquidem,*
 And hath a speciall gift to forme a verbe.
Baldock.   Leave of this jesting, here my lady comes.

52 pedants] Q2; pendants Q1

37

Enter the Ladie [Neece *to the king*].

Neece.   The greefe for his exile was not so much,
As is the joy of his returning home.
This letter came from my sweete *Gaveston*,
What needst thou, love, thus to excuse thy selfe?   60
I know thou couldst not come and visit me.
I will not long be from thee though I die:
This argues the entire love of my Lord.
When I forsake thee, death seaƷe on my heart,
But rest thee here where *Gaveston* shall sleepe.
Now to the letter of my Lord the King,
He wils me to repaire unto the court,
And meete my *Gaveston*: why do I stay,
Seeing that he talkes thus of my mariage day?
Whose there, *Balduck*?   70
See that my coache be readie, I must hence.
Baldock.   It shall be done madam.
Neece.   And meete me at the parke pale presentlie:
Spencer, stay you and beare me companie,   *Exit* [Baldock].
For I have joyfull newes to tell thee of,
My lord of *Cornewall* is a comming over,
And will be at the court as soone as we.
Spencer.   I knew the King would have him home againe.
Neece.   If all things sort out, as I hope they will,
Thy service *Spencer* shalbe thought upon.   80
Spencer.   I humbly thanke your Ladieship.
Neece.   Come lead the way, I long till I am there.

Enter Edward, *the* Queene, Lancaster, Mortimer [*junior*],   [II.ii
        Warwicke, Penbrooke, Kent, *attendants.*

Edward.   The winde is good, I wonder why he stayes,
I feare me he is wrackt upon the sea.
Queene.   Look *Lancaster* how passionate he is,
And still his minde runs on his minion.
Lancaster.   My Lord.

38

Edward.   How now, what newes, is *Gaveston* arrivde?
Mortimer.   Nothing but *Gaveston*, what means your grace?
  You have matters of more waight to thinke upon,
  The King of *Fraunce* sets foote in *Normandie.*
Edward.   A trifle, weele expell him when we please: 10
  But tell me *Mortimer*, whats thy devise,
  Against the stately triumph we decreed?
Mortimer.   A homely one my lord, not worth the telling.
Edward.   Prethee let me know it.
Mortimer.   But seeing you are so desirous, thus it is:
  A loftie Cedar tree faire flourishing,
  On whose top-branches Kinglie Eagles pearch,
  And by the barke a canker creepes me up,
  And gets unto the highest bough of all,
  The motto: *Æque tandem.*   20
Edward.   And what is yours my lord of *Lancaster*?
Lancaster.   My lord, mines more obscure then *Mortimers.*
  Plinie reports, there is a flying Fish,
  Which all the other fishes deadly hate,
  And therefore being pursued, it takes the aire:
  No sooner is it up, but thers a foule,
  That seaseth it: this fish my lord I beare,
  The motto this: *Undique mors est.*
Edward.   Proud *Mortimer*, ungentle *Lancaster*,
  Is this the love you beare your soveraigne?   30
  Is this the fruite your reconcilement beares?
  Can you in words make showe of amitie,
  And in your shields display your rancorous minds?
  What call you this but private libelling,
  Against the Earle of *Cornewall* and my brother?
Queene.   Sweete husband be content, they all love you.
Edward.   They love me not that hate my *Gaveston.*
  I am that Cedar, shake me not too much,
  And you the Eagles, sore ye nere so high,
  I have the gesses that will pull you downe,   40
  And *Æque tandem* shall that canker crie,

---

*35 my brother] *stet* Q1–4   40 gesses] Chappell; gresses Q1–4

Unto the proudest peere of *Britanie*:
Though thou comparst him to a flying Fish,
And threatenest death whether he rise or fall,
Tis not the hugest monster of the sea,
Nor fowlest Harpie that shall swallow him.
Mortimer.   If in his absence thus he favors him,
What will he do when as he shall be present?
Lancaster.   That shall wee see, looke where his lordship comes.

Enter Gaveston.

Edward.   My *Gaveston*,   50
Welcome to *Tinmouth*, welcome to thy friend,
Thy absence made me droope, and pine away,
For as the lovers of faire *Danae*,
When she was lockt up in a brasen tower,
Desirde her more, and waxt outragious,
So did it sure with me: and now thy sight
Is sweeter farre, then was thy parting hence
Bitter and irkesome to my sobbing heart.
Gaveston.   Sweet Lord and King, your speech preventeth mine,
Yet have I words left to expresse my joy: 60
The sheepeherd nipt with biting winters rage,
Frolicks not more to see the paynted springe,
Then I doe to behold your Majestie.
Edward.   Will none of you salute my *Gaveston?*
Lancaster.   Salute him? yes: welcome Lord Chamberlaine.
Mortimer.   Welcome is the good Earle of *Cornewall.*
Warwicke.   Welcome Lord governour of the Ile of *Man.*
Penbrooke.   Welcome maister secretarie.
Kent.   Brother, doe you heare them?
Edward.   Stil wil these Earles and Barrons use me thus?   70
Gaveston.   My Lord I cannot brooke these injuries.
Queene.   Aye me poore soule when these begin to jarre.
Edward.   Returne it to their throtes, ile be thy warrant.
Gaveston.   Base leaden Earles that glorie in your birth,
Goe sit at home and eate your tenants beefe:
And come not here to scoffe at *Gaveston,*

Whose mounting thoughts did never creepe so low,
As to bestow a looke on such as you.
Lancaster.　　Yet I disdaine not to doe this for you.

　　　　　　　　　　　　　　　　[*Draws sword.*]

Edward.　　Treason, treason: whers the traitor?　　　　　80
Penbrooke.　　Heere, here.
Edward.　　Convey hence *Gaveston*, thaile murder him.
Gaveston.　　The life of thee shall salve this foule disgrace.
Mortimer.　　Villaine thy life, unlesse I misse mine aime.

　　　　　　　　　　　　　　　[*Wounds* Gaveston.]

Queene.　　Ah furious *Mortimer* what hast thou done?
Mortimer.　　No more then I would answere were he slaine.

　　　　　　　　　　　　　[*Exit* Gaveston, *attended.*]

Edward.　　Yes more then thou canst answer though he live,
　Deare shall you both abie this riotous deede:
　Out of my presence, come not neere the court.
Mortimer.　　Ile not be barde the court for *Gaveston*.　　90
Lancaster.　　Weele haile him by the eares unto the block.
Edward.　　Looke to your owne heads, his is sure enough.
Warwicke.　　Looke to your owne crowne, if you back him thus.
Kent.　　*Warwicke*, these words do ill beseeme thy years.
Edward.　　Nay all of them conspire to crosse me thus,
　But if I live, ile tread upon their heads,
　That thinke with high lookes thus to tread me down.
　Come *Edmund* lets away, and levie men,
　Tis warre that must abate these Barons pride.

　　　　　　　　　　Exit the King [, Queene, *and* Kent].

Warwicke.　　Lets to our castels, for the king is moovde.　　100
Mortimer.　　Moov'd may he be, and perish in his wrath.
Lancaster.　　Cosin it is no dealing with him now,
　He meanes to make us stoope by force of armes,
　And therefore let us jointlie here protest,
　To prosecute that *Gaveston* to the death.
Mortimer.　　By heaven, the abject villaine shall not live.
Warwicke.　　Ile have his bloud, or die in seeking it.

*81 Here, here.] *stet* Q1-4 (~ ʌ ~ ʌ)
　82 *Edward.*] Dyce²; (*as part of* Penbrooke's *speech*) Q1-4

Penbrooke.   The like oath *Penbrooke* takes.

Lancaster.   And so doth *Lancaster*:

Now send our Heralds to defie the King,   110

And make the people sweare to put him downe.

Enter a Poast.

Mortimer.   Letters, from whence?

Messenger.   From *Scotland* my lord.

Lancaster.   Why how now cosin, how fares all our friends?

Mortimer.   My unckles taken prisoner by the Scots.

Lancaster.   Weel have him ransomd man, be of good cheere.

Mortimer.   They rate his ransome at five thousand pound.

Who should defray the money, but the King,

Seeing he is taken prisoner in his warres?

Ile to the King.   120

Lancaster.   Do cosin, and ile beare thee companie.

Warwicke.   Meane time my lord of *Penbrooke* and my selfe,

Will to *Newcastell* heere, and gather head.

Mortimer.   About it then, and we will follow you.

Lancaster.   Be resolute, and full of secrecie.

Warwicke.   I warrant you.

Mortimer.   Cosin, and if he will not ransome him,

Ile thunder such a peale into his eares,

As never subject did unto his King.

Lancaster.   Content, ile beare my part, holla whose there?   130

[*Enter a Guard.*]

Mortimer.   I marry, such a garde as this dooth well.

Lancaster.   Lead on the way.

Guard.   Whither will your lordships?

Mortimer.   Whither else but to the King.

Guard.   His highnes is disposde to be alone.

Lancaster.   Why, so he may, but we will speake to him.

Guard.   You may not in, my lord.

Mortimer.   May we not?

[*Enter the* King *and* Kent.]

Edward.   How now, what noise is this?
  Who have we there, ist you?   [*Offers to go back.*] 140
Mortimer.   Nay, stay my lord, I come to bring you newes,
  Mine unckles taken prisoner by the Scots.
Edward.   Then ransome him.
Lancaster.   Twas in your wars, you should ransome him.
Mortimer.   And you shall ransome him, or else——
Kent.   What *Mortimer*, you will not threaten him?
Edward.   Quiet your self, you shall have the broad seale,
  To gather for him thoroughout the realme.
Lancaster.   Your minion *Gaveston* hath taught you this.
Mortimer.   My lord, the familie of the *Mortimers*   150
  Are not so poore, but would they sell their land,
  Would levie men enough to anger you.
  We never beg, but use such praiers as these.
                                        [*Lays hand on sword.*]
Edward.   Shall I still be haunted thus?
Mortimer.   Nay, now you are heere alone, ile speake my minde.
Lancaster.   And so will I, and then my lord farewell.
Mortimer.   The idle triumphes, maskes, lascivious showes
  And prodigall gifts bestowed on *Gaveston*,
  Have drawne thy treasure drie, and made thee weake,
  The murmuring commons overstretched hath.   160
Lancaster.   Looke for rebellion, looke to be deposde,
  Thy garrisons are beaten out of *Fraunce*,
  And lame and poore, lie groning at the gates,
  The wilde *Oneyle*, with swarmes of Irish Kernes,
  Lives uncontroulde within the English pale,
  Unto the walles of *Yorke* the Scots made rode,
  And unresisted, drave away riche spoiles.
Mortimer.   The hautie *Dane* commands the narrow seas,
  While in the harbor ride thy ships unrigd.
Lancaster.   What forraine prince sends thee embassadors?   170
Mortimer.   Who loves thee? but a sort of flatterers.
Lancaster.   Thy gentle Queene, sole sister to *Valoys*,

Complaines, that thou hast left her all forlorne.

Mortimer. Thy court is naked, being bereft of those,
That makes a king seeme glorious to the world,
I meane the peeres, whom thou shouldst dearly love:
Libels are cast againe thee in the streete,
Ballads and rimes, made of thy overthrow.

Lancaster. The Northren borderers seeing their houses burnt,
Their wives and children slaine, run up and downe,   180
Cursing the name of thee and *Gaveston*.

Mortimer. When wert thou in the field with banner spred?
But once, and then thy souldiers marcht like players,
With garish robes, not armor, and thy selfe
Bedaubd with golde, rode laughing at the rest,
Nodding and shaking of thy spangled crest,
Where womens favors hung like labels downe.

Lancaster. And thereof came it, that the fleering Scots,
To *Englands* high disgrace, have made this Jig,
   Maids of England, sore may you moorne,   190
   For your lemmons you have lost, at Bannocks borne,
   With a heave and a ho,
   What weeneth the king of England,
   So soone to have woone Scotland,
   With a rombelow.

Mortimer. *Wigmore* shall flie, to set my unckle free.

Lancaster. And when tis gone, our swordes shall purchase more.
If ye be moov'de, revenge it as you can,
Looke next to see us with our ensignes spred. *Exeunt Nobiles.*

Edward. My swelling hart for very anger breakes,   200
How oft have I beene baited by these peeres?
And dare not be revengde, for their power is great:
Yet, shall the crowing of these cockerels,
Affright a Lion? *Edward*, unfolde thy pawes,
And let their lives bloud slake thy furies hunger:
If I be cruell, and growe tyrannous,
Now let them thanke themselves, and rue too late.

Kent. My lord, I see your love to *Gaveston*,

*179 their] Q2; the Q1

44

Will be the ruine of the realme and you,
For now the wrathfull nobles threaten warres,   210
And therefore brother banish him for ever.
Edward.   Art thou an enemie to my *Gaveston?*
Kent.   I, and it greeves me that I favoured him.
Edward.   Traitor be gone, whine thou with *Mortimer.*
Kent.   So will I, rather then with *Gaveston.*
Edward.   Out of my sight, and trouble me no more.
Kent.   No marvell though thou scorne thy noble peeres,
When I thy brother am rejected thus.   *Exit.*
Edward.   Away:
Poore *Gaveston*, that hast no friend but me,   220
Do what they can, weele live in *Tinmoth* here,
And so I walke with him about the walles,
What care I though the Earles begirt us round?
Heere comes she thats cause of all these jarres.

Enter the Queene, *three Ladies* [, *one of these* Neece *to the king*,
        Gaveston], Baldock, *and* Spencer.

Queene.   My lord, tis thought, the Earles are up in armes.
Edward.   I, and tis likewise thought you favour him.
Queene.   Thus do you still suspect me without cause.
Neece.   Sweet unckle speake more kindly to the queene.
Gaveston.   My lord, dissemble with her, speake her faire.
Edward.   Pardon me sweet, I forgot my selfe.   230
Queene.   Your pardon is quicklie got of *Isabell.*
Edward.   The yonger *Mortimer* is growne so brave,
That to my face he threatens civill warres.
Gaveston.   Why do you not commit him to the tower?
Edward.   I dare not, for the people love him well.
Gaveston.   Why then weele have him privilie made away.
Edward.   Would *Lancaster* and he had both carroust,
A bowle of poison to each others health:
But let them go, and tell me what are these.
Neece.   Two of my fathers servants whilst he liv'de,   240
Mait please your grace to entertaine them now.

*226 him] *stet* Q 1–4

Edward.   Tell me, where wast thou borne? What is thine armes?
Baldock.   My name is *Baldock*, and my gentrie
  If fetcht rom Oxford, not from Heraldrie.
Edward.   The fitter art thou *Baldock* for my turne,
  Waite on me, and ile see thou shalt not want.
Baldock.   I humblie thanke your majestie.
Edward.   Knowest thou him *Gaveston*?
Gaveston.   I my lord,
  His name is *Spencer*, he is well alied,
  For my sake let him waite upon your grace,   250
  Scarce shall you finde a man of more desart.
Edward.   Then *Spencer* waite upon me, for his sake
  Ile grace thee with a higher stile ere long.
Spencer.   No greater titles happen unto me,
  Then to be favoured of your majestie.
Edward.   Cosin, this day shalbe your mariage feast,
  And *Gaveston*, thinke that I love thee well,
  To wed thee to our neece, the onely heire
  Unto the Earle of *Gloster* late deceased.
Gaveston.   I know my lord, many will stomack me,   260
  But I respect neither their love nor hate.
Edward.   The head-strong Barons shall not limit me.
  He that I list to favour shall be great:
  Come lets away, and when the mariage ends,
  Have at the rebels, and their complices.

                                        Exeunt omnes.

Enter Lancaster, Mortimer [*junior*], Warwick, Penbrooke, Kent. [II.iii

Kent.   My lords, of love to this our native land,
  I come to joine with you, and leave the king,
  And in your quarrell and the realmes behoofe,
  Will be the first that shall adventure life.
Lancaster.   I feare me you are sent of pollicie,
  To undermine us with a showe of love.
Warwicke.   He is your brother, therefore have we cause
  To cast the worst, and doubt of your revolt.

                                        46

Kent.   Mine honor shalbe hostage of my truth,
  If that will not suffice, farewell my lords.   10
Mortimer.   Stay *Edmund*, never was Plantagenet
  False of his word, and therefore trust we thee.
Penbrooke.   But whats the reason you should leave him now?
Kent.   I have enformd the Earle of *Lancaster.*
Lancaster.   And it sufficeth: now my lords know this,
  That *Gaveston* is secretlie arrivde,
  And here in *Tinmoth* frollicks with the king.
  Let us with these our followers scale the walles,
  And sodenly surprize them unawares.
Mortimer.   Ile give the onset.
Warwicke.   And ile follow thee.   20
Mortimer.   This tottered ensigne of my auncesters,
  Which swept the desart shore of that dead sea,
  Whereof we got the name of *Mortimer*,
  Will I advaunce upon this castell walles,
  Drums strike alarum, raise them from their sport,
  And ring aloude the knell of *Gaveston.*
Lancaster.   None be so hardie as to touche the King,
  But neither spare you *Gaveston*, nor his friends.

                                        Exeunt.

[*Alarums.*] *Enter* [*at several doors*] *the* King *and* Spencer, *to them* [II.iv]
          Gaveston, *&c.* [*the* Queene, Neece, *lords*].

Edward.   O tell me *Spencer*, where is *Gaveston?*
Spencer.   I feare me he is slaine my gratious lord.
Edward.   No, here he comes, now let them spoile and kill:
  Flie, flie, my lords, the earles have got the holde,
  Take shipping and away to *Scarborough,*
  Spencer and I will post away by land.
Gaveston.   O stay my lord, they will not injure you.
Edward.   I will not trust them, *Gaveston* away.
Gaveston.   Farewell my Lord.
Edward.   Ladie, farewell.   10
Neece.   Farewell sweete unckle till we meete againe.

Edward.   Farewell sweete *Gaveston*, and farewell Neece.
Queene.   No farewell, to poore *Isabell*, thy Queene?
Edward.   Yes, yes, for *Mortimer* your lovers sake.

                                        Exeunt omnes, manet Isabella.

Queene.   Heavens can witnesse, I love none but you.
From my imbracements thus he breakes away,
O that mine armes could close this Ile about,
That I might pull him to me where I would,
Or that these teares that drissell from mine eyes,
Had power to mollifie his stonie hart,   20
That when I had him we might never part.

                    Enter the Barons, alarums.

Lancaster.   I wonder how he scapt.
Mortimer.   Whose this, the Queene?
Queene.   I *Mortimer*, the miserable Queene,
Whose pining heart, her inward sighes have blasted,
And body with continuall moorning wasted:
These hands are tir'd, with haling of my lord
From *Gaveston*, from wicked *Gaveston*,
And all in vaine, for when I speake him faire,
He turnes away, and smiles upon his minion.
Mortimer.   Cease to lament, and tell us wheres the king?   30
Queene.   What would you with the king, ist him you seek?
Lancaster.   No madam, but that cursed *Gaveston*.
Farre be it from the thought of *Lancaster*,
To offer violence to his soveraigne,
We would but rid the realme of *Gaveston*,
Tell us where he remaines, and he shall die.   [*Exeunt Barons.*]
Queene.   Hees gone by water unto *Scarborough*,
Pursue him quicklie, and he cannot scape,
The king hath left him, and his traine is small.
Warwicke.   Forslowe no time, sweet *Lancaster* lets march.   40
Mortimer.   How comes it, that the king and he is parted?
Queene.   That this your armie going severall waies,
Might be of lesser force, and with the power
That he intendeth presentlie to raise,

48

Be easilie supprest: and therefore be gone.
Mortimer.   Heere in the river rides a Flemish hoie,
 Lets all aboord, and follow him amaine.
Lancaster.   The wind that bears him hence, wil fil our sailes,
 Come, come aboord, tis but an houres sailing.
Mortimer.   Madam, stay you within this castell here.   50
Queene.   No *Mortimer*, ile to my lord the king.
Mortimer.   Nay, rather saile with us to *Scarborough.*
Queene.   You know the king is so suspitious,
 As if he heare I have but talkt with you,
 Mine honour will be cald in question,
 And therefore gentle *Mortimer* be gone.
Mortimer.   Madam, I cannot stay to answer you,
 But thinke of *Mortimer* as he deserves.   [*Exeunt Barons.*]
Queene.   So well hast thou deserv'de sweete *Mortimer*,
 As *Isabell* could live with thee for ever,   60
 In vaine I looke for love at *Edwards* hand,
 Whose eyes are fixt on none but *Gaveston*:
 Yet once more ile importune him with praiers,
 If he be straunge and not regarde my wordes,
 My sonne and I will over into *France*,
 And to the king my brother there complaine,
 How *Gaveston* hath robd me of his love:
 But yet I hope my sorrowes will have end,
 And *Gaveston* this blessed day be slaine.

                                             Exit.

                    Enter Gaveston *pursued.*   [II.v]

Gaveston.   Yet lustie lords I have escapt your handes,
 Your threats, your larums, and your hote pursutes,
 And though devorsed from king *Edwards* eyes,
 Yet liveth *Pierce* of *Gaveston* unsurprizd,
 Breathing, in hope (*malgrado* all your beards,
 That muster rebels thus against your king)
 To see his royall soveraigne once againe.

Enter the Nobles.

Warwicke.   Upon him souldiers, take away his weapons.

Mortimer.   Thou proud disturber of thy countries peace,

Corrupter of thy king, cause of these broiles,   10

Base flatterer, yeeld, and were it not for shame,

Shame and dishonour to a souldiers name,

Upon my weapons point here shouldst thou fall,

And welter in thy goare.

Lancaster.   Monster of men,

That like the Greekish strumpet traind to armes

And bloudie warres, so many valiant knights,

Looke for no other fortune wretch then death,

King *Edward* is not heere to buckler thee.

Warwicke.   *Lancaster*, why talkst thou to the slave?

Go souldiers take him hence, for by my sword,   20

His head shall off: *Gaveston*, short warning

Shall serve thy turne: it is our countries cause,

That here severelie we will execute

Upon thy person: hang him at a bough.

Gaveston.   My Lord!

Warwicke.   Souldiers, have him away:

But for thou wert the favorit of a King,

Thou shalt have so much honor at our hands.

Gaveston.   I thanke you all my lords, then I perceive,

That heading is one, and hanging is the other,   30

And death is all.

Enter earle of Arundell.

Lancaster.   How now my lord of *Arundell*?

Arundell.   My lords, king *Edward* greetes you all by me.

Warwicke.   *Arundell*, say your message.

Arundell.   His majesty,

Hearing that you had taken *Gaveston*,

Intreateth you by me, yet but he may

See him before he dies, for why he saies,

*18 King] Q2; Kind Q1

And sends you word, he knowes that die he shall,
And if you gratifie his grace so farre,
He will be mindfull of the curtesie.   40
Warwicke.   How now?
Gaveston.   Renowmed *Edward,* how thy name
  Revives poore *Gaveston.*
Warwicke.   No, it needeth not.
  Arundell, we will gratifie the king
  In other matters, he must pardon us in this,
  Souldiers away with him.
Gaveston.   Why my Lord of *Warwicke,*
  Will not these delaies beget my hopes?
  I know it lords, it is this life you aime at,
  Yet graunt king *Edward* this.
Mortimer.   Shalt thou appoint
  What we shall graunt? Souldiers away with him: 50
  Thus weele gratifie the king,
  Weele send his head by thee, let him bestow
  His teares on that, for that is all he gets
  Of *Gaveston,* or else his sencelesse trunck.
Lancaster.   Not so my Lord, least he bestow more cost,
  In burying him, then he hath ever earned.
Arundell.   My lords, it is his majesties request,
  And in the honor of a king he sweares,
  He will but talke with him and send him backe.
Warwicke.   When, can you tell? *Arundell* no,   60
  We wot, he that the care of realme remits,
  And drives his nobles to these exigents
  For *Gaveston,* will if he seaze him once,
  Violate any promise to possesse him.
Arundell.   Then if you will not trust his grace in keepe,
  My lords, I will be pledge for his returne.
Mortimer.   It is honourable in thee to offer this,
  But for we know thou art a noble gentleman,
  We will not wrong thee so,
  To make away a true man for a theefe.   70
Gaveston.   How meanst thou *Mortimer?* that is over base.

Mortimer.   Away base groome, robber of kings renowme,
Question with thy companions and thy mates.
Penbrooke.   My lord *Mortimer*, and you my lords each one,
To gratifie the kings request therein,
Touching the sending of this *Gaveston*,
Because his majestie so earnestlie
Desires to see the man before his death,
I will upon mine honor undertake
To carrie him, and bring him back againe,   80
Provided this, that you my lord of *Arundell*
Will joyne with me.
Warwicke.   *Penbrooke*, what wilt thou do?
Cause yet more bloudshed: is it not enough
That we have taken him, but must we now
Leave him on had-I-wist, and let him go?
Penbrooke.   My lords, I will not over wooe your honors,
But if you dare trust *Penbrooke* with the prisoner,
Upon mine oath I will returne him back.
Arundell.   My lord of *Lancaster*, what say you in this?
Lancaster.   Why I say, let him go on *Penbrookes* word.   90
Penbrooke.   And you lord *Mortimer*?
Mortimer.   How say you my lord of *Warwick*?
Warwicke.   Nay, do your pleasures, I know how twill proove.
Penbrooke.   Then give him me.
Gaveston.   Sweete soveraigne, yet I come
To see thee ere I die.
Warwicke.   Yet not perhaps,   [*Aside.*]
If *Warwickes* wit and policile prevaile.
Mortimer.   My lord of *Penbrooke*, we deliver him you,
Returne him on your honor. Sound, away.   *Exeunt.*

Manent Penbrooke, Arundell, Gaveston, *and* Penbrookes *men, foure*
            souldiers [, *one of them* James].

Penbrooke.   My Lord, you shall go with me,
My house is not farre hence, out of the way   100
A little, but our men shall go along.

*98.1, 104 Arundell] Chappell; *Mat.* Q 1–4

We that have prettie wenches to our wives,
Sir, must not come so neare and balke their lips.
Arundell.   Tis verie kindlie spoke my lord of *Penbrooke*,
  Your honor hath an adamant, of power
  To drawe a prince.
Penbrooke.   So my lord. Come hether *James*,
  I do commit this *Gaveston* to thee,
  Be thou this night his keeper, in the morning
  We will discharge thee of thy charge, be gon.
Gaveston.   Unhappie *Gaveston*, whether goest thou now.   110
                    Exit [Gaveston] *cum servis* Penbrookis.
Horse boy.   My lord, weele quicklie be at *Cobham*.
                    Exeunt ambo [Penbrooke *and* Arundell, *attended*].

          Enter Gaveston *moorning, and the earle of* Penbrookes   [II.vi]
                    men [, James *and three souldiers*].

Gaveston.   O treacherous *Warwicke* thus to wrong thy friend!
James.   I see it is your life these armes pursue.
Gaveston.   Weaponles must I fall and die in bands,
  O must this day be period of my life,
  Center of all my blisse! And yee be men,
  Speede to the king.

                    Enter Warwicke *and his companie.*

Warwicke.   My lord of *Penbrookes* men,
  Strive you no longer, I will have that *Gaveston*.
James.   Your lordship doth dishonor to your selfe,
  And wrong our lord, your honorable friend.
Warwicke.   No *James*, it is my countries cause I follow.   10
  Goe, take the villaine, soldiers come away,
  Weel make quick worke, commend me to your maister
  My friend, and tell him that I watcht it well.
  Come, let thy shadow parley with king *Edward*.
Gaveston.   Treacherous earle, shall I not see the king?

Warwicke.   The king of heaven perhaps, no other king,
Away.

                    Exeunt Warwicke *and his men, with* Gaveston.
                         Manet James *cum cæteris.*

James.   Come fellowes, it booted not for us to strive,
We will in hast go certifie our Lord.

                                   Exeunt.

        Enter king Edward *and* Spencer, [Baldock,] *with*   [III.i]
                 Drummes and Fifes.

Edward.   I long to heare an answer from the Barons
Touching my friend, my deerest *Gaveston.*
Ah *Spencer*, not the riches of my realme
Can ransome him, ah he is markt to die,
I know the malice of the yonger *Mortimer,*
Warwick I know is roughe, and *Lancaster*
Inexorable, and I shall never see
My lovely *Pierce*, my *Gaveston* againe,
The Barons overbeare me with their pride.
Spencer.   Were I king *Edward, Englands* soveraigne,   10
Sonne to the lovelie *Elenor* of *Spaine,*
Great *Edward Longshankes* issue: would I beare
These braves, this rage, and suffer uncontrowld
These Barons thus to beard me in my land,
In mine owne realme? my lord pardon my speeche,
Did you retaine your fathers magnanimitie,
Did you regard the honor of your name,
You would not suffer thus your majestie
Be counterbuft of your nobilitie.
Strike off their heads, and let them preach on poles,   20
No doubt, such lessons they will teach the rest,
As by their preachments they will profit much,
And learne obedience to their lawfull king.
Edward.   Yea gentle *Spencer*, we have beene too milde,
Too kinde to them, but now have drawne our sword,
And if they send me not my *Gaveston,*

                         54

Weele steele it on their crest, and powle their tops.
Baldock.   This haught resolve becomes your majestie,
Not to be tied to their affection,
As though your highnes were a schoole boy still,   30
And must be awde and governd like a child.

    Enter Hugh Spencer *an old man, father to the yong* Spencer,
        with his trunchion, and soldiers.

Spencer pater.   Long live my soveraigne the noble *Edward*,
In peace triumphant, fortunate in warres.
Edward.   Welcome old man, comst thou in *Edwards* aide?
Then tell thy prince, of whence, and what thou art.
Spencer pater.   Loe, with a band of bowmen and of pikes,
Browne bils, and targetiers, foure hundred strong,
Sworne to defend king *Edwards* royall right,
I come in person to your majestie,
Spencer, the father of *Hugh Spencer* there,   40
Bound to your highnes everlastinglie,
For favors done in him, unto us all.
Edward.   Thy father *Spencer?*
Spencer.   True, and it like your grace,
That powres in lieu of all your goodnes showne,
His life, my lord, before your princely feete.
Edward.   Welcome ten thousand times, old man againe.
Spencer, this love, this kindnes to thy King,
Argues thy noble minde and disposition:
Spencer, I heere create thee earle of *Wilshire*,
And daily will enrich thee with our favour,   50
That as the sun-shine shall reflect ore thee:
Beside, the more to manifest our love,
Because we heare Lord *Bruse* dooth sell his land,
And that the *Mortimers* are in hand withall,
Thou shalt have crownes of us, t'out bid the Barons,
And *Spencer*, spare them not, but lay it on.
Souldiers a largis, and thrice welcome all.
Spencer.   My lord, here comes the Queene.

Enter the Queene *and her sonne, and* Levune
a Frenchman.

Edward.   Madam, what newes?
Queene.   Newes of dishonor lord, and discontent,
   Our friend *Levune*, faithfull and full of trust,   60
   Informeth us, by letters and by words,
   That lord *Valoyes* our brother, king of *Fraunce*,
   Because your highnesse hath beene slack in homage,
   Hath seazed *Normandie* into his hands.
   These be the letters, this the messenger.
Edward.   Welcome *Levune*, tush *Sib*, if this be all,
   Valoys and I will soone be friends againe.
   But to my *Gaveston*: shall I never see,
   Never behold thee now? Madam in this matter
   We will employ you and your little sonne,   70
   You shall go parley with the king of *Fraunce*.
   Boye, see you beare you bravelie to the king,
   And do your message with a majestie.
Prince.   Commit not to my youth things of more waight
   Then fits a prince so yong as I to beare,
   And feare not lord and father, heavens great beames
   On *Atlas* shoulder, shall not lie more safe,
   Then shall your charge committed to my trust.
Queene.   A boye, this towardnes makes thy mother feare
   Thou art not markt to many daies on earth.   80
Edward.   Madam, we will that you with speed be shipt,
   And this our sonne, *Levune* shall follow you,
   With all the hast we can dispatch him hence.
   Choose of our lords to beare you companie,
   And go in peace, leave us in warres at home.
Queene.   Unnatural wars, where subjects brave their king,
   God end them once, my lord I take my leave,
   To make my preparation for *Fraunce*.

Enter lord Arundell.

Edward.   What lord *Arundell*, dost thou come alone?
Arundell.   Yea my good lord, for *Gaveston* is dead.   90
Edward.   Ah traitors, have they put my friend to death?
Tell me *Arundell*, died he ere thou camst,
Or didst thou see my friend to take his death?
Arundell.   Neither my lord, for as he was surprizd,
Begirt with weapons, and with enemies round,
I did your highnes message to them all,
Demanding him of them, entreating rather,
And said, upon the honour of my name,
That I would undertake to carrie him
Unto your highnes, and to bring him back.   100
Edward.   And tell me, would the rebels denie me that?
Spencer.   Proud recreants.
Edward.   Yea *Spencer*, traitors all.
Arundell.   I found them at the first inexorable,
The earle of *Warwick* would not bide the hearing,
Mortimer hardly, *Penbrooke* and *Lancaster*
Spake least: and when they flatly had denyed,
Refusing to receive me pledge for him,
The earle of *Penbrooke* mildlie thus bespake.
My lords, because our soveraigne sends for him,
And promiseth he shall be safe returnd,   110
I will this undertake, to have him hence,
And see him redelivered to your hands.
Edward.   Well, and how fortunes that he came not?
Spencer.   Some treason, or some villanie was cause.
Arundell.   The earle of *Warwick* seazde him on his way,
For being delivered unto *Penbrookes* men,
Their lord rode home, thinking his prisoner safe,
But ere he came, *Warwick* in ambush laie,
And bare him to his death, and in a trenche

88.1 *et   seq.*   Arundell]   Chappell;   *and is assigned* Matr. *as speech-*
throughout this scene in Q1–4   *prefix*
Arundell *is addressed as* Matrevis

Strake off his head, and marcht unto the campe.   120
Spencer.   A bloudie part, flatly against law of armes.
Edward.   O shall I speake, or shall I sigh and die!
Spencer.   My lord, referre your vengeance to the sword,
Upon these Barons, harten up your men,
Let them not unrevengd murther your friends,
Advaunce your standard *Edward* in the field,
And marche to fire them from their starting holes.

Edward *kneeles, and saith.*

By earth, the common mother of us all,
By heaven, and all the mooving orbes thereof,
By this right hand, and by my fathers sword,   130
And all the honors longing to my crowne,
I will have heads, and lives, for him as many,
As I have manors, castels, townes, and towers:
Tretcherous *Warwicke*, traiterous *Mortimer*,
If I be *Englands* king, in lakes of gore
Your headles trunkes, your bodies will I traile,
That you may drinke your fill, and quaffe in bloud,
And staine my roiall standard with the same,
That so my bloudie colours may suggest
Remembrance of revenge immortallie,   140
On your accursed traiterous progenie,
You villaines that have slaine my *Gaveston*:
And in this place of honor and of trust,   [*Rises*.]
Spencer, sweet *Spencer*, I adopt thee heere,
And meerely of our love we do create thee
Earle of *Gloster*, and lord Chamberlaine,
Despite of times, despite of enemies.
Spencer.   My lord, here is a messenger from the Barons,
Desires accesse unto your majestie.
Edward.   Admit him neere.   150

148 here is] Dodsley²; heres is Q1–2; heers Q3–4

58

Enter the Herald *from the Barons, with his coate of armes.*

Herald.   Long live king *Edward*, *Englands* lawful lord.
Edward.   So wish not they Iwis that sent thee hither,
  Thou comst from *Mortimer* and his complices,
  A ranker route of rebels never was:
  Well, say thy message.
Herald.   The Barons up in armes, by me salute
  Your highnes, with long life and happines,
  And bid me say as plainer to your grace,
  That if without effusion of bloud,
  You will this greefe have ease and remedie,   160
  That from your princely person you remoove
  This *Spencer*, as a putrifying branche,
  That deads the royall vine, whose golden leaves
  Empale your princelie head, your diadem,
  Whose brightnes such pernitious upstarts dim,
  Say they, and lovinglie advise your grace,
  To cherish vertue and nobilitie,
  And have old servitors in high esteeme,
  And shake off smooth dissembling flatterers:
  This graunted, they, their honors, and their lives,   170
  Are to your highnesse vowd and consecrate.
Spencer.   A traitors, will they still display their pride?
Edward.   Away, tarrie no answer, but be gon.
  Rebels, will they appoint their soveraigne
  His sports, his pleasures, and his companie:
  Yet ere thou go, see how I do devorce   *Embrace* Spencer.
  Spencer from me: now get thee to thy lords,
  And tell them I will come to chastise them,
  For murthering *Gaveston*: hie thee, get thee gone,
  Edward with fire and sword, followes at thy heeles.   180
                                        [*Exit* Herald.]
  My lords, perceive you how these rebels swell:
  Souldiers, good harts, defend your soveraignes right,

*181 lords] Chappell; lord Q1–4

59

For now, even now, we marche to make them stoope,
Away.   *Exeunt.*

Alarums, excursions, a great fight, and a retreate.

Enter the King, Spencer *the father,* Spencer *the sonne,*
and the noblemen of the kings side.

Edward.   Why do we sound retreat? upon them lords,
This day I shall powre vengeance with my sword
On those proud rebels that are up in armes,
And do confront and countermaund their king.
Spencer.   I doubt it not my lord, right will prevaile.
Spencer pater.   Tis not amisse my liege for eyther part,   190
To breathe a while, our men with sweat and dust
All chockt well neare, begin to faint for heate,
And this retire refresheth horse and man.
Spencer.   Heere come the rebels.

Enter the Barons, Mortimer, Lancaster, Warwick,
Penbrooke, *cum cæteris.*

Mortimer.   Looke *Lancaster,*
Yonder is *Edward* among his flatterers.
Lancaster.   And there let him bee,
Till hee pay deerely for their companie.
Warwicke.   And shall or *Warwicks* sword shal smite in vaine.
Edward.   What rebels, do you shrinke, and sound retreat?   200
Mortimer.   No *Edward*, no, thy flatterers faint and flie.
Lancaster.   Th'ad best betimes forsake them and their trains,
For theile betray thee, traitors as they are.
Spencer.   Traitor on thy face, rebellious *Lancaster.*
Penbrooke.   Away base upstart, brav'st thou nobles thus?
Spencer pater.   A noble attempt, and honourable deed,
Is it not, trowe ye, to assemble aide,
And levie armes against your lawfull king?
Edward.   For which ere long, their heads shall satisfie,
T'appeaze the wrath of their offended king.   210

*202 them] Tucker Brooke; thee Q1–4

Mortimer.   Then *Edward*, thou wilt fight it to the last,
   And rather bathe thy sword in subjects bloud,
   Then banish that pernicious companie?
Edward.   I traitors all, rather then thus be bravde,
   Make *Englands* civill townes huge heapes of stones,
   And plowes to go about our pallace gates.
Warwicke.   A desperate and unnaturall resolution,
   Alarum to the fight,
   Saint *George* for *England*, and the Barons right.
Edward.   Saint *George* for *England*, and king *Edwards* right.   220
                                      [*Exeunt severally. Alarums.*]

        Enter Edward, *with the Barons* [*and* Kent] *captives.*

Edward.   Now lustie lords, now not by chance of warre,
   But justice of the quarrell and the cause,
   Vaild is your pride: me thinkes you hang the heads,
   But weele advance them traitors, now tis time
   To be avengd on you for all your braves,
   And for the murther of my deerest friend,
   To whome right well you knew our soule was knit,
   Good *Pierce* of *Gaveston* my sweet favoret,
   A rebels, recreants, you made him away.
Kent.   Brother, in regard of thee and of thy land,   230
   Did they remoove that flatterer from thy throne.
Edward.   So sir, you have spoke, away, avoid our presence.
                                            [*Exit* Kent.]
   Accursed wretches, wast in regard of us,
   When we had sent our messenger to request
   He might be spared to come to speake with us,
   And *Penbrooke* undertooke for his returne,
   That thou proud *Warwicke* watcht the prisoner,
   Poore *Pierce*, and headed him against lawe of armes?
   For which thy head shall over looke the rest,
   As much as thou in rage out wentst the rest.   240
Warwicke.   Tyrant, I scorne thy threats and menaces,
   Tis but temporall that thou canst inflict.

*218 Alarum to the fight.] *stet* Q 1–4

Lancaster.   The worst is death, and better die to live,
  Then live in infamie under such a king.
Edward.   Away with them: my lord of *Winchester*,
  These lustie leaders *Warwicke* and *Lancaster*,
  I charge you roundly off with both their heads,
  Away.
Warwicke.   Farewell vaine worlde.
Lancaster.   Sweete *Mortimer* farewell.
                    [*Barons led off by* Spencer pater.]
Mortimer.   *England*, unkinde to thy nobilitie,   250
  Grone for this greefe, behold how thou art maimed.
Edward.   Go take that haughtie *Mortimer* to the tower,
  There see him safe bestowed, and for the rest,
  Do speedie execution on them all,
  Be gon.
Mortimer.   What *Mortimer*? can ragged stonie walles
  Immure thy vertue that aspires to heaven?
  No *Edward*, *Englands* scourge, it may not be,
  Mortimers hope surmounts his fortune farre.   [*Exit guarded.*]
Edward.   Sound drums and trumpets, marche with me my friends, 260
  Edward this day hath crownd him king a new.   *Exit* [*attended*].
                    Manent Spencer *filius*, Levune *and* Baldock.
Spencer.   *Levune*, the trust that we repose in thee,
  Begets the quiet of king *Edwards* land,
  Therefore be gon in hast, and with advice,
  Bestowe that treasure on the lords of *Fraunce*,
  That therewith all enchaunted like the guarde,
  That suffered *Jove* to passe in showers of golde
  To *Danae*, all aide may be denied
  To *Isabell* the Queene, that now in *France*
  Makes friends, to crosse the seas with her yong sonne,   270
  And step into his fathers regiment.
Levune.   Thats it these Barons and the subtill Queene,
  Long leveld at.
Baldock.   Yea, but *Levune* thou seest,

---

266 therewith all] *possibly* therewithall   273 leveld] Dodsley³ (*qy*), Dyce; levied
    as in Q4   Q1–4

62

These Barons lay their heads on blocks together,
What they intend, the hangman frustrates cleane.
Levune.   Have you no doubts my lords, ile clap so close,
Among the lords of *France* with *Englands* golde,
That *Isabell* shall make her plaints in vaine,
And *Fraunce* shall be obdurat with her teares.
Spencer.   Then make for *Fraunce* amaine, *Levune* away,   280
Proclaime king *Edwards* warres and victories.

Exeunt omnes.

Enter Edmund [*earle of* Kent].   [IV.i]

Kent.   Faire blowes the winde for *Fraunce*, blowe gentle gale,
Till *Edmund* be arrivde for *Englands* good,
Nature, yeeld to my countries cause in this.
A brother, no, a butcher of thy friends,
Proud *Edward*, doost thou banish me thy presence?
But ile to *Fraunce*, and cheere the wronged Queene,
And certifie what *Edwards* loosenes is.
Unnaturall king, to slaughter noble men
And cherish flatterers:
Mortimer I stay thy sweet escape,   10
Stand gratious gloomie night to his device.

Enter Mortimer *disguised.*

Mortimer.   Holla, who walketh there, ist you my lord?
Kent.   *Mortimer* tis I,
But hath thy potion wrought so happilie?
Mortimer.   It hath my lord, the warders all a sleepe,
I thanke them, gave me leave to passe in peace:
But hath your grace got shipping unto *Fraunce*?
Kent.   Feare it not.

Exeunt.

276 clap so] Dodsley[1]; claps Q 1–4

63

Enter the Queene *and her sonne.*   [IV.ii]

Queene.   A boye, our friends do faile us all in *Fraunce,*
   The lords are cruell, and the king unkinde,
   What shall we doe?
Prince.   Madam, returne to *England,*
   And please my father well, and then a Fig
   For all my unckles frienship here in *Fraunce.*
   I warrant you, ile winne his highnes quicklie,
   A loves me better than a thousand *Spencers.*
Queene.   A boye, thou art deceivde at least in this,
   To thinke that we can yet be tun'd together,
   No, no, we jarre too farre. Unkinde *Valoys,*   10
   Unhappie *Isabell,* when *Fraunce* rejects,
   Whether, O whether doost thou bend thy steps?

Enter sir John *of* Henolt.

Sir John.   Madam, what cheere?
Queene.   A good sir *John* of *Henolt,*
   Never so cheereles, nor so farre distrest.
Sir John.   I heare sweete lady of the kings unkindenes,
   But droope not madam, noble mindes contemne
   Despaire: will your grace with me to *Henolt,*
   And there stay times advantage with your sonne?
   How say you my Lord, will you go with your friends,
   And shake off all our fortunes equallie?   20
Prince.   So pleaseth the Queene my mother, me it likes.
   The king of *England,* nor the court of *Fraunce,*
   Shall have me from my gratious mothers side,
   Till I be strong enough to breake a staffe,
   And then have at the proudest *Spencers* head.
Sir John.   Well said my lord.
Queene.   Oh my sweet hart, how do I mone thy wrongs,
   Yet triumphe in the hope of thee my joye?
   Ah sweete sir *John,* even to the utmost verge
   Of *Europe,* or the shore of *Tanaise,*   30
   Will we with thee to *Henolt,* so we will.

The Marques is a noble Gentleman,
His grace I dare presume will welcome me,
But who are these?

Enter Edmund [*earle of* Kent] *and* Mortimer.

Kent.   Madam, long may you live,
  Much happier then your friends in *England* do.
Queene.   Lord *Edmund* and lord *Mortimer* alive?
  Welcome to *Fraunce*: the newes was heere my lord,
  That you were dead, or very neare your death.
Mortimer.   Lady, the last was truest of the twaine,
  But *Mortimer* reservde for better hap,   40
  Hath shaken off the thraldome of the tower,
  And lives t'advance your standard good my lord.
Prince.   How meane you, and the king my father lives?
  No my lord *Mortimer*, not I, I trow.
Queene.   Not sonne, why not? I would it were no worse,
  But gentle lords, friendles we are in *Fraunce*.
Mortimer.   Mounsier *le Grand*, a noble friend of yours,
  Tould us at our arrivall all the newes,
  How hard the nobles, how unkinde the king
  Hath shewed himself: but madam, right makes roome,   50
  Where weapons want, and though a many friends
  Are made away, as *Warwick*, *Lancaster*,
  And others of our partie and faction,
  Yet have we friends, assure your grace, in *England*
  Would cast up cappes, and clap their hands for joy,
  To see us there appointed for our foes.
Kent.   Would all were well, and *Edward* well reclaimd,
  For *Englands* honor, peace, and quietnes.
Mortimer.   But by the sword, my lord, it must be deserv'd.
  The king will nere forsake his flatterers.   60
Sir John.   My Lords of *England*, sith the ungentle king
  Of *Fraunce* refuseth to give aide of armes,
  To this distressed Queene his sister heere,
  Go you with her to *Henolt*: doubt yee not,
  We will finde comfort, money, men, and friends

Ere long, to bid the English king a base.
How say yong Prince, what thinke you of the match?
Prince.   I thinke king *Edward* will out-run us all.
Queene.   Nay sonne, not so, and you must not discourage
Your friends that are so forward in your aide.   70
Kent.   Sir *John* of *Henolt*, pardon us I pray,
These comforts that you give our wofull queene,
Binde us in kindenes all at your commaund.
Queene.   Yea gentle brother, and the God of heaven,
Prosper your happie motion good sir *John.*
Mortimer.   This noble gentleman, forward in armes,
Was borne I see to be our anchor hold.
Sir *John* of *Henolt*, be it thy renowne,
That *Englands* Queene, and nobles in distresse,
Have beene by thee restored and comforted.   80
Sir John.   Madam along, and you my lord, with me,
That *Englands* peeres may *Henolts* welcome see.

                                        [*Exeunt.*]

                 Enter the King, Arundell, *the two* Spencers,   [IV.iii]
                                 with others.

Edward.   Thus after many threats of wrathfull warre,
Triumpheth *Englands Edward* with his friends,
And triumph *Edward* with his friends uncontrould.
My lord of *Gloster*, do you heare the newes?
Spencer.   What newes my lord?
Edward.   Why man, they say there is great execution
Done through the realme, my lord of *Arundell*
You have the note, have you not?
Arundell.   From the lieutenant of the tower my lord.
Edward.   I pray let us see it, what have we there?   10
Read it *Spencer.*   Spencer *reads their names.*
Why so, they barkt a pace a month agoe,
Now on my life, theile neither barke nor bite.
Now sirs, the newes from *Fraunce. Gloster*, I trowe

*81 lord,] *stet* Q1-4 (~ ∧)

                                  66

The lords of *Fraunce* love *Englands* gold so well,
As *Isabella* gets no aide from thence.
What now remaines, have you proclaimed, my lord,
Reward for them can bring in *Mortimer*?
Spencer.   My lord, we have, and if he be in *England*,
A will be had ere long I doubt it not.   20
Edward.   If, doost thou say? *Spencer*, as true as death,
He is in *Englands* ground, our port-maisters
Are not so careles of their kings commaund.

Enter a Poaste.

How now, what newes with thee, from whence come these?
Post.   Letters my lord, and tidings foorth of *Fraunce*,
To you my lord of *Gloster* from *Levune*.
Edward.   Reade.
Spencer *reades the letter.*

My dutie to your honor premised, &c. I have according to instructions in that behalfe, dealt with the king of *Fraunce* his lords, and effected, that the Queene all discontented and discomforted, is 30 gone, whither if you aske, with sir *John* of *Henolt*, brother to the Marquesse, into *Flaunders*: with them are gone lord *Edmund*, and the lord *Mortimer*, having in their company divers of your nation, and others, and as constant report goeth, they intend to give king *Edward* battell in *England*, sooner then he can looke for them: this is all the newes of import.

Your honors in all service, Levune.

Edward.   A villaines, hath that *Mortimer* escapt?
With him is *Edmund* gone associate?
And will sir *John* of *Henolt* lead the round?   40
Welcome a Gods name Madam and your sonne,
England shall welcome you, and all your route.
Gallop a pace bright *Phœbus* through the skie,
And duskie night, in rustie iron carre:
Betweene you both, shorten the time I pray,
That I may see that most desired day,

When we may meet these traitors in the field.
Ah nothing greeves me but my little boye,
Is thus misled to countenance their ils.
Come friends to *Bristow*, there to make us strong,   50
And windes as equall be to bring them in,
As you injurious were to beare them foorth.

[*Exeunt.*]

Enter the Queene, *her sonne,* Edmund [*earle of* Kent],   [IV.iv
Mortimer, *and sir* John.

Queene.   Now lords, our loving friends and countrimen,
Welcome to *England* all with prosperous windes,
Our kindest friends in *Belgia* have we left,
To cope with friends at home: a heavie case,
When force to force is knit, and sword and gleave
In civill broiles makes kin and country men
Slaughter themselves in others and their sides
With their owne weapons gorde, but whats the helpe?
Misgoverned kings are cause of all this wrack,
And *Edward* thou art one among them all,   10
Whose loosnes hath betrayed thy land to spoyle,
And made the channels overflow with blood,
Of thine own people patron shouldst thou be
But thou——
Mortimer.   Nay madam, if you be a warriar,
Ye must not grow so passionate in speeches:
Lords, sith that we are by sufferance of heaven,
Arrivde and armed in this princes right,
Heere for our countries cause sweare we to him
All homage, fealtie and forwardnes,   20
And for the open wronges and injuries
Edward hath done to us, his Queene and land,
We come in armes to wrecke it with the sword:
That *Englands* queene in peace may reposesse
Her dignities and honors, and withall

23 wrecke] *i.e.*, wreak *or* revenge   *23 sword] Q2 (sworde); swords Q1

We may remoove these flatterers from the king,
That havocks *Englands* wealth and treasurie.
Sir John.   Sound trumpets my lord and forward let us martch,
Edward will thinke we come to flatter him.
Kent.   I would he never had bin flattered more.   30

[Exeunt.]

Enter the King, Baldock, *and* Spencer *the sonne,*   [IV.v]
flying about the stage.

Spencer.   Fly, fly, my Lord, the Queene is over strong,
Her friends doe multiply and yours doe fayle,
Shape we our course to *Ireland* there to breath.
Edward.   What, was I borne to flye and runne away,
And leave the *Mortimers* conquerers behind?
Give me my horse and lets r'enforce our troupes:
And in this bed of honor die with fame[7].
Baldock.   O no my lord, this princely resolution
Fits not the time, away, we are pursu'd.

[Exeunt.]

[Enter] Edmund *[earle of* Kent] *alone with a sword and target.* [IV.vi]

Kent.   This way he fled, but I am come too late.
Edward, alas my hart relents for thee,
Proud traytor *Mortimer* why doost thou chase
Thy lawfull king thy soveraigne with thy sword?
Vilde wretch, and why hast thou of all unkinde,
Borne armes against thy brother and thy king?
Raigne showers of vengeance on my cursed head
Thou God, to whom in justice it belongs
To punish this unnaturall revolt:
Edward, this *Mortimer* aimes at thy life: 10
O fly him then, but *Edmund* calme this rage,
Dissemble or thou diest, for *Mortimer*
And *Isabell* doe kisse while they conspire,

7 honor] Q1 (c): honors Q1 (u)

And yet she beares a face of love forsooth:
Fie on that love that hatcheth death and hate.
Edmund away, *Bristow* to *Longshankes* blood
Is false, be not found single for suspect:
Proud *Mortimer* pries neare into thy walkes.

Enter the Queene, Mortimer, *the young* Prince *and*
Sir John *of* Henolt.

Queene.   Succesfull battells gives the God of kings,
    To them that fight in right and feare his wrath: 20
    Since then succesfully we have prevayled,
    Thankes be heavens great architect and you.
    Ere farther we proceede my noble lordes,
    We heere create our welbeloved sonne,
    Of love and care unto his royall person,
    Lord warden of the realme, and sith the fates
    Have made his father so infortunate,
    Deale you my lords in this, my loving lords,
    As to your wisdomes fittest seemes in all.
Kent.   Madam, without offence if I may aske,   30
    How will you deale with *Edward* in his fall?
Prince.   Tell me good unckle, what *Edward* doe you meane?
Kent.   Nephew, your father, I dare not call him king.
Mortimer.   My lord of *Kent*, what needes these questions?
    Tis not in her controulment, nor in ours,
    But as the realme and parlement shall please,
    So shall your brother be disposed of.
    I like not this relenting moode in *Edmund*,   [*To* Queene.]
    Madam, tis good to looke to him betimes.
Queene.   My lord, the Maior of *Bristow* knows our mind.   40
Mortimer.   Yea madam, and they scape not easilie,
    That fled the feeld.
Queene.   *Baldock* is with the king,
    A goodly chauncelor, is he not my lord?
Sir John.   So are the *Spencers*, the father and the sonne.
Kent.   This, *Edward*, is the ruine of the realme.   [*Aside.*]

*45 This, *Edward*,] Q2 (~ ᴧ ~,); ~ ᴧ ~ ᴧ Q1

Enter Rice ap Howell, *and the Maior of* Bristow, *with*
Spencer *the father.*

Rice.   God save Queene *Isabell*, and her princely sonne.
Madam, the Maior and Citizens of *Bristow*,
In signe of love and dutie to this presence,
Present by me this traitor to the state,
Spencer, the father to that wanton *Spencer*,   50
That like the lawles *Catiline* of *Rome*,
Reveld in *Englands* wealth and treasurie.
Queene.   We thanke you all.
Mortimer.   Your loving care in this,
Deserveth princelie favors and rewardes,
But wheres the king and the other *Spencer* fled?
Rice.   *Spencer* the sonne, created earle of *Gloster*,
Is with that smoothe toongd scholler *Baldock* gone,
And shipt but late for *Ireland* with the king.
Mortimer.   Some whirle winde fetche them backe, or sincke them
       all:——   [*Aside.*]
They shalbe started thence I doubt it not.   60
Prince.   Shall I not see the king my father yet?
Kent.   Unhappie *Edward*, chaste from *Englands* bounds. [*Aside.*]
Sir John.   Madam, what resteth, why stand ye in a muse?
Queene.   I rue my lords ill fortune, but alas,
Care of my countrie cald me to this warre.
Mortimer.   Madam, have done with care and sad complaint,
Your king hath wrongd your countrie and himselfe,
And we must seeke to right it as we may,
Meane while, have hence this rebell to the blocke,
Your lordship cannot priviledge your head.   70
Spencer pater.   Rebell is he that fights against his prince,
So fought not they that fought in *Edwards* right.
Mortimer.   Take him away, he prates. You *Rice ap Howell*,
                              [*Spencer led off.*]
Shall do good service to her Majestie,

*45.1 *and the Maior of* Bristow] *stet*   *62 Unhappie] Dodsley[1]; Unhappies
    Q 1–4   Q 1–4

Being of countenance in your countrey here,
To follow these rebellious runnagates.
We in meane while madam, must take advise,
How *Baldocke*, *Spencer*, and their complices,
May in their fall be followed to their end.

Exeunt omnes.

Enter the Abbot, *Monkes*, Edward, Spencer, *and* Baldocke [IV.vii
[*disguised as monks*].

Abbot.   Have you no doubt my Lorde, have you no feare,
As silent and as carefull will we be,
To keepe your royall person safe with us,
Free from suspect, and fell invasion
Of such as have your majestie in chase,
Your selfe, and those your chosen companie,
As daunger of this stormie time requires.
Edward.   Father, thy face should harbor no deceit,
O hadst thou ever beene a king, thy hart
Pierced deeply with sence of my distresse,   10
Could not but take compassion of my state.
Stately and proud, in riches and in traine,
Whilom I was, powerfull and full of pompe,
But what is he, whome rule and emperie
Have not in life or death made miserable?
Come *Spencer*, come *Baldocke*, come sit downe by me,
Make triall now of that philosophie,
That in our famous nurseries of artes
Thou suckedst from *Plato*, and from *Aristotle*.
Father, this life contemplative is heaven,   20
O that I might this life in quiet lead,
But we alas are chaste, and you my friends,
Your lives and my dishonor they pursue,
Yet gentle monkes, for treasure, golde nor fee,
Do you betray us and our companie.
Monk.   Your grace may sit secure, if none but wee

26 *Monk.*] Chappell (*1st Monk.*); *Monks.* Q1–4

72

Doe wot of your abode.

Spencer.　Not one alive, but shrewdly I suspect,
　A gloomie fellow in a meade belowe,
　A gave a long looke after us my lord,　　　　　　　　　30
　And all the land I know is up in armes,
　Armes that pursue our lives with deadly hate.

Baldock.　We were imbarkt for *Ireland*, wretched we,
　With awkward windes, and sore tempests driven
　To fall on shoare, and here to pine in feare
　Of *Mortimer* and his confederates.

Edward.　*Mortimer*, who talkes of *Mortimer*,
　Who wounds me with the name of *Mortimer*
　That bloudy man? good father on thy lap
　Lay I this head, laden with mickle care,　　　　　　　40
　O might I never open these eyes againe,
　Never againe lift up this drooping head,
　O never more lift up this dying hart!

Spencer.　Looke up my lord. *Baldock*, this drowsines
　Betides no good, here even we are betraied.

　　　Enter with Welch hookes, *Rice ap Howell, a* Mower,
　　　　　　and the Earle of Leicester.

Mower.　Upon my life, those be the men ye seeke.

Rice.　Fellow enough: my lord I pray be short,
　A faire commission warrants what we do.

Leister.　The Queenes commission, urgd by *Mortimer*,　[*Aside.*]
　What cannot gallant *Mortimer* with the Queene?　　　50
　Alas, see where he sits, and hopes unseene,
　T'escape their hands that seeke to reave his life:
　Too true it is, *quem dies vidit veniens superbum,*
　Hunc dies vidit fugiens jacentem.
　But *Leister* leave to growe so passionate,
　Spencer and *Baldocke*, by no other names,
　I arrest you of high treason here,
　Stand not on titles, but obay th'arrest,
　Tis in the name of *Isabell* the Queene:
　My lord, why droope you thus?　　　　　　　　　　60

73

Edward.   O day! the last of all my blisse on earth,
  Center of all misfortune. O my starres!
  Why do you lowre unkindly on a king?
  Comes *Leister* then in *Isabellas* name,
  To take my life, my companie from me?
  Here man, rip up this panting brest of mine,
  And take my heart, in reskew of my friends.
Rice.   Away with them.
Spencer.   It may become thee yet,
  To let us take our farewell of his grace.
Abbot.   My heart with pittie earnes to see this sight,   70
  A king to beare these words and proud commaunds.
Edward.   *Spencer*,
  A sweet *Spencer*, thus then must we part.
Spencer.   We must my lord, so will the angry heavens.
Edward.   Nay so will hell, and cruell *Mortimer*,
  The gentle heavens have not to do in this.
Baldock.   My lord, it is in vaine to greeve or storme,
  Here humblie of your grace we take our leaves,
  Our lots are cast, I feare me so is thine.
Edward.   In heaven wee may, in earth never shall wee meete,   80
  And *Leister* say, what shall become of us?
Leister.   Your majestie must go to Killingworth.
Edward.   Must! tis somwhat hard, when kings must go.
Leister.   Here is a Litter readie for your grace,
  That waites your pleasure, and the day growes old.
Rice.   As good be gon, as stay and be benighted.
Edward.   A litter hast thou, lay me in a hearse,
  And to the gates of hell convay me hence,
  Let *Plutos* bels ring out my fatall knell,
  And hags howle for my death at *Charons* shore,   90
  For friends hath *Edward* none, but these, and these,
  And these must die under a tyrants sword.
Rice.   My lord, be going, care not for these,
  For we shall see them shorter by the heads.
Edward.   Well, that shalbe, shalbe: part we must,

*91–2 these, and these, | And these] *stet* Q 1–4

74

Sweete *Spencer*, gentle *Baldocke*, part we must.
Hence fained weeds, unfained are my woes,
Father, farewell: *Leister*, thou staist for me,
And go I must, life farewell with my friends.

Exeunt Edward *and* Leicester.

Spencer.   O is he gone! is noble *Edward* gone,   100
Parted from hence, never to see us more!
Rent sphere of heaven, and fier forsake thy orbe,
Earth melt to ayre, gone is my soveraigne,
Gone, gone alas, never to make returne.
Baldock.   *Spencer*, I see our soules are fleeted hence,
We are deprivde the sun-shine of our life,
Make for a new life man, throw up thy eyes,
And hart and hand to heavens immortall throne,
Pay natures debt with cheerefull countenance,
Reduce we all our lessons unto this,   110
To die sweet *Spencer*, therefore live wee all,
Spencer, all live to die, and rise to fall.
Rice.   Come, come, keepe these preachments till you come to the
place appointed. You, and such as you are, have made wise worke
in *England*.
Will your Lordships away?
Mower.   Your worship I trust will remember me?
Rice.   Remember thee fellow? what else?
Follow me to the towne.

[*Exeunt.*]

Enter the King, Leicester, *with a Bishop* [*of* Winchester] *for the* [V.i]
crowne [*and* Trussell].

Leister.   Be patient good my lord, cease to lament,
Imagine Killingworth castell were your court
And that you lay for pleasure here a space,
Not of compulsion or necessitie.
Edward.   *Leister*, if gentle words might comfort me,
Thy speeches long agoe had easde my sorrowes,
For kinde and loving hast thou alwaies beene:

75

The greefes of private men are soone allayde,
But not of kings: the forrest Deare being strucke
Runnes to an herbe that closeth up the wounds,   10
But when the imperiall Lions flesh is gorde,
He rends and teares it with his wrathfull pawe,
And highly scorning, that the lowly earth
Should drinke his bloud, mounts up into the ayre:
And so it fares with me, whose dauntlesse minde
The ambitious *Mortimer* would seeke to curbe,
And that unnaturall Queene false *Isabell*,
That thus hath pent and mu'd me in a prison,
For such outragious passions cloye my soule,
As with the wings of rancor and disdaine,   20
Full often am I sowring up to heaven,
To plaine me to the gods against them both:
But when I call to minde I am a king,
Me thinkes I should revenge me of the wronges,
That *Mortimer* and *Isabell* have done.
But what are kings, when regiment is gone,
But perfect shadowes in a sun-shine day?
My nobles rule, I beare the name of king,
I weare the crowne, but am contrould by them,
By *Mortimer*, and my unconstant Queene,   30
Who spots my nuptiall bed with infamie,
Whilst I am lodgd within this cave of care,
Where sorrow at my elbow still attends,
To companie my hart with sad laments,
That bleedes within me for this strange exchange.
But tell me, must I now resigne my crowne,
To make usurping *Mortimer* a king?
Bishop.   Your grace mistakes, it is for *Englands* good,
And princely *Edwards* right we crave the crowne.
Edward.   No, tis for *Mortimer*, not *Edwards* head,   40
For hees a lambe, encompassed by Woolves,
Which in a moment will abridge his life:
But if proud *Mortimer* do weare this crowne,

13 And] Dodsley[1]; *omit* Q 1–4

76

cure

Heavens turne it to a blaze of quenchelesse fier,
Or like the snakie wreathe of *Tisiphon*,
Engirt the temples of his hatefull head,
So shall not *Englands* Vine be perished,
But *Edwards* name survives, though *Edward* dies.
Leister.   My lord, why waste you thus the time away,
  They stay your answer, will you yeeld your crowne?   50
Edward.   Ah *Leister*, way how hardly I can brooke
  To loose my crowne and kingdome, without cause,
  To give ambitious *Mortimer* my right,
  That like a mountaine overwhelmes my blisse,
  In which extreame my minde here murthered is:
  But what the heavens appoint, I must obaye,
  Here, take my crowne, the life of *Edward* too,
  Two kings in *England* cannot raigne at once:
  But stay a while, let me be king till night,
  That I may gaze upon this glittering crowne,   60
  So shall my eyes receive their last content,
  My head, the latest honor dew to it,
  And joyntly both yeeld up their wished right.
  Continue ever thou celestiall sunne,
  Let never silent night possesse this clime,
  Stand still you watches of the element,
  All times and seasons rest you at a stay,
  That *Edward* may be still faire *Englands* king:
  But dayes bright beames dooth vanish fast away,
  And needes I must resigne my wished crowne.   70
  Inhumaine creatures, nurst with Tigers milke,
  Why gape you for your soveraignes overthrow?
  My diadem I meane, and guiltlesse life.
  See monsters see, ile weare my crowne againe,
  What, feare you not the furie of your king?
  But haplesse *Edward*, thou art fondly led,
  They passe not for thy frownes as late they did,
  But seekes to make a new elected king,
  Which fils my mind with strange despairing thoughts,

commands sun to stand still

*47 Vine] Oxberry; Vines Q1–4

77

Which thoughts are martyred with endles torments.   80
And in this torment, comfort finde I none,
But that I feele the crowne upon my head,
And therefore let me weare it yet a while.
Trussell.   My Lorde, the parlement must have present newes,
And therefore say, will you resigne or no.

                                        The king rageth.

Edward.   Ile not resigne, but whilst I live, be king.
  Traitors be gon, and joine you with *Mortimer*,
  Elect, conspire, install, do what you will,
  Their bloud and yours shall seale these treacheries.
Bishop.   This answer weele returne, and so farewell.   90
Leister.   Call them againe my lorde, and speake them faire,
  For if they goe, the prince shall lose his right.
Edward.   Call thou them back, I have no power to speake.
Leister.   My lord, the king is willing to resigne.
Bishop.   If he be not, let him choose.
Edward.   O would I might, but heavens and earth conspire
  To make me miserable: heere receive my crowne.
  Receive it? no, these innocent hands of mine
  Shall not be guiltie of so foule a crime.
  He of you all that most desires my bloud,   100
  And will be called the murtherer of a king,
  Take it: what are you moovde, pitie you me?
  Then send for unrelenting *Mortimer*
  And *Isabell*, whose eyes being turnd to steele,
  Will sooner sparkle fire then shed a teare:
  Yet stay, for rather then I will looke on them,
  Heere, heere: now sweete God of heaven,
  Make me despise this transitorie pompe,
  And sit for aye inthronized in heaven,
  Come death, and with thy fingers close my eyes,   110
  Or if I live, let me forget my selfe.
Bishop.   My lorde——

86 be king] Dodsley[1]; *omit* Q1–4   Q1–4
104 being] Q2; beene Q1   112 *Bishop.*] Dyce; *Bartley.* Q1–4
111.1 *omit*] Chappell; *Enter Bartley.*

Edward.   Call me not lorde, away, out of my sight:
Ah pardon me, greefe makes me lunatick.
Let not that *Mortimer* protect my sonne,
More safetie is there in a Tigers jawes,
Then his imbrasements: beare this to the queene,
Wet with my teares, and dried againe with sighes,
If with the sight thereof she be not mooved,
Returne it backe and dip it in my bloud.   120
Commend me to my sonne, and bid him rule
Better then I, yet how have I transgrest,
Unlesse it be with too much clemencie?
Trussell.   And thus, most humbly do we take our leave.
            [*Exeunt Bishop of* Winchester *and* Trussell.]
Edward.   Farewell, I know the next newes that they bring,
Will be my death, and welcome shall it be,
To wretched men death is felicitie.

            [*Enter* Bartley *to* Leister *with letter.*]

Leister.   An other poast, what newes bringes he?
Edward.   Such newes as I expect, come *Bartley*, come,
And tell thy message to my naked brest.   130
Bartley.   My lord, thinke not a thought so villanous
Can harbor in a man of noble birth.
To do your highnes service and devoire,
And save you from your foes, *Bartley* would die.
Leister.   My lorde, the counsell of the Queene commaunds,
That I resigne my charge.
Edward.   And who must keepe mee now, must you my lorde?
Bartley.   I, my most gratious lord, so tis decreed.
Edward.   By *Mortimer*, whose name is written here,
Well may I rent his name, that rends my hart.   140
This poore revenge hath something easd my minde,
So may his limmes be torne, as is this paper,
Heare me immortall *Jove*, and graunt it too.
Bartley.   Your grace must hence with mee to Bartley straight.
Edward.   Whether you will, all places are alike,

117 Then] Q2; This Q1

And every earth is fit for buriall.
Leister.   Favor him my lord, as much as lieth in you.
Bartley.   Even so betide my soule as I use him.
Edward.   Mine enemie hath pitied my estate,
And thats the cause that I am now remoovde.   150
Bartley.   And thinkes your grace that *Bartley* will bee cruell?
Edward.   I know not, but of this am I assured,
That death ends all, and I can die but once.
  Leicester, farewell.
Leister.   Not yet my lorde, ile beare you on your waye.

                             Exeunt omnes.

         Enter Mortimer, *and Queene* Isabell.   [V.i

Mortimer.   Faire *Isabell,* now have we our desire,
The proud corrupters of the light-brainde king,
Have done their homage to the loftie gallowes,
And he himselfe lies in captivitie.
Be rulde by me, and we will rule the realme,
In any case, take heed of childish feare,
For now we hould an old Wolfe by the eares,
That if he slip will seaze upon us both,
And gripe the sorer being gript himselfe.
Thinke therefore madam that imports us much,   10
To erect your sonne with all the speed we may,
And that I be protector over him,
For our behoofe will beare the greater sway
When as a kings name shall be under writ.
Queene.   Sweet *Mortimer,* the life of *Isabell,*
Be thou perswaded, that I love thee well,
And therefore so the prince my sonne be safe,
Whome I esteeme as deare as these mine eyes,
Conclude against his father what thou wilt,
And I my selfe will willinglie subscribe.   20
Mortimer.   First would I heare newes that hee were deposde,
And then let me alone to handle him.

10 us] Q3; as Q1–2

Enter Messenger [and then Bishop of Winchester *with the crown].*

Letters from whence?
Messenger.   From Killingworth my lorde.
Queene.   How fares my lord the king?
Messenger.   In health madam, but full of pensivenes.
Queene.   Alas poore soule, would I could ease his greefe.
Thankes gentle *Winchester*: sirra, be gon.
                              [*Exit Messenger.*]
Bishop.   The king hath willingly resignde his crowne.
Queene.   O happie newes, send for the prince my sonne.
Bishop.   Further, or this letter was sealed, Lord *Bartley* came,   30
So that he now is gone from Killingworth,
And we have heard that *Edmund* laid a plot,
To set his brother free, no more but so.
The lord of *Bartley* is so pitifull,
As *Leicester* that had charge of him before.
Queene.   Then let some other be his guardian.
                              [*Exit* Winchester.]
Mortimer.   Let me alone, here is the privie seale,
Whose there? call hither *Gurney* and *Matrevis*.
To dash the heavie headed *Edmunds* drift,
Bartley shall be dischargd, the king remoovde,   40
And none but we shall know where he lieth.
Queene.   But *Mortimer*, as long as he survives
What safetie rests for us, or for my sonne?
Mortimer.   Speake, shall he presently be dispatch'd and die?
Queene.   I would hee were, so it were not by my meanes.

Enter Matrevis *and* Gurney.

Mortimer.   Inough.
Matrevis, write a letter presently
Unto the Lord of *Bartley* from our selfe,
That he resigne the king to thee and *Gurney*,
And when tis done, we will subscribe our name.   50
Matrevis.   It shall be done my lord.

*36.1 [*Exit* Winchester.] *See Textual Note*

Mortimer.   *Gurney.*
Gurney.   My Lorde.
Mortimer.   As thou intendest to rise by *Mortimer*,
Who now makes Fortunes wheele turne as he please,
Seeke all the meanes thou canst to make him droope,
And neither give him kinde word, nor good looke.
Gurney.   I warrant you my lord.
Mortimer.   And this above the rest, because we heare
That *Edmund* casts to worke his libertie,
Remoove him still from place to place by night,
Till at the last, he come to Killingworth,   60
And then from thence to Bartley back againe:
And by the way to make him fret the more,
Speake curstlie to him, and in any case
Let no man comfort him, if he chaunce to weepe,
But amplifie his greefe with bitter words.
Matrevis.   Feare not my Lord, weele do as you commaund.
Mortimer.   So now away, post thither wards amaine.
Queene.   Whither goes this letter, to my lord the king?
Commend me humblie to his Majestie,
And tell him, that I labour all in vaine,   70
To ease his greefe, and worke his libertie:
And beare him this, as witnesse of my love.
Matrevis.   I will madam.   *A ring.*

      Exeunt Matrevis *and* Gurney. *Manent* Isabell *and* Mortimer.

      Enter the yong Prince, *and the Earle of* Kent *talking*
                      with him.

Mortimer.   Finely dissembled, do so still sweet Queene.
Heere comes the yong prince, with the Earle of *Kent*.
Queene.   Some thing he whispers in his childish eares.
Mortimer.   If he have such accesse unto the prince,
Our plots and stratagems will soone be dasht.
Queene.   Use *Edmund* friendly, as if all were well.
Mortimer.   How fares my honorable lord of *Kent*?   80

60 Till] Q2; And Q1

Kent.   In health sweete *Mortimer*, how fares your grace?
Queene.   Well, if my Lorde your brother were enlargde.
Kent.   I heare of late he hath deposde himselfe.
Queene.   The more my greefe.
Mortimer.   And mine.
Kent.   Ah they do dissemble.   [*Aside.*]
Queene.   Sweete sonne come hither, I must talke with thee.
Mortimer.   Thou being his unckle, and the next of bloud,
    Doe looke to be protector over the prince?
Kent.   Not I my lord: who should protect the sonne,   90
    But she that gave him life, I meane the Queene?
Prince.   Mother, perswade me not to weare the crowne,
    Let him be king, I am too yong to raigne.
Queene.   But bee content, seeing it his highnesse pleasure.
Prince.   Let me but see him first, and then I will.
Kent.   I, do sweete Nephew.
Queene.   Brother, you know it is impossible.
Prince.   Why, is he dead?
Queene.   No, God forbid.
Kent.   I would those wordes proceeded from your heart.   100
Mortimer.   Inconstant *Edmund*, doost thou favor him,
    That wast a cause of his imprisonment?
Kent.   The more cause have I now to make amends.
Mortimer.   I tell thee tis not meet, that one so false
    Should come about the person of a prince.
    My lord, he hath betraied the king his brother,
    And therefore trust him not.
Prince.   But hee repents, and sorrowes for it now.
Queene.   Come sonne, and go with this gentle Lorde and
    me.
Prince.   With you I will, but not with *Mortimer*.   110
Mortimer.   Why yongling, s'dainst thou so of *Mortimer*?
    Then I will carrie thee by force away.
Prince.   Helpe unckle *Kent*, *Mortimer* will wrong me.
Queene.   Brother *Edmund*, strive not, we are his friends,
    Isabell is neerer then the earle of *Kent*.
Kent.   Sister, *Edward* is my charge, redeeme him.

Queene.   *Edward* is my sonne, and I will keepe him. [*Is going off.*]
Kent.   *Mortimer* shall know that he hath wrongde mee.
   Hence will I haste to Killingworth castle,
   And rescue aged *Edward* from his foes,
   To be revengde on *Mortimer* and thee.   120

                                        Exeunt omnes [*severally*].

          Enter Matrevis *and* Gurney *with the* King [*and souldiers*].   [V.iii

Matrevis.   My lord, be not pensive, we are your friends.
   Men are ordaind to live in miserie,
   Therefore come, dalliance dangereth our lives.
Edward.   Friends, whither must unhappie *Edward* go,
   Will hatefull *Mortimer* appoint no rest?
   Must I be vexed like the nightly birde,
   Whose sight is loathsome to all winged fowles?
   When will the furie of his minde asswage?
   When will his hart be satisfied with bloud?
   If mine will serve, unbowell straight this brest,   10
   And give my heart to *Isabell* and him,
   It is the chiefest marke they levell at.
Gurney.   Not so my liege, the Queene hath given this charge,
   To keepe your grace in safetie,
   Your passions make your dolours to increase.
Edward.   This usage makes my miserie increase.
   But can my ayre of life continue long,
   When all my sences are anoyde with stenche?
   Within a dungeon *Englands* king is kept,
   Where I am sterv'd for want of sustenance,   20
   My daily diet, is heart breaking sobs,
   That almost rents the closet of my heart,
   Thus lives old *Edward* not reliev'd by any,
   And so must die, though pitied by many.
   O water gentle friends to coole my thirst,
   And cleare my bodie from foule excrements.
Matrevis.   Heeres channell water, as our charge is given.

Sit downe, for weele be Barbars to your grace.

Edward.   Traitors away, what will you murther me,
  Or choake your soveraigne with puddle water?   30

Gurney.   No, but wash your face, and shave away your beard,
  Least you be knowne, and so be rescued.

Matrevis.   Why strive you thus? your labour is in vaine.

Edward.   The Wrenne may strive against the Lions strength,
  But all in vaine, so vainely do I strive,
  To seeke for mercie at a tyrants hand.

     They wash him with puddle water, and shave his beard away.

Immortall powers, that knowes the painfull cares,
  That waites upon my poore distressed soule,
  O levell all your lookes upon these daring men,
  That wronges their liege and soveraigne, *Englands* king.   40
  O *Gaveston*, it is for thee that I am wrongd,
  For me, both thou, and both the *Spencers* died,
  And for your sakes, a thousand wronges ile take,
  The *Spencers* ghostes, where ever they remaine,
  Wish well to mine, then tush, for them ile die.

Matrevis.   Twixt theirs and yours, shall be no enmitie.
  Come, come, away, now put the torches out,
  Weele enter in by darkenes to Killingworth.

     Enter Edmund [*earle of* Kent].

Gurney.   How now, who comes there?

Matrevis.   Guarde the king sure, it is the earle of *Kent.*   50

Edward.   O gentle brother, helpe to rescue me.

Matrevis.   Keepe them a sunder, thrust in the king.

Kent.   Souldiers, let me but talke to him one worde.

Gurney.   Lay hands upon the earle for this assault.

Kent.   Lay downe your weapons, traitors, yeeld the king.

Matrevis.   *Edmund*, yeeld thou thy self, or thou shalt die.

Kent.   Base villaines, wherefore doe you gripe mee thus?

Gurney.   Binde him, and so convey him to the court.

Kent.   Where is the court but heere, heere is the king,
  And I will visit him, why stay you me?   60

Matrevis.   The court is where lord *Mortimer* remaines,
  Thither shall your honour go, and so farewell.
                          Exeunt Matrevis *and* Gurney, *with the king.*

                Manent Edmund *and the souldiers.*

Kent.   O miserable is that commonweale,
  Where lords keepe courts, and kings are lockt in prison!
Souldier.   Wherefore stay we? on sirs to the court.
Kent.   I, lead me whether you will, even to my death,
  Seeing that my brother cannot be releast.
                                    Exeunt omnes.

                Enter Mortimer *alone.*   [V.iv]

Mortimer.   The king must die, or *Mortimer* goes downe,
  The commons now begin to pitie him,
  Yet he that is the cause of *Edwards* death,
  Is sure to pay for it when his sonne is of age,
  And therefore will I do it cunninglie.
  This letter written by a friend of ours,
  Containes his death, yet bids them save his life.
  Edwardum occidere nolite timere bonum est.
  Feare not to kill the king tis good he die.
  But read it thus, and thats an other sence: 10
  Edwardum occidere nolite timere bonum est.
  Kill not the king tis good to feare the worst.
  Unpointed as it is, thus shall it goe,
  That being dead, if it chaunce to be found,
  Matrevis and the rest may beare the blame,
  And we be quit that causde it to be done:
  Within this roome is lockt the messenger,
  That shall conveie it, and performe the rest,
  And by a secret token that he beares,
  Shall he be murdered when the deed is done.   20
  Lightborn,
  Come forth.

[*Enter* Lightborn.]

Art thou as resolute as thou wast?

Lightborne.   What else my lord? and farre more resolute.

Mortimer.   And hast thou cast how to accomplish it?

Lightborne.   I, I, and none shall know which way he died.

Mortimer.   But at his lookes *Lightborne* thou wilt relent.

Lightborne.   Relent, ha, ha, I use much to relent.

Mortimer.   Well, do it bravely, and be secret.

Lightborne.   You shall not need to give instructions,

Tis not the first time I have killed a man.   30

I learnde in *Naples* how to poison flowers,

To strangle with a lawne thrust through the throte,

To pierce the wind-pipe with a needles point,

Or whilst one is a sleepe, to take a quill

And blowe a little powder in his eares,

Or open his mouth, and powre quick silver downe,

But yet I have a braver way then these.

Mortimer.   Whats that?

Lightborne.   Nay, you shall pardon me, none shall knowe my
    trickes.

Mortimer.   I care not how it is, so it be not spide: 40

Deliver this to *Gurney* and *Matrevis*,

At every ten miles end thou hast a horse.

Take this, away, and never see me more.

Lightborne.   No?

Mortimer.   No,

Unlesse thou bring me newes of *Edwards* death.

Lightborne.   That will I quicklie do, farewell my lord.   [*Exit.*]

Mortimer.   The prince I rule, the queene do I commaund,

And with a lowly conge to the ground,

The proudest lords salute me as I passe,   50

I seale, I cancell, I do what I will,

Feard am I more then lov'd, let me be feard,

And when I frowne, make all the court looke pale,

I view the prince with *Aristarchus* eyes,

Whose lookes were as a breeching to a boye.

They thrust upon me the Protectorship,
And sue to me for that that I desire,
While at the councell table, grave enough,
And not unlike a bashfull puretaine,
First I complaine of imbecilitie,   60
Saying it is, *onus quam gravissimum*,
Till being interrupted by my friends,
Suscepi that *provinciam* as they terme it,
And to conclude, I am Protector now,
Now is all sure, the Queene and *Mortimer*
Shall rule the realme, the king, and none rule us,
Mine enemies will I plague, my friends advance,
And what I list commaund, who dare controwle?
Major sum quam cui possit fortuna nocere.
And that this be the coronation day,   70
It pleaseth me, and *Isabell* the Queene.
The trumpets sound, I must go take my place.

Enter the yong King, [*Arch*]*bishop* [*of* Canterbury], *Champion,*
Nobles, Queene.

Bishop.   Long live king *Edward*, by the grace of God
King of *England*, and lorde of *Ireland*.
Champion.   If any Christian, Heathen, Turke, or Jew,
Dares but affirme, that *Edwards* not true king,
And will avouche his saying with the sworde,
I am the Champion that will combate him!
Mortimer.   None comes, sound trumpets.
King.   Champion, heeres to thee.   [*Drinks.*] 80
Queene.   Lord *Mortimer*, now take him to your charge.

Enter Souldiers with the Earle of Kent *prisoner.*

Mortimer.   What traitor have wee there with blades and billes?
Souldier.   *Edmund* the Earle of *Kent*.
King.   What hath he done?
Souldier.   A would have taken the king away perforce,
As we were bringing him to Killingworth.
Mortimer.   Did you attempt his rescue, *Edmund* speake?

Kent.   *Mortimer,* I did, he is our king,
  And thou compelst this prince to weare the crowne.
Mortimer.   Strike off his head, he shall have marshall lawe.
Kent.   Strike of my head? base traitor I defie thee.   90
King.   My lord, he is my unckle, and shall live.
Mortimer.   My lord, he is your enemie, and shall die.
Kent.   Staie villaines.
King.   Sweete mother, if I cannot pardon him,
  Intreate my lord Protector for his life.
Queene.   Sonne, be content, I dare not speake a worde.
King.   Nor I, and yet me thinkes I should commaund,
  But seeing I cannot, ile entreate for him:
  My lord, if you will let my unckle live,
  I will requite it when I come to age.   100
Mortimer.   Tis for your highnesse good, and for the realmes.
  How often shall I bid you beare him hence?   [*To Souldiers.*]
Kent.   Art thou king, must I die at thy commaund?
Mortimer.   At our commaund, once more away with him.
Kent.   Let me but stay and speake, I will not go,
  Either my brother or his sonne is king,
  And none of both them thirst for *Edmunds* bloud.
  And therefore soldiers whether will you hale me?
      They hale Edmund *away, and carie him to be beheaded.*
King.   What safetie may I looke for at his hands,
  If that my Unckle shall be murthered thus?   110
Queene.   Feare not sweete boye, ile garde thee from thy foes,
  Had *Edmund* liv'de, he would have sought thy death.
  Come sonne, weele ride a hunting in the parke.
King.   And shall my Unckle *Edmund* ride with us?
Queene.   He is a traitor, thinke not on him, come.
           Exeunt omnes.

107 both them] Q2; both, then Q1

Enter Matrevis *and* Gurney.   [V.v]

Matrevis.   *Gurney*, I wonder the king dies not,
  Being in a vault up to the knees in water,
  To which the channels of the castell runne,
  From whence a dampe continually ariseth,
  That were enough to poison any man,
  Much more a king brought up so tenderlie.
Gurney.   And so do I, *Matrevis*: yesternight
  I opened but the doore to throw him meate,
  And I was almost stifeled with the savor.
Matrevis.   He hath a body able to endure,   10
  More then we can enflict, and therefore now,
  Let us assaile his minde another while.
Gurney.   Send for him out thence, and I will anger him.
Matrevis.   But stay, whose this?

Enter Lightborne.

Lightborne.   My lord protector greetes you.
Gurney.   Whats heere? I know not how to conster it.
Matrevis.   *Gurney*, it was left unpointed for the nonce,
  Edwardum occidere nolite timere,
  Thats his meaning.
Lightborne.   Know you this token? I must have the king.
Matrevis.   I, stay a while, thou shalt have answer straight.   20
  This villain's sent to make away the king.
Gurney.   I thought as much.
Matrevis.   And when the murders done,
  See how he must be handled for his labour,
  Pereat iste: let him have the king,
  What else? Heere is the keyes, this is the lake,
  Doe as you are commaunded by my lord.
Lightborne.   I know what I must do, get you away,
  Yet be not farre off, I shall need your helpe,
  See that in the next roome I have a fier,
  And get me a spit, and let it be red hote.   30

25 lake] *i.e.,* lacus *or* dungeon

Matrevis.   Very well.
Gurney.   Neede you any thing besides?
Lightborne.   What else, a table and a fetherbed.
Gurney.   Thats all?
Lightborne.   I, I, so: when I call you, bring it in.
Matrevis.   Feare not you that.
Gurney.   Heeres a light to go into the dungeon.
                              [*Exeunt* Matrevis *and* Gurney.]
Lightborne.   So,
  Now must I about this geare, nere was there any
  So finely handled as this king shalbe.   40
  Foh, heeres a place in deed with all my hart.

            [Edward *comes up or is discovered.*]

Edward.   Whose there, what light is that, wherefore comes thou?
Lightborne.   To comfort you, and bring you joyfull newes.
Edward.   Small comfort findes poore *Edward* in thy lookes,
  Villaine, I know thou comst to murther me.
Lightborne.   To murther you my most gratious lorde?
  Farre is it from my hart to do you harme,
  The Queene sent me, to see how you were used,
  For she relents at this your miserie.
  And what eyes can refraine from shedding teares,   50
  To see a king in this most pittious state?
Edward.   Weepst thou already? list a while to me,
  And then thy heart, were it as *Gurneys* is,
  Or as *Matrevis*, hewne from the *Caucasus*,
  Yet will it melt, ere I have done my tale.
  This dungeon where they keepe me, is the sincke,
  Wherein the filthe of all the castell falles.
Lightborne.   O villaines!
Edward.   And there in mire and puddle have I stood,
  This ten dayes space, and least that I should sleepe,   60
  One plaies continually upon a Drum,
  They give me bread and water being a king,
  So that for want of sleepe and sustenance,
  My mindes distempered, and my bodies numde,

And whether I have limmes or no, I know not.
O would my bloud dropt out from every vaine,
As doth this water from my tattered robes:
Tell *Isabell* the Queene, I lookt not thus,
When for her sake I ran at tilt in *Fraunce*,
And there unhorste the duke of *Cleremont*.   70
Lightborne.   O speake no more my lorde, this breakes my heart.
Lie on this bed, and rest your selfe a while.
Edward.   These lookes of thine can harbor nought but death.
I see my tragedie written in thy browes,
Yet stay a while, forbeare thy bloudie hande,
And let me see the stroke before it comes,
That even then when I shall lose my life,
My minde may be more stedfast on my God.
Lightborne.   What meanes your highnesse to mistrust me thus?
Edward.   What meanes thou to dissemble with me thus?   80
Lightborne.   These handes were never stainde with innocent bloud,
Nor shall they now be tainted with a kings.
Edward.   Forgive my thought, for having such a thought,
One jewell have I left, receive thou this.
Still feare I, and I know not whats the cause,
But everie jointe shakes as I give it thee:
O if thou harborst murther in thy hart,
Let this gift change thy minde, and save thy soule,
Know that I am a king, oh at that name,
I feele a hell of greefe: where is my crowne?   90
Gone, gone, and doe I remaine alive?
Lightborne.   Your overwatchde my lord, lie downe and rest.
Edward.   But that greefe keepes me waking, I shoulde sleepe,
For not these ten daies have these eyes lids closd.
Now as I speake they fall, and yet with feare
Open againe. O wherefore sits thou heare?
Lightborne.   If you mistrust me, ile be gon my lord.
Edward.   No, no, for if thou meanst to murther me,
Thou wilt returne againe, and therefore stay.
Lightborne.   He sleepes.   100

77 even] Dodsley[1]; and even Q1-4

92

Edward.   O let me not die yet, stay, O stay a while.
Lightborne.   How now my Lorde.
Edward.   Something still busseth in mine eares,
  And tels me, if I sleepe I never wake,
  This feare is that which makes me tremble thus,
  And therefore tell me, wherefore art thou come?
Lightborne.   To rid thee of thy life. *Matrevis* come.
Edward.   I am too weake and feeble to resist,
  Assist me sweete God, and receive my soule.

   [*Enter* Matrevis, Gurney, *and exeunt. Return with table.*]

Lightborne.   Runne for the table.   110
Edward.   O spare me, or dispatche me in a trice.
Lightborne.   So, lay the table downe, and stampe on it,
  But not too hard, least that you bruse his body.

                                          [King *dies.*]

Matrevis.   I feare mee that this crie will raise the towne,
  And therefore let us take horse and away.
Lightborne.   Tell me sirs, was it not bravelie done?
Gurney.   Excellent well, take this for thy rewarde.

                    Then Gurney *stabs* Lightborne.

  Come let us cast the body in the mote,
  And beare the kings to *Mortimer* our lord,   120
  Away.

                               Exeunt omnes.

       Enter Mortimer *and* Matrevis [*at different doors*].   [V.vi]

Mortimer.   Ist done, *Matrevis*, and the murtherer dead?
Matrevis.   I my good Lord, I would it were undone.
Mortimer.   *Matrevis*, if thou now growest penitent
  Ile be thy ghostly father, therefore choose,
  Whether thou wilt be secret in this,
  Or else die by the hand of *Mortimer*.
Matrevis.   *Gurney*, my lord, is fled, and will I feare,
  Betray us both, therefore let me flie.
Mortimer.   Flie to the Savages.

101 die∧ yet,] Q4 ~ , ~ ∧ Q1–3

                    93

Matrevis.   I humblie thanke your honour.   [*Exit.*] 10
Mortimer.   As for my selfe, I stand as *Joves* huge tree,
  And others are but shrubs compard to me,
  All tremble at my name, and I feare none,
  Lets see who dare impeache me for his death?

Enter the Queene.

Queene.   A *Mortimer*, the king my sonne hath news,
  His fathers dead, and we have murdered him.
Mortimer.   What if he have? the king is yet a childe.
Queene.   I, I, but he teares his haire, and wrings his handes,
  And vowes to be revengd upon us both,
  Into the councell chamber he is gone,   20
  To crave the aide and succour of his peeres.
  Aye me, see where he comes, and they with him,
  Now *Mortimer* begins our tragedie.

Enter the King, *with the lords.*

1. Lord   Feare not my lord, know that you are a king.
King.   Villaine.
Mortimer.   How now my lord?
King.   Thinke not that I am frighted with thy words,
  My father's murdered through thy treacherie,
  And thou shalt die, and on his mournefull hearse,
  Thy hatefull and accursed head shall lie,   30
  To witnesse to the world, that by thy meanes,
  His kingly body was too soone interrde.
Queene.   Weepe not sweete sonne.
King.   Forbid not me to weepe, he was my father,
  And had you lov'de him halfe so well as I,
  You could not beare his death thus patiently,
  But you I feare, conspirde with *Mortimer.*
1. Lord.   Why speake you not unto my lord the king?
Mortimer.   Because I thinke scorne to be accusde,
  Who is the man dare say I murdered him?   40
King.   Traitor, in me my loving father speakes,

24, 38 *1. Lord.*] Chappell; *Lords.* Q 1–4

94

And plainely saith, twas thou that murdredst him.

Mortimer.　But hath your grace no other proofe then this?

King.　Yes, if this be the hand of *Mortimer.*

Mortimer.　False *Gurney* hath betraide me and himselfe.

Queene.　I feard as much, murther cannot be hid.

Mortimer.　Tis my hand, what gather you by this.

King.　That thither thou didst send a murtherer.

Mortimer.　What murtherer? bring foorth the man I sent.

King.　A *Mortimer*, thou knowest that he is slaine,　　　　50
And so shalt thou be too: why staies he heere?
Bring him unto a hurdle, drag him foorth,
Hang him I say, and set his quarters up,
But bring his head back presently to me.

Queene.　For my sake sweete sonne pittie *Mortimer.*

Mortimer.　Madam, intreat not, I will rather die,
Then sue for life unto a paltrie boye.

King.　Hence with the traitor, with the murderer.

Mortimer.　Base fortune, now I see, that in thy wheele
There is a point, to which when men aspire,　　　　60
They tumble hedlong downe: that point I touchte,
And seeing there was no place to mount up higher,
Why should I greeve at my declining fall?
Farewell faire Queene, weepe not for *Mortimer*,
That scornes the world, and as a traveller,
Goes to discover countries yet unknowne.

King.　What, suffer you the traitor to delay?

　　　　　　　　　　[*Exit* Mortimer *with* 1. Lord *attended.*]

Queene.　As thou receivedst thy life from me,
Spill not the bloud of gentle *Mortimer.*

King.　This argues, that you spilt my fathers bloud,　　　　70
Els would you not intreate for *Mortimer.*

Queene.　I spill his bloud? no.

King.　I, madam, you, for so the rumor runnes.

Queene.　That rumor is untrue, for loving thee,
Is this report raisde on poore *Isabell.*

King.　I doe not thinke her so unnaturall.

77　2. *Lord.* Dyce; *Lords.* Q 1–4

2. Lord.   My lord, I feare me it will proove too true.

King.   Mother, you are suspected for his death,
  And therefore we commit you to the Tower,
  Till further triall may be made thereof.   80
  If you be guiltie, though I be your sonne,
  Thinke not to finde me slack or pitifull.

Queene.   Nay, to my death, for too long have I lived,
  When as my sonne thinkes to abridge my daies.

King.   Awaye with her, her wordes inforce these teares,
  And I shall pitie her if she speake againe.

Queene.   Shall I not moorne for my beloved lord,
  And with the rest accompanie him to his grave?

2. Lord.   Thus madam, tis the kings will you shall hence.

Queene.   He hath forgotten me, stay, I am his mother.   90

2. Lord   That bootes not, therefore gentle madam goe.

Queene.   Then come sweete death, and rid me of this greefe.

                            [*Exit* Queene *and* 2. Lord.]

                    [*Enter* 1. Lord.]

1. Lord.   My lord, here is the head of *Mortimer.*

King.   Goe fetche my fathers hearse, where it shall lie,
  And bring my funerall robes: accursed head,
  Could I have rulde thee then, as I do now,
  Thou hadst not hatcht this monstrous treacherie!

                            [*Enter some with hearse.*]

  Heere comes the hearse, helpe me to moorne, my lords:
  Sweete father heere, unto thy murdered ghost,
  I offer up this wicked traitors head,   100
  And let these teares distilling from mine eyes,
  Be witnesse of my greefe and innocencie.

                    FINIS

89, 91 *2. Lord.* Dyce; *Lords.* Q 1–4   93 *1. Lords.*] Chappell; *Lords.* Q 1–4

II.ii

35 my brother] This phrase led Dyce, followed by Cunningham and Bullen, to
assign lines 29–35 to Edmund. But though such a confusion had occurred at
I.i.107, it is not present here. Edward is merely calling Gaveston his brother to
demonstrate his feelings of close relationship.

81 Heere, here.] Q1–4 read, '*Penbrooke*. Heere, here King: convey . . . .' a crux that
has produced two lines of emendation. Dyce[1], followed by Bullen and Briggs,
ended the speech with 'King' and assigned the remainder to Edward. Dyce[2],
followed by Methuen and later editors including the present, took it that the unceremonious use of 'King' – the only time in the play – was an anomaly and that
Edward's speech-prefix had somehow been confused as part of the text. This seems
to be the correct position despite the difficulty that in Q1 Edward's prefix is always
'*Edward*' and never '*King*'. However, he is 'the king' in several stage-directions,
and Q1 may not reproduce what could have been variable prefixes in the copy. It is
certain, at least, that Edward, not Pembroke, should be the one to give the order to
the guard to protect Gaveston and escort him to safety. Pembroke thus remains in
character as a rebellious baron by pointing at Gaveston, with 'Heere, here', in
answer to Edward's cry, 'Treason, treason: whers the traitor?'

179 their] In Q1 the line is so tightly set to the full measure as to lead to the suspicion that 'their' stood in the copy but was shortened to 'the' as a justifying device.
At any rate, the Q2 emendation is required by the sense, whatever the source of
the Q1 error.

226 him] Quite possibly the usual emendation of Q1–4 'him' to 'them' or to ''em'
or 'hem' is correct in order to secure agreement with the plural 'Earles'. If emendation is required, 'them' would be preferable since nowhere else does Edward use a
colloquialism like ''em' or 'hem'. On the other hand, Isabella's response in line 227
seems to be specifically directed at Edward's suspicion of her relations with Mortimer, a point on which she had spiritedly defended herself against Gaveston's
innuendoes. She has not been accused previously of taking the side of the barons in
general. Hence even though it is admittedly awkward, Edward's jeer could narrow
the uprising of the earls to the Queen's sympathies for Mortimer.

II.v

18 King *Edward*] Although Q2's substitution of 'King' for Q1 'Kind' can have no
authority, the analogues are so numerous in the play to make the emendation con-
vincing. Even though 'Kind' makes sufficient sense, the concordance reveals that
Marlowe had no tendency to employ it as an adjective and the phrase here would
therefore be uncharacteristic whereas 'King *Edward*' would be completely normal.

98.1 Arundell]   See the Introduction for a discussion of the confusion of Arundel and Maltravers (Matrevis).

III.i

181 lords]   The unknown editor of the Chappell edition early saw that Edward here is gathering strength by first addressing the nobles in his train and then appealing to his soldiers. Q1–4 'lord' – although commonly retained by editors – could apply only to Spencer, or, less likely, to Arundel. But nowhere else does the King address Spencer directly in such formal fashion: it is always the intimate 'Spencer'. Thus the plural seems required by the context.

202 them]   The Q1–4 reading 'thee' is possible only if 'Th'ad' means *They had* (actually a desirable meaning for the contraction), in which case the sense would be: *They had best forsake thee soon and also forsake their plots, because you may be sure they are going to forsake you sooner or later.* With this meaning a clash appears between the forsaking of the plots (from the point of view of the barons) and the forsaking the King (from Edward's point of view). It is simpler to conjecture that the thrust is not towards persuading Spencer to leave Edward but, as usual, Edward to leave his favourites. If the compositor misunderstood 'Th'ad' as 'They had', he might have altered 'them' to 'thee'.

218 Alarum to the fight.]   Q1–4 line as 'Alarum...England, | And...right.' Whether in the revised lining of the present edition (following the Chappell re-arrangement) or in that of Q1–4, a short line occurs. According to Elizabethan stage convention it was possible, as at III.i.184.1–3, for the same persons to make an exit and an immediate extrance in a battle scene if the gap were covered by noises appropriate for an off-stage fight. Since no direction is present at line 220.1 in Q1–4, it is at least possible that a stage-direction at the left of the copy, 'Alarum to the fight', was mistaken by the compositor and inserted as the beginning of a text line. If it were removed, Warwick would speak two regular pentameters, and Edward would respond with a single pentameter line before the exits. On the other hand, the phrase 'Alarum to the fight' – although roughly similar to such directions in *1 Tamburlaine* as '*Sound trumpets to the battell*' (II.iv.42.1) or '*They sound to the battaile*' (V.i.402.1) – is also possible as a shout of encouragement or of command; and the fact that it is very likely a part line is of no significance. Moreover, if the lining of the present edition be accepted, a rhyme results. It is this rhymed couplet, fortuitous as it may be, that could slightly tip the scales in favour of retaining the words in the text instead of treating them as a stage-direction, especially since such an error in Q1 cannot be demonstrated but only conjectured.

IV.ii

81 lord]   In the absence of a comma after 'lord' in Q1–4, Dyce's emendation to 'lords' is tempting in view of the occasional confusion in this play between singular and plural as in IV.v.7 or V.i.47. But such an emendation would probably be a sophistication. It is not inappropriate for Hainault to single out Isabella and then the prince. The nobles who followed these two would automatically be included in any invitation. The only emendation needed, then, is a comma after 'lord'.

IV.iv

23 sword]   It is probable that the preceding plural 'armes' has contaminated Q1 'swords' and that the more conventional phrase in the singular, as in Q2–4, is what is needed.

IV.vi

45 This, *Edward*,]   The lack of commas enclosing 'Edward' in Q1 is not unusual, for Q1 often leaves parentheses of this sort unpointed. Many editors follow Q1 and thus in modernized texts accept 'This' as modifying the subject '*Edward*'. Yet the context suggests that '*Edward*' is in fact a vocative. Kent's sympathy for his brother and his revulsion against the barons, as exhibited in IV.vi.1–18, would make it impossible for him at this point to call Edward the ruin of his realm as he had earlier done. His remark must be an aside, like line 62, although not so marked. It would be fanciful to take it, otherwise, that he is protecting himself here by speaking publicly against his brother. Nor, to escape the dilemma, can the line be assigned to Mortimer as Dyce (preceded by Oxberry) attempted.

45.1 *and the Maior of* Bristow]   Alone among editors Dyce queries this stage-direction and points out, correctly, that the conduct of the scene with the Mayor as a mute is odd since at some point he should have been singled out for royal attention. It may be that the person who marked the manuscript for copying out as a prompt-book, reading the references to the Mayor immediately preceding in line 40 and then in line 47, thought that his presence was required and added him. On the other hand, although these references are not entirely superfluous since they indicate the loyalty of the town and countryside to the Queen, nevertheless they probably do serve to justify an original Marlowe direction that would bring in the Mayor, with his chain, as an approving witness. Since Rice ap Howel is the moving agent, in full control by royal authority (in Holinshed), the Mayor may be treated as a mute along with the citizens, and Rice speak for them all.

62 Unhappie]   Q1–4 'Unhappies' for *Unhappy is* is not especially idiomatic. Possibly the possessive '*Englands*' later in the line contaminated 'Unhappie'.

IV.vii

91–2 these, . . . And these]   Editors through Robinson excised 'And these' in line 92, or with Dyce and Cunningham 'and these' in line 91. No difficulty exists in these lines as printed in Q1. In line 91 Edward indicates first Spencer and Baldock and then the monks (or *vice versa*), and then in line 92 distinguishes Spencer and Baldock as doomed to execution.

V.i

47 Vine]   Although Q1–4 'Vines' is not impossible, given the decoration of Edward's crown, the use of the singular 'royall vine' at III.i.163 suggests that the plural here is in error. The crux can scarcely be decided by speculating about Marlowe's unlikely knowledge that in Edward's day the leaves on the crown were strawberry leaves.

V.ii

36 [*Exit* Winchester.]] The Bishop's exit, like his entrance, is unmarked and the cause of some difficulty. As the text now stands, the Messenger's letter from Kenilworth must represent Leicester's report of Edward's resignation, but this letter is not mentioned in the dialogue except as the Bishop anticipates its contents in line 28 and refers to it in line 30 with the information about the arrival of Berkeley. He then adds the curious information about the rumor of Kent's plot although, in fact, this does not seem to be contrived until later in lines 119–21 as the result of the altercation about his influence on the young prince. This being so, it is idle to worry that the Bishop scarcely had the opportunity to observe the kind treatment of Edward by Berkeley. Thus no need exists to assign lines 34–5 to Mortimer, as the text now stands, as did the shrewd editor of Chappell's edition, with the Bishop's exit placed after 'no more but so' of line 33. (However, the Chappell editor's rationalizing of the Queen's 'Thankes gentle *Winchester*' in line 27 is interesting: he has Winchester himself deliver the letter instead of the Messenger.) Good as is 'no more but so' as an exit line, the information about Berkeley's treatment of Edward could not possibly have been in Leicester's letter, and thus is knowledge not otherwise available to Mortimer so long as we assume the letter to be Leicester's as the Bishop's words imply. Tucker Brooke, following Dyce, places the entrance of the Bishop just before the Queen's thanks in line 27; but whereas Dyce and later editors mark his exit after line 37, Tucker Brooke omits a direction and Briggs argues for the presence of the Bishop during the rest of the scene. The failure of Q1 to mark the Bishop's exit is not surprising in view of its parallel failure to indicate his entrance. But that he would remain and thus be privy to the scene with Gurney and Maltravers has never been accepted except by Briggs (and presumably by Tucker Brooke). As the text stands, whether he leaves at line 36 or line 37 is scarcely to be determined. The Queen's 'Then let some other be his guardian' in line 36 is in response to the Bishop but not seemingly an order to him, and it appears to be addressed to Mortimer while the Bishop is withdrawing. Certainly, in line 37 Mortimer's 'Let me alone' is his direct answer to the Queen. An exit after line 37 and 'here is the privie seale' brings in question whether the seal is given to the Bishop (for what purpose?) or is instead relative to the order Mortimer proposes to issue to Gurney and Maltravers. On the whole, an abrupt exit between lines 36 and 37 seems to be a reasonable enough compromise. It will be remarked, however, that the exit is indeed abrupt and that the failure of Q1 to provide directions for the Bishop is suspicious. Instead of the speculation that some text has been dropped, the present editor is of the opinion that the scene has undergone an incomplete revision, not necessarily by Marlowe. Although at first sight the prior announcement of Kent's plot seems related to the disturbance of the text, the evidence of lines 57–61 demonstrates that it must have been there from the start. In the present editor's view the scene originally did not contain the Bishop but had only the arrival of the Messenger. If this be so, line 27 is an addition at least in part, and line 28, now assigned to the Bishop, was Mortimer's announcement to the Queen of the contents of the letter. If then the letter were not from Leicester (as implied by the Bishop's statement in line 30 of its official source) but instead from one of Mortimer's spies, lines 30–5 in their present form or somewhat like it would have been Mortimer's reading aloud from the letter. In this hypothetical reconstruction Mortimer and Isabella are alone, receive the letter and comment on it, and formulate the plan to

remove Berkeley. One could guess that in preparation for the staging it was felt desirable to show the crown being brought back to London, and thus the Bishop's part of the scene was invented chiefly by transfer of lines from Mortimer to him, with some possible recasting. Without the Bishop the scene reads smoothly; with him there is a curious awkwardness.

PRESS-VARIANTS IN Q1

[Drawn from the Malone Society reprint prepared by W. W. Greg.]

SHEET H (*outer forme*)

Corrected: Zurich
Uncorrected: Cassell

Sig. H1
    IV.ii.62 Fraunce] Fraunce,

Sig. H2ᵛ
    IV.iv.19 him] him,

Sig. H3
    IV.v.7 honor] honors
    IV.vi.2 Edward,] Edward
         7 head] head.
         8 God,] God

Sig. H4ᵛ
    IV.vii.4 inuaſion] inuaſion,

EMENDATIONS OF ACCIDENTALS

[NOTE: In the copy-text Q1 names of countries and of cities are invariably in roman, a practice generally followed in Q2–4. Personal names like *Gaveston* and *Spencer* or *Edward* are with only a few exceptions italicized. Titles, like *Warwick* or *Lancaster* are ordinarily printed in roman but occasionally italicized in Q2–4. In this edition all names of countries and cities are silently italicized, as are all personal names and titles. Special notice is given, however, when Q1 breaks its custom and italicizes words that it ordinarily prints in roman.]

I.i

0.1 Gaveston] *Gavestone* Q1–4
1–2 *Roman* in Q1–4
2 *friend.*] Q2; ~ ∧ Q1
11 *Elizium*] Elizium Q1–4
11 soule.] ~ , Q1–4
19 king.] ~ , Q1–4
23.1 *Enter...men.*] Q1–4 *place as line* 24.1
27 *et seq. man*] *omit* Q1–4
37 *3. poore man.*] *Sold.* Q1–4
60 hay.] ~ , Q1–4
70 die.] ~ , Q1–4
71 majestie,] Q3; ~ . Q1–2
74 *et seq. Lancaster*] Lancaster Q1, 2–4±
77 this?—— In] ~ ? ∧ in Q1–4
81 *Mortimer,*] Q4; ~ ∧ Q1–3
82 *et. seq. Mortimer.*] *Mortimer ju.* Q1–4±
90 *Mort*∧] ~ . Q1–4
93 thereat,] ~ ∧ Q1–4
95 stiffe.] ~ , Q1–4
100–1 you,...*Gaveston:*] ~ :...~ , Q1–4

103 *Darbie...Leicester*] roman in Q1–4
105 realme.] ~ , Q1–4
116 face.] Q3; ~ , Q1–2
119 heads?] ~ . Q1–4
122 speake.] ~ , Q1–4
129 friends.] Q3; ~ , Q1–2
142 Q1–4 *line:* kneele, | Knowest
143 *Gaveston.*] ~ , Q1–4
148 friend.] ~ , Q1–4
156 *et seq. Cornewall*] Cornewall Q1, 2–4±
156 *et seq. Man*] Man Q1–4
158 *et seq. Kent.*] *Throughout the play* Kent's *speech-prefixes are forms of* Edmund
160 words:] Q3; ~ , Q1–2
162 hart.] ~ , Q1–4
167 treasurie:]~ , Q1; ~ . Q2–4
175 *et seq. Coventrie*] Coventrie Q1, 2–4±
190 *et seq. Rome*] Rome Q1–4
198 I,] Q3; ~ ∧ Q1–2
203 goods:] Q3; ~ , Q1–2
207 beseeme] Q2; be seeme Q1

I.ii

7 sure,] ~ ∧| Q1–4
10 *et seq. Warwicke*] Warwicke Q1, 2–4±
17 Cornewall∧ now,] ~ , ~ ∧ Q1–3; ~ ∧ ~ ∧ Q4
19 looke.] ~ , Q1–4
33 *et seq. Canterburies*] Canterburies

Q1–4
38 away,] ~ ∧ Q1–4
50 *Gaveston.*] ~ , Q1–4
54 *Gaveston*] Q2; Gaveston Q1
68 speake.]~ , Q1–4
76 Content.] ~ : Q1–4

I.iii

1 *Edmund,...Lancaster*₍] ~ ₍...~ ,   3 *Mortimers,*] ~ ₍ Q1–4
Q1–4

I.iv

4 Q1–4 *line*: lorde, | I
27 king——] Q4; ~ . Q1–3
30 peasant,] Q3; ~ ₍ Q1–2, 4
34 *et seq. Kent*] Q2±; Kent Q1, 2–4±
37 *Warwicke...Lancaster*] Q1–4 *italic*
40 done, our] done, | our Q1–4
47 peeres?] ~ , Q1–4
50 *Inde*] Inde Q1–4
69 *Wales*:] Wales, Q1–4
76 him, whome] him, | whome Q1–4
85 content.] ~ , Q1–4
108 false.] ~ , Q1–4
125 *et seq. Ireland*] Ireland Q1, 2–4±
133–4 greater,...part.] ~ ....~ , Q1–
4
135 *Gaveston,*] Q4; ~ ₍ Q1–3
147 Queene——] ~ , Q1–4
155 exilde.] ~ , Q1–4
181 *Gaveston.*] ~ , Q1–4
204 Madam!] ~ , Q1–4
230 Lords,] ~ ₍ Q1–4
231 Will] Q4; will Q1–3
238 so.] ~ , Q1–4
243 Nay,] ~ ₍ Q1–4
245 him,] ~ ? Q1–4
276 topflag] *possibly* top flag in Q1;

topflag Q2–3; top-flag Q4
281 king.] ~ , Q1–4
288–9 *Gaveston,...hath.*] ~ ....~ ,
Q1–4
298 forlorne.] ~ , Q1–4
302 me.]~ , Q1–4
319 these?] ~ ₍ Q1; ~ . Q2–4
321 *Mortimer?*] ~ . Q1–4
322 *Gaveston,...Lord,*] ~ ₍...~ ₍
Q1–4
336 first.] ~ , Q1–4
342 smile.] ~ , Q1–4
345 *Warwick*₍] Q4; ~ , Q1–3
347 imbrotherie.] ~ , Q1–4
358 *et seq. England*] England Q1–4
359 *Chirke*] Q2; Chirke Q1
368 light.] ~ , Q1–4
379 *et seq. Glosters*] Glosters Q1–4
381 him,] Q2; ~ . Q1
386 *et seq. Scotland*] Scotland Q1–4
386 here.] Q2; ~ , Q1
390 will.] Q3; ~ , Q1–2
396 *Octavius*] Q3; *Octavis* Q1–2
411 appearde.] Q2; ~ , Q1
415 crowne.] ~ , Q1–4

II.i

1–2 *One line in* Q1–4
5 enemies.] ~ , Q1–4
41 men.] ~ , Q1–4
57 *Neece.*] Q1–4 *speech-prefix in this
scene is Lady.*
58 home.] ~ , Q1–4

60 thou,] ~ ₍ Q1–4
61 me.] ~ , Q1–4
62, 64 *Roman in* Q1–4
63 Lord.] ~ , Q1–4
73.1 *Exit.*] Q1–4 *place in line 72*

II.ii

3 *et seq. this scene Lancaster*] *italic*
Q1–4
9 *et seq. Normandie*] Normandie Q1–4
10 trifle] Q2; trifle Q1
22 Mortimers.] Q3; ~ , Q1–2

37 *Gaveston.*] ~ , Q1–4
42 *Britanie*] Britanie Q1–4
50–1 *One line in* Q1–4
51 *Tinmouth*] Tinmouth Q1–4
65 yes:] ~ ₍ Q1–3; ~ , Q4

67 *Man*] man Q1–3; Man Q4
69 Brother,] ~ ₄ Q1–4
94 *Warwicke*] *italic* Q1–4
97 down.] ~ , Q1–4
117 pound.] ~ , Q1–4
123 *Newcastell*] Newcastell Q1–4
137 in,] ~ ₄ Q1–4
138 not?] Q4; ~ . Q1–3
145 else——] ~ . Q1, 4; ~ ? Q2–3
152 you.] ~ , Q1–4
166 *Yorke*] Yorke Q1–4
190–5 *Roman in* Q1–4

197 more.] ~ , Q1–4
219–20 *One line in* Q1–4
219 Away: ~ ₄ Q1–4
223 begirt] Q1 *perhaps* be girt; Q2–4
  begirt
223 round?] Q4; ~ , Q1–3
224.1 *three Ladies*] Q4; *Ladies 3* Q1–3
228 *Neece.*] Q1–4 *speech-prefix in this
  scene is* Lady.
242 Q1–4 *line*: borne? | What
248–9 *One line in* Q1–4

II.iii

17 king.] ~ , Q1–4

II.iv

0.1 King] Q3; king Q1–2
5 *et seq. Scarborough*] Scarborough
  Q1–4
15 you.] ~ , Q1–4

21.1 *Barons,*] ~ ₄ Q1–4
32 *Gaveston.*] ~ , Q1–4
69.1 *Exit.*] *Exeunt.* Q1–4

II.v

14–16 Q1–4: Monster...strumpet |
  Traind...warres, | So...knights,
20–2 Q1–4 *line*: Go...hence, | For...
  off: | Gaveston...turne: | It...
  cause,
23 execute₄] Q3; ~ , Q1–2
24 bough.] ~ : Q1–4
25 Lord!] ~ . Q1–4
34–5 *One line in* Q1–4
42 not.] ~ , Q1–4
49–50 Q1–4 *line*: Shalt...graunt? |
  Souldiers...him:
60–1 Q1–4 *line*: When...wot, | He
  ...remits
60 When,] ~ ₄ Q1–4
63 seaze] Q2; zease Q1

81 *Arundell*] Q2; Arundell Q1
85 had-I-wist] Q4; had-Iwist Q1; had-
  I wist Q2–3
91 *Mortimer?*] ~ . Q1–4
92 *Warwick?*] Q4; ~ . Q1–3
93 Q1–4 *line*: pleasures, | I
97 *Penbrooke*] Q4; Penbrooke Q1–3
98 honor. Sound,] ~ , sound₄ Q1–3;
  ~ ₄ ~ ₄ Q4
100 hence,...way₄] Q4; ~ ₄...~ ,
  Q1–2; ~ ,...~ , Q3
101 along.] ~ , Q1–4
105 adamant,...power₄] ~ ₄...~ ,
  Q1–4
106 lord. Come] ~ , come Q1–4
110.1 Penbrookis] Pen. Q1–4

II.vi

4–5 life,...blisse! And] ~ !...~ ,
  and Q1–4
10 follow.] ~ , Q1–4

13 well.] ~ , Q1–4
17.1 Warwicke] Q2; Warwike Q1
18 *James.*] *omit* Q1–4

III.i

2 *Gaveston.*] ∼ , Q 1–4
10 *Edward,*] Q 3; ∼ ‸ Q 1–2
16–17 magnanimitie,...name,] Q 4;
    ∼ ?...∼ ? Q 1–3
19 nobilitie.] ∼ , Q 1–2
37 four hundred] Q 4; *400* Q 1–3
43 *Spencer.*] *Spencer filius.* Q 1–4
45 life,] ∼ ‸ Q 1–4
46 againe.] Q 3; ∼ , Q 1–2
49 *et seq. Wilshire*] Wilshire Q 1–4
56 *Spencer*] Q 2; *Spenser* Q 1
58.1 Levune] Q 1–4 *s.d. and speech-
    prefixes* Lewne
64 hands.] ∼ , Q 1–4
67 againe.] ∼ , Q 1–4
71 *Fraunce.*] ∼ , Q 1–4
83 hence.] ∼ , Q 1–4
91 death?] ∼ , Q 1–4
105 *Lancaster*] *italic in* Q 1–4
132 lives,] ∼ ‸ Q 1–4
133–4 towers:...*Mortimer,*] ∼ ,...∼ :
    Q 1–4
134 *Warwicke*] *italic in* Q 1–4
141–2 progenie,...*Gaveston:*] ∼ :...
    ∼ , Q 1–4
151, 156 *Herald.*] *Messen.* Q 1–4

173 gon.] ∼ , Q 1–4
180 heeles.] ∼ , Q 1–4
184.2 King] Q 2; king Q 1
189, 194, 204 *Spencer.*] *Spen. son.* Q 1–4
191, 206 *Spencer pater.*] *Spen. fa.* Q 1–4
195–6, 197–8 *One line in* Q 1–4
195, 204 *Lancaster*] *italic in* Q 1–4
199, 237 *Warwicks*] *italic in* Q 1–4
205 thus?] Q 4; ∼ . Q 1–3
207 not,] ∼ ‸ Q 1–4
213 companie?] ∼ . Q 1–4
218–19 Q 1–4 *line:* Alarum...England,
    | And...right.
219, 220 *George*] George Q 1–4
222 cause,] ∼ ‸ Q 1–4
223 pride:] ∼ , Q 1–4
232 presence.] ∼ , Q 1–4
238 armes?] ∼ , Q 1–4
240 rest.] Q 2; ∼ ? Q 1
245 them:] ∼ ‸ Q 1–4
247–8, 254–5 *One line in* Q 1–4
257 heaven?] ∼ , Q 1–4
261.2 *et seq.* Levune] Lewne *or* Lewen
    Q 1–4
280 *Fraunce*‸ amaine,] ∼ , ∼ ‸ Q 1–4

IV.i

7 is.] ∼ , Q 1–4
9–11 Q 1–4 *line:* And...stay | Thy...

device.
13–14 *One line in* Q 1–4

IV.ii

5 *Fraunce.*] ∼ , Q 1–4
10 farre. Unkinde] ∼ , unkinde Q 1–4
12 steps?] Q 4; ∼ . Q 1–3
17–18 *Henolt,*...sonne?] Q 4; ∼ ?...
    ∼ , Q 1–3
20 equallie?] Q 4; ∼ . Q 1–3
21 likes.] ∼ , Q 1–4
27–8 wrongs,...joye?]   ∼ ?...∼ ,
    Q 1–4
31 will.] ∼ , Q 1–4

36 alive?] ∼ , Q 1–4
47 *le Grand*] le Grand Q 1–4
54 grace,...*England*‸] ∼ ‸...∼ , Q 1–
    4
64 *Henolt:*] ∼ , Q 1–4
66 base.] ∼ , Q 1–4
69 sonne] Q 2; soune Q 1
76 gentleman,] ∼ ‸ Q 1–4
77 hold.] ∼ , Q 1–4
81 lord,] ∼ ‸ Q 1–4

IV.iii

3 uncontrould.] ~ , Q1–4
5 *Spencer.*] Q1–4 *speech-prefix in this scene is* Spen. ju.
14 *Fraunce. Gloster,* I trowe‿] ~ , ~ ‿ ~ ~ , Q1–4
16 *Isabella*] Isabell Q1–4

26, 37 *Levune*] Lewne Q1–4
32 *Flaunders*] Flaunders Q1–4
42 route.] ~ , Q1–4
44 carre:] ~ , Q1–4
49 ils.] Q4; ~ , Q1–3
50 *et seq. Bristow*] Bristow Q1–4

IV.iv

3 *Belgia*] Belgia Q1–4
5 knit,...gleave‿] Q3; ~ ‿...~ , Q1–2
6 men‿] Q4; ~ , Q1–2; ~ : Q3

13–14 *One line in* Q1–4
14 thou——] ~ . Q1–4
18 armed] Q2; armde Q1

IV.vi

1 late.] ~ , Q1–4
2 *Edward*] Q2; Edward Q1
11 *Edmund*] Q2; Edmund Q1
16 *Longshankes*] Longshankes Q1–4
22 you.] ~ , Q1–4
37 of.] Q4; ~ , Q1–3

45.1 ap] Q2; up Q1
46 sonne.] ~ , Q1–4
59 all:——] ~ : ‿ Q1–4
73 prates. You] ~ , you Q1–4
73 *Howell*] Q3; howell Q1–2
76 runnagates.] ~ , Q1–4

IV.vii

11 state.] Q4; ~ , Q1–3
13 was,] Q3; ~ ‿ Q1–2, 4
23 pursue,] Q3; ~ ‿ Q1–2
26–7 *Prose in* Q1–4
44 *Spencer.*] Spen. son. Q1–4
45.1 ap] Q2; up Q1
47 enough:] ~ , Q1–4
55 *et seq. Leister*] Q2; Leister Q1, 2–4 ±

68, 74, 100 *Spencer.*] Spen. ju. Q1–4
72–3 *One line in* Q1–4
96 must.] ~ , Q1–4
101 more!] ~ , Q1–4
113–15 Q1–4 *line:* Come...appointed | You...England. | Will...away?
114 appointed.] Q3; ~ ‿ Q1–2
117 else?] Q4; ~ , Q1; ~ ‿ Q2–3

V.i

0.1 King] Q2; king Q1
4 necessitie] Q2; neceissitie Q1
9 kings:] ~ , Q1–4
70 crowne.] Q3; ~ , Q1; ~ ‿ Q2
73 life.] ~ , Q1–4
97 crowne.] ~ , Q1–4
99 crime.] ~ , Q1–4
112 lorde——] ~ . Q1–4
113–14 Q1–4 *line:* Call...lorde, | Away...me, | Greefe...lunatick,

113 sight:] ~ , Q1–4
114 lunatick.] ~ , Q1–4
117 imbrasements:] Q3; ~ , Q1–2
120 bloud.] ~ , Q1–4
140 hart.] ~ , Q1–4
153 once.] ~ , Q1–4
154 *Leister*] Leicester Q1–4
155 *Leister.*] Leist. Q1 *cw;* Leicester Q1–4 *text*

V.ii

4 captivitie.] ~ , Q1–4
9 himselfe.] Q3; ~ , Q1–2
11 with all] Q4; withall Q1–3
23 Letters] *Mor. ju.* Letters Q1–4
26 greefe.] ~ , Q1–4
27 *Winchester*:] Winchester, Q1–4
28 *Bishop.*] Winchester. Q1–4
33 so.] ~ , Q1–4
35 *Leicester*] Q3; Leicester Q1–2
38 there?] ~ , Q1–4

38 *Matrevis.*] ~ , Q1–4
46–7 *One line in* Q1–4
46 Inough.] ~ ∧ Q1–4
61 Bartley] *Bartley* Q1–4
74 Queene.] ~ , Q1–4
75 *et seq. Kent*] Kent Q1, 2–4±
81 grace?] Q3; ~ . Q1; ~ , Q2
89 prince?] ~ . Q1–4
96 I,] ~ ∧ Q1–4
105 prince.] ~ , Q1–4

V.iii

0.1 King] Q2; *king* Q1
1 friends.] ~ , Q1–4
27 given.] ~ , Q1–4
33 thus?...vaine.] ~ ,...~ ? Q1–4
    (~ ∧...~ ? Q2)
34 strength,] Q4; ~ . Q1–3

40 king.] ~ , Q1–4
45 tush,] Q3; ~ ∧ Q1–2
46 enmitie.] ~ , Q1–4
55 traitors,] ~ ∧ Q1–4
63–4 Q1–4 *line*: O...lords | Keepe
    ...prison!

V.iv

5 cunninglie.] ~ , Q1–4
21–2 *One line in* Q1–4
30 man.] ~ , Q1–4
40 spide:] ~ , Q1–4
44 No?] Q2; ~ . Q1
45–6 *One line in* Q1–4
54 *Aristarchus*] Q2 (*Aristarcus*); *Aris-
    torchus* Q1
55 boye.] ~ , Q1–4

59 puretaine] Q3; paretaine Q1–2
68 controwle?] ~ , Q1–4
69 *nocere.*] ~ , Q1–4
71 Queene.] ~ , Q1–4
78 him!] ~ ? Q1–3; ~ . Q4
90 head?] ~ , Q1–4
101 realmes.] Q3; ~ , Q1–2
112 death.] ~ , Q1–4

V.v

19 token?...king.] ~ ,...~ ? Q1–4
20 I,] Q3; ~ ∧ Q1–2
25 else? Heere] ~ , heere Q1–4
34 all?] ~ . Q1–4
35 so:] ~ ∧ Q1–4
38–9 *One line in* Q1–4
40 shalbe.] ~ , Q1–4
46 lorde?] ~ , Q1–4
52 already?] ~ , Q1–4
55 tale.] Q3; ~ , Q1–2

65 not.] ~ , Q1–4
72 while.] Q3; ~ , Q1–2
84 this.] ~ , Q1–4
90 greefe:] ~ , Q1–4
94 closd.] ~ , Q1–4
96 againe.] ~ , Q1–4
107 life. *Matrevis* come.] ~ , ~ ~ ,
    Q1–4
117 rewarde.] Q4; ~ , Q1–3
119–20 *One line in* Q1–4

V.vi

7 *Gurney*,...lord,] Q4; ~ ∧...~ ∧
    Q1–2; ~ ,...~ ∧ Q3
21 peeres.] ~ , Q1–4
23.1 King] Q2; *king* Q1
40 murdered] Q2 (murthered); mur-
    deredd Q1
61 downe:] ~ , Q1–4
63 fall?] Q4; ~ , Q1–3

73 I,] ~ ∧ Q1–4
73 madam,] Q4; ~ ∧ Q1–3
80 thereof.] ~ , Q1–4
87 lord,] ~ ? Q1–4
88 grave?] Q4; ~ . Q1–3
97 treacherie!] ~ ? Q1–3; ~ . Q4
98 moorne,] ~ ∧ Q1–4

HISTORICAL COLLATION

[NOTE: The following editions are herein collated: Q1 (1594); Q2 (1598); Q3 (1612); Q4 (1622); Dd¹ (*Old Plays*, 1744); Dd² (*Old Plays*, 1780); S (*Ancient British Drama*, 1810); Ch (*Edward the Second*, sold by J. Chappell, Jr, 1818); Ox (*Edward* the Second, ed. William Oxberry, 1818); Dd³ (*Old Plays*, ed. J. P. Collier, 1825); R (*Works*, ed. Robinson, 1826); D¹ (*Works*, ed. Dyce, 1850); D² (*Works*, ed. Dyce, 1858); C (*Works*, ed. Cunningham, 1870); B (*Works*, ed. Bullen, 1885); TB (*Works*, ed. Tucker Brooke, 1910); Bgs (*Edward the Second*, ed. Briggs, 1914); M (*Edward the Second*, ed. Charlton and Waller, 1933); K (*Plays*, ed. Kirschbaum, 1962); Ri (*Plays*, ed. Ribner, 1963); Gl (*Edward the Second*, ed. Gill, 1967). Reference is also made to Q2 MS, transcript in the Dyce copy of Q2; Br MS: Broughton's annotations in the BM copy of Robinson; Coll MS: Collier's annotations in the BM copy of Dyce¹; and Gg: *Edward the Second*, Malone Society Reprints, prepared by W. W. Greg.]

I.i

0.1 *on*] of Q2 MS
6 these these] these Q2 MS
7 swum] swam Dd¹, Ox, R
9 thy] thine Q2–4, Q2 MS, Dd¹–B, K
10 my] mine Ch, Dd³
14 die] lie S–C
19 knee] knees Q4
20 As] Its Q2 MS
20 that] they Dd¹–R, C
21 Rakt] Bakt Q2 MS
22 *Tanti*] *tantum* Q2 MS
22 fawne] fanne Q1–4, Dd¹⁻², S, Ch, Dd³, Bgs, Gl
25 *Poore men.*] *1st Poor Man.* Ch
25 Such] Poor men, such K
25 your] your your Q2
28 horses] horse Q2–4, Dd¹–B
31 time] *omit* Q2 MS
40 should] would R, C, B, K
40 Porpintine] Porcupine O2–4, Dd¹+ (–Bgs)
41 dart] eate Q2 MS
43 these] them Q2 MS
49 We] I Q2 MS
49 *Exeunt.*] exit 3 Q2 MS
54 is] are Q2 MS, Dd¹–R, C
58 *Sylvian*] Sylvan Q2 MS, Dd²+ (–B, Bgs)

59 grazing] gasing Q2 MS
60 Goate] Goates Q2 MS
60 an] the Q2–4, Dd¹–B
61 Sometime] Sometimes Dd¹–R, C
65 which] as Q2 MS
66 hard] *omit* Q2 MS
70 and] shall Dd¹–C
71–2 majestie, | My lord. Heere comes] ~ . | My lord, heere comes Q1–2; ~ , | My Lord, here comes Q3–4; majesty. | Here comes Dd¹; majesty. | Here come Ox; majesty. | My lord here comes Dd²⁻³; majesty. | My lord here come S; majesty. | But soft; here come Ch, Br MS; majesty. | By'r lord ! here comes R, C; majesty. | Here come my lord D, B; majesty. My lord ! Here comes M, K, Ri
72 and] here and B
72 the nobles] nobles Dd¹, Ch, Ox
83 to] unto Dd¹–R, C
94 plane] plaine Q2–4, Dd¹⁻², S, Dd³
107 *Kent.*] *Edm.* Q1–3; *Ed.* Q4; *Edward.* Dd¹–B (–D)
107 me mute] me n Q2
110 *Percie*] *Peirce* Q2
118 preach] perch Dd¹, Dd³ (*qy*)

125 the] this Ch
128 love] leave D, C
129 *Gaveston*] *Lancaster* Ch, Ox, R, D, C
135 Am] And Dd², S, Dd³
140 kis] nay, kiss Ch
144 of] for Q2, Dd¹, S; for of O3-4, D; by Ox
152 orewhelme] overwhelme Q2-3
152 my] the Ch
154 thee] the Q2
163 be envied] should'st be envied Ch;

envied be Ox
168 seale] seals C
170 What so] Whate'er Ch
173 streete] streets Ch
180 these] those Ch
189 violent] valiant S
193 No] Well Ch
200 to] unto Coll MS
201 true, true] Do, do Dd¹-R; Prut, prut D (*qy*); Tut, tut Coll MS
207 may] may best Q3-4, Dd²-R, C, B, K

I.ii

20 dooth] do Ch; To Dd³ (*qy*), Coll MS
25 exceptions] exception Ch
27 Ah] Ay Dd¹, Ox, R, C
27, 34 bewraies] betrays Ch
29 Weele] We'd Ch, R, D, C, B, TB; Weeld Gg (*qy*)
36 him, next_∧] ~ _∧ ~ , Q1-4

46 *et seq.* whether] whither Q4, Dd¹+ (−Bgs)
51 cheekes] cheek Ox, R, C, B
62 weele] we will Coll MS, D², C, B
62 *Gaveston*] that Gaveston Ch, Br MS
65 by] with Q2-4, Dd¹-B
77 *Bishop.*] omit Q-4, Dd¹, Ox, TB
83 I] Ah Dd²-³

I.iii

0.1 *and the earle of* Kent] *omit* Ox

I.iv

9 we] and we C, B
20, 21 on] upon Ch, Dd³ (*qy*), Coll MS
36 in] on Ox, R
41 upstart] upstart's Ch, D
42 stops] stop Ch
43 my] good my Ch
47 overdaring] overbearing B
49 fleete] float Ch
61 lords] lord Q2, Ch
62 due] *omit* Ch
65 you] ye Q3-4
66 our] the C, B
80 be] are Q3-4, Ox, R, C
80 noble] nobly Ch
98 For] With Dd¹, Ox, R, D, C
101 The] Thy Dd¹-R
102 make] may Q1-4, Dd², S, Ch, Dd³, Bgs, M, K, Ri, Gl

103 raisd] raise Dd¹-², Ox, Dd³, R; rise S, Ch, C
108 were it] were it were it Q3-4, Dd², S, Dd³
111 of] on Dd¹, Ox, R
133 makes] make Ch
136 lord,] ~ _∧ Q1-4, Bgs, K, Ri; love_∧ Dd¹-³, S, Ch, D, C
143.1 *Queen* Isabell] *Edmund and Queen Isabell* Q1-4, Dd¹-², S, Ox, Dd³, R, C
147 with] on Ox
161 you] thou Ox
161 rob] robs S; robb'st Ox
168 repeald] recalled Ch
172 *Circes*] Circe Dd¹+ (−TB, Bgs, K)
173 at] that Q3-4, Ox, R, C
180 doted *Jove*] Jove doated Ch

182–5 *Omit* Ch, Ox
187 sister] daughter Dd³ (*qy*)
189 ill intreated] ill-treated Dd², S, Ox, Dd³, R; sore ill-treated Ch
190 injures] injuries Q2, B
198 ye] you D¹
201 unto] upon C, B
201, 204, 227, 241 repeale] recall Ch
205 shipwrack] shipwrackt Q2–4, Dd¹–B
211 tendrest] honourest Ch
212 unto these] upon the C
213 ye] you Q2–4, Dd¹–B
214 he] *omit* Q2–4, Dd¹, Ox, R–B, K
234 No?] ~ , Q1–4, Dd¹⁻², Ox, Dd³, R, TB
237 I] ay Dd¹
246 true] good Ch
249 be true] agree Ch
267 murtherer] murther Q3–4
268 that] the Ch
282 shall we] we shall Ox, R, C, B, M, K
282 of] on Q3–4, Dd¹–R
286 us downe] down us Ch
293 *Penbrooke* and I] I and Pembroke Ch
300 brought] ta'en Ch

301 new] news Q3–4; now Ch
303 lov'd] love B
322, 323 repeald] recalled Ch
328 thy] my Q3–4
332 treasurie] treasure Dd¹–R
342 soveraignes] soveraigne Q1–2
352 *Penbrooke* wil] will Pembroke Ch
357 so] all Q3–4
360 warre] wars Ch
361 Deserves] Deserve Dd¹–C
361 nor] or Ch
378 wot] wote Q2–3; wrote Q4
379 our] your Ch
382 the] *omit* Q3–4
393 *Hercules*ᴧ] *Hector*, Q1–4, Dd¹, K
393 for] did for Q4, Ox; for his Dd¹⁻², S, Dd³, R, C, B
393 wept] weepe Q4, Ox
405 it] *omit* Dd¹–R
405–6 realme,...paie.] ~ ,...~ , Q1–2; ~ ....~ , Dd¹–R, C, Ri
410 make] makes Q4
416 other] others Q3–4, Dd¹–C, K, Ri
418 jest] jet S, Ch
419 that] *omit* C, B
419 impatient] so impatient Ch

II.i

18 repeald] recalled Ch
30 she] I Ch
44 formall] *omit* Q3–4
45 of] as Q4
47 exceptions] exception Ch
48 the] their Ch

52 these] those Ch
52 pedants] pendants Q1
54 *quandoquidem*] *quando quidem* Q4
65 But rest] I put Dd¹
65 rest] *omit* Q2; stay Q3–4, Dd²–B, K
73 pale] -pail Dd¹, S

II.ii

19 unto] into C, B
23 a] *omit* Q2, Dd¹
29 *Edward.*] *Kent.* D–B
39 ye] you Q4
40 gesses] gresses Q1–4, Dd¹⁻², S (*i.e.,* jesses], Dd³, R
51 *Tinmouth*] Chester Ch
56 sure] fare Q4, Dd¹–B
60 left] *omit* Ox
72 Aye] Ah Dd¹–R, C

81 here.] here King: Q1–4, Dd¹–B, Bgs (−D²)
82 *Edward.*] *omit* Q1–4, Dd¹–D¹, C
86 were] where Ch
88 abie] abide Q2–4, Dd¹–B, K
114 fares] fare Dd², S, Ch, Dd³, R, D, C
117 pound] pounds Ch, Ox
133 lordships] lordship Ox
142 unkles] uncle is Dd¹–Dd³
144 wars, you] wars and you Ch

148 gather] gather gold Ch
152 Would] 'Twoul'd Q3–4, D, C, B, K; Could Dd¹–R
154 haunted] taunted Ox, R
159 treasure] treasurie Q3–4, Ox, R, D, C, B, K
160 hath] break Dd¹–B
165 lives] live Dd¹⁻², S, Ch, Dd³
165 within] with Dd³
166 made] make Dd¹–C
167 drave] draw Dd¹–R; drive D, C, B
175 makes] make Dd²–B, K (−Ox)
177 againe] against Q3–4, Dd¹–R, C
179 borderers] brothers Dd¹
179 their] the Q1
182 banner] banners Q4, R, C
184 not] nor Dd²
188 thereof] therefore Q3–4
193 *weeneth*] weened Dd¹, Ch, Ox, R
198 ye] you Q4, Ox, D
198 as] if Q4, Ox, R, C
200 for] with Q4, Ox, R
202 power is] power's so Ch
208 to] for Ox, R, C
212 my] *omit* Dd¹
217 though] that Dd¹–R
217 scorne] scorn'st] Ch
220 hast] has Ox, R, C, B, K
221 *Tinmoth*] Chester Ch
224 comes] cometh Dd¹–B, K (−D)
224 thats] that is D
226 him] them Dd¹–R, C; 'em D, B, TB, Bgs, Ri; hem Gg (*qy*)
230 forgot] had forgot R, C
242 thine armes] thy name and arms Ch
244 fetcht] fetch Q2–4, Dd¹–B, K
246 shalt] shall B, K
252 me,...sake‚] ~ ‸...~ , Q3–4; ~ ‸...~ ; Ch, Ox, D, K
254 titles] title Ch

II.iii

2 with] *omit* Ch
3 and] for Ch
9 shalbe] should be Q4
24 this] thes TB; these M
24 castell] castle's Dd¹–B, K
25 raise] rouse Coll MS
27 to] *omit* Q2–3

II.iv

15 Heavens] Heaven Ch, Ox, R, C, B, K
41 is] are Dd¹–R, C
42 this] thus Dd¹–B, K
45 and] *omit* Q4, Dd¹–B
63 praiers] prayer Q2–4, Dd¹–B

II.v

2 larums] alarms Dd¹, Ox
5 your] you Q2
6 king] kind Dd³
7 see] these Q2
15 traind] trainest Ch
18 King] Kind Q1, TB, Bgs, M, K, Gl
24 at] upon Dd¹⁻², S, Dd³; on Ch
25 Lord] lords Dd¹–R, C, B, K
26 have] heave Ch
35 that] *omit* D (*qy*), C
36 yet but] but that Dd¹–R, C
42 No] Nay Ch
47 Will not...hopes?] Will these delays beget me any hopes? Dd¹–R; Will now these short delays...D
48 it] my Ch
55 Lord] lords Dd², S, Ch, Dd³, R, C, B, K
58 in] on Dd¹–R, D¹, C
61 that] that hath Q3–4
61 realme] his realm Dd¹–B, K
61 realme remits] Realme-remits Q3–4
63 seaze] zease Q1, Bgs; sees C, M, Ri
65 in keepe] *omit* Dd¹

71 that] this Dd¹–R, C
73 thy mates] mates Q2–4, D, C, B, K
74 My] *omit* Ch
79 mine] my Q3–4
83 is it] it is Dd¹, Ox
88 mine] my Dd¹–R
95 Yet not] Not yet Dd², Ch, Ox, Dd³, R, C

97 you] *omit* Ch; to you Ox, R, C
98.1 Arundell] Mat. Q1–4, Dd¹⁻², S, Ox, Dd³, R
99 Lord] Lord of *Arundel* D (*qy*), C, B
102 to] for Ch
103 and] to Q2–4, Dd¹–B, K
111 *Horse boy*.] *1st Servant.* Ch; *Pembroke.* Gl

II.vi

5 all] *omit* Q3–4
7 longer] more Dd¹⁻², S, Ox, Dd³, R, C
7 that] *omit* Ch
8 doth] does B, K

15 I not] not I Q2–4, Dd¹⁻², S, D
17 Away] *omit* Ch
18 booted] booteth Q3–4, Dd¹⁻², S, Ox, Dd³, R; boots Ch
19.1 *Exeunt.*] *omit* Q3–4

III.i

8 *Pierce*, my] *Pierce* of Q2–4, Dd¹–C
12 *Edward*] *Edwards* Q2
20 preach] perch Dd¹
21 teach the rest] profit much Ox
22 *Omit* Ox
22 As by their preachments] That by their preaching Ch
25 have] we've Ch
27 crest] crests Ch, D²
28 haught] high Dd¹, Ox
29 Not] You ought not Dd¹⁻², S, Ch, Dd³
35 thy] the Q2–4, Dd¹–R (−Ch)
42 favors] favor Q2–4, Dd¹–B
52 Beside] Besides Dd¹–R, C
55 t'] to Q3–4
56 but] *omit* Q2–4, Dd¹–D, B (−Ch)
57 largis] large Dd¹
58 comes] come Q2
58.1 *et seq.* Levune] Lewne Q1–4; Lejeune Ch; Lewen Ox
62 lord] *omit* Dd¹–R
62 brother] dear brother Ch
69 thee] him Ch
69 now] more Dd¹–R, Coll MS, C
75 Then] That C
75 fits] suits Ox, R
75 a prince…I] so young a prince as I Ch

81 you] thou Ch
88.1 *et seq.* Arundell] Matre Q1–3; Matrevis Q4, Dd¹–R
90 Yea] Yes Q3–4
91 Ah] Oh Ch
103 the] *omit* Ox, R, C
106 Spake] Speake Q2–3
107 me] my Q4
111 this] *omit* Dd¹
113 fortunes] fortunes it D, C, B
114 cause] the cause Dd¹–R, C, B
120 strake] stroke Q3–4; struck Dd¹–R
121 against] 'gainst Q4, Dd¹–B
140 immortallie] immortalitie Q3
143 this] his C, B
145 of] out of Ox, R
147 times] time Ox, R
148 here is] heres is Q1–2; heer's Q3–4, Dd¹, Ox, R, D², C, TB, M, Ri
153 complices] accomplices Dd¹–R
154 route] roote Q3–4, Dd¹–R, D¹
156 armes] arm Ox
159 bloud] more blood Ch
160 this greefe] of this Q4, Ox
163 leaves] leave Q2 (BM *copy*)
173 tarrie] await for Ch
181 lords] lord Q1–4, Dd¹–R, TB, Bgs, M, K, Ri, Gl
183 stoope] stop Ox

185 lords] my lords Dd¹
202 Th'ad] They'd Ch–B, M, K; Thou'd
     Ri
202 them] thee Q1–4, Dd¹–B, M, K
204 on] in S
207 Is it] It is Q2
211 wilt] will Q2
214 thus be] be thus Ch
221 now] *omit* Ox, R
221 chance] the chance Ox, R
223 Vaild] Veil'd Dd¹
224 advance] exalt Ch
227 knew] know Ch
228 *Pierce*] Piercy Dd¹
234 messenger] messengers Q3–4, Dd²,
     Ox, Dd³, R
237 watcht] snatch'd K

238 against] 'gainst Q4, Dd¹–B
240 in rage] *omit* Ox, R
242 Tis] It is Dd¹–B, K
243 to] than Dd¹–S, Dd³
244 Then] To Dd¹–S, Dd³
259 hope] hopes Dd³
259 his] hie Q3–4
265 treasure] pleasure B
266 therewith all] therewithall Q4
271 into] unto S
272 it] is Q3
273 leveld] levied Q1–4, Dd¹–R (Dd³
     qy leveled)
276 doubts] doubte Q2–4, Dd¹–B, K
276 clap so] claps Q1–4; creep Ox
279 with] 'gainst Ch

IV.i

1 gale] gales Ch
4 thy] his Ch
10 sweet] swift Coll MS

14 thy] my R
17 unto] into Q4

IV.ii

3 doe] goe Q3
7 A] He Dd¹–R, C
12 doost] must D (*qy*)
20 shake off all] share of all TB, Gg
     (*qy*), Ri; share with us Ch, Br MS
20 our] your R
22 nor] not Dd¹–², S, Dd³
23 have] heave Ch, Br MS
27 wrongs] wrong Dd²–³
30 or] on D
31 Will we] We will R, C, B, K
33 dare] *omit* Dd¹
34 who] what Dd¹
42 t'] to Q3–4, S

44 not I] not so Ch
51 want] won't Dd¹–², S, Ch, Dd³, R;
     wont Ox, C
51 a] so Dd¹–R, C
53 partie] part D, C
53 faction] our faction Ch, Br MS
59 deserv'd] earn'd Ch, Br MS
66 a base] abase Q4, Dd¹–R
67 How say] How say'st D; Now say
     D (*qy*), C
67 yong] you Ox, R
67 you] *omit* Q3
67 match] march Dd¹
81 lord] lords D, B

IV.iii

0.1, 9 Arundell] Matr. Q1–4, Dd¹–S,
     Dd³, R
3 with his friends] henceforth Ch, Br
     MS
3 his] *omit* C
10 there] here Ch
12 a month] not long Q3–4, Ox

16 As] That Ch
16 *Isabella*] Isabell Q1–4, Dd¹–R, Bgs
16 gets] will get Ch, Br MS
18 can] that Ch
20 A] He Dd¹–R, C
20 be] he R
24 come] comes Ox

26 lord] lords Dd²
27.1 *letter*] *letters* Q 3–4, Dd¹⁻², S, Dd³
28 premised] promised Q 1, 3, BGs, K; præmised Q 2

28 instructions] my instructions Ch
29 his] and his Ch
44 duskie] dusty Ox, R, C
47 these] those Ch, Ox, R, C

IV.iv

3 *Belgia*] Belgium Ch
6 makes] make Q 2–4, Dd¹–B, K
8 gorde] gore Dd¹–R, C
12 And] Who R, D, C, B
12 channels] channell Q 2–4, Dd¹–B
12–13 blood,...people‸] ∼ ,...∼ ; Q 3; ∼ ‸...∼ ; Q 4, Dd², S, Dd³, D, C, B, K

16 Ye] You Q 4, D, B, M, K, Gl
17 that] *omit* Ox, D (*qy*), C
23 sword] swords Q 1, TB, Bgs, M, Ri, Gl
26 these] those Ch, Ox, R, C
27 havocks] havock Dd¹–B
28 trumpets] trumpets them Ch

IV.v

6 and] *omit* Dd¹–R, C

7 honor] honors Q 1 (u), TB, Bgs, M

IV.vi

5 unkinde] mankind Ch
7 my] thy C
18 into] unto Ch, B, K
19 Succesful] Succesfulls Q 2–3
19 battells] battel Q 2–4, Dd¹–B, K
21 succesfully] successively Q 4
22 Thankes] Thankt Q 2–3; Thanked Q 4, Dd¹–B
27 infortunate] unfortunate Q 4, Dd¹–R, Ri
30–1 *Kent. Madam...fall?*] *preceded in* Q 2 *by lines in error:* Edm. Madam ...you deale...fall? *then correct text follows*

41 scape] scapt Q 3
45 *Kent.*] *Y. Mor.* Ox, D
45 This, *Edward,*] ∼ ‸ ∼ ‸ Q 1, 4, Dd¹–C, TB, Bgs, Gl; ∼ ‸ ∼ , Q 2–3
45.1 *and the Maior of* Bristow] *omit* D
62 Unhappie] Unhappies Q 1–4, B, Bgs, Gl; Unhappy is M, Ri
63 ye] you D, C, B, M, K
69 have] heave Ch
70 Your...head.] *omit* Q 2–4, Dd¹–B
71 his] the Q 2–4, Dd¹–B
79 fall] flight Coll MS

IV.vii

0.1 *Monkes*] Monke Q 3
2 will we] we will Q 2–4, Dd¹–B
6 *Omit* Dd¹, Ox
6 those] these Ch
10 sence] a sense Dd¹–B, K (−D)
14 emperie] empire Dd¹
16 come *Baldocke*] Baldock Ch, C
17 that] *omit* Q 3; thy Q 4, Ox, R, C
19 suckedst] suck'st Dd¹–R
26 *Monk.*] *Monks.* Q 1–4, Dd¹⁻², S, Dd³, Bgs, M, K, Ri

30 A] He Dd¹–R, C
34 sore] with sore Q 4, D; surly Dd¹; sorest Ox
34 tempests] tempest Ox, R
37 who talkes of *Mortimer*] *omit* Ch
41 open] ope Q 3–4, Dd¹–B
45 here even] even here Ch, Ox, R, C
45.2 of] *omit* Q 2
46 those] these Q 2–4, Dd¹–B
50 gallant] *omit* Q 3–4, Dd²–R
50 with] doe with Q 4, Ch, Ox, R

57 arrest] do arrest Ch, Ox, R, D (*qy*), C, B, K
64 Comes] Come Q2, Ox; Came O3–4
70 earnes] yearns Dd¹–R, C
73 A] *omit* Dd¹, Ch, Ox, R, D (*qy*), C
76 not...in] nought...with S, Ch
77 in] *omit* Ch
80 never shall wee] we ne'er shall Ch
83 somwhat] something Ch
87 in] on Q3–4, C

91 friends] friend Ox, R, C
91 *Edward*] hapless Edward D (*qy*), C
91 and these] *omit* D, C
92 And these] *omit* Dd¹–R
95 that] what Dd¹, Ox, R
95 ¹shalbe] which must be Ch
99.1 Leicester] Lancaster Q2–4
104 fleeted] fleeting Q2–4, Dd¹–B
108 hand] hands C, B
117 worship] Lordship Q2–4, Dd¹–B, K

V.i

4 of] for Ox, R
7 hast thou alwaies] always hast thou Ox
13 And] *omit* Q1–24
14 into] to Q2–4, Dd¹–B (−Ch)
19 cloye] claw Dd¹, Ox
21 often] oft Q2–4, Dd¹–², S, Ch, Dd³, D¹
21 heaven] high heaven Dd¹–R (−Ch)
21 sowring] for soaring Ch
24 the] my Q2–4, D, B, K
39 crave] claim Ch
41 by] with Ch
44 Heavens] Heaven Ch, Ox, R, C
47 Vine] Vines Q1–4, Dd¹–², Ch, Dd³, Bgs, K, Gl
48 survives] survies Q3; survive Q4, Dd¹–C
55 extreame] extreams Q3–4, Dd²–R C,
56 what] that Q2–4, D
59 be] *omit* Q2
62 dew] done Ch
69 beames] beame Q2–4, Dd¹–B
77 passe] care Ch
78 seekes] seeke Q4, Dd¹–B
81 this torment] these torments Ch
84, 124 *Trussell*.] *Trusty* Dd¹–², S, Dd³, R; Bishop Ch, Ox

86 but] not Q3–4, C
86 I live] I'll live M
86 be king] *omit* Q1–4, C, Bgs, K
87 and] *omit* C
87 you] *omit* Dd²–R, D (*qy*)
88 conspire] confirm Dd¹, S, R
96 heavens] heav'n Dd¹–R
104 being] beene Q¹
109 aye] ever Dd¹, Ox, R, C
111.1 *omit*] *Enter Bartley.* Q1–4, Dd¹–R (−Ch)
112 *Bishop.*] *Bartley.* Q1–4, Dd¹–², S, Ox, Dd³, R; *Leicester.* Ch
116 is there] there is Q2–4, Dd¹–², S, Dd³, D, B, K
116 jawes] paws Ch
117 Then] This Q1
117 imbrasements] embracement Dd³
124 our] out R
127.1 *Enter* Bartley.] *omit* Q1–4, Dd¹–R (−Ch)
134 *Bartley* would] would Berkley Ch
135 of] and Q3–4, Dd², S, Ch, Dd³
135 commaunds] command S, Ch
143 immortall] immorrall Q3
149 Mine] My Q3–4
152 am I] I am Ch

V.ii

7 eares] eare Q3–4
10 that] it Dd², Ch, Ox, R, D¹, C
10 us] as Q1–2, Dd²,³
11 erect] elect Ch, Ox

13 will] twill Q3–4, Dd²–B
14 as] that Ch
21 newes] the news S, Ch
21 that] *omit* Q2–4, Dd¹–R, D, B, K

30 letter] *omit* D (*qy*)
34 so] as Ch, Ox, R, D (*qy*), C, B (*qy*); *omit* S
34 The lord] *Mortimer*. The Lord Ch
41 lieth] doth lie Ch
44 and die] *omit* Ch
57 we] *omit* S
60 Till] And Q 1, K

60 he] be K
86 they] how they Ch
88 Thou] You Q 2–4, Dd¹–B
94 it] it is Q 3–4, Dd²–R, K; 'tis D, C, B
111 s'dainst] dain'st Dd¹; disdain'st S, Ox
116 redeeme] release Ch

V.iii

3 dangereth] endangereth Ch
13 this] us Ch
14 To] Only to D (*qy*), C
15 dolours] choler Dd¹–R
15 to] *omit* Q 4
16 increase] to increase B
22 rents] rend Dd¹–B
27 our] your B
37 knowes] know Dd¹–C
38 waites] wait Dd¹–C, K

39 all] *omit* Ox, D (*qy*), C
39 O] *omit* Ch
40 wronges] wrong Dd¹–C
41 that] *omit* C
48 to] into Ch
49 there] here Ch, Ox
54 this] his O 2–4, Dd²–B, K
58 Binde] Blind Ox
58 so] *omit* R

V.iv

21 thou as] thou so Q 2–4, Dd¹–B, K
23 and] nay Ch
32 through] downe Q 3–4, D, C
33 a] the B
37 But] And B, K
42 miles] mile Q 2–3, Dd¹–B, K
46 bring] bring'st Ch
48 do I] I do Ch
48 commaund] mand Dd³
57 that that] that which Dd¹–R
65 is all] all is Ch

66 the king] and king Ch
66 rule us] rules us Q 2–4, B
73 Canterbury] Winchester Ch
76 Dares] Dare Ox, R, C, B, K
84 A] He Dd¹–R, C
88 this] the Ch
103 king] a king Q 3–4
107 none of both them] none of both, then Q 1, 3, K (both‿ then); neither of them S, Ch, Ox, R

V.v

3 castell] Bastell Q 3–4; castles Ox
3 runne] runs Q 4
15 conster] construe Q 2–4, Dd¹–B
19 you] ye Dd¹–R, C, B, K
25 Heere is] heer's Q 3–4
25 keyes] key Ch, M, (*after* Verity), K
25 lake] lock Coll MS, B (*qy*)
29 See that] See Ch
29 roome] room that Ch
30 And] *omit* Ch
30 spit] spet Q 2
33 What else,] *omit* Dd¹–R, C

36 you] thou Q 2–4, Dd¹–B, K
37 to] *omit* Ox, R, C
42 comes] com'st Q 2–4, Dd¹–B, K
60 dayes] day' R
66 dropt] drop Dd¹⁻², S, Ch, Dd³, R
77 even] and even Q 1–4, Bgs
80 meanes] mean'st Q 2, Dd¹–B, K
83 my thought] me then Ch
91 remaine] still remain Dd¹, Ox, D; yet remain Ch
91 alive] *omit* Q 3–4, Dd², S, Ch, Dd³, R, C
94 eyes lids] eye-lids Q 4, Dd¹–C, K

101 die, yet,] ~ , ~ , Q 1–3, Dd¹⁻², S,
    Ox, Dd³, R, C, Bgs, K
101 stay, O stay] O stay Q 4, D
104 never] ne'er shall Ch

113 that you] thou Ox, R, C
116 it] is Q 2
119 kings] news Ch

V.vi

3 now] *omit* Q 3–4
15 A] Oh Ox
18 I, I] Ay Ch, Ox, D, C; I B
22 Aye] Ah Dd¹-R, C
24, 38 *1. Lord.*] *Lords.* Q 1–4, Dd¹-R
    (−Ch), TB, Bgs
26 How] Ho Q 2, D
27 frighted] frightened Ox, R
32 too] so Dd², S, Ch, Dd³
34 not me] me not B
39 thinke] think it Coll MS, D² (*qy*)
39 be] be so S
40 dare] dares Q 2–4, Dd¹-D, B, K
42 murdredst] murdrest Q 2, Dd¹⁻²,
    Ox, Dd³, R, K; murdered S, Ch
47 Tis] It is Ch, D, B

50 A] Aye Dd¹-R, C
55 For...sonne] Sweet son, for my
    sake Ch
72 no] *omit* Q 3–4
77, 89, 91 *2. Lord.*] *Lords.* Q 1–4, Dd¹⁻²,
    S, Dd³, TB, Bgs; *1. Lord.* Ch, Ox;
    Lord. R
80 may] *omit* Q 3–4
88 his] the Q 3–4
89 Thus] Tush D (*qy*)
93 *1. Lord.*] *Lords.* Q 1–4, Dd¹⁻²,
    TB, Bgs; *2nd Lord.* Ox; *Lord.* R, C
99 ghost] head Ox
100 head] ghost Ox
102 innocencie] innocence Dd¹-R

DOCTOR FAUSTUS

TEXTUAL INTRODUCTION

The earliest theatrical references to *Doctor Faustus*[1] start in Henslowe's records where on 30 September 1594 (*i.e.*, 2 October, according to Greg) receipts were £3 12s., a large sum for a play not marked as 'ne'. Over twenty performances are recorded between this date and 5 January 1597, an indication that *Faustus* was one of the more popular of the Admiral's plays. The Henslowe inventory of 10 March 1958 mentions 'j dragon in fostes', a possible backdrop 'the sittie of Rome', and, in Alleyn's inventory of about the same date, 'faustus Ierkin [and] his clok'. The drop to 5s. for the receipts on 5 January 1597 seems to have led to the withdrawal of the play from repertory, but on 22 November 1602 on behalf of the Admiral's company Henslowe paid £4 to William Birde, or Borne, and Samuel Rowley 'for ther adicyones in doctor fostes', a revival that Greg conjectures coincided with the return of Alleyn to the company after his retirement late in 1597.[2]

The date of composition lies under some dispute, with 1588–9 and 1592–3 being the years most frequently suggested. Crucial in the argument is the obvious source of the play, *The Historie of the Damnable Life and Deserved Death of Doctor John Faustus*, an English translation of the German *Historia* (or *Faust-Buch*) which had been published in late 1587. The first known edition of the *Historie* is dated 1592, although the existence of an earlier edition is implied by its titlepage statement, 'newly imprinted, and in convenient places imperfect matter added: according to the true Copie printed at Franckfort, and translated into English by P. F. Gent.'[3]

---

[1] A reference appearing in *The Black Book* by T. M. (1604) – 'like one of my Diuells in Dr. Faustus when the old Theater crackt and frighted the audience' – implies that the play was acted at the Theatre in Shoreditch. The date of such a performance is uncertain except that it was almost certainly before September 1594 when the play appears in the repertory of the Admiral's company at the Rose.

[2] W. W. Greg, *Marlowe's 'Doctor Faustus' 1604–1616: Parallel Texts* (1950), pp. 11–12. Hereafter all references to Greg are to this edition.

[3] The existence of a lost earlier edition is also suggested by a copyright dispute recorded in the Court Book of the Stationers' Company on 18 December 1592, for which see Greg, p. 3ff.

That the P. F. translation of about May 1592 was the immediate source for the play is generally accepted, and this opinion enables Greg (pp. 5–10) to argue strongly for the writing of *Faustus* in the last year of Marlowe's life, May 1592–May 1593. This view may well be the true one, for the mature style of Marlowe's part certainly agrees with a late instead of an early date.[1]

Almost two years before the record of payment to Rowley and Birde for the additions, Thomas Bushell entered for his copy of the play on 7 January 1601. However, no edition is known before his quarto of 1604, printed by Valentine Simmes. Since this is preserved in a single copy, in the Bodleian Library, at least the possibility exists that it is not the first edition, for a delay of three years between entry and publication might be thought an unusual procedure. (For a discussion of the bibliographical evidence, see below, pp. 146–7.) Greg remarks (p. 13) that the 1604 title suggests that it is a reprint of an earlier quarto since the acting company is given as 'the Earle of Nottingham his seruants' (*i.e.*, the Lord Admiral's men) whereas the company had passed under the patronage of Prince Henry before the end of 1603. However, if Bushell for some reason had delayed publication he might easily have retained the original title proposed in 1601. The 1604 (A1) edition represents a distinctive textual version commonly identified as the A-text. It was reprinted in 1609 (A2) by George Eld for John Wright[2] and again by Eld for Wright in 1611 (A3). The first edition of the B-text version appeared in 1616 for John Wright (B1). The printer was not mentioned in the imprint but may have been George Eld.[3] This version was reprinted for Wright in 1619 (B2) with a titlepage that for the first time mentioned 'With new Additions', in 1620 (B3), in 1624 (B4), in 1628 (B5), and in 1631 (B6), all for Wright. Each was

[1] The evidence is not completely certain, however. It is possible that P.F. chiefly added to the lost (imperfect) edition, and that what is taken to be the play's source passages might therefore have been present in substantially the same form in the earlier version. No demonstration is possible, but one may note that the facts as we know them point to a derivation from the 1592 text. We have no knowledge of the preceding text.

[2] The transfer from Bushell to Wright was not recorded in the Register until 13 September 1610.

[3] See Robert Ford Welsh, *The Printing of the Early Editions of Marlowe's Plays* (University Microfilms, 1964), pp. 128–9.

printed from its immediate predecessor except that B 5 seems to have used as copy a mixture of B 2 and B 4. Finally, in 1663 the last early edition appeared, published by W. Gilbertson 'with New Additions as it is now Acted. With several New Scenes'. This, being a much altered and debased text, is not considered in the present edition.

Ever since Leo Kirschbaum's pioneering article in 1946,[1] it has been generally accepted that the A-text represents a so-called 'bad quarto', which is to say a memorial reconstruction of some acting version, contrived without direct reference to any manuscript in the authorial line. Each 'bad quarto' of an Elizabethan play seems to be something of a law to itself, and the 1604 *Doctor Faustus* aligns itself more with such Shakespearean 'bad quartos' as *Romeo and Juliet*, *Richard III*, and *King Lear* than with the classic case of *Hamlet* which was cobbled up chiefly from the memory of a subsidiary actor, a 'hired man'. That is, in the main the tragic action of *Faustus* involving the central character appears to be better reported than the comic scenes.[2] In his important, searching discussion of the 'Nature of the A-text', Greg (pp. 29–62) offered evidence to suggest, first, that the B-text cannot contain the 1602 additions (the present editor believes otherwise); second, that the A-text represents on the whole a shortened version of the 1616 B-text (this view must be somewhat modified if the 1602 additions are actually present in B); and third that *Doctor Faustus* (like *Edward II*) was originally a play for Pembroke's men who may have been formed from Strange's men, and that in January 1593, during a brief abatement of the plague, Pembroke's company acted the play at the Theatre on the occasion recorded in *The Black Book*. But the company did not

---

[1] 'The Good and Bad Quartos of *Doctor Faustus*', *The Library*, n.s. XXVI (1946), 272–94.

[2] That this difference could be more apparent than real might be argued if the 'norm' of the B-text comic and farcical scenes were not representative of the early play's scenes but if they were instead revised or added in 1602 and are therefore untrustworthy for comparison, as will be suggested below. All one can say with any certainty about the state of the text of the farcical scenes in the A-text is that there are at least two examples of post-Marlovian gag dating from about 1594–5 in the reference to French crowns and to Doctor Lopez (see Appendix: A-text Scene iv, 30–5, and Scene ix, 127–8). One might normally expect the reporting of the farcical scenes to be cruder; but if the B-text is an unreliable witness for these, we have little that can act as evidence. However, what evidence we have suggests that the comic and farcical scenes in the A-text are inferior in their fidelity to the reporting of the tragic action.

prosper and by the end of September they were in such difficulties that a question arose of pawning their wardrobe; and it would appear that at least four of their plays about this time (including *Edward II*) came into the hands of the booksellers. It is possible that their promptbook was sold to the Admiral's in the autumn of 1593, the company that acted *Faustus* in the autumn of 1594. Greg also points out that three of the five plays that we know belonged to Pembroke's company have come down to us in bad quartos, and he conjectures that if Pembroke's men carried on some sort of provincial existence subsequently (they were found at Oxford in 1595–6) they reconstructed their sold promptbooks from memory for acting in the country, including *Doctor Faustus*. Although highly speculative, this hypothesis is a reasonable one and would establish the A-text as a 1594–5 memorial version of the original production of the play, even though faulty by consequence of the transmission and perhaps altered in some respects for provincial audiences. Some one person may have taken it upon himself to bring the results together to make as coherent a play as possible out of the memorial production of the parts, and indeed the stage-directions often appear to reproduce an actual performance.[1]

The problem of the B-text is more complex and less subject to detailed hypothesis. Except for some lines in Act V no question now

[1] All difficulties are not solved by the hypothesis of memorial reconstruction. Greg seems to think of the process as performed by one man, whereas in the present editor's opinion a communal operation by members of the company (with or without all of the original comic actors) seems better to fit the results. Even so, the details of the bond and possibly of the Friars' Dirge present problems. It may be that what Greg thinks are revisions in the promptbook, especially those that seem to refer back independently to the *Historie*, are in fact – like the Emperour Carolus scene – memorial versions of the original play (Greg's whole view being vitally affected in its details by his belief that the 1602 additions are not present in the B-text and thus that it is a reliable witness to the A-text original). Others could be the work of some one person charged with putting together the communal reconstruction to make up an acceptable play. It would not be impossible for such a person, indeed, to run together as one scene the two B-text scenes of Robin's theft of the magic book and his conjuring of Mephostophilis from Turkey (providing the splitting of this scene were not part of the B-text revision, as seems more likely). These are details, however, which need not affect the general rightness of the hypothesis that the A-text is a bad quarto. (For some remarks on details, see Bowers, 'The Text of Marlowe's *Faustus*', *Modern Philology*, XLIX (1952), 197–8; this article errs, however, in agreeing that the 1602 additions are not present in the B-text, and thus its assumptions, in turn, are coloured by the false hypothesis that the A-text is substantially a report of the present B-text.)

exists of the general superiority of the B to the A-text in the tragic sections and of the fact that it appears to be more complete (some 2121 lines versus 1517 lines of print in each quarto) although the 1602 additions, believed by the present editor to be present in the B-version, must account for some of the extra length.[1] On the other hand Greg has demonstrated that some portions of the 1616 B-text rely heavily on the A3 quarto of 1611 and reproduce certain of its readings that are either unique or differ from A1 of 1604 by agreeing with A2 variants. In either case the A3 variants from A1 followed by B1 can have no authority. Nevertheless, a manuscript was available for the major part if not for all of the play. By Greg's liberal calculations (p. 74) for the direct influence of A3 copy,[2] except for Scene viii (779–802) and the amplified Chorus 2 (the longer form of which is found from manuscript at 753.1–778.1), A3 was utilized for the Chorus 1 (1–28.1), Scene i (28.2–193.1), Scene iii (228.2–342.1), Scene v (388.1–402, 484–500), Scene xvii (1680.1–1696.2), Scene xviii (1837–89, 1925.1–1982.1), and Chorus 4 (2001.2–2009.2). Since the comic and farcical scenes in which the A-text is either wanting or else differs materially usurp the major action of Scenes vii to xvi (the generally assigned Acts III and IV), there was less opportunity to make direct use of A3 in this midsection; hence the unequal division appears to have no significance. In Greg's view the underlying manuscript and a copy of A3 were given to the printer,

---

[1] In the early editorial history when only the B-text was known, little question was raised, but after the A-text became available it was at first thought to represent the original play in all detail and consequently was selected by Bullen and by Tucker Brooke as their copy-text. This interregnum was interrupted only by Boas until the Kirschbaum article and the Greg analysis established the peculiar memorial nature of the A-text and elevated the B-text to paramount authority. It was peculiarly unfortunate that Kirschbaum felt the demonstration of the memorial nature of the A-text involved the hypothesis that it was a redaction of the whole of the present B-text so that one in effect proved the other and that this linking of two essentially discrete problems powerfully affected the thinking of Sir Walter Greg, who had already been working on parallel lines before Kirschbaum published his results. The two problems are in fact independent; and where the evidence appears to overlap in certain comic scenes, the hypothesis of B-text revision as synonymous with the 1602 additions is as satisfactory as A-text memorial corruption and shortening where this evidence concerns the identifiable revisions.

[2] To be more exact, these are the passages that Greg believes were printed in B1 directly from A3 copy. The present editor holds to another hypothesis about the nature of the printer's copy while not denying the consultation or even the basic use of the A3 quarto.

with directions in the manuscript at certain points requesting the printer to insert such and such a passage from A3 that had been crossed out in MS. In some cases these passages of A3 had already been editorially emended by comparison with the lines in MS[1]. It is, instead, the opinion of the present editor that the printer's copy was a fresh inscription that had been made up from an underlying manuscript by some person hired by Wright[2] who for convenience sometimes used an example of A3 as his central authority when the texts were close (usually comparing A3 with his basic manuscript and occasionally altering its readings to bring them into conformity). The evidence is too lengthy to reproduce here but may be consulted in 'The Text of Marlowe's *Faustus*', pp. 198–203. In the course of writing out the copy this inscriber seems to have censored most references by name to God,[3] to have altered phrases or lines he did

---

[1] It may be remarked that another method by which some printers seem to have set revised editions was apparently not employed here, on the evidence of the nature of the specific alterations in A3 passages. That is, a printer faced with a difficult manuscript seems occasionally to have secured a copy of an earlier printed edition (even though corrupt, like a bad quarto) fixed both manuscript and printed copy above his cases, and made his way through the manuscript with whatever help the printed edition could offer, or *vice versa*. Some reason exists to conjecture that this was the procedure for printing Act I of the good Q2 *Hamlet*.

[2] It would accord better with censorship for the stage if the printer's copy had, instead, been a manuscript prepared from the same materials but intended to replace a lost promptbook after 1611. On the one hand, such a theory would explain more satisfactorily Wright's late purchase of the original papers preserved over a considerable length of time in the theatre, as well as the deletion and alteration of tender material for the stage (less tender apparently for publication) under the Act Against Abuses. On the other, such a supposed theatrical manuscript would need to have been an intermediate copy from which a promptbook was subsequently transcribed afresh; the question always arises in such a case whether conditions were such as to require a copy in this intermediate form before the promptbook was made up. Moreover, any such guess would require the further guess that the original promptbook had been lost and had to be reconstructed from the authors' original papers with the convenient assistance of the 1611 quarto for those earliest papers which might have had their legibility affected by storage for about twenty years. Fortunately, for editorial purposes speculation of this nature is of no assistance. As will be suggested below, the evidence favors B printer's copy transcribed from the authors' papers. Whether this was done by a theatrical scribe or by someone working for Wright makes little or no difference.

[3] As examples, he substituted 'all godlinesse' in 281 for A3 'the Trinity', 'Why' in 398 for 'To God', 'power' in 414 for 'god', 'heaven' at 563 for 'God', and – the supreme example of all – he excised 1939, 'See see where Christs bloud streames in the firmament'.

not understand or thought were corrupt,[1] and he sometimes tinkered with A3's metre (as in 'and Galen come' in line 40) and grammar. Although the evidence demonstrates that he could be scrupulous, often, in changing a word in A3 by reference to his manuscript (as when on some occasions he restored A1 readings from A3 variation), in other examples of unauthoritative interference he seems to have failed to consult his manuscript, or chose to tinker anyway, even when he found that it agreed with the A3 text or else – less likely at least to the extent that Greg is forced to conjecture – the manuscript may sometimes have been damaged or missing. Nevertheless, the history of his unauthoritative changes, except for the heavy and constant censorship, is far outweighed by his substitution of what appear to be authorial readings for A-text corruptions, even in very small matters. In the opinion of the present editor the reference he made to MS, even when he was presumably copying chiefly from the A3 printed text, was relatively thorough.[2] It is true that he failed to correct a certain number of A3 printer's variants from A1, so that B1 a few times follows the faulty A3 copy, but such oversights may be balanced by the number of times that he restored from MS the readings corrupted in A3.[3] It is also true, however, that just as he sometimes failed to settle cruxes in his A3 copy by satisfactory reference to the original manuscript, he also passed over examples of

[1] As examples, he changed A3 'whose sweete delight's disputes' to 'and sweetly can dispute' in 18, and 'suppositions' in 606 to 'questions'. He omitted 790, A's ' Quarters the towne in foure equivolence' apparently because it made no sense to him, and so presumably with A3 'spirits' for A1 'speeches' in 273.

[2] Random examples are the B1 substitution of 'petty' for A3 'pretty' in 57, 'spirits' for 'subjects' in 149, 'bushy' for 'little' (A1 'lustie') in 178, or 'which' for 'that' in 202. This last is particularly interesting because it repairs what seems to have been a tendency of Simmes's Compositor *A* who set the A1 quarto here to substitute 'that' for 'who' or 'which' as shown in other Simmes plays. See also A1 and B1 'who' in 305 but A3 'that'.

[3] Examples of his overlooking A3 departures from A1 (supposedly to be revealed by his manuscript) are A3 and B1 'the' but A1 'our' in 121, and 'to aid' in 324 for A1 'aid'. Yet in 99 he returned to A1 'wrath' from A3 'rod', in 102 to A1 'treasury' from A3 'treasure', and in 170 to A1 'heeretofore' from A3 'hetherto'. Such scrupulousness when a control is present to authenticate the change gives one considerable confidence in the general run of B1 variants when special circumstances have not intervened. For Compositor *A* and his corruptions of text, one may consult Alan Craven, 'Simmes' Compositor *A*: The Compositor of Five Shakespeare Quartos,' *Studies in Bibliography*, XXVI (1973), 37–60.

limping lines, distorted syntax, and even possible omissions in his A-text so that the true readings of the manuscript never can be discovered. These errors are visible. What we do not know, of course, and never shall discover is how much the original manuscript may have differed when B1 repeats what seems to be relatively satisfactory A-text.

Two main problems are present in the B-text. First, as sketched above, there lies the question of the purity of the text of the sections from the original play in their B- as against their A-form, owing on the one part to the effect of the printed A-text on the printer's copy for B and on the other to the effect of the independent editorial work (advertent as well as inadvertent) of the inscriber of the B-text's copy. These concern the scenes or part-scenes present in both texts in relatively close form. Secondly, there lies the moot question of the status and transmission of the sections that are unique to the B-text, including some that expand and revise basic material present also in the A-text but only in roughly parallel form. For over twenty years following the enquiries of Kirschbaum and of Greg it has been commonly accepted that the unique B-scenes are subtractions in the A-text from the original full form of the play substantially as represented by the 1616 B-text.[1] As a consequence modern criticism has proceeded on the assumption that the form and content of the original play put together by Marlowe and an unknown collaborator in 1592–3 can safely be reconstructed from the B-text with only occasional reference to A, and that the Rowley–Birde additions of 1602 have been permanently lost. Analysis discloses that the Kirschbaum–Greg hypothesis to this effect rests on a more narrow and ambiguous factual basis than is commonly supposed and that evidence of greater weight suggests the opposite: the older view of Bullen and of Tucker Brooke was correct, that the 1602 additions are indeed present in the B-text and thereby account for its marked disparity with sections of the A-text well beyond the effects of the

[1] One qualifies this statement by 'substantially' not only to cover the alterations of the B-text editor as well as his various failures to bring the A-text into conformity with his manuscript, but also to cover certain areas of B, perhaps inferior to A, which Greg is forced to conjecture must represent Marlowe's subsequent revision of the prompt-book so that a superior text is preserved in the A-report from that in the B-text based on the original foul papers.

A-text memorial transmission combined with the exigencies of provincial performance.[1] The present editor has come to this conclusion slowly and – at first – reluctantly during the course of his attempts to apply to the textual situation the accepted view that the B-text represents the unified original play and nothing more. So many difficulties and anomalies resulted, and so much incredible complexity of hypothesis, that in the course of a fresh examination he was led to believe that the internal evidence of the B-text itself enforced the conclusion that it could not be taken either as a unified whole or as the original play but must have been produced by a considerable expansion and revision at some subsequent time. At this point only two choices could be made. Greg himself had been much troubled by the difficulties created from the rejection of the Rowley–Birde additions as present in the B-text and had seriously contemplated the possibility that the original play might have been revised when, conjecturally, the Admiral's men took it over from the failing Pembroke's company in late 1593 or early 1594 (pp. 92–7). He finally came to believe that the weight of the evidence was insufficient to bear so speculative a theory, at which point he was caught on the other horn of the dilemma – that one set of internal evidence and two pieces of external evidence seemed to forbid placing the construction of the B-text later than 1593–1601 and thus appeared to rule out the presence of the Rowley–Birde additions of 1602. It followed that he felt he had no choice but to accept the unity of the B-text as the form of the original play in 1592–3 and to proceed to explain the difficulties as best he could on the basis of that hypothesis.[2]

Because of the weight of the evidence for revision within the B-text, and in some part because of the inherent improbability that in 1616 John Wright would put out a new text (advertised in 1619 as

---

[1] Tucker Brooke and earlier editors were of course unaware of the memorial transmission of the A-text, a fact that can now be held to be established and one that reduces for us their faith in the literal reproduction of the original manuscript of the early play by the 1604 quarto.

[2] An amazing feat of logical argumentation resulted – if one accepted its premise – that was given the acclaim that was its due, including that of the present editor's review in 1952, 'The Text of Marlowe's *Faustus*', despite some querying of the technical details of the transmission of the B-text to print; but at the time this review did not see the difficulty with the premise.

'with new additions')[1] that would not include the substantial £4's worth of added 1602 matter, the present editor was led to question the only serious barrier, the external evidence, and came to the conclusion that it was not solid enough to hold against the clearcut evidence for revision. Since doubt could be cast upon its validity, a strong case could be made that the revisions in the B-text were those of Rowley–Birde, not of some earlier and unrecorded major operation on the play as Greg had been tempted to suggest. The working-out of this problem, with the detailed presentation of evidence, went beyond the limits suitable for an introduction to the present text and so has been published elsewhere.[2] What follows here is a condensed presentation of the major evidence and the new conclusions that may be drawn from it. The case must necessarily rest on the fuller presentation, not on this digest.

In brief, the material that is unique to the B-text is as follows:

(1) Lines [831–5], 836–980 which represent much of the opening of Scene viii (III.i) and concern themselves with Faustus' decision to forgo the sights of Rome in favour of disrupting the Pope's feast, the rescue of Bruno, and the exit of the Pope and his train to prepare for the banquet.

(2) The beginning of Scene xi (IV.i), lines 1154.2–1203.1, which introduces the new B-text characters Martino, Frederick, and Benvolio, and no doubt lines 1316–20, Benvolio's threats at the conclusion of the scene which prepare for the action of Scenes xii–xiii.[3]

(3) Scenes xii–xiii (IV.ii, iii), lines 1324.2–1456.1, comprising Benvolio's revenge and Faustus' retaliation.

(4) Scene xv (IV.v), lines 1504.2–1557.1, the meeting of the clowns in the tavern with the conclusion of this episode in lines 1588.1–1668 of expanded Scene xvi (IV.vi) in which they interrupt Faustus' exhibition at Vanholt and are humiliated.

(5) The start of Scene xviii (V.ii), lines 1796.2–1819, in which Lucifer, Belzebub and Mephistophilis exult over Faustus' imminent doom and Wagner thanks Faustus for the bequests in his will. Also, lines 1879.1–1925 later in the scene, Mephistophilis' confession that it was he who tempted Faustus, followed by the visions of heaven and of hell under the direction of the Good and Bad Angels.

(6) Scene xix (V.iii), lines 1982.3–2001.1, the Scholars' discovery of Faustus' body.

[1] The failure to add this advertisement in 1616 appears to have no significance since it was probably due to the influence of the 1611 quarto's title on the printer, an error that Wright corrected in the next edition.

[2] 'Marlowe's *Doctor Faustus*: The 1602 Additions', *Studies in Bibliography*, XXVI (1973), 1–18.

[3] Associated with these additions are the revisions of the A-scene action in respect to the Injurious Knight that turn him into Benvolio, 1227–9, 1241–5, 1274–1315. In this scene how much of the text relating to Faustus and Carolus is a revised form and how much the pure text of the original play is problematic, except for the lines relating to Saxon Bruno that are definitely part of the revision.

Stylistic evidence sets these additions in Scenes viii, xi, xii, xiii, and xviii apart from all the other comic or tragic scenes in which the A-text and the B-text join and which thus must represent the original play. The best test for the author of the new material is his penchant for rhyming couplets, at least ten in Scene viii; one in the addition to Scene xi and two in the rewritten part; fourteen in Scene xii; nine in Scene xiii; and one in the first addition in Scene xviii and ten in the second. Nowhere else in the play, whether in A or in B, is there a single couplet. This couplet writer also liked occasionally to complete a part line by the opening part line of a new speech, a device that is found only once (and then perhaps accidentally) in the rest of the play. However, one such line is present in Scene viii, one in Scene xii, four in Scene xiii, and four in Scene xviii. The style of Scene viii, in particular, is distinctive in its free use of adjectives in -al to end verse lines, one of which is also found in Scene xi,[1] and is so characteristic of the work of Samuel Rowley in *When You See Me You Know Me* (1605) as to lead Greg (pp. 133–6) to conjecture that Rowley (and perhaps even Birde) was the original collaborator with Marlowe in 1592–3 and at that time worked on these scenes. However, Rowley's special characteristics are found only in the unique B-scenes and never in the work of Marlowe's original collaborator when the A- and B-texts coincide.[2] In addition, clumsy joins in two places mark the B-text additions. The most prominent is the utter confusion at the start of the new material in Scene viii in which Faustus repeats the narrative of his eight days' trip through the heavens already provided in the Chorus before the scene; Mephostophilis repeats in expanded form the last two lines of the Chorus in order to change the A-text occasion from St Peter's feast (already accepted by B) to the Pope's victory over the Emperor and his capture of Saxon Bruno (the Foxe source material); and then the original situation (found also in A) is reversed whereby it was Mephostophilis who restrained Faustus' impatience to be off and

---

[1] Cf. in Scene viii 'State Pontificall', 870; 'Statutes Decretall', 883; 'authority Apostolicall', 923; 'blessing Apostolicall', 973; and, in Scene xi, 'state Majesticall', 1233.

[2] That is, if one excepts 'demonstrations Magicall' in 177. It is also of interest that in Scene vii use is made of source material from Foxe's *Book of Martyrs*, also utilized in Rowley's *When You See Me*, but the only time in *Faustus* that anything other than the *Historie* appears as source.

advised him to sightsee after the feast, now changed to Faustus' urgent request to be allowed to stay to disrupt the papal banquet. It is difficult to argue that this series of contradictions and non sequiturs marked the original composition of the scene and that the simple and unified A-text action was its memorial reconstruction. Another repetition of material resulting from the B-text additions comes in Wagner's added thanks for the bequest which repeats the information already given in his opening soliloquy and moves his farewell to Faustus to join that of the Scholars.

The crucial facts once these unique B-scenes are surveyed as a unit are, first, that they *are* unique in B without any clear reason for subtraction;[1] second, that they are stylistically different from all the other scenes that by their coincidence in A and B indicate that they come from the original play; thirdly, that they alone – except for certain other actions assignable as Rowley–Birde revisions of the A-text – show awkward joins; and, last, that generally admitted stylistic characteristics point with some degree of certainty to the authorship of Scenes vii and xi (and of the other couplet scenes and passages) by Samuel Rowley, whose hand is certainly not that of Marlowe's collaborator in the non-Marlovian sections present in both A and B.

Briefly, the present editor takes it that the revisions are these:

(1) In preparation for Scenes xii–xiii of Benvolio's revenge, Rowley–Birde elaborated comic Scene xi by altering the simple account of the Injurious Knight in A's dramatization of the *Historie* to the relatively elaborate Benvolio action which includes mention of Saxon Bruno that links the expansion with the addition in Scene viii.

(2) In preparation for the expansion of comic Scene xvi at Vanholt by the farcical action of the clowns, the revisers contrived the new farcical tavern Scene xv. To prepare for the final jest about Faustus' wooden leg (which continues the Horse-courser action beyond its termination in the A-text), they recapitulated in this scene the Horse-courser's theft of Faustus' leg, adding new material from the *Historie* about the eating of the hay and the charming of some yokels. In order to avoid excessive repetition in the narrative of the same event, the revisers cut and altered B-text Scene xiv, transferring some of its original material as found in A to build up the new Scene xv.[2]

[1] To posit memorial failure in A every time a stylistically distinctive scene appears in B is a desperate expedient. The last Scene xix is perhaps arguable as a production cut, but the suggestion that the visions of heaven and of hell were cut because of the limited facilities of a provincial stage will not stand close scrutiny because their descriptive nature in fact scarcely needs the props except for two or three lines in all.

[2] This transfer of material from Scene xiv to xv included the A-text lines (see Appendix: A-text Scene ix continued, 131–2), 'now, I thinking my horse had had some

(3) It would seem that Rowley–Birde worked over the continuous A-text scene of Robin's theft of the magic book, the incident of the silver goblet, and the conjuring of Mephistophilis (see Appendix: A-scene vii), splitting the scene into two parts (Scenes vii, x) and renaming A-text Rafe as Dick, who appears in Scenes xv, xvi of new B-text material.

(4) The difficulties in the B-text exhibition of Helen in Scene xvii, 1680.1–1706, not all to be attributed to memorial reconstruction in A, suggest the possibility that the revisers tinkered with these lines and that in some respects the A-text is closer to the original play.[1]

(5) In the same scene, xvii, the first speech of the Old Man, 1707–23, is so different in both versions as to go beyond memorial corruption and to suggest rewriting in the B-text.

(6) Scene xix, 1982.3–2001.1, presents a difficult problem. Not un-understandable as a possible production cut, it stands as the only example of material unique to B about which there can reasonably be a question. Nevertheless, the style is not so clearly Marlowe's as to demonstrate its presence in the original[2] nor, because of the final Chorus (which after Scene xix becomes slightly repetitious in its effect on the assimilation of experience by the audience), is a conventional ending in peace required after the terrors of Faustus' great soliloquy.

The evidences for addition and revision in the B-text seem not to be reversible and the alterations might well have been extensive enough to warrant the substantial payment to Rowley and Birde of £4. The question then arises whether this cumulative evidence (including that for Rowley's hand in the unique B-text material), difficult to explain on any premise except that the Rowley–Birde additions of 1602 appear in the B1 quarto of 1616, is strong enough

rare Qualitie that he would not have had me knowne of', and the mention of the Horse-courser's 'Oastrie' (161). (In the revised B-text of Scene xiv the Horse-courser proposed to throw the leg into some ditch or other, but in Scene xv he took it home to his hostry.) This last 'echo' in Scene xv of A-text material revised out of B-text xiv suggests that the original play, as in the A-text, had Mephistophilis present in this scene and that his name in the B-text opening stage-direction was an oversight of the revisers. This hypothesis of transferred material by revision also explains what to Kirschbaum and to Greg was the important evidence in the A-text Scene ix continuation: an echo of unique B-scene xv missing in A and therefore demonstration that the A-text was a memorial reconstruction of the original play in the B-text form as we have it.

[1] Otherwise one might need to conjecture, with Greg, that Marlowe revised this scene in the promptbook. But the present editor has reservations about the authorship of this action and inclines to the view that it was written by Marlowe's collaborator.

[2] Against 'selfe time' in line 1993 may be placed Marlowe's 'selfe place' in 511. Yet it is disturbing that the phrase 'the Doctor' in line 1987 is elsewhere exclusively a characteristic of the added scenes in the B-text, as in lines 1183, 1222, 1294, 1553, 1557, 1658. Marlowe *could* have written this scene but he *need* not have. The present editor is inclined with some tentativeness to assign it to the Rowley–Birde additions. For some faintly possible support, see the textual note to line 1968.

to outweigh the external evidence that may be brought against it. This evidence consists of two supposed allusions to the unique B-text Scenes xii and xiii in plays to be dated respectively 1594 and 1600–1. Four paraphrases or relatively exact reproductions of lines common to A and to B in *Faustus* are made by *The Taming of A Shrew* (entered and printed in 1594), often taken as being a bad quarto of a Pembroke play. As to these no question can exist. However, the suggestion that a fifth, *A Shrew*, IV.ii.60–1, 'This angrie sword should rip thy hatefull chest, | And hewd thee smaller than the *Libian* sands' is a paraphrase of *Faustus*, 1397–8, 'And had you cut my body with your swords, | Or hew'd this flesh and bones as small as sand' in Scene xii is, in Greg's words (p. 28), 'One of the least convincing of the parallels, and cannot be taken by itself to prove anything at all'. But Greg continues, 'It is, however, supported by a curious point relating to another of the scenes peculiar to B', and he describes the allusion in *The Merry Wives of Windsor*, IV.v.67ff. (TLN 2283–7) in Bardolph's speech, 'for so soone as I came beyond *Eaton*, they threw me off, from behinde one of them, in a slough of myre; and set spurres, and away; like three *Germane*-divels; three *Doctor Faustasses*.' This is taken to refer to the same scene, in which Benvolio, Frederick, and Martino are punished by the three devils, with special reference to Martino. Faustus commands, 'Go *Belimothe*, and take this caitife hence,| And hurle him in some lake of mud and durt' (1408–9), and shortly in Scene xiii (IV.iii) Martino re-enters bewailing that he is 'Halfe smother'd in a Lake of mud and durt, | Through which the Furies drag'd me by the heeles' (1434–5). Greg concludes, 'Since, then, *The Merry Wives* was probably written in 1600 or 1601, it follows that the scene in question was at any rate no part of the Rowley–Birde additions of November 1602.'

Although by no means so certain as Kirschbaum and Greg of the precise application of this reference to B-text Scenes xii–xiii instead of to Faustus' magic-making in general with his speedy transfer from place to place, the present editor is not prepared to deny it out of hand; but even if it were to be accepted, the conclusion does not follow by necessity that the Rowley–Birde additions are automatically disproved. Although *The Merry Wives* was probably composed about 1600, the text we have comes to us from the Folio of 1623, almost certainly printed from a Crane transcript of the promptbook current at that date. A bad-quarto text registered on 18 January 1602 (almost a year before the Henslowe payment) may offer only doubtful testimony about the form of the original play but at least it does not preserve the allusion. A number of anomalies in the Folio text, including a change of Ford's alias from Brooke to Broome and a clear rewriting of parts of the fifth act, constitute a warning that the Folio text cannot be relied on in all its details to provide us with an exact record of the 1600–1 text. The differences between the Folio and the bad quarto, moreover, in the matter of the Germans suggest some caution in assigning to 1600–1 anything to do with this puzzling German material in its Folio form. The possibility holds, therefore, that the *Faustus* allusion, whether or not specifically to B-text Scenes xii–xiii, was a part of the rewriting that produced the altered Folio text as we have it, just possibly for the court performance of November 1604 when the award of the Garter insignia to the Count of Mömpelgart was a year old and the joke was less touchy and more reminiscent.

In the midst of these uncertainties about the precise form of the Shakespeare text, no one can say for sure that the *Faustus* allusion was present in *The Merry Wives* on its initial composition in 1600–1, given the known facts about Folio alteration of the play. Under these circumstances, the one keystone piece of evidence that is supposed to demonstrate the impossibility of the Rowley–Birde additions in the B-text of *Faustus* is too uncertain, and even suspect, to bear the major weight of excluding these additions contrary to the general run of probability and also contrary to the specific evidence for the distinctive quality as well as the unity of the added B-text material, the evidence that it does not always fit smoothly into the original context, the generally accepted relation of its style to that of Samuel Rowley, and the inexplicable reasons behind its omission by A if the A-text were a memorial reconstruction of the present B-text. Moreover, a piece of evidence not previously recognized as pertinent to the problem seems to enforce the writing of the Rowley–Birde addition to and revision of related Scene xi after the stage production of *Hamlet* in 1600–1. This is line 1174, 'He took his rouse with stopes of Rhennish wine', which is clearly a borrowing from *Hamlet*, I.iv.8–10 (TLN 612–14), 'The King doth wake to night, and takes his rouse, | Keepes wassels and the swaggering upstairs reeles, | And as he dreines his draughts of Rhenish downe'. This is, in fact, better evidence for date than the *Merry Wives* reference since it is a quotation and not a rather vague allusion of doubtful specific application. The only alternatives to line 1174 as written in 1602 are to speculate that Shakespeare was drawing on his memory of *Faustus* or to place the I.iv lines in the *Ur-Hamlet*, both rather desperate expedients to avoid a straightforward conclusion. Once the additions and revisions are accepted as the 1602 reworking, Greg's extreme complexity of material is simplified,[1] and is made editorially workable. The numerous textual problems are not automatically solved, but various of them are materially clarified; and except for the details of the contamination of the manuscript text from the 1611 quarto and the ministrations of the editor–inscriber we now know pretty well where we stand. The problem resolves itself, in fact, to that of a slightly more complex example than usual where – as in *Richard III*, *Henry V*, *King Lear* – a good text has replaced a bad quarto but has not escaped contamination from the bad edition used in some manner to help make up the printer's copy for the replacement.

The working hypothesis behind the present text, therefore, is that sometime in 1592–3, probably, Marlowe wrote some scenes for *Doctor Faustus* and that a collaborator for the rest, with or without Marlowe's assistance, put together the play largely in the form reproduced memorially by the A-text. This A-text was perhaps made up in 1594–5 by Pembroke's men as a promptbook for provincial performance and contains some instances of actor's gag as in the references to French crowns and to Doctor Lopez or in Wagner's

[1] Analysis suggests that every major difficulty in Greg's reconstruction of the history of the texts ultimately refers back to the denial of the evidence of revision as applying to the Rowley–Birde additions. Acceptance of these, for example, removes all need to argue that Marlowe must have reworked the play in the promptbook, that the passages peculiar to B in Act V are original drafts discarded in the final make-up for performance, that – contrary to the evidence of the A-text – Rowley was probably Marlowe's original collaborator, and so on.

retort after line 204. The bad quarto is unusual, however, in the apparent closeness with which much of the verse of the tragic action is recalled. It is possible that the comic and farcical parts are not so debased as has been commonly supposed, but their reconstruction was probably of inferior quality. Signs of revision in the B-text are present in every comic scene after the first, Scene iv, which (although to a lesser extent than Scene ii) may have escaped comparatively untouched and thus could furnish the closest control we have to test the general relation of the A-text reporting of the farcical scenes to the original.[1] However, since the generally good quality of the reporting of the tragic sections is probably due to one man – the important actor who took the part of Faustus and perhaps to the assistance of other actors like the one who played Mephistophilis – it is possible that the original farcical actors save for Wagner were less concerned with the reconstruction or else that they recalled their parts with less fidelity – a natural assumption. (These actors would also probably double parts in the comic action.) Hence even despite the revisions in the B-text which make it an untrustworthy guide to the language of the original farcical scenes, it is probable that the dialogue of the A-text farce is more corrupt than that of the tragic action. The comic action where it has not been so revised in B as to make comparison with A of little service appears to occupy a middle ground in A between the generally good reporting of the tragic and the inferior reconstruction of the farcical parts. Again because of the revision in B, the A-text quality may be somewhat better than is commonly supposed[2].

[1] Even this is very speculative, however, for the correspondences are not always so exact for the differences to be attributable to the memorial transmission of the A-text. Moreover, some actor's gag is clearly derived from the later acting version from which the A-text descends. It is not evident whether some of the language common to this Scene iv in the B-text and to the other farcical scenes resulted from the Rowley–Birde revision or from their use in other scenes of some of the phrases and locutions of the original, not always preserved in the parallel A reconstruction but coming down to us in the 1602 version. On the whole the latter is somewhat the more probable, and the comparative freedom of Scene iv in the B-text from revision is at least a tenable hypothesis.

[2] For instance, the A-text prose of Scene xi at the Emperour's court may be largely original since it is clear that the verse of the B-text is that of the reviser, Samuel Rowley. For the excellent possibility that lines 1009–1087.3 in comic Scene ix were not revised by Rowley–Birde and hence can offer a control for the reporting, see below p. 141, fn. 2.

The nature of the manuscript behind the B-text then comes in question. The late date of the conflation of this manuscript with the A3 quarto suggests that the copy behind B1 of 1616 was being put together for the printer and was not some theatrical copy that had come into the printer's hands (but see above, p. 126, fn. 1). If so, the general characteristics of the manuscript of the original play – as distinguished from the manuscript of the Rowley–Birde additions and revisions – so far as these original characteristics can be separated from the influence of A3 on the text of B1, do not suggest a promptbook. No bar seems to exist, therefore, for conjecturing that the manuscript could well have been the foul papers (or possibly a fair copy of these that had been sold to the company) of Marlowe and his collaborator. The papers of the Rowley–Birde additions and revisions do suggest a theatrical influence in their precise stage-directions, but if the promptbook was not available to Wright for the serious sections of the play, it would not have been available for the additions. Thus it seems reasonable to conjecture that, in turn, these were the original papers, whether in foul or in fair form, but written directly for the theatre by two actors who inserted the directions for the action that they required. Evidence exists in the several bad joins, particularly in the one towards the opening of Scene viii, that whereas Rowley and Birde were aware of the original play (no doubt in its promptbook form), their own papers were written out not directly as a new promptbook joining the old material but instead independently for subsequent linking-up with the older retained text when the new promptbook was to be copied out.[1] The evidence such as it is for the influence of the A-text stage-

[1] See 'Marlowe's *Doctor Faustus*: The 1602 Additions'. For example, there is some indication that Rowley–Birde proposed to scrap Chorus 2 before Scene viii and incorporate its material in their revised text. The change in purpose from St Peter's feast to one celebrating the Pope's victory, together with the altered discussion between Faustus and Mephistophilis about their purposes in Rome, seems to have resulted from the joining by the B-text inscriber of independent papers from the early play with the new 1602 additions. The chief problem in this matter comes in Act V. The 1602 papers hypothesized for the revision of Scene xvii between lines 1681 and 1723 constitute a unit and could have been intercalated with the early manuscript by the B-text inscriber, just as the new opening of Scene xviii, lines 1796.2–1820, and then the addition of lines 1880–1925 could have been worked-in. The problem arises whether in this act lines 1724–87 and 1821–79 were also copied out in the Rowley–Birde papers and thus with or without the assistance of A3. It seems clear that in Scene ix such snippets of

directions on B at 1680.1–1680.2, 1696.1–1696.2, and 1725.1 suggest that the Act V Rowley–Birde revisions were separate and that the two did not themselves copy-out and revise this intercalated matter taken from the original play. In this area textual evidence is almost wholly wanting. Against a minor agreement of B1 with A3 in 'my' for A1 'mine' at 1765 could be placed the non-evidential A3 unique reading 'I would' at 1841 in which B1 follows A1 in 'would'.

It would appear, then, that the manuscript purchased by Wright between 1611 and 1616 was the discarded papers of Marlowe and his collaborator from which the original promptbook had been made as well as the discarded papers of Rowley–Birde from which the 1602 promptbook had been copied. Marlowe's and his collaborator's papers being about ten years older, and perhaps in true foul-papers form, were apparently in a less legible condition than the Rowley–Birde papers. Hence when Wright hired some person to put this purchase into shape for the printer, Wright's 1611 edition (presumably still regarded as an authority for the sections of the original play) was utilized to assist the editor in making a fair copy of the original papers for the printer. Without a highly technical and perhaps inconclusive study of the characteristics of the two B-text compositors in setting the respective parts, not at present available, nothing more than a guess can be made whether the editor also found it advisable to recopy the added and revised 1602 sections or to mix-in these papers as convenient with his recopying of the original manuscript. One might perhaps guess at the latter, but it would be strictly a guess since evidence from the use of the A-text is necessarily wanting. (Perhaps his treatment of the additions and revisions in Act V was – in part or in whole – different.) But against such a guess must be placed the evidence (see below) from the

the original papers as 991–3 and 1004–5 had been incorporated by Rowley–Birde in their expansion and were not printed in B1 direct from the early manuscript or from A3. Yet it is interesting that the B-text inscriber went back to A3 for part of the stage-direction at 980.2 when the Rowley–Birde papers began new Scene ix, that was shortly to be taken over by the parallel A-version, evidence it would seem that from 1009–1087.3 the copy for the B-text was the early papers and that Rowley–Birde had not interfered. If so, we have again something of a control about the quality of the A reporting of comic scenes, which is certainly less exact than that of the tragic action spelling *Mephastophilis* in Rowley–Birde material, that he may well have re-inscribed the whole manuscript for the printer, as he was certainly doing in the area 980.3–991 in Scene ix.

The editorial problem resolves itself into two major parts:

(1) *Should the A- or the B-text be selected as copy-text?* To this the answer is simple. The whole of the A-text has no direct link with any authorial manuscript and hence its accidentals can have no authority whatever. Under these circumstances the B-text must be taken as the copy-text since it derives, even through the inter-mediaries of inscriber and compositor – and even despite contamination from A3 – from a manuscript that appears to be the authors' papers.

(2) *Should the edited text be based on the A- or on the B-version?* A strong argument could be made that scholars and critical readers are likely to be more interested in an edited text that would confine itself to a reconstruction of the original play than in a later version that includes the 1602 additions which could have had no part in Marlowe's original design – granting that he had anything to say about this design as it applied to the parts of the play written by his collaborator. (We must not allow sentiment about Marlowe to interfere with an estimate of how this play was originally put together.) Several major difficulties stand in the way of the logical practicability of such a proposal. It is true that the simple additions could be omitted since they can be isolated except where revision of the A-text has occurred at the joins, as in Scene viii. However, the 1602 revisions of the A-text present an insuperable problem. An example can be drawn from the farcical Scene xiv in which the presence of Mephostophilis has been suppressed and the scene re-written in preparation for the new 1602 Scene xv, yet no doubt with some of the original play's lines still embedded in the revised version in a different form from those found in the memorial A-text. If an editor were to confine himself to the A-text scenes, he would be forced to take over at this point the corrupt A-text which probably in its general action approximated that of the original play but scarcely in its language or in all its business, as the example of Scene iv (just possibly untouched in the main by revision) illustrates, and probably the example of Scene ix, 1009–1087.3. Similarly, a choice

would need to be made between the B-text's farcical Scenes vii and x or the combined A-text original. If the A-text were chosen, the result would be relatively distant from anything that could be said to reproduce the original play's language. If the B-text is printed, probable 1602 revision (not to be distinguished) would be offered as if it were the original, which likely it is not. In expanded and revised Scene xi part of the exchange between Carolus and Faustus is manifestly a 1602 revision. To remove this in order to substitute the A-text memorial version of the original is not entirely to return to the early play as it was first presented, and so perhaps with the Vanholt comic action. It would seem that a text consisting in part of debased A-text scenes, even though they derive ultimately from the original, and in part of the B-text's purer form of the earlier play would be convenient occasionally for the specialist but would not satisfy many needs of the general scholarly or critical reader. The case would be altered, of course, if the A-text were not a memorial version, a bad quarto; but facts are facts. Hence it has seemed best to the present editor to attempt in the main to offer a critically edited text in its 1602 form, which is at least textually coherent and historically a unit. If we are interested in Marlowe's own intentions we have them in the B-version in a textually superior form on the whole, or at least generally recoverable by emendation from A. No trustworthy evidence suggests that the B-text revisions concerned themselves in any significant part to alter Marlowe's contributions to the play; instead they operated chiefly on the work of his collaborator, even in Act V. How much Marlowe's original views about the play influenced the work of his collaborator cannot be known, or whether he ever concerned himself with the other parts of the play.[1] Under

[1] We cannot know, indeed, whether the play resulted from a planned and simultaneous collaboration or whether another playwright took over a play that Marlowe had started, with sketched-in parts of the last act, and himself reorganized the material and in a sense constructed a play called *Doctor Faustus*, using such parts of Marlowe's original work as pleased him. The intervention of the collaborator in Act V is disturbing because it suggests later tinkering with Marlowe's scene. It may be strictly a speculation, but the present editor inclines to the view that the function of Wagner in the play could be significant in this matter. If we grant that Scene ii is Marlowe's and that Marlowe may have had something to say about Scene iv, it would seem to have been his intention to associate Wagner with the action more intimately than the development of the later farcical scenes permits. Otherwise, the bequest to Wagner in

these circumstances – since the major interest of the play lies in Marlowe's own contribution – it may seem better for general study to take the play as we have it in 1602, in a viable form. The critic cannot be misled about Marlowe's intentions if he will confine his analysis to Marlowe's own lines;[1] and he can reconstruct the general course of the original comic and farcical action concentrated in Acts III and IV from what is certainly a Rowley–Birde improvement on the work of his collaborator. It would be possible, then, to edit the

the fifth act has little point, or even the possibility (from the misplaced short Chorus 2 in the B-text assigned to Wagner) that Wagner was kept in the audience's eye by acting as the choral presenter. It seems possible that the collaborator went his own way in dropping Wagner contrary to Marlowe's original design and that this may be a straw in the wind as to the nature of the collaboration. However, if one really wants to guess, it is intriguing that in the A-text Horse-courser action of A's Scene viii (B-text Scene xiv), line 137, the Horse-courser says, 'O yonder is his snipper snapper, do you heare? you, hey, passe, where's your maister?' and then engages in a dialogue with Mephistophilis. Despite what seems to be a vestigial stage-direction in the B-text of Scene xiv for the entrance with Faustus of Mephistophilis, who is not present in the revised scene, the 'snipper snapper' would apply better to Wagner and in view of Scene iv the 'hey, passe' is at least as appropriate. To introduce this speculation would of course involve the hypothesis that in the A-text provincial version Mephistophilis (perhaps largely mute in the original as he had been in Scene xi) took over Wagner's lines upon his disappearance and that Wagner was dropped not only in the A-text Scene xi but also in the revision of the original by Rowley–Birde. These are dangerous seas and can be sailed only as exercises in a dream-world of what might have been, especially since Wagner's entrance in both texts with the invitation to Vanholt introduces a problem, although not an insuperable one, if the A-text production had made the change. However, they indicate the faint possibility that in fact the collaborator could have kept Wagner more in mind than the strict evidence of the texts suggests and that the A acting version may in some part be responsible for his general lack of participation in Acts III and IV. But any such speculation involves a number of difficulties and the matter is very obscure. Nevertheless, the address of the Horse-courser to Mephistophilis is anomalous though natural enough if it had been Wagner.

[1] For instance, it would seem to be anomalous for Greg to apply lines 1886–9, which are part of a major Rowley–Birde addition in Act V, to any meaningful interpretation of Marlowe's lines 65–74. The chief exception would be the question of Scene xix, the close of the play. The present editor's own opinion – held with some diffidence but nevertheless held – is that this scene was very likely part of the Rowley–Birde additions. But if on stylistic or other grounds a critic chooses to think differently and to include it in his over-view of the original play and of Marlowe's Act V, that must remain his privilege, given the uncertain status of the scene. A minor exception would be the apparently revised version in B of the Old Man's first speech, lines 1707–23, which has every appearance of being well reported from the original play in the A-text (see Appendix: A-text Scene xi continued, lines 34–45). Again, Marlowe's authorship of these lines is not certain and they may be part of the collaborator's work in V.i.

text exclusively on the basis of the 1616 quarto copy-text with only such verbal emendations from A as seem required to restore the conjectured original from B's corruptions and sophistications. However, when the B-text cuts passages from A that may well have been present in the original play, these have been restored even though the unity of texture suffers thereby.[1] In such cases the risk of omitting original material weighs more heavily that the virtues of mechanical consistency.

The A1 quarto of 1604 collating A–F⁴ (F4 wanting, blank?) was printed for Bushell by Valentime Simmes. Two compositors set this play, for convenience identified as Compositor A and Compositor C.[2] The alternation of the two workmen was irregular and their stints coincide with the beginning and end of a type-page only in the first sheet and part of the second. Compositor C set sigs A2^r– B2^r, B3^v, C1^r–C2^r (upper), C3^r (lower)–C3^v (upper), C4^v (lower), D1^r (lower)–D2^r (upper), D2^v (lower), E2^r (lower)–E2^v (upper), E3^v (upper)–E4^v (upper). Compositor A set sig. B2^v–B3^r, B4^{r-v}, C2^r–(lower)–C3^r (upper), C3^v (lower)–C4^v (upper), C4^v (lowest)– D1 (upper), D2^r (lower)–D2^v (upper), D2^v (lowest)–E2^r (upper), E2^v (lower)–E3^v (upper), E3^v (upper)–F3^v. In terms of the A-text

---

[1] Like the lines after Mephistophilis' original presentation of the magic book which may be the work of Marlowe's collaborator cut by Rowley–Birde (551.0.1–13) although the possibility cannot be overlooked that they are an expansion in the performance from which the A memorial text derives. Such doubtful passages have not been included in the continuous line-numbering although more certain cases like the restoration of the B-text omission of Chorus 3 (1138–54) have been continuously numbered. It is an interesting speculation that, on the evidence of Chorus 2, Rowley and Birde may have planned to omit the two internal Choruses, leaving only the prologue and the epilogue, although we cannot be sure even of these.

[2] The basic bibliographical facts about the printing of A1 and of B1 are drawn from Robert Ford Welsh, *The Printing of the Early Editions of Marlowe's Plays*, pp. 85–157. Because Compositor A has been identified as A in other investigations of Simmes's compositors, the editor has preferred to substitute A for Dr Welsh's Y and C for his X, thus leaving Simmes's also identified Compositor B out of the picture. The editor's own assignment of the shares differs in a few minor respects from that of Dr Welsh since the analysis of Compositor A by subsequent scholars has expanded and refined the information about the characteristics that serve to identify him; however, the editor is not equally confident of all the assignments, especially of the shorter stints. For more information about Compositor A, see W. Craig Ferguson, *Valentine Simmes* (1968) chapter 3, pp. 27–37; also, Alan E. Craven, 'Simmes' Compositor A: The Compositor of Five Shakespeare Quartos', *Studies in Bibliography*, XXVI (1973).

comparable to the line-numbering of the present edition, Compositor *C* set 0.1–300; A-text Scene iv, 32–64; 451–531; 597–635; 694 (| and the divell)–707; 778.2–980.1; 1137.1–1154.1; A-text Scene viii, 120–63; 1680.1–1742. Compositor *A* set 301–42.1, plus A-text Scene iv, 0.1–31; A-text Scene iv, 65–73, plus 389–450; 532–96; 635.1–694 (pention, |); 708–78.1; A-text Scene vi, (end) 1–41.2; A-text Scene vii, 0.1–34, plus A-text Scene viii, 1–119.1; A-text Scene viii, 164–72, plus A-text Scene ix, 0.1–34, plus A-text Scene xi, 0.1–8; 1743–2009.1.

Nothing is as yet known about Compositor *C*, but Compositor *A* has been studied by Dr Craven in relation to his setting of Q2 *Richard II* and discovered to be a careless workman likely to make an unauthoritative substantive change once in every seventeen lines of text, with substitutions heading the list, followed by omissions, interpolations, sophistications, and transpositions. In so far as possible the present editor has endeavoured to take account of this compositor in the decisions about emendations from the A-text in the B copy-text.

The evidence for the setting and printing of A1 brought together by Dr Welsh shows that the quarto was printed with two skeleton-formes throughout, these skeletons switching formes in sheet E but returning in final sheet F to their original positions. The evidence of the running-titles suggests to the present editor that sheet A was not cast-off and set last but was instead the first to be composed. Dr Welsh's evidence for type-shortages (pp. 107–13) indicates that in sheets C–E each compositor set his stint seriatim, a conclusion strongly supported by the nature of the stints which are not confined to formes. Dr Welsh was admittedly hampered by his inability to identify precise types from photographs of the unique Bodleian copy, and thus the remainder of his evidence is suspect (based largely on the shortages of black-letter 'W', a congenital difficulty in founts of Continental origin) that whereas each compositor had his own set of roman cases they were forced to share only one pair of cases of the black-letter fount (pp. 115–20). If this were so, not only would each compositor set his stint seriatim (which is certain) but also the stints would have been alternated instead of being set simultaneously. Given the absence of more precise findings from the distribution and setting of identified types, the present editor takes it that, instead, Compositor C probably set sheet A by formes, and almost certainly started sheet B by setting sigs B1^v, 2^r, 3^v of the inner forme. Then Compositor A became available and completed the inner forme with sig. B4^r (probably while C was setting B3^v), at which point Compositor C went back to B1^r of the outer forme and then on to sheet C while Compositor A composed the remaining pages B2^v, 3^r, 4^v. Thereafter, it may be conjectured, each set simultaneously in irregular stints until Compositor A took over the setting of sheet F, which he set by formes.

The irregularity of the stints is interesting and most unusual. If A1 had been a reprint one would have expected the compositors, working either simultaneously or by alternation, to set complete pages. Instead, once sheet B set by pages had been disposed of, after Compositor A entered to assist his fellow in completing the sheet with greatest expedition, no stint in sheets C–E begins and ends with a page except for the part of sheet C set seriatim by Compositor C while waiting for A to finish with sheet B. On the contrary there is a general tendency to select as a dividing point some prominent place in the text, often the beginning of a new scene but sometimes the stage-direction for the entrance of a character within a scene. This practice is so consistent and so odd as to call for explanation. The editor's conjecture is that the procedure is not consistent with setting from printed copy but is most explicable if the compositors were setting from manuscript that had not been cast off but where arbitrary joins could be marked at readily identifiable points. It would follow almost by necessity that they were generally setting without thought of complete pages. Only after their galleys had been transferred to the imposing stone was the type divided into the proper pages, by formes, when the time came for imposition. This method is so unusual as to suggest that the copy was not an easy one to cast off for exact operation by two simultaneously setting compositors even though – on the probable evidence of sheet B – a single compositor could work by formes from cast-off copy. If this is so, and an explanation for the procedure based on printed copy is hard to come by, the conjecture is possible that A1 was composed from manuscript and hence that it is the true first edition. The case is speculative, but the bibliographical evidence can be interpreted in that direction.

The 1616 black-letter quarto B1 collating A–H⁴ (H4 blank) was more conventionally set by two compositors, perhaps in the shop of George Eld who frequently printed for Wright. Compositor *Y* (Welsh's Compositor *A*) may be distinguished chiefly by his spelling *deuil* and *I'le* and *Benuolio* but also by his preference for *do, go, 'tis, e're, ne're, o're, he'le* or *hee'le*, by endings usually in *-y*, by his setting *Germane* in roman, and by a frequent use of ligatures in *ee* and *oo*. Compositor *X* (Welsh's Compositor *B*) set *diuel, Il'e, Benvolio*, and preferred *doe, goe, tis, ere, nere, ore, hee'l, wee'l*, endings in *-ie, Germane* in black letter, and unligatured *ee* and *oo*. Compositor *X* set sigs A3ᵛ–D2ʳ, D3ʳ, E1ʳ–E2ᵛ, F2ᵛ–G2ᵛ, H2ᵛ–H3ᵛ. Compositor *Y* set sigs A2ʳ–A3ʳ, D2ᵛ, D3ᵛ–D4ᵛ, E3ʳ–F2ʳ, G3ʳ–H2ʳ. In terms of the line-numbering of the present edition, Compositor *Y* set 0.1–99, 873–908, 944–1047, 1192–1419.1, 1676 (| golden)–1919. Compositor *X* set 100–872, 909–943, 1048–1191, 1419.2–1676 (store of |), 1920–2009.2. A survey of the basic emendations needed in the B-text that may reasonably be attributed to compositorial error suggests that Compositor *X* was the less trustworthy workman in respect to substitutions and sophistications but that Compositor *Y* had some tendency to omit words. In so far as possible what can be determined about the characteristics of these compositors has guided the editor in certain of his emendations.

Although the analysis of the running-titles is hampered by the trimming of the leaves in the only known copy, in the British Museum, it seems clear that sheets B–C were machined by only one skeleton-forme, that a second was added with sheet D (the start of the fairly regular alternation of stints by the two compositors), and that sheets D–H were regularly imposed by the two skeletons but sheet A was machined using only the second or added skeleton for both formes. Dr Welsh (p. 150ff.) from the interpretation of this evidence supported by the evidence of the setting and distribution of identifiable types finds that Compositor *X* set sheets B and C by formes from cast-off copy and that in sheet D when Compositor *Y* first appears the copy was also set by formes. It is less certain that Dr Welsh's further conjecture that sheets E–H were set by formes is correct, for his evidence is not strong and the allocation of copy is odd for such a procedure. (Indeed, Beaumont and Fletcher's *Cupid's Revenge*, which exhibits much the same pattern, can be shown to have had its pages set seriatim by two alternating compositors each setting about one-half of the sheet as in *Faustus*.) It would seem more probable that each compositor was given copy for approximately half a sheet, that he set it seriatim, and that the formes for each sheet were imposed as completed. Whether the compositors worked simultaneously or by spelling each other is not to be determined from the available evidence. However, Dr Welsh shows that sheet A was imposed only from the second skeleton that had been made-up for sheet D, and that its pages contain identifiable types from outer D and outer E. It follows almost by necessity (supported by the compositorial stints) that the copy for sheet A had been cast off and was set and printed last of all after sheet H, a method adopted, for example, in the first edition of *Edward II*. One may remark that on this evidence it seems clear that the 1616 quarto is indeed the first edition as usually supposed.

The evidence of the ease and accuracy with which copy was cast off suggests that this copy was not likely to be the mixture of manuscript and annotated A3 printed pages, with directions back and forth for the insertion first of manuscript pages and then of printed copy, that Greg has envisaged. This evidence can now be added to that in 'The Text of Marlowe's *Faustus*' which indicates that an editor–scribe prepared the printer's copy throughout and that the printer's copy was exclusively in manuscript form.[1]

Two small points need summary discussion. The first concerns the spelling of Mephostophilis' name. In the German and in the translated *Historie* it is *Mephostophiles*. The usual A-text form is *Mephastophilis*, although the almost invariable B-text form *Mephostophilis* is found in the A-text twice – both times in stage-directions

---

[1] To the evidence of the repeated error in the B-text of *euening Starres* but A3 correct *erring Starres* and the other examples of handwriting misreadings in copy thought by Greg to have been set directly from A3 may be added *watch* in 821 for correct A3 *match*, this also in the work of Compositor *X* who set *euening* twice. It was also *X* who set the B misreading *Sworne* for A3 *Swarme* in 142. See also the discussion below of the Compositor *Y* spellings *Mephastophilis* which bear heavily on the side of a total inscription of the copy for B1 even for the Rowley–Birde additions.

and hence possibly by another hand – set by Compositor *C* on sig. B1^v and by Compositor *A* on sig. D3^v. However, the A-text has a sprinkling of the form *Mephastophilus* in the work of both compositors although chiefly in Compositor *A*: Compositor *A* set it on B4^r (once), B4^v (five times), C2^v (twice), C3^v (once); Compositor *C* set it on C3 (once), C3^v (once), and D1^r (twice). Whether these are compositorial aberrations or, more likely, variation in the copy is not to be determined. The cluster on sigs B4^r–4^v is odd but the pattern throughout does not seem to derive from the copying of differences in a hypothetical lost earlier edition set by two compositors with different spellings of the name. Being memorial, the A-text spellings can have no authority about the form in the original manuscript of the play; moreover, the *Mephastophilis* variant with *a* is unique in the history of the name although *Mephostophilus* is known in *The Merry Wives* and in Shirley's *Young Admiral* (1637), for which see Greg, p. 40n.

In the B-text on the first two occurrences of the name – in the Latin conjuration (247, 250) – Compositor *X* set *Mephostophilis* although the A-text read *Mephastophilis*. As Greg remarks (p. 313), this spelling in B ought to have repeated here the form in the manuscript.[1] The first time Compositor *Y* encounters the name is in 891 in the Rowley–Birde addition in Scene viii not present in the A-text. If this addition had been set from the 1602 papers and not copied by the inscriber, the spelling *Mephostophilis* here would confirm the name as Rowley and Birde had seen it in the promptbook; but the evidence is against such direct setting. On his second encounter *Y* sets the abbreviation *Mephosto.* still in the 1602 addition, but only a few lines later, in the stage-direction at 980.3 it is spelled *Mephastophilis* even though the name is not present in the parallel A-text direction that comes a little after (see Appendix: A-text Scene vi, 0.1–2) but was almost certainly added by the inscriber. The spelling with *a* cannot be compositorial (unless a most fortuitous a:o confusion) since Compositor *Y* had not previously seen it in his copy. Within a few lines *Y* sets the abbreviation *Mephasto:* (991) in a

[1] From the intrusion in B's conjuration text of stage-directons not present in A, the presence of the original manuscript here is strongly suggested, no matter what other dependence the inscriber may have placed on A3 in this invocation.

passage originally written by Marlowe's collaborator but in the B copy only a bridge of five lines between the two parts of the 1602 addition and therefore almost surely copied-out in 1602 as part of the text of these papers. Moreover, the name is not present in the A-text for this brief passage. Shortly, in *Y* it is *Mephosto:* (1006) in a Rowley couplet, but it is *Mephastophilis* again at 1314 in a passage from the original play by the collaborator (here the A-text has the same and could have influenced B), but thereafter *Mephostophilis* in 1402 and 1412 in Rowley–Birde additions, and later in 1680.1 and 1696.1, until once more *Mephasto:* (as in A3) at 1747. Subsequently in the one remaining occurrence in *Y* it is *Mephostophilis*. This is curious evidence. The only time Compositor *X* sets the A-text form is in the bond (495) where A-text contamination of the copy is possible. The remaining four examples are all in the work of Compositor *Y*, but in two of these (both in the Rowley–Birde addition) the example of the A-text could not have affected the form as it may have in the final two cases.

From this evidence three tentative conclusions may be drawn: (1) Since the A-text form could not have derived to B by direct contamination at 980.3 and 991, it must have been present in the copy; this being so, the other *Y* occurrences are not necessarily to be imputed to the A-text parallels at 1314 and 1747. (2) It is probable that Compositor *X*, who made only one slip, was less influenced by his copy than was *Y*, and that *Y*'s slips are not necessarily the only times that the variants appeared in his or in *X*'s copy; if so, the copy could have been more irregular than the five appearances of *Mephastophilis* in the B-text would indicate. (3) Since two of the A-text forms appear in a 1602 addition and also at a point where no opportunity had as yet developed for Compositor *Y* to be influenced by preceding examples, the copy for the play at that place was an inscription, not the original Rowley–Birde papers.[1] Hence it would appear that the inscriber of the printer's copy for the B-text normally read *Mephostophilis* in his manuscripts but under the influence

---

[1] The logic is not altered even if Scene viii passages in B not present in A are denied as 1602 additions and accepted as original but omitted passages in the A-text production.

of A3, which he was closely consulting in his preparation of parts of the play, he picked up the alternative spelling *Mephastophilis* and from time to time wrote it thus even when the A-text was not present to influence him directly.

The second point is the question of the authority of the various 1619 (B2) quarto variations from 1616, including some that return to A1 readings.[1] Greg took these returns[2] so seriously that he devoted a special appendix to the question of their possible authority (pp. 140–50). In this he argued on bibliographical grounds that it is impossible for the B2 variants to have arisen in any major part from formes of B1 in a different state of press-correction from those known in the only preserved copy. Of the 112 verbal variants listed in Greg's parallel-text edition,[3] he disposes of all but a dozen as accidental, attempted unauthoritative corrections, or else errors in the transmission. Of the six or seven in this dozen that he takes to be truly significant, he states, 'The conclusion, I think, must stand that the most likely source of the reviser's independent knowledge was a recollection of a current performance of the play' (p. 150). It follows that these key variants, for an editor, are 'entitled to the respect due, not merely to a persuasive contemporary emendation, but to one that may actually derive from an authoritative source' (*ibid.*).[4] Greg's sole reason for assuming that the reviser of B2 did not have a copy of A1 before him (the possibility of a manuscript is dismissed) is, 'Had he done so it is inconceivable that he would have restored the line already mentioned (2048+, and that in a slightly

---

[1] The editor has been able to check these variants against the unique copy of the 1619 quarto formerly in private hands but now in the Princeton University Library.

[2] Only once, in 556, and then fortuitously, did the B2 quarto return to a reading of A2–3 not present in A1. If the A1 readings result from consultation, as the present editor believes, the copy referred to was definitely A1.

[3] This includes a number of such minor variants as *hath-has, mongst-amongst*, and the like.

[4] See also p. 149: 'If, therefore, his knowledge was derived from A, the whole question becomes unimportant. We possess A and can judge of its readings for ourselves; nothing that the reviser happened to remember of it or approve in it can add to our knowledge or affect our judgement. If, on the other hand, he derived his knowledge from current performance, his recollections, whether always accurate or not, are of considerable importance, since they may include corrections of the printed tradition; and of particular interest will be his restoration of readings of A when these differ from B1.'

different form)[1] without also restoring the line that followed it to its obviously original reading; and it is highly probable that he would have undone some of the other mischief due to censoring' (p. 149). The present editor does not find the failure to alter the hypermetrical line 1940 after adding 1939 (even without the second 'see') inconceivable, and prefers the hypothesis of casual consultation of A1 to 'correct' the printer's copy for B2 (probably a part of Wright's preparation for the second edition) to the – to him – untenable hypothesis that the memory of a performance would enable the B2 reviser to restore the A1 readings in such cases as 'againe' at 371 but more particularly of 'rare' at 1542, this latter in the new Rowley–Birde Scene xv where material was being transferred from the original A-scene equivalent of Scene xiv and in the process 'rare' (if authoritative as the editor assumes) got dropped. These trivia, and others, are truly inconceivable as recollections of a performance but they are not inconceivable for an alert reader of A1 who was not charged with restoring all A1 readings that he preferred but was picking up things here and there at his pleasure.[2] This reviser was quite unsystematic in that he made no effort to restore missing lines in B1 other than the striking line 1939 and he left most B1 textual tangles alone. His independent alterations give the best clue to his intentions in that he was more concerned to 'correct' his copy according to his own views than he was to restore A1 readings – in fact, only eleven of these are put back, as against perhaps seven or eight times the number of independent alterations he made that are not to be attributed to the B2 compositor. This suggests that his main motive was to prepare copy for the second edition that would improve it for readers; hence he went

[1] The line is 1939 in the present edition, 'See see where Christs bloud streamed in the firmament', omitted in B1 owing to the censorship though present in A1–3, with the consequential change in B1 1940 of 'One drop of bloud will save me; oh my Christ' for A1–3 'One drop would save my soule, halfe a drop, ah my Christ'. B2, actually, prints 'See where', not 'See see where'.

[2] If, as we must assume, Wright did not secure some outside person's annotated copy of B1 (such as gave rise to the 1679 Beaumont and Fletcher Folio's variants) but as happened with the second and third editions of Dekker's *Shoemakers' Holiday* made some small effort to improve his second-edition text, the failure to restore censorship is not, as Greg takes it, significant, for given the origin of the B1 printer's copy it seems clear that this censorship was performed by the inscriber of the B1 copy for the press.

over the 1616 text and tinkered with it as ideas occurred to him with no intention of ferreting out all its errors.[1] That he knew the A1 text well is attested by his occasional memory for small details, such as the emendation of 1114 *demogorgon* to agree with AB1 *demigorgon* at 246[2] or his recollection of *rare qualities* at 1542. It is quite clear that he was not engaged in collating B1 against A1 but instead had A1 at his elbow and occasionally consulted it when he felt something was wrong that he could not readily deal with (as perhaps at 408) but more often, it would seem, when his memory was tickled. It may be that he occasionally read through an A1 passage before tackling his text. (See his added 'meere' in line 516 under the influence of line 524.) Yet as remarked, the changes were unsystematic. The occasions on which he did in fact restore A1 readings[3] are very few indeed in comparison with the number of his own changes and they should not be overemphasized or the true proportion is unbalanced. The present editor, with some certitude, believes that these few restorations were made from A1 and from no other authority (least of all from memory of a performance) and thus that they have no extrinsic authority beyond that of A1. In the treatment of emendations the fact that B2 may read with A1 has not influenced editorial choice.[4]

[1] Typical is his treatment of 833–4. The B1 repetition (A is wanting)

> The which this day with high solemnity
> This day is held through *Rome* and *Italy*

is obviously inept; the B2 corrector, therefore, altered 833 to read *The which in state and high solemnity*, which certainly smooths out the two lines but without authority. In 1170 he refined *warlike semblances* to *perfect semblances* in order to avoid the literal application of *warlike* to Alexander's paramour. He gilded the lily at 1182 by increasing the number of attendant devils from B1's *a thousand* to *ten thousand*. In 403 a similar expansion took place from *that famous Art* to *that most famous Art*, and in 462 he preferred *attaine* to *obtaine*. In 516 Faustus' remark that hell is *a fable* becomes *a meere fable*. In the light of these changes, this editor cannot take seriously the respect that Greg gives to B2 *whole* for B1 *huge Argosies* (157) or even Greg's liking for B2 *divers* instead of AB1 *thousand* in line 50.

[2] This is Greg's suggestion. In fact, since they are both in farcical conjuring scenes, the memory of the B2 corrector was more likely stimulated by '*demygorgon*' (misprinted in B1 as '*denygorgon*') in line 728 so that memory of A1 is not required here.

[3] These occur in lines 90, 142, 159, 240, 558, 821, 1079, 1542, 1786, 1839, 1939.

[4] As a convenience only and in part as a means of securing some consistency of notation, the footnotes that detail the emendations accepted from A1 in this edition will also list B2 in the cases where B2 agrees. No intention is present in this notation to give B2 any more authority than would be present if an emendation were drawn, say, from B6.

The following chart is offered to assist in clarifying the structure of the A-text play, which is to say a form as close as we shall ever come to the original production, as well as the relationship to it of the B-text. Assignment of authorship on the basis of scenes or passages by Marlowe, by his original collaborator, and by Rowley and Birde[1] has been added. The absolute distinction of all of Marlowe's share is perhaps not possible, and opinion may well differ here and there as to whether he or his colllaborator wrote some of the lines. The present editor is inclined to the belief that here and there the collaborator tinkered with Marlowe's work, but in the nature of the case these pieces of text are difficult to distinguish from A's memorial expansion and alteration which on occasion may have been followed by the B-text inscriber.[2]

The B- and the A-Texts

B-TEXT	A-TEXT
Chorus 1 0.1–28.1 *Marlowe*	Chorus 1 Same
Scene i (I.i) 28.2–193.1 Faustus rejects divinity and embraces magic with Valdes and Cornelius *Marlowe*	Scene i Same
Scene ii (I.ii) 193.2–228.1 The Scholars and Wagner *Marlowe*	Scene ii Same
Scene iii (I.iii) 228.2–342.1 Faustus raises Mephistophilis *Marlowe*	Scene iii Same

[1] It would be tempting to assign the comic additions and revisions to Rowley and the farcical to Birde despite the fact that we have no identified writings by Birde for comparison. The additions and revisions containing couplets and the completions of part lines are almost surely Rowley's. One might speculate that the revision of the Old Man's speech does not sound much like Rowley and that it might be given to Birde, who might even have written the last Scene xix; but guesswork of this kind is idle and it is safer not to try to distinguish all of the couplet passages from the non-couplet additions and revisions.

[2] Greg's attribution of authorship may be found in the chart on pp. 138–9 of his parallel-text edition.

Scene iv (I.iv) 342.2–388.1
Wagner hires Robin
Collaborator

Scene iv Parallel; see Appendix for
text

Scene v (II.i) 388.2–551.1
Faustus signs contract and receives
  magic book from Mephistophilis
*Marlowe, with scattered alterations or
additions by collaborator or from A-
text; 550–551 revised by editor or by
Rowley–Birde*
[*Chorus 2 short A-version out of place*]

Scene v Generally same but makes one
continuous scene of B-text Scenes v–
vi; 551.0.1–551.0.13 may represent
original play cut in B

Scene vi (II.ii) 551.2–721.1
Conversations with Mephistophilis,
  regrets, Angels, Seven Deadly Sins
*Marlowe, but A-text contamination in
645–6. Collaborator possibly responsible
for 635.1–712 but certainly for 713–21
unless this is A-text contamination.
Rowley–Birde may have touched up
Seven Deadly Sins*

Scene v continued (Greg, Sc. vi)

Scene vii (II.iii) 721.2–753.1
Robin and Dick with conjuring book
*Collaborator; revised by Rowley–Birde
and A-version split into Scenes vii, x*

[A-text Scene vii joining B-text Scenes
vii, x]

Chorus 2
Marlowe

Chorus 2
Short text

Scene viii (III.i) 778.2–980.1
779–835 Description of Rome
Collaborator

Scene vi (Greg, Sc. vii)
Same

836–980.1 Rescue of Bruno
*Rowley–Birde; 856–60 copied out from
  collaborator*

Wanting, except 856–60 parallel

Scene ix (III.ii) 980.2–2–1087.2
980.2–1036 Discovery of Bruno's rescue
*Rowley–Birde, except 989–93, 1004–5
copied out from collaborator*

Scene vi continued
Wanting, except 989–93, 1004–5
parallel

1037–1087.2 Disruption of feast
Collaborator

Parallel; see Appendix for text

Scene x (III.iii) 1087.3–1137.1
Robin, Dick, Vintner. Punishment by
  Mephistophilis
Collaborator

Scene vii (Greg, Sc. viii–ix)
Parallel to B-text. Scenes vii, x; see
  Appendix for text

[Chorus 3, 1137.2–1154.1, omitted;
  probably cut by Rowley–Birde;
  written by collaborator]

Chorus 3   1136.2–1154.1 *Collaborator*

Scene xi (IV.i) 1154.2–1324.1
Magic before Carolus; Benvolio horned
1154.2–1203.1
Rowley–Birde addition

Scene viii (Greg, Sc. x)
Parallel for magic, knight
Wanting

1203.2–1324.1
Collaborator, revised by Rowley–Birde

Parallel; see Appendix for text to
  1504.1

Scene xii (IV.ii) 1324.2–1430.4
Revenge of Benvolio; its punishment
Rowley–Birde addition

Wanting

Scene xiii (IV.iii) 1430.5–1456.1
Return of knights horned
Rowley–Birde addition

Wanting

Scene xiv (IV.iv) 1456.2–1504.1
Horse-courser episode; invitation to
  Vanholt
Collaborator, revised by Rowley–Birde

Scene viii continued (Greg, Sc. xi)
Parallel

Scene xv (IV.v) 1504.2–1557.1
Tavern scene of clowns
*Rowley–Birde addition, with some
  material drawn from A-form of revised
  Scene xiv*

Wanting

Scene xvi (IV.vi) 1557.2–1673.1
Vanholt magic and interference by
  clowns
1557.2–1588, 1669–1673.1
Collaborator, revised by Rowley–Birde

Scene ix (Greg Sc. xii)

Parallel; see Appendix for text

1588.1–1668
Rowley–Birde addition

Wanting

Scene xvii (V.i) 1673.2–1796.1
Faustus, Scholars, Helen, Old Man
1673.2–1706
*Marlowe(?), or collaborator, or Marlowe
  with collaborator's alterations*

Scene x (Greg, Sc. xiii)

Same; see Appendix for A-text of
  1673.2–1680

157

1706.1–1723 *Rowley–Birde revision of Marlowe(?) or* *of collaborator*	Parallel; see Appendix for text
1724–87 *Marlowe*	Same
[1788–1796.1 *Marlowe(?) or collaborator, cut by* *Rowley–Birde*]	1788–1796.1 *Marlowe(?) or collaborator*

Scene xviii (V.ii) 1796.2–1982.2
Devils exult, Wagner receives bequest,
  Scholars visit Faustus, damnation of
  Faustus
	Scene xi (Greg, Sc. xiv)

1796.2–1820 *Rowley–Birde addition*	Wanting
1820–79 *Marlowe*	Same
1879.1–1925 *Rowley–Birde addition*	Wanting
1925.1–1982.2 *Marlowe*	Same
Scene xix (V.iii) 1982.3–2001.1 Scholars discover Faustus' body *Rowley–Birde addition, or Marlowe(?)*	Wanting
Chorus 4 2001.2–2009.1 *Marlowe*	Same

In the preparation of this edition, A1 (1604) in the unique
Bodleian copy was collated against A2 (1611) from the Staats-
bibliothek Hamburg and A3 (1611) at the Henry E. Huntington
Library, and then its variants from B1 (1616) were recorded. B1
(1616) in the unique British Museum copy (C.34.d.26) was collated
against B2 (1619), formerly the Garrett copy but now at Princeton
University, B3 (1620) in the British Museum copy (C.39.c.26), B4
(1624) in the British Museum copy (C.34.d.27), B5 (1628) in the
copy at Lincoln College, Oxford, and B6 (1631) in the British
Museum copy (644.e.69). The following modern editions have been
recorded in the Historical Collation: *Old English Plays*, ed. Dilke

(1814), the 1818 edition published by J. Chappell Jr, the 1818 edition edited by Oxberry, *Works*, edited by Robinson (1824), *Works*, edited by Dyce (1850, revised 1858), *Works*, edited by Cunningham (1870), *Works*, edited by Bullen (1885), *Works*, edited by Tucker Brooke (1910), the edition by Boas (Methuen, 1932), by Greg (1950, the modernized text), *Plays*, edited by Kirschbaum (1962), the edition by Jump (Revels, 1962), *Complete Plays*, edited by Ribner (1963). For those editions like Dyce and Cunningham which print both texts, only the B1 text was fully collated and recorded, but variants in their edited A-texts are recorded in the footnotes to the Appendix diplomatic reprint of the parallel A-text scenes and passages that could not be handled in the formal Historical Collation based on the B copy-text.

DRAMATIS PERSONÆ

Doctor Faustus
Wagner, his servant
Valdes } Students of
Cornelius } magic
Three Scholars
Mephostophilis
An Old Man
Pope Adrian
Raymond, King of Hungary
Bruno, the rival Pope
Cardinals of France
  and Padua
Archbishop of Rheims
Charles V, Emperor of
  Germany
Martino }
Frederick } Knights at his
Benvolio } court
Duke of Saxony
Duke of Vanholt
Duchess of Vanholt
Robin, the Clown
Dick
Vintner

Horse-courser
Carter
Hostess
Good Angel
Bad Angel
Lucifer
Beelzebub
Pride }
Covetousness }
Envy } the Seven
Wrath } Deadly
Gluttony } Sins
Sloth }
Lechery }
Alexander the }
  Great }
His Paramour }
Darius, King of } Spirits
  Persia }
Helen }
Two Cupids }
Bishops, Monks, Friars,
  Soldiers, Attendants, Devils,
  a Piper

The Tragedie of Doctor Faustus.

Enter Chorus.   [Chorus 1]

Not marching in the fields of *Thrasimen*,
Where *Mars* did mate the warlicke *Carthagens*,
Nor sporting in the dalliance of love
In Courts of Kings, where state is over-turn'd,
Nor in the pompe of proud audacious deeds,
Intends our Muse to vaunt his heavenly verse;
Onely this, Gentles: we must now performe
The forme of *Faustus* fortunes, good or bad,
And now to patient judgements we appeale,
And speake for *Faustus* in his infancie.   10
Now is he borne, of parents base of stocke,
In *Germany*, within a Towne cal'd *Rhode*:
At riper yeares to *Wittenberg* he went,
Whereas his kinsmen chiefly brought him up;
So much he profits in Divinitie,
The fruitfull plot of Scholerisme grac'd,
That shortly he was grac'd with Doctors name,
Excelling all, whose sweete delight's dispute
In th' heavenly matters of Theologie,
Till swolne with cunning of a selfe conceit,   20
His waxen wings did mount above his reach,
And melting, heavens conspir'd his over-throw:
For falling to a divellish exercise,
And glutted now with learnings golden gifts,
He surfets upon cursed Necromancie:
Nothing so sweet as Magicke is to him,
Which he preferres before his chiefest blisse;
And this the man that in his study sits.

Exit.

12 *Rhode*] Methuen; *Rhodes* AB 1–6
16 The   fruitfull...grac'd,]   A 1–3;
   omit B 1–6
*18 whose sweete delight's dispute] and
sweetly can dispute B 1–6; whose
sweete delight disputes A 1–3
28.1 *Exit.*] A 1–3; *omit* B 1–6

[Scene i]

Enter Faustus *in his study.* [I.i]

Faustus.   Settle thy studies *Faustus*, and begin
To sound the depth of that thou wilt professe,   30
Having commenc'd, be a Divine in shew,
Yet levell at the end of every Art,
And live and die in *Aristotles* workes.
Sweet *Analitikes*, tis thou hast ravisht me,
Bene disserere est finis logices.
Is to dispute well Logickes chiefest end?
Affoords this Art no greater miracle?
Then read no more, thou hast attain'd that end;
A greater subject fitteth *Faustus* wit:
Bid *on kai me on* farewell, *Galen* come: 40
Seeing *ubi desinit philosophus, ibi incipit medicus.*
Be a Phisitian *Faustus*, heape up gold,
And be eterniz'd for some wondrous cure:
Summum bonum medicinæ sanitas,
The end of Physicke is our bodies health:
Why *Faustus*, hast thou not attain'd that end?
Is not thy common talke sound Aphorismes?
Are not thy bils hung up as monuments,
Wherby whole Cities have escap't the plague,
And thousand desperate maladies beene cur'd?   50
Yet art thou still but *Faustus*, and a man.
Couldst thou make men to live eternally,
Or being dead, raise them to life againe,
Then this profession were to be esteem'd.
Physicke farewell: where is *Justinian*?
Si una eademque res legatur duobus, alter rem, alter valorem rei, &c.
A petty case of paltry Legacies:
Exhereditare filium non potest pater, nisi——

28.2 *Enter*] A 1–3; *omit* B 1–6
40 *on kai me on*] Bullen; *Oncaymæon*
    A 1; *Oeconomy* A 2–3, B 1–6
40 *Galen*] A 1–3; *and Galen* B 1–6

41 Seeing...*medicus.*] A 1–3 (Seeing,);
    omit B 1–6
47 Is...Aphorismes?] A 1–3; *omit* B 1–6
*52 men] *stet* A 3, B 1–6; man A 1–2

Such is the subject of the *Institute*,
And universall body of the law. 60
This study fits a Mercenarie drudge,
Who aims at nothing but externall trash,
Too servile and illiberall for mee.
When all is done, *Divinitie* is best:
Jeromes Bible *Faustus*, view it well:
Stipendium peccati mors est: ha, *Stipendium, &c.*
The reward of sin is death? that's hard:
Si peccasse negamus, fallimur, et nulla est in nobis veritas:
If we say that we have no sinne we deceive our selves, and there
is no truth in us. 70
Why then belike
We must sinne, and so consequently die,
I, we must die, an everlasting death.
What doctrine call you this? *Che sera, sera*:
What will be, shall be; *Divinitie* adeiw.
These Metaphisicks of Magitians,
And Negromantick bookes are heavenly.
Lines, Circles, Signes, Letters, and Characters,
I these are those that *Faustus* most desires.
O what a world of profite and delight, 80
Of power, of honour, and omnipotence,
Is promised to the Studious Artizan?
All things that move betweene the quiet Poles
Shall be at my command: Emperors and Kings,
Are but obey'd in their severall Provinces:
Nor can they raise the winde, or rend the cloudes:
But his dominion that exceeds in this,
Stretcheth as farre as doth the mind of man:
A sound Magitian is a Demi-god,
Here tire my braines to get a Deity. 90

78 Signes] Greg; *omit* B 1–6; sceanes   *86 Nor...cloudes:] A 1–3; *omit* B 1–6
  A 1–3   *90 tire] *stet* B 1–6; trie A 1–3
78 and] A 1–3; *omit* B 1–6

Enter Wagner.

Wagner, commend me to my deerest friends,
The Germane *Valdes* and *Cornelius*,
Request them earnestly to visit me.
Wagner. I will sir. *Exit.*
Faustus.　Their conference will be a greater helpe to me,
Then all my labours, plod I ne're so fast.

Enter the Angell *and* Spirit [Bad Angel].

Good Angel.　O *Faustus*, lay that damned booke aside,
And gaze not on it least it tempt thy soule,
And heape Gods heavy wrath upon thy head.
Reade, reade the Scriptures: that is blasphemy. 100
Bad Angel.　Go forward *Faustus* in that famous Art
Wherein all natures treasury is contain'd:
Be thou on earth as *Jove* is in the skye,
Lord and Commander of these elements. *Exeunt* Angels.
Faustus.　How am I glutted with conceipt of this?
Shall I make spirits fetch me what I please?
Resolve me of all ambiguities?
Performe what desperate enterprise I will?
I'le have them flie to *India* for gold;
Ransacke the Ocean for Orient Pearle, 110
And search all corners of the new-found-world
For pleasant fruites, and Princely delicates.
I'le have them read me strange Philosophy,
And tell the secrets of all forraine Kings:
I'le have them wall all *Germany* with Brasse,
And make swift *Rhine*, circle faire *Wittenberge*:
I'le have them fill the publique Schooles with silke,
Wherewith the Students shall be bravely clad.
I'le leavy souldiers with the coyne they bring,
And chase the Prince of *Parma* from our Land, 120

102 treasury] A1–2; treasure A3, B1–6　　117 silke] Dyce; skill AB1–6
109 *India*] A1–3, B2–6; *Indian* B1

And raigne sole King of all our Provinces.
Yea stranger engines for the brunt of warre,
Then was the fiery keele at *Antwerpe* bridge,
I'le make my servile spirits to invent.
Come *Germane Valdes* and *Cornelius,*
And make me blest with your sage conference.

Enter Valdes *and* Cornelius.

Valdes, sweete *Valdes,* and *Cornelius,*
Know that your words have won me at the last,
To practise Magicke and concealed Arts.
Yet not your words onely, but mine owne fantasie,   130
That will receive no object, for my head
But ruminates on Negromantique skill.
Philosophy is odious and obscure,
Both Law and Physicke are for petty wits:
Divinitie is basest of the three,
Unpleasant, harsh, contemptible and vilde:
'Tis magick, magick, that hath ravisht me.
Then gentle friends aid me in this attempt,
And I, that have with concise Sillogismes
Gravel'd the Pastors of the Germane Church,   140
And made the flowring pride of *Wittenberg*
Swarme to my Problemes, as th'infernall spirits
On sweet *Musæus* when he came to hell,
Will be as cunning as *Agrippa* was,
Whose shadows made all *Europe* honour him.
Valdes.   *Faustus,* these bookes, thy wit, and our experience,
Shall make all Nations to Canonize us:
As Indian *Moores,* obey their Spanish Lords,
So shall the spirits of every element,
Be alwaies serviceable to us three: 150

121 our] A1; the A2–3, B1–6
123 *Antwerpe*] B6; *Anwerpe* B1–5
130–2 Yet...skill.] A1–3 (object^ ...
   head,...skill,); *omit* B1–6
135–6 Divinitie...vilde:] A1–3; *omit*
   B1–6

139 concise Sillogismes] Dyce; subtle
   A3 (subtile), B1–6 Sillogismes;
   Consissylogismes A1–2
142 Swarme] A1–3, B2–6; Sworne B1
145 shadows] A1–3; shadow B1–6

Like Lyons shall they guard us when we please,
Like *Almaine* Rutters with their horsemens staves,
Or Lapland Giants trotting by our sides:
Sometimes like women or unwedded Maides,
Shadowing more beauty in their Airie browes,
Then has the white breasts of the Queene of love.
From *Venice* shall they drag huge *Argosies*,
And from *America* the Golden Fleece,
That yearely stuffes old *Phillips* treasury,
If learned *Faustus* will be resolute.   160
Faustus.   *Valdes*, as resolute am I in this,
As thou to live, therefore object it not.
Cornelius.   The miracles that magick will performe,
Will make thee vow to study nothing else.
He that is grounded in Astrology,
Inricht with tongues, well seene in Minerals,
Hath all the Principles Magick doth require:
Then doubt not *Faustus* but to be renowm'd,
And more frequented for this mysterie,
Then heeretofore the *Delphian* Oracle.   170
The spirits tell me they can dry the sea,
And fetch the treasure of all forraine wrackes:
Yea all the wealth that our fore-fathers hid,
Within the massy entrailes of the earth:
Then tell me *Faustus* what shall we three want?
Faustus.   Nothing *Cornelius*; O this cheeres my soule:
Come, shew me some demonstrations Magicall,
That I may conjure in some bushy Grove,
And have these joies in full possession.
Valdes.   Then hast thee to some solitary Grove,   180
And beare wise *Bacons*, and *Abanus* workes,
The *Hebrew* Psalter, and new Testament;
And whatsoever else is requisite,
We will informe thee e're our conference cease.

159 stuffes] A1–3, B2–6; stuff'd B1   *181 *Abanus*] Greg (*after* Düntzer);
*178 bushy] *stet* B1–6; lustie A1; little   *Albanus* AB1–6
    A2–3

Cornelius.   Valdes, first let him know the words of Art,
  And then all other ceremonies learn'd,
  Faustus may try his cunning by himselfe.
Valdes.   First I'le instruct thee in the rudiments,
  And then wilt thou be perfecter then I.
Faustus.   Then come and dine with me, and after meate   190
  We'le canvase every quidditie thereof:
  For e're I sleep, I'le try what I can do:
  This night I'le conjure tho I die therefore.

                                                   Exeunt omnes.

                                                  [Scene ii]
                          Enter two Schollers.   **[I.ii]**

1. Scholler.   I wonder what's become of *Faustus* that
  Was wont to make our schooles ring, with *sic probo*.

                          Enter Wagner.

2. Scholler.   That shall we presently know, here comes his boy.
1. Scholler.   How now sirra, where's thy Maister?
Wagner.   God in heaven knowes.
2. Scholler.   Why, dost not thou know then?
Wagner.   Yes, I know, but that followes not.   200
1. Scholler.   Go to sirra, leave your jesting, and tell us where he is.
Wagner.   That followes not by force of argument, which you,
  being *Licentiats*, should stand upon; therefore acknowledge your
  errour, and be attentive.
2. Scholler.   Then you will not tell us?
Wagner.   You are deceiv'd, for I will tell you: yet if you were not
  dunces, you would never aske me such a question: For is he not
  Corpus naturale? and is not that *Mobile*? Then wherefore should
  you aske me such a question? But that I am by nature flegmatique,
  slow to wrath, and prone to letcherie (to love I would say) it were   210
  not for you to come within fortie foot of the place of execution,
  although I do not doubt but to see you both hang'd the next
  Sessions. Thus having triumpht over you, I will set my countenance like a Precisian, and begin to speake thus: Truely my deere

brethren, my Maister is within at dinner, with *Valdes* and *Cornelius*,
as this wine, if it could speake, would informe your Worships:
and so the Lord blesse you, preserve you, and keepe you, my deere
brethren.   *Exit.*

1. Scholler.   O *Faustus,*
Then I feare that which I have long suspected: 220
That thou art falne into that damned Art
For which they two are infamous through the world.

2. Scholler.   Were he a stranger, not allyed to me,
The danger of his soule would make me mourne:
But come, let us go, and informe the *Rector*:
It may be his grave counsell may reclaime him.

1. Scholler.   I feare me, nothing will reclaime him now.

2. Scholler.   Yet let us see what we can do.

                                                        Exeunt.

Thunder. Enter Lucifer *and foure devils* [*above*],   [I.iii
Faustus *to them with this speech.*

Faustus.   Now that the gloomy shadow of the night,
Longing to view *Orions* drisling looke,   230
Leapes from th'Antarticke world unto the skie,
And dyms the *Welkin*, with her pitchy breathe:
Faustus, begin thine Incantations,
And try if devils will obey thy Hest,
Seeing thou hast pray'd and sacrific'd to them.
Within this circle is *Jehova's* Name,
Forward, and backward, *Anagramatis'd*:
Th'abreviated names of holy Saints,
Figures of every adjunct to the heavens,
And Characters of Signes, and erring Starres,   240
By which the spirits are inforc'd to rise:
Then feare not *Faustus* to be resolute
And try the utmost Magicke can performe.

*230 looke] *stet* AB 1–6   240 erring] A 1–3, B 2–6; evening B 1

Thunder.

Sint mihi Dei Acherontis propitii, valeat numen triplex Jehovæ, Ignei,
Aerii, Aquatici, Terreni, spiritus salvete: Orientis Princeps Lucifer,
Belzebub inferni ardentis monarcha, et Demogorgon, propitiamus vos,
ut appareat, et surgat Mephostophilis.

Dragon.

Quid tu moraris; per Jehovam, Gehennam, et consecratam aquam
quam nunc spargo; signumque crucis quod nunc facio; et per vota
nostra ipse nunc surgat nobis dicatus Mephostophilis.   250

Enter a Devill.

I charge thee to returne, and change thy shape,
Thou art too ugly to attend on me:
Go and returne an old *Franciscan* Frier,
That holy shape becomes a devill best.   *Exit* Devill.
I see there's vertue in my heavenly words.
Who would not be proficient in this Art?
How pliant is this *Mephostophilis?*
Full of obedience and humility,
Such is the force of Magicke, and my spels.
Now *Faustus*, thou art Conjurer laureate   260
That canst commaund great *Mephostophilis,*
Quin redis Mephostophilis fratris imagine.

Enter Mephostophilis.

Mephostophilis.   Now *Faustus* what wouldst thou have me do?
Faustus.   I charge thee waite upon me whilst I live
To do what ever *Faustus* shall command:
Be it to make the Moone drop from her Sphere,

243.1 Thunder.] Dilke; B1–6 *place this*
    stage-direction in roman (i.e. italic)
    with a comma as if the first word of
    the text of 244
245 *Aquatici*] Tucker Brooke; *Aquatani*
    AB1; *Aquitani* B2–6
*245 *Terreni*] Greg; *omit* AB1–6
245 *Lucifer*,] Greg; *omit* AB1–6
*247.1 Dragon.]Methuen;B1–6 *print this*
    stage-direction with a comma as part

of the text, preceding quod tumeraris
248 *Quid tu moraris*] Bullen (*qy*), Meth-
    uen; *quod tumeraris* AB1–6
*260–3 Now...*imagine.*] A1–3; *omit*
    B1–6
260 Now] Wagner (*after* Albers),
    Bullen; No A1–3
262 *redis*] Methuen (*after* Root); *regis*
    A1–3

Or the Ocean to overwhelme the world.

Mephostophilis.   I am a servant to great *Lucifer*,
And may not follow thee without his leave;
No more then he commands, must we performe.   270

Faustus.   Did not he charge thee to appeare to me?

Mephostophilis.   No, I came now hether of mine owne accord.

Faustus.   Did not my conjuring speeches raise thee? speake.

Mephostophilis.   That was the cause, but yet *per accidens*:
For when we heare one racke the name of God,
Abjure the Scriptures, and his Saviour Christ:
We flye in hope to get his glorious soule;
Nor will we come unlesse he use such meanes,
Whereby he is in danger to be damn'd:
Therefore the shortest cut for conjuring   280
Is stoutly to abjure the Trinity,
And pray devoutely to the Prince of hell.

Faustus.   So *Faustus* hath already done, and holds this principle,
There is no chiefe but onely *Beelzebub*:
To whom *Faustus* doth dedicate himselfe.
This word Damnation, terrifies not me,
For I confound hell in *Elizium*:
My Ghost be with the old Phylosophers.
But leaving these vaine trifles of mens soules,
Tell me, what is that *Lucifer*, thy Lord?   290

Mephostophilis.   Arch-regent and Commander of all Spirits.

Faustus.   Was not that *Lucifer* an Angell once?

Mephostophilis.   Yes *Faustus*, and most deerely lov'd of God.

Faustus.   How comes it then that he is Prince of Devils?

Mephostophilis.   O: by aspiring pride and insolence,
For which God threw him from the face of heaven.

Faustus.   And what are you that live with *Lucifer*?

Mephostophilis.   Unhappy spirits that fell with *Lucifer*,
Conspir'd against our God with *Lucifer*,
And are for ever damn'd with *Lucifer*.   300

273 speeches] A1; spirits A2–3; *omit*   godlinesse B1–6
    B1–6   286 me] *stet* B1–6; him A1–3
281 the Trinity] A1 (Trinitie), 2–3; all   298 fell] A1–3; live B1–6

Faustus.　　Where are you damn'd?

Mephostophilis.　　In hell.

Faustus.　　How comes it then that thou art out of hell?

Mephostophilis.　　Why this is hell: nor am I out of it.
　Think'st thou that I who saw the face of God,
　And tasted the eternall Joyes of heaven,
　Am not tormented with ten thousand hels,
　In being depriv'd of everlasting blisse?
　O *Faustus* leave these frivolous demandes,
　Which strike a terror to my fainting soule.　　　　　　310

Faustus.　　What, is great *Mephostophilis* so passionate
　For being deprived of the Joyes of heaven?
　Learne thou of *Faustus* manly fortitude,
　And scorne those Joyes thou never shalt possesse.
　Go beare these tydings to great *Lucifer*,
　Seeing *Faustus* hath incur'd eternall death,
　By desperate thoughts against *Joves* Deity:
　Say he surrenders up to him his soule,
　So he will spare him foure and twenty yeares,
　Letting him live in all voluptuousnesse,　　　　　　　320
　Having thee ever to attend on me,
　To give me whatsoever I shall aske;
　To tell me whatsoever I demand:
　To slay mine enemies, and aid my friends,
　And alwaies be obedient to my will.
　Go, and returne to mighty *Lucifer*,
　And meet me in my Study, at Midnight,
　And then resolve me of thy Maisters mind.

Mephostophilis.　　I will *Faustus*.　　　　　　　　*Exit.*

Faustus.　　Had I as many soules, as there be Starres,　　330
　I'de give them all for *Mephostophilis*.
　By him, I'le be great Emperour of the world,
　And make a bridge, thorough the moving Aire,
　To passe the Ocean with a band of men,

305 who] A 1; that A 2–3, B 1–6　　　334 Ocean $_\wedge$ ...men,] A 1–3; $\sim$: ... $\sim$ $_\wedge$
310 strike] A 1–3, B 5–6; strikes B 1–4　　　B 1
324 aid] A 1; to aid A 2–3, B 1–6

I'le joyne the Hils that bind the *Affrick* shore,
And make that Country, continent to *Spaine*,
And both contributary to my Crowne.
The Emperour shall not live, but by my leave,
Nor any Potentate of *Germany*.
Now that I have obtain'd what I desir'd   340
I'le live in speculation of this Art
Till *Mephostophilis* returne againe.

> *Exeunt* [Faustus; Lucifer *and devils above*].

                                        [Scene iv]
Enter Wagner *and* [Robin] *the Clowne*.   [I.iv

Wagner.   Come hither sirra boy.
Robin.   Boy? O disgrace to my person: Zounds, boy in your face,
you have seene many boyes with such pickadevaunts I am sure.
Wagner.   Sirra, hast thou no commings in?
Robin.   Yes, and goings out too, you may see sir.
Wagner.   Alas poore slave, see how poverty jests in his nakednesse,
I know the Villaines out of service, and so hungry, that he would
give his soule to the devill, for a shoulder of Mutton, tho it were 350
bloud raw.
Robin.   Not so neither; I had need to have it well rosted, and good
sauce to it, if I pay so deere, I can tell you.
Wagner.   Sirra, wilt thou be my man and waite on me? and I will
make thee go, like *Qui mihi discipulus.*
Robin.   What, in Verse?
Wagner.   No slave, in beaten silke, and staves-aker.
Robin.   Staves-aker? that's good to kill Vermine: then belike if I
serve you, I shall be lousy.
Wagner.   Why so thou shalt be, whether thou dost it or no: for 360
sirra, if thou dost not presently bind thy selfe to me for seven
yeares, I'le turne all the lice about thee into Familiars, and make
them tare thee in peeces.

342.2–388.1 *For the* A-text *of this scene,*   *345 such pickadevaunts] A 1–3; beards
see *Appendix: A-text, Scene iv   B 1–6
                                                  *349 that he] that I know he AB 1–6

172

Robin.   Nay sir, you may save your selfe a labour, for they are as
familiar with me, as if they payd for their meate and drinke, I
can tell you.

Wagner.   Well sirra, leave your jesting, and take these Guilders.

Robin.   Yes marry sir, and I thanke you to.

Wagner.   So, now thou art to bee at an howres warning, when-
soever, and wheresoever the devill shall fetch thee.   370

Robin.   Here, take your Guilders againe, I'le none of 'em.

Wagner.   Not I, thou art Prest, prepare thy selfe, for I will
presently raise up two devils to carry thee away: *Banio, Belcher.*
                                                    [*Calls.*]

Robin.   *Belcher?* and *Belcher* come here, I'le belch him: I am not
afraid of a devill.

                         Enter two devils.

Wagner.   How now sir, will you serve me now?

Robin.   I good *Wagner*, take away the devill then.

Wagner.   Spirits away.   *Exeunt.*
Now sirra follow me.

Robin.   I will sir; but hearke you Maister, will you teach me this 380
conjuring Occupation?

Wagner.   I sirra, I'le teach thee to turne thy selfe to a Dog, or a
Cat, or a Mouse, or a Rat, or any thing.

Robin.   A Dog, or a Cat, or a Mouse, or a Rat? O brave *Wagner*.

Wagner.   Villaine, call me Maister *Wagner*, and see that you walke
attentively, and let your right eye be alwaies *Diametrally* fixt upon
my left heele, that thou maist, *Quasi vestigiis nostris insistere.*

Robin.   Well sir, I warrant you.

                                                    Exeunt.

*371 againe] A 1–3, B 2–6; *omit* B 1

[Scene v]
Enter Faustus *in his Study.*   [II.i]

Faustus.   Now *Faustus*, must thou needs be damn'd,
And canst not now be sav'd.   390
What bootes it then to thinke on God or Heaven?
Away with such vaine fancies, and despaire,
Despair in GOD, and trust in *Belzebub*:
Now go not backward: no, *Faustus*, be resolute.
Why waverst thou? O something soundeth in mine eares,
Abjure this Magicke, turne to God againe.
I and *Faustus* will turne to God againe.
To God? he loves thee not:
The god thou serv'st is thine owne appetite,
Wherein is fixt the love of *Belzebub*,   400
To him, I'le build an Altar and a Church,
And offer luke-warme bloud, of new borne babes.

Enter the two Angels.

Bad Angel.   Go forward *Faustus* in that famous Art.
Good Angel.   Sweete *Faustus* leave that execrable Art.
Faustus.   Contrition, Prayer, Repentance? what of these?
Good Angel.   O they are meanes to bring thee unto heaven.
Bad Angel.   Rather illusions, fruits of lunacy,
That makes men foolish that do use them most.
Good Angel.   Sweet *Faustus* think of heaven, and heavenly things.
Bad Angel.   No *Faustus*, thinke of honour and of wealth.   410
                                        Exeunt Angels.

Faustus.   Wealth?
Why, the Signory of *Embden* shall be mine:
When *Mephostophilis* shall stand by me,
What god can hurt me? *Faustus* thou art safe.

390 And] A1–3; *omit* B1–6   397 I…againe.] A1–3; *omit* B1–6
*390 not now] thou not AB1–6   398 To God?] A1–3; Why B1–6
394 backward: no, *Faustus*,] A1–3   408 makes] A1–2; makee A3; make
  (no∧); backward *Faustus* B1–2;   B1–6
  backe *Faustus* B3–6   *408 men] A1–3, B2–6; them B1
*395 eares] A1–3; eare B1–6   *414 god] A1–3 (God); power B1–6

Cast no more doubts; *Mephostophilis* come
And bring glad tydings from great *Lucifer*.
Ist not midnight? come *Mephostophilis*.
Veni veni Mephostophilis.

Enter Mephostophilis.

Now tell me what saith *Lucifer* thy Lord.
Mephostophilis.   That I shall waite on *Faustus* whilst he lives,   420
So he will buy my service with his soule.
Faustus.   Already *Faustus* hath hazarded that for thee.
Mephostophilis.   But now thou must bequeath it solemnly,
And wright a Deed of Gift with thine owne bloud;
For that security craves *Lucifer*.
If thou deny it I must backe to hell.
Faustus.   Stay *Mephostophilis*
And tell me, what good will my soule do thy Lord?
Mephostophilis.   Enlarge his Kingdome.
Faustus.   Is that the reason why he tempts us thus?   430
Mephostophilis.   *Solamen miseris socios habuisse doloris*.
Faustus.   Why, have you any paine that torture other?
Mephostophilis.   As great as have the humane soules of men.
But tell me *Faustus*, shall I have thy soule?
And I will be thy slave and waite on thee,
And give thee more then thou hast wit to aske.
Faustus.   I *Mephostophilis*, I'le give it him.
Mephostophilis.   Then *Faustus* stab thy Arme couragiously,
And bind thy soule, that at some certaine day
Great *Lucifer* may claime it as his owne,   440
And then be thou as great as *Lucifer*.
Faustus.   Loe *Mephostophilis*, for love of thee
Faustus hath cut his arme, and with his proper bloud
Assures his soule to be great *Lucifers*,
Chiefe Lord and Regent of perpetuall night.
Veiw here this bloud that trickles from mine arme,

418 *Mephostophilis*] B 2–6; *Mephosto-*   432 that] *i.e.*, you who (other is *normal*
    phile AB 1   *plural*)
420 *Mephostophilis*.] A 1–3, B 2–6; *omit*   *443 proper] *stet* AB 1–6
    B 1

175

And let it be propitious for my wish.
Mephostophilis.   But *Faustus*
Write it in manner of a Deed of Gift.
Faustus.   I so I do; but *Mephostophilis*,   450
My bloud congeales, and I can write no more.
Mephostophilis.   I'le fetch thee fire to dissolve it streight.   *Exit*.
Faustus.   What might the staying of my bloud portend?
Is it unwilling I should write this byll?
Why streames it not, that I may write a fresh?
Faustus gives to thee his soule: ah there it staid.
Why shouldst thou not? is not thy soule thine owne?
Then write againe: *Faustus* gives to thee his soule.

Enter Mephostophilis *with the Chafer of Fire.*

Mephostophilis.   See *Faustus* here is fire, set it on.
Faustus.   So, now the bloud begins to cleere againe: 460
Now will I make an end immediately.
Mephostophilis [*aside*].   What will not I do to obtaine his soule?
Faustus.   *Consummatum est*: this byll is ended,
And *Faustus* hath bequeath'd his soule to *Lucifer*.
But what is this Inscription on mine Arme?
Homo fuge: whether should I flye?
If unto God, hee'le throw me downe to hell.
My sences are deceiv'd, here's nothing writ:
O yes, I see it plaine, even heere is writ
Homo fuge: yet shall not *Faustus* flye.   470
Mephostophilis.   I'le fetch him somewhat to delight his minde.
                                                            Exit.

Enter Devils, giving Crownes and rich apparell to
Faustus: *they dance, and then depart.*

Enter Mephostophilis.

Faustus.   What meanes this shew? speake *Mephostophilis*.
Mephostopihilis.   Nothing *Faustus* but to delight thy mind,

455 a fresh] *i.e.*, afresh, *as in* A 1–3   saucer, *as in the History*, ch. 6
*456 ah] A 1–3; O B 1–6   heading
459 Set it on] *i.e.*, over the coals, in a   467 God] A 1–3; heaven B 1–6

And let thee see what Magicke can performe.

Faustus.　　But may I raise such spirits when I please?

Mephostophilis.　　I *Faustus*, and do greater things then these.

Faustus.　　Then *Mephostophilis* receive this scrole,
A Deed of Gift, of body and of soule:
But yet conditionally, that thou performe
All Covenants, and Articles, betweene us both.　　　　　　　480

Mephostophilis.　　*Faustus*, I sweare by *Hell* and *Lucifer*,
To effect all promises betweene us made.

Faustus.　　Then heare me read it *Mephostophilis*.
On these conditions following:

　First, that Faustus *may be a spirit in forme and substance.*

　Secondly, that Mephostophilis *shall be his servant, and be by him commanded.*

　Thirdly, that Mephostophilis *shall doe for him, and bring him whatsoever.*

　Fourthly, that he shall be in his chamber or house invisible.　　490

　Lastly, that hee shall appeare to the said John Faustus, *at all times, in what forme or shape soever he please.*

　I John Faustus *of* Wittenberg, *Doctor, by these presents, doe give both body and soule to* Lucifer, *Prince of the East, and his Minister* Mephostophilis, *and furthermore grant unto them that foure and twentie yeares being expired, and these Articles above written being inviolate, full power to fetch or carry the said* John Faustus, *body and soule, flesh and bloud, into their habitation wheresoever.*

　　　　　　　　　　　　　　By me John Faustus. 500

Mephostophilis.　　Speake *Faustus*, do you deliver this as your
Deed?

Faustus.　　I, take it, and the devill give thee good of it.

Mephostophilis.　　So, now *Faustus* aske me what thou wilt.

Faustus.　　First, I will question with thee about hell:
Tell me, where is the place that men call Hell?

Mephostophilis.　　Under the heavens.

---

482 made] A1–3; both B1–6　　　　　498² *and*] B2; *omit* AB1
*486–7 *by him commanded*] stet B1–6　　504 with] A1; *omit* A2–3, B1–6
492 *or*] A1; *and* A2–3, B1–6

Faustus.   I, so are all things else; but whereabouts?

Mephostophilis.   Within the bowels of these Elements,
Where we are tortur'd, and remaine for ever.
Hell hath no limits, nor is circumscrib'd,   510
In one selfe place: but where we are is hell,
And where hell is there must we ever be.
And to be short, when all the world dissolves,
And every creature shall be purifi'd,
All places shall be hell that is not heaven.

Faustus.   I thinke Hel's a fable.

Mephostophilis.   I, thinke so still, till experience change thy mind.

Faustus.   Why, dost thou think that *Faustus* shall be damn'd?

Mephostophilis.   I, of necessity, for here's the scrowle
In which thou hast given thy soule to *Lucifer*.   520

Faustus.   I, and body too, but what of that:
Think'st thou that *Faustus*, is so fond to imagine,
That after this life there is any paine?
Tush, these are trifles, and meere old wives Tales.

Mephostophilis.   But I am an instance to prove the contrary:
For I tell thee I am damn'd, and now in hell.

Faustus.   Nay, and this be hell, I'le willingly be damn'd.
What, sleeping, eating, walking and disputing?
But leaving this, let me have a wife, the fairest Maid in *Germany*,
for I am wanton and lascivious, and cannot live without a wife. 530

Mephostophilis.   Well *Faustus*, thou shalt have a wife.

                              He fetches in a woman devill.

Faustus.   What sight is this?

Mephostophilis.   Now *Faustus* wilt thou have a wife?

Faustus.   Here's a hot whore indeed; no, I'le no wife.

Mephostophilis.   Marriage is but a ceremoniall toy,
And if thou lovest me thinke no more of it.
I'le cull thee out the fairest Curtezans,
And bring them every morning to thy bed:
She whom thine eye shall like, thy heart shall have,
Were she as chaste as was *Penelope*,   540
As wise as *Saba*, or as beautifull

*524 Tush] A1–3; No B1–6

178

As was bright *Lucifer* before his fall.
Hold, take this booke, peruse it thoroughly:
The iterating of these lines brings gold;
The framing of this circle on the ground
Brings Thunder, Whirle-winds, Storme and Lightning:
Pronounce this thrice devoutly to thy selfe,
And men in harnesse shall appeare to thee,
Ready to execute what thou commandst.

Faustus.   Thankes *Mephostophilis* for this sweete booke.   550
This will I keepe, as chary as my life.
Yet faine would I have a booke wherein I might beholde al spels 551.0.1
and incantations, that I might raise up spirits when I please.

Mephostophilis.   Here they are in this booke.

> *There turne to them.*

Faustus.   Now would I have a booke where I might see al characters
of planets of the heavens, that I might knowe their motions and
dispositions.

Mephostophilis.   Heere they are too.   *Turne to them.*

Faustus.   Nay let me have one booke more, and then I have done,
wherein I might see al plants, hearbes and trees that grow upon
the earth.   551.0.10

Mephostophilis.   Here they be.

Faustus.   O thou art deceived.

Mephostophilis.   Tut I warrant thee.   *Turne to them.*

> *Exeunt.*

[Scene vi]

Enter Faustus *in his Study, and* Mephostophilis.   [II.ii]

Faustus.   When I behold the heavens then I repent
And curse thee wicked *Mephostophilis*,
Because thou hast depriv'd me of those Joyes.

---

*543 Hold] A1–3; Here B1–6
543 peruse...thoroughly] A1–3; and
    peruse...well B1–6
551.0.1–1 3 *Added in* A1–3; *omit* B1–6
551.0.5 of planets] Greg; and planets
    A1–3

551.1 *Exeunt.*] B1–6; A1–3 *omit the
    direction and continue the scene
    without a break*
551.2 *Before* Scene vi B1–6 *print the
    short form of* Chorus 2 *from* A-text
    (*for the long form, see* 753.2–778.1)

Mephostophilis. 'Twas thine owne seeking *Faustus*, thanke thy
    selfe.
But think'st thou heaven is such a glorious thing?
I tell thee *Faustus* it is not halfe so faire
As thou, or any man that breathes on earth.
Faustus. How prov'st thou that?
Mephostophilis. 'Twas made for man; then he's more excellent.   560
Faustus. If Heaven was made for man, 'twas made for me:
I will renounce this Magicke and repent.

Enter the two Angels.

Good Angel. *Faustus* repent, yet God will pitty thee.
Bad Angel. Thou art a spirit, God cannot pity thee.
Faustus. Who buzzeth in mine eares I am a spirit?
Be I a devill yet God may pitty me,
Yea, God will pitty me if I repent.
Bad Angel. I, but *Faustus* never shall repent.   *Exeunt* Angels.
Faustus. My heart is hardned, I cannot repent:
Scarce can I name salvation, faith, or heaven,   570
But feareful ecchoes thunder in mine eares,
Faustus, thou art damn'd, then swords and knives,
Gunnes, poyson, halters, and invenomb'd steele,
Are laid before me to dispatch my selfe:
And long e're this, I should have done the deed,
Had not sweete pleasure conquer'd deepe despaire.
Have not I made blind *Homer* sing to me
Of *Alexanders* love, and *Oenons* death?
And hath not he that built the walles of *Thebes*
With ravishing sound of his melodious Harpe,   580
Made musicke with my *Mephostophilis*?
Why should I die then, or basely despaire?
I am resolv'd, *Faustus* shall not repent.
Come *Mephostophilis* let us dispute againe,

558 breathes] A 1–3, B 2–6; breathe B 1
570 heaven,] A 1–3, B 3–4; ~ . B 1–2;
   ~ : B 5–6
571–2 But...knives,] A 1–3; *omit* B 1–
   6

571 thunder] Dyce (1604 *version*);
   thunders A 1–3
*573 Gunnes, poyson] Swords, poyson
   B 1–6; Poyson, gunnes A 1–3

And reason of divine Astrology.
Speake, are there many Spheares above the Moone?
Are all Celestiall bodies but one Globe,
As is the substance of this centricke earth?
Mephostophilis.   As are the elements, such are the heavens,
Even from the Moone unto the Emperiall Orbe,   590
Mutually folded in each others Spheares,
And jointly move upon one Axle-tree,
Whose termine, is tearmed the worlds wide Pole.
Nor are the names of *Saturne*, *Mars*, or *Jupiter*,
Fain'd, but are erring Starres.
Faustus.   But have they all
One motion, both *situ et tempore?*
Mephostophilis.   All move from East to West in foure and twenty
houres, upon the poles of the world, but differ in their motions
upon the poles of the Zodiacke.
Faustus.   These slender questions *Wagner* can decide: 600
Hath *Mephostophilis* no greater skill?
Who knowes not the double motion of the Planets?
That the first is finisht in a naturall day?
The second thus: *Saturne* in thirty yeares, *Jupiter* in twelve, *Mars*
   in foure, the *Sun*, *Venus*, and *Mercury* in a yeare; the Moone in
   twenty eight daies. Tush, these are fresh mens suppositions:
But tell me, hath every Spheare a Dominion, or *Intelligentia?*
Mephostophilis.   I.
Faustus.   How many Heavens, or Spheares, are there?
Mephostophilis.   Nine, the seven Planets, the Firmament, and the 610
Emperiall heaven.
Faustus.   But is there not *Cælum igneum*, and *Christalinum?*
Mephostophilis.   No *Faustus* they be but Fables.
Faustus.   Resolve me then in this one question:
Why are not Conjunctions, Oppositions, Aspects, Eclipses, all at
one time, but in some years we have more, in some lesse?
Mephostophilis.   *Per inæqualem motum respectu totius.*
Faustus.   Well, I am answer'd: now tell me who made the world?

595 erring] A 1–3; evening B 1–6   606 suppositions] A 1–3; questions B 1–6
606 Tush] A 1–3; *omit* B 1–6   *612 and] Greg; & B 1–6

Mephostophilis.   I will not.

Faustus.   Sweet *Mephostophilis* tell me.   620

Mephostophilis.   Move me not *Faustus.*

Faustus.   Villaine, have I not bound thee to tell me any thing?

Mephostophilis.   I, that is not against our Kingdome: this is.
Thou art damn'd, think thou of hell.

Faustus.   Thinke *Faustus* upon God, that made the world.

Mephostophilis.   Remember this.——   *Exit.*

Faustus.   I, go accursed spirit to ugly hell:
'Tis thou hast damn'd distressed *Faustus* soule.
Ist not too late?

Enter the two Angels.

Bad Angel.   Too late.   630

Good Angel.   Never too late, if *Faustus* will repent.

Bad Angel.   If thou repent, devils will teare thee in peeces.

Good Angel.   Repent and they shall never raise thy skin.

Exeunt Angels.

Faustus.   Ah Christ my Saviour, my Saviour,
Helpe to save distressed *Faustus* soule.

Enter Lucifer, Belzebub, *and* Mephostophilis.

Lucifer.   Christ cannot save thy soule, for he is just,
There's none but I have interest in the same.

Faustus.   O what art thou that look'st so terrible.

Lucifer.   I am *Lucifer,*
And this is my companion Prince in hell.   640

Faustus.   O *Faustus* they are come to fetch thy soule.

Belzebub.   We are come to tell thee thou dost injure us.

Lucifer.   Thou calst on Christ contrary to thy promise.

Belzebub.   Thou should'st not thinke on God.

Lucifer.   Thinke of the devill.

Belzebub.   And his dam to.

Faustus.   Nor will I henceforth: pardon me for this,

622 I not] A1; not I A2–3, B1–6   645 of] A1–2; on A3, B1–6
633 raise] *i.e.,* race *as in* A1   647 I...me] A1–3; *Faustus*...him
634 Ah] A1–3; O B1–6   B1–6
638 terrible] A1–3; terribly B1–6

182

And *Faustus* vowes never to looke to heaven,
Never to name God, or to pray to him,
To burne his Scriptures, slay his Ministers,　　　　　　650
And make my spirites pull his churches downe.
Lucifer.　So shalt thou show thy selfe an obedient servant,
And we will highly gratify thee for it.
Belzebub.　*Faustus* we are come from hell in person to shew thee
some pastime: sit downe and thou shalt behold the seven deadly
sinnes appeare to thee in their owne proper shapes and likenesse.
Faustus.　That sight will be as pleasant to me, as Paradise was to
Adam the first day of his creation.
Lucifer.　Talke not of Paradice or Creation, but marke the shew.
Go *Mephostophilis*, fetch them in.　　　　　　660

　　　　Enter the Seven Deadly Sinnes [*led by a* Piper].

Belzebub.　Now *Faustus*, question them of their names and
dispositions.
Faustus.　That shall I soone: What art thou the first?
Pride.　I am *Pride*; I disdaine to have any parents: I am like to
Ovids Flea, I can creepe into every corner of a Wench: Sometimes,
like a Perriwig, I sit upon her Brow: next, like a Neckelace I hang
about her Necke: Then, like a Fan of Feathers, I kisse her lippes;
And then turning my selfe to a wrought Smocke do what I list. But
fye, what a smell is heere? I'le not speake a word more for a
Kings ransome, unlesse the ground be perfum'd, and cover'd with 670
cloth of Arras.
Faustus.　Thou art a proud knave indeed: What art thou the
second?
Covetousnesse.　I am *Covetousnesse*: begotten of an old Churle in a
leather bag; and might I now obtaine my wish, this house, you
and all, should turne to Gold, that I might locke you safe into my
Chest: O my sweete Gold!
Faustus.　And what art thou the third?
Envy.　I am *Envy*, begotten of a Chimney-sweeper, and an
Oyster-wife: I cannot read, and therefore wish all books burn'd. 680

*649–51 Never...downe.] A1–3; *omit*　　667 lippes] A1–3; *omit* B1·
　B1–6

183

I am leane with seeing others eate: O that there would come a famine over all the world, that all might die, and I live alone, then thou should'st see how fat I'de be. But must thou sit, and I stand? come downe with a vengeance.

Faustus. Out envious wretch: But what art thou the fourth?

Wrath. I am *Wrath*: I had neither father nor mother, I leapt out of a Lyons mouth when I was scarce an houre old, and ever since have runne up and downe the world with these case of Rapiers, wounding my selfe when I could get none to fight withall: I was borne in hell, and look to it, for some of you shall be my 690 father.

Faustus. And what are thou the fift?

Gluttony. I am *Gluttony*; my parents are all dead, and the devill a peny they have left me, but a bare pention, and that buyes me thirty meales a day, and ten Beavers: a small trifle to suffice nature. I come of a Royall Pedigree, my father was a Gammon of Bacon, and my mother was a Hogshead of Claret Wine. My godfathers were these: Peter Pickeld-herring, and Martin Martlemasse-beefe: But my godmother, O she was an ancient Gentlewoman, her name was Margery March-beere: Now *Faustus* thou hast heard all 700 my progeny, wilt thou bid me to supper?

Faustus. Not I.

Gluttony. Then the devill choke thee.

Faustus. Choke thy selfe Glutton: What are thou the sixt?

Sloth. Hey ho; I am *Sloth*: I was begotten on a sunny bank: where I have laine ever since, and you have done me great injury 705.0 to bring me from thence, let me be carried thither againe by Gluttony and Letchery, 705.0

hey ho: I'le not speake an other word.

Faustus. And what are you Mistris Minkes, the seventh and last?

Letchery. Who I sir? I am one that loves an inch of raw Mutton, better then an ell of fryde Stockfish: and the first letter of my name begins with *Letchery*. 710

---

*694 bare] A1–3; small B1–6
705.0.1–705.0.3 where...Letchery,] A
1–3 *omit* B1–6
*706 an other word] A1–3 (an other

word for a Kings raunsome.); a
word more for a kings ransome.
B1–6
708 I sir] A1–3, B2–6; I I sir B1

Lucifer.   Away to hell, away: on piper.

Exeunt the Seven Sinnes.

Faustus.   O how this sight doth delight my soule.

Lucifer.   Tut *Faustus*, in hell is all manner of delight.

Faustus.   O might I see hell, and returne againe safe, how happy
were I then.

Lucifer.   *Faustus*, thou shalt, at midnight I will send for thee;
Meane while peruse this booke, and view it throughly,
And thou shalt turne thy selfe into what shape thou wilt.

Faustus.   Thankes mighty *Lucifer*.
This will I keepe as chary as my life.   719.0.1

Lucifer.   Now *Faustus* farewell.   720

Faustus.   Farewell great *Lucifer*: come *Mephostophilis*.

Exeunt omnes, severall waies.

[Scene vii]

Enter [Robin] *the Clowne.*

[II.iii.]

Robin.   What *Dick*, looke to the horses there till I come againe.
I have gotten one of Doctor *Faustus* conjuring bookes, and now
we'le have such knavery, as't passes.

Enter Dick.

Dick.   What *Robin*, you must come away and walk the horses.

Robin.   I walke the horses, I scorn't 'faith, I have other matters
in hand, let the horses walk themselves and they will. *A per se, a,
t. h. e. the: o per se, o, demy orgon, gorgon*: keepe further from me
O thou illiterate, and unlearned Hostler.

Dick.   'Snayles, what hast thou got there, a book? why thou   730
canst not tell ne're a word on't.

Robin.   That thou shalt see presently: keep out of the circle, I say,
least I send you into the Ostry with a vengeance.

Dick.   That's like, 'faith: you had best leave your foolery, for an
my Maister come, he'le conjure you 'faith.

713 Tut] A1–3; But B1–6   721.2–753.1 *For the* A-text *of* Scene vii,
*719.0.1 This...life.] *stet* AB1   *see* Appendix: A-text, Scene vii
                                           728 demy] Dyce; *deny* B1–6

185

Robin.   My Maister conjure me? I'le tell thee what, an my Maister
come here, I'le clap as faire a paire of hornes on's head as e're thou
sawest in thy life.

Dick.   Thou needst not do that, for my Mistresse hath done it.

Robin.   I, there be of us here, that have waded as deepe into   740
matters, as other men, if they were disposed to talke.

Dick.   A plague take you, I thought you did not sneake up and
downe after her for nothing. But I prethee tell me, in good sadnesse
Robin, is that a conjuring booke?

Robin.   Do but speake what thou't have me to do, and I'le do't:
If thou't dance naked, put off thy cloathes, and I'le conjure thee
about presently: Or if thou't go but to the Taverne with me, I'le
give thee white wine, red wine, claret wine, Sacke, Muskadine,
Malmesey and Whippincrust, hold belly hold, and wee'le not pay
one peny for it.   750

Dick.   O brave, prethee let's to it presently, for I am as dry as a
dog.

Robin.   Come then let's away.

                                                     Exeunt.

                    Enter the Chorus.   [Chorus 2]

Learned *Faustus*
To find the secrets of Astronomy,
Graven in the booke of *Joves* high firmament,
Did mount him up to scale *Olimpus* top.
Where sitting in a Chariot burning bright,
Drawne by the strength of yoked Dragons neckes;
He viewes the cloudes, the Planets, and the Starres,   760
The Tropicks, Zones, and quarters of the skye,
From the bright circle of the horned Moone,
Even to the height of *Primum Mobile*:
And whirling round with this circumference,
Within the concave compasse of the Pole,
From East to West his Dragons swiftly glide,
And in eight daies did bring him home againe.
Not long he stayed within his quiet house,

761 Tropicks,] Greg; Tropick, B1; Tropicke‸ B2–6

To rest his bones after his weary toyle,
But new exploits do hale him out agen,   770
And mounted then upon a Dragons backe,
That with his wings did part the subtle aire,
He now is gone to prove *Cosmography*,
That measures costs, and kingdomes of the earth:
And as I guesse will first arrive at *Rome*,
To see the Pope and manner of his Court,
And take some part of holy *Peters* feast,
The which this day is highly solemnized.

                                                    Exit.

                                          [Scene viii]
          Enter Faustus *and* Mephostophilis.   [III.i]

Faustus.   Having now my good *Mephostophilis*,
Past with delight the stately Towne of *Trier*:   780
Invironed round with airy mountaine tops,
With wals of Flint, and deepe intrenched Lakes,
Not to be wonne by any conquering Prince:
From *Paris* next, costing the Realme of *France*,
We saw the River *Maine*, fall into *Rhine*,
Whose bankes are set with Groves of fruitfull Vines.
Then up to *Naples* rich *Campania*,
The buildings faire, and gorgeous to the eye,
Whose streetes straight forth, and paved with finest bricke,
Quarter the towne in foure equivolence.   790
There saw we learned *Maroes* golden tombe:
The way he cut, an English mile in length,
Thorough a rocke of stone in one nights space:
From thence to *Venice*, *Padua*, and the rest,
In midst of which a sumptuous Temple stands,
That threates the starres with her aspiring top,

774 costs] *i.e.*, coasts   790 Quarter...equivolence] A1–3
*787 *Naples*ᴧ] Chappell (Naples'); ~ ,   (Quarters); *omit* B1–6
     AB1–6   794 rest] A1–3; East B1–6
*788 The] Whose AB1–6   *795 midst] A1–3; one B1–6
789 Whose] Greg; The AB1–6

Whose frame is paved with sundry coloured stones,
And roof't aloft with curious worke in gold.
Thus hitherto hath *Faustus* spent his time.
But tell me now, what resting place is this? 800
Hast thou, as earst I did command,
Conducted me within the walles of *Rome*?
Mephostophilis.   I have my *Faustus*, and for proofe thereof,
This is the goodly Palace of the Pope:
And cause we are no common guests,
I chuse his privy chamber for our use.
Faustus.   I hope his Holinesse will bid us welcome.
Mephostophilis.   All's one, for wee'l be bold with his Venison.
But now my *Faustus*, that thou maist perceive,
What *Rome* contains for to delight thine eyes, 810
Know that this City stands upon seven hils,
That underprop the ground-worke of the same:
Just through the midst runnes flowing *Tybers* streame,
With winding bankes that cut it in two parts;
Over the which foure stately Bridges leane,
That make safe passage, to each part of *Rome*.
Upon the Bridge, call'd *Ponte Angelo*,
Erected is a Castle passing strong,
Where thou shalt see such store of Ordinance,
As that the double Cannons forg'd of brasse, 820
Do match the number of the daies contain'd,
Within the compasse of one compleat yeare:
Beside the gates, and high Pyramydes,
That *Julius Cæsar* brought from *Affrica*.
Faustus.   Now by the Kingdomes of Infernall Rule,
Of *Stix*, of *Acheron*, and the fiery Lake,
Of ever-burning *Phlegeton*, I sweare,
That I do long to see the Monuments
And situation of bright splendent *Rome*,
Come therefore, let's away. 830
Mephostophilis.   Nay stay my *Faustus*: I know you'd see the Pope
And take some part of holy *Peters* feast,

815 foure] A1–3; two B1–6   821 match] A1–3, B2–6; watch B1

The which this day with high solemnity,
This day is held through *Rome* and *Italy*,
In honour of the Popes triumphant victory.
Faustus.   Sweete *Mephostophilis*, thou pleasest me:
Whilst I am here on earth let me be cloyd
With all things that delight the heart of man.
My foure and twenty yeares of liberty
I'le spend in pleasure and in daliance,   840
That *Faustus* name, whilst this bright frame doth stand,
May be admired through the furthest Land.
Mephostophilis.   'Tis well said *Faustus*, come then stand by me
And thou shalt see them come immediately.
Faustus.   Nay stay my gentle *Mephostophilis*,
And grant me my request, and then I go.
Thou know'st within the compasse of eight daies,
We veiw'd the face of heaven, of earth and hell.
So high our Dragons soar'd into the aire,
That looking downe the earth appear'd to me,   850
No bigger then my hand in quantity.
There did we view the Kingdomes of the world,
And what might please mine eye, I there beheld.
Then in this shew let me an Actor be,
That this proud Pope may *Faustus* cunning see.
Mephostophilis.   Let it be so my *Faustus*, but first stay,
And view their triumphs, as they passe this way.
And then devise what best contents thy minde,
By cunning in thine Art to crosse the Pope,
Or dash the pride of this solemnity;   860
To make his Monkes and Abbots stand like Apes,
And point like Antiques at his triple Crowne:
To beate the beades about the Friers Pates,
Or clap huge hornes, upon the Cardinals heads:
Or any villany thou canst devise,
And I'le performe it *Faustus*: heark they come:
This day shall make thee be admir'd in *Rome*.

836–988 *Omitted in* A 1–3   855, 859 cunning] B 4–6; comming
836–7 me:...earth͵ let] B 2 (me,);   B 1–3
    ~ ͵...~ : Let B 1   862 Antiques] *i.e.*, antics

Enter the Cardinals *and* Bishops, *some bearing Crosiers, some*
the Pillars, Monkes *and* Friers, *singing their Procession:*
Then the Pope, *and* Raymond *King of* Hungary,
with Bruno *led in chaines.*

Pope.   Cast downe our Foot-stoole.
Raymond.   Saxon *Bruno* stoope,
  Whilst on thy backe his hollinesse ascends
  Saint *Peters* Chaire and State Pontificall.   870
Bruno.   Proud *Lucifer,* that State belongs to me:
  But thus I fall to *Peter,* not to thee.
Pope.   To me and *Peter,* shalt thou groveling lie,
  And crouch before the Papall dignity:
  Sound Trumpets then, for thus Saint *Peters* Heire,
  From *Bruno's* backe, ascends Saint *Peters* Chaire.
                              A Flourish while he ascends.
  Thus, as the Gods creepe on with feete of wool,
  Long ere with Iron hands they punish men,
  So shall our sleeping vengeance now arise,
  And smite with death thy hated enterprise.   880
  Lord Cardinals of *France* and *Padua,*
  Go forth-with to our holy Consistory,
  And read amongst the Statutes Decretall,
  What by the holy Councell held at *Trent,*
  The sacred Sinod hath decreed for him,
  That doth assume the Papall government,
  Without election, and a true consent:
  Away and bring us word with speed.
1. Cardinal.   We go my Lord.   *Exeunt* Cardinals.
Pope.   Lord *Raymond*——   [*They talk apart*]. 890
Faustus.   Go hast thee gentle *Mephostophilis,*
  Follow the Cardinals to the Consistory;
  And as they turne their superstitious Bookes,
  Strike them with sloth, and drowsy idlenesse;
  And make them sleepe so sound, that in their shapes,
  Thy selfe and I, may parly with this Pope:
  This proud confronter of the Emperour,

And in despite of all his Holinesse
Restore this *Bruno* to his liberty,
And beare him to the States of *Germany*.   900
Mephostophilis.   *Faustus*, I goe.
Faustus.   Dispatch it soone,
  The Pope shall curse that *Faustus* came to *Rome*.
                              Exeunt Faustus *and* Mephostophilis.
Bruno.   Pope *Adrian* let me have some right of Law,
  I was elected by the Emperour.
Pope.   We will depose the Emperour for that deed,
  And curse the people that submit to him;
  Both he and thou shalt stand excommunicate,
  And interdict from Churches priviledge,
  And all society of holy men: 910
  He growes to prowd in his authority,
  Lifting his loftie head above the clouds,
  And like a Steeple over-peeres the Church.
  But wee'le pul downe his haughty insolence:
  And as Pope *Alexander* our Progenitour,
  Trode on the neck of Germane *Fredericke*,
  Adding this golden sentence to our praise;
  That *Peters* heires should tread on Emperours,
  And walke upon the dreadfull Adders backe,
  Treading the Lyon, and the Dragon downe,   920
  And fearelesse spurne the killing Basiliske:
  So will we quell that haughty Schismatique;
  And by authority Apostolicall
  Depose him from his Regall Government.
Bruno.   Pope *Julius* swore to Princely *Sigismond*,
  For him, and the succeeding Popes of *Rome*,
  To hold the Emperours their lawfull Lords.
Pope.   Pope *Julius* did abuse the Churches Rites,
  And therefore none of his Decrees can stand.
  Is not all power on earth bestowed on us?   930
  And therefore tho we would we cannot erre.
  Behold this Silver Belt whereto is fixt

928 Rites] *i.e.*, rights *as in* Dyce

191

Seven golden keys fast sealed with seven seales,
In token of our seven-fold power from heaven,
To binde or loose, lock fast, condemne, or judge,
Resigne, or seale, or what so pleaseth us.
Then he and thou, and all the world shall stoope,
Or be assured of our dreadfull curse,
To light as heavy as the paines of hell.

Enter Faustus *and* Mephostophilis *like the* Cardinals.

Mephostophilis.   Now tell me *Faustus*, are we not fitted well?   940
Faustus.   Yes *Mephostophilis*, and two such Cardinals
Ne're serv'd a holy Pope, as we shall do.
But whilst they sleepe within the Consistory,
Let us salute his reverend Father-hood.
Raymond.   Behold my Lord, the Cardinals are return'd.
Pope.   Welcome grave Fathers, answere presently,
What have our holy Councell there decreed,
Concerning *Bruno* and the Emperour,
In quittance of their late conspiracie
Against our State, and Papall dignitie?   950
Faustus.   Most sacred Patron of the Church of *Rome*,
By full consent of all the reverend Synod
Of Priests and Prelates, it is thus decreed:
That *Bruno*, and the Germane Emperour
Be held as Lollords, and bold Schismatiques,
And proud disturbers of the Churches peace.
And if that *Bruno* by his owne assent,
Without inforcement of the German Peeres,
Did seeke to weare the triple Dyadem,
And by your death to clime Saint *Peters* Chaire,   960
The Statutes Decretall have thus decreed,
He shall be streight condemn'd of heresie,
And on a pile of Fagots burnt to death.
Pope.   It is enough: here, take him to your charge,
And beare him streight to *Ponte Angelo*,

933 keys] Chappell; seales B1–2;   *952 reverend] *omit* B1–6
    scales B3–6

And in the strongest Tower inclose him fast.
To morrow, sitting in our Consistory,
With all our Colledge of grave Cardinals,
We will determine of his life or death.
Here, take his triple Crowne along with you,   970
And leave it in the Churches treasury.
Make haste againe, my good Lord Cardinalls,
And take our blessing Apostolicall.
Mephostophilis.   So, so, was never Diuell thus blest before.
Faustus.   Away sweet *Mephostophilis* be gone,
The Cardinals will be plagu'd for this anon.
                    Exeunt Faustus *and* Mephostophilis [*with* Bruno].
Pope.   Go presently, and bring a banket forth,
That we may solemnize Saint *Peters* feast,
And with Lord *Raymond*, King of *Hungary*,
Drinke to our late and happy victory.   980
                                        Exeunt.

                                        [Scene ix]
    A Senit while the Banquet is brought in; and then Enter   [III.ii]
        Faustus *and* Mephostophilis *in their owne shapes.*

Mephostophilis.   Now *Faustus*, come prepare thy selfe for mirth,
The sleepy Cardinals are hard at hand,
To censure *Bruno*, that is posted hence,
And on a proud pac'd Steed, as swift as thought,
Flies ore the Alpes to fruitfull *Germany*,
There to salute the wofull Emperour.
Faustus.   The Pope will curse them for their sloth to day,
That slept both *Bruno* and his crowne away.
But now, that *Faustus* may delight his minde,
And by their folly make some merriment,   990
Sweet *Mephostophilis* so charme me here,
That I may walke invisible to all,
And doe what ere I please, unseene of any.
Mephostophilis.   *Faustus* thou shalt, then kneele downe presently,

Whilst on thy head I lay my hand,
And charme thee with this Magicke wand,
First weare this girdle, then appeare
Invisible to all are here:
The Planets seven, the gloomy aire,
Hell and the Furies forked haire,   1000
Pluto's blew fire, and Hecat's tree,
With Magicke spels so compasse thee,
That no eye may thy body see.

So *Faustus*, now for all their holinesse,
Do what thou wilt, thou shalt not be discern'd.
Faustus.   Thankes *Mephostophilis*: now Friers take heed,
Lest *Faustus* make your shaven crownes to bleed.
Mephostophilis.   *Faustus* no more: see where the Cardinals come.

Enter Pope *and all the Lords. Enter the* Cardinals
with a Booke.

Pope.   Welcome Lord Cardinals: come sit downe.
Lord *Raymond*, take your seate, Friers attend,   1010
And see that all things be in readinesse,
As best beseemes this solemne festivall.
1. Cardinal.   First, may it please your sacred Holinesse,
To view the sentence of the reverend Synod,
Concerning *Bruno* and the Emperour.
Pope.   What needs this question? Did I not tell you,
To morrow we would sit i'th Consistory,
And there determine of his punishment?
You brought us word even now, it was decreed,
That *Bruno* and the cursed Emperour   1020
Were by the holy Councell both condemn'd
For lothed Lollords, and base Schismatiques:
Then wherefore would you have me view that booke?
1. Cardinal.   Your Grace mistakes, you gave us no such charge.
Raymond.   Deny it not, we all are witnesses
That *Bruno* here was late delivered you,

1008.1–1087.2 *For the* A-text *of* Scene ix, *see* Appendix: A-text, Scene vi

With his rich triple crowne to be reserv'd,
And put into the Churches treasury.
Both Cardinals.   By holy *Paul* we saw them not.
Pope.   By *Peter* you shall dye,   1030
Unlesse you bring them forth immediatly:
Hale them to prison, lade their limbes with gyves:
False Prelates, for this hatefull treachery,
Curst be your soules to hellish misery.

> [*Exeunt* Cardinals *attended.*]

Faustus.   So, they are safe: now *Faustus* to the feast,
The Pope had never such a frolicke guest.
Pope.   Lord Archbishop of *Reames*, sit downe with us.
Archbishop.   I thanke your Holinesse.
Faustus.   Fall to, the Divell choke you an you spare.
Pope.   Who's that spoke? Friers looke about.   1040
Lord *Raymond* pray fall too, I am beholding
To the Bishop of *Millaine*, for this so rare a present.
Faustus.   I thanke you sir.   *Snatch it.*
Pope.   How now? who snatch't the meat from me!
Villaines why speake you not?
My good Lord Archbishop, heres a most daintie dish,
Was sent me from a Cardinall in *France*.
Faustus.   I'le have that too.   [*Snatch it.*]
Pope.   What Lollards do attend our Hollinesse,
That we receive such great indignity?   1050
Fetch me some wine.
Faustus.   I, pray do, for *Faustus* is a dry.
Pope.   Lord *Raymond*, I drink unto your grace.
Faustus.   I pledge your grace.   [*Snatch it.*]
Pope.   My wine gone too? yee Lubbers look about
And find the man that doth this villany,
Or by our sanctitude you all shall die.
I pray my Lords have patience at this troublesome banquet.
Archbishop.   Please it your holinesse, I thinke it be some Ghost
crept out of Purgatory, and now is come unto your holinesse for 1060
his pardon.

1043 *Snatch it.*] A1–3; *omit* B1–6

Pope.   It may be so:
Go then command our Priests to sing a Dirge,
To lay the fury of this same troublesome ghost.

> *The* Pope *crosseth himselfe.*

Faustus.   How now?
Must every bit be spiced with a Crosse?
Nay then take that.

> Faustus *hits him a boxe of the eare.*

Pope.   O I am slaine, help me my Lords:
O come and help to beare my body hence:
Damb'd be this soule for ever, for this deed.   1070

> *Exeunt the* Pope *and his traine.*

Mephostophilis.   Now *Faustus,* what will you do now?
for I can tell you, you'le be curst with Bell, Booke, and
Candle.

Faustus.   Bell, Booke, and Candle; Candle, Booke, and Bell,
Forward and backward, to curse *Faustus* to hell.

> *Enter the* Friers *with Bell, Booke, and Candle,*
> *for the Dirge.*

1. Frier.   Come brethren, let's about our businesse with good
devotion.
Cursed be he that stole away his holinesse meate from the Table.
> *Maledicat Dominus.*
Cursed be he that stroke his holinesse a blow on the face.
> *Maledicat Dominus.*   1080

> [Faustus *strikes a friar.*]
Cursed be he that strucke fryer Sandelo a blow on the pate.
> *Maledicat Dominus.*
Cursed be he that disturbeth our holy Dirge.
> *Maledicat Dominus.*

1064.1 *The...himselfe.*] A1–3; *omit*   1077 *away*] A1; *omit* A2–3, B1–6
B1–6   1079 *on*] A1–3, B2–6; *omit* B1
1067.1 Faustus...*eare.*] A1–3; *omit*
B1–6

Cursed be he that tooke away his holinesse wine.
             Maledicat Dominus.
    Et omnes sancti. Amen.

        Beate the Friers, *fling fire workes among them,*
                 and Exeunt.

                                              Exeunt.

                                        [Scene x]

    Enter [Robin *the*] *Clowne and* Dicke, *with a Cup.*   [III.iii]

Dick.   Sirra *Robin*, we were best looke that your devill can
answere the stealing of this same cup, for the Vintners boy followes
us at the hard heeles.   1090
Robin.   'Tis no matter, let him come; an he follow us, I'le so
conjure him, as he was never conjur'd in his life, I warrant him:
let me see the cup.

                    Enter Vintner.

Dick.   Here 'tis: Yonder he comes: Now *Robin*, now or never
shew thy cunning.
Vintner.   O, are you here? I am glad I have found you, you are a
couple of fine companions: pray where's the cup you stole from
the Taverne?
Robin.   How, how? we steale a cup? take heed what you say, we
looke not like cup-stealers I can tell you.   1100
Vintner.   Never deny't, for I know you have it, and I'le search you.
Robin.   Search me? I and spare not: hold the cup *Dick*, come,
come, search me, search me.
Vintner.   Come on sirra, let me search you now.
Dick.   I, I, do, do, hold the cup *Robin*, I feare not your searching;
we scorne to steale your cups I can tell you.
Vintner.   Never out face me for the matter, for sure the cup is
betweene you two.
Robin.   Nay there you lie, 'tis beyond us both.

1087 *Et…Amen.*] A 1–3; *omit* B 1–6   1087.4–1137.1 *For the* A-text *of* Scene
1087.3.0 *For* Chorus 3 *that follows here*   x, *see* Appendix: A-text, Scene
    in A 1–3, *see* 1137.2–1154.1   vii

Vintner.   A plague take you, I thought 'twas your knavery to 1110
take it away: Come, give it me againe.

Robin.   I much: when, can you tell? *Dick*, make me a circle, and
stand close at my backe, and stir not for thy life, *Vintner* you
shall have your cup anon, say nothing *Dick*: *O per se o, demogorgon,
Belcher* and *Mephostophilis*.

        Enter Mephostophilis. [*Exit* Vintner *running*.]

Mephostophilis.   You Princely Legions of infernall Rule,
How am I vexed by these villaines Charmes?
From *Constantinople* have they brought me now,
Onely for pleasure of these damned slaves.

Robin.   By Lady sir, you have had a shroud journey of it, will it 1120
please you to take a shoulder of Mutton to supper, and a Tester
in your purse, and go backe againe.

Dick.   I, I pray you heartily sir; for wee cal'd you but in jeast
I promise you.

Mephostophilis.   To purge the rashnesse of this cursed deed,
First, be thou turned to this ugly shape,
For Apish deeds transformed to an Ape.

Robin.   O brave, an Ape? I pray sir, let me have the carrying of
him about to shew some trickes.

Mephostophilis.   And so thou shalt: be thou transformed to   1130
A dog, and carry him upon thy backe;
Away be gone.

Robin.   A dog? that's excellent: let the Maids looke well to their
porridge-pots, for I'le into the Kitchin presently: come *Dick*, come.

                                Exeunt the two Clownes.

Mephostophilis.   Now with the flames of ever-burning fire,
I'le wing my selfe and forth-with flie amaine
Unto my *Faustus* to the great Turkes Court.

                                                Exit.

            Enter Chorus.   [Chorus 3]

When *Faustus* had with pleasure tane the view
Of rarest things, and royal courts of kings,

1137.2–1154.1 Chorus 3] A 1–3; *omit* B 1–6

Hee stayde his course, and so returned home,   1140
Where such as beare his absence but with griefe,
I meane his friends and nearest companions,
Did gratulate his safetie with kinde words,
And in their conference of what befell,
Touching his journey through the world and ayre,
They put forth questions of Astrologie,
Which *Faustus* answerd with such learned skill,
As they admirde and wondred at his wit.
Now is his fame spread forth in every land,
Amongst the rest the Emperour is one,   1150
Carolus the fift, at whose pallace now
Faustus is feasted mongst his noblemen.
What there he did in triall of his art,
I leave untold, your eyes shall see performd.

                                                    Exit.

                                    [Scene xi]

        Enter Martino, *and* Frederick *at severall dores.*   [IV.i]

Martino.   What ho, Officers, Gentlemen,
  Hye to the presence to attend the Emperour.
  Good *Fredericke* see the roomes be voyded straight,
  His Majesty is comming to the Hall;
  Go backe, and see the State in readinesse.
Fredericke.   But where is *Bruno* our elected Pope,   1160
  That on a furies back came post from *Rome*,
  Will not his grace consort the Emperour?
Martino.   O yes,
  And with him comes the Germane Conjurer,
  The learned *Faustus*, fame of *Wittenberge*,
  The wonder of the world for Magick Art;
  And he intends to shew great *Carolus*,
  The race of all his stout progenitors;
  And bring in presence of his Majesty,
  The royall shapes and warlike semblances   1170

1154.2–1203.1 *Omitted in* A 1–3

                                    199

Of *Alexander* and his beauteous Paramour.

Fredericke.   Where is *Benvolio?*

Martino.   Fast a sleepe I warrant you,
He took his rouse with stopes of Rhennish wine,
So kindly yesternight to *Bruno's* health,
That all this day the sluggard keepes his bed.

Fredericke.   See, see his window's ope, we'l call to him.

Martino.   What hoe, *Benvolio.*

Enter Benvolio *above at a window,
in his nightcap: buttoning.*

Benvolio.   What a devill ayle you two?

Martino.   Speak softly sir, least the devil heare you: 1180
For *Faustus* at the Court is late arriv'd,
And at his heeles a thousand furies waite,
To accomplish what soever the Doctor please.

Benvolio.   What of this?

Martino.   Come leave thy chamber first, and thou shalt see
This Conjurer performe such rare exploits,
Before the Pope and royall Emperour,
As never yet was seene in *Germany*.

Benvolio.   Has not the Pope enough of conjuring yet? He was
upon the devils backe late enough; and if he be so farre 1190
in love with him, I would he would post with him to *Rome*
againe.

Fredericke.   Speake, wilt thou come and see this sport?

Benvolio.   Not I.

Martino.   Wilt thou stand in thy Window, and see it then?

Benvolio.   I, and I fall not asleepe i'th meane time.

Martino.   The Emperour is at hand, who comes to see
What wonders by blacke spels may compast be.

Benvolio.   Well, go you attend the Emperour: I am content for
this once to thrust my head out at a window: for they say, if 1200
a man be drunke over night, the Divell cannot hurt him in the
morning: if that bee true, I have a charme in my head, shall
controule him as well as the Conjurer, I warrant you.

Exeunt [Martino *and* Fredericke.]

200

A Senit. [*Enter*] Charles *the Germane Emperour*, Bruno, [*Duke of*]
Saxony, Faustus, Mephostophilis, Fredericke, Martino, *and*
Attendants.

Emperour.　Wonder of men, renown'd Magitian,
　　Thrice learned *Faustus*, welcome to our Court.
　　This deed of thine, in setting *Bruno* free
　　From his and our professed enemy,
　　Shall adde more excellence unto thine Art,
　　Then if by powerfull Necromantick spels,
　　Thou couldst command the worlds obedience:　　　　　　　1210
　　For ever be belov'd of *Carolus*.
　　And if this *Bruno* thou hast late redeem'd,
　　In peace possesse the triple Diadem,
　　And sit in *Peters* Chaire, despite of chance,
　　Thou shalt be famous through all *Italy*,
　　And honour'd of the Germane Emperour.
Faustus.　These gracious words, most royall *Carolus*,
　　Shall make poore *Faustus* to his utmost power,
　　Both love and serve the Germane Emperour,
　　And lay his life at holy *Bruno's* feet.　　　　　　　　1220
　　For proofe whereof, if so your Grace be pleas'd,
　　The Doctor stands prepar'd, by power of Art,
　　To cast his Magicke charmes, that shall pierce through
　　The Ebon gates of ever-burning hell,
　　And hale the stubborne Furies from their caves,
　　To compasse whatsoere your grace commands.
Benvolio.　Bloud, he speakes terribly: but for all that, I doe not
　　greatly beleeve him, he lookes as like a Conjurer as the Pope to
　　a Coster-monger.
Emperour.　Then *Faustus* as thou late didst promise us,　　　1230
　　We would behold that famous Conquerour,
　　Great *Alexander*, and his Paramour,
　　In their true shapes, and state Majesticall,
　　That we may wonder at their excellence.

1203.2–1324.1 *For the* A-text *of* Scene xi, *see* Appendix: A-text, Scene viii
1228 a Conjurer] B2–6; conjurer B1

Faustus. Your Majesty shall see them presently.

Mephostophilis away,
And with a solemne noyse of trumpets sound,
Present before this royall Emperour,
Great *Alexander* and his beauteous Paramour.

Mephostophilis. *Faustus* I will. [*Exit.*] 1240

Benvolio. Well Master Doctor, an your Divels come not away quickly, you shall have me asleepe presently: zounds I could eate my selfe for anger, to thinke I have beene such an Asse all this while, to stand gaping after the divels Governor, and can see nothing.

Faustus. Il'e make you feele something anon, if my Art faile me not.

My Lord, I must forewarne your Majesty,
That when my Spirits present the royall shapes
Of *Alexander* and his Paramour, 1250
Your grace demand no questions of the King,
But in dumbe silence let them come and goe.

Emperour. Be it as *Faustus* please, we are content.

Benvolio. I, I, and I am content too: and thou bring *Alexander* and his Paramour before the Emperour, Il'e be *Acteon*, and turne my selfe to a Stagge.

Faustus. And Il'e play *Diana*, and send you the hornes presently.

[*Enter* Mephostophilis.]

Senit. Enter at one dore the Emperour Alexander, *at the other* Darius; *they meete,* Darius *is throwne downe,* Alexander *kils him; takes off his Crowne, and offering to goe out, his Paramour meetes him, he embraceth her, and sets* Darius *Crowne upon her head; and comming backe, both salute the Emperour, who leaving his State, offers to embrace them, which* Faustus *seeing, suddenly staies him. Then trumpets cease, and Musicke sounds.*

My gracious Lord, you doe forget your selfe,
These are but shadowes, not substantiall.

Emperour. O pardon me, my thoughts are ravished so 1260

1257.2 dore] B2–6; *omit* B1
1260 ravished so] Greg; so ravished B1–6

With sight of this renowned Emperour,
That in mine armes I would have compast him.
But *Faustus*, since I may not speake to them,
To satisfie my longing thoughts at full,
Let me this tell thee: I have heard it said,
That this faire Lady, whilest she liv'd on earth,
Had on her necke a little wart, or mole;
How may I prove that saying to be true?

Faustus.   Your Majesty may boldly goe and see.

Emperour.   *Faustus* I see it plaine,   1270
And in this sight thou better pleasest me,
Then if I gain'd another Monarchie.

Faustus.   Away, be gone.   *Exit Show.*
See, see, my gracious Lord, what strange beast is yon, that thrusts
his head out at the window.

Emperour.   O wondrous sight: see Duke of *Saxony*,
Two spreading hornes most strangely fastened
Upon the head of yong *Benvolio*.

Saxony.   What, is he asleepe, or dead?

Faustus.   He sleeps my Lord, but dreames not of his hornes.   1280

Emperour.   This sport is excellent: wee'l call and wake him.
What ho, *Benvolio*.

Benvolio.   A plague upon you, let me sleepe a while.

Emperour.   I blame thee not to sleepe much, having such a head
of thine owne.

Saxony.   Looke up *Benvolio*, tis the Emperour calls.

Benvolio.   The Emperour? where? O zounds my head.

Emperour.   Nay, and thy hornes hold, tis no matter for thy head,
for that's arm'd sufficiently.

Faustus.   Why how now sir Knight, what, hang'd by the hornes? 1290
this is most horrible: fie, fie, pull in your head for shame, let not
all the world wonder at you.

Benvolio.   Zounds Doctor, is this your villany?

Faustus.   O say not so sir: the Doctor has no skill,
No Art, no cunning, to present these Lords,
Or bring before this royall Emperour

1275 the window] B2–6; window B1   1291 is] B2–6; *omit* B1

The mightie Monarch, warlicke *Alexander*.
If *Faustus* do it, you are streight resolv'd,
In bold *Acteons* shape to turne a Stagge.
And therefore my Lord, so please your Majesty,   1300
Il'e raise a kennell of Hounds shall hunt him so,
As all his footmanship shall scarce prevaile,
To keepe his Carkasse from their bloudy phangs.
Ho, *Belimoth, Argiron, Asteroth*.

Benvolio.   Hold, hold: zounds hee'l raise up a kennell of Divels
I thinke anon: good my Lord intreate for me: 'sbloud I am never
able to endure these torments.

Emperour.   Then good Master Doctor,
Let me intreate you to remove his hornes,
He has done penance now sufficiently.   1310

Faustus.   My gracious Lord, not so much for injury done to me,
as to delight your Majesty with some mirth, hath *Faustus* justly
requited this injurious knight, which being all I desire, I am
content to remove his hornes. *Mephostophilis*, transforme him;
and hereafter sir, looke you speake well of Schollers.

Benvolio.   Speake well of yee? 'sbloud and Schollers be such
Cuckold-makers to clap hornes of honest mens heades o'this
order, Il'e nere trust smooth faces, and small ruffes more. But an
I be not reveng'd for this, would I might be turn'd to a gaping
Oyster, and drinke nothing but salt water.   [*Exit.*] 1320

Emperour.   Come *Faustus* while the Emperour lives.
In recompence of this thy high desert,
Thou shalt command the state of *Germany*,
And live belov'd of mightie *Carolus*.

                                        Exeunt omnes.

                                        [Scene xii]

            Enter Benvolio, Martino, Fredericke, *and Souldiers*.   [IV.ii

Martino.   Nay sweet *Benvolio*, let us sway thy thoughts
From this attempt against the Conjurer.
Benvolio.   Away, you love me not, to urge me thus,

1324.2–1430.4 Scene xii] *omit* A 1–3

Shall I let slip so great an injury,
When every servile groome jeasts at my wrongs,
And in their rusticke gambals proudly say,   1330
Benvolio's head was grac't with hornes to day?
O may these eye-lids never close againe,
Till with my sword I have that Conjurer slaine.
If you will aid me in this enterprise,
Then draw your weapons, and be resolute:
If not, depart: here will *Benvolio* die,
But *Faustus* death shall quit my infamie.
Fredericke.   Nay, we will stay with thee, betide what may,
  And kill that Doctor if he come this way.
Benvolio.   Then gentle *Fredericke* hie thee to the grove,   1340
  And place our servants, and our followers
  Close in an ambush there behinde the trees,
  By this (I know) the Conjurer is neere,
  I saw him kneele, and kisse the Emperours hand,
  And take his leave, laden with rich rewards.
  Then Souldiers boldly fight; if *Faustus* die,
  Take you the wealth, leave us the victorie.
Fredericke.   Come souldiers, follow me unto the grove,
  Who kils him shall have gold, and endlesse love.
                        Exit Frederick *with the Souldiers*.
Benvolio.   My head is lighter then it was by th' hornes,   1350
  But yet my heart's more ponderous then my head,
  And pants untill I see that Conjurer dead.
Martino.   Where shall we place our selves *Benvolio*?
Benvolio.   Here will we stay to bide the first assault,
  O were that damned Hell-hound but in place,
  Thou soone shouldst see me quit my foule disgrace.

                  Enter Fredericke.

Fredericke.   Close, close, the Conjurer is at hand,
  And all alone, comes walking in his gowne;
  Be ready then, and strike the Peasant downe.

1351 heart's] B2–6; heart B1

Benvolio.   Mine be that honour then: now sword strike home,   1360
For hornes he gave, Il'e have his head anone.

Enter Faustus *with the false head.*

Martino.   See, see, he comes.
Benvolio.   No words: this blow ends all,
Hell take his soule, his body thus must fall.
Faustus.   Oh.
Fredericke.   Grone you Master Doctor?
Benvolio.   Breake may his heart with grones: deere *Frederik* see,
Thus will I end his griefes immediatly.
Martino.   Strike with a willing hand, his head is off.
Benvolio.   The Divel's dead, the Furies now may laugh.
Fredericke.   Was this that sterne aspect, that awfull frowne,   1370
Made the grim monarch of infernall spirits,
Tremble and quake at his commanding charmes?
Martino.   Was this that damned head, whose heart conspir'd
Benvolio's shame before the Emperour?
Benvolio.   I, that's the head, and here the body lies,
Justly rewarded for his villanies.
Fredericke.   Come, let's devise how we may adde more shame
To the blacke scandall of his hated name.
Benvolio.   First, on his head, in quittance of my wrongs,
Il'e naile huge forked hornes, and let them hang   1380
Within the window where he yoak'd me first,
That all the world may see my just revenge.
Martino.   What use shall we put his beard to?
Benvolio.   Wee'l sell it to a Chimny-sweeper: it will weare out
ten birchin broomes I warrant you.
Fredericke.   What shall his eyes doe?
Benvolio.   Wee'l put out his eyes, and they shall serve for buttons
to his lips, to keepe his tongue from catching cold.
Martino.   An excellent policie: and now sirs, having divided him,
what shall the body doe?   [Faustus *rises.*] 1390
Benvolio.   Zounds the Divel's alive agen.
Fredericke.   Give him his head for Gods sake.

---

*1373 heart] *stet* B1   1386 his] B2–6; *omit* B1

206

Faustus.   Nay keepe it: *Faustus* will have heads and hands,
I, all your hearts to recompence this deed.
Knew you not Traytors, I was limitted
For foure and twenty yeares, to breathe on earth?
And had you cut my body with your swords,
Or hew'd this flesh and bones as small as sand,
Yet in a minute had my spirit return'd,
And I had breath'd a man made free from harme.   1400
But wherefore doe I dally my revenge?
Asteroth, Belimoth, Mephostophilis,

Enter Mephostophilis *and other Divels.*

Go horse these traytors on your fiery backes,
And mount aloft with them as high as heaven,
Thence pitch them headlong to the lowest hell:
Yet stay, the world shall see their miserie,
And hell shall after plague their treacherie.
Go *Belimothe*, and take this caitife hence,
And hurle him in some lake of mud and durt:
Take thou this other, dragge him through the woods,   1410
Amongst the pricking thornes, and sharpest briers,
Whilst with my gentle *Mephostophilis*,
This Traytor flies unto some steepie rocke,
That rowling downe, may breake the villaines bones,
As he intended to dismember me.
Fly hence, dispatch my charge immediatly.
Fredericke.   Pitie us gentle *Faustus*, save our lives.
Faustus.   Away.
Fredericke.   He must needs goe that the Divell drives.

Exeunt Spirits with the knights.

Enter the ambusht Souldiers.

1. Soldier.   Come sirs, prepare your selves in readinesse,   1420
Make hast to help these noble Gentlemen,
I heard them parly with the Conjurer.
2. Soldier.   See where he comes, dispatch, and kill the slave.

1394 I, all] Chappell; I call B1–6

Faustus.   What's here? an ambush to betray my life:
Then *Faustus* try thy skill: base pesants stand,
For loe these Trees remove at my command,
And stand as Bulwarkes twixt your selves and me,
To sheild me from your hated treachery:
Yet to encounter this your weake attempt,
Behold an Army comes incontinent.   1430

*Faustus strikes the dore, and enter a devill playing on a Drum, after
him another bearing an Ensigne: and divers with weapons, Mephostophilis with fire-workes; they set upon the Souldiers and drive them
out.*   [*Exeunt omnes.*]

                                    [Scene xiii]

    Enter at severall dores, Benvolio, Fredericke, *and* Martino,   [IV.iii
        *their heads and faces bloudy, and besmear'd with
            mud and durt; all having hornes on their heads.*

Martino.   What ho, *Benvolio.*
Benvolio.   Here, what *Frederick*, ho.
Fredericke.   O help me gentle friend; where is *Martino?*
Martino.   Deere *Frederick* here,
    Halfe smother'd in a Lake of mud and durt,
    Through which the Furies drag'd me by the heeles.
Fredericke.   *Martino* see,
    Benvolio's hornes againe.
Martino.   O misery.
    How now *Benvolio?*
Benvolio.   Defend me heaven, shall I be haunted still?
Martino.   Nay feare not man, we have no power to kill.   1440
Benvolio.   My friends transformed thus: O hellish spite,
    Your heads are all set with hornes.
Fredericke.   You hit it right,
    It is your owne you meane, feele on your head.
Benvolio.   'Zons, hornes againe.
Martino.   Nay chafe not man, we all are sped.

1430.5–1456.1 Scene xiii] *omit* A 1–3

Benvolio.   What devill attends this damn'd Magician,
  That spite of spite, our wrongs are doubled?
Fredericke.   What may we do, that we may hide our shames?
Benvolio.   If we should follow him to worke revenge,
  He'd joyne long Asses eares to these huge hornes,
  And make us laughing stockes to all the world.   1450
Martino.   What shall we then do deere *Benvolio*?
Benvolio.   I have a Castle joyning neere these woods,
  And thither wee'le repaire and live obscure,
  Till time shall alter this our brutish shapes:
  Sith blacke disgrace hath thus eclipst our fame,
  We'le rather die with griefe, then live with shame.

                                                    Exeunt omnes.

                                          [Scene xiv]

        Enter Faustus, *and the* Horse-courser.   [IV.iv]

Horse-courser.   I beseech your Worship accept of these forty
  Dollors.
Faustus.   Friend, thou canst not buy so good a horse, for so small
  a price: I have no great need to sell him, but if thou likest him for 1460
  ten Dollors more, take him, because I see thou hast a good minde
  to him.
Horse-courser.   I beseech you sir accept of this; I am a very poore
  man, and have lost very much of late by horse flesh, and this
  bargaine will set me up againe.
Faustus.   Well, I will not stand with thee, give me the money:
  now sirra I must tell you, that you may ride him o're hedge and
  ditch, and spare him not; but do you heare? in any case, ride
  him not into the water.
Horse-courser.   How sir, not into the water? why will he not drink 1470
  of all waters?
Faustus.   Yes, he will drinke of all waters, but ride him not into the
  water; o're hedge and ditch, or where thou wilt, but not into

---

1456.2–1504.1 *For the* A-text *of* Scene   1456.2 Horse-courser] Chappell; *Horse-*
    xiv, *see* Appendix: A-text, Scene   *courser, and Mephostophilis* B1–6
    viii (*continued*) *line* 90*ff.*

the water: Go bid the Hostler deliver him unto you, and remember
what I say.

Horse-courser. I warrant you sir; O joyfull day: Now am I a
made man for ever.   *Exit.*

Faustus. What art thou *Faustus* but a man condemn'd to die?
Thy fatall time drawes to a finall end;
Despaire doth drive distrust into my thoughts.   1480
Confound these passions with a quiet sleepe:
Tush, Christ did call the Theefe upon the Crosse,
Then rest thee *Faustus* quiet in conceite.   *He sits to sleepe.*

Enter the Horse-courser *wet.*

Horse-courser. O what a cosening Doctor was this? I riding my
horse into the water, thinking some hidden mystery had beene
in the horse, I had nothing under me but a little straw, and had
much ado to escape drowning: Well I'le go rouse him, and make
him give me my forty Dollors againe. Ho sirra Doctor, you
cosening scab; Maister Doctor awake, and rise, and give me my
mony againe, for your horse is turned to a bottle of Hay,—Maister 1490
Doctor.   *He puls off his leg.*
Alas I am undone, what shall I do? I have puld off his leg.

Faustus. O help, help, the villaine hath murder'd me.

Horse-courser. Murder or not murder, now he has but one leg,
I'le out-run him, and cast this leg into some ditch or other.
                                                      [*Exit.*]

Faustus. Stop him, stop him, stop him—ha, ha, ha, *Faustus* hath
his leg againe, and the Horse-courser a bundle of hay for his forty
Dollors.

Enter Wagner.

How now *Wagner* what newes with thee?

Wagner. If it please you, the Duke of *Vanholt* doth earnestly 1500
entreate your company, and hath sent some of his men to attend
you with provision fit for your journey.

Faustus. The Duke of *Vanholt*'s an honourable Gentleman, and
one to whom I must be no niggard of my cunning; Come, away.
                                                  Exeunt.

[Scene xv]

Enter [Robin *the*] *Clowne,* Dick, Horse-courser, *and a* Carter. [IV.v]

Carter.   Come my Maisters, I'le bring you to the best beere in
Europe, what ho, Hostis; where be these Whores?

Enter Hostis.

Hostesse.   How now, what lacke you? What my old Guesse?
welcome.
Robin.   Sirra *Dick,* dost thou know why I stand so mute?
Dick.   No *Robin,* why is't?   1510
Robin.   I am eighteene pence on the score, but say nothing, see
if she have forgotten me.
Hostesse.   Who's this, that stands so solemnly by himselfe: what
my old Guest?
Robin.   O Hostisse how do you? I hope my score stands still.
Hostesse.   I there's no doubt of that, for me thinkes you make no
hast to wipe it out.
Dick.   Why Hostesse, I say, fetch us some Beere.
Hostesse.   You shall presently: looke up into th' hall there ho.
Exit.

Dick.   Come sirs, what shall we do now till mine Hostesse comes? 1520
Carter.   Marry sir, I'le tell you the bravest tale how a Conjurer
serv'd me; you know Doctor *Fauster*?
Horse-courser.   I, a plague take him, heere's some on's have cause
to know him; did he conjure thee too?
Carter.   I'le tell you how he serv'd me: As I was going to *Witten-*
berge t'other day, with a loade of Hay, he met me, and asked me
what he should give me for as much Hay as he could eate; now
sir, I thinking that a little would serve his turne, bad him take as
much as he would for three-farthings; so he presently gave me my
mony, and fell to eating; and as I am a cursen man, he never left 1530
eating, till he had eate up all my loade of hay.
All.   O monstrous, eate a whole load of Hay!

1504.2–1557.1 Scene xv] *omit* A 1–3   1507 Guesse] *i.e.,* guests *as in* B 2

Robin.   Yes, yes, that may be; for I have heard of one, that ha's
eate a load of logges.

Horse-courser.   Now sirs, you shall heare how villanously he serv'd
mee: I went to him yesterday to buy a horse of him, and he would
by no meanes sell him under forty Dollors; so sir, because I
knew him to be such a horse, as would run over hedge and ditch,
and never tyre, I gave him his money; so when I had my horse,
Doctor *Fauster* bad me ride him night and day, and spare him no   1540
time; but, quoth he, in any case ride him not into the water. Now
sir, I thinking the horse had had some rare quality that he would not
have me know of, what did I but rid him into a great river,
and when I came just in the midst my horse vanisht away, and I
sate straddling upon a bottle of Hay.

All.   O brave Doctor.

Horse-courser.   But you shall heare how bravely I serv'd him for it;
I went me home to his house, and there I found him asleepe; I
kept a hallowing and whooping in his eares, but all could not wake
him: I seeing that, tooke him by the leg, and never rested pulling,   1550
till I had pul'd me his leg quite off, and now 'tis at home in mine
Hostry.

Dick.   And has the Doctor but one leg then? that's excellent, for
one of his devils turn'd me into the likenesse of an Apes face.

Carter.   Some more drinke Hostesse.

Robin.   Hearke you, we'le into another roome and drinke a while,
and then we'le go seeke out the Doctor.

                                            Exeunt omnes.

                                            [Scene xvi]

        Enter the Duke *of* Vanholt; *his* Dutches,   [IV.vi]
               Faustus, *and* Mephostophilis.

Duke.   Thankes Maister Doctor, for these pleasant sights, nor
know I how sufficiently to recompence your great deserts
in erecting that inchanted Castle in the Aire: the sight where-   1560

---

*1542 rare] A 1–3, B 2–6; *omit* B 1   1557.2–1673.1 *For the* A-text of Scene
1553 *Dick.*] Methuen; *Clow.* B 1–6   xvi, *see* Appendix: A-text, Scene
                                              ix. *The* A-text *omits* 1587.1–1668

of so delighted me, as nothing in the world could please me
more.

Faustus.   I do thinke my selfe my good Lord, highly recompenced,
in that it pleaseth your grace to thinke but well of that which
Faustus hath performed. But gratious Lady, it may be, that you
have taken no pleasure in those sights; therefor I pray you tell me,
what is the thing you most desire to have? be it in the world, it
shall be yours: I have heard that great bellyed women, do long
for things, are rare and dainty.

Lady.   True Maister Doctor, and since I finde you so kind I will   1570
make knowne unto you what my heart desires to have, and were
it now Summer, as it is January, a dead time of the Winter, I
would request no better meate, then a dish of ripe grapes.

Faustus.   This is but a small matter: Go *Mephostophilis*, away.

                                        Exit Mephostophilis.

Madam, I will do more then this for your content.

            Enter Mephostophilis *agen with the grapes.*

Here, now taste yee these, they should be good, for they come
from a farre Country I can tell you.

Duke.   This makes me wonder more then all the rest, that at this
time of the yeare, when every Tree is barren of his fruite, from   1580
whence you had these ripe grapes.

Faustus.   Please it your grace, the yeare is divided into two circles
over the whole world, so that when it is Winter with us, in the
contrary circle it is likewise Summer with them, as in *India*, *Saba*,
and such Countries that lye farre East, where they have fruit twice
a yeare.   From whence, by meanes of a swift spirit that I have, I
had these grapes brought as you see.

Lady.   And trust me, they are the sweetest grapes that e're I tasted.

                The Clownes bounce at the gate, within.

Duke.   What rude disturbers have we at the gate?
Go pacifie their fury, set it ope,
And then demand of them, what they would have.   1590

        They knocke againe, and call out to talke with Faustus.

1587.1 *Clownes*] Dyce; *Clowne* B 1–6

A Servant.   Why how now Maisters, what a coyle is there?
  What is the reason you disturbe the Duke?
Dick.   We have no reason for it, therefore a fig for him.
Servant.   Why saucy varlets, dare you be so bold.
Horse-courser.   I hope sir, we have wit enough to be more bold
  then welcome.
Servant.   It appeares so, pray be bold else-where,
  And trouble not the Duke.
Duke.   What would they have?
Servant.   They all cry out to speake with Doctor *Faustus.*   1600
Carter.   I, and we will speake with him.
Duke.   Will you sir? Commit the Rascals.
Dick.   Commit with us, he were as good commit with his father,
  as commit with us.
Faustus.   I do beseech your grace let them come in,
  They are good subject for a merriment.
Duke.   Do as thou wilt *Faustus*, I give thee leave.
Faustus.   I thanke your grace.

  Enter [Robin] *the Clowne,* Dick, Carter, *and* Horse-courser.

                    Why, how now my good friends?
  'Faith you are too outragious, but come neere,
  I have procur'd your pardons: welcome all.   1610
Robin.   Nay sir, we will be wellcome for our mony, and we will
  pay for what we take: What ho, give's halfe a dosen of Beere
  here, and be hang'd.
Faustus.   Nay, hearke you, can you tell me where you are?
Carter.   I marry can I, we are under heaven.
Servant.   I but sir sauce box, know you in what place?
Horse-courser.   I, I, the house is good enough to drink in: Zons
  fill us some Beere, or we'll breake all the barrels in the house, and
  dash out all your braines with your Bottles.
Faustus.   Be not so furious: come you shall have Beere.   1620
  My Lord, beseech you give me leave a while,
  I'le gage my credit, 'twill content your grace.

1608 good] B2-6; goods B1

Duke.   With all my heart kind Doctor, please thy selfe,
Our servants, and our Courts at thy command.

Faustus.   I humbly thanke your grace: then fetch some Beere.

Horse-courser.   I mary, there spake a Doctor indeed, and 'faith Ile
drinke a health to thy woodden leg for that word.

Faustus.   My woodden leg? what dost thou meane by that?

Carter.   Ha, ha, ha, dost heare him *Dick*, he has forgot his legge.

Horse-courser.   I, I, he does not stand much upon that.   1630

Faustus.   No faith, not much upon a woodden leg.

Carter.   Good Lord, that flesh and bloud should be so fraile with
your Worship: Do not you remember a Horse-courser you sold
a horse to?

Faustus.   Yes, I remember I sold one a horse.

Carter.   And do you remember you bid he should not ride him
into the water?

Faustus.   Yes, I do verie well remember that.

Carter.   And do you remember nothing of your leg?

Faustus.   No in good sooth.   1640

Carter.   Then I pray remember your curtesie.

Faustus.   I thank you sir.

Carter.   'Tis not so much worth; I pray you tel me one thing.

Faustus.   What's that?

Carter.   Be both your legs bedfellowes every night together?

Faustus.   Wouldst thou make a *Colossus* of me, that thou askest
me such questions?

Carter.   No truelie sir, I would make nothing of you, but I would
faine know that.

Enter Hostesse [*brought hither by magic*] *with drinke.*

Faustus.   Then I assure thee certainelie they are.   1650

Carter.   I thanke you, I am fully satisfied.

Faustus.   But wherefore dost thou aske?

Carter.   For nothing sir: but me thinkes you should have a
wooden bedfellow of one of 'em.

Horse-courser.   Why, do you heare sir, did not I pull off one of
your legs when you were asleepe?

1636 him] B 2–6; *omit* B 1

Faustus. But I have it againe now I am awake: looke you heere sir.
All. O horrible, had the Doctor three legs?
Carter. Do you remember sir, how you cosened me and eat up
my load of—— Faustus *charmes him dumb.* 1660
Dick. Do you remember how you made me weare an Apes——
[Faustus *charmes him dumb.*]
Horse-courser. You whoreson conjuring scab, do you remember
how you cosened me with a ho——
[Faustus *charmes him dumb.*]
Robin. Ha' you forgotten me? you thinke to carry it away with
your *Hey-passe*, and *Re-passe*: do you remember the dogs fa——
[Faustus *charmes him dumb.*] *Exeunt Clownes.*
Hostesse. Who payes for the Ale? heare you Maister Doctor,
now you have sent away my guesse, I pray who shall pay me for
my A—— ? [Faustus *charmes her dumb.*] *Exit* Hostesse.
Lady. My Lord,
We are much beholding to this learned man. 1670
Duke. So are we Madam, which we will recompence
With all the love and kindnesse that we may.
His Artfull sport, drives all sad thoughts away.

Exeunt.

[Scene xvii]

Thunder and lightning: Enter devils with cover'd dishes; [V.i
Mephostophilis *leades them into* Faustus *Study:*
Then enter Wagner.

Wagner. I think my Maister means to die shortly, he has made
his will, and given me his wealth, his house, his goods, and store
of golden plate; besides two thousand duckets ready coin'd: I
wonder what he meanes, if death were nie, he would not frolick
thus: hee's now at supper with the schollers, where ther's such
belly-cheere, as *Wagner* in his life nere saw the like: and see where
they come, belike the feast is done. *Exit.* 1680

1673.2–1680 *For the* A-text, *see* Appendix: A-text, Scene xx

Enter Faustus, Mephostophilis, *and two or three*
Schollers.

1. Scholler.　Master Doctor *Faustus*, since our conference about
faire Ladies, which was the beautifullest in all the world, we have
determin'd with our selves, that *Hellen* of *Greece* was the admir-
ablest Lady that ever liv'd: therefore Master Doctor, if you will
doe us so much favour, as to let us see that peerelesse dame of
Greece, whom all the world admires for Majesty, we should thinke
our selves much beholding unto you.

Faustus.　Gentlemen,
For that I know your friendship is unfain'd,
And *Faustus* custome is not to deny　　　　　　　　　　　　1690
The just requests of those that wish him well,
You shall behold that peerelesse dame of *Greece*,
No otherwaies for pompe or Majesty,
Then when sir *Paris* crost the seas with her,
And brought the spoyles to rich *Dardania*:
Be silent then, for danger is in words.

Musicke sound, Mephostophilis *brings in* Hellen,
she passeth over the stage.

2. Scholler.　Too simple is my wit to tell her worth,
Whom all the world admires for majesty.

3. Scholler.　No marvel tho the angry Greekes pursu'd
With tenne yeares warre the rape of such a queene,　　　　1700
Whose heavenly beauty passeth all compare.

1. Scholler.　Now we have seene the pride of Natures worke,
And only Paragon of excellence,
Let us depart, and for this blessed sight

---

*1690 And...not] A1–3; It is not
　　　Faustus custome B1–6
1691 requests] A1; request A2–3, B1–6
1693 otherwaies] A1–3; otherwise B1–6
1696.2 *Followed in* B1–6 *by* 2 Was this
　　　faire *Hellen*, whose admired worth
　　　| Made *Greece* with ten yeares
　　　warres afflict [B1: afslict] poore

Troy? Omit A1–3
1697 2. *Scholler.*] A1–3; *3* B1–6
1699–1701 *3. Scholler.* No...compare.]
　　　A1–3; *omit* B1–6
1703 And...excellence,] A1–3; *omit*
　　　B1–6
1704 Let us depart] A1–3; Wee'l take
　　　our leaves B1–6

217

Happy and blest be *Faustus* evermore.   *Exeunt Schollers.*
Faustus.   Gentlemen farewell: the same wish I to you.

Enter an Old Man.

Old Man.   O gentle *Faustus* leave this damned Art,
  This Magicke, that will charme thy soule to hell,
  And quite bereave thee of salvation.
  Though thou hast now offended like a man,   1710
  Doe not persever in it like a Divell;
  Yet, yet, thou hast an amiable soule,
  If sin by custome grow not into nature:
  Then *Faustus*, will repentance come too late,
  Then thou art banisht from the sight of heaven;
  No mortall can expresse the paines of hell.
  It may be this my exhortation
  Seemes harsh, and all unpleasant; let it not,
  For gentle sonne, I speake it not in wrath,
  Or envy of thee, but in tender love,   1720
  And pitty of thy future miserie.
  And so have hope, that this my kinde rebuke,
  Checking thy body, may amend thy soule.
Faustus.   Where art thou *Faustus*? wretch, what hast thou done?
  Damned art thou *Faustus*, damned, despaire and die,
                 Mephostophilis gives him a dagger.
  Hell claimes his right, and with a roaring voice,
  Saies *Faustus* come, thine houre is almost come,
  And *Faustus* now will come to do thee right.
                      [Offers to stab himself.]
Old Man.   Ah stay good *Faustus*, stay thy desperate steps.
  I see an Angell hover ore thy head,   1730
  And with a vyoll full of pretious grace,
  Offers to poure the same into thy soule,
  Then call for mercy, and avoyd despaire.
Faustus.   Ah my sweete friend,

1706.1–1723 *Enter* . . . *thy soule.*] *For*   1725 Damned . . . die,] A 1–3; *omit* B 1–6
  the A-text, *see* Appendix: A-text,   1729, 1734 Ah] A 1–3; O B 1–6
  Scene x, *continuation, lines* 34–45   *1730 hover] *stet* B 1–6
*1715 Then] *stet* B 1–6   1734 my sweete] A 1–3; *omit* B 1–6

I feele thy words to comfort my distressed soule,
Leave me a while, to ponder on my sinnes.
Old Man.   *Faustus* I leave thee, but with griefe of heart,
Fearing the enemy of thy haplesse soule.   *Exit.*
Faustus.   Accursed *Faustus*, where is mercy now?
I do repent, and yet I doe despaire,   1740
Hell strives with grace for conquest in my breast:
What shall I doe to shun the snares of death?
Mephostophilis.   Thou traytor *Faustus*, I arrest thy soule,
For disobedience to my soveraigne Lord,
Revolt, or I'le in peece-meale teare thy flesh.
Faustus.   I do repent I ere offended him,
Sweet *Mephostophilis*, intreat thy Lord
To pardon my unjust presumption,
And with my bloud againe I will confirme
The former vow I made to *Lucifer*.   1750
Mephostophilis.   Do it then *Faustus*, with unfained heart,
Lest greater dangers do attend thy drift.
Faustus.   Torment sweet friend, that base and crooked age,
That durst disswade me from thy *Lucifer*,
With greatest torments that our hell affoords.
Mephostophilis.   His faith is great, I cannot touch his soule;
But what I may afflict his body with,
I will attempt, which is but little worth.
Faustus.   One thing good servant let me crave of thee,
To glut the longing of my hearts desire,   1760
That I may have unto my paramour,
That heavenly *Hellen*, which I saw of late,
Whose sweet embraces may extinguish cleare,
Those thoughts that do disswade me from my vow,
And keepe mine oath I made to *Lucifer*.
Mephostophilis.   This, or what else my *Faustus* shall desire,
Shall be perform'd in twinkling of an eye.

1739 where...now] A1–3;   wretch   1753 crooked age] A1–3; aged man
     what hast thou done B1–6   B1–6
1751 *Mephostophilis.*]   A1–3,   B5–6;   1755 torments] A1–3; torment B1–6
     omit B1–4   *1763 cleare] *stet* B1–6
1753 *Faustus.*] A1–3; *omit* B1–6   1765 mine oath] A1–3; my vow B1–6

Enter Hellen *againe, passing over betweene two Cupids.*

Faustus.   Was this the face that Launcht a thousand ships,
And burnt the toplesse Towers of *Ilium?*
Sweet *Hellen* make me immortall with a kisse: 1770
Her lips sucke forth my soule, see where it flies.
Come *Hellen*, come, give me my soule againe,
Here will I dwell, for heaven is in these lippes,
And all is drosse that is not *Helena*.

Enter Old Man [*aloof*].

I will be *Paris*, and for love of thee,
In stead of *Troy* shall *Wittenberg* be sack't,
And I will combat with weake *Menelaus*,
And weare thy colours on my plumed crest.
Yea, I will wound *Achilles* in the heele,
And then returne to *Hellen* for a kisse.   1780
O thou art fairer then the evenings aire,
Clad in the beauty of a thousand starres:
Brighter art thou then flaming *Jupiter*,
When he appear'd to haplesse *Semele*:
More lovely then the Monarch of the sky,
In wanton *Arethusa's* azur'd armes,
And none but thou shalt be my Paramour.   *Exeunt.*
Old Man.   Accursed *Faustus*, miserable man,
That from thy soule exclud'st the grace of heaven,
And fliest the throne of his tribunall seate.   1790

Enter the Divelles.

Sathan begins to sift me with his pride:
As in this furnace God shal try my faith,
My faith, vile hell, shall triumph over thee,
Ambitious fiends, see how the heavens smiles
At your repulse, and laughs your state to scorne,
Hence hell, for hence I flie unto my God.

Exeunt.

1774.1 *Enter* Old Man.] A1–3; *omit*   azure B1
    B1–6   1788–96 *Old Man....*God.] A1–3;
*1786 azur'd] A1–3 (azurde), B2–6;   *omit* B1–6

[Scene xviii]

Thunder. Enter [above] Lucifer, Belzebub, *and* Mephostophilis.   [V.ii]

Lucifer.   Thus from infernall *Dis* do we ascend
  To view the subjects of our Monarchy,
  Those soules which sinne seales the blacke sonnes of hell,
  'Mong which as chiefe, *Faustus* we come to thee,   1800
  Bringing with us lasting damnation,
  To wait upon thy soule; the time is come
  Which makes it forfeit.
Mephostophilis.   And this gloomy night,
  Here in this roome will wretched *Faustus* be.
Belzebub.   And here wee'l stay,
  To marke him how he doth demeane himselfe.
Mephostophilis.   How should he, but in desperate lunacie.
  Fond worldling, now his heart bloud dries with griefe;
  His conscience kils it, and his labouring braine,
  Begets a world of idle fantasies,   1810
  To over-reach the Divell, but all in vaine;
  His store of pleasures must be sauc'd with paine.
  He and his servant *Wagner* are at hand,
  Both come from drawing *Faustus* latest will.
  See where they come.

Enter Faustus *and* Wagner.

Faustus.   Say *Wagner*, thou hast perus'd my will,
  How dost thou like it?
Wagner.   Sir, so wondrous well,
  As in all humble dutie, I do yeeld
  My life and lasting service for your love.

Enter the Scholers.

Faustus.   Gramercies *Wagner*. Welcome gentlemen.   1820
                                    [*Exit* Wagner.]
1. Scholler.   Now worthy *Faustus*: me thinks your looks are
  chang'd.

Faustus. Ah gentlemen.

2. Scholler. What ailes *Faustus?*

Faustus. Ah my sweet chamber-fellow, had I liv'd with thee, then had I lived still, but now must dye eternally.

Looke sirs, comes he not, comes he not?

1. Scholler. O my deere *Faustus* what imports this feare?

2. Scholler. Is all our pleasure turn'd to melancholy?

3. Scholler. He is not well with being over solitarie.

2. Scholler. If it be so, wee'l have Physitians,   1830
And *Faustus* shall bee cur'd.

3. Scholler. Tis but a surfet sir, feare nothing.

Faustus. A surfet of deadly sin, that hath damn'd both body and soule.

2. Scholler. Yet *Faustus* looke up to heaven, and remember Gods mercy is infinite.

Faustus. But *Faustus* offence can nere be pardoned, the serpent that tempted *Eve* may be saved, but not *Faustus.* Ah gentlemen, heare me with patience, and tremble not at my speeches. Though my heart pant and quiver to remember that I have beene a student 1840
here these thirty yeares, O would I had never seene *Wittenberg,* never read book: and what wonders I have done, all *Germany* can witnesse, yea all the world: for which *Faustus* hath lost both *Germany* and the world, yea heaven it selfe: heaven the seate of God, the Throne of the Blessed, the Kingdome of Joy, and must remaine in hell for ever. Hell, ah hell for ever. Sweet friends, what shall become of *Faustus* being in hell for ever?

2. Scholler. Yet *Faustus* call on God.

Faustus. On God, whom *Faustus* hath abjur'd? on God, whom *Faustus* hath blasphem'd? Ah my God, I would weepe, but the 1850
Divell drawes in my teares. Gush forth bloud in stead of teares, yea life and soule: oh hee stayes my tongue: I would lift up my hands, but see they hold 'em, they hold 'em.

All. Who, *Faustus?*

1822, 1838, 1846, 1850, 1856 Ah] A1–   1835 Gods] A1–3 (gods); *omit* B1–
3; O B1–6   6
1824–5 Ah...eternally.] A1–3; B1–6   1839 me] A1–3, B2–6; *omit* B1
line thee, | Then

Faustus.   Why, *Lucifer* and *Mephostophilis*:
Ah gentlemen, I gave them my soule for my cunning.
All.   O God forbid.
Faustus.   God forbade it indeed, but *Faustus* hath done it: for
the vaine pleasure of foure and twenty yeares hath *Faustus* lost
eternall joy and felicitie. I writ them a bill with mine owne bloud,   1860
the date is expired: this is the time, and he will fetch mee.
1. Scholler.   Why did not *Faustus* tell us of this before, that
Divines might have prayd for thee?
Faustus.   Oft have I thought to have done so: but the Divel
threatned to teare me in peeces if I nam'd God: to fetch me body
and soule, if I once gave eare to Divinitie: and now 'tis too late.
Gentlemen away, least you perish with me.
2. Scholler.   O what may we do to save *Faustus*?
Faustus.   Talke not of me, but save your selves and depart.
3. Scholler.   God will strengthen me, I will stay with *Faustus*.   1870
1. Scholler.   Tempt not God sweet friend, but let us into the next
roome, and there pray for him.
Faustus.   I, pray for me, pray for me: and what noyse soever you
heare, come not unto me, for nothing can rescue me.
2. Scholler.   Pray thou, and we will pray, that God may have mercie
upon thee.
Faustus.   Gentlemen farewell: if I live till morning, Il'e visit you:
if not, *Faustus* is gone to hell.
All.   *Faustus*, farewell.   *Exeunt* Schollers.

[*Enter* Mephostophilis *below.*]

Mephostophilis.   I, *Faustus*, now thou hast no hope of heaven,   1880
Therefore despaire, thinke onely upon hell;
For that must be thy mansion, there to dwell.
Faustus.   O thou bewitching fiend, 'twas thy temptation,
Hath rob'd me of eternall happinesse.
Mephostophilis.   I doe confesse it *Faustus*, and rejoyce;
'Twas I, that when thou wer't i'the way to heaven,
Damb'd up thy passage; when thou took'st the booke,

1866 'tis A1–3, B2; 'tis B1; it is B3–6   1880–1925 *Omit* A1–3
1872 there] A1; *omit* A2–3, B1–6

To view the Scriptures, then I turn'd the leaves
And led thine eye.
What, weep'st thou? 'tis too late, despaire, farewell,   1890
Fooles that will laugh on earth, must weepe in hell.   *Exit.*

Enter the Good Angell, *and the* Bad [Angell]
at severall doores.

Good Angel.   Oh *Faustus*, if thou hadst given eare to me,
Innumerable joyes had followed thee.
But thou didst love the world.
Bad Angel.   Gave eare to me,
And now must taste hels paines perpetually.
Good Angel.   O what will all thy riches, pleasures, pompes,
Availe thee now?
Bad Angel.   Nothing but vexe thee more,
To want in hell, that had on earth such store.
                    Musicke while the Throne descends.
Good Angel.   O thou hast lost celestiall happinesse,
Pleasures unspeakeable, blisse without end.   1900
Hadst thou affected sweet divinitie,
Hell, or the Divell, had had no power on thee.
Hadst thou kept on that way, *Faustus* behold,
In what resplendant glory thou hadst set
In yonder throne, like those bright shining Saints,
And triumpht over hell: that hast thou lost,
And now poore soule must thy good Angell leave thee,
The jawes of hell are open to receive thee.
                    Exit. [*Throne ascends.*]
                    Hell is discovered.
Bad Angel.   Now *Faustus* let thine eyes with horror stare
Into that vaste perpetuall torture-house,   191
There are the furies tossing damned soules,
On burning forkes: their bodies boyle in lead.
There are live quarters broyling on the coles,
That ner'e can die: this ever-burning chaire,
Is for ore-tortur'd soules to rest them in.

1891 must] B2; most B1   1912 boyle] B3; broyle B1–2

These, that are fed with soppes of flaming fire,
Were gluttons, and lov'd only delicates,
And laught to see the poore starve at their gates:
But yet all these are nothing, thou shalt see
Ten thousand tortures that more horrid be.   1920
Faustus.   O, I have seene enough to torture me.
Bad Angel.   Nay, thou must feele them, taste the smart of all.
He that loves pleasure, must for pleasure fall:
And so I leave thee *Faustus* till anon,
Then wilt thou tumble in confusion.   *Exit.* [*Hell closes.*]
                                            The Clock strikes eleven.

Faustus.   Ah *Faustus,*
Now hast thou but one bare houre to live,
And then thou must be damn'd perpetually.
Stand still you ever moving Spheares of heaven,
That time may cease, and midnight never come.   1930
Faire natures eye, rise, rise againe and make
Perpetuall day: or let this houre be but
A yeare, a month, a weeke, a naturall day,
That *Faustus* may repent, and save his soule.
O lente lente currite noctis equi:
The Stars move still, Time runs, the Clocke will strike,
The devill will come, and *Faustus* must be damn'd.
O I'le leape up to my God: who puls me downe?
See see where Christs bloud streames in the firmament,
One drop would save my soule, halfe a drop, ah my Christ.   1940
Rend not my heart, for naming of my Christ,
Yet will I call on him: O spare me *Lucifer.*
Where is it now? 'tis gone. And see where God
Stretcheth out his Arme, and bends his irefull Browes:
Mountaines and Hils, come, come, and fall on me,
And hide me from the heavy wrath of God.

1926, 1940 Ah] A1–3; O B1–6
1938 my God] A1–3; heaven B1–
 6
1939 See...firmament,] A1–3 (blood),
 B2–6; *omit* B1
1940 One drop...drop,] A1–3; One

drop of bloud will save me; B1–6
*1943–4 where God...Browes:] A1–3
 (browes); a threatning Arme, an
 angry Brow. B1–6
1946 God] A1–3; heaven B1–6

No, no?
Then will I headlong run into the earth:
Gape earth; O no, it will not harbour me.
You Starres that raign'd at my nativity,   1950
Whose influence hath allotted death and hell;
Now draw up *Faustus* like a foggy mist,
Into the entrals of yon labouring cloud,
That when you vomite forth into the aire,
My limbes may issue from your smoky mouthes,
So that my soule may but ascend to heaven.

                       The Watch strikes.

Ah halfe the houre is past: 'twill all be past anone:
O God, if thou wilt not have mercy on my soule,
Yet for Christs sake, whose bloud hath ransom'd me,
Impose some end to my incessant paine: 1960
Let *Faustus* live in hell a thousand yeares,
A hundred thousand, and at last be sav'd.
No end is limited to damned soules.
Why wert thou not a creature wanting soule?
Or why is this immortall that thou hast?
Ah *Pythagoras Metemsycosis*; were that true,
This soule should flie from me, and I be chang'd
Unto some brutish beast.
All beasts are happy, for when they die,
Their soules are soone dissolv'd in elements,   1970
But mine must live still to be plagu'd in hell.
Curst be the parents that ingendred me;
No *Faustus*, curse thy selfe, curse *Lucifer*,
That hath depriv'd thee of the joies of heaven.

                    The clocke striketh twelve.

It strikes, it strikes; now body turne to aire,
Or *Lucifer* will beare thee quicke to hell.

1947 No, no?] A1–3 (No no,); No?   1958–9 O God...me,] A1–3 (Oh);
    B1–6   O, if my soule must suffer for my
*1956 So that...but] A1–3; But let my   sinne, B1–6
    soule mount, and B1–6   1966, 1982 Ah] A1–3; Oh B1–6
1957 Ah] A1–3; O B1–6   *1968 Unto] A1–3; Into B1–6

O soule be chang'd into little water drops,
And fall into the Ocean, ne're be found.
Thunder, and enter the devils.

My God, my God, looke not so fierce on me;
Adders and serpents, let me breathe a while:　　　　1980
Ugly hell gape not; come not *Lucifer*,
I'le burne my bookes; ah *Mephostophilis*.

Exeunt with him.
[*Exeunt* Lucifer *and devils above.*]

[Scene xix]

Enter the Schollers.　　　　　　　　　[V.iii]

1. Scholler.　Come Gentlemen, let us go visit *Faustus*,
For such a dreadfull night, was never seene,
Since first the worlds creation did begin.
Such fearefull shrikes, and cries, were never heard,
Pray heaven the Doctor have escapt the danger.
2. Scholler.　O help us heaven, see, here are *Faustus* limbs,
All torne asunder by the hand of death.
3. Scholler.　The devils whom *Faustus* serv'd have torne him thus: 1990
For twixt the houres of twelve and one, me thought
I heard him shreeke and call aloud for helpe:
At which selfe time the house seem'd all on fire,
With dreadfull horror of these damned fiends.
2. Scholler.　Well Gentlemen, tho *Faustus* end be such
As every Christian heart laments to thinke on:
Yet for he was a Scholler, once admired
For wondrous knowledge in our Germane schooles,
We'll give his mangled limbs due buryall:
And all the Students clothed in mourning blacke,　　　2000
Shall waite upon his heavy funerall.

Exeunt.

*1977 little] A1–3; small B1–6　　　　1981.1 *with him*] A1–3; *omit* B1–6
1979 My God, my God,] A1–3; O
　　mercy heaven, B1–6

Enter Chorus. [Chorus 4].

Cut is the branch that might have growne full straight,
And burned is *Apollo's* Lawrell bough,
That sometime grew within this learned man:
Faustus is gone, regard his hellish fall,
Whose fiendfull fortune may exhort the wise
Onely to wonder at unlawfull things,
Whose deepnesse doth intice such forward wits,
To practise more then heavenly power permits.

[*Exit.*]

Terminat hora diem, Terminat Author opus.

FINIS.

APPENDIX

[A-text, Scene iv; Greg 360–436. See this edition, Scene iv, 342.2–388.1]

Enter Wagner and the Clowne.

Wag. Sirra boy, come hither.

Clo. How, boy? swowns boy, I hope you have seene many boyes with such pickadevaunts as I have. Boy quotha?

Wag. Tel me sirra, hast thou any commings in?

Clo. I, and goings out too, you may see else.

Wag. Alas poore slave, see how poverty jesteth in his naked-nesse, the vilaine is bare, and out of service, and so hungry, that I know he would give his soule to the Divel for a shoulder of mutton, though it were blood rawe.

Clo. How, my soule to the Divel for a shoulder of mutton though 10 twere blood rawe? not so good friend, burladie I had neede have it wel roasted, and good sawce to it, if I pay so deere.

Wag. wel, wilt thou serve me, and Ile make thee go like *Qui mihi discipulus?*

Clo. How, in verse?

Wag. No sirra, in beaten silke and staves acre.

Clo. how, how, knaves acre? I, I thought that was al the land his father left him: Doe yee heare, I would be sorie to robbe you of your living.

Wag. Sirra, I say in staves acre.   20

Clo. Oho, oho, staves acre, why then belike, if I were your man, I should be ful of vermine.

Wag. So thou shalt, whether thou beest with me, or no: but sirra, leave your jesting, and binde your selfe presently unto me for seaven yeeres, or Ile turne al the lice about thee into familiars, and they shal teare thee in peeces.

Clo. Doe you heare sir? you may save that labour, they are too

3 quotha] quoth ha A3   18 yee] you D, C, Bn
13 me] us C

229

familiar with me already, swowns they are as bolde with my flesh, as if they had payd for my meate and drinke.

Wag.   wel, do you heare sirra? holde, take these gilders.   30

Clo.   Gridyrons, what be they?

Wag.   Why french crownes.

Clo.   Mas but for the name of french crownes a man were as good have as many english counters, and what should I do with these?

Wag.   Why now sirra thou art at an houres warning when-soever or wheresoever the divell shall fetch thee.

Clo.   No, no, here take your gridirons againe.

Wag.   Truly Ile none of them.

Clo.   Truly but you shall.   40

Wag.   Beare witnesse I gave them him.

Clo.   Beare witnesse I give them you againe.

Wag.   Well, I will cause two divels presently to fetch thee away *Baliol* and *Belcher*.

Clo.   Let your *Balio* and your *Belcher* come here, and Ile knocke them, they were never so knocht since they were divels, say I should kill one of them, what would folkes say? do ye see yonder tall fellow in the round slop, hee has kild the divell, so I should be cald kill divell all the parish over.

Enter two divells, and the clowne runnes up and downe crying.

Wag.   *Balioll* and *Belcher*, spirits away.   *Exeunt.* 50

Clow.   what, are they gone? a vengeance on them, they have vilde long nailes, there was a hee divell and a shee divell, Ile tell you how you shall know them, all hee divels has hornes, and all shee divels has clifts and cloven feete.

Wag.   Well sirra follow me.

Clo.   But do you hear? if I should serve you, would you teach me to raise up *Banios* and *Belcheos*?

29 my] their D, C, Bn
33 for] in C, Bn
41 him] to him C
47 ye] you Bn

48 the divell] y^e *or* y^t divel A2; that divell A3
49.2 *crying*] *the Stage* A2–3

Wag. I will teach thee to turne thy selfe to anything, to a dogge, or a catte, or a mouse, or a ratte, or any thing.

Clo. How? a Christian fellow to a dogge or a catte, a mouse or ⁶⁰ a ratte? no, no sir, if you turne me into any thing, let it be in the likenesse of a little pretie frisking flea, that I may be here and there and every where, O Ile tickle the pretie wenches plackets Ile be amongst them ifaith.

Wag. Wel sirra, come.

Clo. But doe you heare *Wagner*?

Wag. How *Balioll* and *Belcher*.

Clo. O Lord I pray sir, let *Banio* and *Belcher* go sleepe.

Wag. Vilaine, call me Maister *Wagner*, and let thy left eye be diametarily fixt upon my right heele, with *quasi vestigias nostras* ⁷⁰ *insistere*.   *exit*

Clo: God forgive me, he speakes Dutch fustian: well, Ile folow him, Ile serve him, thats flat.   *exit*

[A-text, end of Scene vi; Greg, 878–928. See this edition, Scene ix, 1008.1–1087.2]

Sound a Sonnet, enter the Pope and the Cardinall of Lorraine to the banket, with Friers attending.

Pope My Lord of *Lorraine*, wilt please you draw neare.

Fau. Fall too, and the divel choake you and you spare.

Pope How now, whose that which spake? Friers looke about.

Fri. Heere's no body, if it like your Holynesse.

Pope. My Lord, here is a daintie dish was sent me from the Bishop of *Millaine*.

Fau. I thanke you sir.   *Snatch it.*

Pope. How now, whose that which snatcht the meate from me? will no man looke? My Lord, this dish was sent me from the Cardinall of Florence.   ₁₀

Fau. You say true, Ile hate.

Pope. What againe? my Lord Ile drinke to your grace

---

62 little] *omit* A2–3   0.1 *Sonnet*] *Sinet* A2–3
70 *vestigias, nostras*] *vestigiis nostris* D,   0.1 ²*the*] *omit* A2–3
  C

Fau. Ile pledge your grace.

Lor.   My Lord, it may be some ghost newly crept out of Purgatory come to begge a pardon of your holinesse.

Pope   It may be so, Friers prepare a dirge to lay the fury of this ghost, once again my Lord fall too.

The Pope crosseth himselfe.

Fau.   What, are you crossing of your selfe?
Well use that tricke no more, I would advise you.

Crosse againe.

Fau.   Well, theres the second time, aware the third, I give you 20 faire warning.

Crosse againe, and Faustus hits him a boxe of the eare, and they all runne away.

Fau.   Come on Mephastophilis, what shall we do?

Me.   Nay I know not, we shalbe curst with bell, booke, and candle.

Fau.   How? bell, booke, and candle, candle, booke, and bell,
Forward and backward, to curse *Faustus* to hell.
Anon you shal heare a hogge grunt, a calfe bleate, and an asse braye, because it is S. *Peters* holy day.

Enter all the Friers to sing the Dirge.

Frier.   Come brethren, lets about our businesse with good devotion.   30

Sing this.   *Cursed be hee that stole away his holinesse meate from the table. maledicat dominus.*

Cursed be hee that strooke his holinesse a blowe on the face.
maledicat dominus.

Cursed be he that tooke Frier Sandelo a blow on the pate.
male, &c.

Cursed be he that disturbeth our holy Dirge.
male, &c.

21.1 *of*] *on* A2–3   28.1 ²*the*] *omit* A2–3
23 bell, booke] bel-booke A3   31 *away*] *omit* A2–3
27 and] *omit* C, Bn

Cursed be he that tooke away his holinesse wine.

maledicat dominus.   40

Et omnes sancti Amen.

Beate the Friers, and fling fier-workes among them,
and so Exeunt.

[A-text, Scene vii; Greg Scenes viii–ix, 948–1037. See this edition, Scene vii, 721.2–753.1; Scene x, 1087.3–1137.1. Continuous A-text, Scene vii is placed in A after Chorus 3]

Enter Robin the Ostler with a booke in his hand

Robin   O this is admirable! here I ha stolne one of doctor Faustus conjuring books, and ifaith I meane to search some circles for my owne use: now wil I make al the maidens in our parish dance at my pleasure starke naked before me, and so by that meanes I shal see more then ere I felt, or saw yet.

Enter Rafe calling Robin.

Rafe   *Robin,* prethee come away, theres a Gentleman tarries to have his horse, and he would have his things rubd and made cleane: he keepes such a chafing with my mistris about it, and she has sent me to looke thee out, prethree come away.

Robin   Keepe out, keep out, or else you are blowne up, you 10 are dismembred *Rafe,* keepe out, for I am about a roaring peece of worke.

Rafe   Come, what doest thou with that same booke thou canst not reade?

Robin   Yes, my maister and mistris shal finde that I can reade, he for his forehead, she for her private study, shee's borne to beare with me, or else my Art failes.

Rafe   Why *Robin* what booke is that?

Robin   What booke? why the most intollerable booke for conjuring that ere was invented by any brimstone divel.   20

Rafe   Canst thou conjure with it?

3 my] mine A2–3   13 that] the A2–3
3 wil I] I will A3

Robin   I can do al these things easily with it: first, I can make thee druncke with ipocrase at any taberne in Europe for nothing, thats one of my conjuring workes.

Rafe   Our maister Parson sayes thats nothing.

Robin   True *Rafe*, and more *Rafe*, if thou hast any mind to *Nan Spit* our kitchin maide, then turne her and wind hir to thy owne use, as often as thou wilt, and at midnight.

Rafe   O brave *Robin*, shal I have *Nan Spit*, and to mine owne use? On that condition Ile feede thy divel with horse-bread as long as   30 he lives, of free cost.

Robin   No more sweete *Rafe*, letts goe and make cleane our bootes which lie foule upon our handes, and then to our conjuring in the divels name.   *exeunt.*

[A-text, Scene vii; Greg 985–1037. See this edition, Scene x, 1087.4–1137.1]

> *Enter Robin and Rafe with a silver Goblet.*

Robin   Come *Rafe*, did not I tell thee, we were for ever made by this doctor Faustus booke? *ecce signum*, heeres a simple purchase for horse-keepers, our horses shal eate no hay as long as this lasts.

> *enter the Vintner.*

Rafe   But *Robin*, here comes the vintner.

Robin   Hush, Ile gul him supernaturally: Drawer, I hope al is payd, God be with you, come *Rafe*.

Vintn.   Soft sir, a word with you, I must yet have a goblet payde from you ere you goe.

Robin   I a goblet *Rafe*, I a goblet? I scorne you: and you are but a &c. I a goblet? search me.   10

Vintn.   I meane so sir with your favor.

Robin   How say you now?

Vintner   I must say somewhat to your felow, you sir.

Rafe   Me sir, me sir, search your fill: now sir, you may be ashamed to burden honest men with a matter of truth.

27 her] *omit* A2–3   30 Ile] I'd C, Bn
27 thy] thine A2–3

Vintner Wel, tone of you hath this goblet about you.

Ro. You lie Drawer, tis afore me: sirra you, Ile teach ye to impeach honest men: stand by, Ile scowre you for a goblet, stand aside you had best, I charge you in the name of Belzabub: looke to the goblet *Rafe*. 20

Vintner what meane you sirra?

Robin Ile tel you what I meane. *He reades.*
Sanctobulorum Periphrasticon: nay Ile tickle you Vintner, looke to the goblet *Rafe, Polypragmos Belseborams framanto pacostiphos tostu Mephastophilis, &c.*

> *Enter Mephostophilis: sets squibs at their backes:*
> *they runne about.*

Vintner *O nomine Domine*, what meanst thou *Robin?* thou hast no goblet.

Rafe *Peccatum peccatorum*, heeres thy goblet, good Vintner.

Robin *Misericordia pro nobis*, what shal I doe? good divel 30 forgive me now, and Ile never rob thy Library more.

> *Enter to them Meph.*

Meph. Vanish vilaines, th'one like an Ape, an other like a Beare, the third an Asse, for doing this enterprise.

Monarch of hel, under whose blacke survey
Great Potentates do kneele with awful feare,
Upon whose altars thousand soules do lie,
How am I vexed with these vilaines charmes?
From *Constantinople* am I hither come,
Onely for pleasure of these damned slaves.

Robin How, from *Constantinople?* you have had a great 40 journey, wil you take sixe pence in your purse to pay for your supper, and be gone?

Me. wel villaines, for your presumption, I transforme thee into an Ape, and thee into a Dog, and so be gone. *exit.*

17 ye] you D, C, Bn   32 an other] another A3
23 *Sanctobulorum*] *Sanctabulorum* A2–3   32–3 *Omit* D, Bn, TB
25.1 *Mephostophilis*] *Mephastophilis* A3   37 these] this A2–3
26 *Domine*] *Domini* D, C, Bn

Rob.   How, into an Ape? thats brave, Ile have fine sport with the boyes, Ile get nuts and apples enow.

Rafe   And I must be a Dogge.   *exeunt.*

Robin   Ifaith thy head will never be out of the potage pot.

[A-text, Scene viii; Greg 1038–133. See this edition Scene xi, 1203.2–1324.1] Scene xiv, 1456.2–1504.1]

Enter Emperour, Faustus, and a Knight, with Attendants.

Em.   Maister doctor Faustus, I have heard strange report of thy knowledge in the blacke Arte, how that none in my Empire, nor in the whole world can compare with thee, for the rare effects of Magicke: they say thou hast a familiar spirit, by whome thou canst accomplish what thou list, this therefore is my request, that thou let me see some proofe of thy skil, that mine eies may be witnesses to confirme what mine eares have heard reported, and here I sweare to thee, by the honor of mine Imperial crowne, that what ever thou doest, thou shalt be no wayes prejudiced or indamaged.   10

Knight   Ifaith he lookes much like a conjurer.   *aside.*

Fau.   My gratious Soveraigne, though I must confesse my selfe farre inferior to the report men have published, and nothing answerable to the honor of your Imperial majesty, yet for that love and duety bindes me thereunto, I am content to do whatsoever your majesty shall command me.

Em.   Then doctor Faustus, marke what I shall say, As I was sometime solitary set, within my Closet, sundry thoughts arose, about the honour of mine auncestors, how they had wonne by prowesse such exploits, gote such riches, subdued so many king-   20 domes, as we that do succeede, or they that shal hereafter possesse our throne, shal (I feare me) never attaine to that degree of high

47 be] *omit* A 2–3   15 whatsoever] what A 2–3
 1 report] reports A 2–3   18 sometime] sometimes A 3
 6 mine] my A 2–3   19 wonne] done D² (*qy*)
13 men] of men A 3

renowne and great authoritie, amongest which kings is *Alexander*
the great, chiefe spectacle of the worldes prehemince,
The bright shining of whose glorious actes
Lightens the world with his reflecting beames,
As when I heare but motion made of him,
It grieves my soule I never saw the man:
If therefore thou, by cunning of thine Art,
Canst raise this man from hollow vaults below,   30
where lies intombde this famous Conquerour,
And bring with him his beauteous Paramour,
Both in their right shapes, gesture, and attire
They usde to weare during their time of life,
Thou shalt both satisfie my just desire,
And give me cause to praise thee whilst I live.

Fau: My gratious Lord, I am ready to accomplish your
request, so farre forth as by art and power of my spirit I am
able to performe.

Knight   Ifaith thats just nothing at all.   *aside.*   40

Fau.   But if it like your Grace, it is not in my abilitie to present
before your eyes, the true substantiall bodies of those two deceased
princes which long since are consumed to dust.

Knight   I mary master doctor, now theres a signe of grace in
you, when you will confesse the trueth.   *aside.*

Fau: But such spirites as can lively resemble *Alexander* and his
Paramour, shal appeare before your Grace, in that manner that
they best liv'd in, in their most florishing estate, which I doubt not
shal sufficiently content your Imperiall majesty.

Em   Go to maister Doctor, let me see them presently.   50

Kn.   Do you heare maister Doctor? you bring *Alexander* and
his paramour before the emperor?

Fau.   How then sir?

Kn.   Ifaith thats as true as *Diana* turned me to a stag.

Fau: No sir, but when *Acteon* died, he left the hornes for you:
Mephastophilis be gone.   *exit Meph.*

Kn.   Nay, and you go to conjuring, Ile be gone.   *exit Kn:*

26 *Omit* A2–3   32 *Omit* A2–3
27 motion] mention M (*qy*) 48 best] both D, C, Bn

Fau. Ile meete with you anone for interrupting me so: heere
they are my gratious Lord.

Enter Meph: with Alexander and his paramour.

emp. Maister Doctor, I heard this Lady while she liv'd had 60
a wart or moale in her necke, how shal I know whether it be so
or no?

Fau: Your highnes may boldly go and see.   *exit Alex:*

emp: Sure these are no spirites, but the true substantiall bodies
of those two deceased princes.

Fau: wilt please your highnes now to send for the knight that
was so pleasent with me here of late?

emp: One of you call him foorth.

Enter the Knight with a paire of hornes on his head.

emp. How now sir knight? why I had thought thou hadst
beene a batcheler, but now I see thou hast a wife, that not only gives 70
thee hornes, but makes thee weare them, feele on thy head.

Kn: Thou damned wretch, and execrable dogge,
Bred in the concave of some monstrous rocke:
How darst thou thus abuse a Gentleman?
Vilaine I say, undo what thou hast done.

Fau: O not so fast sir, theres no haste but good, are you remem-
bred how you crossed me in my conference with the emperour?
I thinke I have met with you for it.

emp: Good Maister Doctor, at my intreaty release him, he hath
done penance sufficient.   80

Fau: My Gratious Lord, not so much for the injury hee offerd
me heere in your presence, as to delight you with some mirth, hath
Faustus worthily requited this injurious knight, which being all
I desire, I am content to release him of his hornes: and sir knight,
hereafter speake well of Scholers: *Mephastophilis*, transforme him
strait. Now my good Lord having done by duety, I humbly take
my leave.

61 wart or moale] moale or wart A 2–3   67 here] *omit* A 2–3
65 those] these A 2–3   76 haste‸] ~ ; D, C, Bn

emp: Farewel maister Doctor, yet ere you goe, expect from me a bounteous reward.   *exit Emperour.*

[A-text, Scene viii, continued; Greg 1134–226. See this edition, Scene xiv, 1456.2–1504.1]

Fau: Now Mephastophilis, the restlesse course that time 90 doth runne with calme and silent foote,
Shortning my dayes and thred of vitall life,
Calls for the payment of my latest yeares,
Therefore sweet Mephastophilis, let us make haste to *Wertenberge.*
Me: what, wil you goe on horse backe, or on foote?
Fau: Nay, til I am past this faire and pleasant greene, ile walke on foote.

enter a Horse-courser

Hors: I have beene al this day seeking one maister Fustian: masse see where he is, God save you maister doctor.
Fau: What horse-courser, you are wel met.   100
Hors: Do you heare sir? I have brought you forty dollers for your horse.
Fau: I cannot sel him so: if thou likst him for fifty, take him.
Hors: Alas sir, I have no more, I pray you speake for me.
Me: I pray you let him have him, he is an honest felow, and he has a great charge, neither wife nor childe.
Fau: Wel, come give me your money, my boy wil deliver him to you: but I must tel you one thing before you have him, ride him not into the water at any hand.
Hors: why sir, wil he not drinke of all waters?   110
Fau: O yes, he wil drinke of al waters, but ride him not into the water, ride him over hedge or ditch, or where thou wilt, but not into the water.
Hors: Wel sir, Now am I made man for ever, Ile not leave my horse for fortie: if he had but the qualitie of hey ding, ding, hey, ding, ding, Ide make a brave living on him; hee has a buttocke so

96 I am] I'm D, C, Bn   115 fortie] twice forty D (*qy*), C, Bn
114 made] a made A 2–3   116 so] as D, C, Bn

slicke as an Ele; wel god buy sir, your boy wil deliver him me: but
hark ye sir, if my horse be sick, or ill at ease, if I bring his water to
you, youle tel me what is?

Exit Horsecourser.

Fau.   Away you villaine: what, doost thinke I am a horse- 120
doctor? what art thou Faustus but a man condemnd to die?
Thy fatall time doth drawe to finall ende,
Dispaire doth drive distrust unto my thoughts,
Confound these passions with a quiet sleepe:
Tush, Christ did call the thiefe upon the Crosse,
Then rest thee Faustus quiet in conceit. *Sleepe in his chaire.*

Enter Horsecourser all wet, crying.

Hors.   Alas, alas, Doctor Fustian quoth a, mas Doctor *Lopus*
was never such a Doctor, has given me a purgation, has purg'd
me of fortie Dollers, I shall never see them more: but yet like
an asse as I was, I would not be ruled by him, for he bade me 130
I should ride him into no water; now, I thinking my horse had had
some rare qualitie that he would not have had me knowne of, I like
a ventrous youth, rid him into the deepe pond at the townes ende,
I was no sooner in the middle of the pond, but my horse vanisht
away, and I sat upon a bottle of hey, never so neare drowning in my
life: but Ile seeke out my Doctor, and have my fortie dollers againe,
or Ile make it the dearest horse: O yonder is his snipper snapper,
do you heare? you, hey, passe, where's your maister?

Me.   why sir, what would you? you cannot speake with him.

Hors. But I wil speake with him.   140

Me.   Why hee's fast asleepe, come some other time.

Hors.   Ile speake with him now, or Ile breake his glasse-
windowes about his eares.

Me.   I tell thee he has not slept this eight nights.

Hors.   And he have not slept this eight weekes Ile speake
with him.

117 buy] b'wi'ye D, C, Bn
118 ye] you A2–3
119 is] it is D, C, Bn
120 horse-|doctor] ~ - | ~ A1–3
123 unto] into D, C

132 knowne] know D, C
135 my] al my A2–3
142 glasse-|windowes] ~ - | ~ A1–3
144, 145 this] these A2

Me. See where he is fast asleepe.

Hors. I, this is he, God save ye maister doctor, maister doctor, maister doctor Fustian, fortie dollers, fortie dollers for a bottle of hey.   150

Me. Why, thou seest he heares thee not.

Hors. So, ho, ho: so, ho, ho.   *Hallow in his eare.*
No, will you not wake? Ile make you wake ere I goe.
                            Pull him by the legge, and pull it away.
Alas, I am undone, what shall I do:

Fau. O my legge, my legge, helpe *Mephastophilis*, call the Officers, my legge, my legge.

Me. Come villaine to the Constable.

Hors. O Lord sir, let me goe, and Ile give you fortie dollers more.

Me. Where be they?   160

Hors. I have none about me, come to my Oastrie, and Ile give them you.

Me. Be gone quickly.   *Horsecourser runnes away.*

Fau. What is he gone? farwel he, Faustus has his legge againe, and the Horsecourser I take it, a bottle of hey for his labour; wel, this tricke shal cost him fortie dollers more.

Enter Wagner.

How now *Wagner*, what's the newes with thee?

Wag. Sir, the Duke of *Vanholt* doth earnestly entreate your company.

Fau. The Duke of *Vanholt*! an honourable gentleman, to whom   170
I must be no niggard of my cunning, come *Mephastophilis*, let's away to him.   *exeunt.*

148 ye] you D, C, Bn   152 *eare*] *eares* A3

[A-text, Scene ix; Greg, 1227–65. See this edition, Scene xvi, 1557.2–1587, 1669–1673.1]

Enter to them the Duke, and the Dutches,
the Duke speakes.

Du: Beleeve me maister Doctor, this merriment hath much pleased me.

Fau: My gratious Lord, I am glad it contents you so wel: but it may be Madame, you take no delight in this, I have heard that great bellied women do long for some dainties or other, what is it Madame? tell me, and you shal have it.

Dutch. Thankes, good maister doctor.
And for I see your curteous intent to pleasure me, I wil not hide from you the thing my heart desires, and were it nowe summer, as it is January, and the dead time of the winter, I would desire no better 10 meate then a dish of ripe grapes.

Fau: Alas Madame, thats nothing, *Mephastophilis,* be gone: *exit Meph.*   were it a greater thing then this, so it would content you, you should have it

enter Mephasto:
with the grapes.

here they be madam, wilt please you taste on them.

Du: Beleeve me master Doctor, this makes me wonder above the rest, that being in the dead time of winter, and in the month of January, how you shuld come by these grapes.

Fau: If it like your grace, the yeere is divided into twoo circles over the whole worlde, that when it is heere winter with us, in the 20 contrary circle it is summer with them, as in *India, Saba,* and farther countries in the East, and by means of a swift spirit that I have, I had them brought hither, as ye see, how do you like them Madame, be they good?

Dut: Beleeve me Maister doctor, they be the best grapes that ere I tasted in my life before.

Fau: I am glad they content you so Madam.

11 ripe] *omit* A2–3

242

Du: Come Madame, let us in, where you must wel reward
this learned man for the great kindnes he hath shewd to you.

Dut: And so I wil my Lord, and whilst I live,   30
Rest beholding for this curtesie.

Fau: I humbly thanke your Grace.

Du: Come, maister Doctor follow us, and receive your
reward.

                                                    exeunt.

[A-text, Scene x, Greg 1266–74. See this edition, Scene xvii,
1673.2–1680]   *enter Wagner solus.*

Wag. I thinke my maister meanes to die shortly,
For he hath given to me al his goodes,
And yet me thinkes, if that death were neere,
He would not banquet, and carowse, and swill
Amongst the Students, as even now he doth,   5
who are at supper with such belly-cheere,
As *Wagner* nere beheld in all his life.
   See where they come: belike the feast is ended.

[A-text, Scene x, later continuation; Greg 1302–13. See this edition,
Scene xvii, 1706.1–1723]

                         Enter an old man.

Old. Ah Doctor Faustus, that I might prevaile,   34
To guide thy steps unto the way of life,
By which sweete path thou maist attaine the gole
That shall conduct thee to celestial rest.
Breake heart, drop bloud, and mingle it with teares,
Teares falling from repentant heavinesse
Of thy most vilde and loathsome filthinesse,   40
The stench whereof corrupts the inward soule
With such flagitious crimes of hainous sinnes,
As no commiseration may expel,
But mercie Faustus of thy Saviour sweete,
Whose bloud alone must wash away thy guilt.

1 means...shortly] shortly means to   3 neere] so near C, Bn
  die C, Bn   42 sinnes] sin D, C

18 whose...dispute] Critics usually take it that the B1 editor thought the A-text corrupt or obscure here, but finding no acceptable alternative in his manuscript he pieced out the line to suit himself. That A is closer to the original than B may be suggested by the *Historie*, 'none for his time was able to argue with him in Divinity', which like A pinpoints Faustus' excelling in theological disputes. Yet A's syntax seems corrupt. The simplest emendation is to add the contraction for 'is' to 'delight'.

52 men] The A3 variant 'men' for A1–2 'man', A3 being followed by B1, is clearly unauthoritative, and it is anyone's guess whether B1's manuscript read 'men' or whether the inscriber was merely following A3. A3's reason for alteration is clear enough in that it establishes the plural with 'them' of line 53. One may be tempted to suggest that this only seeming anomaly in A1 was present in the original, and that in the jump from 'man' as *mankind* to its individual members 'them' would be easy enough by Elizabethan standards. Indeed, this would be the opinion of the present editor were it not for the stronger possibility that 'man' in line 51 contaminated line 52 in the actor's memory. Since 'man' in line 51 is manifestly right, 'men' in line 52 is almost required in order to avoid a really inapposite shift.

86 Nor...cloudes:] The omission of this A1 line by B1 makes one suspicious since the only doubtful sense that could justify B's smoothing out the text would be the question of the referent for 'this'. It is just possible that the B editor took 'this' as applying narrowly to raising the winds or rending the clouds as a simple concrete action with no other significance and quite naturally objected that such 'dominion' did not stretch as far as does the mind of man. He might even have thought it a blasphemous doctrine. Line 86 is not impossible as an A-text vulgarized expansion absent in the manuscript; but the possibility of B's misunderstanding and consequent editorial tinkering is strong enough to lead an editor, with some misgivings, to import the A reading. Support may perhaps be given by lines 545–6 'The framing of this circle on the ground | Brings Thunder, Whirle-winds, Storme and Lightning', which are also in a Marlowe passage. It may be too ingenious to suggest that the 'this' may refer directly to raising the winds and rending the clouds quite legitimately if in turn the line is a partial gloss on 83–4, 'All things that move betweene the quiet Poles | Shall be at my command', a reference back that the B-inscriber did not recognize. To establish dominion over the forces of Nature certainly stretches the mind of man farther than imperial sway; and wind and clouds may be taken as representative of the most difficult to control of the 'things that move betweene the quiet Poles'.

90 tire] Editors unquestioningly accept this B reading for A1 'trie', but 'try' appears in Marlowe lines at 192, 234, and 243 in circumstances that suggest that 'trie' (or 'try') would by no means be impossible here. Unfortunately the spelling is of no assistance, for the later occurrences of 'try' come in passages set by Compositor *X* whereas this is Compositor *Y*, who sometimes sets *-ie* and sometimes *-y* endings. However, transposition of letters is not a very viable hypothesis, and it seems clear

that *Y* felt the word was 'tire'. It may be some small comfort that *Y* is a little less likely than *X* to substitute words. It is also interesting, however, that in Elegy I.v.24 correct O 1–2 'tyrde' appears in O 3 as the error 'tride'. Still, some doubt must rest with the B reading here.

178 bushy] Greg followed by Jump prefers A 1 'lustie', Greg suggesting that 'lustie' meaning *pleasant* was ceasing to be a common usage and thus called forth the A 2 compositor's 'little' which in turn (through A 3) produced the B editor's conventional 'bushy'. Greg was aware that the *Historie* 'thicke Wood' encouraged 'bushy' but he insisted that Faustus had no especial reason to choose a grove for conjuring and that Valdes' assent is not only clumsy but silly. In fact, without referring to druidical ceremonies among trees, one may take it that anyone practising forbidden magic had better conceal himself, as fortified by Valdes' 'solitary Grove'. Marlowe liked adjectives in *-y*, and *bushy woods* is quoted in *O.E.D.* from 1575. The B 1 editor must have referred to manuscript to alter A 3's 'little'; one has no reason not to respect his reading.

181 *Abanus*] Greg identifies this writer as Pietro d'Abano. The AB corruption 'Albanus' may be original or an A-text memorial error transferred to B. This confusion is more likely than one with Albertus Magnus.

230 looke] In the *A Shrew* version of these lines the reading is 'lookes' in a passage that correctly quotes the unusual 'unto' of line 231. The sense is indifferent, and the *A Shrew* authority is insufficient to justify emendation despite the ever-present possibility that B 1 merely repeated the singular from A.

245 *Terreni*] This addition by Greg, as also that of '*Lucifer*' in the same line, may well repair accidental omissions in B 1 under the influence of A 3, even though the B 1 stage-directions 'Thunder' and 'Dragon', confused as text, demonstrate reference to manuscript.

247.1 Dragon.] This object appears, unseen by Faustus, and presumably has a suitable opportunity to exhibit itself while Faustus is awaiting an answer to his appeal. One would suppose that the Dragon made its exit when he resumes '*Quid tu moraris*'. If the exit were delayed until the end of the invocation, an exit might detract from the attention given the entrance of the devil at line 250.1.

260–2 Now...*imagine.*] Since no reason can be suggested for B 1's omission of these A 1 lines except that they were not present in the manuscript, they can be admitted – as is customary – only with reservations. They do seem to be repetitious and rather suspect in their tone, although Marlowe could have intended the jejune hubris they express to contrast with the comparative delicacy of lines 255–9. Probably the Latin is the best reason to regard them as genuine, this being unlikely as an actor's expansion.

345 such pickadevaunts] The *A Shrew* reference 'you have many boies with such Pickadevantes' establishes the correctness of the A reading and the sophistication of the B editor.

349 that he] The repetition of 'I know' in the B 1 text seems to be an error. Greg omits the first 'I know' as in A 1, but this memorial version is scarcely to be trusted in a parallel text and the present emendation more naturally applies 'I know' to the

two statements not just to the one. One can only guess that an error of anticipation in the B inscription is a trifle less likely than an echo, although in fact no choice in such a situation can really hold. More to the point, in case the A-text here exerted any influence on the B inscriber, he could have inserted the first 'I know' from his manuscript and taken over the second from A 3.

371 againe] The accidental omission of this word in the B1 inscription is suggested by its occurrence in *A Shrew*, 'Here here take your two shillings again', which, as Boas noted, comes shortly after the *pickadevants* quotation of line 345.

390 not now] B1 seems to have copied A 3 without reference to manuscript in reading 'Canst thou not be sav'd?' where the reporter's faulty recollection of a query has shaped his syntax. Something closer to an exclamation seems to be required. Editors have sometimes suppressed the query; Greg runs-on 'canst not be sav'd' as part of line 390. The present editor's emendation merely smooths the line and makes no pretense at recovering original authority.

395 eares] It is a small point, but the A1 plural here seems to be more correct than the B1 singular in view of the Marlovian line 571 'But feareful ecchoes thunder in mine eares.' Line 1549 'kept a hallowing and whooping in his eares' has no application (except for the idiom) since it is not Marlowe's.

408 men] Greg's argument for A1 'men' instead of B1 'them' is largely based on his belief in B2 authority, which picks 'men' up from A1. The present editor having no faith in B2's return to A1 except as casual editing for the second edition, makes the emendation with some reservations on the shaky hypothesis of an error of anticipation either by the B inscriber or by Compositor X. One cannot be sure, however, that a flower of rhetoric has not been crushed by emendation.

414 god] In view of the B1 inscriber's usual delicacy in finding paraphrases for 'God', the preference of Boas, Greg, and Jump for B1 'power' instead of A1–3 'God' (properly 'god') on the grounds that 'god' would impute polytheism to Faustus seems odd. One may suppose that the inscriber mistook 'god' (if that were the manuscript form) or else 'God' in A 3 and felt he had to remove it. It should be remarked that Faustus freely mixes classical and Christian references to deity.

443 proper] Some temptation exists to omit this extra-metrical word, as did early editors, as a piece of A-text expansion taken over by B1. However, one can point to line 656 'appeare to thee in their owne proper shapes' (if this is Marlowe's), and to the five occurrences of 'proper' in the two parts of *Tamburlaine*. But the idiom is a common one, and the early editors may have been right.

456 ah] This is the first of the various times that the B-text reads 'O' where the A-text has 'ah'. We know from *Edward II* that Marlowe frequently wrote 'ah', and we have this form in the manuscript fragment of *The Massacre at Paris* to confirm it. The present editor has restored throughout, with only one or two exceptions, the 'ah' readings of A1 on the theory that the B inscriber usually changed them except for one slip in line 1824 where Compositor Y set 'ah'. The one contrary piece of evidence would be the unique spelling 'oh', not the usual 'O', in line 1940 where the inscriber is rewriting a line.

486–7 *by him commanded*] This is the first of the six substantive disagreements between A and B in the bond; lines 492 and 498 join the present in being closer in A1 than in B1 to the *Historie*. The fidelity of the A-text would be most unusual if the bond were reported throughout. Hence one might speculate that the person who put together the reported parts turned to the *Historie* here, where the bond is given almost in full. The B variants may be in part compositorial or the editorial work of the B inscriber but there is no necessity to assume so any more than that they represent manuscript readings. (Fidelity to the *Historie* in A, especially in such a passage, is not necessarily a valid test of non-authority in B if the A-text inscriber returned to the *Historie* for assistance.) Greg's hypothesis that the bond was written on a separate piece of paper apart from the manuscript so that it was lost, thereby necessitating B's reliance exclusively on A except for its unauthoritative variants, is unnecessarily elaborate and speculative to explain what could be a relatively simple situation.

524 Tush] The present editor takes it that A1 'Tush' fell here under the B1 inscriber's censorship of oaths as well as divine references and thus that 'No' is an unauthoritative substitution. One may compare the omission of A1 'Tush' in line 606 but especially the inept substitution of 'But' in line 713 for A1 'Tut', mild enough but just possibly reading 'Tush' in the manuscript despite the similarity between A and B forms. 'Tush' appears in *Edward II*.

543 Hold] The B-text variation in this line seems due to the revision consequent upon the cut of 551.0.1–551.0.13 and the transfer of material from lines 717–19 to round off the scene. Under these consequences the odds favour the authority of the A-text.

573 Gunnes, poyson] Corruption may have entered the B-text here, just possibly from the B inscriber's censorship. The case is moot, however, for Greg's objection that an excessive awkwardness in the thought-sequence results in B is not necessarily true if the lines are read aright. That is, 'Scarce can I name salvation, faith, or heaven' may be taken as illustrating the hardening of Faustus' heart. Nothing more need follow. His inability to name heavenly things could sufficiently account for his resulting despair without the need for thunder in his ears and a voice prophesying damnation. The A lines, then, could be an actor's expansion, but this explanation is perhaps not a wholly satisfying one. (What actually stood in the manuscript may be a matter of legitimate doubt, for if lines are actually wanting in B the A-text may not precisely reproduce them.) Most editors accept the A-text without change, and that is perhaps the safest course although there is much to be said for Greg's ingenious retention of B's line 573 beginning 'Swords, poyson, halters' by emending the A-text line 572 to read 'gunnes and knives' instead of 'swords and knives'. The A-text's hexameter in line 573 is not necessarily wrong but it need not be scanned so since a pentameter can be managed by reading 'and invenom'd steele' as an anapest followed by an iamb, an expedient also required by the line in the present text. The rationale behind the editor's version is a wish to preserve the order of the B-text items while substituting 'Gunnes' for B's 'Swords' (supposed to have been the inscriber's substitution when he dropped line 572). This has the added virtue of placing the two adjacent stresses initially (as Marlowe often preferred) instead of internally. This passage may just possibly have some relationship to the *Faerie Queene*'s episode of Despair, especially I.x.50, but guns are not listed there.

612 and] In his original note to this line on p. 398 Greg remarked that '&' being in italic (*i.e.*, roman in a black-letter text) should stand for *et*. But he corrected himself in the edition's errata slip: 'But if & is interpreted as *et* it seems to imply that the fiery and crystalline spheres are one, whereas as Mephostophilis' reply shows, they are in fact distinct. This would be clearer if & were interpreted as *and*.'

649–51 Never...downe.] It is natural to assume that these lines disappeared in B1 because of censorship. If, instead, one thought them an A-text expansion not in the B manuscript, a difficulty would arise in that lines 650–1 – the most natural expansion – are not the only ones wanting but also line 649 with its mention of God. To hypothesize that lines 650–1 were not present in the manuscript but that 649 was, though censored, is far too elaborate.

694 bare] A1 'bare' here for B1 'small' removes the feeble anticipation of 'small' from line 695. If Marlowe wrote the parade of the Sins originally, one might cite as pertinent 'one bare houre' in line 1927.

706 an other word.] Sloth's B-text 'I'le not speak a word more for a kings ransome' seems in great part to be authenticated as from the original play by A1's 'Ile not speak an other word for a Kings raunsome.' If so, the previous statement of Pride, lines 669–70, who in the A-text declines to 'speake an other worde, except the ground were perfumde and covered with cloth of arras' could well be a Rowley–Birde revision in the B-text where she will 'not speake a word more for a Kings ransome, unlesse the ground' *etc.* One of the two asseverations should be cut from a critical edition of the B-text since only half of the exchange was made, and that imperfectly. In many respects it would seem most natural to undo the conjectural revision in Pride's speech and to restore the original text from A1. But since in other places there is little chance of identifying and restoring the original from the 1602 revision, it would be inconsistent to interfere here. (The editorial policy about the difficulties of editing the revised B-text is discussed in the Textual Introduction.) However, if as in this text an editor makes the cut that Rowley–Birde inadvertently omitted in Sloth's ending, it is almost incumbent on him to complete the exchange and to transfer Pride's original 'an other word' in A1 (replaced by Sloth's 'a word more') ahead to Sloth, but without the repetition for a kings ransome'. That for Sloth A1 reads 'Ile not speake an other word' is helpful but not the reason for the emendation, since A1 here merely repeats the same phrase ('an other word') that it had already used for Pride, and this does not, seemingly, agree with what the manuscript had for Sloth.

719.0.1 This...life.] Present both in A and B, this appears to be an original line that should have been excised consequent upon the revision of 551.0.1–551.0.13, presumably by Rowley–Birde. For a similar case see the textual note above to line 706.

787 Naples∧] Greg followed by Jump retains the AB1 comma after '*Naples*' and remarks (p. 347) that 'Marlowe seems to identify *Campania* appositionally with *Naples*, and this is indeed suggested by the wording of *EFB*'. On the contrary, the *Historie* source implies that Campania is a city within the larger area of Naples: 'but went to *Campania* in the Kingdome of *Neapolis*, in which he saw...great and high houses of stone'. One may speculate that the comma got into the B-text when the inscriber, uncertain of the reference, followed the A-text comma, itself a simple

appositional error. If Marlowe, as likely, was following the *Historie* here, he intended *Naples* to be in the possessive case. The present text, then, follows the shrewd interpretation of the editor of the previously uncollated Chappell edition and by removing the comma restores what should have been the original genitive.

788   The buildings... | Whose streetes]   The B-text seems to have followed the A1 corruption here so that the reading of the manuscript cannot be recovered with any confidence. A halting sense would be achieved if we were to read an elided 'are' after 'buildings', but the transition would still be abrupt. (Chappell's editor tried for this by emending to 'building's'.) Followed by Jump, Greg most ingeniously rewrote to 'With buildings... | Whose streets...', which implies a transposition error as the mainspring of the A1 corruption. It seems to the present editor that a simple transposition, not a modified one, has perhaps occurred, whether by the reporter or by Compositor *C*. The source of the error could well be a false parallel structure with lines 785–6, so that 'Whose' following the place, the river Rhine, got itself transferred in 788 also to follow the place Campania. The true parallel with the structure of 788–9 is actually 794–7 in which the place is given, the detail of the temple, and then 'Whose'. In 788–9 if the editor's emendation is right, 'The buildings...eye,' is a parenthesis that intervenes between the referent Campania and the 'Whose'. The omission of line 790 in B1 seems to be attributable, as Greg remarks, to the B1 editor's confusion over the A version of 'form equivolent'. In the present text A1 'Quarters' has been emended to 'Quarter' on the analogy of B1's usual practice in dealing with A's lax Elizabethan grammar as at 812 and 816.

795   midst]   This A1 reading may be corrupt, but B1 'one' is worse. Once the B1 inscriber read 'East' for 'rest' in line 794 he could make nothing of 'in the midst' and seems to have substituted the neutral but weak 'one' as his best course. It is true, of course, that the addition of '*Padua*, and the rest' makes precise reference difficult to St Marks, as being in the city of Venice. If one wanted to be ingenious one could argue that since Padua and the rest was part of the Venetian Republic (if Marlowe knew that), Venice the city with its St Marks might be taken as 'in the midst' of the Republic of Venice. Some such contortion would be required to justify A1 as authoritative, unless Marlowe actually did not know for certain where St Marks was and so was writing with deliberate vagueness. Whatever the rights of the case, it is clear that *rest–midst* and *East–one* must be treated as units and accepted or rejected as such.

952   reverend]   Some word is missing here. Dyce queried 'holy' on the example of line 882, which is certainly acceptable. One could also choose 'sacred' from line 885, or, with this editor, 'reverend' from line 1014. In all probability the original reading would have been one of these three.

1373   heart]   Dilke's emendation of B1 'heart' to 'art' is tempting and has been followed by most editors, including Greg, though rejected by Tucker Brooke, Jump, and Ribner. The many references to Faustus' art as in lines 1208, 1222, 1246, 1295 in this area of Rowley–Birde addition and revision certainly encourage such an emendation. With some diffidence the editor retains the B1 reading since it can be defended without unduly straining the sense. The other references to 'art' are conventional in comparison, for here the *art* would be specifically attributed to the head. That the head as the residence of reason could be said to possess the *art* to retaliate on Benvolio is possible enough although the language elsewhere does not encourage the idiom. (The closest parallel comes in Marlowe's lines 131–2, 'for my head | But ruminates on Negromantique skill'.) On the other hand, the heart as the source of emotion and thus the instigator of all action has already been referred to in line 1351 – 'But yet my heart's more ponderous than my head' – and it is therefore the apt organ to conceive resentment and thus to 'conspire' the revenge on Benvolio. (An illustration of the idea may come from the Marlovian line 1751, 'Do it *Faustus*, with unfained heart'.) To associate the heart and the action generated by it is no more than to say that the head's reason approved of the heart's impulse and possibly contrived the exact means to put the heart's impulse into action. The distinction between head and heart (or body) in line 1375 implies that both have been punished for their action as equally guilty. It would seem that 'art' strains the idiom more than 'heart' and could well be a sophistication. As for the appropriateness of 'conspir'd' uniting head and heart in an action, see *O.E.D.* 5. *trans*: 'To unite in producing, to concur to'.

1542 rare] It seems probable that in the process of the Rowley–Birde writing of new Scene xv by transferring some of the material from the original version of Scene xiv, this 'rare', preserved now only in the A-text, got inadvertently dropped.

1690 And...not] As Greg points out (p. 70), the omission in A 2–3 of 'And' from the A 1 line may well have forced the B-text editor to alter the construction, including the placement of the colon after 'well' in line 1691 for A's comma, in order to buttress his new version.

1730 hover] Most modern editors may be right in believing that the B 1 reading 'hover' (for A 1 'hovers') clashes with AB 1 'Offers' in 1732 and is a compositional (or editorial) instinctive alteration. But when in 1840 one sees B 1 'though my heart pant and quiver' for A 1 'pants...quivers' one cannot be sure which is the corrupting agent. B 1 often appears to normalize such A 1 usage, but whether by editorial or compositorial preference or because the B 1 manuscript so read is not to be determined. It does appear that A 1 uses the singular forms more consistently than is Marlowe's usual practice.

1786 azur'd] The question here is between A 1 'azurde' and B 1 'azure'. No story of classical mythology is referred to but instead the mirroring of the sun in the blue waters of the fountain. Neptune may be conceived of as 'saphir visag'd' and his court under the waves as 'the stately azure Pallace' (*Hero and Leander*, II.155, 165), but nothing in mythology suggests that fresh-water nymphs were solid blue. Hence the waters (arms) are coloured blue only by the temporary reflection of the sky and the image should in exact terms be 'azur'd'. This may be taking too literal a view of the metaphor, of course, but, even so, 'azur'd' was used for 'azure', as Greg points out (p. 389) in such quotations as 'twixt the greene Sea and the azur'd vault' in *The Tempest*, V.i.43 (TLN 1994). He also cites 'an azured stone' from 1604 in *O.E.D.*, and lists Ward's citation from Peele's *Edward I*, line 1127, 'Azured silke'. These last may or may not refer to objects made azure by veining, but if they do they are not pertinent as signifying that Arethusa had blue-veined arms, as has been suggested, for the waters made blue by the sky are central to Marlowe's image. That B 2 printed 'azur'd' from A 1 has nothing to do with its authority, of course; but there would seem to be every reason to take it that B 1 made a simple error here, either compositorial or scribal.

1943–4 where God...Browes] One might worry a bit about accepting the A1 expanded version of the B1 condensed and not ineffective 'a threatning Arme, an angry Brow' were it not clear that, as at line 1946, the B inscriber was censoring the name of God. It is a good illustration of his operations and his ability to contrive a new metrically exact line by rewriting.

1956 So that...but] This emendation from A1 is the most doubtful of all in the soliloquy, chiefly because the reason is obscure why the B inscriber would wish to change A1 unless the repetition of 'that' troubled him, or else the true meaning of 'So that' as Greg suggests (p. 399). That 'mount' as in B1 is used in Chorus 2, line 757, means very little in establishing B1's authority. The editor is frank to say that he is here playing the odds. Since retention of the B1 reading would make this the sole major variant in the soliloquy where the A1 report has not been preferred, we may as well bet on A1 once more and be consistent in treating its text even though the causes for B1 variance are more obscure here than elsewhere. However, see the relatively easy rejection of A1 at 1977 and the more doubtful acceptance at 1968.

1968 Unto] B1 here reads 'Into' and the pull of this parallelism with AB1 'chang'd into' in line 1977 is a strong one in favour of rejecting the A1 variant 'Unto' and adhering to B1. Yet it just may be that the last page or two of Marlowe's early papers were missing and that all of the B1 variants in the soliloquy are automatically suspect, even though most of them can be rationalized as the normal operations of the inscriber whether or not he had the manuscript. If the manuscript were indeed missing as Greg would have it, one would be forced most interestingly into rejecting Scene xix as Marlowe's (for such a gap would be too convenient, to be followed by more of his papers) or even perhaps as his collaborator's, and would almost be impelled to accept it, as the editor is inclined to believe, as Rowley and Birde's. However, as between the virtues of 'Into' or 'Unto' and the possibility that in such a neutral word the reporting actor could have slipped one may as well toss a coin, although 'unto' in line 231 is a useful parallel and could be decisive. Greg's argument that 'into' in line 1977 was picked up by anticipation of 'into' in line 1978 and should be 'to' is special pleading that by attacking the credibility of the A-text reporter gets around the parallel between lines 1968 and 1977. Hence he uses it to support his faith in 'Unto' as the more unusual expression and thereby the less likely to be a reportorial error. The pyramiding of speculation in this manner, however, can scarcely influence editorial decision. Moreover, to read 'to hell' in 1976 and 'to little water drops' in 1977 is not well advised.

1977 little] The argument here for restoring A1 'little' for B1 'small' is that the A1 metrics troubled the B inscriber. Given other possible B inscriber interference in this soliloquy, the point seems to be well taken. It may be that *Dido*, IV.iv.63 'As in the Sea are little water drops' could support the A1 reading. One notes the borrowing of line 1770 from *Dido* IV.iv.123, 'And heele make me immortall with a kisse'. On the other hand, *1 Tamburlaine*, III.i.11, has 'Small drops of water'.

[NOTE: Because of the complex textual transmission of this play, a few changes are made in this section of the apparatus. Although the copy-text is B1 (1616), the readings of A1 (1604), A2 (1609), and A3 (1611) are provided for emendations as well as the readings of the later quartos in the line of the B-text: B1 in some part derives from A3 and is thus affected by the readings of the A-text. However, the reading to the left of the bracket, which is that of the present edited text, is given in its B1 forms on the various occasions when emendation is not total. That is, in notation of lineation variants the punctuation is that of B1 even though in the record, say, of AB1–6 the A-text for convenience appears before the B-text. Similarly, in other AB combinations, as in the emendation at line 568, the B form is given, not the exact form of A (which in the case of 568 would have read '*Evil*', not '*Evill*' with B1–2. The condensed notation AB means that A1–3 are in agreement with B.]

4 over-turn'd,] A1–3; ~ ᴧ B1; ~ : B2–6

6 verse;] ~ ᴧ B1; ~ : AB2–6

26 him,] A3, B2; ~ ; B1; ~ ᴧ A1–2

27 blisse;] ~ , AB1–6

35 *logices*] B4 (*Logices*); *logicis* A1–3; *Logicis* B1–3

44 *bonum*ᴧ] AB2; ~ , B1

56 *Si...rei, &c.*] AB1–6 *line: duobus,* | *Alter*

56 *legatur*] *legatus* AB1–6

57 Legacies:] A1–3 (legacies); Legacies, B1–6

58 *Exhereditare*] *Ex hæreditari* A1; *Exhereditari* A2–3, B1–6

59 *Institute*] institute AB1–6

63 and] AB2; aad B1

66 *peccati*ᴧ] AB2; ~ , B1

66 ha] AB2; *ha* B1

68 *peccasse*ᴧ] AB2; ~ , B1

69–71 AB1–6 *line:* If...sinne | We... us. | Why...sinne, | And...die,

77–8 heavenly....Characters,] ~ ᴧ... ~ : A1–3; ~ ,...~ . B1; ~ ,... ~ : B2–6

126.1 Enter...Cornelius.] A1–3 *place as* 127.1; B1–6 ±*place to right of* 126–7

127 sweete *Valdes*,] A1; ~ ~ ᴧ A2–3, B1–6

128 last,] AB2; ~ . B1

133–4 obscure,...wits:] ~ ,...~ , A1–3; ~ :...~ , B1–6

140 Germane] A1–3 (Germaine); *Germane* B1–6

147 Shall] AB2–6; shall B1

147–8 us:...Lords,] ~ ,...~ , A1–3; ~ ,...~ : B1–5; ~ ....~ : B6

148 Indian...Spanish] AB4; *Indian...Spanish* B1–3

153 Lapland] A1–3; Lopland B1–6

153–4 sides:...Maides,] ~ ,...~ , ~ ,...~ : B1; ~ ....~ , B2–6

194–5 *Prose in* AB1–6

199 Why,...then?] AB2; ~ ᴧ...~ ! B1

203 upon;] ~ , AB1–6

212 hang'd] A1–3; hangd'd B1; hanged B2–6

215 Maister] A1–3 (maister); Mr. B1; Master B2–6

219–20 *One line in* B1–6

228.2 *foure*] B2; 4 B1

244 *Dei*] A1–3 (*dei*); Dii B1–6

244 *Ignei*,] A1, B2 (*ignei,*); *ignei*ᴧ A2–3, B1

245 *Aquatici*,] ~ ᴧ AB1–6

246 *Belʒebub*ᴧ] ~ , AB1–6

246 *monarcha*,] ~ ᴧ AB1–6

246 Demogorgon] demigorgon AB1; Demigorgon B2–6

247 *Mephostophilis.*] ~ , A1–3; ~ ∧
 B1–6

248 ¶ *Quid*] *no*¶ AB1–6

248 *Gehennam*] AB3–6 (*gehennam*); *ge-
hennan* B1–2

248 *aquam*∧] A1–3; ~ , B1–6

250 *dicatus*] B2; *dicætis* A1; *dicatis* A2–
3, B1

254 Devill] A2–3, B2 (*Divell*); devill
 B1

261, 262 *Mephostophilis*] *Mephastophilis*
 A1–3

272 accord] AB2; accdred B1

274 *accidens*] B4; *accident* AB1–3

311 What,] A1; ~ ∧ A2–3, B1–6

333 thorough] through AB1–6

342.1 *Exeunt*] *Exit* AB1–6

344 *Robin.*] *speech-prefixes in* AB1–6 *are
forms of* Clowne

344 Zounds,] ~ ∧ AB1–6

346 in] AB2; In B1

371 againe,] ~ . A1–3; *omit* B1–6

375.1 *two*] AB2; 2 B1

376 sir,] B2; ~ ∧ B1

377 *Wagner,*] B3; ~ ∧ B1–2

378–9 *One line in* B1–6 (away; now)

378 *Exeunt.*] A1–3; *omit* B1–6

386 attentively] B2: atttentively B1

387 *vestigiis nostris*] *vestigias nostras*
 AB1–6

389 damn'd,] A1–3; ~ ? B1–6

390 sav'd.] ~ ? AB1–6

393 *Belzebub:*] A1–3; ~ , B1–6

395 eares,] B2; ~ : A1–2; ~ ∧ A3; ~ .
 B1

398–9 not: | The] A1–3; *one line in* B1–6

399 god] A1; God A2–3, B1–6

399 appetite,] AB2; ~ ∧ B1

403 *Bad*] *Evill* B1–6

407 lunacy,] AB2; ~ . B1

410 *Faustus,*] AB2; ~ ∧ B1

411–12 Wealth? | Why] A1–3; *one line in*
 B1–6

412 Why,] ~ ∧ AB1–6

415 *Mephostophilis*] B2; *Mepho:* B1

427–8 *Prose in* A1–3; B1–6 *line:* me, |
 What

427 *Mephostophilis*] B2; *Mephosto.* B1

431 *miseris*∧] A1–3, B2; ~ , B1

442–4 *Lined as in* A1–3; B1–6 *lines:*
 arme, | And . . . *Lucifers.*

442 *Mephostophilis,*] A1; ~ ∧ A2–3;
 Mephosto: B1–6±

466, 470 *fuge:*] ~ , AB1–6

484 *On . . . following*] *roman in* AB1–6

484 *following:*] ~ . AB1–6 (A3 ~ ,)

494 *the*] A1–3, B2; *rhe* B1

495 *Mephostophilis*] B2; *Mephastophilis*
 AB1

498 *flesh*∧] B2; ~ , AB1

502 I,] AB2; ~ ∧ B1

528 What,] ~ ∧ AB1–6

536 it.] A1; ~ , A2–3, B1; ~ : B2–6

540 *Penelope,*] AB3; ~ ; B1–2

544 iterating] AB2; Iterating B1

568 *Bad*] B3; *Evill* AB1–2

568 *Exeunt*] AB3; *Exit* B1–2

579 *Thebes*∧] ~ , AB1–6

592 jointly] AB2; jontly B1

595–6 But . . . *tempore?*] *one line in* AB1–6

604–7 AB1–6 *line:* The . . . yeares; |
 Jupiter . . . and | Mercury . . . daies. |
 These . . . every | Spheare . . . *Intelli-
gentia?*

604 thus:] ~ , AB1–6

604–5 thirty . . . twelve . . . four] 30 . . .
 12 . . . 4 AB1–6

604 yeares,] A1–3; ~ ; B1–6

606 Tush,] ~ ∧ A1–3

617 *motum*∧] AB2 ~ , B1

623 *One line in* A1–3; B1–6 *line:* King-
dome. | This is: Thou

623 Kingdome: This is.] ~ . . . . ~ :
 B1–6

628–9 'Tis . . . late?] A1–3; *one line in*
 B1–6

630 *et seq. Angel*] A1–3; *omit* B1–6

633.1 *Exeunt*] A1–3; *Ex.* B1–6

639–40 *One line in* AB1–6

648 heaven,] A1–3; ~ . B1–6

659–60 *Prose in* AB1–6

659 shew.] ~ , AB1–6

660.1 Seven] AB2 (seaven); 7 B1

675 house,] B2; ~ ∧ B1

698 Peter Pickeld-] A1–3; Peter- | pick-
eld- B1–6±

703 choke] A1–3 (choake), B2; chooke
 B1

705 sunny bank] A 1–3 (banke); sunny-| bank B 1–6

711 away:] ∼ ∧ B 1; ∼ , B 2–6

711 *Exeunt*] A 1–3; *Ex.* B 1–6

722 *Robin.*] omit B 1–6

727 *per se*] B 2; *perse* B 1

727 *se,*] ∼ ∧ B 1–6

728 *e.*] B 2; ∼ ∧ B 1

728 *se, o,*] ∼ ∧ ∼ ∧ B 1; ∼ ∧ ∼ , B 2–6

730 there,] ∼ ∧ B 1; ∼ ? B 2–6

754–5 Learned...Astronomy,] A 1–3; *one line in* B 1–6

783 Prince:] ∼ , AB 3–6; ∼ . B 1–2

785 *Rhine*] AB 3; *Rhines* B 1–2

793 Thorough] B 6 (Thorow); Through AB 1–5

808 Venison] B 2; Venson B 1

810 eyes,] ∼ . B 1; ∼ : B 1–6

817 *Ponte*] *Ponto* AB 1–6

836 *Mephostophilis,*] B 2; *Mephosto.* B 1

877 Gods∧] B 3; ∼ , B 1–2

890 *Raymond*——] ∼ . B 1–5; ∼ , B 6

902 Dispatch] B 2; Dispath B 1

903.1 *Exeunt*] *Exit* B 1–6

916 Germane] B 4; *Germane* B 1–3

920 downe,] B 5; ∼ . B 1–4

939.1 Mephostophilis] B 6; Mephosto. B 1–5

941 *Mephostophilis,*] B 3; *Mephosto.* B 1–2

960 Saint] B 2; S. B 1

960 Chaire,] B 2; ∼ ., B 1

965 *Ponte*] *Ponto* B 1–6

966 fast.] ∼ , B 1; ∼ ; B 2–6

975 *Mephostophilis∧*] *Mephosto.* B 1–6

978 Saint] B 3; S. B 1–2

980.3 Mephostophilis] B 2; Mephasto- philis B 1

985 *Germany*] B 3; Germany B 1–2

987–8 day,...away.] B 2 (away); ∼ . ...∼ , B 1

991 *Mephostophilis∧*] B 2; *Mephasto:* B 1

1006 *Mephostophilis:*] B 6; *Mephosto:* B 1–5

1029 *Both*] *Amb.* B 1–6

1038, 1059 *Archbishop.*] *Bishop.* B 1–6

1040 about.] B 3; ∼ , B 1–2

1047 *France*] B 6; France B 1–5

1050–1 *One line in* B 1–6

1053 *Raymond*] B 2; *Kaymond* B 1

1058 B 1 *lines*: this | Troublesome; B 2–6 *line*: patience | At

1065–6 *One line in* B 1–6

1071–2 Now...Candle.] B 3; B 1–2 *line*: you | You'le

1082, 1084, 1086 *Dominus*] Dom. B 1–6

1087.1 workes] AB 2; worke B 1

1112 much: when,...tell?] B 3; ∼ , ∼ ∧ ...∼ : B 1–2

1130–2 And so...gone] *Prose in* B 1–6

1130 transformed] transform'd B 1–6

1156 Emperour.] ∼ , B 1–6

1162 Emperour?] B 2; ∼ . B 1

1163–4 *One line in* B 1–6

1164 Germane] *Germane* B 1–6

1164 Conjurer,] B 2; ∼ . B 1

1187 and] B 2; snd B 1

1189–92 B 1–6 *line*: Has...yet? | He... enough; | And...him, | I... againe.

1203.1 *Exeunt*] *Exit* B 1–6

1203.3 Fredericke,] B 2; ∼ ∧ B 1

1227 Bloud,] ∼ ∧ B 1–6

1235–6 presently....away,] ∼ ,...∼ . B 1–5; ∼ ,...∼ , B 6

1236 *Mephostophilis*] B 2; *Mephosto* B 1

1241, 1308 Master] M. B 1–6

1257.6 comming] B 2; *commig* B 1

1279, 1290 What,] ∼ ∧ B 1–6

1301 kennell] B 2; kennelll B 1

1304 *Belimoth...Asteroth*] *Belimote... Asterote* B 1–6

1312 mirth,] B 4; ∼ : B 1–3

1314 *Mephostophilis*] B 2; *Mephasto- philis* B 1

1342 Close] B 2; close B 1

1366 see,] B 2; ∼ ∧ B 1

1374 Emperour?] B 3; ∼ . B 1–2

1437–8 *One line in* B 1–6

1437 misery.] ∼ , B 1–6

1443 meane,] B 2; ∼ ∧ B 1

1455 fame,] B 2; ∼ . B 1

1482 Tush,] AB 6; ∼ ∧ B 1–5

1494–5 B 1–6 *line*: leg, | I'le

1504 Come,] ∼ ∧ B 1–6

1507 Guesse?] B 2; ∼ ∧ B 1

1509 *et seq. this scene* Robin.] *Clowne.* B 1–6

1537 forty] B2; 40 B1
1554 me₍] B2; ~ , B1
1558–62 B1 *lines*: Nor...the | Sight...
one, | As...more.; B2–6 *line*:
Nor...Aire: | The...me, | As...
more.
1567 have?] ~ , B1–6
1576–7 B1–6 *line*: good | For
1576 good,] B3; ~ ₍ B1–2
1589 fury,] B3; ~ ₍ B1–2
1608 B1–6 *line*: grace: | Why
1608 grace.] B2; ~ : B1
1611 *et seq. this scene Robin.*] *Clowne.*
B1–6
1630 I, I,] B2; ~ , ~ . B1
1663 you] B2; yo B1
1681, 1684 Master] M. B1–6
1683, 1692 *Greece*] A1–3; Greece B1–6
1688–9 *One line in* AB1–6
1691 well,] A1–3; ~ : B1–6
1699 pursu'd] A2; pursude A1
1734–5 A1–3 *line*: Ah...words, | To
...soule,; B1–6 *as one line*
1747 *Mephostophilis,*] AB2; *Mephasto:*
B1
1791 *Sathan*] Sathan A1–3
1791 pride:] ~ , A1–3
1793, 1796 hell] A2; hel A1
1799 sinne₍] B3; ~ , B1–2
1821 *et seq. 1. Scholler.*] B1–6 *speech-
prefixes are*: 1. *or* 2. *or* 3.
1824–5 Ah...eternally.] A1–3; B1–6
line: thee, | Then

1830–1 *Prose in* AB1–6
1837–8 AB1–6 *line*: But...pardoned, |
The...saved, | But
1839 speeches. Though] ~ , though
AB1–6
1841 thirty] A1–3; 30 B1–6
1841 yeares,] A1–3; ~ . B1–6
1842 book:] A1; ~ , A2–3, B1–6
1843 witnesse,] A1–3; ~ : B1; ~ ; B2–6
1843 world:] B2; ~ , AB1
1854 Who,] ~ ₍ AB1–6
1855–6 Why...cunning] A1–3; *prose in*
B1–6
1880 I,] ~ ₍ B1–6
1887] passage;] ~ , B1–6
1890 What,] ~ ₍ B1–6
1892 *et seq. Angel*] *omit* B1–6
1906 hell:] B3; ~ , B1–2
1920 Ten] B2; ten B1
1932–3 AB1–6 *line*: yeare, | A
1936 strike,] AB3; ~ . B1–2
1941 Christ,] AB3; ~ , B1–2
1943–4 A1–3 *line*: Where...gone: |
And...arme, | And...browes:
1947–8 *One line in* AB1–6
1959 ransom'd] A2–3; ransomd A1
1974.1 *striketh*] A1–2; *strikes* A3, B1–6
1978 And] AB2; and B1
1978 Ocean,] A1; ~ ₍ A2–3, B1–6
1980 serpents,] A1; ~ ₍ A2–3, B1–6
1998 Germane] B4; *Germane* B1–3
2004 man:] A1–2, B2; ~ , A3, B1
2007 things,] A1–3; ~ : B1–6

HISTORICAL COLLATION

Chorus 1

1 marching] marching now A1–3, Bn, Tb

1 the fields] fields A1–3, Bn, TB

1 *Thrasimen*] Tharsimen B3–6, Dk, Ox, R

2 warlicke] omit A1–3, Bn, TB

2 *Carthagens*] Carthaginians A1–3, Bn, TB; Carthagen B6, Dk–R

6 vaunt] daunt A1–3, TB

6 his] her D, C

7 Gentles] Gentlemen A1–3, Bn, TB

7 now] omit A1–3, Bn, TB

9 And now] omit A1–3, Bn, TB; And so Gg

9 appeale] appeale our plaude A1–3, Bn, TB

11 is he] he is Ch

12 *Rhode*] Rhodes AB1–6, Dk–TB

13 At] Of A1–3, Bn, TB

13 *Wittenberg*] *Wertenberg* A1, Bn, TB; *Wirtenberg* A2

14 kinsmen] kinsman Dk, Ox, R

15 much] soone A1–3, Bn, TB

16 The fruitfull…grac'd,] omit B1–6, Dk–C, K

18 whose sweete delight's dispute] whose sweete delight disputes A1–3, Bn, TB, Gg, Ri; and sweetly can dispute B1–6, Dk–C, M, K, Rv

19 th'] omit A1–3, Bn, TB

19 of] in Coll MS

20 of] and B2–6, Dk–R, C

22 melting,] ~ ∧ A1–3, Dk–R, TB

24 now] more A1–3

25 upon] on the B2–6, Dk–R, C

28.1 *Exit*.] omit B1–6

Scene i

28.2 Enter] omit B1–6

34 *Analitikes*] Anulatikes A1

34 tis] omit Ch

35 est] et Ox

37 miracle] miracles Ox

38 that] the A1–3, Bn, TB

40 *on kai me on*] *Oncaymæon* A1; *Oeconomy* A2–3, B1–6, Dk–C

40 *Galen*] and *Galen* B1–6, Dk–C, M, K

41 Seeing…*medicus*.] omit B1–6, Dk–C, K

47 Is...Aphorismes?] *omit* B1–6, Dk–C, K

47 sound] found Bn

50 thousand] divers B2–6, Ch, Ox, Gg, Ri

50 cur'd] easde A1–3, Bn, TB

52 Couldst] wouldst A1–3, TB

52 men] man A1–2, Bn, TB

53 them] men B3–6

57 petty] pretty A1–3, Ox, Bn, TB

58 *nisi*——] *nisi &c.* B2–6, Dk–Bn

60 law] Church A1–3

61 This] His A1–3, TB

63 Too servile] The devill A1–3

69–70 there is] theres A1–3, Bn, TB, Gg, Rv, Ri

78 Signes] *omit* B1–6, Dk–R, M, K, Rv; sceanes A1–3, D–TB

78 and] *omit* B2–6, Dk–R, K

81 and] of A1–3, Bn, TB, Gg, Rv, Ri

86 Nor...cloudes:] *omit* B1–6, Dk–C, K

87 exceeds] excells Gg

89 Demi-god] mighty god A1–3, Bn, TB

90 Here] Heere *Faustus* A1–3, Bn, TB

90 tire my] trie thy A1–3, Bn, TB, Ri

90 get] gaine AB2–6, D, Bn, TB

91 *Wagner,*] *as speech-prefix* A2

95 to me] *omit* Dk–Ox

96.1 Angel *and* Spirit] *good Angell and the evill Angell* A1–3

99 wrath] rod A2–3

101 *et seq. Bad Angel.] Evill A.* A1–3

102 treasury] treasure A2–3, B1–6, Dk–Bn, M

104 these] the Ch

108 enterprise] enterprises B4–6

109 *India] Indian* B1

112 pleasant] pleasants A3

116 make] with B2–6, Gg

116 faire] all B4–6

116 *et seq. Wittenberge] Wertenberge* A1–3, Bn, TB

117 silke] skill AB1–6, Dk–R

121 our] the A2–3, B1–6, Dk–C, M

123 *Antwerpe] Anwerpe* B1–5; *Antwarpes* A1; *Antwerpes* A2–3, Bn, TB, Gg–Ri

126 blest] wise B2–6, Ox

126.1 *Enter...*] B1–6± *place to right of lines* 126–7; A1–3 *print as line* 127.1

130–2 Yet...skill.] *omit* B1–6, Dk–C

135–6 Divinitie...vilde:] *omit* B1–6, Dk–C

139 concise Sillogismes] subtle Sillogismes A3 (subtile), B1–6, Dk–C, M, K, Ri; Consissylogismes A1–2

142 Swarme] Sworne B1

145 shadows] shadow B1–6, Dk–C

146 *Faustus*] *omit* Dk, Ox, R, C

147 to] *omit* B3–6, Ox

149 spirits] subjects A1–3, TB

152 Rutters] Ritters Ox

156 has] have B2–6, Dk–Bn; in A1–3, Gg, Rv, Ri

157 From] For A1

157 shall they] they shall Dk–R

157 they] the A2

157 drag] dregge A1, TB

157 huge] whole B2–6, Dk, R, Gg

159 stuffes] stuff'd B1

161, 185 *Valdes*] *omit* Ox, R, C

166 in] *omit* A1

167 Principles] principals A2

170 heeretofore] hetherto A2–3

170 *Delphian] Dolphian* A1

173 Yea] I A1–3, Bn, TB, Rv

177 some] *omit* Ch

178 bushy] lustie A1, TB, Gg, Rv, Ri; little A2–3; lofty Coll MS

181 *Abanus] Albanus* AB1–6, Dk–R, TB; Albertus D (*after* Mitford), C, Bn, M, K

187 may] my A3

Scene ii

195.1 *Enter* Wagner.] *omit* B1; A1–3 *print as line* 196.1

196 presently] *omit* A1–3, Bn, TB

196 here] for see here A1–3, Bn, TB

199 not thou] thou not Ch

199 then] *omit* A1–3, Bn, TB

201 us] *omit* Dk–R

202 by force] necessary by force A1–3, Bn, TB

202 which] that A1–3, Bn, TB

203 *Licentiats*] licentiate A1–3, TB

203 upon] upon't A1, TB; upon it A2–3

204.1 A1–3, Bn, TB *add*: *2. Why, didst thou not say thou knewst?* | *Wag. Have you any witnesse on't?* | *1. Yes sirre, I heard you.* | *Wag. Aske my fellow if I be a thiefe.* (Bn fellows)

205 Then] Well,] A1–3, Bn, TB

206 You...for] Yes sir, A1–3, Bn, TB

207 me] *omit* Dk–R

207 he not] not he A1–3, Bn, TB

211 foot] feet Dk–R, Bn

212 but] *omit* A1–3, Bn, TB

216 could] would Dk, Ox, R, C

216 would] it would A1–3, TB; could Dk, Ox, R

216 Worships] worshipe A2–3

218 brethren] brethren, my deare brethren A1–3, Bn, TB

219 O *Faustus*] Nay A1–3, Bn, TB

220 that...suspected:] *omit* A1–3, Bn, TB

221 That thou art] he is A1–3, Bn, TB

221 that damned] the damned B6, Dk, Ox, R, C

223 not] and not A1–3, Bn, TB

224 The...mourne] yet should I grieve for him A1–3, Bn, TB

226 It may be] and see if hee by A1–3, Bn, TB

226 may] can A1–3, Bn, TB

226 him] *omit* B2–6

227 I...will] O but I...can A1–3, Bn, TB

227 now] *omit* A1–3, Bn, TB

228 see] trie A1–3, Bn, TB

Scene iii

228.2–228.3 *Thunder...speech.*] *Enter Faustus to conjure.* A1–3

229 night] earth A1–3, Bn, TB

230 looke] looks Gg

231 th'] the B4–6, Dk, Ox, R, C

232 her] his B3–6, Dk–R, C

237 *Anagramatis'd*] and Agramithist A1–3

238 Th'abreviated] The breviated A1–3, C, Bn, TB, Gg, Rv

240 erring] evening B1

242 to] but A1–3, Bn, TB

243 utmost] uttermost A1–3, Bn, TB, Gg, K, Rv

244 Thunder.] *omit* A1–3, TB; *as part of text, with comma* B1–6

245 *Aquatici*] *Aquatani* AB1, D, C, Br, Ri; *Aquitani* B2–6, Dk–R; *aquæ* M

245 *Terreni*] *omit* AB1–6, Dk–TB, K, Ri; *terræ* M

246 *Lucifer,*] *omit* AB1–6, Dk–M, K, Ri

248 Dragon.] *omit* A1–3, Bn, TB, Ri; *as part of text with comma* B1–6, Dk–C

248 *Quid tu moraris*] *quod tumeraris* AB1–6, Dk–Bn; *quid timeraris* or *temeraris* Coll MS

250 *vota*] *rota* Dk, Ox, R

250.1 *a*] *omit* B4–6

257 pliant] playnt B6

260–3 Now...*imagine.*] *omit* B1–6, Dk–C, K

260 Now] No A1–3

262 *redis*] *regis* A1–3, Bn, TB

263 do] to do Bn

272 now] *omit* B2–6, Dk–Bn, Gg, Rv, Ri

273 speeches] *omit* B1–6, Dk–C, K; spirits A2–3

281 the Trinity] all godlinesse B1–6, Dk–C, K

283 *Faustus* hath already...holds] I have...hold Gg

285 *Faustus* doth] doth *Faustus* Ch, Br MS

286 me] him A1–3, Bn, TB, Rv

287 I confound] He confounds A1–3, Bn, TB, Rv

288 My] His A1–3, Bn, TB, Rv

291 all] *omit* B6

298 fell] live B1–6, Dk–R

305 who] that A2–3, B1–6, Dk–C, M

309 these] those B2–6

310 strike] strikes B1–4, M
310 soule] heart Dk–R, C
315 these] those A1–3, TB
316 hath] had R, C
318 up] omit A2–3
319 foure and twenty] 24. A1–2, TB
322 me] omit A2–3
324 aid] to aid A2–3, B1–6, Dk–C, M,
K

334 Ocean$_\wedge$...men,] ~:...~ $_\wedge$ B1;
~ $_\wedge$...~ $_\wedge$ B2; ~ $_\wedge$...~ . B3–6,
Ch ~ $_\wedge$...~ ; Dk, Ox±
336 Country] land A1–3, TB
339–40 Germany...desir'd$_\wedge$] ~ ,...~ .
Dk, Ox, R, C
340 desir'd] desire A1–3, Bn, TB, Gg,
Rv, Ri

Scene iv (B-text)

342.2–388.1 For the A-text and collation
of its variants, see Appendix: A-
text, Scene iv
345 such pickadevaunts] beards B1–6,
Dk–C, Bn (Ap), TB (Ap), M
346 Sirra] omit B3–6, Dk–R
347 Yes] omit Dk–R, C
349 I know] omit Gg

349 that he] that I know he AB1–6, Dk–
Ri
360 it] omit Ch
364 save] spare B6, Dk–R
371 your] you Dk
371 againe] omit B1, TB (Ap), K
372 for] or D²
377 devill] devils Ch, D, C, Bn (Ap)

Scene v

390 And] omit B1–6, Dk–C, K
390 not now] thou not AB1–6, Dk–M,
K, Rv, Ri; not Gg
391 on] of A1–3, Bn, TB, Rv
394 backward: no, Faustus] backward
Faustus B1–2, D, M, K, Ri; backe
Faustus B3–6, Dk–R, C; backward;
no Gg
395 Why] omit B4–6, Ox
395 thou? O] omit Gg
395 eares] eare B1–6; Dk–C, M, K
395 soundeth] roundeth Br MS
397 I...againe.] omit B1–6, Dk–C, K
398 To God?] Why B1–6, Dk–C, K
400 fixt] first Ch, Ox, R
402.1 Enter...Angels.] Enter good
Angell, and Evill. A1–3
403 Bad...Art.] omit A1–3, Bn, TB, Gg
403 famous] most famous B2–6, Dk, Ox,
R
405 of] be B2–6, Ch, Ox
405 these] them A1–3, Bn, TB
408 makes] makee A3; make B1–6, Dk–
C, M–Ri
408 men] them B1, Ch
408 use] trust A1–3, Bn, TB

410 honour] honours C
410 of wealth] wealth A1
411 Wealth] Of Wealth A1–3, Bn, TB
412 mine:] ~ , A1–3, TB
414 god] God A1–3, Bn, TB; power
B1–6, Dk–C, M–Ri
414 me? Faustus] thee Faustus? A1–3,
TB (~ $_\wedge$ ~ , A2–3); Bn (~ ? ~ $_\wedge$)
415 Cast] Come A3
415 Mephostophilis come] come Mephastophilis A1–3, Bn, TB
418 Mephostophilis] Mephostophile AB1
(Mephastophile A1–3), D–M
419 me] omit A1–3
419 saith] sayes A1–3, Bn, TB
420 Mephostophilis.] omit B1
421 he will...his] thou wilt...thy Dk–
R
423 now] Faustus, thou A1–3, Bn, TB
425 Lucifer] great Lucifer A1–3, Bn, TB
426 must] wil A1–3, Bn, TB
428 And] omit M, Gg, Rv
430 why] omit A1–3, TB
432 Why,] omit A1–3
432 torture] tortures A1–3, Bn, TB
432 other] others A1–3, B4–6, Dk–M, Ri

433 soules] spirits Dk, Ox, R

433 men] man Ox, R, C

437 I'le] I A1–3, Bn, TB

437 him] thee A1–3, D, Bn, TB

438 *Faustus*] omit A1–3, TB

438 thy] thine A1–3, B3–6, Ox–Bn

441 And] omit B3–6

443 *Faustus...his...his*] I cut mine... my A1–3, Bn, TB, M, Gg, Ri

443 proper] omit Dk–R, C

444 Assures his] Assure my A1–3, Bn, TB, M, Gg, Ri

444 his soule] himself Dk, Ox, R, C

446 this] the A1–3, Bn, TB

447 my] thy B4–6, Dk, Ox, R, C

449 Write] thou must write A1–3, Bn, TB

450 I so] Ah, so Dk, Ox, R, C

450 do] will A1–3, Bn, TB

454 Is it] It is B2–6, Dk, Ox, R

456 ah] O B1–6, Dk–C, K, Rv, Ri

457 thy] this C

458 soule] omit B4–6

458.1 *the Chafer of fire*] a chafer of coles A1–3

459 See...fire] Heres fier, come *Faustus*, A1–3, Bn, TB

461 an] omit B4

462 not I] I not A2–3

462 obtaine] attaine B2

465 mine] my A2–3

466 should] shall B6

467 God] heaven B1–6, Dk–R, C, K

467 me] thee A1–3, TB

469 O yes] omit A1–3, Bn, TB

469 even heere] here in this place A1–3, Bn, TB

471 somewhat] something Dk, Ox, R

471.2 *Devils*] with divels A1–3

471.3 they] and A1–3

471.4 *Enter* Mephostophilis.] omit A1–3

472 What...*Mephostophilis*] Speake Mephastophilis, what meanes this shewe? A1–3, Bn, TB

473 mind] minde withall A1–3, Bn, TB

474 let thee see] shewe thee A1–3, Bn TB

475 such] up A1–3, Bn, TB

477 Then *Mephostophilis*] Then theres inough for a thousand soules, | Here Mephastophilis A1–3, Bn, TB, M

477 this scrole] omit B4–6

479 performe] perform'st Dk–R

480 Covenants, and Articles,] All articles prescrib'd A1–3, Bn, TB, M; covenant-articles Gg

482 made] both B1–6, Dk–C, K

483 it] omit C

483 it *Mephostophilis*] them A1–3, Bn, TB

486–7 *be by him commanded*] *at his command* A1–3, Bn, TB, M, Gg, Rv, Ri

489 *whatsoever*] whatsoever he requireth Dk–R, C; *whatsoever he desires* D, Bn

490 *chamber or house*] house or chamber Dk, Ox, R, C

491 *that*] omit Dk, Ox, R, C

492 *shape...forme*] *forme...shape* A1–3, Bn, TB, M, Gg, Rv, Ri

492 or] and A2–3, B1–6, Dk, Ox, R

495 *that*] omit Br MS

496 *foure and twentie*] 24. A1–2, TB; twenty-four Bn

496 *being*] omit A1–3, Bn, TB, Gg, Rv, Ri

496 *and these*] *the* A1–3, Bn, TB, Gg, Rv, Ri

498 *flesh and bloud*] omit Dk–R

498 *and bloud,*] bloud, B1; *bloud, or goods* A1–3, Bn–Gg, Rv, Ri

502 of it] on't A1–3, Bn, TB, Rv

503 So,] omit A1–3, Bn, TB, Gg, Rv

503 me] omit A1–3, Bn, TB, Gg, Rv

504 I will] will I A1–3, Bn, TB, Gg–Ri

504 with] omit A2–3, B1–6, Dk, Ox, R, C

505 the] that B4–6

507 so...else] omit A1–3, Bn, TB

507 whereabouts] where about A1–3, Bn, TB

508 these] the Ch

511 but] for A1–3, Bn, TB

512 there] omit A1–3, TB

513 be short] conclude A1–3, Bn, TB

515 is] are B2–6, Dk–C

516 I] Come, I A1–3, Bn, TB
516 fable] meere fable B2–6, Dk–R
517 I] Ah Dk, Ox, R, C
518 dost thou think] think'st thou then A1–3, Bn, TB
520 In which] Wherein A1–3, Bn, TB
521 but] and Dk–R, C
524 Tush] No B1–6, Dk–C, M–Ri
524 meere] omit A2–3
525 But] But *Faustus* A1–3, Bn, TB
526 I tell thee] omit A1–3, Bn, TB
526 now] am now A1–3, Bn, TB
527 Nay] How? now in hell? nay A1–3, Bn, TB
527 damn'd] damned here A1–3, Bn, TB
528 sleeping, eating] omit A1–3, Bn, TB
528 and disputing] disputing, &c A1–3, Bn, TB
529 leaving] leaving off A1–3, Bn, TB, Ri
530 wife.] wife. | *Me.* How, a wife? I prithee *Faustus* talke not of a wife. | *Fau.* Nay sweete *Mephastophilis* fetch me one, for I will have one. A1–3, Bn, TB, Gg (*omit* How, a wife?), Rv, Ri (*like* Gg)
531 Well...wife.] Well thou wilt have one, sit [A2–3 stay] there till I come, Ile fetch thee a wife in the divels name. A1–3, Bn, TB, Rv
531 wife.] wife; sit there till I come. Gg, Ri
531.1 *He...devill.*] *Enter with a divell*

drest like a woman, with fier workes. A1–3
532 *Faustus.* What...this?] omit A1–3, Bn, TB
533 Now...wife?] Tel *Faustus*, how dost thou like thy wife? A1–3, TB; Tell me *Faustus*.... Bn, Rv; Now *Faustus* Gg
534 Here's...wife.] A plague on her for a hote whore. A1–3, Bn, TB
535 Marriage] Tut *Faustus*, marriage A1–3, Bn, TB
536 And] omit A1–3, TB
536 no] omit A1
539 thine] thy A2–3, B5–6
539 thy] thine B2–6
540 Were] Be A1–3, Bn, TB
540 as was] as were B4–6
543 Hold] Here B1–6, Dk–C, M, K
543 peruse it thoroughly] and peruse it well] B1–6, Dk–C, M, K..
546 Thunder...Storme] whirlewindes, tempests, thunder A1–3, Bn, TB
548 harnesse] armour A1–3, Bn, TB
549 commandst] desirst A1–3, Bn, TB
550–1 for this...life] omit A1–3, Bn TB, Gg, Rv
551.0.1–551.0.13] omit B1–6, Dk–C, M, K, Ri
551.0.1 might] may A2–3
551.0.5 of planets] and planets A1–3, Bn, TB
551.1 Exeunt.] omit A1–3, *which continue the scene without break*

552.0.0–552.0.11 B1–6 *here reprint, as follows, the short form of* Chorus 2 *as found in* A1–3 *at* 754:

Wag. Learned *Faustus*　　　*Enter Wagner solus.*
To know the secrets of Astronomy
Graven in the booke of *Joves* high firmament,
Did mount himselfe to scale *Olympus* top,
Being seated in a chariot burning bright,
Drawne by the strength of yoaky Dragons necks,
He now is gone to prove Cosmography,
And as I gesse will first arrive at *Rome*,
To see the Pope and manner of his Court;
And take some part of holy *Peters* feast,
That to this day is highly solemnized.　　　*Exit Wagner.*
552.0.6 yoaky] yoaked B4–6, Dk, Ch, R
552.0.6 necks] necke B2
552.0.11 to] on B2–6, Dk, R

Scene vi

551.2 *Enter...Mephostophilis.*] *omit* A1–3
554 those] these Dk, Ox, R, C
555 'Twas...selfe.] *omit* A1–3, Bn, TB
555 thine] thy B6
556 But] why *Faustus* A1–3, Bn, TB
556 is] *omit* A2–3, B2–6, Dk, Ox, R, C
557 *Faustus,*] *omit* A1–3, Bn, TB
557 it is] tis A1–3, Bn, TB, Ri
558 breathes] breathe B1, K
560 'Twas] It was A1–3, TB
560 then he's] therefore is man A1–3, Bn, TB
561 Heaven was] it were A1–3, Bn, TB
562.1 *Enter...Angels.*] *Enter good Angel, and evill Angel.* A1–3 (A3: *omit* ²*Angel*)
563 repent, yet]] ~ ∧ ~ , A1–3
563 God] heaven Dk–R
565 eares] eare B4
567 Yea] I A1–3, Bn, TB
568 I] Ah Dk, Ox, R
568 shall] will Dk–R, C
568 Angels] *omit* A1–3
569 heart is] hearts so A1–3, Bn, TB
570 heaven,] ~ . B1–2; ~ : B5–6, Dk, Ox, R, D, C
571–2 But...knives,] *omit* B1–6, Dk–C, M, K
571 thunder] thunders A1–3, TB, Rv
572 swords] guns Gg, Rv
573 Gunnes, poyson] Swords, poyson B1–6, Dk–C, Gg, K, Rv, Ri; Poyson, gunnes A1–3, Bn (gun), TB, M
573 poyson] poysons B2–6, Dk–C
575 this] this time B4
575 I should] should I Ox
575 done the deed] slaine my selfe A1–3, Bn, TB
577 not I] I not Dk–R
583 not] nere A1–3, Bn, TB
585 reason] argue A1–3, Bn, TB
586 Speake] Tel me A1–3, Bn, TB
586 Spheares] heavens A1–3, Bn, TB
589 such] so Ch
589 heavens] spheares A1–3, Bn, TB
590 Even...Orbe,] *omit* A1–3, Bn, TB

591 Spheares] orbe A1–3, Bn, TB
592 jointly] *Faustus* all jointly A1–3, Bn, TB
593 termine] terminine A1–3, Bn, TB; terminus C
594 or] and Dk–R, C
595 erring] evening B1–6, Dk–R
595 But] But tell me A1–3, Bn, TB
597 move] joyntly move A1–3, Bn, TB
597 foure and twenty] 24. A1–3; twenty-four Bn
598 motions] motion A1–3, Bn, TB, M
599 poles] place Dk–R
600 These] Tush, these A1–3, Bn, TB
600 questions] trifles A1–3, Bn, TB
602 motion] motions B4
603 That] *omit* A1–3, Bn, TB
604 *Saturne*] as *Saturne* A1–3, Bn, TB
606 Tush] *omit* B1–6, Dk–C, M, Gg–Ri
606 suppositions] questions B1–6, Dk–C, M
607 *Intelligentia*] *Intelligentij* A1–3
612–13 *Faustus.* But...Fables.] *omit* A1–3, Bn, TB
612 not] none Dk, Ox; no R, C
612 and] & B1–6; et Dk–C, M, Rv, Ri
613 be] are Dk–R
614 Resolve me then] Well, resolve me A1–3, Bn, TB
614, 616 in] *omit* Dk–R
614 one] *omit* A1–3, Dk–R, Bn, TB
615 are not] have wee not A1–3, Bn, TB
616 ²in] *omit* A2–3, Dk–R, C
618 now] *omit* A1–3, Bn, TB
621 *Faustus*] for I will not tell thee A1–3, A1–3, Bn, TB
622 I not] not I A2–3, B1–6, Dk–C, M, Gg–Ri
623 I] *omit* B3–6
623 This] but this A1–3, Bn, TB
624 Thou...hell.] Thinke thou on hell *Faustus,* for thou art damnd. A1–3, Bn, TB
627 I] Ah Dk–R, C
629 Ist...late?] *omit* Dk–R, C
629.1 *Enter...Angels.*] *Enter good Angell and evill.* A1–3 (A3: *evil Angel*)

631 will] can A1–3, Bn, TB

632 will] shall A1–3, Bn, TB

633.1 Angels] *omit* A1–3

634 Ah] O B1–6, Dk–C, Gg–Ri

634 my Saviour, my Saviour,] my Saviour, A1–3, Bn, TB

635 Helpe] seeke A1–3, Bn, TB; Help
help! C

638 terrible] terribly B1–6, Dk–C, M,
K, Rv, Ri

641 fetch] fetch away A1–3, Bn, TB

641 thy soule] thee Ox, R

642 *Belzebub.*] *Lucifer.* A1–3, Bn, TB

642 are come] come A1–2, Bn, TB;
came A3

643, 645 *Lucifer.*] *omit* A1–3, Bn, TB

643 calst on] talkst of A1–3, Bn, TB

644, 646, 654 *Belzebub.*] *omit* A1–3, Bn,
TB

644 on] of A1–3, Bn, TB

645 of] on A3, B1–6, Ch–C, M, Gg–Ri

646 his dam] of his dame A1–3, Bn, TB

647 I...me] *Faustus*...him B1–6, R
(omit *Faustus*), D, C, M, K; he...
him Dk–R (*omit* he)

647 for] in A1–3, Bn, TB, M, Gg, Rv,
Ri

649–51 Never...downe] *omit* B1–6,
Dk–C, K

652 So...servant] Do so A1–3, Bn, TB

652 shalt thou] *omit* Dk, Ox, R, C

653 for it] *omit* A1–3, Bn, TB

654 in person] *omit* A1–3, Dk, Ox, R,
Bn, TB

655 some] *omit* Dk, Ox, R

655 downe] *omit* Dk, Ox, R

655 behold] see al A1–3, Bn, TB

655 seven] *omit* Dk, Ox, R

656 to thee] *omit* A1–3, Bn, TB

656 owne] *omit* A1–3, Bn, TB

656 and likenesse] *omit* A1–3, Dk, Ox,
R, Bn, TB

657 pleasant] pleasing A1–3, Bn, TB

657 to] unto A1–3, B3–6, Dk–TB

657 was] *omit* Dk, Ox, R

658 the first...his] on Dk, Ox, R

659 or] nor A1–3, Bn, TB

659 or Creation] *omit* Dk, Ox, R, C

659 the] this A1–3, Bn, TB

660 Go...in] talke of the divel, and
nothing else: come away A1–3, Bn,
TB

660 fetch] and fetch B6, Dk–C

661 *Belzebub.*] *omit* A1–3, Bn, TB

661 question] examine A1–3, Bn, TB

661 names] several names A1–3, Bn, TB

663 That...soone:] *omit* A1–3, Bn, TB

666–7 next...Necke:] *omit* A1–3, Bn,
TB

667 Then] or A1–3, Bn, TB

667 lippes] *omit* B1–6, Dk–R, C, K

667 And] *omit* R

667–8 And...list] indeede I doe, what
doe I not? A1–3, Bn, TB

669 smell] scent A1–3, Bn, TB

669–70 a word...ransome, unlesse] an
other worde, except A1–3, Bn, TB,
Gg; another word unless M, Rv, Ri

670 be] were A1–3, Bn, TB; is Dk–R

672 Thou...indeed:] *omit* A1–3, Bn,
TB

674 in a] in an olde A1–3, Bn, TB

675 leather] leatherne A1–3, Dk–R, C,
Bn, TB

675 now obtaine] have A1–3, Bn, TB

675–6 this...turne] I would desire, that
this house, and all the people in it
were turnd A1–3, Bn, TB

676 safe into] uppe in my good A1–3,
Bn, TB

678 And] *omit* A1–3, Bn, TB

679–85 A1–3, Bn, TB *exchange with
lines* 686–91 *to make* Wrath *the third
and* Envy *the fourth*

680 burn'd] were burnt A1–3, Bn, TB

682 over] through A1–3, Bn, TB

683 I'de] I would A1–3, Bn, TB

685 Out...But] Away envious rascall:
A1–3, Bn, TB

687 an houre] half an houre A1–3, Bn,
TB

687–8 ever since have] have ever since
B3–6; I have ever since Dk–R, C

688 have] I have A1–3, Bn, TB

688 these] this A1–3, Dk–TB, Ri

689 could get none] had no body A1–3,
Bn, TB

692 And] *omit* A1–3, Bn, TB

693 I] who I sir, I] A 1–3, Bn, TB
694 bare] small B 1–6, Dk–C, M–Ri
694 buyes me] is A 1–3, Bn, TB
696 I] O I A 1–3, Bn, TB
696 come] came B 3–6; am Dk–R
696 Pedigree] parentage A 1–3, Bn, TB
696 father] grandfather A 1–3, Bn, TB
697 and] *omit* A 1–3, Bn, TB
697 mother was] grandmother A 1–3, Bn, TB
698 Pickeld-] Pickle- A 1–3, Bn, TB
699 But] O but A 1–3, Bn, TB
699 O] *omit* A 1–3, Bn, TB
699 an ancient Gentlewoman,] a jolly gentlewoman, and welbeloved in every good towne and Citie, A 1–3, Bn, TB, Gg, Rv, Ri
700 Margery] mistress Margery A 1–3, Bn, TB, Gg, Ri; *omit* Ch
702 Not I.] No, Ile see thee hanged, thou wilt eate up all my victualls. A 1–3, Bn, TB, Rv (A 2–3: hang'd first); Not I; thou wilt...victuals. Gg, Ri
703 Then] *omit* Ox, R, C
705 Hey ho;] *omit* A 1–3, Bn, TB
705.0.1–705.0.3 where...Letchery] *omit* B 1–6, Bk–C
706 an other word] an other word for a King's raunsome A 1–3, Bn, TB; a

word more for a kings ransome B 1–6, Dk–C, M–Ri
707 And] *omit* A 1–3, Bn, TB
707 are you] art thou Dk–R, C
708 I sir] I I sir B 1
710 Letchery] L. Coll MS, D², C, Bn
711 *Lucifer.*] *omit* A 1–3
711 away: on piper.] to hel. | *Lu.* Now Faustus, how dost thou like this? A 1–3, Bn (± *Lucifer.*), TB (*ditto*)
712 how...delight] this feedes A 1–3, Bn, TB
713 Tut] But B 1–6, Dk–R
713 is...delight] are delights Dk–R, C
714 safe] *omit* A 1–3, Bn, TB
716 *Faustus,*] *omit* A 1–3, Bn, TB
716 at...thee] I wil send for thee at midnight A 1–3, Bn, TB
717 Meane...throughly] in mean time take this booke, peruse it throwly A 1–3, Bn, TB
718 thy selfe] *omit* Bn (*qy*)
719 Thankes] Great thankes A 1–3, Bn, TB
720 Now *Faustus* farewell.] Farewel Faustus, and thinke on the divel. A 1–3, Bn, TB
721.1 *severall waies*] *omit* A 1–3

Scene vii

721.2–753.1 *For the* A-text *and collation of its variants, see the* Appendix: A-text, Scene vii, *which in the* B-text *order follows* Scene ix
726 scorn't] scorn Dk, Ox, R
726, 734, 735 'faith] ifaith B 2–6, Dk–R, C
727 and] an B 2–6, Dk–Bn (Ap), K
728 *demy*] *deny* B 1–6, Dk, Ch, Ox, M–Ri
731 not] *omit* B 2–6
731 tell] *omit* B 3–6
732 thou shalt] shalt thou Dk–R, C
734 best] better Dk–R
737 as faire a] a faire B 2–6, Dk–R, C
739 needst] needs B 6
740 I] Ah Dk–R, C
745, 746, 747 thou't] thou'lt B 2–6, Dk–Bn (Ap), M
749 Whippincrust] Whippincurst B 2
751 prethee] I prithee B 2–6
753 let's] let us B 2–6, Dk–R, C

Chorus 2

753.2 *the* Chorus] *Wagner solus* A 1–3
754 Learned] *Wag.* Learned A 1–3, TB; *omit* Ch, R
755 find] know A 1–3, Bn, TB
757 him up] himselfe A 1–3, Bn, TB; up B 6
758 Where sitting] Being seated A 1–3, Bn, TB
759 yoked] yoky A 1–3, Bn, TB, Gg
760–71 He…backe,] *omit* A 1–3, Bn, TB

760 He viewes] To view B 3–6
761 Tropicks,] Tropick, B 1; Tropicke‸ B 2–6, Dk–C, M
764 with] of Dk, Ox, R
764 this] his B 4
767 did] do Ch
769 ²his] this Dk–R
774 That…earth:] *omit* A 1–3, Bn, TB
778 The which] That to A 1–3, Bn, TB
778.1 *Exit.*] *exit Wagner.* A 1–3

Scene viii

781 round] *omit* B 4–6
785 *Rhine*] *Rhines* B 1–2
787 up to] unto B 3–6, Dk–R, C
787 *Naples*‸] ~ , A B 1–6, D–M, Ri; ~ ; Dk, Ox, R, C, Gg, K, Rv
788 The] Whose A B 1–6, Dk–M, K, Ri; With Gg, Rv
788 buildings] building's Ch
789 Whose] The A B 1–6, Dk–M, K, Ri
790 Quarter…equivolence] *omit* B 1–6, Dk–R
790 Quarter] Quarters A 1–3, TB, M, K
790 equivolence] forme equivolent A 3
794 rest] East B 1–6, Dk–R, C, M
795 midst] one B 1–6, Dk–M, K
797–8 Whose…gold] *omit* A 1–3, Bn, TB
800 me] *omit* B 4
803–6 I have…use.] Faustus I have, and because we wil not be unprovided, I have taken up his holinesse privy chamber for our use. A 1–3, Bn, TB
807 us] you B 3–6, Dk, Ox, R
808 All's one for] Tut, tis no matter man, A 1–3, Bn, TB
808 Venison] good cheare A 1–3, Bn, TB
809 But] And A 1–3, Bn, TB
810 containes…eyes] containeth to delight thee with A 1–3, Bn, TB
811 upon] on Ch
812 underprop] underprops A 1–3, TB

813–14 Just…parts;] *omit* A 1–3
815 foure] two B 1–6, Dk–R, C
816 make] makes A 1–3, TB
819–22 Where…yeare:] Within whose walles such store of ordnance are, | And double Canons, fram'd [Bn: formed] of carved brasse, | As match the dayes within one compleate yeare, A 1–3, Bn, TB
821 match] watch B 1
823 Beside] Besides A 1–3, Bn, TB
824 That] which A 1–4, Bn, TB
826 of] *omit* A 1–3, Bn, TB
828 the] those B 2–6
831 stay my *Faustus*] Faustus stay A 1–3, Bn, TB
831 you'd] you'd faine A 1–3, TB
833–5 The which…victory.] Where thou shalt see a troupe of bald-pate Friers, | Whose *summum bonum* is in belly-cheare. A 1–3, Bn, TB
833 this day] *omit* B 1
833 this day with] in state and B 2–6, Ch, D–M, Gg, Ri
836–988 *Faustus.* Sweete…away.] *omit* A 1–3, Bn, TB
837 be] *omit* B 6
841 whilst] while B 2–6
842 through] thorow B 6, Ch, D, C
846 my] one D (*qy*)
855 cunning] comming B 1–3, Dk, Ox, R
859 cunning] comming B 1–3

859 in] of Gg
860 this] his B4–6, Ox, C
862 at] to B4–6, Ch
866 it] *omit* B2–6
867.2 *pillars*] pillows Ox
880 And...enterprise] *omit* B2–6
881 *France*] Florence Gg (*qy*)
882 our] the B2–6
888 word] word again Gg
896 this] the B2–6
904 some] *omit* B4–6, Dk–Bn (Ap), M
908 shalt] shall B3–6, Dk–Bn (Ap)

927 Emperours] Emperour Dk–R, C
928 Rites] rights D, Bn (Ap), Gg, Rv
933 keys] seales B1–2, Dk, Ox, R–TB
    (Ap); scales B3–6
947 have] hath B3–6, D, C
952 reverend] *omit* B1–6, Dk–R, D
    (*but qy* holy), TB (Ap), M, K, Rv,
    Ri; holy C, Bn (Ap), Gg
953 Priests] Priest Dk, Ox, R
969 or] and R, C
970 his] this B3–6
971 treasury] consistory Ch

Scene ix

980.2 *Senit*] Sonet B4–6
984 on] one B6
989–93 But...any.] *Fau.* Well, I am
    content, to compasse then some
    sport, | And by their folly make us
    merriment. | Then charme me that
    I may be invisible, to do what I
    please unseene of any whilst I stay
    in Rome. A1–3, Bn, TB
994 *Mephostophilis.*] *omit* B2
994–1003 *Faustus* thou...*see.*] *omit* A1–
    3, Bn, TB
1002 *tree*] *three* M (*qy*)
1004 now...holinesse] *omit* A1–3, Bn,
    TB
1006–8 *Faustus.* Thankes...come.] *omit*
    A1–3, Bn, TB
1008.1–1087.2 *Enter...Exeunt.*] *For the*
    A-text *and collation of its variants,
    see the* Appendix: A-text, Scene vi
1009 sit] sit ye Ch
1011 be] are B5–6
1030, 1031, 1039 you] ye B6
1032 them] them forth B3–6
1039 ¹you] *omit* B4–5
1040 about.] about. | *Fri.* Heere's no
    body if it like your Holynesse.

A1–3, Bn, TB, Gg (*as* 1045.1), Rv,
    Ri
1041 beholding] beholden B3–6, Ox,
    Ch, R
1043 *Snatch it.*] *omit* B1–6
1045, 1057 you] ye B2–6
1050 such] this B4
1059 ¹it] *omit* B2–6
1064 same] *omit* C
1064 ghost.] ghost. | once again my
    Lord fall to. A1–3, Bn, TB, Gg,
    Rv, Ri
1064.1 *The Pope...himselfe.*] *omit* B1–6
1066 Crosse?] crosse? | Well, use...
    fair warning. A1–3, Bn, TB, Gg,
    Rv
1067.1 Faustus...*eare.*] *omit* B1–6
1070 ¹this] his B2–6, Dk–Bn (Ap), M
1070.1 the] *omit* B2–6
1077 away] *omit* A2–3, B1–6, Dk–Bn
    (Ap), M, Rv, Ri
1079 on] *omit* B1
1081 *strucke*] tooke A1–3, Bn, TB, Gg, Rv
1087 *Et...Amen.*] *omit* B1–6, Dk–R,
    C, K
1087.3.0 *For* Chorus 3 *that follows here in*
    A1–3, *see* 1137.2–1154.1

Scene x

1087.4–1137.1 *For the* A-text *and colla-
    tion of its variants, see* Appendix:
    A-text Scene vii
1089 same] *omit* B6

1090 at...heeles] hard at the heels Ch,
    Ox
1091 an] and B2–6
1093.1 *et seq.* Vintner] Vinter's Boy K

1106 your] *omit* B4
1112 I] Ah Dk–R, C
1114 *demogorgon*] *Demigorgon* B2–6, Dk–R, C
1116 You...Rule,] Gg, Ri *print* A-text
1118 have...now] am I hither brought Gg
1120 By Lady] By our lady Ox; By'r Lady Ch, R, C
1121 to take] take B5–6
1123 I, I] Aye, aye. I M

Chorus 3

1137.2–1154.1 *Enter* Chorus...*Exit.*] omit B1–6; *supplied from* A-text *positioned after* B-text 1087.3
1141 beare] bare Gg–Ri
1149 his] the A3
1152 mongst] amongst A2–3
1153 *Omit* A2–3

Scene xi

1154.2–1203.1 *Omit* A1–3, Bn, TB
1162 consort] comfort B3–4
1170 warlike] perfect B2–6, D, C, Bn (Ap)
1177 window's] window Ox
1179 ayle] ails Dk–R, C
1182 a] ten B2–6
1200 a] the B5–6
1203.2–1324.1 *A Senit. Enter* Martino ...*Exeunt.*] *For the* A-text *and collation of its variants, see* Appendix: A-Text, Scene viii
1217 These] Those B2–6
1228 a Conjurer] Conjurer B1
1237 trumpets] trumpets' Ch, R+
1238 this] the B2–6
1241 an] and B2–6
1251 demand] demands B4
1257.2 *dore*] *omit* B1
1257.6 *State*] *Seate* B3–4
1259 These] They B2–6
1260 ravished so] so ravished B1–6, Dk–M, K, Ri
1264 thoughts] thought B4
1266 whilest] while B2–6
1268 How] Now Dk–R, C, Bn (Ap)
1272 I gain'd] I had gain'd B3–4; I'd gain'd Dk–R, C
1274 thrusts] thrust Dk, Ox
1275 the window] window B1, Dk–M, Ri
1291 is] *omit* B1
1291 fie, fie] fie Ox, R, C, Bn (Ap)
1293 is...villany?] this is your villany. B4, D, C
1300 so] so't Ch
1302 As] And B2, 5–6; That B3–4, Ch
1310 has] hath B2–6, Ox
1314 hornes] horne B4
1315 sir] *omit* B4
1317 of] on Dk–R, C

Scene xii

1324.2–1430.4 *Omit* 1–3, Bn, TB
1325 sway] stay B4
1333, 1339 that] the B3–6
1337 my] thy B3–6, Dk, Ox
1342 an] *omit* B2–6
1346 boldly] bravely B3–6
1351 heart's] heart B1, TB (Ap), K
1352 that] the B2–6
1354 bide] hide Dk, R, C, Bn (Ap)
1357 Conjurer] hated Conjurer Gg
1359 the] that B3–6
1361.1 *the*] *his* B2–6
1369 now] *omit* B3–6
1373 heart] art Dk–D (*qy* heart), C, Bn (Ap), M, K, Gg
1375 here] there B3–6
1386 his] *omit* B1, K
1387 put] pull B3–6, D, Gg

1394 I, all] I call B 2–6, Dk, Ox, D¹, TB
(Ap); And all R, C
1395 you] ye B 2–6
1405 Thence] Then B 2–6

1411 Amongst] Among B 2–6
1419.2 *ambusht*] *ambush* B 5–6
1426 these] the B 4–6

Scene xiii

1430.5–1456.1 *Omit* A 1–3, Bn, TB
1430.7 *all having*] *having all* B 2–6
1440 we] they C, TB (Ap)
1444 all are] are all B 2–6

1447 shames] shame Ch
1451 then do] do then Ch
1454 this] these B 2–6, D, C, Bn (Ap),
M, Rv, Ri

Scene xiv

1456.2–1504.1 *For the* A-text *and its
collation of variants, see* Appendix:
A-text, Scene viii, *continued,* line
90ff.
1456.2 -Courser] -Courser, *and Mephistophilis* B 1–6
1464 horse] horses- Ox
1473 or] and Dk–R, C
1476–7 a made man] made a man Dk,

Ox, R
1480 my] thy Ch
1487 escape] scape B 4, C
1493 hath] has B 5–6
1494 has] hath B 5–6
1500 *et seq. Vanholt*] Anholt M, Ri
1500 you] *omit* B 6
1502 you] *omit* B 2–6
1502 provision] provisions C

Scene xv

1504.2–1557.1 *Omit* A 1–3, Bn, TB
1507 Guesse] guests B 2–6, Dk–R, C,
K, Ri
1509 thou] *omit* B 3–6
1512 have] has Dk–R, C
1515 you] you do C
1519 into] in M
1519 hall there] hall. There Gg
1519.1 *Exit.*] *omit* B 2–6
1520 now] *omit* B 2–6
1521 sir] sirs Dk–R, D (*qy*), C

1522, 1540 *Fauster*] *Faustus* B 2–6, Dk–
Bn (Ap)
1528 that] *omit* Dk–R, C
1529 my] *omit* B 2–6
1533 of] *omit* B 2–3
1537, 1542 sir] sirs C
1542 had had] had Ox, R, C, Bn (Ap)
1542 rare] *omit* B 1, Dk–TB, K
1543 rid] ride B 4, 6, Dk–R
1553 *Dick.*] *Clow.* B 1–6, Dk, Ch, R;
Robin. Ox, D, Bn (Ap)

Scene xvi

1557.2–1673.1 *Enter . . . Exeunt.*] *For the*
A-text *and collation of its variants,
see* Appendix: A-text, Scene ix
1561 delighted] delighteth B 2–6
1564 pleaseth] hath pleased B 3–6
1576 taste] take Dk–R
1577 come] came B 3–6
1580 ripe] *omit* B 3–6

1587.1–1673.1 *The . . . Exeunt.*] *Omit*
A 1–3, Bn, TB
1587.1 *Clownes*] *Clowne* B 1–6
1587.1 *bounce*] *bounceth* B 3–6
1606 for] to B 3–6
1608 good] goods B 1
1610 pardons] pardon B 4
1614 me] *omit* B 3–6

1626 I] Ah Dk–R, C
1626 spake] spoke B 4
1628 dost] dost thou B 2–6
1636 him] *omit* B 1, Bn (Ap), TB (Ap)
1641 pray] pray you B 3–6
1642 I] *omit* B 3–6
1647 such questions] such a question Dk–R, C

1653 thinkes] thinke B 6
1655 not I] I not B 4
1663 me] *omit* R, C
1663 with] of Gg
1664 Ha'] Have B 2–6
1667 guesse] guests B 2–6, Dk–R, C
1673 sport] sports B 2–6
1673 drives] drive B 5–6

Scene xvii

1673.2–1680 *Thunder . . . done. Exit.*] *For the A-text and collation of its variants, see* Appendix: A-text, Scene x
1675 goods] good B 4
1676 besides] beside B 2
1676–9 I wonder . . . like:] Gg A-text *but* And yet I wonder; for if . . . nigh *from B-text;* Rv (A-text)
1679 nere] never B 3–6, Ch
1680 done] ended B 2–6, Ch
1680.1 Mephostophilis] *omit* A 1–3
1685 so much] that A 1–3, Bn, TB, Gg, Rv
1686 whom . . . Majesty] *omit* M
1687 beholding] beholden Dk, Ch, Ox
1690 And] *omit* A 2–3
1690 And *Faustus . . . not*] It is not *Faustus* custome B 1–6, Dk–C, M, K, Ri
1691 requests] request A 2–3, B 1–6, Dk–C, M, K
1693 otherwaies] otherwise B 1–6, Dk–C, M, K, Ri
1693 or] and A 1–3, Bn, TB, Gg, Rv, Ri
1694 with] for Gg
1696.1–1696.2 Mephostophilis . . . *she*] *and Helen* A 1–3
1696.2 *stage.*] stage. | *2* Was this faire *Hellen,* whose admired worth | Made *Greece* with ten yeares warres afflict poore *Troy?* B 1–6, Dk–C, M, K, Ri (Ox–C, Ri: war)
1697 *2. Scholler.*] *3* B 1–6, Dk–C, M, K, Ri
1697 wit] will B 6
1697 worth] praise A 1–3, Bn, TB, M, Gg, Rv, Ri

1699–1701 *3. Scholler.* No . . . compare.] *omit* B 1–6, Dk–C, K
1702 Now] Since A 1–3, Bn, TB, Gg, Rv, Ri
1702 worke] workes A 1–3, Bn, TB, Rv, Ri
1703 And . . . excellence,] *omit* B 1–6, Dk–C, K
1704 Let us depart] Wee'l take our leaves B 1–6, Dk–C, M, K, Ri (Dk–R, C: leave)
1704 blessed sight] glorious deed A 1–3, Bn, TB, Rv
1706 wish I] I wish A 1–3, Dk–R, Bn, TB, Gg, K
1706.1–1723 *Enter . . . thy soule.*] *For the A-text and collation of its variants, see* Appendix, A-text, Scene x, *continuation, lines 34–45*
1720 envy of] of envie to B 3–6
1723 soule.] M *adds* A-text, Scene xi, *lines 38–45 (see* Appendix)
1725 Damned . . . die,] *omit* B 1–6, Dk–C, K
1726 claimes his] calls for A 1–3, Bn, TB
1727 almost] *omit* A 1–3, TB
1728 now] *omit* A 1–3, TB
1728 thee] the Bn
1729, 1734 Ah] O B 1–6, Dk–C, M–Ri (Ri: 1734 Ah)
1730 hover] hovers A 1–3, Bn, TB, Gg, Rv, Ri
1734 my sweete] *omit* B 1–6, Dk–M, K, Rv
1735 to] do C, Bn
1737 *Faustus . . . heart*] I goe sweete *Faustus,* but with heavy cheare A 1–3, Bn, TB

1738 enemy] ruine A1–3, Bn, TB
1738 haplesse] hopelesse A1–3, Bn, TB
1738 *Exit.*] omit A1–3
1739 where...now] wretch what hast thou done B1–6, Dk–C, K
1746 I...him,] omit A1–3, Bn, TB
1750 The] My A1–3, Bn, TB
1751 *Mephostophilis.*] omit B1–4
1751 *Faustus*] quickely A1–3, Bn, TB
1752 dangers] danger A1–3, Bn, TB
1753 *Faustus.*] omit B1–6
1753 crooked age] aged man B1–6, Dk–C, M–Ri
1755 torments] torment B1–6, K, Rv, Ri
1757 may] omit B2–4; can B5–6
1761 may] might A1–3, Bn, TB
1763 embraces] imbracings A1–3, Bn, TB, Ri
1763 cleare] cleane A1–3, D, Bn, TB, Gg

1764 Those] These A1–3, Bn, TB
1765 mine] my A2–3, B1–6, Dk–M; the Gg, K
1765 oath] vow B1–6, Dk–R
1766 This] *Faustus,* this A1–3, Bn, TB
1766 my *Faustus* shall] thou shalt A1–3, Bn, TB
1767.1 *Enter...Cupids.*] enter *Helen.* A1–3
1771 sucke] suckes A1–3, Bn, TB
1773 is] be A1–3, TB
1774.1 *Enter* Old Man.] omit B1–6, Dk–C, K
1775 *Paris*] *Pacis* A1
1781 evenings] evening A1–3: Dk, Ox, R–TB
1785 sky] sea Ch, Br MS
1786 azur'd] azure B1, Dk–R, C
1788–96 *Old Man.* Accursed...God.] omit B1–6, Dk–D
1795 laughs] leave C; laugh Bn

Scene xviii

1796.2–1819 *Thunder...love.*] omit A1–3, Bn, TB
1800 'Mong] Mongst B6
1807 in] with Gg
1809 ²his] omit B4
1819.1 *Enter the* Scholers.] *Enter Faustus with the Schollers.* A1–3
1820–1 *Faustus.* Gramercies...chang'd.] omit A1–3, Bn, TB
1820 Gramercies] Gramercy B2–6, Dk–C
1822 Ah] Oh B1–6, Dk–C, M, K
1823 *2. Scholler.*] *1. Scholler.* A1–3, Bn, TB
1825 must] I A1–3, Bn, TB
1826 sirs] omit A1–3, Bn, TB
1827–8 *1. Scholler.* O...melancholy?] *2. Sch:* what meanes *Faustus?* A1–3, Bn, TB
1829 He...with] Belike he is growne into some sicknesse, by A1–3, Bn, TB
1831–2 And...nothing.] to cure him, tis but a surffet, never feare man. A1–3, Bn, TB

1832 sir] omit B5–6
1833 deadly] a deadly B4–6, Dk–R, C
1835 Gods] omit B1–6, Dk–R, C, K
1836 mercy is] mercies are A1–3, Bn, TB
1838, 1846, 1850, 1856 Ah] O B1–6, Dk–C, K
1839 me] omit B1, K
1840 pant and quiver] pants and quivers A1–3, Bn, TB, Gg, Rv, Ri
1841 would] I would A3
1841 never] nere B2–6
1848 *2. Scholler.*] *3. Sch.* A1–3, Bn, TB, Rv
1850 would] could Ch
1853 'em...'em] them...them A1–3, Bn, TB, Rv
1855 Why,] omit A1–3, Bn, TB
1857 O] omit A1–3, Bn, TB, Gg, Rv, Ri
1859 the] omit A1–3, Bn, TB
1859 foure and twenty] 24. A1–3, TB; twenty-four Bn
1861 this is the time] the time wil come A1–3, Bn, TB
1865 me body] both body A1–3, Bn, TB
1866 'tis] 'ts; it is B3–6

1868 may] shal A1–3, Bn, TB
1868 save] *omit* A1–3
1872 there] *omit* A3, B1–6, Dk–C, M, K
1873 I] Ah Bn
1873 you] yee A1–3, Bn, TB, Rv
1875 may] *omit* C
1880–1925 *Mephostophilis.* I,...confusion. *Exit.*] *omit* A1–3, Bn, TB
1880 I] Ah, Dk, Ox, R, C
1891 must] most B1
1892 Oh] Ah Gg, Ri
1895 hels] hell B3–6
1904 set] sit B2–6, D, M, Gg, Rv; sat Ch, R, C, K, Ri
1908 are open] is ready B3–6
1912 boyle] broyle B1–2
1917 Were] Where B6
1917 and] that B4–6
1925 tumble] tremble Dk–R, C
1926 Ah] O B1–6, Dk–Bn, K
1932 be but] but be Gg
1938 to] unto A2–3
1938 my God] heaven B1–6, Dk–C, K
1939 See...firmament,] *omit* B1
1939 See see] See B2–6, Dk–C
1940 One drop...drop,] One drop of bloud will save me; B1–6, Dk–C, K
1940 ah] oh B1–6, Dk–C, K
1941 Rend] Ah rend A1–3, Bn, TB, M
1943–4 where...Browes] a threatning Arme, an angry Brow B1–6, Dk–C, K (B4–6, Ch: and angry)
1944 out] forth A2–3
1946 God] heaven B1–6, Dk–C, K

1947 No, no] No B1–6, Dk–C, K
1949 Gape earth] Earth gape A1–3, Bn, TB, M, Gg, Rv, Ri
1950 raign'd] raing'd B3
1951 hath] have B2–6
1953 entrals] entrance A3
1953 yon] your B3–6
1953 cloud] clouds D²
1954 you] ye R, C
1954–5 you...your] they...their D² (*qy*), Gg
1956 So that...but] But let my soule mount and B1–6, Dk–C, Bn, TB, K
1957 Ah] O B1–6, Dk–C, K
1958–9 O God...me,] O, if my soule must suffer for my sinne, B1–6, Dk–C, K
1962 last] the last B4–6
1963 No] O no A1–3, Bn, TB, M, Gg, Rv, Ri
1966, 1982 Ah] Oh B1–6, Dk–C, K
1966 *Metemsycosis*] *metem su cossis* A1; *metemsucossis* A2
1966 true] but true C
1968 Unto] Into Dk–C, K, Ri
1975 It] O it A1–3, Bn, TB, M, Rv, Ri
1976 hell.] hel: | *Thunder and lightning.* A1–3
1977 into] to Gg, Ri
1977 little] small B1–6, Dk–C, K
1979 My God, my God] O mercy heaven B1–6, Dk–C, K
1982.1 *Exeunt with him.*] *Exeunt.* B1; *omit* B2–6

Scene xix

1982.3–2001.1 *Enter...funerall. Exeunt.*] *omit* A1–3, Bn, TB
1982.3 *the*] *omit* B2–6
1988 heaven] heavens B2–6, Dk–C

1990 devils] Divill B2–6
1990 have] hath B3–6
1993 selfe] same B4–6, Ch; said Ox

THE FIRST BOOK OF LUCAN
TRANSLATED INTO ENGLISH

The earliest mention of Marlowe's translation of the First Book of Lucan's *Pharsalia* is an entry in the Stationers' Register for 28 September 1593 in which John Wolf entered for his copy 'a booke intituled Lucans *firste booke of the famous Civill warr betwixt* POMPEY *and* CESAR Englished by CHRISTOPHER MARLOW'. Immediately below is Wolf's entry for *Hero and Leander*.

The first and only known early edition is a quarto-form octavo collating A² B–D⁴ E² (E 2 wanting, blank?), 'Printed by P. Short, and are to be ſold by Walter | Burre at the Signe of the Flower de Luce in | Paules Churchyard, 1600.' To this is attached a dedication by the publisher Thomas Thorpe to Edward Blount in which he remarks, 'This spirit was sometime a familiar of your own, *Lucans first booke translated*; which (in regard of your old right in it) I have rais'd in the circle of your Patronage.' Blount was the publisher in 1598 of the earliest known edition of *Hero and Leander*; its dedication to Sir Thomas Walsingham may imply that Blount had some claim on Marlowe's literary remains, although perhaps the application is only to that poem. So far as is known Wolf did not publish the *Lucan*, and no record exists of his transfer of his rights in it (or in *Hero and Leander*) if in fact they proved to be valid. At any rate, Blount in some manner secured copy for both books, published *Hero and Leander* in 1598, and on 2 March 1598 transferred copy on it (without mention of *Lucan*) to Paul Linley. Linley published a 1598 edition of Marlowe's part of *Hero and Leander* that reprinted Blount's, but also added the first printing of Chapman's continuation. He then transferred his rights both to *Hero and Leander* and to *Lucan* to John Flasket on 26 June 1600, who in that year reprinted Linley's edition of *Hero and Leander* advertising *Lucan* on the title-page but not mentioning Chapman. It is generally assumed (although there are some difficulties in this hypothesis) that Flasket had originally intended to print only the Marlowe part of *Hero and Leander* and to eke it out with the translation of *Lucan*, but when the Chapman continuation became available to him he dropped the idea of adding *Lucan* and substituted Chapman instead. The manuscript of *Lucan* seems then without record to have found its way into Thomas Thorpe's hands, who put out the first edition in 1600, advertising it on the title as translated line for line. Walter Burr was apparently only the bookseller.

The early date at which the manuscript was secured, four months after Marlowe's death, and what seems to have been its parallel progress with the *Hero and Leander* manuscript to Blount,[1] suggests the strong possibility that *Lucan* was set from Marlowe's holograph. Some slight internal evidence may corroborate this hypothesis. In general, the numerous errors made by the compositors, including difficulty with the punctuation, indicate something less than a fair copy, and certain of the spellings are not inconsistent with what we know of Marlowe's practice in the brief fragment of *The Massacre at Paris*. More to the point, however, is the interesting anomaly in lines 440–1 where '(*Jove*)' set after '*Mercury*' seems to be a misplaced insert in line 440 to substitute for 'it' in line 441, perhaps as a result of Marlowe's change when the Lucan allusion to Taranis was clarified by his reading of Sulpitius's note identifying him with Jupiter. If this is so, it may be that what at first sight seems a sidenote to Leuca in line 585, reading '*or Luna*' may be a reproduction of a note in the manuscript that Marlowe made for himself.

The quarto, as it is convenient to call it (although properly a 4°-form 8° printed as a quarto but from cut double sheets), was set by one compositor from the start of its text on sig. B 1 through sig. D 2ʳ or line 528. Lines 529–56 on sig. D 2ᵛ cannot be assigned with certainty, but a second compositor took over on sig. D 3ʳ (just possibly on D 2ᵛ) with line 557 and set to the end of the text on sig. E 1ʳ. Compositor *X* set thirty-four occurrences of the city Rome invariably as 'Roome', and 'Roman' as noun or adjective was always in roman type in its eight appearances. The exclamation *oh* in its four occurrences is invariably 'O' and the four times 'rage' is found in its various forms it is always 'rage'. In contrast, in the few pages set by Compositor *Y*, starting on sig. D 3, the spelling is in-

---

[1] It must be noticed, however, that no external evidence exists to trace the manuscript that Wolf entered as in fact the manuscript that Blount possessed, but it is a natural inference that they were the same document.

variably 'Rome' (four times); the single occurrence of 'Romans' (line 673) is set in italic. The form 'O' appears three times on sig. $D4^{r-v}$, but twice on E1 as 'ô' (whether through conviction or type-shortage one cannot say). Most interestingly, because of the possibility that it may be a spelling copied from the manuscript (see Textual Note for line 642), 'rage' is set in its three occurrences as 'radge' although 'enrag'd' is found in line 659. It is an easy conjecture that Compositor Y was brought in to complete the setting of the last pages of the text while Compositor X transferred to setting the title and dedication so that these would be ready without delay to join with the text on sig. E1 to machine A^2 and E^2 together by twin half-sheet imposition. Since setting a title was work only for a superior compositor (see the Textual Introduction to *Edward II*), it is possible that Compositor Y was a less experienced workman than X, although his stint is too brief to make a proper evaluation of his abilities. However, the pattern of the running-titles as these reflect the imposition of the formes and the method of printing suggests that Compositor X was faster than Y in his composition. Sheets B and C were machined with separate skeleton-formes imposing the inner and outer formes, C making use of the two skeletons that had imposed sheet B. However, both inner and outer D were imposed from a single skeleton drawn from inner C, a shift of this nature usually signifying that the compositor had been unable to keep up with the swifter and more efficient method of printing reflected in the use of two skeleton-formes.[1]

Professor Millar MacLure, the editor of the Revels edition of the *Poems*, has determined (p. xxxv) that the edition of Lucan published in Frankfurt in 1551 is the text that seems to satisfy most of the doubtful readings in Marlowe. Lucan's text was closer in its early editions to the modern versions than was the text of Ovid's *Amores*.

Only three copies of the 1600 quarto are known to be preserved: British Museum (237.l.1), Bodleian Library (Mal. 133[10]), and a

[1] Not too much weight can be put on this evidence, but it should be remarked that the press-corrections in both formes of sheet D look more like a second than a first round of proofreading, and thus may possibly show more care devoted to the work of Compositor Y. Incidentally, the proofreading of inner B may well have been against copy, perhaps a slight corroboration of the hypothesis that the manuscript was not an easy one.

copy in the Folger Shakespeare Library. These have been collated and their press-variants found in the inner formes of sheets B and D have been recorded. Dyce mentions a press-variant he observed in line 101 on sig. B2ᵛ of the outer forme (*Aeʒean* for *Aegean*), but this is not present in any of the three collated copies. Modern editions collated and their substantive variants recorded in the Historical Collation are *Works*, ed. Robinson (1826), *Works*, ed. Dyce (1850), *Works*, ed. Dyce (1858), *Works*, ed. Cunningham (1870), *Works*, ed. Bullen (1885), *Works*, ed. Tucker Brooke (1910), *Poems*, ed. Martin (Methuen, 1931), and *Poems*, ed. MacLure (Revels, 1968).

TO HIS KIND, AND TRUE FRIEND:
EDWARD BLUNT

Blount: *I purpose to be blunt with you, and out of my dulnesse to encounter you with a* Dedication *in the memory of that pure Elementall wit* Christopher Marlow; *whose ghoast or* Genius *is to be seene walke the* Churchyard *in (at the least) three or foure sheets. Me thinks you should presently looke wilde now, and growe humorously frantique upon the tast of it. Well, least you should, let mee tell you. This spirit was sometime a familiar of your own,* Lucans first booke translated; *which (in regard of your old right in it) I have rais'd in the circle of your Patronage. But stay now* Edward (*if I mistake not*) *you are to accommodate your selfe with some fewe instructions, touching the* property of a Patron, *that you are not yet possest of; and to study them for your better grace as our Gallants do fashions. First you must be proud and thinke you have merit inough in you, though you are ne're so emptie; then when I bring you the booke take physicke, and keepe state, assigne me a time by your man to come againe, and afore the day be sure to have chang'd your lodging; in the meane time sleepe little, and sweat with the invention of some pittiful dry jest or two which you may happen to utter, with some litle (or not at al) marking of your friends when you have found a place for them to come in at: or if by chance something has dropt from you worth the taking up, weary all* that come to you with the often repetition of it; Censure scornefully inough, and somewhat like a travailer; commend nothing least you discredit your (that which you would seeme to have) judgement. These things if you can mould your selfe to them* Ned *I make no question but they will not become you. One speciall vertue in our Patrons of these daies I have promist my selfe you shall fit excellently, which is to give nothing; Yes, thy love I will challenge as my peculiar Object both in this, and (I hope) manie more succeeding offices: Farewell, I affect not the world should measure my thoughts to thee by a scale of this Nature: Leave to thinke good of me when I fall from thee.* 10 20 30

Thine in all rites of perfect friendship,
THOMAS THORPE.

THE FIRST BOOKE OF LUCAN

TRANSLATED INTO ENGLISH

Wars worse then civill on *Thessalian* playnes,
And outrage strangling law and people strong,
We sing, whose conquering swords their own breasts launcht,
Armies alied, the kingdoms league uprooted,
Th'affrighted worlds force bent on publique spoile,
Trumpets and drums, like deadly threatning other,
Eagles alike displaide, darts answering darts.
Romans, what madnes, what huge lust of warre
Hath made *Barbarians* drunke with *Latin* bloud?   10
Now *Babilon*, (proud through our spoile) should stoop,
While slaughtred *Crassus* ghost walks unreveng'd,
Will ye wadge war, for which you shall not triumph?
   Ay me, O what a world of land and sea,
Might they have won whom civil broiles have slaine,
As far as *Titan* springs where night dims heaven,
I to the *Torrid Zone* where midday burnes,
And where stiffe winter whom no spring resolves,
Fetters the *Euxin* sea, with chaines of yce:
Scythia and wilde *Armenia* had bin yoakt,   20
And they of *Nilus* mouth (if there live any.)
Roome, if thou take delight in impious warre,
First conquer all the earth, then turne thy force
Against thy selfe: as yet thou wants not foes.
   That now the walles of houses halfe rear'd totter,
That rampiers fallen down, huge heapes of stone
Lye in our townes, that houses are abandon'd,
And few live that behold their ancient seats;
Italy many yeares hath lyen until'd,
And choakt with thorns, that greedy earth wants hinds,   30
Fierce *Pirhus*, neither thou nor *Hanniball*

---

3 launcht] *i.e.*, lanced   21 *Roome*] *i.e.*, Rome

Art cause, no forraine foe could so afflict us,
  These plagues arise from wreake of civill power.
But if for *Nero* (then unborne) the fates
Would find no other meanes, (and gods not sleightly
Purchase immortal thrones; nor *Jove* joide heaven
Untill the cruel Giants war was done)
We plaine not heavens, but gladly beare these evils
For *Neros* sake: *Pharsalia* grone with slaughter;
And *Carthage* soules be glutted with our blouds;
At *Munda* let the dreadfull battailes joyne;   40
Adde, *Cæsar*, to these illes *Perusian* famine;
The *Mutin* toyles; the fleet at *Leuca* suncke;
And cruel field, nere burning *Aetna* fought:
  Yet *Room* is much bound to these civil armes,
  Which made thee Emperor; thee (seeing thou being old
  Must shine a star) shal heaven (whom thou lovest,)
  Receive with shouts; where thou wilt raigne as King,
  Or mount the sunnes flame bearing charriot,
  And with bright restles fire compasse the earth,
  Undaunted though her former guide be chang'd.   50
Nature, and every power shal give thee place,
  What God it please thee be, or where to sway:
But neither chuse the north t'erect thy seat;
Nor yet the adverse reking southerne pole,
Whence thou shouldst view thy *Roome* with squinting beams.
If any one part of vast heaven thou swayest,
The burdened axes with thy force will bend;
The midst is best; that place is pure, and bright,
There *Cæsar* may'st thou shine and no cloud dim thee;
Then men from war shal bide in league, and ease,   60
Peace through the world from *Janus Phane* shal flie,
And boult the brazen gates with barres of Iron.
Thou *Cæsar* at this instant art my God,
Thee if I invocate, I shall not need
To crave *Apolloes* ayde, or *Bacchus* helpe;
Thy power inspires the *Muʒe* that sings this war.

57 axes] *i.e.*, axis (*obs. by-form*)   59 There] Robinson; Their Q

The causes first I purpose to unfould
Of these garboiles, whence springs a long discourse,
And what made madding people shake off peace.
The fates are envious, high seats quickly perish,   70
Under great burdens fals are ever greevous;
Roome was so great it could not beare it selfe:
So when this worlds compounded union breakes,
Time ends and to old *Chaos* all things turne;
Confused stars shal meete, celestiall fire
Fleete on the flouds, the earth shoulder the sea,
Affording it no shoare, and *Phœbe's* waine
Chace *Phœbus* and inrag'd affect his place,
And strive to shine by day, and ful of strife
Disolve the engins of the broken world.   80
    All great things crush themselves, such end the gods
    Allot the height of honor, men so strong
    By land, and sea, no forreine force could ruine:
    O *Roome* thy selfe art cause of all these evils,
    Thy selfe thus shivered out to three mens shares:
    Dire league of partners in a kingdome last not.
O faintly joyn'd friends with ambition blind,
Why joine you force to share the world betwixt you?
While th'earth the sea, and ayre the earth sustaines;
While *Titan* strives against the worlds swift course;   90
Or *Cynthia* nights Queene waights upon the day;
Shall never faith be found in fellow kings.
Dominion cannot suffer partnership;
This need no forraine proofe, nor far fet story:
Roomes infant walles were steept in brothers bloud;
Nor then was land, or sea, to breed such hate,
A towne with one poore church set them at oddes.
    Cæsars, and *Pompeys* jarring love soone ended,
    T'was peace against their wils; betwixt them both
    Stept *Crassus* in: even as the slender *Isthmos*,   100
    Betwixt the *Aegean* and the *Ionian* sea,
    Keepes each from other, but being worne away

68 a long] Robinson; along Q

282

They both burst out, and each incounter other:
So when as *Crassus* wretched death who stayd them,
Had fild *Assirian Carras* wals with bloud,
His losse made way for Roman outrages.
Parthians y'afflict us more then ye suppose,
Being conquered, we are plaugde with civil war.
Swords share our Empire, fortune that made *Roome*
Governe the earth, the sea, the world it selfe,   110
Would not admit two Lords: for *Julia*
Snatcht hence by cruel fates with ominous howles,
Bare downe to hell her sonne, the pledge of peace,
And all bands of that death presaging aliance.
   Julia, had heaven given thee longer life
    Thou hadst restrainde thy headstrong husbands rage,
    Yea and thy father to, and swords thrown down,
    Made all shake hands as once the *Sabines* did;
    Thy death broake amity and trainde to war,
    These Captaines emulous of each others glory.   120
Thou feard'st (great *Pompey*) that late deeds would dim
Olde triumphs, and that *Cæsars* conquering *France*,
Would dash the wreath thou wearst for Pirats wracke.
Thee wars use stirde, and thoughts that alwaies scorn'd
A second place; *Pompey* could bide no equall,
Nor *Cæsar* no superior, which of both
Had justest cause unlawful tis to judge:
Each side had great partakers; *Cæsars* cause,
The gods abetted; *Cato* likt the other;
Both differ'd much, *Pompey* was strooke in yeares,   130
And by long rest forgot to manage armes,
And being popular sought by liberal gifts,
To gaine the light unstable commons love,
And joyed to heare his *Theaters* applause;
He liv'd secure boasting his former deeds,
And thought his name sufficient to uphold him,
Like to a tall oake in a fruitfull field,
Bearing old spoiles and conquerors monuments,
Who though his root be weake, and his owne waight

Keepe him within the ground, his armes al bare,   140
His body (not his boughs) send forth a shade;
Though every blast it nod, and seeme to fal,
When all the woods about stand bolt up-right,
Yet he alone is held in reverence.
    Cæsars renowne for war was lesse, he restles,
Shaming to strive but where he did subdue,
When yre, or hope provokt, heady, and bould,
At al times charging home, and making havock;
Urging his fortune, trusting in the gods,
Destroying what withstood his proud desires,   150
And glad when bloud, and ruine made him way:
So thunder which the wind teares from the cloudes,
With cracke of riven ayre and hideous sound,
Filling the world, leapes out and throwes forth fire,
Affrights poore fearefull men, and blasts their eyes
With overthwarting flames, and raging shoots
Alongst the ayre and nought resisting it
Falls, and returnes, and shivers where it lights.
Such humors stirde them up; but this warrs seed,
    Was even the same that wrack's all great dominions.   160
When fortune made us lords of all, wealth flowed,
And then we grew licencious and rude,
The soldiours pray, and rapine brought in ryot,
Men tooke delight in Jewels, houses, plate,
And scorn'd old sparing diet, and ware robes
Too light for women; Poverty (who hatcht
Roomes greatest wittes) was loath'd, and al the world
Ransackt for golde, which breeds the world decay;
And then large limits had their butting lands,
The ground which *Curius* and *Camillus* till'd,   170
Was stretcht unto the fields of hinds unknowne;
Againe, this people could not brooke calme peace,
Them freedome without war might not suffice,
Quarrels were rife, greedy desire stil poore
Did vild deeds, then t'was worth the price of bloud,

157 nought] Br MS, Tucker Brooke; not Q

And deem'd renowne to spoile their native towne,
Force mastered right, the strongest govern'd all.
Hence came it that th'edicts were overrul'd,
That lawes were broake, *Tribunes* with *Consuls* strove,
Sale made of offices, and peoples voices   180
Bought by themselves and solde, and every yeare
Frauds and corruption in the field of *Mars*;
Hence interest and devouring usury sprang,
Faiths breach, and hence came war to most men welcom.
Now *Cæsar* overpast the snowy *Alpes*,
His mind was troubled, and he aim'd at war,
And comming to the foord of *Rubicon*,
At night in dreadful vision fearefull *Roome*,
Mourning appear'd, whose hoary hayres were torne,
And on her Turret-bearing head disperst,   190
And armes all naked, who with broken sighes,
And staring, thus bespoke: what mean'st thou *Cæsar*?
Whether goes my standarde? Romans if ye be,
And beare true harts, stay heare: this spectacle
Stroake *Cæsars* hart with feare, his hayre stoode up,
And faintnes numm'd his steps there on the brincke:
He thus cride out: Thou thunderer that guardst
Roomes mighty walles built on *Tarpeian* rocke,
Ye gods of *Phrigia* and *Iúlus* line,
Quirinus rites and *Latian Jove* advanc'd   200
On *Alba* hill, ô *Vestall* flames, ô *Roome*,
My thoughts sole *goddes*, aide mine enterprise,
I hate thee not, to thee my conquests stoope,
Cæsar is thine, so please it thee, thy soldier;
He, he afflicts *Roome* that made me *Roomes* foe.
This said, he laying aside all lets of war,
Approcht the swelling streame with drum and ensigne,
Like to a Lyon of scortcht desart *Affricke*,
Who seeing hunters pauseth till fell wrath
And kingly rage increase, then having whiskt   210
His taile athwart his backe, and crest heav'd up,
With jawes wide open ghastly roaring out;

(Albeit the *Moores* light Javelin or his speare
Sticks in his side) yet runs upon the hunter.
    In summer time the purple *Rubicon*,
    Which issues from a small spring, is but shallow,
    And creepes along the vales, deviding just
    The bounds of *Italy*, from *Cisalpin Fraunce*;
    But now the winters wrath and wat'ry moone,
    Being three daies old inforst the floud to swell,   220
    And frozen *Alpes* thaw'd with resolving winds.
The thunder hov'd horse in a crooked line,
To scape the violence of the streame first waded,
Which being broke the foot had easie passage.
    As soone as *Cæsar* got unto the banke
    And bounds of Italy; here, here (saith he)
An end of peace; here end polluted lawes;
Hence leagues, and covenants; Fortune thee I follow,
Warre and the destinies shall trie my cause.
    This said, the restles generall through the darke   230
    (Swifter then bullets throwne from Spanish slinges,
    Or darts which *Parthians* backward shoot) marcht on
    And then (when *Lucifer* did shine alone,
    And some dim stars) he *Arriminum* enter'd:
    Day rose and viewde these tumultes of the war;
    Whether the gods, or blustring south were cause
    I know not, but the cloudy ayre did frown;
    The soldiours having won the market place,
    There spred the colours, with confused noise
    Of trumpets clange, shril cornets, whistling fifes;   240
    The people started; young men left their beds,
    And snatcht armes neer their houshold gods hung up
    Such as peace yeelds; wormeaten leatherne targets,
    Through which the wood peer'd, headles darts, olde swords
    With ugly teeth of blacke rust fouly scarr'd:
But seeing white Eagles, and *Roomes* flags wel known,
And lofty *Cæsar* in the thickest throng,
They shooke for feare, and cold benumm'd their lims,
    And muttering much, thus to themselves complain'd:

O wals unfortunate too neere to *France*,   250
Predestinate to ruine; all lands else
Have stable peace, here wars rage first begins,
We bide the first brunt, safer might we dwel,
Under the frosty beare, or parching East,
Wagons or tents, then in this frontire towne.
We first sustain'd the uproares of the *Gaules*,
And furious *Cymbrians* and of *Carthage* Moores,
As oft as *Roome* was sackt, here gan the spoile:
Thus sighing whispered they, and none durst speake
And shew their feare, or griefe: but as the fields   260
When birds are silent thorough winters rage;
Or sea far from the land, so all were whist.
    Now light had quite dissolv'd the mysty night,
    And *Cæsars* mind unsetled musing stood;
    But gods and fortune prickt him to this war,
    Infringing all excuse of modest shame,
    And laboring to approve his quarrell good.
The angry Senate urging *Grachus* deeds,
From doubtfull *Roome* wrongly expel'd the *Tribunes*,
That crost them; both which now approacht the camp,   270
And with them *Curio*, sometime *Tribune* too,
One that was feed for *Cæsar*, and whose tongue
Could tune the people to the Nobles mind:
Cæsar (said he) while eloquence prevail'd,
And I might pleade, and draw the Commons minds
To favour thee, against the Senats will,
Five yeeres I lengthned thy commaund in *France*:
But law being put to silence by the wars,
We from our houses driven, most willingly
Suffered exile: let thy sword bring us home.   280
Now while their part is weake, and feares, march hence,
„Where men are ready, lingering ever hurts:
In ten yeares wonst thou *France*; *Roome* may be won
With farre lesse toile, and yet the honors more;
Few battailes fought with prosperous successe

263 night] Robinson; might Q

May bring her downe, and with her all the world;
Nor shalt thou triumph when thou comst to *Roome*;
Nor capitall be adorn'd with sacred bayes:
Envy denies all, with thy bloud must thou   290
Abie thy conquest past: the sonne decrees
To expel the father; share the world thou canst not;
Injoy it all thou maiest: thus *Curio* spake,
And therewith *Cæsar* prone enough to warre,
Was so incenst as are *Eleius* steedes
With clamors: who though lockt and chaind in stalls,
Souse downe the wals, and make a passage forth:
Straight summon'd he his severall companies
Unto the standard: his grave looke appeasd
The wrastling tumult, and right hand made silence:
And thus he spake: you that with me have borne   300
A thousand brunts, and tride me ful ten yeeres,
See how they quit our bloud shed in the North;
Our friends death; and our wounds; our wintering
Under the *Alpes*; *Roome* rageth now in armes
As if the *Carthage Hannibal* were neere;
Cornets of horse are mustered for the field;
Woods turn'd to ships; both land and sea against us:
Had forraine wars ill thriv'd; or wrathful *France*
Pursu'd us hither, how were we bestead
When comming conqueror, *Roome* afflicts me thus?   310
Let come their leader whom long peace hath quail'd;
Raw soldiours lately prest; and troupes of gownes;
Brabbling *Marcellus*; *Cato* whom fooles reverence;
Must *Pompeis* followers with strangers ayde,
(Whom from his youth he bribde) needs make him king?
And shal he triumph long before his time,
And having once got head still shal he raigne?
What should I talke of mens corne reapt by force,
And by him kept of purpose for a dearth?
Who sees not warre sit by the quivering Judge;   320

302 bloud shed] Br MS, Rv;ᵣbloudshed   *311 leader] Dyce; leaders Q
Q

288

And sentence given in rings of naked swords,
And lawes assailde, and arm'd men in the *Senate?*
Twas his troupe hem'd in *Milo* being accusde;
And now least age might waine his state, he casts
For civill warre, wherein through use he's known
To exceed his maister, that arch-traitor *Sylla.*

   As brood of barbarous *Tygars* having lapt
   The bloud of many a heard, whilst with their dams
   They kennel'd in *Hircania,* evermore
   Wil rage and pray: so *Pompey* thou having lickt   330
   Warme goare from *Syllas* sword art yet athirst,
   Jawes flesht with bloud continue murderous.
Speake, when shall this thy long usurpt power end?
What end of mischiefe? *Sylla* teaching thee,
At last learne wretch to leave thy monarchy;
What, now *Scicillian* Pirats are supprest,
And jaded king of *Pontus* poisoned slaine,
Must *Pompey* as his last foe plume on me,
Because at his commaund I wound not up
My conquering Eagles? say I merit nought,   340
Yet for long service done, reward these men,
And so they triumph, be't with whom ye wil.
Whether now shal these olde bloudles soules repaire?
What seates for their deserts? what store of ground
For servitors to till? what *Colonies*
To rest their bones? say *Pompey,* are these worse
Then Pirats of *Sycillia?* they had houses:
Spread, spread these flags that ten years space have conquer'd,
Lets use our tried force, they that now thwart right
In wars wil yeeld to wrong: the gods are with us,   350
Neither spoile, nor kingdom seeke we by these armes,
But *Roome* at thraldoms feet to rid from tyrants.

   This spoke none answer'd, but a murmuring buz
   Th'unstable people made: their houshold gods

327 As] Dyce; A Q   337 jaded‸] Robinson; *Jaded,* Q
332 Jawes‸ flesht‸] Dyce; Jawes, flesh,   348 Spread] Robinson; Spead Q
   Q

And love to *Room* (thogh slaughter steeld their harts
And minds were prone) restrain'd them; but wars love
And *Cæsars* awe dasht all: then *Lælius*
The chiefe *Centurion* crown'd with Oaken leaves,
For saving of a Romaine Citizen,
Stept forth, and cryde: chiefe leader of *Rooms* force,   360
So be I may be bold to speake a truth,
We grieve at this thy patience and delay:
What doubtst thou us? even nowe when youthfull bloud
Pricks forth our lively bodies, and strong armes
Can mainly throw the dart; wilt thou indure
These purple groomes? that *Senates* tyranny?
Is conquest got by civill war so hainous?
Well, leade us then to *Syrtes* desart shoare;
Or *Scythia*; or hot *Libiaes* thirsty sands.
This band that all behind us might be quail'd,   370
Hath with thee past the swelling Ocean;
And swept the foming brest of *Artick Rhene*.
Love over-rules my will, I must obay thee,
Cæsar; he whom I heare thy trumpets charge
I hould no Romaine; by these ten blest ensignes
And all thy several triumphs, shouldst thou bid me
Intombe my sword within my brothers bowels;
Or fathers throate; or womens groning wombe;
This hand (albeit unwilling) should performe it;
Or rob the gods; or sacred temples fire;   380
These troupes should soone pull down the church of *Jove*.
If to incampe on *Thuscan Tybers* streames,
Ile bouldly quarter out the fields of *Rome*;
What wals thou wilt be leaveld with the ground,
These hands shall thrust the ram, and make them flie,
Albeit the Citty thou wouldst have so ra'st
Be *Roome* it selfe. Here every band applauded,
And with their hands held up, all joyntly cryde
  They'ill follow where he please: the showts rent heaven,
  As when against pine bearing *Ossa's* rocks,   390

---

*370 band] Dyce; hand Q   372 *Artick*] Robinson; *Articks* Q

Beates *Thracian Boreas*; or when trees bowe down,
  And rustling swing up as the wind fets breath.
When *Cæsar* saw his army proane to war,
And fates so bent, least sloth and long delay
Might crosse him, he withdrew his troupes from *France*,
And in all quarters musters men for *Roome*.
  They by *Lemannus* nooke forsooke their tents;
  They whom the *Lingones* foild with painted speares,
  Under the rockes by crooked *Vogesus*;
  And many came from shallow *Isara*,   400
  Who running long, fals in a greater floud,
  And ere he sees the sea looseth his name;
  The yellow *Ruthens* left their garrisons;
  Mild *Atax* glad it beares not Roman boats;
  And frontier *Varus* that the campe is farre,
  Sent aide; so did *Alcides* port, whose seas
  Eate hollow rocks, and where the north-west wind
  Nor *Zephir* rules not, but the north alone,
  Turmoiles the coast, and enterance forbids;
  And others came from that uncertaine shore,   410
  Which is nor sea, nor land, but oft times both,
  And changeth as the Ocean ebbes and flowes:
  Whether the sea roul'd alwaies from that point,
  Whence the wind blowes stil forced to and fro;
  Or that the wandring maine follow the moone;
  Or flaming *Titan* (feeding on the deepe)
  Puls them aloft, and makes the surge kisse heaven,
  Philosophers looke you, for unto me
  Thou cause, what ere thou be whom God assignes
  This great effect, art hid. They came that dwell   420
  By *Nemes* fields, and bankes of *Satirus*,
  Where *Tarbels* winding shoares imbrace the sea,
  The *Santons* that rejoyce in *Cæsars* love,
  Those of *Bituriges* and light *Axon* pikes;
  And they of *Rhene* and *Leuca*, cunning darters,
  And *Sequana* that well could manage steeds;

*391 bowe] D¹ (*qy*), D²; bowde Q   404 boats] Robinson; bloats Q

The *Belgians* apt to governe *Brittish* cars;
Th'*Averni* too, which bouldly faine themselves
The Romanes brethren, sprung of *Ilian* race;
The stubborne *Nervians* staind with *Cottas* bloud;   430
And *Vangions* who like those of *Sarmata*,
Were open slops: and fierce *Batavians*,
Whome trumpets clang incites, and those that dwel
By *Cyngas* streame, and where swift *Rhodanus*
Drives *Araris* to sea; They neere the hils,
Under whose hoary rocks *Gebenna* hangs;
And *Trevier*; thou being glad that wars are past thee;
And you late shorne *Ligurians*, who were wont
In large spread heire to exceed the rest of *France*;
And where to *Hesus*, and fell *Mercury*   440
They offer humane flesh, and where *Jove* seemes
Bloudy like *Dian*, whom the *Scythians* serve;
And you French *Bardi*, whose immortal pens
Renowne the valiant soules slaine in your wars,
Sit safe at home and chaunt sweet *Poesie*.
And *Druides* you now in peace renew
Your barbarous customes, and sinister rites,
In unfeld woods, and sacred groves you dwell,
And only gods and heavenly powers you know,
Or only know you nothing. For you hold   450
That soules passe not to silent *Erebus*
Or *Plutoes* bloodles kingdom, but else where
Resume a body: so (if truth you sing)
Death brings long life. Doubtles these northren men
Whom death the greatest of all feares affright not,
Are blest by such sweet error, this makes them
Run on the swords point and desire to die,
And shame to spare life which being lost is wonne.
You likewise that repulst the *Caicke* foe,
March towards *Roome*; and you fierce men of *Rhene*   460

432 Were] *i.e.*, wear   440 *Mercury*] Robinson; *Mercury*
439 heire] *i.e.*, hair   (Jove) Q
                              441 *Jove*] Dyce; it Q

Leaving your countrey open to the spoile.
These being come, their huge power made him bould
To mannage greater deeds; the bordering townes
He garrison'd; and *Italy* he fild with soldiours.
    Vaine fame increast true feare, and did invade
The peoples minds, and laide before their eies
Slaughter to come, and swiftly bringing newes
Of present war, made many lies and tales.
One sweares his troupes of daring horsemen fought
Upon *Mevanias* plaine, where Buls are graz'd;   470
Other that *Cæsars* barbarous bands were spread
Along *Nar* floud that into *Tiber* fals,
And that his owne ten ensignes, and the rest
Marcht not intirely, and yet hide the ground,
And that he's much chang'd, looking wild and big,
And far more barbarous then the French (his vassals)
And that he lags behind with them of purpose,
Borne twixt the *Alpes* and *Rhene*, which he hath brought
From out their Northren parts, and that *Roome*
He looking on by these men should be sackt.   480
Thus in his fright did each man strengthen Fame,
And without ground, fear'd, what themselves had faind:
Nor were the Commons only strooke to heart
With this vaine terror; but the Court, the Senate;
The fathers selves leapt from their seats; and flying
Left hateful warre decreed to both the *Consuls*.
Then with their feare, and danger al distract,
Their sway of fleight carries the heady rout
That in chain'd troupes breake forth at every port;
You would have thought their houses had bin fierd   490
Or dropping-ripe, ready to fall with Ruine,
So rusht the inconsiderate multitude
Thorough the Citty hurried headlong on,
As if, the only hope (that did remaine
To their afflictions) were t'abandon *Roome*.
Looke how when stormy *Auster* from the breach
Of *Libian Syrtes* roules a monstrous wave,

Which makes the maine saile fal with hideous sound;
The Pilot from the helme leapes in the sea;
And Marriners, albeit the keele be sound,   500
Shipwracke themselves: even so the Citty left,
All rise in armes; nor could the bed-rid parents
Keep back their sons, or womens teares their husbands;
They stai'd not either to pray or sacrifice,
Their houshould gods restrain them not, none lingered,
As loath to leave *Roome* whom they held so deere,
Th'irrevocable people flie in troupes.
    O gods that easie grant men great estates,
    But hardly grace to keepe them: *Roome* that flowes
    With Citizens and Captives, and would hould   510
    The world (were it together) is by cowards
    Left as a pray now *Cæsar* doth approach:
    When Romans are besieg'd by forraine foes,
    With slender trench they escape night stratagems,
    And suddaine rampire raisde of turfe snatcht up
    Would make them sleepe securely in their tents.
    Thou *Roome* at name of warre runst from thy selfe,
    And wilt not trust thy Citty walls one night:
    Wel might these feare, when *Pompey* fear'd and fled.
    Now evermore least some one hope might ease   520
    The Commons jangling minds, apparant signes arose,
    Strange sights appear'd, the angry threatning gods
    Fill'd both the earth and seas with prodegies;
    Great store of strange and unknown stars were seene
    Wandering about the North, and rings of fire
    Flie in the ayre, and dreadfull bearded stars,
    And Commets that presage the fal of kingdoms.
The flattering skie gliter'd in often flames,
And sundry fiery meteors blaz'd in heaven;
Now spearlike, long; now like a spreading torch: 530
Lightning in silence, stole forth without clouds,
And from the northren climat snatching fier
Blasted the Capitoll: The lesser stars

*510 Captives] Dyce; Captaines Q

Which wont to run their course through empty night
At noone day mustered; *Phœbe* having fild
Her meeting hornes to match her brothers light,
Strooke with th'earths suddaine shadow waxed pale,
Titan himselfe throand in the midst of heaven,
His burning chariot plung'd in sable cloudes,
And whelm'd the world in darknesse, making men   540
Dispaire of day; as did *Thiestes* towne
(*Mycenæ*), *Phœbus* flying through the East:
Fierce *Mulciber* unbarred *Ætna's* gate,
Which flamed not on high; but headlong pitcht
Her burning head on bending *Hespery*.
Cole-blacke *Charibdis* whirl'd a sea of bloud;
Fierce Mastives hould; the vestall fires went out,
The flame in *Alba* consecrate to *Jove*,
Parted in twaine, and with a double point
Rose like the *Theban* brothers funerall fire;   550
The earth went off hir hinges; And the *Alpes*
Shooke the old snow from off their trembling laps.
The Ocean swell'd, as high as Spanish *Calpe*,
Or *Atlas* head; their saints and houshold gods
Sweate teares to shew the travailes of their citty.
Crownes fell from holy statues, ominous birds
Defil'd the day, and wilde beastes were seene,
Leaving the woods, lodge in the streetes of *Rome*.
Cattell were seene that muttered humane speech:
Prodigious birthes with more and ugly jointes   560
Then nature gives, whose sight appauls the mother,
And dismall Prophesies were spread abroad:
And they whom fierce *Bellonaes* fury moves
To wound their armes, sing vengeance, *Sibils* priests,
Curling their bloudy lockes, howle dreadfull things,
Soules quiet and appeas'd sigh'd from their graves,
Clashing of armes was heard, in untrod woods
Shrill voices schright, and ghoasts incounter men.

*557 and wilde beastes] *stet* Q   566 sigh'd] sight Q
564 *Sibils*] *i.e.,* Cybel's

295

Those that inhabited the suburbe fieldes
Fled, fowle *Erinnis* stalkt about the wals,   570
Shaking her snakie haire and crooked pine
With flaming toppe, much like that hellish fiend
Which made the sterne *Lycurgus* wound his thigh,
Or fierce *Agave* mad; or like *Megæra*
That scar'd *Alcides*, when by *Junoes* taske
He had before lookt *Pluto* in the face.
Trumpets were heard to sound; and with what noise
An armed battaile joines, such and more strange
Blacke night brought forth in secret: *Sylla's* ghost
Was seene to walke, singing sad Oracles,   580
And *Marius* head above cold *Tav'ron* peering
(His grave broke open) did affright the Boores.
To these ostents (as their old custome was)
They call th'*Etrurian Augures*, amongst whom
The gravest, *Aruns*, dwelt in forsaken *Leuca,   * or Luna
Well skild in *Pyromancy*; one that knew
The hearts of beasts, and flight of wandring foules;
First he commands such monsters *Nature* hatcht
Against her kind (the barren Mules loth'd issue)
To be cut forth and cast in dismall fiers: 590
Then, that the trembling Citizens should walke
About the City; then the sacred priests
That with divine lustration purg'd the wals,
And went the round, in, and without the towne.
Next, an inferiour troupe, in tuckt up vestures,
After the *Gabine* manner: then the Nunnes
And their vaild Matron, who alone might view
Minervas statue; then, they that keepe, and read
Sybillas secret works, and wash their saint
In *Almo's* floud: Next learned *Augures* follow;   600
Apolloes southsayers; and *Joves* feasting priests;
The skipping *Salii* with shields like wedges;
And *Flamins* last, with networke wollen vailes.
While these thus in and out had circled *Roome*,

599 wash] Dyce; washt Q

Looke what the lightning blasted, *Aruns* takes
And it inters with murmurs dolorous,
And cals the place *Bidentall*: on the Altar
He laies a ne're-yoakt Bull, and powers downe wine,
Then crams salt levin on his crooked knife;
The beast long struggled, as being like to prove   610
An aukward sacrifice, but by the hornes
The quick priest pull'd him on his knees and slew him:
No vaine sprung out but from the yawning gash,
In steed of red bloud wallowed venemous gore.
These direfull signes made *Aruns* stand amaz'd,
And searching farther for the gods displeasure,
The very cullor scard him; a dead blacknesse
Ranne through the bloud, that turn'd it all to gelly,
And stain'd the bowels with darke lothsome spots:
The liver swell'd with filth, and every vaine   620
Did threaten horror from the host of *Cæsar*;
A small thin skinne contain'd the vital parts,
The heart stird not, and from the gaping liver
Squis'd matter; through the cal, the intralls pearde,
And which (aie me) ever pretendeth ill,
At that bunch where the liver is, appear'd
A knob of flesh, whereof one halfe did looke
Dead, and discoulour'd; th'other leane and thinne.
By these he seeing what myschiefes must ensue,
Cride out, O gods! I tremble to unfould   630
What you intend, great *Jove* is now displeas'd,
And in the brest of this slaine Bull are crept,
Th'infernall powers. My feare transcends my words,
Yet more will happen then I can unfold;
Turne all to good, be *Augury* vaine, and *Tages*
Th'arts master falce. Thus in ambiguous tearmes,
Involving all, did *Aruns* darkly sing.
But *Figulus* more seene in heavenly mysteries,
Whose like *Aegiptian Memphis* never had

*624 matter;...cal_∧] Methuen; ~ _∧ ... ~ ; Q

297

For skill in stars, and tune-full planeting,   640
   In this sort spake. The worlds swift course is lawlesse
   And casuall; all the starres at randome radge:
   Or if *Fate* rule them, *Rome* thy Cittizens
   Are neere some plague: what mischiefe shall insue?
   Shall townes be swallowed? shall the thickned aire,
   Become intemperate? shall the earth be barraine?
   Shall water be conjeal'd and turn'd to ice?
   O Gods what death prepare ye? with what plague
   Meane ye to radge? the death of many men
   Meetes in one period. If cold noysome *Saturne*   650
   Were now exalted, and with blew beames shinde,
   Then *Gaynimede* would renew *Deucalions* flood,
   And in the fleeting sea the earth be drencht.
   O *Phœbus* shouldst thou with thy rayes now sing
   The fell *Nemean* beast, th'earth would be fired,
   And heaven tormented with thy chafing heate,
   But thy fiers hurt not; *Mars*, 'tis thou enflam'st
   The threatning Scorpion with the burning taile
   And fier'st his cleyes. Why art thou thus enrag'd?
   Kind *Jupiter* hath low declin'd himselfe;   660
   Venus is faint; swift *Hermes* retrograde;
   Mars onely rules the heaven: why doe the Planets
   Alter their course; and vainly dim their vertue?
   Sword-girt *Orions* side glisters too bright.
   Wars radge draws neare; and to the swords strong hand,
   Let all Lawes yeeld, sinne beare the name of vertue,
   Many a yeare these furious broiles let last,
   Why should we wish the gods should ever end them?
   War onely gives us peace, ô *Rome* continue
   The course of mischiefe, and stretch out the date   670
   Of slaughter; onely civill broiles make peace.
These sad presages were enough to scarre
The quivering Romans, but worse things affright them.
As *Mænas* full of wine on *Pindus* raves,

*642 radge] *stet* Q   667 furious] Robinson; firious Q
  654 sing] *i.e.,* singe   672 scarre] *i.e.,* scare

So runnes a Matron through th'amazed streetes,
Disclosing *Phœbus* furie in this sort:
Pean whither am I halde? where shall I fall,
Thus borne aloft? I see *Pangeus* hill,
With hoarie toppe, and under *Hemus* mount
Philippi plaines; *Phœbus* what radge is this? 680
Why grapples *Rome*, and makes war, having no foes?
Whither turne I now? thou lead'st me toward th'east,
Where *Nile* augmenteth the *Pelusian* sea:
This headlesse trunke that lies on *Nylus* sande
I know: now throughout the aire I flie,
To doubtfull *Sirtes* and drie *Affricke*, where
A fury leades the *Emathian* bandes, from thence
To the pine bearing hils, hence to the mounts
Pirene, and so backe to *Rome* againe.
Se impious warre defiles the Senat house, 690
New factions rise; now through the world againe
I goe; ô *Phœbus* shew me *Neptunes* shore,
And other Regions, I have seene *Philippi*:
This said, being tir'd with fury she sunke downe.

677–8 fall,...aloft?] Dyce; ~ ?... ~ , Q

FINIS.

311 leader]   Although the English context suggests that Q 'leaders' is right, it appears to be a compositorial misunderstanding. The Latin is *dux* and the reference is to Pompey. Cf. line 131.

370 band]   Q 'hand' makes nonsense here. The Latin is *manus* but as the Methuen editor points out this Latin word can be used in the sense of 'band'. A compositorial error (or foul case) is by no means certain, therefore, and we may have a mistranslation.

391 bowe   Q 'bowde' here makes some sense but the structure calls for 'bowe' as parallel to 'swing up'. Editors retaining 'bowde' usually make 'bow'd down and rustling' a parenthesis between the subject 'trees' and its verb 'swing up' but the logic of this structure is uncertain; the rustling must be associated with the springing up when the wind dies down to fetch its breath. The Latin reads, *curvato robore pressae | Fit sonus aut rursus redeuntis in aethera silvae.*

510 Captives]   Latin *victisque* justifies this Dyce emendation of Q 'Captaines', which is a not impossible misreading of 'Captiues', aided, perhaps, by what at first seems the obvious sense of military and civil men. But the number of captives attests to Rome's military prowess.

557 and wilde beastes]   Cunningham's conjecture 'at night wild beasts' is intended to mend the metre by inserting Lucan's *sub nocte* not otherwise accounted for in the line. However, the metre may not be deficient. If the caesural pause were to take the place of the unaccented syllable of the third iamb, the line would scan. An error here is not easy to account for in the necessary terms.

624 matter;...cal$_\Lambda$]   In the Methuen edition Martin justifies the emendation from Q 'Squised matter through the cal; the intrails pearde,' by the Latin *Cor iacet, et saniem per hiantes viscera rimas | Emittunt, produntque suas omenta latebras* – the cauls, or membranes, showed their hiding-places. Martin also points out that 'peard' is more likely the obsolete aphetic form of 'appeared' than the 'peered' or *looked* to which it is often emended.

642 radge]   Dyce's emendation 'range' is very tempting for Latin *et incerto discurrunt sidera motu*, in which there is no suggestion of 'to move or rush violently' which is the nearest that *O.E.D.* vb.4 comes. However, it is possible that Marlowe is touching up the milder Lucan description. The relation of lines 641–2 to 660–3 is not altogether certain; that is, 660–3 might be a more detailed description of the general situation mentioned in 641–2 – in which case it is Mars alone that is raging and the other planets have altered their course to avoid Mars and dimmed their virtues. If this is true, Dyce's 'range' is almost inevitable. But the lawlessness described in 641–2 in fact seems to have no very intimate relation to the specific detail of the particular planet Mars that is in power at the moment in 660–3 except as the withdrawal of the normal modifying influences gives Mars a control over

earthly matters it would not otherwise have. If the two descriptions are to be taken as mainly discrete, 'radge' is possible in line 642. From the point of view of meaning alone, then, 'range' is superior but 'radge' is possible. Other evidence can be brought to bear with a shade more certainty, perhaps, in attacking the crux. The spelling 'radge' is an unusual one, but is repeated in lines 649 and 665. It is clear, then, that in line 642 the word is not a misprint for 'range' but that the compositor thought he was setting the word 'rage'. The question that is posed is whether or not 'radge' is a copy spelling. If it is what the compositor was reproducing from the manuscript in 642, as in 649 and 665, then the Q reading in 642 must be retained as authoritative. If on the other hand it is a compositorial spelling, emendation could be admitted, if necessary, for if the compositor for some reason mistook 'range' and thought it was 'rage', he would spell the word in his own way as 'radge'. Line 642 comes on sig. D4^{v} in the stint of Compositor Y, who took over from X on sig. D3 (see Textual Introduction). Compositor X spells 'rage' exclusively: 'rage' in lines 252 and 261, 'raging' in 156, and 'rageth' in 304. On the other hand, Compositor Y sets the three noticed spellings 'radge' and once 'enrag'd' in line 659. Whether the latter is variant because of its form is not to be determined, nor whether it is a copy or a compositorial spelling. One might argue that such an exceptional spelling is more likely to come from copy than to be a compositorial characteristic (*O.E.D.* cites no examples of *radge*), but that is scarcely evidence. However, one small piece of evidence exists. On sig. B1, in line 12 Compositor X sets 'wadge' (for *wage*). Since in many respects he is a relatively consistent speller, and in the five examples present he had set 'rage' invariably, something may be said for 'wadge' as a copy spelling. If this is so, it may be taken in connection with the single example of 'enraged' in Y's work to suggest that in the three 'radge' spellings Y was in fact following copy, not his own normal habit for this word. Such as it is, then, the evidence may lean slightly towards an acceptance of 'radge' as what Marlowe wrote in line 642, providing the manuscript was holograph (as seems quite possible) and thus that 'radge' was not a scribal blunder as well as a scribal spelling.

PRESS-VARIANTS IN (4°-FORM)
8° (1600)

[Copies collated: BM (237.l.1), Bodl (Bodleian Mal. 133[10], DFo (Folger Shakespeare Library).]

SHEET B (*inner forme*)

Corrected: BM, DFo
Uncorrected: Bodl

Sig. B1v
  24 reaer'd] reafer'd
  44 bound] bouud
  48 flame] plume
Sig. B3v
  160 dominions.] dominion
Sig. B4
  167 wittes)] wittes

SHEET D (*inner forme*)

Corrected: BM, Bodl
Uncorrected: DFo

Sig. D2
  516 in] iu

SHEET D (*outer forme*)

Corrected: BM, Bodl
Uncorrected: DFo

Sig. D3
  562 Prophesies] Prhphesies

EMENDATIONS OF ACCIDENTALS

Dedication

3 Christopher] Chr.　　　　32 Thomas] Thom.
20 *up*,] ~ ∧

Text

3 launcht,] ~ ∧ |
4 uprooted,] ~ ∧
5 force∧] ~ :
10 *Babilon*] Babilon
10 stoop,] ~ ∧ |
11 unreveng'd,] ~ .
18 *Euxin*] Euxin
21 *Roome*,] Roome∧
23 foes.] ~ ,
24 rear'd] reaer'd Q (c); reafer'd Q (u)
29 hinds,] ~ ∧
36 done∧)] ~ .)
41 Adde, *Cæsar*,] ~ ∧ ~ ;
44 *Room*] Room
45 Emperor;] ~ ,
50 chang'd.] ~ ,
55 *et seq. Roome*] Roome
55 beames.] ~ ∧ |
56 swayest,] Q *point uncertain*
65 *Apolloes*] *Appolles*
77 waine∧] ~ ,
81 gods∧] ~ ,
82 strong∧] ~ .
85 shares:] ~ ,
89 earth∧...ayre∧] ~ ,...~,
99 wils;] ~ ,
100 in:] ~ ,
108 war.] ~ ,
110 selfe,] ~ ∧
113 sonne,] ~ ∧
117 down,] ~ .
121 *Pompey*)...dim∧] ~ ∧...~)
122 *et seq. France*] France (except *France* line 218)
123 wracke.] ~ ∧
149 gods,] ~ ∧
168 Ransackt] Ransanckt

177 all.] ~ ,
180 voices∧] ~ ,
190 Turret-bearing] ~ , ~
192 bespoke:] ~ ,
200 advanc'd∧] ~ ,
216 spring,] ~ ∧
217 vales,] ~ ∧
232 shoot)] ~ (
241 beds,] ~ ;
249 complain'd: ~
255 towne.] ~ ,
257 Moores] moores
271 *Curio*,] ~ ;
276 will,] ~ .
278 wars,] ~ ;
281 hence,] ~ ∧
300 spake:] ~ ;
303 our wintering] onr wintering
310 conqueror,] ~ ∧
319 dearth?] ~ ,
322 *Senate*?] ~ ;
329 *Hircania*,] ~ ∧
353 answer'd,] ~ ∧
357 *Lælius*] *Lalius*
360 cryde:] ~ ,
361–2 truth,...delay:] ~ :...~ ,
372 *Rhene*.] ~ ,
374 *Cæsar*;] ~ ,
380 fire;] ~ :
381 *Jove*.] ~ ,
382 streames;] ~ ;
389 please:] ~ ,
407 wind∧] ~ ;
415 moone;] ~ ?
416 deepe)] ~ ,
419 cause,...assignes∧] ~ ∧...~ ,
425 *Rhene*∧...*Leuca*,] ~ ,...~ ∧

428 *Averni*ᴧ too,] ∼ , ∼ ᴧ
428 themselvesᴧ] ∼ ;
431 *Vangions*] vangions
445 Poesie.] ∼ ,
458 wonne.] ∼ ;
468 tales.] ∼ ,
477 purpose,] ∼ ;
486 *Consuls*] Consuls
500 sound,] ∼ ᴧ
519 fled.] ∼ ,
529 heaven;] ∼ :
541 towneᴧ] ∼ ;
542 (Mycenæ),] (∼)ᴧ
543 unbarredᴧ] ∼ ;
549 twaine.] ∼ ;
553–4 *Calpe*,...head;] ∼ ;...∼ ,
563 movesᴧ] ∼ ,
567 woodsᴧ] ∼ ,
568 men.] ∼ ,

572 fiendᴧ] ∼ ;
584 amongst] amonst
585 *Leuca*,] ∼ ᴧ
595 vestures,] ∼ ;
601 southsayers;] ∼ ,
602 *Salii*] Salij
607 *Bidentall*:] ∼ ,
614 gore.] ∼ ,
619–20 spots:...filth,] ∼ ,...∼ :
633 words,] ∼ ᴧ |
634 unfold;] ∼ ,
640 planeting,] ∼ ᴧ
644 plague:] ∼ ?
673 Romans] *Romans*
673 them.] ∼ ,
674 *Mænas*] Maenus
685 know:] ∼ ,
691 againeᴧ] ∼ :
694 said,] ∼ ᴧ

HISTORICAL COLLATION

[NOTE: The following editions are herewith collated. Q (1600); R (*Works*, ed. Robinson, 1826); D¹ (*Works*, ed. Dyce, 1850); D² (*Works*, ed. Dyce, 1858); C (*Works*, ed. Cunningham, 1870); B (*Works*, ed. Bullen, 1885); TB (*Works*, ed. Tucker Brooke, 1910); M (*Poems*, ed. Martin, Methuen, 1931); Rv (*Poems*, ed. MacLure, Revels, 1968). Reference is also made to Br MS: Broughton's manuscript notes and queries in the BM copy of Robinson; and Coll MS: Collier's notes and queries in the BM copy of Dyce¹.]

Dedication

2 *the*] omit R, C, B
24 *but*] that B

31 rites] rights R, B

Text

3 launcht] lanc'd D, C
19 had] have C
20 mouth] source *or* fount TB (*qy*)
24 rear'd] reaer'd Q (c); reafer'd Q (u), R
32 wreake] wreck R
39 blouds] blood R
42 *Leuca*] Leucas D (*qy*), Lucas B
48 flame] plume Q (u), R, TB
57 axes] axles R; axis C, Rv
57 thy] omit R
59 There] Their Q
68 a long] along Q
86 last] lasts R
94 need] needs R, D, C, B
105 *Carras*] Carras' R; Carra's D (*i.e.*, Carræ's *or* Carrhæ's), C–Rv
123 wearst] wear'dst R; war'st D–M
157 Alongst] Along R
157 nought] not Q, R–B
160 wrack's] racks R; wrecks D, B
160 dominions] dominion Q (u), R, TB
168 world] world's D, B
240 trumpets] trumpets' D, B; trumpet's R, C, M, Rv
263 night] might Q
268 Grachus] *i.e.*, Gracchi's D
279 our] her B

294 *Eleius*] Eleus' R, D (*qy* Elean), C; Elean B
302 bloud shed] bloudshed Q, R–M
303 friends] friend's R; friends' D–Rv (−TB)
311 leader] leaders Q, R, TB, M, Rv
313 Brabbling] Babbling R–B
327 As] A Q, R, Coll MS, TB, M, Rv
332 Jawes▲ flesht] Jawes, flesh, Q; Jaws fresh R
336 *Scicillian*] *i.e.*, Cilician D
337 jaded▲] *Jaded*, Q
345 servitors] survivors TB (*qy*)
347 *Sycillia*] *i.e.*, Cilicia D
348 Spread] Spead Q, TB
350 wars] war R
370 band] hand Q, R, TB
372 *Artick*] *Articks* Q, TB, Rv
378 womens groning] groaning women's D¹ (*qy*); groaning woman's D²
383 Ile] He R
384 with] to M
391 bowe] bowde Q, R, C, TB, Rv
392 fets] sets R
404 boats] bloats Q
421 *Nemes*] Neme's R; Nemes' D–Rv (−TB)

421 *Satirus*] Aturus R
425 *Rhene*ᴧ and *Leuca*,] ~ ᴧ...~ ᴧ Q, R
428 *Averni*] *i.e.,* Arverni D
429 Romanes] Roman's R; Romans'
　　D–Rv (–TB)
433 trumpets] trumpet's R–B; trumpets'
　　M, Rv
440 *Mercury*] *Mercury* (*Jove*) Q
441 *Jove*] it Q, R; Juno Coll MS
447 rites,] ~ ᴧ R
455 affright] affrights R
459 repulst] repulse R
466 peoples] peoples' R; people's D–
　　Rv (–TB)
474 hide] hid R, D, C
478 twixt] betwixt R
510 Captives] Captaines Q, R, TB
515 rampire] rampart R
521 Commons] common R
550 brothers] brother's R; brothers' D–
　　Rv (–TB)
552 laps] tops D¹ (*qy*), D²
557 Defil'd the day] The day defil'd D
　　(*qy*)
557 and] at night C (*qy*), B (*qy*), M
561 sight] sigh R
564 *Sibils*] Cybel's D, C, B, M

566 sigh'd] sight Q, TB; sigh R
585 *Leuca*] Luna R; Luca D, C, Rv
585 **or *Luna*] *omit* R, D, C
587 flight] flights R
589 Mules] mule's D, B, Rv; mules'
　　R, C, M (*read* mule's: mulam *in*
　　Sulpitius)
599 wash] washt Q, R, TB, Rv
616 gods] gods' D, B, Rv; god's R, C,
　　M
624 matter;...cal,] ~ ,...~ ; Q, TB;
　　~ ᴧ...~ ; R–B
624 pearde] peer'd D, C, B, Rv
641 this] his M
642 radge] range D, C, B
654 sing] sing R, TB; singe D, C, B, M,
　　Rv
667 furious] firious Q
669 War onely Onely Q *cw* D 4ᵛ)
671 civill] cruel R
672 scarre] scar R; scare D+ (–TB)
674 *Mænas*] *Mænus* Q, TB
677–8 fall,...aloft?] ~ ?...~ , Q, R,
　　TB
686 drie] dire R
688 hence] thence R–B

OVID'S ELEGIES

TEXTUAL INTRODUCTION

The earliest known appearance of Marlowe's *Ovid's Elegies* is in an octavo (O1) preserved uniquely in the Henry E. Huntington Library in which a selection of ten of the more erotic verses[1] was preceded by Sir John Davies' Epigrams, which were to be joined to Marlowe for the rest of the publishing history of the Elegies. This octavo collates A–G⁴ (A1, G4 blank and wanting), with the title-page on sig. A2 reading 'EPIGRAMMES | and | ELEGIES. | By I. D. and | C. M | [two blocks of type-orns. arranged horizontally] | *At Middleborough*.' The text of Davies begins on sig. A3 and ends on D3ᵛ with 'FINIS. I. D.' The second section starts on sig. E1 with the title 'CERTAINE | *OF OVIDS* | ELEGIES | By C. Marlow. | [type-orns. as on A2] | *At Middleborough*.' Marlowe's text begins on sig. E2 and ends on G3ᵛ. Sig. D4ʳ⁻ᵛ contains three amorous poems headed 'Ignoto'. Except for signed sigs. A3 and E2, the second and third leaves of the gatherings are signed only with the arabic numerals '2' and '3'. This system is a characteristic of the Edinburgh printer Robert Waldegrave but was also used on occasion by the London printer Thomas Scarlet. However, a further peculiarity in that only the verso of the fourth or final leaves of the gatherings has a catchword is not characteristic of their work. Thus not only is the date unknown (usually assigned to *c.* 1594–5) but also whether the Middleburgh imprint—a conventional device for putting objectionable books on the market – is in this case accurate or not. This edition was reprinted substantially page for page in a second edition (O2) with the imprint reading '*At Middleborugh*.' Copies are preserved in the British Museum (C.34.a.28) and in the Carl H. Pforzheimer Library. The order of the two editions can be established by strictly bibliographical evidence such as misprints in O2 deriving from broken types in O1.[2] No fresh authority is present in this O2.

---

[1] The Elegies selected were I.i, ii, iii, v, xiii, xv; II.iv, x; III.vi, xiii. The order was I.i, I.iii, I.v, III.xiii, I.xv (misnumbered II.xv), I.xiii, II.iv, II.x, III.vi, and I.ii.

[2] The order of the six editions of this text, the relations of O3 to O1, and the apparent authority of the two basic textual lines are worked out in detail in Bowers, 'The Early Editions of Marlowe's *Ovid's Elegies*, '*Studies in Bibliography*, xxv

The third edition (O3) begins a new tradition by printing all of the three books of Elegies,[1] omitting the Ignoto poems, and placing the Davies' Epigrams at the end instead of the beginning. This octavo collates A–F^8 G^4, with the title-page 'ALL | OVIDS ELEGIES: | 3. BOOKES. | *By C. M.* | Epigrams by *I. D* | [double row of three asterisk orns, each row within square brackets] | *At Middlebourgh.*' Included after Marlowe's I.xv is Ben Jonson's version, reprinted from the text published in his *Poetaster*, 1602. Copies are preserved in the Bodleian Library (Mason AA.207), in the Dyce Collection of the Victoria and Albert Museum, and in the Huntington Library.

This O3 contains the substantive text for the previously unprinted elegies and has a matching authority with O1 in respect to to the selected ten elegies that had already appeared. The textual relationship of these ten elegies in O3 and O1 offers a complex problem. The Epigrams in O3 were reprinted with considerable tinkerings from O2, but the readings establish that O2 had no relation to the O3 text of the Elegies. Instead, the O3 printer seems to have made some use of O1, as indicated by various common errors and slight evidence for a bibliographical relationship between the two editions. The exact nature of this use is in doubt; but on the whole the evidence suggests that instead of using a copy of O1 annotated and brought into general conformity with the manuscript behind O3, the O3 printer seems to have placed both O1 and the manuscript above his cases and thus made use of the printed copy as a reference in setting largely from the manuscript.

The remaining three editions are simple reprints without authority. That denominated O4 exists in a single known copy in the Bodleian Library (Douce O.31). It stems from O3 but is a terminal edition since no other known edition descends from it. This octavo is a paginal reprint also collating A–F^8 G^4, with a unique title-page omitting 'All' and reading '[row of type-orns.] | Ouids Elegies: | *Three Bookes.* | By C. M. | *Epigrames by I. D.* |

(1972), 149–72. The present introduction merely summarizes the findings presented there with full evidence.

[1] Since III.v in modern editions was not present in the edition Marlowe used, the numbering of the elegies in the present edition differs by one beginning with III.v, which is properly III.vi.

[narrow orn. with fish] | At Middlebourgh.' The fifth edition (O 5) appears to be somewhat later and derives directly from O 3 in the condensed format 8°: A–F⁸. It is recognizable by the leaf type-ornaments on its title-page above two fists, the right inverted. The imprint reads 'AT MIDDLEBOVRGH.' Copies are known in the British Museum (C.57.i.42), the Bodleian, the Dyce Collection in the Victoria and Albert Museum, the Huntington, Folger (3 copies), Pierpont Morgan, Carl H. Pforzheimer, Harvard, Yale, and University of Illinois Libraries. The sixth edition (O 6) is a relatively late paginal reprint of O 5, collating A–F⁸ but with a block of four lace type-ornaments on its title and the imprint 'AT MIDDLE-BOVRGH.' Alternate elegies are likely to be set in italic. Copies are known in the British Museum (1068.6.20[2]), and in the Bodleian, Huntington, Folger, Newberry, Harvard, Yale, and University of Hull Libraries.

The translations are generally credited to Marlowe's Cambridge years and are sometimes thought to be the earliest of his preserved writings, but no proper evidence is available to substantiate these opinions. Any hypothesis that the selection first printed in the *Certaine Elegies* represents his early trials is not to be entertained in view of the relatively minor differences between the versions in O 1 and O 3, which do not appear to bear the marks of revision. The nature of the selection, the association with the Davies' Epigrams, but particularly the appearance of the three Ignoto poems suggest instead that O 1 was printed from someone's collection of amorous and satiric verse. If so, the manuscript behind O 1 is at least at one remove from Marlowe's papers.

The relationship to Marlowe's autograph of the manuscript from which O 3 was set is even more obscure and few if any assumptions are possible. The record in the Stationers' Register of the ecclesiastical order on 1 June 1599 to call in and burn 'Davyes Epigrams, with Marlowes Elegys' probably refers to O 2. On the evidence of the Jonson version of I.xv in O 3 that clearly is drawn from Marlowe in the O 1 or O 2 text, O 3 could not have been printed before 1602. The later the printing of O 3, the less probability for the preservation of Marlowe's papers, of course, and if perhaps twenty years or so intervened it may be that the manuscript secured by the O 3 publisher was a copy, or a copy of a copy. Practically no signs of Marlowe's spellings as represented in the Folger fragment of *The Massacre of Paris* appear in O 3, but this is scarcely evidence since the single compositor who set the octavo was fairly uniform in his characteristics (although occasionally influenced by O 1) and may have thoroughly overlaid the spelling system of his manuscript. One interesting fact develops, however, in that the publisher seems to have had the Epigrams worked over seemingly in an attempt to 'improve' an old-fashioned text; and it is a normal assumption that this agent's concern to revise metrical irregularity and obscure senses of words would also have led him to the same operation in the manuscript of the Elegies. Some sophistication in the O 3 text is to be expected, therefore, of the same nature as that found in the Epigrams. In the verses printed for the first time these alterations cannot be identified, but in the ten selected elegies a number of the variants from the O 1 text, even allowing for some corruption in the O 1 transmission, reveal much the same pattern as that found in the Epigrams. One curious feature is to be observed in the midst of some fairly obvious sophistication of the O 1 text. This is the occasional literal fidelity to the Latin in the O 3 variants, even though O 3 repeats certain of O 1's errors.[1] Of the approximately twenty such cases, some of the very minor readings may represent corruption in O 1 of authority reproduced in O 3. Examples would be the O 3 preterite for the O 1 present in *meant* (I.i.5), the O 3 singular *triumph* for O 1's plural (I.ii.28), *All* in O 3 for O 1's *This* (I.x.iii.25), *And* for O 1 *The* (I.xv.34), *that being* for O 1's *and being* (III.vi.19), *And* for O 1's *Or* (III.xiii.8), and even *heldst* for O 1's *hadst* (I.xiii.39). On the other hand, the O 3 bland *With Muse prepar'd* (I.i.5) for O 1's *With muse upreard* (*Arma gravi numero violentaque bella parabam | edere*) could be taken only with difficulty as a Marlowe revision in the O 3 manuscript or else an O 1 corruption in view of Jonson's *phrase Accius high-reard straine* (I.xv.19), despite the greater fidelity of the O 3 verb to the Latin. An odd cluster comes in

---

[1] These errors are to be distinguished from those that Marlowe made because of the corruption of the Latin text he used. This edition has been identified as *P. Ovidii Nasonis Amatoria...Additis Guidonis Morilloni in Heroid...Basileae* [1568]: see Marlowe's *Poems*, edited by Millar MacLure (Revels edition, 1968), p. xxxiii.

III.xiii.40–7. First, in line 38, O 3 correctly mends the metre by reading *thorough* for O 1's *through*. The change of O 1 *dying* to *dead* in line 40 (*And would be dead, but dying, with thee remaine*) adds crispness but may actually be as much a metrical smoothing as a closer rendering of *tunc ego, sed tecum, mortuus esse velim*. Metrical considerations may also have dictated in line 47 the substitution of *palme* in O 3 for O 1's *garland* despite the Latin *palma*. Whatever the suspect motive of these O 3 variants, however, and whatever their closer relation to the Latin, it is not easy to associate these O 1 readings with transmissional corruption and the O 3 forms with original authority. And in line 45 the case would appear to be confirmed by the O 3 switch from O 1's typical Marlowe phrase *yeeld not* to *deny* (*negato*). It would seem that someone with a knowledge of the Latin text made casual revisions here and there, and that these are combined with indifferent readings in O 3 that are more readily assignable to O 1 lapses than to scrupulous O 3 tinkering. (Something could be said, of course, although there is contrary evidence, for the hypothesis that the manuscript behind O 1 was copied from Marlowe's papers in a somewhat later state than is represented by the manuscript behind O 3. But the treatment given the Davies' Epigrams suggests, instead, editorial ministrations in O 3 as an explanation for at least some of the variants.) Yet this same hypothetical editor allowed such corruptions in the O 3 manuscript to stand as *Temple* for O 1 *tempe* I.i.19.

These considerations weigh heavily against a general acceptance of all O 3 variants that are not obvious errors and force an editor to survey each variant on its merits. The overall working hypothesis adopted by the present editor favors the general purity of the O 3 text in the more indifferent variants between it and O 1, especially when some evidence may account for possible corruption in O 1, as in the adoption of O 3 *doth* for O 1 *shall* at I.xv.10 because of the possibility of contamination in O 1 from *shall* in the preceding line. But on the whole the major variants have been given careful scrutiny in an attempt to weed out the more probable and explicable of the O 3 editor's sophistications of the kind observed in the control text of the Epigrams, where no fresh authority could have entered. Complicating the editorial problem is the question of the fidelity of the O 3 compositor if he were indeed setting by reference to the two copies. Even if the compositor were setting from an annotated example of O 1 (an unlikely hypothesis), the fidelity of the scribe preparing the copy would come in question.

For the elegies first printed in the complete text, O 3 is taken as the copy-text since it is the only authority, O 4–6 being mere reprints. The case is more troublesome for the ten elegies first printed in O 1. Ordinarily the fidelity to the substantive readings of one or other copy has no bearing on the choice of copy-text since the selection is supposed to be made of the edition that can be shown to be nearer to the author's papers and thus, in theory, more faithful to his system of accidentals. That O 1 was not set from Marlowe's own papers seems a reasonable hypothesis given the nature of the mixed volume. Whether or not O 3 derived directly from holograph is not to be demonstrated although in the editor's private opinion the odds favor at least one intervening transcript. Hence the case appears to be a stand-off; but for the ten selected elegies O 1 has been chosen as the copy-text on the grounds that its considerably earlier date insures a texture of accidentals that (the question of transmissional distance being obscure) at least is historically closer to Marlowe than the later O 3's texture.

The Pforzheimer and British Museum copies of O 2 have been collated and shown to be invariant. The Bodleian, Dyce, and Huntington copies of O 3 have also been collated and their press-variants recorded. The unique Bodleian (Douce O.31) copy of O 4, the British Museum (C.57.i.42) copy of O 5, and the Huntington copy of O 6 were collated for the variants recorded in the apparatus. The following editions have been collated as well: *Works*, ed. Robinson (1826), *Works*, ed. Dyce, 1850 and 1858, *Works*, ed. Cunningham (1870), *Works*, ed. Bullen (1885), *Works*, ed. Tucker Brooke (1910), *Poems*, ed. Martin (Methuen, 1931), and *Poems*, ed. MacLure (Revels, 1968). The Robinson edition reprinted the text of O 2 as well as of O 4 (O 3 not being known to the editor), but only the second is here collated. Dyce did not know of O 4 or O 6. The first editor to utilize the readings from O 1 was Tucker Brooke, but he and Martin drew their knowledge of this text from the Edmonds reprint of 1870.

P. Ovidii Nasonis Amorum
Liber Primus
ELEGIA 1

*Quemadmodum a Cupidine, pro bellis
amores scribere coactus sit*

We which were *Ovids* five books, now are three,
For these before the rest preferreth he:
If reading five thou plainst of tediousnesse,
Two tane away, thy labor will be lesse:
With Muse upreard I meant to sing of armes,
Choosing a subject fit for feirse alarmes:
Both verses were alike till Love (men say)
Began to smile and tooke one foote away.
Rash boy, who gave thee power to change a line?
We are the Muses prophets, none of thine.   10
What if thy Mother take *Dianas* bowe,
Shall *Dian* fanne when love begins to glowe?
In wooddie groves ist meete that *Ceres* Raigne,
And quiver bearing *Dian* till the plaine:
Who'le set the faire treste sunne in battell ray,
While *Mars* doth take the *Aonian* harpe to play?
Great are thy kingdomes, over strong and large,
Ambitious Imp, why seekst thou further charge?
Are all things thine? the Muses *Tempe* thine?
Then scarse can *Phœbus* say, this harpe is mine.   20
When in this workes first verse I trod aloft,
Love slackt my Muse, and made my numbers soft.
I have no mistris, nor no favorit,
Being fittest matter for a wanton wit,

I.i O1 *copy-text*
*5 upreard] O1–2; prepar'd O3
5 meant] O3; meane O1–2
8 tooke] O3; take O1–2
11 What] O3; That O1–2

15 sunne] O3; sonne O1–2
19 *Tempe*] O1–2 (tempe); *Temple* O3
21 workes] O3; worke O1–2
22 Love] O3; I O1–2
22 numbers] O3; number O1–2

Thus I complaind, but Love unlockt his quiver,
Tooke out the shaft, ordaind my hart to shiver:
And bent his sinewy bow upon his knee,
Saying, Poet heers a worke beseeming thee.
Oh woe is me, he never shootes but hits,
I burne, love in my idle bosome sits.   30
Let my first verse be sixe, my last five feete,
Fare well sterne warre, for blunter Poets meete.
Elegian Muse, that warblest amorous laies,
Girt my shine browe with sea banke mirtle praise.

ELEGIA 2

Quod primo Amore correptus, in triumphum
duci se a Cupidine patiatur

What makes my bed seem hard seeing it is soft?
Or why slips downe the Coverlet so oft?
Although the nights be long, I sleepe not tho,
My sides are sore with tumbling to and fro.
Were Love the cause, it's like I shoulde descry him,
Or lies he close, and shoots where none can spie him?
T'was so, he stroke me with a slender dart,
Tis cruell love turmoyles my captive hart.
Yeelding or striving doe we give him might,
Lets yeeld, a burden easly borne is light.   10
I saw a brandisht fire increase in strength,
Which being not shakt, I saw it die at length.
Yong oxen newly yokt are beaten more,
Then oxen which have drawne the plow before.
And rough jades mouths with stubburn bits are torne,
But managde horses heads are lightly borne,
Unwilling Lovers, love doth more torment,
Then such as in their bondage feele content.

*34 praise] *stet* O 1–6   7 so,] O 3; ~ ˄ O 1–2
    I.ii O 1 *copy-text*   9 striving] O 1–2; strugling O 3
    3 tho,] O 2; ~ ˄ O 1 (*i.e.*, then)   12 shakt] O 1–2; slackt O 3

316

Loe I confesse, I am thy captive I,
And hold my conquered hands for thee to tie.   20
What needes thou warre, I sue to thee for grace,
With armes to conquer armlesse men is base,
Yoke *Venus* Doves, put Mirtle on thy haire,
Vulcan will give thee Chariots rich and faire.
The people thee applauding thou shalte stand,
Guiding the harmelesse Pigeons with thy hand.
Yong men and women, shalt thou lead as thrall,
So will thy triumph seeme magnificall.
I lately cought, will have a new made wound,
And captive like be manacled and bound.   30
Good meaning, shame, and such as seeke loves wrack
Shall follow thee, their hands tied at their backe.
Thee all shall feare and worship as a King,
Io, triumphing shall thy people sing.
Smooth speeches, feare and rage shall by thee ride,
Which troopes hath alwayes bin on *Cupids* side:
Thou with these souldiers conquerest gods and men,
Take these away, where is thy honor then?
Thy mother shall from heaven applaud this show,
And on their faces heapes of Roses strow.   40
With beautie of thy wings, thy faire haire guilded,
Ride golden Love in Chariots richly builded.
Unlesse I erre, full many shalt thou burne,
And give woundes infinite at everie turne.
In spite of thee, forth will thy arrowes flie,
A scorching flame burnes all the standers by.
So having conquerd *Inde*, was *Bacchus* hew,
Thee Pompous birds and him two tygres drew.
Then seeing I grace thy show in following thee,
Forbeare to hurt thy selfe in spoyling mee.   50
Beholde thy kinsmans *Cæsars* prosperous bandes,
Who gardes the conquered with his conquering hands.

28 triumph] O3; triumphs O1-2   *42 Chariots] *stet* O1-6
31 meaning,] Robinson; ~ ∧ O1-6   *52 the] Dyce; theee O1-6
38 thy] O1-2; thine O3

ELEGIA 3

Ad amicam

I aske but right: let hir that cought me late,
Either love, or cause that I may never hate:
I aske too much, would she but let me love hir,
Love knowes with such like praiers, I dayly move hir:
Accept him that will serve thee all his youth,
Accept him that will love with spotlesse truth:
If loftie titles cannot make me thine,
That am descended but of knightly line,
Soone may you plow the little lands I have,
I gladly graunt my parents given to save,   10
Apollo, Bacchus, and the Muses may,
And *Cupide* who hath markt me for thy pray,
My spotlesse life, which but to Gods gives place,
Naked simplicitie, and modest grace.
I love but one, and hir I love change never,
If men have Faith, Ile live with thee for ever.
The yeares that fatall destenie shall give,
Ile live with thee, and die, or thou shalt grieve.
Be thou the happie subject of my Bookes,
That I may write things worthy thy faire lookes: 20
By verses horned *Io* got hir name,
And she to whom in shape of Swanne *Jove* came.
And she that on a faind Bull swamme to land,
Griping his false hornes with hir virgin hand:
So likewise we will through the world be rung,
And with my name shall thine be alwaies sung.

I.iii O 1 *copy-text*   *13 gives] O 3; give O 1–2
1 hir] O 1–2; he O 3   18 or] O 1–2 (*i.e.,* ere); ere O 3–6
4 Love] O 1–2; *Jove* O 3   18 shalt] O 1–2; shall O 3
*9 lands] *stet* O 1–2   22 Swanne] O 3; Bull O 1–2

ELEGIA 4

Amicam, qua arte, quibusve nutibus in cæna, præsente
viro uti debeat, admonet

Thy husband to a banquet goes with me,
Pray God it may his latest supper be,
Shall I sit gazing as a bashfull guest,
While others touch the damsell I love best?
Wilt lying under him his bosome clippe?
About thy neck shall he at pleasure skippe?
Marveile not though the faire Bride did incite
The drunken *Centaures* to a sodaine fight.
I am no halfe horse, nor in woods I dwell,
Yet scarse my hands from thee containe I well.   10
But how thou shouldst behave thy selfe now know;
Nor let the windes away my warnings blowe.
Before thy husband come, though I not see
What may be done, yet there before him bee.
Lie with him gently, when his limbes he spread
Upon the bed, but on my foote first tread.
View me, my becks, and speaking countenance:
Take, and receive each secret amorous glaunce.
Words without voyce shall on my eye browes sit,
Lines thou shalt read in wine by my hand writ.   20
When our lascivious toyes come in thy minde,
Thy Rosie cheekes be to thy thombe inclinde.
If ought of me thou speak'st in inward thought,
Let thy soft finger to thy eare be brought.
When I (my light) do or say ought that please thee,
Turne round thy gold-ring, as it were to ease thee.
Strike on the boord like them that pray for evill,
When thou doest wish thy husband at the devill.
What wine he fills thee, wisely will him drinke,
Aske thou the boy, what thou enough doest thinke.   30

I.iv O3 *copy-text*
*7 though] *stet* O3–6   *18 receive] *stet* O3–6

When thou hast tasted, I will take the cup,
And where thou drinkst, on that part I will sup.
If hee gives thee what first himselfe did tast,
Even in his face his offered Gobbets cast.
Let not thy necke by his vile armes be prest,
Nor leane thy soft head on his boistrous brest.
Thy bosomes Roseat buds let him not finger,
Chiefely on thy lips let not his lips linger.
If thou givest kisses, I shall all disclose,
Say they are mine, and hands on thee impose. 40
Yet this Ile see, but if thy gowne ought cover,
Suspitious feare in all my veines will hover,
Mingle not thighes, nor to his legge joyne thine,
Nor thy soft foote with his hard foote combine.
I have beene wanton, therefore am perplext,
And with mistrust of the like measure vext.
I and my wench oft under clothes did lurke,
When pleasure mov'd us to our sweetest worke.
Do not thou so, but throw thy mantle hence,
Least I should thinke thee guilty of offence. 50
Entreat thy husband drinke, but do not kisse,
And while he drinkes, to adde more do not misse,
If hee lyes downe with Wine and sleepe opprest,
The thing and place shall counsell us the rest.
When to go homewards we rise all along,
Have care to walke in middle of the throng.
There will I finde thee, or be found by thee,
There touch what ever thou canst touch of mee.
Aye me I warne what profits some few howers,
But we must part, when heav'n with black night lowers. 60
At night thy husband clippes thee, I will weepe
And to the dores sight of thy selfe will keepe:
Then will he kisse thee, and not onely kisse
But force thee give him my stolne honey blisse.
Constrain'd against thy will give it the pezant,

34 Gobbets] Dyce; Goblets O 3–6   62 will] Robinson; *omit* O 3–6
36 leane] O 5; leave (leaue) O 3–4

320

Forbeare sweet wordes, and be your sport unpleasant.
To him I pray it no delight may bring,
Or if it do, to thee no joy thence spring:
But though this night thy fortune be to trie it,
To me to morrow constantly deny it.　　　　　　　　　70

ELEGIA 5

Corinnæ concubitus

In summers heate, and midtime of the day,
To rest my limbes, uppon a bedde I lay,
One window shut, the other open stood,
Which gave such light, as twincles in a wood,
Like twilight glimps at setting of the sunne,
Or night being past, and yet not day begunne.
Such light to shamefaste maidens must be showne,
Where they may sport, and seeme to be unknowne.
Then came *Corinna* in a long loose gowne,
Her white necke hid with tresses hanging downe,　　　10
Resembling faire *Semiramis* going to bed,
Or *Layis* of a thousand lovers sped.
I snatcht her gowne: being thin, the harme was small,
Yet strivde she to be covered therewithall,
And striving thus as one that would be cast,
Betrayde her selfe, and yeelded at the last.
Starke naked as she stood before mine eie,
Not one wen in her bodie could I spie,
What armes and shoulders did I touch and see,
How apt her breasts were to be prest by me,　　　　20
How smoothe a bellie, under her waste sawe I,
How large a legge, and what a lustie thigh?
To leave the rest, all likt me passing well,
I clinged her naked bodie, downe she fell,
Judge you the rest, being tyrde she bad me kisse.
Jove send me more such afternoones as this.

I.v O1 *copy-text*　　　　　　　　12 sped] O3; spread O1–2
*12 lovers] O1–2; wooers O3　　　25 tyrde] O1–2; tride O3

ELEGIA 6

Ad Janitorem, ut fores sibi aperiat

Unworthy porter, bound in chaines full sore,
On mooved hookes set ope the churlish dore.
Little I aske, a little entrance make,
The gate halfe ope my bent side in will take.
Long Love my body to such use makes slender
And to get out doth like apt members render.
He shewes me how unheard to passe the watch,
And guides my feete least stumbling falles they catch.
But in times past I fear'd vaine shades, and night,
Wondring if any walked without light.   10
Love hearing it laugh'd with his tender mother
And smiling sayed, be thou as bold as other.
Forth-with Love came, no darke night-flying spright
Nor hands prepar'd to slaughter, me affright.
Thee feare I too much: only thee I flatter,
Thy lightning can my life in pieces batter.
Why enviest me, this hostile denne unbarre,
See how the gates with my teares wat'red are.
When thou stood'st naked ready to be beate,
For thee I did thy mistris faire entreate.   20
But what entreates for thee some-times tooke place,
(O mischiefe) now for me obtaine small grace.
Gratis thou maiest be free, give like for like,
Night goes away: the dores barre backeward strike.
Strike, so againe hard chaines shall binde thee never,
Nor servile water shalt thou drinke for ever.
Hard-hearted *Porter* doest and wilt not heare?
With stiffe oake propt the gate doth still appeare.
Such rampierd gates beseiged Cittyes ayde,
In midst of peace why art of armes afraide?   30
Excludst a lover, how wouldst use a foe?
Strike backe the barre, night fast away doth goe.

With armes or armed men I come not guarded,
I am alone, were furious Love discarded.
Although I would, I cannot him cashiere
Before I be divided from my geere.
See Love with me, wine moderate in my braine,
And on my haires a crowne of flowers remaine.
Who feares these armes? who wil not go to meete them?
Night runnes away; with open entrance greete them. 40
Art carelesse? or ist sleepe forbids thee heare,
Giving the windes my words running in thine eare?
Well I remember when I first did hire thee,
Watching till after mid-night did not tire thee.
But now perchaunce thy wench with thee doth rest,
Ah howe thy lot is above my lot blest:
Though it be so, shut me not out therefore,
Night goes away: I pray thee ope the dore.
Erre we? or do the turned hinges sound,
And opening dores with creaking noyse abound? 50
We erre: a strong blast seem'd the gates to ope:
Aie me how high that gale did lift my hope!
If *Boreas* beares *Orithyas* rape in minde,
Come breake these deafe dores with thy boysterous wind.
Silent the Cittie is: nights deawie hoast
March fast away: the barre strike from the poast.
Or I more sterne then fire or sword will turne,
And with my brand these gorgeous houses burne.
Night, Love, and wine to all extreames perswade:
Night shamelesse, wine and Love are fearelesse made. 60
All have I spent: no threats or prayers move thee,
O harder then the dores thou gardest I prove thee.
No pritty wenches keeper maist thou bee:
The carefull prison is more meete for thee.
Now frosty night her flight beginnes to take,
And crowing Cocks poore soules to worke awake.
But thou my crowne, from sad haires tane away,

---

53 If *Boreas* beares] i.e., If, *Boreas*,   *60 Night_∧ shamelesse, wine_∧] ~ , ~ _∧
   thou bear'st   ~ , O 3–6

On this hard threshold till the morning lay.
That when my mistresse there beholds thee cast,
She may perceive how we the time did wast: 70
What ere thou art, farewell, be like me paind,
Carelesse, farewell, with my falt not distaind.
And farewell cruell posts, rough thresholds block,
And dores conjoynd with an hard iron lock.

ELEGIA 7

Ad pacandam amicam, quam verberaverat

Binde fast my hands, they have deserved chaines,
While rage is absent, take some friend the paynes.
For rage against my wench mov'd my rash arme,
My Mistresse weepes whom my mad hand did harme.
I might have then my parents deare misus'd,
Or holy gods with cruell strokes abus'd.
Why? *Ajax*, maister of the seven-fould shield,
Butcherd the flocks he found in spatious field,
And he who on his mother veng'd his sire,
Against the destinies durst sharpe darts require.   10
Could I therefore her comely tresses teare?
Yet was she graced with her ruffled hayre.
So fayre she was, *Atalanta* she resembled,
Before whose bow th'*Arcadian* wild beasts trembled.
Such *Ariadne* was, when she bewayles
Her perjur'd *Theseus* flying vowes and sayles,
So chast *Minerva* did *Cassandra* fall,
Deflowr'd except, within thy Temple wall.
That I was mad, and barbarous all men cried,
She nothing said, pale feare her tongue had tyed.   20
But secretlie her lookes with checks did trounce mee,
Her teares, she silent, guilty did pronounce me.
Would of mine armes, my shoulders had beene scanted,
Better I could part of my selfe have wanted.
To mine owne selfe have I had strength so furious?

I.vii O 3 *copy-text*

And to my selfe could I be so injurious?
Slaughter and mischiefs instruments, no better,
Deserved chaines these cursed hands shall fetter,
Punisht I am, if I a *Romaine* beat,
Over my Mistris is my right more great?　　　　　　30
Tydides left worst signes of villanie,
He first a Goddesse strooke; an other I.
Yet he harm'd lesse, whom I profess'd to love,
I harm'd: a foe did *Diomedes* anger move.
Go now thou Conqueror, glorious triumphs raise,
Pay vowes to *Jove*, engirt thy hayres with baies,
And let the troupes which shall thy Chariot follow,
Io, a strong man conquerd this Wench, hollow.
Let the sad captive formost with lockes spred
On her white necke but for hurt cheekes be led.　　40
Meeter it were her lips were blewe with kissing
And on her necke a wantons marke not missing.
But though I like a swelling floud was driven,
And as a pray unto blinde anger given,
Wa'st not enough the fearefull Wench to chide?
Nor thunder in rough threatings haughty pride?
Nor shamefully her coate pull ore her crowne,
Which to her wast her girdle still kept downe.
But cruelly her tresses having rent,
My nayles to scratch her lovely cheekes I bent.　　50
Sighing she stood, her bloodlesse white lookes shewed
Like marble from the *Parian* Mountaines hewed.
Her halfe dead joynts, and trembling limmes I sawe,
Like *Popler* leaves blowne with a stormy flawe,
Or slender eares, with gentle *Zephire* shaken,
Or waters tops with the warme south-winde taken.
And downe her cheekes, the trickling teares did flow,
Like water gushing from consuming snowe.
Then first I did perceive I had offended,
My bloud, the teares were that from her descended.　　60
Before her feete thrice prostrate downe I fell,
My feared hands thrice back she did repell.

But doubt thou not (revenge doth griefe appease)
With thy sharpe nayles upon my face to seaze.
Bescratch mine eyes, spare not my lockes to breake,
(Anger will helpe thy hands though nere so weake.)
And least the sad signes of my crime remaine,
Put in their place thy keembed haires againe.

ELEGIA 8

*Exæcratur lenam, quæ puellam suam meretricia
arte instituebat*

There is, who ere will knowe a bawde aright
Give eare, there is an old trot *Dipsas* hight.
Her name comes from the thing: she being wise,
Sees not the morne on rosie horses rise.
She magick arts and *Thessale* charmes doth know,
And makes large streams back to their fountaines flow,
She knows with gras, with thrids on wrong wheeles spun
And what with Mares ranck humour may be done.
When she will, cloudes the darckned heav'n obscure,
When she will, day shines every where most pure.   10
(If I have faith) I sawe the starres drop bloud,
The purple moone with sanguine visage stood.
Her I suspect among nights spirits to fly,
And her old body in birdes plumes to lie.
Fame saith as I suspect, and in her eyes
Two eye-balles shine, and double light thence flies.
Great grand-sires from their antient graves she chides
And with long charmes the solide earth divides.
She drawes chast women to incontinence,
Nor doth her tongue want harmefull eloquence.   20
By chaunce I heard her talke, these words she sayd
While closely hid betwixt two dores I layed.
Mistris thou knowest, thou hast a blest youth pleas'd,
He staide, and on thy lookes his gazes seaz'd.

I.viii O3 *copy-text*   *7 wrong wheeles] *stet* wrŏg O3–6

326

And why shouldst not please? none thy face exceedes,
Aye me, thy body hath no worthy weedes.
As thou art faire, would thou wert fortunate,
Wert thou rich, poore should not be my state.
Th'opposed starre of *Mars* hath done thee harme,
Now *Mars* is gone: *Venus* thy side doth warme,   30
And brings good fortune, a rich lover plants
His love on thee, and can supply thy wants.
Such is his forme as may with thine compare,
Would he not buy thee thou for him shouldst care.
She blusht: red shame becomes white cheekes, but this
If feigned, doth well; if true it doth amisse.
When on thy lappe thine eyes thou dost deject,
Each one according to his gifts respect.
Perhaps the *Sabines* rude, when *Tatius* raignde,
To yeeld their love to more then one disdainde.   40
Now *Mars* doth rage abroad without all pitty,
And *Venus* rules in her *Æneas* Citty.
Faire women play, shee's chast whom none will have,
Or, but for bashfulnesse her selfe would crave.
Shake off these wrinckles that thy front assault,
Wrinckles in beauty is a grievous fault.
Penelope in bowes her youths strength tride,
Of horne the bowe was that approv'd their side.
Time flying slides hence closely, and deceaves us,
And with swift horses the swift yeare soone leaves us.   50
Brasse shines with use; good garments would be worne,
Houses not dwelt in, are with filth forlorne.
Beauty not exercisde with age is spent,
Nor one or two men are sufficient.
Many to rob is more sure, and lesse hatefull,
From dog-kept flocks come preys to woolves most gratefull.
Behold what gives the Poet but new verses?
And thereof many thousand he rehearses.
The Poets God arayed in robes of gold,
Of his gilt Harpe the well tun'd strings doth hold.   60
Let *Homer* yeeld to such as presents bring,

(Trust me) to give, it is a witty thing.
Nor, so thou maist obtaine a wealthy prize,
The vaine name of inferiour slaves despize.
Nor let the armes of antient lines beguile thee,
Poore lover with thy gransires I exile thee.
Who seekes, for being faire, a night to have,
What he will give, with greater instance crave.
Make a small price, while thou thy nets doest lay,
Least they should fly, being tane, the tirant play.   70
Dissemble so, as lov'd he may be thought,
And take heed least he gets that love for nought.
Deny him oft, feigne now thy head doth ake:
And *Isis* now will shew what scuse to make.
Receive him soone, least patient use he gaine,
Or least his love oft beaten backe should waine.
To beggers shut, to bringers ope thy gate,
Let him within heare bard out lovers prate.
And as first wrongd the wronged some-times banish,
Thy fault with his fault so repuls'd will vanish.   80
But never give a spatious time to ire,
Anger delaide doth oft to hate retire.
And let thine eyes constrained learne to weepe,
That this, or that man may thy cheekes moist keepe.
Nor, if thou couzenst one, dread to for-sweare,
„*Venus* to mockt men lendes a sencelesse eare.
Servants fit for thy purpose thou must hire
To teach thy lover, what thy thoughts desire.
Let them aske some-what, many asking little,
Within a while great heapes grow of a tittle.   90
And sister, Nurse, and mother spare him not,
By many hands great wealth is quickly got.
When causes fale thee to require a gift,
By keeping of thy birth make but a shift.
Beware least he unrival'd loves secure,
Take strife away, love doth not well endure.

65 lines] Dyce] lives (liues) O3–6   *97 bed mens] Dyce (men's); beds men
                                                                O3–6

On all the bed mens tumbling let him viewe
And thy neck with lascivious markes made blew.
Chiefely shew him the gifts, which others send:
If he gives nothing, let him from thee wend.   100
When thou hast so much as he gives no more,
Pray him to lend what thou maist nere restore.
Let thy tongue flatter, while thy minde harme-workes:
Under sweete hony deadly poison lurkes.
If this thou doest, to me by long use knowne,
Nor let my words be with the windes hence blowne,
Oft thou wilt say, live well, thou wilt pray oft,
That my dead bones may in their grave lie soft.
As thus she spake, my shadow me betraide,
With much a do my hands I scarsely staide.   110
But her bleare eyes, balde scalpes thin hoary flieces
And riveld cheekes I would have puld a pieces.
The gods send thee no house, a poore old age,
Perpetuall thirst, and winters lasting rage.

ELEGIA 9

Ad Atticum, amantem non oportere desidiosum
esse, sicuti nec militem

All Lovers warre, and *Cupid* hath his tent,
Atticke, all lovers are to warre farre sent.
What age fits *Mars*, with *Venus* doth agree,
Tis shame for eld in warre or love to be.
What yeares in souldiours Captaines do require,
Those in their lovers, pretty maydes desire.
Both of them watch: each on the hard earth sleepes:
His Mistris dores this; that his Captaines keepes.
Souldiers must travaile farre: the wench forth send,
Her valiant lover followes without end.   10
Mounts, and raine-doubled flouds he passeth over,

111 thin] Dyce; thine O3–6   *8 dores] *stet* O3–6
I.ix O3 *copy-text*

And treades the deserts snowy heapes do cover.
Going to sea, *East* windes he doth not chide
Nor to hoist saile attends fit time and tyde.
Who but a souldiour or a lover is bould
To suffer storme mixt snowes with nights sharpe cold?
One as a spy doth to his enemies goe,
The other eyes his rivall as his foe.
He Citties greate, this thresholds lies before:
This breakes Towne gates, but he his Mistris dore.   20
Oft to invade the sleeping foe tis good
And arm'd to shed unarmed peoples bloud.
So the fierce troupes of *Thracian Rhesus* fell
And Captive horses bad their Lord fare-well.
Sooth Lovers watch till sleepe the hus-band charmes,
Who slumbring, they rise up in swelling armes.
The keepers hands and corps-dugard to passe
The souldiours, and poore lovers worke ere was.
Doubtfull is warre and love, the vanquisht rise
And who thou never think'st should fall downe lies.   30
Therefore who ere love sloathfulnesse doth call,
Let him surcease: love tries wit best of all.
Achilles burnd *Briseis* being tane away:
Troianes destroy the *Greeke* wealth, while you may.
Hector to armes went from his wives embraces,
And on *Andromache* his helmet laces.
Great *Agamemnon* was, men say, amazed,
On *Priams* loose-trest daughter when he gazed.
Mars in the deed the black-smithes net did stable,
In heaven was never more notorious fable.   40
My selfe was dull, and faint, to sloth inclinde,
Pleasure, and ease had mollifide my minde.
A faire maides care expeld this sluggishnesse,
And to her tentes wild me my selfe addresse.
Since maist thou see me watch and night warres move:
He that will not growe slothfull let him love.

12 do] Robinson; to O3–6
*41 faint, to] O3(c) (faint‸ to); to faint O3(u)

ELEGIA 10

Ad puellam, ne pro amore præmia poscat

Such as the cause was of two husbands warre,
Whom *Troiane* ships fecht from *Europa* farre.
Such as was *Leda*, whom the God deluded
In snowe-white plumes of a false swanne included.
Such as *Amimone* through the drie fields strayed
When on her head a water pitcher laied.
Such wert thou, and I fear'd the Bull and Eagle
And what ere love made *Jove* should thee invegle.
Now all feare with my mindes hot love abates,
No more this beauty mine eyes captivates.　　　　　　10
Ask'st why I chaunge? because thou crav'st reward:
This cause hath thee from pleasing me debard.
While thou wert plaine, I lov'd thy minde and face:
Now inward faults thy outward forme disgrace.
Love is a naked boy, his yeares saunce staine,
And hath no cloathes, but open doth remaine.
Will you for gaine have *Cupid* sell himselfe?
He hath no bosome, where to hide base pelfe.
Love and Loves sonne are with fierce armes to oddes;
To serve for pay beseemes not wanton gods.　　　　　20
The whore stands to be bought for each mans mony
And seekes vild wealth by selling of her Cony,
Yet greedy Bauds command she curseth still,
And doth constraind, what you do of good will.
Take from irrationall beasts a president,
Tis shame their wits should be more excelent.
The Mare askes not the Horse, the Cowe the Bull,
Nor the milde Ewe gifts from the Ramme doth pull.
Only a Woman gets spoiles from a Man,
Farmes out her-self on nights for what she can.　　　　30
And lets what both delight, what both desire,
Making her joy according to her hire.

I.x O3 *copy-text*　　　　　　　*2 Europa*] *stet* O3–6

The sport being such, as both alike sweete try it,
Why should one sell it, and the other buy it?
Why should I loose, and thou gaine by the pleasure
Which man and woman reape in equall measure?
Knights of the post of perjuries make saile,
The unjust Judge for bribes becomes a stale.
Tis shame sould tongues the guilty should defend
Or great wealth from a judgement seate ascend.   40
Tis shame to grow rich by bed merchandize,
Or prostitute thy beauty for bad prize.
Thankes worthely are due for things unbought,
For beds ill hyr'd we are indebted nought.
The hirer payeth al, his rent discharg'd
From further duty he rests then inlarg'd.
Faire Dames for-beare rewards for nights to crave,
Ill gotten goods good end will never have.
The Sabine gauntlets were too dearely wunne
That unto death did presse the holy Nunne.   50
The sonne slew her, that forth to meete him went,
And a rich neck-lace caus'd that punnishment.
Yet thinke no scorne to aske a wealthy churle,
He wants no gifts into thy lap to hurle.
Take clustred grapes from an ore-laden vine,
May bounteous lome *Alcinous* fruite resigne.
Let poore men show their service, faith, and care;
All for their Mistrisse, what they have, prepare.
In verse to praise kinde Wenches tis my part,
And whom I like eternize by mine art.   60
Garments do weare, jewells and gold do wast,
The fame that verse gives doth for ever last.
To give I love, but to be ask't disdayne,
Leave asking, and Ile give what I refraine.

56 May] Dyce; Many O3–6   56 lome] Methuen (loam); loue O3–6

ELEGIA 11

Napen alloquitur, ut paratas tabellas ad
Corinnam perferat

In skilfull gathering ruffled haires in order,
Nape free-borne, whose cunning hath no border,
Thy service for nights scapes is knowne commodious
And to give signes dull wit to thee is odious.
Corinna clips me oft by thy perswasion,
Never to harme me made thy faith evasion.
Receive these lines, them to my Mistrisse carry,
Be sedulous, let no stay cause thee tarry.
Nor flint, nor iron, are in thy soft brest
But pure simplicity in thee doth rest.   10
And tis suppos'd Loves bowe hath wounded thee,
Defend the ensignes of thy warre in mee.
If, what I do, she askes, say hope for night,
The rest my hand doth in my letters write.
Time passeth while I speake, give her my writ
But see that forth-with shee peruseth it.
I charge thee marke her eyes and front in reading,
By speechlesse lookes we guesse at things succeeding.
Straight being read, will her to write much backe,
I hate faire *Paper* should writte matter lacke.   20
Let her make verses, and some blotted letter
On the last edge to stay mine eyes the better.
What neede she tyre her hand to hold the quill,
Let this word, come, alone the tables fill.
Then with triumphant laurell will I grace them
And in the midst of *Venus* temple place them.
Subscribing that to her I consecrate
My faithfull tables being vile maple late.

I.xi O3 *copy-text*   23 tyre] Duce; try O3–6
1 skilfull] O4; skilfuld O3

333

ELEGIA 12

Tabellas quas miserat execratur, quod amica
noctem negabat

Bewaile my chaunce, the sad booke is returned,
This day denyall hath my sport adjourned.
Presages are not vaine, when she departed
Nape by stumbling on the thre-shold started.
Going out againe passe forth the dore more wisely
And som-what higher beare thy foote precisely.
Hence luck-lesse tables, funerall wood be flying
And thou the waxe stuft full with notes denying,
Which I thinke gather'd from cold hemlocks flower
Wherein bad hony *Corsicke* Bees did power.   10
Yet as if mixt with red leade thou wert ruddy,
That colour rightly did appeare so bloudy.
As evill wood throwne in the high-waies lie,
Be broake with wheeles of chariots passing by.
And him that hew'd you out for needfull uses
Ile prove had hands impure with all abuses.
Poore wretches on the tree themselves did strangle,
There sat the hang-man for mens neckes to angle.
To hoarse scrich-owles foule shadowes it allowes,
Vultures and furies nestled in the boughes.   20
To these my love I foolishly committed
And then with sweete words to my Mistrisse fitted.
More fitly had they wrangling bondes contained
From barbarous lips of some Atturney strained.
Among day bookes and billes they had laine better
In which the Merchant wayles his banquerout debter.
Your name approves you made for such like things,
The number two no good divining bringes.
Angry, I pray that rotten age you wrackes
And sluttish white-mould overgrowe the waxe.   30

I.xii O 3 *copy-text*   23 they] Robinson; thy O 3–6

334

ELEGIA 13

Ad Auroram ne properet

Now on the sea from her old love comes shee,
That drawes the day from heavens cold axletree.
Aurora whither slidest thou? downe againe,
And birds for *Memnon* yearly shall be slaine.
Now in her tender armes I sweetly bide,
If ever, now well lies she by my side.
The aire is colde, and sleepe is sweetest now,
And birdes send forth shrill notes from everie bow.
Whither runst thou, that men, and women, love not?
Hold in thy rosie horses that they move not.   10
Ere thou rise starres teach seamen where to saile,
But when thou comest they of their courses faile.
Poore travailers though tierd, rise at thy sight,
And souldiours make them ready to the fight,
The painfull Hinde by thee to field is sent,
Slow oxen early in the yoake are pent.
Thou coosnest boyes of sleepe, and dost betray them
To Pedants, that with cruell lashes pay them.
Thou makste the suretie to the lawyer runne,
That with one worde hath nigh himselfe undone,   20
The lawier and the client hate thy view,
Both whom thou raisest up to toyle anew.
By thy meanes women of their rest are bard,
Thou setst their labouring hands to spin and card.
All could I beare, but that the wench should rise,
Who can indure, save him with whom none lies?
How oft wisht I night would not give thee place,
Nor morning starres shunne thy uprising face.
How oft, that either wind would breake thy coche,
Or steeds might fal forcd with thick clouds approch.   30

I.xiii O1 *copy-text*   4 for] Dyce; from O1–6
1 on] O1–2; ore O3   21 client] O3; client both do O1–2
1 love] O1–2; Love O3   *25 All] O3; This O1–2

Whither gost thou hateful nimph? *Memnon* the elfe
Received his cole-blacke colour from thy selfe.
Say that thy love with *Cæphalus* were not knowne,
Then thinkest thou thy loose life is not showne?
Would *Tithon* might but talke of thee a while,
Not one in heaven should be more base and vile.
Thou leav'st his bed, because hees faint through age,
And early mountest thy hatefull carriage:
But heldst thou in thine armes some *Cæphalus*,
Then wouldst thou cry, stay night and runne not thus. 40
Punish ye, because yeares make him waine?
I did not bid thee wed an aged swaine.
The Moone sleepes with *Endemion* everie day,
Thou art as faire as shee, then kisse and play.
Jove that thou shouldst not hast but wait his leasure,
Made two nights one to finish up his pleasure.
I chid no more, she blusht, and therefore heard me,
Yet lingered not the day, but morning scard me.

ELEGIA 14

Puellam consolatur cui præ nimia cura
comæ deciderant

Leave colouring thy tresses I did cry,
Now hast thou left no haires at all to die.
But what had beene more faire had they beene kept?
Beyond thy robes thy dangling lockes had sweept.
Feardst thou to dresse them? being fine and thinne
Like to the silke the curious *Seres* spinne,
Or thrids which spiders slender foote drawes out
Fastning her light web some old beame about.
Not black, nor golden were they to our viewe,
Yet although neither, mixt of eithers hue, 10

39 heldst] O3; hadst O1–2
41 Punish ye] O1–2; Doest Punish
O3
47 chid] O1; chide O2–3

I.xiv O3 *copy-text*
4 lockes] O5; lackes O3–4
10 neither] Robinson; either O3–6

Such as in hilly *Idas* watry plaines,
The Cedar tall spoyld of his barke retaines.
Ad they were apt to curle an hundred waies,
And did to thee no cause of dolour raise.
Nor hath the needle, or the combes teeth reft them,
The maide that kembd them ever safely left them.
Oft was she drest before mine eyes, yet never,
Snatching the combe, to beate the wench out drave her.
Oft in the morne her haires not yet digested,
Halfe sleeping on a purple bed she rested,   20
Yet seemely like a *Thracian Bacchinall*
That tyr'd doth rashly on the greene grasse fall.
When they were slender, and like downy mosse,
Thy troubled haires, alas, endur'd great losse.
How patiently hot irons they did take
In crooked tramells crispy curles to make.
I cryed, tis sinne, tis sinne, these haires to burne,
They well become thee, then to spare them turne.
Farre off be force, no fire to them may reach,
Thy very haires will the hot bodkin teach.   30
Lost are the goodly lockes, which from their crowne
Phœbus and *Bacchus* wisht were hanging downe.
Such were they as *Diana* painted stands
All naked holding in her wave-moist hands.
Why doest thy ill kembd tresses losse lament?
Why in thy glasse doest looke being discontent?
Bee not to see with wonted eyes inclinde,
To please thy selfe, thy selfe put out of minde.
No charmed herbes of any harlot skathd thee,
No faithlesse witch in *Thessale* waters bath'd thee.   40
No sicknesse harm'd thee, farre be that a way,
No envious tongue wrought thy thicke lockes decay.
By thine owne hand and fault thy hurt doth growe,
Thou mad'st thy head with compound poyson flow.

---

*13 Ad] *stet* O 3   *26 tramells]   Robinson   (trammels);
  18 drave] drive O 3–6   trannels O 3–6
  24 Thy] Dyce; They O 3–6

Now *Germany* shall captive haire-tyers send thee,
And vanquisht people curious dressings lend thee,
Which some admiring, O thou oft wilt blush
And say he likes me for my borrowed bush,
Praysing for me some unknowne *Guelder* dame,
But I remember when it was my fame.   50
Alas she almost weepes, and her white cheekes,
Died red with shame, to hide from shame she seekes.
She holds, and viewes her old lockes in her lappe,
Aye me rare gifts unworthy such a happe.
Cheere up thy selfe, thy losse thou maiest repaire,
And be heereafter seene with native haire.

ELEGIA 15

Ad invidos, quod fama poetarum sit perennis

Envie, why carpest thou my time is spent so ill,
And tearmes my works fruits of an idle quill?
Or that unlike the line from whence I sprong,
Wars dustie honors are refused being yong,
Nor that I studie not the brawling lawes,
Nor set my voyce to sale in everie cause?
Thy scope is mortall, mine eternall fame,
That all the world may ever chaunt my name.
Homer shall live while *Tenedos* stands and *Ide*,
Or into sea swift *Symois* doth slide.   10
Ascreus lives, while grapes with new wine swell,
Or men with crooked sickles corne downe fell.
The world shall of *Callimachus* ever speake,
His Arte excelld, although his witte was weake.
For ever lasts high *Sophocles* proud vaine,
With sunne and moone *Aratus* shall remaine.
While bond-men cheat, fathers be hard, bawds hoorish,

I. xv O1 *copy-text*
2 tearmes] O1–2; termst O3
2 my] O3; our O1–2
*3 sprong] Dyce; come O1–6
4 dustie] O1–2; rustie O3

8 may] O3; might O1–2
*10 into] O3; to the O1–2
10 doth] O3; shall O1–2
13–14 The...weake.] O3; *omit* O1–2
17 be hard] Dyce; hoord O1–6

And strumpets flatter, shall *Menander* flourish.
Rude *Ennius*, and *Plautus* full of wit,
Are both in Fames eternall legend writ.   20
What age of *Varroes* name shall not be tolde,
And *Jasons Argos*, and the fleece of golde?
Loftie *Lucretius* shall live that houre,
That Nature shall dissolve this earthly bowre.
Æneas warre, and *Titerus* shall be read,
While *Rome* of all the conquered world is head.
Till *Cupids* bow, and fierie shafts be broken,
Thy verses sweet *Tibullus* shall be spoken.
And *Gallus* shall be knowne from East to West,
So shall *Licoris* whom he loved best: 30
Therefore when flint and yron weare away,
Verse is immortall, and shall nere decay.
Let Kings give place to verse, and kingly showes,
And banks ore which gold bearing *Tagus* flowes.
Let base conceited wits admire vilde things,
Faire *Phœbus* leade me to the Muses springs.
About my head be quivering Mirtle wound,
And in sad lovers heads let me be found.
The living, not the dead can envie bite,
For after death all men receive their right: 40
Then though death rackes my bones in funerall fier,
Ile live, and as he puls me downe, mount higher.

The same by B.J.

Envie, why twitst thou me, my Time's spent ill?
And call'st my verse fruites of an idle quill?
Or that (unlike the line from whence I sprong)
Wars dustie honors I pursue not young?
Or that I studie not the tedious lawes;
And prostitute my voyce in every cause?
Thy scope is mortall; mine eternall Fame,

26 conquered] O3; conquering O1–2   34 And] O3; The O1–2
*33 Let Kings...to verse] O1–2; To   *41 rackes] *stet* O1 (*i.e.*, rakes *as in* O3)
verse let Kings give place O3

Which through the world shall ever chaunt my name.
Homer will live, whil'st *Tenedos* stands, and *Ide*,
Or to the sea, fleete *Simoïs* doth slide: 10
And so shall *Hesiod* too, while vines doe beare,
Or crooked sickles crop the ripened eare.
Callimachus, though in Invention lowe,
Shall still be sung, since he in Arte doth flowe.
No losse shall come to *Sophocles* proud vaine,
With Sunne and Moone *Aratus* shall remaine.
Whil'st Slaves be false, Fathers hard, and Bauds be whorish,
Whilst Harlots flatter, shall *Menander* florish.
Ennius, though rude, and *Accius* high-reard straine,
A fresh applause in every age shall gaine.   20
Of *Varro's* name, what eare shall not be tolde?
Of *Jasons* Argo? and the *Fleece* of *golde*?
Then, shall *Lucretius* loftie numbers die,
When Earth, and Seas in fire and flames shall frie.
Titirus, Tillage, *Æney* shall be read,
Whil'st *Rome* of all the conquer'd world is head.
Till *Cupids* fires be out, and his bowe broken,
Thy verses (neate *Tibullus*) shall be spoken.
Our *Gallus* shall be knowne from East to west: 30
So shall *Licoris*, whom he now loves best.
The suffering Plough-share or the flint may weare:
But heavenly *Poësie* no death can feare.
Kings shall give place to it, and Kingly showes,
The bankes ore which gold-bearing *Tagus* flowes.
Kneele hindes to trash: me let bright *Phœbus* swell,
With cups full flowing from the *Muses* well.
The frost-drad myrtle shall impale my head,
And of sad lovers Ile be often read.
,,Enuy the living, not the dead, doth bite.   40
,,For after death all men receive their right.
Then when this body falls in funeral fire,
My name shall live, and my best part aspire.

P. Ovidii Nasonis Amorum
Liber Secundus

ELEGIA 1

Quod pro gigantomachia amores scribere
sit coactus

I *Ovid* Poet of my wantonnesse,
Borne at *Peligny*, to write more addresse.
So *Cupid* wills, farre hence be the severe,
You are unapt my looser lines to heare.
Let Maydes whom hot desire to husbands leade,
And rude boyes toucht with unknowne love me reade,
That some youth hurt as I am with loves bowe
His owne flames best acquainted signes may knowe,
And long admiring say by what meanes learnd
Hath this same Poet my sad chaunce discernd?   10
I durst the great celestiall battells tell,
Hundred-hand *Gyges*, and had done it well,
With earthes revenge and how *Olimpus* toppe
High *Ossa* bore, mount *Pelion* up to proppe.
Jove and *Joves* thunderbolts I had in hand
Which for his heaven fell on the Gyants band.
My wench her dore shut, *Joves* affares I left,
Even *Jove* himselfe out off my wit was reft.
Pardon me *Jove*, thy weapons ayde me nought,
Her shut gates greater lightning then thyne brought.   20
Toyes, and light Elegies my darts I tooke,
Quickly soft words hard dores wide open strooke.
Verses deduce the horned bloudy moone
And call the sunnes white horses backe at noone.
Snakes leape by verse from caves of broken mountaines
And turned streames run back-ward to their fountaines.
Verses ope dores, and lockes put in the poast

II.i O3 *copy-text*   *23 deduce] Methuen (*qy*) reduce O3–6
1 my] Robinson; thy O3–6   24 backe] Robinson; blacke O3–6

Although of oake, to yeeld to verses boast.
What helpes it me of fierce *Achill* to sing?
What good to me wil either *Ajax* bring?   30
Or he who war'd and wand'red twenty yeare?
Or wofull *Hector* whom wilde jades did teare?
But when I praise a pretty wenches face
Shee in requitall doth me oft imbrace.
A great reward: *Heroes* of famous names
Farewel, your favour nought my minde inflames.
Wenches apply your faire lookes to my verse
Which golden love doth unto me rehearse.

ELEGIA 2

*Ad Bagoum, ut custodiam puellæ sibi commissæ
laxiorem habeat*

Bagous whose care doth thy Mistrisse bridle,
While I speake some fewe, yet fit words be idle.
I sawe the damsell walking yesterday
There where the porch doth *Danaus* fact display.
Shee pleas'd me, soone I sent, and did her woo,
Her trembling hand writ back she might not doo.
And asking why, this answeare she redoubled,
Because thy care too much thy Mistresse troubled.
Keeper if thou be wise cease hate to cherish,
Beleeve me, whom we feare, we wish to perish.   10
Nor is her husband wise, what needes defence
When un-protected ther is no expence?
But furiously he follow his loves fire
And thinke her chast whom many doe desire.
Stolne liberty she may by thee obtaine,
Which giving her, she may give thee againe.

*35 *Heroes* of] Robinson; *Heroes*, O   12 un-protected] Robinson (unpro-
   O3–6   tected]); un-protested O3–6
  II.ii O3 *copy-text*   13 he follow] *i.e.*, let him follow
*5 me, soone∧] ~ ∧ ~ , O3–6   14 thinke] O4; thinkes O3
8 thy care] O5; they care O3–4

Wilt thou her fault learne, she may make thee tremble,
Feare to be guilty, then thou maiest desemble.
Thinke when she reades, her mother letters sent her,
Let him goe forth knowne, that unknowne did enter,   20
Let him goe see her though she doe not languish
And then report her sicke and full of anguish.
If long she stayes, to thinke the time more short
Lay downe thy forehead in thy lap to snort.
Enquire not what with *Isis* may be done
Nor feare least she to th' theater's runne.
Knowing her scapes thine honour shall encrease,
And what lesse labour then to hold thy peace?
Let him please, haunt the house, be kindly usd,
Enjoy the wench, let all else be refusd.   30
Vaine causes faine of him the true to hide,
And what she likes, let both hold ratifide.
When most her husband bends the browes and frownes,
His fauning wench with her desire he crownes.
But yet sometimes to chide thee let her fall
Counterfet teares: and thee lewd hangman call.
Object thou then what she may well excuse,
To staine all faith in truth, by false crimes use.
Of wealth and honour so shall grow thy heape,
Do this and soone thou shalt thy freedome reape.   40
On tell-tales neckes thou seest the linke-knitt chaines,
The filthy prison faithlesse breasts restraines.
Water in waters, and fruite flying touch
Tantalus seekes, his long tongues gaine is such.
While *Junos* watch-man *Io* too much eyde,
Him timelesse death tooke, she was deifide.
I sawe ones legges with fetters blacke and blewe,
By whom the husband his wives incest knewe.
More he deserv'd, to both great harme he fram'd,
The man did grieve, the woman was defam'd.   50
Trust me all husbands for such faults are sad
Nor make they any man that heare them glad.
If he loves not, deafe eares thou doest importune,

Or if he loves, thy tale breedes his misfortune.
Nor is it easily prov'd though manifest,
She safe by favour of her judge doth rest.
Though himselfe see; heele credit her denyall,
Condemne his eyes, and say there is no tryall.
Spying his mistrisse teares, he will lament
And say this blabbe shall suffer punnishment.   60
Why fightst gainst oddes? to thee being cast do happe
Sharpe stripes, she sitteth in the judges lappe.
To meete for poyson or vilde facts we crave not,
My hands an unsheath'd shyning weapon have not.
Wee seeke that through thee safely love we may,
What can be easier then the thing we pray?

ELEGIA 3

Ad Eunuchum servantem dominam

Aye me an *Eunuch* keepes my mistrisse chaste,
That cannot *Venus* mutuall pleasure taste.
Who first depriv'd yong boyes of their best part,
With selfe same woundes he gave, he ought to smart.
To kinde requests thou wouldst more gentle prove,
If ever wench had made luke-warme thy love:
Thou wert not borne to ride, or armes to beare,
Thy hands agree not with the warlike speare.
Men handle those, all manly hopes resigne,
Thy mistrisse enseignes must be likewise thine.   10
Please her, her hate makes others thee abhorre,
If she discardes thee, what use servest thou for?
Good forme there is, yeares apt to play togither,
Unmeete is beauty without use to wither.
Shee may deceive thee, though thou her protect,
What two determine never wants effect.
Our prayers move thee to assist our drift,
While thou hast time yet to bestowe that gift.

II.iii O 3 *copy-text*

ELEGIA 4

Quod amet mulieres, cuiuscunque formæ sint

I meane not to defend the scapes of any,
Or justifie my vices being many,
For I confesse, if that might merite favour,
Heere I display my lewd and loose behaviour.
I loathe, yet after that I loathe, I runne:
Oh how the burthen irkes, that we should shun.
I cannot rule my selfe, but where love please
Am driven like a ship upon rough seas,
No one face likes me best, all faces moove,
A hundred reasons makes me ever love.   10
If any eie mee with a modest looke,
I burne, and by that blushfull glance am tooke:
And she thats coy I like for being no clowne,
Me thinkes she should be nimble when shees downe.
Though her sowre looks a *Sabines* browe resemble,
I thinke sheele doe, but deepely can dissemble.
If she be learned, then for her skill I crave her,
If not, because shees simple I would have her.
Before *Callimachus* one preferres me farre,
Seeing she likes my bookes, why should we jarre?   20
Another railes at me, and that I write,
Yet would I lie with her if that I might.
Trips she, it likes me well, plods she, what than?
She would be nimbler, lying with a man.
And when one sweetely sings, then straight I long,
To quaver on her lippes even in her song,
Or if one touch the lute with art and cunning,
Who would not love those hands for their swift running?
And she I like that with a majestie,
Foldes up her armes, and makes low curtesie.   30

II.iv O1 *copy-text*   12 glance] O3; glasse O1-2
8 Am] O3; And O1-2   14 should] O1-2; would O3
10 makes] O1-2; make O3   29 she] O1-2; her O3
12 burne] Dyce; blushe O1-6

To leave my selfe, that am in love with all,
Some one of these might make the chastest fall.
If she be tall, shees like an *Amazon*,
And therefore filles the bed she lies uppon:
If short, she lies the rounder: to speake troth,
Both short and long please me, for I love both:
I thinke what one undeckt would be, being drest;
Is she attired, then shew her graces best.
A white wench thralles me, so doth golden yellowe,
And nut-browne girles in doing have no fellowe.   40
If her white necke be shadowde with blacke haire,
Why so was *Ledas*, yet was *Leda* faire.
Amber trest is shee, then on the morne thinke I,
My love alludes to everie historie:
A yong wench pleaseth, and an old is good,
This for her looks, that for her woman-hood:
Nay what is she that any *Romane* loves,
But my ambitious ranging mind approoves?

ELEGIA 5

Ad amicam corruptam

No love is so dere (quiverd *Cupid* flie)
That my chiefe wish should be so oft to die.
Minding thy fault, with death I wish to revill,
Alas a wench is a perpetuall evill.
No intercepted lines thy deedes display,
No gifts given secretly thy crime bewray.
O would my proofes as vaine might be withstood,
Aye me poore soule, why is my cause so good.
He's happy, that his love dares boldly credit,
To whom his wench can say, I never did it.   10
He's cruell, and too much his griefe doth favour

31 with all] O3; withall O1–2
35 speake] O1–2; say O3
37–40 I thinke...fellowe.] O3; *omit*
   O1–2

37 drest;] O6 (~ .); ~ ͜ O3–5
*43 Amber] O3; Yellow O1–2
II.v O3 *copy-text*

That seekes the conquest by her loose behaviour.
Poore wretch I sawe when thou didst thinke I slumbred,
Not drunke, your faults in the spilt wine I numbred.
I sawe your nodding eye-browes much to speake,
Even from your cheekes parte of a voice did breake.
Not silent were thine eyes, the boord with wine
Was scribled, and thy fingers writ a line.
I knew your speech (what do not lovers see?)
And words that seem'd for certaine markes to be.   20
Now many guests were gone, the feast being done,
The youthfull sort to divers pastimes runne.
I sawe you then unlawfull kisses joyne,
(Such with my tongue it likes me to purloyne).
None such the sister gives her brother grave,
But such kinde wenches let their lovers have.
Phœbus gave not *Diana* such tis thought,
But *Venus* often to her *Mars* such brought.
What doest, I cryed, transportst thou my delight?
My lordly hands ile throwe upon my right.   30
Such blisse is onely common to us two,
In this sweete good, why hath a third to do?
This, and what grife inforc'd me say I say'd,
A scarlet blush her guilty face arayed.
Even such as by *Aurora* hath the skie,
Or maides that their betrothed husbands spie.
Such as a rose mixt with a lilly breedes,
Or when the Moone travailes with charmed steedes.
Or such, as least long yeares should turne the die,
Arachne staynes *Assyrian* ivory.   40
To these, or some of these like was her colour,
By chaunce her beauty never shined fuller.
She viewed the earth: the earth to viewe, beseem'd her.
She looked sad: sad, comely I esteem'd her.
Even kembed as they were, her lockes to rend,
And scratch her faire soft cheekes I did intend.

*13 wretch] Dyce; wench O 3–6   *14 in] on O 3–6

347

Seeing her face, mine upreard armes discended,
With her owne armor was my wench defended.
I that ere-while was fierce, now humbly sue,
Least with worse kisses she should me indue.   50
She laught, and kissed so sweetely as might make
Wrath-kindled *Jove* away his thunder shake.
I grieve least others should such good perceive,
And wish hereby them all unknowne to leave.
Also much better were they then I tell,
And ever seemed as some new sweete befell.
Tis ill they pleas'd so much, for in my lips,
Lay her whole tongue hid, mine in hers she dips.
This grieves me not, no joyned kisses spent,
Bewaile I onely, though I them lament.   60
No where can they be taught but in the bed,
I know no maister of so great hire sped.

ELEGIA 6

In mortem psittaci

The parrat from east *India* to me sent,
Is dead, al-fowles her exequies frequent.
Go goodly birdes, striking your breasts bewaile,
And with rough clawes your tender cheekes assaile.
For wofull haires let piece-torne plumes abound,
For long shrild trumpets let your notes resound.
Why *Philomele* doest *Tereus* leudnesse mourne?
All wasting years have that complaint out worne.
Thy tunes let this rare birdes sad funerall borrowe,
Itis is great, but auntient cause of sorrowe.   10
All you whose pineons in the cleare aire sore,
But most thou friendly turtle-dove, deplore.
Full concord all your lives was you betwixt,
And to the end your constant faith stood fixt.
What *Pylades* did to *Orestes* prove,

II.vi O3 *copy-text*   8 out] Tucker Brooke; not O3–6
*3, 58 goodly] *stet* O3–6   10 *Itis* is] Methuen; It is as O3–6

Such to the parrat was the turtle dove.
But what availde this faith? her rarest hue?
Or voice that howe to change the wilde notes knew?
What helpes it thou wert given to please my wench,
Birdes haples glory, death thy life doth quench.　　　　　20
Thou with thy quilles mightst make greene *Emeralds* darke,
And passe our scarlet of red saffrons marke.
No such voice-feigning bird was on the ground,
Thou spokest thy words so well with stammering sound.
Envy hath rapt thee, no fierce warres thou movedst,
Vaine babling speech, and pleasant peace thou lovedst.
Behould how quailes among their battailes live,
Which do perchance old age unto them give.
A little fild thee, and for love of talke,
Thy mouth to taste of many meates did balke.　　　　　30
Nuts were thy food, and Poppie causde thee sleepe,
Pure waters moisture thirst away did keepe.
The ravenous vulture lives, the Puttock hovers
Around the aire, the Cadesse raine discovers,
And Crowes survive armes-bearing *Pallas* hate,
Whose life nine ages scarce bring out of date.
Dead is that speaking image of mans voice,
The Parrat given me, the farre worlds best choice.
The greedy spirits take the best things first,
Supplying their voide places with the worst.　　　　　40
Thersites did *Protesilaus* survive,
And *Hector* dyed his brothers yet alive.
My wenches vowes for thee what should I show,
Which stormie South-windes into sea did blowe?
The seventh day came, none following mightst thou see,
And the fates distaffe emptie stood to thee,
Yet words in thy benummed palate rung,
Farewell *Corinna* cryed thy dying tongue.
Elisium hath a wood of holme trees black,
Whose earth doth not perpetuall greene-grasse lacke,　　　　　50

*35 Crowes survive] Crowes survives　　38 worlds] Robinson; words O3–6
　　O3–6

349

There good birds rest (if we beleeve things hidden)
Whence uncleane fowles are said to be forbidden.
There harmelesse Swans feed all abroad the river,
There lives the *Phœnix* one alone bird ever.
There *Junoes* bird displayes his gorgious feather,
And loving Doves kisse eagerly together.
The Parrat into wood receiv'd with these,
Turnes all the goodly birdes to what she please.
A grave her bones hides, on her corps great grave,
The little stones these little verses have.   60
This tombe approoves, I pleasde my mistresse well,
My mouth in speaking did all birds excell.

ELEGIA 7

Amicæ se purgat, quod ancillam non amet

Doost me of new crimes alwayes guilty frame?
To over-come, so oft to fight I shame.
If on the Marble Theater I looke,
One among many is to grieve thee tooke.
If some faire wench me secretly behold,
Thou arguest she doth secret markes unfold.
If I praise any, thy poore haires thou tearest,
If blame, dissembling of my fault thou fearest.
If I looke well, thou thinkest thou doest not move,
If ill, thou saiest I die for others love.   10
Would I were culpable of some offence,
They that deserve paine, beare't with patience.
Now rash accusing, and thy vaine beliefe,
Forbid thine anger to procure my griefe.
Loe how the miserable great eared *Asse*,
Duld with much beating slowly forth doth passe.
Behold *Cypassis* wont to dresse thy head,
Is charg'd to violate her mistresse bed.
The Gods from this sinne rid me of suspition,

II.vii O 3 *copy-text*
*59 great] *stet* O 3–6

350

To like a base wench of despisd condition.   20
With *Venus* game who will a servant grace?
Or any back made rough with stripes imbrace?
Adde she was diligent thy locks to braide,
And for her skill to thee a gratefull maide.
Should I sollicit her that is so just:
To take repulse, and cause her shew my lust?
I sweare by *Venus*, and the wingd boyes bowe,
My selfe unguilty of this crime I know.

ELEGIA 8

Ad Cypassim ancillam Corinnæ

Cypassis that a thousand wayes trimst haire,
Worthy to keembe none but a Goddesse faire,
Our pleasant scapes shew thee no clowne to be,
Apt to thy mistrisse, but more apt to me.
Who that our bodies were comprest bewrayde?
Whence knowes *Corinna* that with thee I playde?
Yet blusht I not, nor usde I any saying,
That might be urg'd to witnesse our false playing.
What if a man with bond-women offend,
To prove him foolish did I ere contend?   10
Achilles burnt with face of captive *Briseis*,
Great *Agamemnon* lov'd his servant *Chriseis*.
Greater then these my selfe I not esteeme,
What graced Kings, in me no shame I deeme.
But when on thee her angry eyes did rush,
In both thy cheekes she did perceive thee blush,
But being present, might that worke the best,
By *Venus* Deity how did I protest.
Thou Goddesse doest command a warme South-blast,
My false oathes in *Carpathian* seas to cast.   20
For which good turne my sweete reward repay,
Let me lie with thee browne *Cypasse* to day.

II.viii O3 *copy-text*   20 false] Tucker Brooke; selfe O3–6
16 thy] Dyce; my O3–6

Ungrate why feignest new feares? and doest refuse;
Well maiest thou one thing for thy Mistresse use.
If thou deniest foole, Ile our deeds expresse,
And as a traitour mine owne fault confesse.
Telling thy mistresse, where I was with thee,
How oft, and by what meanes we did agree.

ELEGIA 9

Ad Cupidinem

O *Cupid* that doest never cease my smart,
O boy that lyest so slothfull in my heart.
Why me that alwayes was thy souldiour found,
Doest harme, and in thy tents why doest me wound?
Why burnes thy brand, why strikes thy bow thy friends?
More glory by thy vanquisht foes assends.
Did not *Pelides* whom his Speare did grieve,
Being requirde, with speedy helpe relieve?
Hunters leave taken beasts, pursue the chase,
And then things found do ever further pace.   10
We people wholy given thee, feele thine armes,
Thy dull hand stayes thy striving enemies harmes.
Doest joy to have thy hooked Arrowes shaked,
In naked bones? love hath my bones left naked.
So many men and maidens without love,
Hence with great laude thou maiest a triumph move.
Rome if her strength the huge world had not fild,
With strawie cabins now her courts should build.
The weary souldiour hath the conquerd fields,
His sword layed by, safe, though rude places yeelds.   20
The Docke in harbours ships drawne from the flouds,
Horse freed from service range abroad the woods.
And time it was for me to live in quiet,
That have so oft serv'd pretty wenches dyet.
Yet should I curse a God, if he but said,

II.ix O 3 *copy-text*   *4 thy tents] *stet* O 3–4

352

Live without love, so sweete ill is a maide.
For when my loathing it of heate deprives me,
I know not whether my mindes whirle-wind drives me.
Even as a head-strong courser beares away,
His rider vainely striving him to stay,   30
Or as a sodaine gale thrustes into sea,
The haven touching barcke now nere the lea,
So wavering *Cupid* brings me backe amaine,
And purple Love resumes his dartes againe.
Strike boy, I offer thee my naked brest,
Heere thou hast strength, here thy right hand doth rest.
Here of themselves thy shafts come, as if shot,
Better then I their quiver knowes them not.
Haples is he that all the night lies quiet
And slumbring, thinkes himselfe much blessed by it.   40
Foole, what is sleepe but image of cold death,
Long shalt thou rest when Fates expire thy breath.
But me let crafty damsells words deceive,
Great joyes by hope I inly shall conceive.
Now let her flatter me, now chide me hard,
Let me enjoy her oft, oft be debard.
Cupid by thee, *Mars* in great doubt doth trample,
And thy step-father fights by thy example.
Light art thou, and more windie then thy winges,
Joyes with uncertaine faith thou takest and brings.   50
Yet Love, if thou with thy faire mother heare,
Within my brest no desert empire beare.
Subdue the wandring wenches to thy raigne,
So of both people shalt thou homage gaine.

32 haven] O5: heaven O3-4   *46 me...her] Dyce; her...me O3-6

ELEGIA 10

Ad Græcinum quod eodem tempore duas amet

Græcinus (well I wot) thou touldst me once,
I could not be in love with twoo at once,
By thee deceived, by thee surprisde am I,
For now I love two women equallie:
Both are wel favoured, both rich in array,
Which is the loveliest it is hard to say:
This seemes the fairest, so doth that to mee,
And this doth please me most, and so doth she.
Even as a boate, tost by contrarie winde,
So with this love and that, wavers my minde.   10
Venus, why doublest thou my endlesse smart?
Was not one wench inough to greeve my heart?
Why addst thou starres to heaven, leaves to greene woods,
And to the vast deep sea fresh water flouds?
Yet this is better farre then lie alone,
Let such as be mine enemies have none,
Yea, let my foes sleepe in an emptie bed,
And in the midst their bodies largely spread:
But may soft love rowse up my drowsie eies,
And from my mistris bosome let me rise: 20
Let one wench cloy me with sweete loves delight,
If one can doote, if not, two everie night,
Though I am slender, I have store of pith,
Nor want I strength, but weight to presse her with:
Pleasure addes fuell to my lustfull fire,
I pay them home with that they most desire:
Oft have I spent the night in wantonnesse,
And in the morne beene lively nerethelesse.
Hees happie who loves mutuall skirmish slayes,
And to the Gods for that death *Ovid* prayes.   30

II.x O1 *copy-text*   14 vast deep] O3; deep vast O1-2
*8 And this] O3; This O1-2   29 slayes] O1-2; layes O3

Let souldiour chase his enemies amaine,
And with his bloud eternall honour gaine,
Let marchants seeke wealth, and with perjured lips,
Being wrackt, carowse the sea tir'd by their ships:
But when I die, would I might droope with doing,
And in the midst thereof, set my soule going,
That at my funeralles some may weeping crie,
Even as he led his life, so did he die.

ELEGIA 11

Ad amicam navigantem

The lofty Pine from high mount *Pelion* raught
Ill waies by rough seas wondring waves first taught,
Which rashly twixt the sharpe rocks in the deepe,
Caried the famous golden-fleeced sheepe.
O would that no Oares might in seas have suncke,
The *Argos* wrackt had deadly waters drunke.
Loe country Gods, and known bed to forsake,
Corinna meanes, and dangerous wayes to take.
For thee the East and West winds make me pale,
With Icy *Boreas*, and the Southerne gale: 10
Thou shalt admire no woods or Citties there,
The unjust seas all blewish do appeare.
The Ocean hath no painted stones or shelles,
The sucking shore with their aboundance swels.
Maides on the shore, with marble white feete tread,
So farre 'tis safe, but to go farther dread.
Let others tell how winds fierce battailes wage,
How *Scyllaes* and *Caribdis* waters rage.
And with what rockes the feard *Cerannia* threat,
In what gulfe either *Syrtes* have their seate.   20

*31–2 souldiour...his...his]   O 1–2;   II.xi O 3 *copy-text*
    souldiours...their...their O 3–6   7 known] Robinson; know O 3–6
  33 and] Cunningham] *omit* O 1–6   19 rockes] Dyce; rocke O 3–6
*34 Being] Cunningham] And being   *19 *Cerannia*] stet O 3–6
    O 1–6

Let others tell this, and what each one speakes
Beleeve, no tempest the beleever wreakes.
Too late you looke back, when with anchors weighd,
The crooked Barque hath her swift sailes displayd.
The carefull ship-man now feares angry gusts,
And with the waters sees death neere him thrusts,
But if that *Triton* tosse the troubled floud,
In all thy face will be no crimsen bloud.
Then wilt thou *Lædas* noble twinne-starres pray,
And he is happy whom the earth holds, say.   30
It is more safe to sleepe, to read a booke,
The *Thracian* Harpe with cunning to have strooke,
But if my words with winged stormes hence slip,
Yet *Galatea* favour thou her ship.
The losse of such a wench much blame will gather,
Both to the Sea-nimphes, and the Sea-nimphes father.
Go, minding to returne with prosperous winde,
Whose blast may hether strongly be inclinde,
Let *Nereus* bend the waves unto this shore,
Hether the windes blowe, here the spring-tide rore.   40
Request milde *Zephires* helpe for thy availe,
And with thy hand assist the swelling saile.
I from the shore thy knowne ship first will see,
And say it brings her that preserveth me;
Ile clip and kisse thee with all contentation,
For thy returne shall fall the vowd oblation,
And in the forme of beds weele strowe soft sand,
Each little hill shall for a table stand:
There wine being fild, thou many things shalt tell,
How almost wrackt thy ship in maine seas fell.   50
And hasting to me, neither darkesome night,
Nor violent South-windes did thee ought affright.
Ile thinke all true, though it be feigned matter.
Mine owne desires why should my selfe not flatter?
Let the bright day-starre cause in heaven this day be,
To bring that happy time so soone as may be.

42 the] Robinson; thy O 3–6

ELEGIA 12

Exultat, quod amica potitus sit

About my temples go triumphant bayes,
Conquer'd *Corinna* in my bosome layes.
She whom her husband, guard, and gate as foes,
Least Arte should winne her, firmely did inclose.
That victory doth chiefely triumph merit,
Which without bloud-shed doth the pray inherit.
No little ditched townes, no lowlie walles,
But to my share a captive damsell falles.
When *Troy* by ten yeares battle tumbled downe,
With the *Atrides* many gainde renowne.   10
But I no partner of my glory brooke,
Nor can an other say his helpe I tooke.
I guide and souldiour wunne the field and weare her,
I was both horse-man, foote-man, standard bearer.
Nor in my act hath fortune mingled chance,
O care-got triumph hetherwards advance.
Nor is my warres cause new, but for a Queene
Europe, and *Asia* in firme peace had beene.
The *Laphithes*, and the *Centaures* for a woman,
To cruell armes their drunken selves did summon.   20
A woman forc'd the *Troyanes* new to enter
Warres, just *Latinus*, in thy kingdomes center:
A woman against late-built *Rome* did send
The *Sabine* Fathers, who sharpe warres intend.
I saw how Bulls for a white Heifer strive,
Shee looking on them did more courage give.
And me with many, but yet me without murther,
Cupid commands to move his ensignes further.

II.xii O3 *copy-text*

ELEGIA 13

Ad Isidem, ut parientem Corinnam iuvet

While rashly her wombes burthen she casts out,
Wearie *Corinna* hath her life in doubt.
She secretly with me such harme attempted,
Angry I was, but feare my wrath exempted.
But she conceiv'd of me, or I am sure
I oft have done, what might as much procure.
Thou that frequents *Canopus* pleasant fields,
Memphis, and *Pharos* that sweete date trees yeelds,
And where swift *Nile* in his large channell slipping,
By seaven huge mouthes into the sea is skipping,   10
By fear'd *Anubis* visage I thee pray,
So in thy Temples shall *Osiris* stay,
And the dull snake about thy offrings creepe,
And in thy pompe hornd *Apis* with thee keepe,
Turne thy lookes hether, and in one spare twaine,
Thou givest my mistris life, she mine againe.
Shee oft hath serv'd thee upon certaine dayes,
Where the *French* rout engirt themselves with Bayes.
On labouring women thou doest pitty take,
Whose bodies with their heavy burthens ake.   20
My wench, *Lucina*, I intreat thee favour,
Worthy she is, thou shouldst in mercy save her.
In white, with incense Ile thine Altars greete,
My selfe will bring vowed gifts before thy feete,
Subscribing, *Naso* with *Corinna* sav'd:
Do but deserve gifts with this title grav'd.
But if in so great feare I may advize thee,
To have this skirmish fought, let it suffice thee.

II.xiii O 3 *copy-text*   10 skipping] Dyce; slipping O 3–6
*9 slipping] stet O 3–6

ELEGIA 14

In amicam, quod abortivum ipsa fecerit

What helpes it Woman to be free from warre?
Nor being arm'd fierce troupes to follow farre?
If without battell selfe-wrought wounds annoy them,
And their owne privie weapon'd hands destroy them.
Who unborne infants first to slay invented,
Deserv'd thereby with death to be tormented.
Because thy belly should rough wrinckles lacke,
Wilt thou thy wombe-inclosed off-spring wracke?
Had ancient Mothers this vile custome cherisht,
All humaine kinde by their default had perisht.   10
Or stones, our stockes originall, should be hurld,
Againe by some in this unpeopled world.
Who should have *Priams* wealthy substance wonne,
If watry *Thetis* had her childe fordone?
In swelling wombe her twinnes had *Ilia* kilde?
He had not beene that conquering *Rome* did build.
Had *Venus* spoilde her bellies *Troyane* fruite,
The earth of *Cæsars* had beene destitute.
Thou also, that wert borne faire, hadst decayed,
If such a worke thy mother had assayed.   20
My selfe that better dye with loving may
Had seene, my mother killing me, no day.
Why takest increasing grapes from Vine-trees full?
With cruell hand why doest greene Apples pull?
Fruites ripe will fall, let springing things increase,
Life is no light price of a small surcease.
Why with hid irons are your bowels torne?
And why dire poison give you babes unborne?
At *Cholcis* stain'd with childrens bloud men raile,
And mother-murtherd *Itis* they bewaile,   30
Both unkinde parents, but for causes sad,

II.xiv O3 *copy-text*   22 no] Dyce; to O3–6
11 Or] Dyce; On O3–6   30 they] Robinson; thee O3–6

Their wedlocks pledges veng'd their husbands bad.
What *Tereus*, what *Jason* you provokes,
To plague your bodies with such harmefull strokes?
Armenian Tygers never did so ill,
Nor dares the Lyonesse her young whelpes kill.
But tender Damsels do it, though with paine,
Oft dyes she that her paunch-wrapt child hath slaine.
Shee dyes, and with loose haires to grave is sent,
And who ere see her, worthily lament.   40
But in the ayre let these words come to nought,
And my presages of no weight be thought.
Forgive her gratious Gods this one delict,
And on the next fault punishment inflict.

ELEGIA 15

Ad annulum, quem dono amicæ dedit

Thou ring that shalt my faire girles finger binde,
Wherein is seene the givers loving minde:
Be welcome to her, gladly let her take thee,
And her small joynts incircling round hoope make thee.
Fit her so well, as she is fit for me:
And of just compasse for her knuckles bee.
Blest ring thou in my mistris hand shalt lye,
My selfe poore wretch mine owne gifts now envie.
O would that sodainly into my gift,
I could my selfe by secret Magicke shift.   10
Then would I wish thee touch my mistris pappe,
And hide thy left hand underneath her lappe.
I would get off though straight, and sticking fast,
And in her bosome strangely fall at last.
Then I, that I may seale her privy leaves,
Least to the waxe the hold-fast drye gemme cleaves,
Would first my beautious wenches moist lips touch,
Onely Ile signe nought, that may grieve me much.
I would not out, might I in one place hit,

II.xv O 3 *copy-text*

But in lesse compasse her small fingers knit.   20
My life, that I will shame thee never feare,
Or be a loade thou shouldst refuse to beare.
Weare me, when warmest showers thy members wash,
And through the gemme let thy lost waters pash.
But seeing thee, I thinke my thing will swell,
And even the ring performe a mans part well.
Vaine things why wish I? go small gift from hand,
Let her my faith with thee given understand.

ELEGIA 16

Ad amicam, ut ad rura sua veniat

Sulmo, Pelignies third part me containes,
A small, but wholesome soyle with watrie veynes.
Although the sunne to rive the earth incline,
And the *Icarian* froward Dog-starre shine,
Pelignian fields with liqued rivers flowe,
And on the soft ground fertile greene grasse growe.
With corne the earth abounds, with vines much more,
And some few pastures *Pallas* Olives bore.
And by the rising herbes, where cleare springs slide,
A grassie turffe the moistened earth doth hide.   10
But absent is my fire, lyes ile tell none,
My heate is heere, what moves my heate is gone.
Pollux and *Castor*, might I stand betwixt,
In heaven without thee would I not be fixt.
Upon the cold earth pensive let them lay,
That meane to travaile some long irkesome way.
Or els will maidens, yong-mens mates, to go
If they determine to persever so.
Then on the rough *Alpes* should I tread aloft,
My hard way with my mistrisse would seeme soft.   20
With her I durst the *Lybian Syrtes* breake through,
And raging Seas in boistrous South-winds plough.

22 be] Robinson; by O3–6   5 with] O5; which O3–4
  II.xvi O3 *copy-text*

No barking Dogs that *Syllaes* intrailes beare,
Nor thy gulfes crooked *Malea*, would I feare.
No flowing waves with drowned ships forth poured,
By cloyed *Charibdis*, and againe devoured.
But if sterne *Neptunes* windie powre prevaile,
And waters force, force helping Gods to faile,
With thy white armes upon my shoulders seaze,
So sweete a burthen I will beare with eaze.   30
The youth oft swimming to his *Hero* kinde,
Had then swum over, but the way was blinde.
But without thee, although vine-planted ground
Conteines me, though the streames in fields surround,
Though *Hindes* in brookes the running waters bring,
And coole gales shake the tall trees leavy spring,
Healthfull *Peligny* I esteeme nought worth,
Nor do I like the country of my birth.
Sythia, Cilicia, Brittaine are as good,
And rockes dyed crimson with *Prometheus* bloud.   40
Elmes love the Vines, the Vines with Elmes abide,
Why doth my mistresse from me oft devide?
Thou swearest, devision should not twixt us rise,
By me, and by my starres, thy radiant eyes.
Maides words more vaine and light then falling leaves,
Which as it seemes, hence winde and sea bereaves.
If any godly care of me thou hast,
Adde deeds unto thy promises at last.
And with swift Naggs drawing thy little Coach,
(Their reines let loose) right soone my house approach.   50
But when she comes, you swelling mounts sinck downe,
And falling vallies be the smooth-wayes crowne.

43 swearest] *i.e., probably* swarest *as in*   51 you] Dyce; your O 3–6
Tucker Brooke

ELEGIA 17

Quod Corinnæ soli sit serviturus

To serve a wench if any thinke it shame,
He being Judge, I am convinc'd of blame.
Let me be slandered, while my fire she hides,
That *Paphos*, and the floud-beate *Cithera* guides.
Would I had beene my mistresse gentle prey,
Since some faire one I should of force obey.
Beauty gives heart, *Corinnas* lookes excell,
Aye me why is it knowne to her so well?
But by her glasse disdainefull pride she learnes,
Nor she her selfe but first trim'd up discernes. 　　　10
Not though thy face in all things make thee raigne,
(O face most cunning mine eyes to detaine)
Thou oughtst therefore to scorne me for thy mate,
Small things with greater may be copulate.
Love-snarde *Calypso* is supposde to pray,
A mortall nimphes refusing Lord to stay.
Who doubts, with *Pelius*, *Thetis* did consort,
Egeria with just *Numa* had good sport,
Venus with *Vulcan*, though smiths tooles laide by,
With his stumpe-foote he halts ill-favouredly. 　　　20
This kinde of verse is not alike, yet fit,
With shorter numbers the heroicke sit.
And thou my light accept me how so ever,
Lay in the mid bed, there be my law giver.
My stay no crime, my flight no joy shall breede,
Nor of our love to be asham'd we need,
For great revenews I good verses have,
And many by me to get glory crave.
I know a wench reports her selfe *Corinne*,
What would not she give that faire name to winne? 　　　30
But sundry flouds in one banke never go,
Eurotas cold, and poplar-bearing *Po*.
Nor in my bookes shall one but thou be writ,
Thou doest alone give matter to my wit.

II.xvii O 3 *copy-text*

ELEGIA 18

Ad Macrum, quod de amoribus scribat

To tragick verse while thou *Achilles* trainst,
And new sworne souldiours maiden armes retainst,
Wee *Macer* sit in *Venus* slothfull shade,
And tender love hath great things hatefull made.
Often at length, my wench depart, I bid,
Shee in my lap sits still as earst she did.
I sayd it irkes me: halfe to weping framed,
Aye me she cries, to love, why art a shamed?
Then wreathes about my necke her winding armes,
And thousand kisses gives, that worke my harmes: 10
I yeeld, and back my wit from battells bring,
Domesticke acts, and mine owne warres to sing.
Yet tragedies, and scepters fild my lines,
But though I apt were for such high deseignes,
Love laughed at my cloak, and buskines painted,
And rule so soone with private hands acquainted.
My Mistris deity also drewe me fro it,
And Love triumpheth ore his buskind Poet.
What lawfull is, or we professe Loves art,
(Alas my precepts turne my selfe to smart)   20
We write, or what *Penelope* sends *Ulysses*,
Or *Phillis* teares that her *Demophoon* misses,
What thanklesse *Jason*, *Macareus*, and *Paris*,
Phedra, and *Hipolite* may read, my care is,
And what poore *Dido* with her drawne sword sharpe,
Doth say, with her that lov'd the *Aonian* harpe.
As soone as from strange lands *Sabinus* came,
And writings did from diverse places frame,
White-cheekt *Penelope* knewe *Ulisses* signe,
The stepdame read *Hyppolitus* lustlesse line.   30
Eneas to *Elisa* answere gives,
And *Phillis* hath to reade; if now she lives.
Jasons sad letter doth *Hipsipile* greete,

Sappho her vowed harpe laies at *Phœbus* feete.
Nor of thee *Macer* that resoundst forth armes,
Is golden love hid in *Mars* mid alarmes.
There *Paris* is, and *Helens* crymes record,
With *Laodameia* mate to her dead Lord.
Unlesse I erre to these thou more incline,
Then warres, and from thy tents wilt come to mine.   40

ELEGIA 19

Ad rivalem, cui uxor curæ non erat

Foole if to keepe thy wife thou hast no neede,
Keepe her for me, my more desire to breede.
Wee skorne things lawfull, stolne sweetes we affect,
Cruell is he, that loves whom none protect.
Let us both lovers hope, and feare a like,
And may repulse place for our wishes strike.
What should I do with fortune that nere failes me?
Nothing I love, that at all times availes me.
Wily *Corinna* sawe this blemish in me,
And craftily knowes by what meanes to winne me.   10
Ah often, that her hale head aked, she lying,
Wild me, whose slowe feete sought delay, be flying.
Ah oft how much she might she feignd offence;
And doing wrong made shew of innocence.
So having vext she nourisht my warme fire,
And was againe most apt to my desire.
To please me, what faire termes and sweet words ha's shee,
Great gods what kisses, and how many gave she?
Thou also that late tookest mine eyes away,
Oft couzen me, oft being wooed say nay.   20
And on thy thre-shold let me lie dispred,
Suffring much cold by hoary nights frost bred.
So shall my love continue many yeares,
This doth delight me, this my courage cheares.
Fat love, and too much fulsome me annoyes,

Even as sweete meate a glutted stomacke cloyes.
In brazen tower had not *Danae* dwelt,
A mothers joy by *Jove* she had not felt.
While *Juno Io* keepes when hornes she wore,
Jove liked her better then he did before.   30
Who covets lawfull things takes leaves from woods,
And drinkes stolne waters in surrownding floudes.
Her lover let her mocke, that long will raigne,
Aye me, let not my warnings cause my paine.
What ever haps, by suffrance harme is done,
What flies, I followe, what followes me I shunne.
But thou of thy faire damsell too secure,
Beginne to shut thy house at evening sure.
Search at the dore who knocks oft in the darke,
In nights deepe silence why the ban-dogges barke.   40
Whether the subtile maide lines bringes and carries,
Why she alone in empty bed oft tarries.
Let this care some-times bite thee to the quick,
That to deceits it may me forward pricke.
To steale sands from the shore he loves alife,
That can effect a foolish wittalls wife.
Now I forewarne, unlesse to keepe her stronger,
Thou doest beginne, she shall be mine no longer.
Long have I borne much, hoping time would beate thee
To guard her well, that well I might entreate thee.   50
Thou suffrest what no husband can endure,
But of my love it will an end procure.
Shall I poore soule be never interdicted?
Nor never with nights sharpe revenge afflicted?
In sleeping shall I fearelesse drawe my breath?
Wilt nothing do, why I should wish thy death?
Can I but loath a husband growne a baude?
By thy default thou doest our joyes defraude.
Some other seeke that may in patience strive with thee,
To pleasure me, for-bid me to corive with thee.   60

46 effect] *i.e.*, affect (*amare*) *as in* Robinson

P. Ovidii Nasonis Amorum
Liber tertius

ELEGIA 1

Deliberatio poetæ, utrum elegos pergat scribere
an potius tragedias

An old wood, stands uncut of long yeares space,
Tis credible some god-head haunts the place.
In midst thereof a stone-pav'd sacred spring,
Where round about small birdes most sweetely sing.
Heere while I walke hid close in shadie grove,
To finde, what worke my muse might move, I strove.
Elegia came with haires perfumed sweete,
And one, I thinke, was longer, of her feete.
A decent forme, thinne robe, a lovers looke,
By her footes blemish greater grace she tooke.　　　　　10
Then with huge steps came violent *Tragedie*,
Sterne was her front, her cloake on ground did lie.
Her left hand held abroad a regal scepter,
The *Lydian* buskin in fit paces kept her.
And first she sayd, when will thy love be spent,
O Poet carelesse of thy argument?
Wine-bibbing banquets tell thy naughtinesse,
Each crosse waies corner doth as much expresse.
Oft some points at the prophet passing by,
And this is he whom fierce love burnes, they cry.　　　　　20
A laughing stocke thou art to all the citty,
While without shame thou singst thy lewdnesse ditty.
Tis time to move grave things in lofty stile,
Long hast thou loyterd, greater workes compile.
The subject hides thy wit, mens acts resound,
This thou wilt say to be a worthy ground.

III.i O3 *copy-text*　　　　　　14 in] Robinson; *omit* O3–6
　2 god-head] Robinson; good head　　14 paces] Robinson; places O3–6
　　O3–6　　　　　　　　　　　　　15 she] Br MS, Dyce; he O3–6
*12 cloake] Dyce; looke O3–6

Thy muse hath played what may milde girles content,
And by those numbers is thy first youth spent.
Now give the *Roman* Tragedie a name,
To fill my lawes thy wanton spirit frame. 30
This saied, she mov'd her buskins gaily varnisht,
And seaven times shooke her head with thicke locks garnisht.
The other smilde, (I wot) with wanton eyes,
Erre I? or mirtle in her right hand lies.
With lofty wordes stout *Tragedie* (she sayd)
Why treadst me downe? art thou aye gravely plaied?
Thou deignst unequall lines should thee rehearse,
Thou fightst against me using mine owne verse.
Thy lofty stile with mine I not compare,
Small doores unfitting for large houses are. 40
Light am I, and with me, my care, light love,
Not stronger am I, then the thing I move.
Venus without me should be rusticall,
This goddesse company doth to me befall.
What gate thy stately words cannot unlocke,
My flatt'ring speeches soone wide open knocke.
And I deserve more then thou canst in verity,
By suffring much not borne by thy severity.
By me *Corinna* learnes, cousening her guard,
To get the dore with little noise unbard. 50
And slipt from bed cloth'd in a loose night-gowne,
To move her feete unheard in setting downe.
Ah howe oft on hard doores hung I engrav'd,
From no mans reading fearing to be sav'd.
But till the keeper went forth, I forget not,
The maide to hide me in her bosome let not.
What gift with me was on her birth day sent,
But cruelly by her was drown'd and rent.
First of thy minde the happy seedes I knewe,
Thou hast my gift, which she would from thee sue. 60
She left; I say'd, you both I must beseech,

32 times] O5; time O3–4
52 setting] Dyce; sitting O3–6

55 keeper] Robinson; keepes O3–4;
keepers O5–6

To empty aire may go my fearefull speech.
With scepters, and high buskins th'one would dresse me,
So through the world shold bright renown expresse me.
The other gives my love a conquering name,
Come therefore, and to long verse shorter frame.
Graunt *Tragedie* thy Poet times least tittle,
Thy labour ever lasts, she askes but little.
She gave me leave, soft loves in time make hast,
Some greater worke will urge me on at last.   70

ELEGIA 2

Ad amicam cursum equorum spectantem

I sit not here the noble horse to see,
Yet whom thou favourst, pray may conquerour be.
To sit, and talke with thee I hether came,
That thou maiest know with love thou mak'st me flame.
Thou viewst the course, I thee: let either heed
What please them, and their eyes let either feede.
What horse-driver thou favourst most is best,
Because on him thy care doth hap to rest.
Such chaunce let me have: I would bravely runne,
On swift steedes mounted till the race were done.   10
Now would I slacke the reines, now lash their hide,
With wheeles bent inward now the ring-turne ride.
In running if I see thee, I shall stay,
And from my hands the reines will slip away.
Ah *Pelops* from his coach was almost feld,
Hippodameias lookes while he beheld.
Yet he attain'd by her support to have her,
Let us all conquer by our mistris favour.
In vaine why flyest backe? force conjoynes us now:
The places lawes this benefit allowe.   20
But spare my wench thou at her right hand seated,
By thy sides touching ill she is entreated.
And sit thou rounder, that behind us see,

III.ii O3 *copy-text*

For shame presse not her backe with thy hard knee.
But on the ground thy cloathes too loosely lie,
Gather them up, or lift them loe will I.
Envious garments so good legges to hide,
The more thou look'st, the more the gowne envide.
Swift *Atalantas* flying legges like these,
Wish in his hands graspt did *Hippomenes*.   30
Coate-tuckt *Dianas* legges are painted like them,
When strong wilde beasts, she stronger hunts to strike them.
Ere these were seene, I burnt: what will these do?
Flames into flame, flouds thou powrest seas into.
By these I judge, delight me may the rest,
Which lie hid under her thinne veile supprest.
Yet in the meane time wilt small windes bestowe,
That from thy fanne, mov'd by my hand may blow?
Or is my heate, of minde, not of the skie?
Ist womens love my captive brest doth frie?   40
While thus I speake, blacke dust her white robes ray:
Foule dust, from her faire body, go away.
Now comes the pompe; themselves let all men cheere:
The shout is nigh; the golden pompe comes heere.
First Victory is brought with large spred wing,
Goddesse come here, make my love conquering.
Applaud you *Neptune*, that dare trust his wave,
The sea I use not: me my earth must have.
Souldiour applaud thy *Mars*: no warres we move,
Peace pleaseth me, and in mid peace is love.   50
With *Augures Phœbus, Phœbe* with hunters standes,
To thee *Minerva* turne the craftes-mens hands.
Ceres and *Bacchus* Country-men adore,
Champions pleace *Pollux, Castor* love horsemen more.
Thee gentle *Venus*, and the boy that flies,
We praise: great goddesse ayde my enterprize.
Let my new mistris graunt to be beloved:
She beckt, and prosperous signes gave as she moved.

41 speake] *i.e., probably* spake *as in* O6   *54 pleace] *stet* O3–4
   (*see* III.v.85)   54 love] loves O3–6

What *Venus* promisd, promise thou we pray,
Greater then her, by her leave th'art, Ile say.   60
The Gods, and their rich pompe witnesse with me,
For evermore thou shalt my mistris be.
Thy legges hang-downe: thou maiest, if that be best,
A while thy tiptoes on the foote-stoole rest.
Now greatest spectacles the *Prætor* sends,
Fower chariot-horses from the lists even ends.
I see whom thou affectest: he shall subdue,
The horses seeme, as thy desire they knewe.
Alas he runnes too farre about the ring,
What doest? thy wagon in lesse compasse bring.   70
What doest, unhappy? her good wishes fade,
Let with strong hand the reine to bend be made.
One slowe we favour, *Romans* him revoke:
And each give signes by casting up his cloake.
They call him backe: least their gownes tosse thy haire,
To hide thee in my bosome straight repaire.
But now againe the barriers open lye;
And forth the gay troupes on swift horses flie.
At least now conquer, and out-runne the rest:
My mistris wish confirme with my request.   80
My mistris hath her wish, my wish remaine:
He holdes the palme: my palme is yet to gaine.
She smilde, and with quicke eyes behight some grace:
Pay it not heere, but in an other place.

ELEGIA 3

De amica, quæ periuraverat

What, are there Gods? her selfe she hath forswore,
And yet remaines the face she had before.
How long her lockes were, ere her oath she tooke:
So long they be, since she her faith forsooke.
Faire white with rose red was before commixt:

64 A] Dyce; Or O3–6   68 thy] Robinson; they O3–6
    III.iii O3 *copy-text*

Now shine her lookes pure white and red betwixt.
Her foote was small: her footes forme is most fit:
Comely tall was she, comely tall shee's yet.
Sharpe eyes she had: radiant like starres they be,
By which she perjurd oft hath lyed to me.　　　　　10
Insooth th'eternall powers graunt maides society
Falsely to sweare, their beauty hath some deity.
By her eyes I remember late she swore,
And by mine eyes, and mine were pained sore.
Say gods: if she unpunisht you deceive,
For others faults, why do I losse receive?
But did you not so envy *Cepheus* Daughter,
For her ill-beautious Mother judgd to slaughter?
Tis not enough, she shakes your record off,
And unrevengd mockt Gods with me doth scoffe.　20
But by my paine to purge her perjuries,
Couzend, I am the couzeners sacrifice.
God is a name, no substance, feard in vaine,
And doth the world in fond beliefe deteine.
Or if there be a God, he loves fine wenches,
And all things too much in their sole power drenches.
Mars girts his deadly sword on for my harme:
Pallas launce strikes me with unconquerd arme.
At me *Apollo* bends his pliant bowe:
At me *Joves* right-hand lightning hath to throwe.　30
The wronged Gods dread faire ones to offend,
And feare those, that to feare them least intend.
Who now will care the Altars to perfume?
Tut, men should not their courage so consume.
Jove throwes downe woods, and Castles with his fire:
But bids his darts from perjurd girles retire.
Poore *Semele*, among so many burn'd;
Her owne request to her owne torment turnd.
But when her lover came, had she drawne backe,
The fathers thigh should unborne *Bacchus* lacke.　40
Why grieve I? and of heaven reproches pen?

10 to] Robinson; by O3–6

The Gods have eyes, and brests as well as men.
Were I a God, I should give women leave,
With lying lips my God-head to deceave,
My selfe would sweare, the wenches true did sweare,
And I would be none of the Gods severe.
But yet their gift more moderately use,
Or in mine eyes good wench no paine transfuse.

ELEGIA 4

Ad virum servantem conjugem

Rude man, 'tis vaine, thy damsell to commend
To keepers trust: their wits should them defend.
Who, without feare, is chaste, is chast in sooth:
Who, because meanes want, doeth not, she doth.
Though thou her body guard, her minde is staind:
Nor, least she will, can any be restrainde.
Nor canst by watching keepe her minde from sinne.
All being shut out, th'adulterer is within.
Who may offend, sinnes least; power to do ill,
The fainting seedes of naughtinesse doth kill.   10
Forbeare to kindle vice by prohibition,
Sooner shall kindnesse gaine thy wills fruition.
I saw a horse against the bitte stiffe-neckt,
Like lightning go, his strugling mouth being checkt.
When he perceivd the reines let slacke, he stayde,
And on his loose mane the loose bridle laide.
How to attaine, what is denyed, we thinke,
Even as the sicke desire forbidden drinke.
Argus had either way an hundred eyes,
Yet by deceit Love did them all surprize.   20
In stone, and Yron walles *Danae* shut,
Came forth a mother, though a maide there put.
Penelope, though no watch look'd unto her,
Was not defilde by any gallant wooer.
What's kept, we covet more: the care makes theft:

III.iv O 3 *copy-text*

373

Few love, what others have unguarded left.
Nor doth her face please, but her husbands love;
I know not, what men thinke should thee so move.
She is not chaste, that's kept, but a deare whore:
Thy feare is, then her body, valued more.   30
Although thou chafe, stolne pleasure is sweet play,
She pleaseth best, I feare, if any say.
A free-borne wench, no right 'tis up to locke:
So use we women of strange nations stocke.
Because the keeper may come say, I did it,
She must be honest to thy servants credit.
He is too clownish, whom a lewd wife grieves,
And this townes well knowne customes not beleeves,
Where *Mars* his sonnes not without fault did breed,
Remus and *Romulus*, *Ilias* twinne-borne seed.   40
Cannot a faire one, if not chast, please thee?
Never can these by any meanes agree.
Kindly thy mistris use, if thou be wise.
Looke gently, and rough husbands lawes despise.
Honour what friends thy wife gives, sheele give many:
Least labour so shall winne great grace of any.
So shalt thou go with youths to feasts together,
And see at home much, that thou nere broughtst thether.

ELEGIA 5

Ad amnem, dum iter faceret ad amicam

Floud with reede-growne slime bankes, till I be past
Thy waters stay: I to my mistris hast.
Thou hast no bridge, nor boate with ropes to throw,
That may transport me without oares to rowe.
Thee I have pass'd, and knew thy streame none such,
When thy waves brim did scarse my anckles touch.

II.v O3 *copy-text. From here on the*   *editions of* III.v (Nox erat). *The*
numbering is one less than in modern   *present* III.v *is modern* III.vi *etc.*
texts owing to the omission in early   1 reede-] Dyce; redde-O3-6

With snow thaw'd from the next hill now thou rushest,
And in thy foule deepe waters thicke thou gushest.
What helpes my hast: what to have tane small rest?
What day and night to travaile in her quest?   10
If standing here I can by no meanes get,
My foote upon the further banke to set.
Now wish I those wings noble *Perseus* had,
Bearing the head with dreadfull Adders clad,
Now wish the chariot, whence corne seedes were found,
First to be throwne upon the untill'd ground.
I speake old Poets wonderfull inventions,
Nere was, nor shall be, what my verse mentions.
Rather thou large banke over-flowing river,
Slide in thy bounds, so shalt thou runne for ever.   20
(Trust me) land-streame thou shalt no envie lack,
If I a lover bee by thee held back.
Great flouds ought to assist young men in love,
Great flouds the force of it do often prove.
In mid *Bithynia* 'tis said *Inachus*,
Grew pale, and in cold foords hot lecherous.
Troy had not yet beene ten yeares siege out-stander,
Whem nimph-*Neæra* rapt thy lookes *Scamander*.
What? not *Alpheus* in strange lands to runne,
Th'*Arcadian* Virgins constant love hath wunne?   30
And *Crusa* unto *Zanthus* first affide,
They say *Peneus* neere *Phthias* towne did hide.
What should I name *Æsope*, that *Thebe* lov'd,
Thebe who Mother of five Daughters prov'd?
If *Achelous*, I aske where thy hornes stand,
Thou saiest broke with *Alcides* angry hand.
Not *Calydon*, nor *Ætolia* did please:
One *Deianira* was more worth then these.
Rich *Nile* by seaven mouthes to the vast sea flowing,
Who so well keepes his waters head from knowing,   40

---

8 gushest] Tucker Brooke; rushest   15 seedes] Tucker Brooke; fields O 3–6
O 3–6   33 *Æsope*] i.e., *the river* Asopus, *as in*
14 Adders] Dyce; Arrowes O 3–6   Dyce (Asop)

Is by *Evadne* thought to take such flame,
As his deepe whirle-pooles could not quench the same.
Drye *Enipeus*, *Tyro* to embrace,
Flye backe his streame chargd, the streame chargd, gave place.
Nor passe I thee, who hollow rocks downe tumbling,
In *Tiburs* field with watry fome art rumbling,
Whom *Ilia* pleasd, though in her lookes griefe reveld,
Her cheekes were scratcht, her goodly haires discheveld.
She wailing *Mars* sinne, and her uncles crime,
Strayd bare-foote through sole places on a time.   50
Her, from his swift waves, the bold floud perceav'd,
And from the mid foord his hoarse voice upheav'd,
Saying, why sadly treadst my banckes upon,
Ilia, sprung from *Idæan Laomedon*?
Where's thy attire? why wand'rest heere alone?
To stay thy tresses white veyle hast thou none?
Why weepst? and spoilst with teares thy watry eyes?
And fiercely knockst thy brest that open lyes?
His heart consists of flint, and hardest steele,
That seeing thy teares can any joy then feele.   60
Feare not: to thee our Court stands open wide,
There shalt be lov'd: *Ilia* lay feare aside.
Thou ore a hundreth Nimphes, or more shalt raigne:
For five score Nimphes, or more our flouds conteine.
Nor *Romane* stocke scorne me so much (I crave)
Gifts then my promise greater thou shalt have.
This said he: shee her modest eyes held downe,
Her wofull bosome a warme shower did drowne.
Thrice she prepar'd to flie, thrice she did stay,
By feare depriv'd of strength to runne away.   70
Yet rending with enraged thumbe her tresses,
Her trembling mouth these unmeete sounds expresses.
O would in my fore-fathers tombe deepe layde,
My bones had beene, while yet I was a maide.
Why being a vestall am I wooed to wed,
Deflowr'd and stained in unlawfull bed?

44 his streame] Robinson; his shame O3–6

376

Why stay I? men point at me for a whore,
Shame, that should make me blush, I have no more.
This said: her coate hood-winckt her fearefull eyes,
And into water desperately she flies.   80
Tis said the slippery streame held up her brest,
And kindly gave her, what she liked best.
And I beleeve some wench thou hast affected:
But woods and groves keepe your faults undetected.
While thus I speake, the waters more abounded:
And from the channell all abroad surrounded.
Mad streame, why doest our mutuall joyes deferre?
Clowne, from my journey why doest me deterre?
How wouldst thou flowe wert thou a noble floud,
If thy great fame in every region stood?   90
Thou hast no name, but com'st from snowy mountaines;
No certaine house thou hast, nor any fountaines.
Thy springs are nought but raine and melted snowe:
Which wealth, cold winter doth on thee bestowe.
Either th'art muddy in mid winter tide:
Or full of dust doest on the drye earth slide.
What thirstie traveller ever drunke of thee?
Who sayd with gratefull voyce perpetuall bee?
Harmefull to beasts, and to the fields thou proves:
Perchance these, others, me mine owne losse mooves.   100
To this I fondly loves of flouds told plainly:
I shame so great names to have usde so vainly:
I know not what expecting, I ere while
Nam'd *Achelaus*, *Inachus*, and *Nile*,
But for thy merits I wish thee, white streame,
Drye winters aye, and sunnes in heate extreame.

104 *Nile*] Robinson; *Ile* O 3–6

ELEGIA 6

Quod ab amica receptus, cum ea coire non
potuit, conqueritur

Either she was foule, or her attire was bad,
Or she was not the wench I wisht t'have had.
Idly I lay with her, as if I lovde not,
And like a burthen greevde the bed that mooved not.
Though both of us performd our true intent,
Yet could I not cast ancor where I meant,
She on my necke her Ivorie armes did throw,
That were as white as is the *Scithean* snow,
And eagerlie she kist me with her tongue,
And under mine her wanton thigh she flong,   10
Yea, and she soothde me up, and calde me sir,
And usde all speech that might provoke and stirre.
Yet like as if cold hemlocke I had drunke,
It mocked me, hung down the head and suncke,
Like a dull Cipher, or rude blocke I lay,
Or shade, or body was I, who can say?
What will my age do, age I cannot shunne,
Seeing in my prime my force is spent and done?
I blush, that being youthfull, hot, and lustie,
I prove neither youth nor man, but old and rustie.   20
Pure rose shee, like a Nun to sacrifice,
Or one that with her tender brother lies,
Yet boorded I the golden *Chie* twise,
And *Libas*, and the white cheek'de *Pitho* thrise,
Corinna cravde it in a summers night,
And nine sweete bouts had we before day light.
What, wast my limbs through some *Thesalian* charms,

III.vi O1 *copy-text*   16 I] O3; Io O1–2
3 lovde] O3; lovde her O1–2   18 Seeing] O1–2; When O3
8 That...is] O1–2; Her armes farre   19 that] O3; and O1–2
  whiter, then O3–6   26 had we] O1–2; we had O3
11 sir] O1–2; sire O3

378

May spelles and droughs do sillie soules such harmes?
With virgin waxe hath some imbast my joynts,
And pierst my liver with sharpe needle poynts?　　　　　　30
Charmes change corne to grasse, and makes it dye,
By charmes are running springs and fountaines drie,
By charmes maste drops from okes, from vines grapes fall,
And fruit from trees, when ther's no wind at al.
Why might not then my sinews be inchanted,
And I grow faint, as with some spirit haunted?
To this ad shame, shame to performe it quaild mee,
And was the second cause why vigor failde mee:
My idle thoughts delighted her no more,
Then did the robe or garment which she wore,　　　　　　40
Yet might her touch make youthfull *Pilius* fire,
And *Tithon* livelier then his yeeres require.
Even her I had, and she had me in vaine,
What might I crave more if I aske againe?
I thinke the great Gods greeved they had bestowde
This benefite, which lewdly I forslowd:
I wisht to be received in, in I get me,
To kisse, I kisse, to lie with her shee let me.
Why was I blest? why made king to refuse it?
Chuf-like had I not gold, and could not use it?　　　　　　50
So in a spring thrives he that told so much,
And lookes uppon the fruits he cannot touch.
Hath any rose so from a fresh yong maide,
As she might straight have gone to church and praide:
Well, I beleeve she kist not as she should,
Nor usde the slight nor cunning which she could,
Huge okes, hard Adamantes might she have moved,
And with sweete words cause deafe rockes to have loved,
Worthy she was to move both Gods and men,
But neither was I man, nor lived then.　　　　　　　　　　60

28 droughs]　O 1-2　(*i.e.*,　draughts);　　46 This] O 1-2; The O 3
　　drugges O 3　　　　　　　　　　　　　　　47 in I get] O 3; and in I got O 1-2
30 needle] O 1-2; needles O 3　　　　　　49 to refuse] O 3; and refusde O 1-2
31 makes] O 1; make O 2-3　　　　　　　56 nor] O 1-2; and O 3
40 wore] O 1-2; more O 3　　　　　　　　58 loved] O 1-2; moned O 3

Can deafe eares take delight when *Phemius* sings,
Or *Thamiras* in curious painted things?
What sweete thought is there but I had the same?
And one gave place still as another came.
Yet notwithstanding, like one dead it lay,
Drouping more then a Rose puld yesterday:
Now when he should not jette, he boults upright,
And craves his taske, and seekes to be at fight.
Lie downe with shame, and see thou stirre no more,
Seeing now thou wouldst deceive me as before: 70
Thou cousenst mee, by thee surprizde am I,
And bide sore losse, with endlesse infamie.
Nay more, the wench did not disdaine a whit,
To take it in her hand and play with it.
But when she saw it would by no meanes stand,
But still droupt downe, regarding not her hand,
Why mockst thou me she cried, or being ill,
Who bad thee lie downe here against thy will?
Either th'art witcht with blood of frogs new dead,
Or jaded camst thou from some others bed.   80
With that her loose gowne on, from me she cast her,
In skipping out her naked feete much grac'd her.
And least her maide should know of this disgrace,
To cover it, spilt water in the place.

ELEGIA 7

Quod ab amica non recipiatur, dolet

What man will now take liberall arts in hand,
Or thinke soft verse in any stead to stand?
Wit was some-times more pretious then gold,
Now poverty great barbarisme we hold.
When our bookes did my mistris faire content,

61 eares] Dyce; yeares O1–2; eare
   O3–6
70 now] O1–2; *omit* O3
71 cousenst] O3 (cousenest); cous-

endst O1–2
84 in] O1–2; on O3
III.vii O3 *copy-text*

I might not go, whether my papers went.
She prais'd me, yet the gate shutt fast upon her,
I heere and there go witty with dishonour.
See a rich chuffe whose wounds great wealth inferr'd,
For bloudshed knighted, before me preferr'd.   10
Foole canst thou him in thy white armes embrace?
Foole canst thou lie in his enfolding space?
Knowest not this head a helme was wont to beare,
This side that serves thee, a sharpe sword did weare.
His left hand whereon gold doth ill alight,
A target bore: bloud sprinckled was his right.
Canst touch that hand wherewith some one lie dead?
Ah whether is thy brests soft nature fled?
Behold the signes of antient fight, his skarres,
What ere he hath his body gaind in warres.   20
Perhaps he'ele tell howe oft he slewe a man,
Confessing this, why doest thou touch him than?
I the pure priest of *Phœbus* and the muses,
At thy deafe dores in verse sing my abuses.
Not what we slouthfull knowe, let wise men learne,
But follow trembling campes, and battailes sterne,
And for a good verse drawe the first dart forth,
Homer without this shall be nothing worth.
Jove being admonisht gold had soveraigne power,
To winne the maide came in a golden shewer.   30
Till then, rough was her father, she severe,
The posts of brasse, the walles of iron were.
But when in gifts the wise adulterer came,
She held her lap ope to receive the same.
Yet when old *Saturne* heavens rule possest,
All gaine in darknesse the deepe earth supprest.
Gold, silver, irons heavy weight, and brasse,
In hell were harbourd, here was found no masse.
But better things it gave, corne without ploughes,
Apples, and hony in oakes hollow boughes.   40

18 thy] O4; they O3   25 knowe] Robinson; knewe O3–6
18 fled] O4; sled O3

With strong plough shares no man the earth did cleave,
The ditcher no markes on the ground did leave.
Nor hanging oares the troubled seas did sweepe,
Men kept the shoare, and sailde not into deepe.
Against thy selfe, mans nature, thou wert cunning,
And to thine owne losse was thy wit swift running.
Why gird'st thy citties with a towred wall?
Why letst discordant hands to armour fall?
What doest with seas? with th'earth thou wert content,
Why seek'st not heav'n the third realme to frequent?   50
Heaven thou affects, with *Romulus*, temples brave
Bacchus, *Alcides*, and now *Cæsar* have.
Gold from the earth in steade of fruits we pluck,
Souldiours by bloud to be inricht have lucke.
Courts shut the poore out; wealth gives estimation,
Thence growes the Judge, and knight of reputation.
All, they possesse: they governe fieldes, and lawes,
They manadge peace, and rawe warres bloudy jawes,
Onely our loves let not such rich churles gaine,
Tis well, if some wench for the poore remaine.   60
Now, *Sabine*-like, though chast she seemes to live,
One her commands, who many things can give.
For me, she doth keeper, and husband feare,
If I should give, both would the house forbeare.
If of scornd lovers god be venger just,
O let him change goods so ill got to dust.

ELEGIA 8

Tibulli mortem deflet

If *Thetis*, and the morne their sonnes did waile,
And envious fates great goddesses assaile,
Sad *Elegia* thy wofull haires unbinde:
Ah now a name too true thou hast, I finde.

---

*62 her] Dyce; she O3–6   2 goddesses] O4; goodesses O3
     III.viii O3 *copy-text*

Tibullus, thy workes Poet, and thy fame,
Burnes his dead body in the funerall flame.
Loe *Cupid* brings his quiver spoyled quite,
His broken bowe, his fire-brand without light.
How piteously with drouping wings he stands,
And knocks his bare brest with selfe-angry hands. 10
The locks spred on his necke receive his teares,
And shaking sobbes his mouth for speeches beares.
So at *Æneas* buriall men report,
Faire-fac'd *Iulus*, he went forth thy court.
And *Venus* grieves, *Tibullus* life being spent,
As when the wilde boare *Adons* groine had rent.
The gods care we are cald, and men of piety,
And some there be that thinke we have a deity.
Outrageous death profanes all holy things
And on all creatures obscure darcknesse brings. 20
To *Thracian Orpheus* what did parents good?
Or songs amazing wilde beasts of the wood?
Where *Linus* by his father *Phœbus* layed
To sing with his unequald harpe is sayed.
See *Homer* from whose fountaine ever fild,
Pierian deawe to Poets is distild.
Him the last day in black *Averne* hath drownd,
Verses alone are with continuance crown'd.
The worke of Poets lasts *Troyes* labours fame,
And that slowe webbe nights fals-hood did unframe. 30
So *Nemesis*, so *Delia* famous are,
The one his first love, th'other his new care.
What profit to us hath our pure life bred?
What to have laine alone in empty bed?
When bad fates take good men, I am forbod,
By secreat thoughts to thinke there is a god.
Live godly, thou shalt die, though honour heaven,
Yet shall thy life be forcibly bereaven.
Trust in good verse, *Tibullus* feeles deaths paines,
Scarse rests of all what a small urne conteines. 40
Thee sacred Poet could sad flames destroy?

Nor feared they thy body to annoy?
The holy gods gilt temples they might fire,
That durst to so great wickednesse aspire.
Eryx bright *Empresse* turnd her lookes aside,
And some, that she refrain'd teares, have deni'd.
Yet better ist, then if *Corcyras* Ile
Had thee unknowne interr'd in ground most vile.
Thy dying eyes here did thy mother close,
Nor did thy ashes her last offrings lose.   50
Part of her sorrowe heere thy sister bearing,
Comes forth her unkeembd locks a sunder tearing.
Nemesis and thy first wench joyne their kisses,
With thine, nor this last fire their presence misses.
Delia departing, happier lov'd, she saith,
Was I: thou liv'dst, while thou esteemdst my faith.
Nemesis answeares, what's my losse to thee?
His fainting hand in death engrasped mee.
If ought remaines of us but name, and spirit,
Tibullus doth *Elysiums* joy inherit.   60
Their youthfull browes with Ivie girt to meete him,
With *Calvus* learnd *Catullus* comes and greete him.
And thou, if falsely charged to wrong thy friend,
Gallus that car'dst not bloud, and life to spend.
With these thy soule walkes, soules if death release,
The godly, sweete *Tibullus* doth increase.
Thy bones I pray may in the urne safe rest,
And may th'earths weight thy ashes nought molest.

52 unkeembd] O5; unkeembe O3–4   64 car'dst] Robinson; carst O3–6
*61–2 Their...comes] *stet* O3–6   *66 The] *stet* O3–6

ELEGIA 9

Ad Cererem, conquerens quod eius sacris cum amica
concumbere non permittatur

Come were the times of *Ceres* sacrifize,
In emptie bed alone my mistris lies.
Golden-hair'd *Ceres* crownd with eares of corne,
Why are our pleasures by thy meanes forborne?
Thee, goddesse, bountifull all nations judge,
Nor lesse at mans prosperity any grudge.
Rude husband-men bak'd not their corne before,
Nor on the earth was knowne the name of floore.
On mast of oakes, first oracles, men fed,
This was their meate, the soft grasse was their bed. 10
First *Ceres* taught the seede in fields to swell,
And ripe-earde corne with sharpe-edg'd sithes to fell.
She first constraind bulles necks to beare the yoake,
And untild ground with crooked plough-shares broake.
Who thinkes her to be glad at lovers smart,
And worshipt by their paine, and lying apart?
Nor is she, though she loves the fertile fields,
A clowne, nor no love from her warme brest yeelds.
Be witnesse *Crete* (nor *Crete* doth all things feigne)
Crete proud that *Jove* her nourcery maintaine. 20
There, he who rules the worlds starre-spangled towers,
A little boy druncke teate-distilling showers.
Faith to the witnesse *Joves* praise doth apply,
Ceres, I thinke, no knowne fault will deny.
The goddesse sawe *Iasion* on *Candyan Ide*,
With strong hand striking wild-beasts brist'led hyde.
She sawe, and as her marrowe tooke the flame,
Was divers waies distract with love, and shame.
Love conquer'd shame, the furrowes dry were burnd,
And corne with least part of it selfe returnd. 30

III.ix O3 *copy-text*   10 their meate] O4; there meate O3

When well-toss'd mattocks did the ground prepare,
Being fit broken with the crooked share,
And seedes were equally in large fields cast,
The plough-mans hopes were frustrate at the last.
The graine-rich goddesse in high woods did stray,
Her long haires eare-wrought garland fell away.
Onely was *Crete* fruitfull that plenteous yeare,
Where *Ceres* went each place was harvest there.
Ida the seate of groves did sing with corne,
Which by the wild boare in the woods was shorne.   40
Law-giving *Minos* did such yeares desire;
And wisht the goddesse long might feele loves fire.
Ceres what sports to thee so grievous were,
As in thy sacrifize we them forbeare?
Why am I sad, when *Proserpine* is found,
And *Juno* like with *Dis* raignes under ground?
Festivall dayes aske *Venus*, songs, and wine,
These gifts are meete to please the powers divine.

ELEGIA 10

Ad amicam, a cuius amore discedere non potest

Long have I borne much, mad thy faults me make:
Dishonest love my wearied brest forsake,
Now have I freed my selfe, and fled the chaine,
And what I have borne, shame to beare againe.
We vanquish, and tread tam'd love under feete,
Victorious wreathes at length my Temples greete.
Suffer, and harden: good growes by this griefe,
Oft bitter juice brings to the sicke reliefe.
I have sustainde so oft thrust from the dore,
To lay my body on the hard moist floore.   10
I know not whom thou lewdly didst imbrace,
When I to watch supplyed a servants place.
I saw when forth a tyred lover went,

III.x O3 *copy-text*

His side past service, and his courage spent.
Yet this is lesse, then if he had seene me,
May that shame fall mine enemies chance to be.
When have not I fixt to thy side close layed?
I have thy husband, guard, and fellow plaied.
The people by my company she pleasd,
My love was cause that more mens love she seazd.   20
What should I tell her vaine tongues filthy lyes,
And to my losse God-wronging perjuries?
What secret becks in banquets with her youths,
With privy signes, and talke dissembling truths?
Hearing her to be sicke, I thether ranne,
But with my rivall sicke she was not than.
These hardned me, with what I keepe obscure,
Some other seeke, who will these things endure.
Now my ship in the wished haven crownd,
With joy heares *Neptunes* swelling waters sound.   30
Leave thy once powerfull words, and flatteries,
I am not as I was before, unwise.
Now love, and hate my light brest each way move;
But victory, I thinke, will hap to love.
Ile hate, if I can; if not, love gainst my will:
Bulles hate the yoake, yet what they hate have still.
I flie her lust, but follow beauties creature;
I loath her manners, love her bodies feature.
Nor with thee, nor without thee can I live,
And doubt to which desire the palme to give.   40
Or lesse faire, or lesse lewd would thou mightst bee,
Beauty with lewdnesse doth right ill agree.
Her deeds gaine hate, her face entreateth love:
Ah, she doth more worth then her vices prove.
Spare me, O by our fellow bed, by all
The Gods who by thee to be perjurde fall,
And by thy face to me a powre divine,
And by thine eyes whose radiance burnes out mine.
What ere thou art mine art thou: choose this course,
Wilt have me willing, or to love by force?   50

Rather Ile hoist up saile, and use the winde,
That I may love yet, though against my minde.

ELEGIA 11

*Dolet amicam suam ita suis carminibus innotuisse
ut rivales multos sibi pararit*

What day was that, which all sad haps to bring,
White birdes to lovers did not alwayes sing.
Or is I thinke my wish against the starres?
Or shall I plaine some God against me warres?
Who mine was cald, whom I lov'd more then any,
I feare with me is common now to many.
Erre I? or by my bookes is she so knowne?
'Tis so: by my witte her abuse is growne.
And justly: for her praise why did I tell?
The wench by my fault is set forth to sell.   10
The bawde I play, lovers to her I guide:
Her gate by my hands is set open wide.
'Tis doubtfull whether verse availe, or harme,
Against my good they were an envious charme.
When *Thebes*, when *Troy*, when *Cæsar* should be writ,
Alone *Corinna* moves my wanton wit.
With Muse oppos'd would I my lines had done,
And *Phœbus* had forsooke my worke begun.
Nor, as use will not Poets record heare,
Would I my words would any credit beare.   20
Scylla by us her fathers rich haire steales,
And *Scyllaes* wombe mad raging dogs conceales.
Wee cause feete flie, wee mingle haires with snakes,
Victorious *Perseus* a wingd steedes back takes.
Our verse great *Tityus* a huge space out-spreads,
And gives the viper curled Dogge three heads.
We make *Enceladus* use a thousand armes,

III.xi O3 *copy-text*   7 bookes] Dyce; lookes O3–6
3 starres] O5; starre O3–4

388

And men inthralld by Mermaids singing charmes.
The East winds in *Ulisses* baggs we shut,
And blabbing *Tantalus* in mid-waters put.   30
Niobe flint, *Callist* we make a Beare,
Bird-changed *Progne* doth her *Itys* teare.
Jove turnes himselfe into a Swanne, or gold,
Or his Bulles hornes *Europas* hand doth hold.
Proteus what should I name? teeth, *Thebes* first seed?
Oxen in whose mouthes burning flames did breede?
Heav'n starre *Electra* that bewaild her sisters?
The ships, whose God-head in the sea now glisters?
The Sunne turnd backe from *Atreus* cursed table?
And sweet toucht harpe that to move stones was able?   40
Poets large power is boundlesse, and immense,
Nor have their words true histories pretence,
And my wench ought to have seem'd falsely praisd,
Now your credulity harme to me hath raisd.

ELEGIA 12

De Junonis festo

When fruite fild *Tuscia* should a wife give me,
We toucht the walles, *Camillus* wonne by thee.
The Priests to *Juno* did prepare chaste feasts,
With famous pageants, and their home-bred beasts.
To know their rites, well recompenc'd my stay,
Though thether leades a rough steepe hilly way.
There stands an old wood with thick trees darke clouded,
Who sees it, graunts some deity there is shrowded.
An Altar takes mens incense, and oblation,
An Altar made after the ancient fashion.   10
Here when the Pipe with solemne tunes doth sound,
The annuall pompe goes on the covered ground.
White Heifers by glad people forth are led,
Which with the grasse of *Tuscane* fields are fed.

III.xii O3 *copy-text*

389

And calves from whose feard front no threatning flyes,
And little Piggs, base Hog-sties sacrifice,
And Rams with hornes their hard heads wreathed back.
Onely the Goddesse hated Goate did lack,
By whom disclosd, she in the high woods tooke,
Is said to have attempted flight forsooke.   20
Now is the goat brought through the boyes with darts,
And give to him that the first wound imparts.
Where *Juno* comes, each youth, and pretty maide,
Shew large wayes with their garments there displayed.
Jewels, and gold their Virgin tresses crowne,
And stately robes to their gilt feete hang downe.
As is the use, the Nunnes in white veyles clad,
Upon their heads the holy mysteries had.
When the chiefe pompe comes, lowd the people hollow,
And she her vestall virgin Priests doth follow.   30
Such was the *Greeke* pompe, *Agamemnon* dead,
Which fact, and country wealth *Halesus* fled.
And having wandred now through sea and land,
Built walles high towred with a prosperous hand.
He to th'*Hetrurians Junoes* feast commended,
Let me, and them by it be aye be-friended.

ELEGIA 13

Ad amicam si peccatura est, ut occulte peccet

Seeing thou art faire, I barre not thy false playing,
But let not mee poore soule know of thy straying.
Nor do I give thee counsaile to live chaste,
But that thou wouldst dissemble when tis paste.
She hath not trode awrie that doth denie it,
Such as confesse, have lost their good names by it.
What madnesse ist to tell night prankes by day,
And hidden secrets openlie to bewray?

III.xiii O 1 *copy-text*   7 night] O 1–2; nights O 3
5 trode] O 1–2; tred O 3

The strumpet with the stranger will not do,
Before the roome be cleere, and doore put too.   10
Will you make shipwracke of your honest name,
And let the world be witnesse of the same?
Be more advisde, walke as a puritane,
And I shall thinke you chaste, do what you can.
Slippe still, onely denie it when tis done,
And before folke immodest speeches shunne,
The bed is for lascivious toyings meete,
There use all tricks, and tread shame under feete.
When you are up and drest, be sage and grave,
And in the bed hide all the faults you have,   20
Be not ashamed to strippe you being there,
And mingle thighs, yours ever mine to beare.
There in your rosie lippes my tongue intombe,
Practise a thousand sports when there you come,
Forbare no wanton words you there would speake,
And with your pastime let the bedsted creake,
But with your robes, put on an honest face,
And blush, and seeme as you were full of grace.
Deceive all, let me erre, and thinke I am right,
And like a wittall thinke thee voyde of slight.   30
Why see I lines so oft receivde and given,
This bed, and that by tumbling made uneven,
Like one start up your haire tost and displast,
And with a wantons tooth, your necke new raste?
Graunt this, that what you do I may not see,
If you wey not ill speeches, yet wey mee:
My soule fleetes when I thinke what you have done,
And thorough everie vaine doth cold bloud runne,
Then thee whom I must love I hate in vaine,
And would be dead, but dying with thee remaine.   40
Ile not sift much, but hold thee soone excusde,
Say but thou wert injuriously accusde.
Though while the deede be doing you be tooke,

*8 And] O3; Or O1–2   yours O1–2
22 yours ever mine] O3; mine ever   *40 dying] O1–2; dead O3

And I see when you ope the two leavde booke:
Sweare I was blinde, yeeld not, if you be wise,
And I will trust your words more then mine eies.
From him that yeelds the garland is quickly got,
Teach but your tongue to say, I did it not,
And being justified by two words, thinke
The cause acquits you not, but I that winke.   50

ELEGIA 14

Ad Venerem, quod elegis finem imponat

Tender loves Mother a new Poet get,
This last end to my *Elegies* is set,
Which I *Pelignis* foster-child have framde,
(Nor am I by such wanton toyes defamde)
Heire of an antient house, if helpe that can,
Not onely by warres rage made Gentleman.
In *Virgil Mantua* joyes: in *Catul Verone*,
Of me *Pelignis* nation boasts alone,
Whom liberty to honest armes compeld,
When carefull *Rome* in doubt their prowesse held.   10
And some guest viewing watry *Sulmoes* walles,
Where little ground to be inclosd befalles,
How such a Poet could you bring forth, sayes,
How small so ere, Ile you for greatest praise.
Both loves to whom my heart long time did yeeld,
Your golden ensignes plucke out of my field,
Horned *Bacchus* graver furie doth distill,
A greater ground with great horse is to till.
Weake Elegies, delightfull Muse farewell;
A worke, that after my death, heere shall dwell   20

FINIS.

45 yeeld not] O 1–2; deny O 3   III.xiv O 3 *copy-text*
47 garland] O 1–2; palm O 3   16 plucke] Dyce; pluckt O 3–6

TEXTUAL NOTES

I.i.

5 upreard] Ovid's *parabam edere* is closer to O3's 'prepared' in its first element but to O1's 'upreard' in its second. But when one compares Ben Jonson's '*Accius* high-reard straine' in his version of I.xv.19, it is difficult not to believe that 'up-reard' is Marlowe's word and 'prepared' a sophistication that got into the copy behind O3.

34 praise] Dyce's emendation 'sprays' for O1–6 'praise' has been followed by all later editors and may well be right, an error caused by confusion of the sound aided, conjecturally, by a misreading. It is certainly true that in Ovid's *cingere litorea flaventia tempora myrto* (*surround with shore-loving myrtle your shining temples* in the Loeb Classics translation) no suggestion is present that the wreath is in praise of the Muse or of the poet, nor is the wearing of the myrtle wreath else-where in these elegies associated with specific praise of anyone or of anything. Moreover, if O1 'praise' were an error, its presence also in O3 could be imputed to the direct transmissional connection between the two texts sometimes exhibited in common error as most notably in O1–3 'thee' for 'the' in I.ii.52 and 'hoord' for 'hard' in I.xv.17. Hence there is much to be said for the adoption of 'sprays'. With some uncertainty, nevertheless, the present editor opts to follow 'praise'. In a sense of course, the myrtle wreath *is* worn in praise of Venus; but if the wreath itself is to be taken as the 'praise', it is more likely that the Muse is being urged to place it on Ovid's brows (in Marlowe's view) as a reward for his service. In various elegies Ovid insists that he has little wealth but can offer the love verses of his Elegian Muse as a gift of greater value. On the other hand, another possibility, closer to the Latin, weighs with the editor. That is, one could conjecture that *shore-loving myrtle* is being translated rather obscurely as 'sea banke mirtle praise', with 'praise' being the praise or love that the myrtle gives the sea banks. Since this interpretation is at least a possibility, it may seem wiser to retain the O1–3 'praise' in the hope that it is not, in fact, an error. If this reading seems too strained to accept, one can fall back on the association of the myrtle wreath as the poet's wealth in the Latin verses, probably by Marlowe, to the Countess of Pembroke: *Sic nos, quorum opes tenuissimae, littorea sunt Myrtus Veneris.*

I.ii

42 Chariots] Strictly speaking, this should be singular, the Latin *rotis* (plural for wheels) signifying a chariot. Possibly Marlowe misunderstood the idiom. On the other hand, the difficulty O1 had with singular and plural (as shown by 'triumphs', I.ii.28, and less certainly 'lands', I.iii.9) creates some doubt here, particularly in view of the plural 'Chariots' at I.ii.24 where the Latin *currum* is clearly intended to be the singular accusative. If in line 42 the plural is a Marlowe mistranslation, it must stand; but emendation would be called for if it could be determined (which it cannot) that it was a scribal or compositorial error.

393

52 the conquered] Dyce's emendation for O 1–6 'thee conquered' is required by
Ovid's *qua vicit, victos protegit ille manu*. That is, Caesar shields those whom he has
conquered; but no intimation is present that Cupid is among Caesar's conquests.
This common error seems to have been transmitted from O 1 to O 3, perhaps along
with preceding 'kinsmans', although this last cannot be taken necessarily as a mistake and its genitive is retained by the more recent editors.

I.iii

9 lands] In view of O 1's difficulties with singular and plural (see above, note to
I.ii.42), some temptation exists to take the easy path and follow O 3 'land' instead
of O 1–2 'lands'. The Latin *campus*, although often translated 'lands', could bear
either reading. However, straw though it may be, in the Huntington O 1 the final
's' of 'lands' is scarcely inked at the top; given a more lightly impressed copy it is
possible that the O 3 compositor may not have seen this final 's', without regard
for what the manuscript may have read at this point (which could have been either
'land' or 'lands'). Incidentally, lines 7–12 cause some difficulty in reading because
it is not as clear as it might be that three parallel statements are present, each intended to be prefaced by *if*: (1) if I am only of knightly birth, (2) if my lands are so
small that numberless ploughshares are not needed to till them, (3) if my parents are
penurious and therefore not generous to me – yet at least I shall have on my side
Apollo, etc.

13 gives] The O 1 reading 'give' may mean 'may give' (like 'follow' in II.ii.13–14),
in which case it is correct. On the other hand, perhaps a stronger chance exists that
'gives', which as in O 3 goes back to 'life', has been contaminated by its proximity
to 'Gods'. In fact, the O 4 error 'give' seems to have occurred for precisely this
reason.

I.iv

7 though] Ovid's *desine mirari...quod* does not encourage the meaning of 'although' here as in *although the fair bride incited, cease marvelling*. The application of
'though' is closer to *then* as in 'tho' of I.ii.3, mistaken by Cunningham for *although*;
but what would seem to be an exact parallel occurs in *Edward II*, II.ii.217, 'No
marvell though thou scorne thy noble peeres' in which the meaning is close to *that*.
In order to clarify this sense, the comma after 'not' and before 'though' in O 3–6
has been removed.

18 receive] Editors customarily gloss this word as *return*, but the *O.E.D.* gives no
support for such a sense. Instead, *O.E.D.* lists various senses that are acceptable,
such as *accept, give heed to, understand, harbour*, and *credit* or *believe*.

I.v

12 lovers] That O 3 'wooers' is correct and O 1 'lovers' corrupt is difficult to
believe. The term 'wooers' is properly used in III.iv.24 for those who sought
Penelope; but to seek Lais was to find her. The Latin is *Lais amata viris*, which is
closer to 'lovers'.

I.vi

60 Night shamelesse, wine]   All editors have followed the O3 corruption which
places a comma after 'Night', and thus makes 'shamelesse' an adjective modifying
'Love and wine'. However, the Latin is decisive in calling 'Night' the shameless
one, and Love and wine the fearless: *nox et Amor vinumque nihil moderabile suadent;* |
illa pudore vacat, Liber Amorque metu.

I.viii

7 wrong wheeles]   Ovid wrote *quid torto concita rhombo* | *licia*, which Marlowe may
have thought meant crooked or bent wheels (although the meaning is actually
magic wheels). Dyce's emendation 'wrung' does not improve matters.

97 bed mens]   The O3–6 'beds' may be the compositor's misunderstanding of the
sense but is perhaps more likely a memorial transposition of 'bed mens' to 'beds
men'. The Latin is singular: *ille viri videat toto vestigia lectto.*

I.ix

8 dores]   Ovid's word is *fores*, which would in fact be the two halves of a door, or a
double door, the plural also being used as a word for *the entrance*. Cunningham's
emendation of O3 'dores' to 'dore' would be literally more accurate but the O3
reading almost certainly originated with Marlowe and must be retained.

41 faint, to sloth]   This is the reading of the press-correction; the original setting
had 'to faint sloth'. Normally one is suspicious of a proofreader's alteration but in
the present case the change seems to have been made with reference to copy and to
remove the compositor's corruption. Ovid's words are *ipse ego segnis eram discinc-
taque in otia natus.* By placing the comma after 'faint' editors customarily emend
O3's 'dull, and faint to sloth'.

I.x

2 *Europa*]   The correct Latin reads *ab Eurota* (from the Eurotas river), but Marlowe's
edition had *Europa*, which he followed.

I.xiii

25 All]   In some respects O1's 'This' migh tbe thought more typical but in view
of Ovid's *omnia* it would seem to be an O1 corruption, and the O3 'All' is therefore
retained. In line 39 below it is worth nothing that O3 'heldst' is closer to the Latin
conplexa teneres than O1 'hadst', although in this case the O1 variant is more
explicable.

I.xiv

13 Ad]   This is the O3 reading. Unaccountably, all editors but Dyce and Tucker
Brooke follow the reprint O4 'And', which is corrupt on the evidence of Latin
adde.

26 tramells]   This has been since Robinson the conventional emendation of O3
'trannells' although Dyce, Bullen, and Tucker Brooke follow O3. On the evidence
of *The Faerie Queene* 'Her golden lockes she roundly did uptye | In breaded tramels'
it would seem that tramells means braids or tresses, or even curls. On the other
hand, 'trannels' means pins or bodkins, which could make some sense here were it
not that Ovid's *torto* seems to apply to the hair itself and not to some instrument:
ut fieret torto nexilis orbe sinus.

I.xv

3 sprong]   The Dyce emendation for O1–6 'come' is taken from the Jonson version
and seems plausible since an assonance like this instead of a rhyme is unknown else-
where. Of course, the Jonson reading has no authority as indicating what stood in
Marlowe's papers if, as is likely, Jonson imitated Marlowe's translation from either
O1 or O2 and not from some manuscript when he introduced the elegy into his
Poetaster, acted 1601.

10 into sea]   This variant from O3 is slightly 'harder' than the O1 'to the sea'; it is
perhaps not evidence that the O1 continuation 'shall slide' for O3 'doth slide'
seems to be corrupt by contamination with 'shall' of line 9 above. Analogues in the
elegies suggest the correctness of O3, however, as a translation of Ovid's *in mare
volvet*. For instance, II.ix.31 reads 'into sea' (*in alta*), and II.xiii.9–10 '*Nile*. . .into
the sea' (*in maris*). II.vi.44 may also be cited although the parallel is not exact and
the Latin differs.

33 Let. . .verse]   It is more than possible that the O3 slightly uncharacteristic inver-
sion of O1's 'Let Kings give place to verse' is one of the tinkerings to which the O3
copy was subjected. In its favor is the slightly closer approximation to the Latin
reges regumque triumphe and the fact that in the next line the first word 'And' in O3
also reproduces the Latin whereas the O1 'The' does not and may thereby betray a
misunderstanding of the sense, even though Jonson retained it. Yet the very neat-
ness of the syntax in the O3 version may be thought suspicious, given the operations elsewhere of the O3 editor as in III.xiii in the Elegies but particularly in the
Epigrams.

41 rackes]   The meaning here, as sufficiently illustrated in *O.E.D.* vb. II.4 and 5b,
seems to be *rake*, for which O1's 'racke' is an obsolete rare spelling. One may also
compare *Edward II*, I.i.20–1: 'As for the multitude that are but sparkes, | Rakt up
in embers of their povertie'. It would probably be fanciful to defend *rack* in the
vb. 2b sense of 'to pull or tear apart, to separate by force, to break up'. Jonson uses
the neutral verb 'falls in funeral fire'. Ovid, if anything, does not support *rake: cum
me supremus adederit ignis*, which the Loeb Classics translator renders as 'when the
final fires have eaten up my frame', a version that would at least permit *rack*. But
the commonness of the *rake* metaphor makes it reasonably certain that that is word
intended in line 33.

II.i

23 deduce]   In the Methuen edition L. C. Martin queries 'deduce' although printing
O3 'reduce'. He points out that Marlowe could have written 'deduce' translating
carmina. . .*deducunt cornua lunae*, and he notes (for the meaning *draw down*) the

O.E.D. citation of Sandys's Ovid's *Metamorphoses* (1626), XII, 244: 'Orion's mother...Could with her charms deduce the strugling Moone' translating *deduxisse.*

35 *Heroes* of] Robinson's emendation of O3's '*Heroes*, O' is supported by *heroum clara valete | nomina.*

II.ii

5 me, soone‸] The reading 'me‸ soone,' followed by all editors is an O3 compositorial mistake that associates 'soone' with 'pleas'd' instead of with 'sent'. The reading adopted in the present edition is supported by Ovid's *protinus, ut placuit, misi scriptoque rogavi.*

II.iv

43 Amber] O1–2 'Yellow' versus O3 'Amber' constitutes a difficult crux. If one were to argue that in some unknown manner lines 37–40 are missing in O1 because of some mistake, then O1 'Yellow' could have been a contaminated reading from missing O3 'so doth golden yellowe'. On the other hand, at first sight it would also seem that O3 preserves with more apparent faithfulness in line 39 'golden yellowe' for *flava*, and O1 in line 43 'Yellow' for *flavent*. The contrast is certainly between yellow–black (lines 39–40 *flava puella–fusco...colore Venus*, here 'golden yellowe' and 'nut-browne', *fusco* meaning dark or swarthy) and black–yellow (lines 41, 43 *nigra* for 'blacke haire' in Leda and *flavent* for 'Yellow trest'. But in fact O3's 'Amber trest' comes from the continuation *seu flavent, placuit croceis Aurora capillis*, where it is Aurora that has the *croceis* or saffron-coloured hair that could be called 'Amber' rather than yellow. Although certainty here is impossible, it may be thought that on the whole the Latin is decisive in justifying O3's 'Amber', particularly since the O1 text has suffered disruption just before this line.

II.v

13 *wretch*] Dyce's emendation for O3 'wench' has been challenged and is not demonstrably correct but it does seem to render *ipse miser vidi*; and 'wench' is readily explicable as a compositorial misreading or misunderstanding.

14 in the spilt wine] All texts and all editors read 'on the spilt wine', which makes little sense. The Latin here is of no help – *sobrius adposito crimina vestra mero*, translated in Loeb as 'with sober eye when the wine had been placed'. However, the reference would seem to be to Ovid writing down her faults in the spilt wine, just as in lines 17–18 he accuses her of writing messages in the same medium. For a possible confusion of 'on' with 'in', see III.vi.84 where O1 reads 'in the place' but O3 'on the place'.

II.vi

3, 58 goodly] The phrase 'goodly birds' in O3, repeated again in line 58, was emended by Dyce to 'godly birds' as a reading of *piae volucres*, and has been followed by subsequent editors. There is a strong possibility that Dyce was right, for the confusion of *god* and *good* is a common one in Elizabethan texts and is present elsewhere in O3: in III.viii.2, for example, O3 reads 'goodesses' where 'goddesses' is required, and in III.i.2 O3 prints the corruption 'good head' for 'god-head'. Moreover, elsewhere Marlowe conventionally translates *pius* as 'godly', as in 'godly care' in II.xvi.47 for *pia cura*, 'Live godly' in III.viii.37 for *vive pius*, and 'godly, sweete *Tibullus*' in III.viii.66 for *culte Tibulle, pios*. That the first reading 'goodly' is repeated in II.vi.58 is perhaps not evidence if the compositor were in error but recalled what he had set earlier. Yet the repetition does suggest the possibility, at least, that 'goodly' was what Marlowe wrote for what is, after all, a quite acceptable translation of *pius*, in intention much like the Loeb phrase 'feathered faithful'. What clinches the matter for the present editor, however, is line 51 in which Marlowe writes 'There good birds rest' for Ovid's *volucrum locus ille piarum* where no chance exists of compositorial confusion of 'god' with 'good' and where 'good' is manifestly his word for *pius*. If here, then presumably in lines 3 and 58 also.

II.vi

35 Crowes survive] All editors have adopted Robinson's emendation of 'crow'. This has the virtue of agreeing with the singular used for the other birds and with the Latin *cornix*, and it also provides a singular subject for the O3 verb 'survives'. However, each of the other birds' names is prefaced by 'the' and if 'Crow' had been in the singular one would have expected the same for it: 'The' could readily replace 'And' without altering the metre. The main difficulty with the O3 plural is the singular verb 'survives'. Although loose Elizabethan grammar might permit 'Crowes survives', the O3 edition usually smooths out all such free-wheeling grammar as is found in O1 (for example, in *have* for *hath* in I.ii.36 or 'make' for 'makes' in II.iv.10). Since the 'And' of line 35 is authorized by the Latin, and since 'Crowe' without the 'the' as elsewhere is unidiomatic here, the difficulty may lie not with the noun but with the verb 'survives', which is more likely to be a misprint or misreading than 'Crowes'. (It is also possible that the O3 compositor thought that 'hate' was the subject of 'survives' and so put it into the singular.) Hence the present editor takes it as the more logical choice to emend O3 'survives' to 'survive' and to retain 'Crowes' without a preceding 'the'. That 'life' is a singular referent back to 'Crowes' is of no significance.

59 great] The Methuen editor emends O3 'great' to 'small' on the basis of *tumulus pro corpore magnus* (as large a mound as is his body's size). But 'great grave' is scarcely to be held a compositorial or editorial error and is instead probably a Marlowe lapse in incorrectly relating *magnus* to the fact that it was a parrot to which *pro corpore* applied.

II.ix

4 thy tents] Marlowe's edition read *castris . . . tuis*, not *meis* as in later texts. The unauthoritative O5 alteration of 'thy' to 'my' probably came from context as in the error in line 52.

46 me . . . her] Dyce's emendation of O3 'Let her enjoy me oft' is required by the Latin *saepe fruar domina, saepe repulsus eam*. In view of this, the Methuen editor's objection (although he follows Dyce) has no pertinence that 'Marlowe is probably

using enjoy in the sense "give pleasure to" as illustrated in *O.E.D.*' The origin of the error is obviously by contamination from the preceding line, 'Now let her flatter me, now chide me hard'.

II.x

8 And this]   The reading is the O 3 variant from O 1 'This'. Not only does the Latin *et* encourage the authority of the O 3 form but also the fact that nine-syllable lines are almost unknown in Marlowe's translation. It would seem that the O 1 compositor was influenced by the start of the preceding line 7 with 'This'.

31–2 souldiour...his...his]   O 1 is faithful to the Latin singular here (where O 3 has the plural) but then departs from the continued Latin singular with the plural 'marchants'. The shift is odd. However, if O 1 is authoritative here, the O 3 change must be laid to a desire to regularize the seeming anomaly. If the singular were to be assigned to O 1 sophistication, on the other hand, one could argue that it was to avoid the ambiguity of 'their bloud' which in the O 3 English could be either that of the soldiers or of their enemies, although in Ovid it is the soldier's. That this ambiguity is serious enough to have led a scribe or compositor to change what he read in his copy is to be doubted, however. Whether Marlowe wrote both in the plural originally but changed the verse about the soldiers to the singular to avoid the ambiguity is – given the choice – more likely. If perhaps incomplete revision is to be conjectured here in Marlowe's papers, one may notice that lines 33–4 about the merchants (plural) are also imperfect.

34 Being]   Cunningham's emendation which mends O1, O3 agreement in an irregular hexameter in line 34 and a limping line 33 (unless 'perjured' should be trisyllabic) not only straightens out the metre but also conforms to the Latin, in which the perjured lips are associated with 'carowsing' the sea, not – as in O1–3 – with seeking wealth (there being no comma after 'wealth' in O1–3).

II.xi

19 *Cerannia*]   That O3's spelling is not a natural compositorial error for correct '*Ceraunia*' may be suggested by *Dido* I.i.147, 'grim *Ceranias* seate'.

II.xiii

9 slipping]   That there is contamination here and one of the rhyme words 'slipping' in lines 9 and 10 is wrong is practically certain. What the correct word was that is obscured by the 'slipping' reading, and which line it occurred in, can be a matter only for conjecture, and Dyce's 'skipping' in line 10 is as good a guess as any. Yet Cunningham, followed by the Revels editor, takes it that the first line of the couplet is in error and so would emend line 9 to 'skipping'. From the sense this switch has something to be said for it, since 'skipping' is an appropriate enough word for the action of water in a broad channel. On the other hand, the Latin *delapsus*, or 'sliding', is firmly related to the river's waters in the channel, and thus if Marlowe is translating exactly we must read 'slipping' in line 9. This position may be

strengthened by reference to III.v.20 'slide in thy bounds', where 'bounds' means channel, and perhaps to III.v.39 for Nile 'by seaven mouthes to the vast sea flowing'. The conjectural 'skipping' in line 10 was no doubt forced on Marlowe by the exigencies of rhyme, for Ovid reads merely *in maris exat aquas*.

III.i

12 cloake]   Although O 3–6 'looke' for Tragedy's presumed melancholy would be suitable enough, Dyce's emendation 'cloake' is required by the Latin *palla iacebat humi*, which shows 'looke' to be a printer's error.

III.ii

54 pleace]   According to the *O.E.D.* this is an obsolete form of 'please'. However, the use of 'please' in the sense required here is a strained one even though it is close to Ovid's *pugilis...placet*. One would scarcely know it from the English, but the object of 'please' is 'Pollux', and thus the word must be taken as 'pleased by'. In the next clause 'horsemen' is the subject in Ovid, and therefore the O 3 error 'loves' must be emended to 'love'. The context shows without question that it is not Castor and Pollux who are pleased by their devotees but instead the devotees who are cheering the images of the gods in the procession.

III.vii

62 her]   The O 3 reading 'she' may be Marlowe's misunderstanding of *imperat ut captae qui dare multa potest*, yet 'keeper' makes sense only if the text reads 'One her commands' as emended by Dyce. It is probable that 'she' in line 63 contaminated 'her' in the typesetting.

III.viii

61–2 Their...comes]   The Methuen editor's emendation 'Your...come', followed by the Revels editor, conforms to the Latin vocative, but the agreement of 'Their' and 'comes' seems to show what Marlowe actually wrote since the change is scarcely likely to be the printer's. Any emendation produces a sophistication.

66 The]   Properly this should read 'Thee, godly *Tibullus*' (*culte Tibulle*), but 'doth' indicates that Marlowe was not following the Latin vocative. For an analogy, see *1 Tamburlaine*, V.i.516.

III.xiii

8 And]   The Latin makes it clear that 'And' as in O 3 is required, not O 1 'Or': *quis furor est, quae nocte latent, in luce fateri, | et quae clam facias facta referre palam?*

40 dying]   Here as in lines 45 and 47 O 3 is metrically regular where the O 1 lines have extra syllables, and O 3 may be more literally exact as in line 47 O 3 'the palme is quickly got' (*vincere palma est*) for O 1 'garland'. In line 45 O 1 'yeeld not' is certainly more typical of Marlowe's use of 'yeeld' than the regular O 3 'deny', despite

some slight possibility that 'yeeld' could have been influenced by 'yeeld' from line 47. On the whole the O3 variants in this cluster appear to be editorial instead of errors by the scribe behind the O1 copy, and O1 seems to preserve the Marlovian expansiveness. In the case in point in line 40, O3 'And would be dead, but dead with thee remaine' reproduces *tunc ego, sed tecum, mortuus esse velim*. Yet O1 'dying' is difficult to assign to anything but the reading of Marlowe's papers, and it may preserve the possibility of word-play on the sexual sense of 'dying', even though this is without precedent in Ovid. It would seem that either one accepts the authority of the three variants in O1 lines 40, 45, and 47, or rejects them all in favor of the smoother O3 readings. As a package, the present editor opts for the authority of O1.

PRESS-VARIANTS IN O3

[Copies collated: Bodl (Bodleian Mason AA.27), Dyce (Victoria and Albert Museum), CSmH (Huntington).]

SHEET B (*outer forme*)

Corrected: Bodl, Dyce

Uncorrected: CSmH

Sig. B2^v
  I.ix.41 faint to] to faint
Sig. B8^v
  II.ii.12 expence] expenne

SHEET B (*inner forme*)

Corrected: Bodl, Dyce

Uncorrected: CSmH

Sig. B7^v
  Jonson I.xv.39 liuing] liuiung

EMENDATIONS OF ACCIDENTALS

I.i

(O$_{1-2}$ *present*)
O$_{1-2}$ *read* Amorum lib. 1. Elegia 1.
0.2 *bellis*] O$_3$; *bell*. O$_{1-2}$
1 *et seq. Ovids*] O$_3$; Ovids O$_{1-2}$.
 All names in O$_{1-2}$ *are in roman*
1 three,] O$_3$; ~ $_\wedge$ O$_{1-2}$
4 away,] O$_3$; ~ $_\wedge$ O$_{1-2}$
5 Muse] O$_3$; muse O$_{1-2}$

7 Love] love O$_{1-6}$
11 bowe,] O$_4$; ~ ? O$_{1-3}$
12 glowe?] ~ . O$_{1-6}$
15 Who'le] O$_3$; Whole O$_{1-2}$
16 Aonian] O$_3$; *Aonion* O$_{1-2}$
16 play?] ~ , O$_{1-2}$; ~ . O$_{3-6}$
19 *Tempe*] *tempe* O$_{1-2}$; *Temple* O$_{3-6}$
25 Love] O$_6$; love O$_{1-5}$

I.ii

(O$_{1-2}$ *present*)
O$_{1-2}$ *read* Amorum lib. 1. Elegia 2.
5, 42 Love] love O$_{1-6}$
6 him?] ~ . O$_{1-6}$
9 Yeelding] O$_3$; yeelding O$_{1-2}$
9 might,] O$_2$; ~ $_\wedge$ O$_1$
13 Yong] O$_3$ (Young); yong O$_{1-2}$
15 torne,] O$_3$; ~ $_\wedge$ O$_{1-2}$
23 *et seq. Venus*] O$_3$; Venus O$_{1-2}$. *All*

names in O$_{1-2}$ *are in roman*
25 The] O$_2$; the O$_1$
28 magnificall.] O$_3$; ~ , O$_{1-2}$
33 Thee] O$_2$; thee O$_1$
37 Thou] O$_3$; thou O$_{1-2}$
38 Take] O$_3$; take O$_{1-2}$
39 Thy] O$_2$; thy O$_1$
43 erre,] O$_2$; ~ $_\wedge$ O$_1$

I.iii

(O$_{1-2}$ *present*)
0 O$_{1-2}$ *read* Amorum lib. 1. Elegia 3.
0.1 *amicam*] O$_2$; *amicum* O$_1$
1 right:] O$_3$; ~ $_\wedge$ O$_{1-2}$
8 line,] O$_3$; ~ . O$_{1-2}$

10 given$_\wedge$] ~ , O$_{1-6}$
11 *et seq. Apollo*] O$_3$; Apollo O$_{1-2}$.
 All names in O$_{1-2}$ *are in roman*
12 pray,] ~ . O$_1$, 4; ~ $_\wedge$ O$_2$; ~ ; O$_3$,
 5–6

I.iv

7 not$_\wedge$] ~ , O$_{3-6}$
15 spread$_\wedge$] O$_6$; ~ , O$_{3-5}$
17 countenance:] ~ $_\wedge$ O$_3$, 5; ~ , O$_4$, 6
24–5 brought. . . .thee,] O$_4$; ~ , . . .~
 . O$_3$
27 evill,] O$_4$; ~ . O$_3$
65 pezant,] O$_5$; ~ $_\wedge$ O$_3$; O$_4$ *point*

uncertain
66 wordes,] O$_4$; ~ . O$_3$
67 bring,] O$_4$; ~ $_\wedge$ O$_3$
68 do,] O$_6$; ~ : O$_{3-5}$
68 spring:] ~ $_\wedge$ O$_3$; ~ . O$_4$; ~ , O$_5$–
 6
69 it,] O$_4$; ~ $_\wedge$ O$_3$

I.v

(O 1–2 *present*)
0 O 1–2 *read* Amorum lib. 1. Elegia 5.
8 unknowne.] O2; ~ ‸ O1
9 *et seq. Corinna*] O3; Corinna O1–2.
    All names in O1–2 *are in roman*

13 gowne: ~ ‸ O1–6
13 small,] O3; ~ ‸ O1; ~ . O2
16 last.] O2; ~ , O1
22 thigh?] O3; ~ , O1; ~ . O2

I.vi

1 sore,] O4; ~ ‸ O3
3 make,] O4; ~ ‸ O3
5 Love] love O3–6
11 laugh'd] O6; laug'd O3–5
13 Love] O6 (*Love*); love O1–5
17 denne] dende O3–5; dend O6
17 unbarre,] O4; ~ ‸ O3
23 free,] O6; ~ ‸ O3–5
23 like,] O4; ~ ‸ O3
27 heare?] ~ , O3–6
34, 37, 59, 60 Love] love O3–6
39 them?] O6; ~ ‸| O3, 5; ~ , O4

40 them.] O5; ~ ? O3–4
41 heare,] O4; ~ ‸ O3
42 running] O4; run-ning O3
42 eare?] ~ . O3–5; ~ , O6
43 thee,] O4; ~ ‸ O3
47 therefore,] O4; ~ ‸ O3
53 minde,] O4; ~ ‸ O3
67 crowne,] ~ ‸ O3–6
72 Carelesse,] ~ ‸ O3–6
72 farewell,] O4; ~ ‸ O3
73 posts,] O6; ~ ‸ O3–5

I.vii

1 chaines,] O4; ~ ‸ O3
7 *Ajax*,] ~ ‸ O3–6
8 field,] ~ ‸ O3; ~ . O4; ~ ; O5–6
9 sire,] O4; ~ ‸ O3
10 durst‸] O6; ~ , O3–5
14 th'] O5; *th'* O3–4
17 fall,] O4; ~ ‸ O3
34 a foe] O4; afoe O3

35 Conqueror,] O4; ~ ‸ O3
36 *Jove*,] O6; ~ ,: O3; ~ : O4–5
38 *Io*,] O4; ~ ‸ O3
43 floud] O4 (fllood); flould O3
49 rent,] O4; ~ ‸ O3
54 flawe,] ~ . O3–5; ~ ; O6
59 offended,] O4; ~ ‸ O3
62 repell.] O4; ~ ‸ O3

I.viii

0 8] 5 O3–6
6 flow,] O4; ~ ‸ O3
16 flies.] O4; ~ ‸ O3
23 pleas'd,] O4; ~ ‸ O3
30 warme,] O4; ~ . O3
37 deject,] O4; ~ ‸ O3
39 raignde,] O4; ~ . O3

61 bring,] O4; ~ ‸ O3
76 waine.] O4; ~ ‸ O3
77 gate,] O4; ~ . O3
78 heare‸] ~ : O3, 5; ~ ; O4; ~ , O6
105 doest,] O6; ~ ‸ O3–5
106 blowne,] ~ . O3–6
109 betraide,] O4; ~ ‸ O3

404

I.ix

1 tent,] O4; ~ ∧ O3
3 agree,] O4; ~ ∧ O3
5 require,] O4; ~ ∧ O3
9 send,] O6; ~ ∧ O3–5
17 goe,] O4; ~ ∧ O3
22 bloud] O4 (blood); bould O3
36 *Andromache*] O6; *Adromache* O3–5

37 say,] O6; ~ ∧ O3–5
39 stable,] O6; ~ ∧ O3–5
41 faint,] O5; ~ ∧ O3–4
42 minde.] O4; ~ ∧ O3
45 watch] O4; wacth O3
45 move:] ~ ∧ O3, 5; ~ , O4, 6

I.x

9 abates,] O4; ~ ∧ O3
15 staine,] O4; ~ ∧ O3
27 Bull,] O4; ~ ∧ O3
29 Man,] O6; ~ ∧ O3–5
33 it,] O6; ~ ∧ O3–5
37 saile,] O6; ~ ∧ O3–5
43 unbought,] O4; ~ ∧ O3
46 inlarg'd.] O6; ~ ∧ O3–5

47 crave,] O6; ~ ∧ O3–5
53 scorne] O4; scrone O3
53 churle,] O4; ~ ∧ O3
55 vine,] O4; ~ ∧ O3
57 care;] ~ ∧ O3–6
61 wast,] O4; ~ ∧ O3
63 disdayne,] O4; ~ ∧ O3

I.xi

1 order,] O4; ~ ∧ O3
2 -borne,] -~ ∧ O3–6
2 border,] O4; ~ . O3
5 perswasion,] O4; ~ ∧ O3
7 carry,] O4; ~ ∧ O3
11 Loves] O6; loves O3–5

11 thee,] O4; ~ ∧ O3
13 night,] O4; ~ ∧ O3
17 reading,] O6; ~ ∧ O3–5
21 letter∧] ~ , O3–6
23 quill,] O6; ~ ∧ O3–5

I.xii

0.1 *quas*] O4; *qas* O3
1 chaunce,] O6; ~ ∧ O3–5
1 returned,] O4; ~ ∧ O3
4 started.] O4; ~ ∧ O3
8 denying,] ~ . O3–6

17 strangle,] O6; ~ ∧ O3–5
19 scrich-] O4; scrith- O3
19 allowes,] O6; ~ ∧ O3–5
27 things,] O6; ~ ∧ O3–5

I.xiii

(O1–2 *present*)
0 O1–2 *read* Amorum.lib.1.Elegia.13.
0.1 *Auroram*] O3; *auroram* O1–2
3 *et seq. Aurora*] O3; Aurora O1–2.

All names in O1–2 *are in roman*
34 showne?] ~ . O1–6
41 waine?] ~ , O1–6

I.xiv

0.1 *nimia*] O4; *mimia* O3
5 them?] ~ ∧ O3–6
9 viewe,] O4; ~ ∧ O3

10 hue,] ~ . O3–5; ~ : O6
20 rested,] ~ . O3–6
23 mosse,] O4; ~ ∧ O3

27 cryed,] O4; ~ ∧ O3
27 burne,] O4; ~ ∧ O3
29 reach,] O4; ~ ∧ O3
32 *Phœbus*] O4; *Phœbus* O3
37 inclinde,] O4; ~ ∧ O3

48 bush,] O6; ~ . O3-5
52 shame,] O6; ~ ∧ O3-5
53 lappe,] O4; ~ ∧ O3
56 haire.] O4; ~ , O3

I.xv

(O1-2 *present*)
0 O1-2 *read* Amorum lib.2. Elegia 15.
1-2 ill,...quill?] O6; ~ ?...~ , O1-2; ~ ,...~ . O3-5
6 cause?] ~ . O1-3, 5-6; ~, O4
9 *et seq. Homer*] O3; Homer O1-2. *All names in* O1-2 *are in roman*
12 fell.] O3; ~ , O1-2

15 vaine,] O3; ~ . O1; ~ : O2
16 *Aratus*] O3; Æratus O1; Eratus O2
17 hoorish,] O3; ~ ∧ O1-2
22 golde?] O6; ~ . O1,3,5; ~ , O2,4
23 *Lucretius*] O3; Lucresius O1-2
30 *Licoris*] O3; Licorus O1-2
35 wits∧] O2; ~ , O1

By B. J.

12 eare.] O6; ~ , O3-4; *point uncertain in* O5

35 *Phœbus*] O4; Phœbus O3

II.i

1 wantonnesse,] O4; ~ ∧ O3
2 *Peligny,*] ~ ∧ O3-6
3 severe,] O4; ~ ∧ O3
6 reade,] O6; ~ . O3-5
8 knowe,] O5; ~ . O3-4
11 tell,] O4; ~ ∧ O3
12 well,] O5; ~ . O3-4

14 bore,] ~ ∧ O3-6
15, 17, 18, 19 *Jove...Jove*] O5; Jove ...Jove O3-4
17 left,] O4; ~ ∧ O3
19 nought,] O4; ~ ∧ O3
21 tooke,] O4; ~ ∧ O3
28 boast.] ~ ∧ O3,5; ~; O4, ~ , O6

II.ii

0.2 *laxiorem*] Laxiorem O3-6
1 bridle,] O4; ~ ∧ O3
7 redoubled,] O6; ~ ∧ O3-5
10 perish.] O6; ~ ∧ O3-5
11 wise,] O4; ~ ∧ O3
12 expence?] ~ ∧ O3-5; ~ . O6
15 obtaine,] ~ ∧ O3-5; ~ . O6
17 tremble,] O6; ~ ∧ O3-5
18 guilty,] O4; ~ ∧ O3
19 her,] ~ ∧ O3-5; ~ ; O6

23 stayes,] O5; ~ ∧ O3-4
29 usd,] O6; ~ ∧ O3-5
31 him∧] ~ , O3-6
31 hide,] ~ ∧ O3-5; ~ . O6
33 frownes,] O4; ~ ∧ O3
43 fruite∧flying] O6; ~ - ~ O3-5
49 fram'd,] O6; ~ ∧ O3-5
57 denyall,] O6; ~ ∧ O3-5
63 not,] O6; ~ ∧ O3-5
66 pray?] O5; ~ . O3-4

II.iii

7 beare,] O4; ~ . O3

II.iv

(O1–2 *present*)
0 O1–2 *read* Amorum lib.2. Elegia 4.
0.1 *cuiuscunque*] O3; *Cuiscunque* O1–2
4 behaviour.] O3; ~ , O1–2
6 shun.] O2; ~ , O1
7 selfe,] O3; ~ ₳ O1–2
7 please₳] ~ , O1–6
13 like₳] O3; ~ , O1–2
14 downe.] O2; ~ , O1
15 *Sabines*] sabins O1; sabines O2
16 dissemble.] O3; ~ , O1; ~ ₳ O2
18 her.] O3; ~ , O1–2
19 *Callimachus*] O3; Calimecus O1–2.
All names in O1–2 *are in roman*

24 man.] O2; ~ , O1
28 running?] O3; ~ , O1; ~ ₳ O2
30 curtesie.] O3; ~ , O1–2
32 fall.] O3; ~ , O1–2
33 *Amazon*] O3; amazon O1–2
34 uppon:] O2; ~ , O1
35 rounder:] ~ ₳ O1–6
39 yellowe] O6; ~ ₳ O3–5
42 *Ledas...Leda*] O3; Ledas...Leda
O1–2
42 faire.] O2; ~ , O1
47 *Romane*] O3; Romane O1–2

II.v

6 bewray.] O4; ~ ₳ O3
8 soule,] ~ ₳ O3–6
13 slumbred,] O6; ~ ₳ | O3, 5; ~ .
O4
14 drunke,] O4; ~ ₳ O3
19 see?)] O4; ~)? O3

27 *Phœbus*] O6; *Phœbus* O3–5
27 thought,] O4; ~ ₳ O3
36 betrothed] O4; bethrothed O3
40 *Arachne*] O4; *Arachine* O 3, 5–6
43 her.] O4; ~ ₳ O3

II.vi

7 leudnesse] O4; leudesse O3
12 -dove,] ~ ₳ O3–6
27 Behould] O3 *cw*; Behold O3 *text*

33 hovers₳] O4; ~ , O3
45 see,] O4; ~ ₳ O3
55 feather,] O5; ~ . O3; ~ : O4

II.vii

2 shame.] O6; ~ , O3–5
25–6 just:...lust?] O4; ~ ?...~ :

26 repulse,] O4; ~ . O3

O3

II.ix

23 quiet,] O4; ~ . O3
28 me.] O4; ~ ₳| O3
30 stay,] ~ . O3–6
32 lea,] ~ . O3–4; ~ : O5–6

34, 51 Love] love O3–6
38 I₳] O4~ , O3
46 oft,] O4; ~ ₳ O3

II.x

(O1–2 *present*)
0 O1–2 *read* Amorum lib.2. Elegia 10.
0.1 *Grœcinum*] O3; Grecinum O1–2
1 *Grœcinus*] O3; Grecinus O1–2. *All
names in* O1–2 *are in roman*
8 she.] O3; ~ , O1–2

10 love₳] O2; ~ , O1
10 that,] O3; ~ ₳ O1–2
21 delight,] O6; ~ ₳ O1–5
28 nerethelesse.] O3; ~ , O1–2
30 prayes] O3; ~ , O1–2
33 wealth,] ~ ₳ O1–6

II.xi

5 suncke,] O5; ~ . O3–4
17 others] O4; othets O3

30 say.] ~ , O3–6

II.xii

4 inclose.] ~ , O3, 5–6; ~ : O4

23 send‸] ~ , O3–6

II.xiii

14 keepe,] ~ . O3–6
21 wench,] ~ ‸ O3–6
24 feete,] ~ : O3, 5–6; ~ . O4

25 Subscribing,] ~ ‸ O3–6
25 sav'd:] ~ , O3–6
26 grav'd.] O4; ~ , O3

II.xiv

6 tormented.] O4; ~ , O3

11 originall,] ~ ‸ O3–6

II.xv

7 lye,] O4; ~ . O3
16 cleaves,] O6; ~ . O3–5

19 hit,] O4; ~ . O3

II.xvi

3 incline,] O4; ~ . O3
5 *Pelignian*] Pelig- O3 *cw*; *Pilignian*
    O3 *text*

6 soft] O4; sofr O3
30 eaze.] O4; ~ , O3
34 surround,] ~ . O3–5; ~ : O6

II.xviii

7 sayd] O3 *text*; said O3 *cw*
7 me:] ~ , O3–4; ~ ‸ O5–6
11 I yeeld] O6; I-yeeld O3–5
14 deseignes,] O5; ~ . O3–4
18 Love] love O3–6
19 Loves] loves O3–6

22 *Demophoon*] O4; *Domoophon* O3
26 harpe.] O4; ~ ‸ O3
29 signe,] O4; ~ ‸ O3
34 *Phœbus*] O4; *Phœbus* O3
37 record,] O5; ~ . O3–4
39 incline] O4; inclnie O3

II.xix

11 hale] haole O3–6
12 delay,] ~ ‸ O3–6
17 shee,] O5; ~ ‸ | O3–4

25 me,] O4; ~ ‸ O3
57 baude?] ~ , O3–6

III.i

15–16 spent,...argument?] O6; ~ ?
    ...~ . O3–5
32 garnisht.] O5; ~ ‸ | O3–4
35 *Tragedie*] O6 (*Tragedy*); Tragedie

O3–5
55 not,] O4; ~ ‸ O3
67 *Tragedie*] Tragedie O3–6
69 hast,] O6; ~ ‸ O3, 5; ~ . O4

III.ii

0.1 spectantem] O4; spactantem O3
4 flame.] O4; ~ ₐ| O3
5 heed₍ₐ₎] ~ , O3–6
32 them.] O5; ~ ₐ| O3; ~ , O4
34 flouds] O4; floulds O3
45 Victory] O6; victory O3–5
51 Phœbus, Phœbe] Phœbus, Phœbe O3–6

57 beloved:] ~ , O3–6
63 -downe:] ~ , O3–6
66 Fower ₐ chariot-horses]   Fower-
    chariot horses O3–6
71 doest,] ₐ ~O3–6
75 backe:] ~ , O3–6
82 gaine.] O4; ~ , O3

III.iii

1 What,] ~ ₐ O3–6
11 society₍ₐ₎] ~ , O3–6
16 receive?] O6; ~ . O3–5

18 slaughter?] ~ . O3–6
21 perjuries,] O4; ~ ₐ O3

III.iv

3 chast,] O6; ~ : O3–5
3 sooth:] O4; ~ ₐ O3
4 not,] ~ ₐ O3–6
20 Love] O5; love O3–4
29 kept,] O3 point uncertain; ~ , O5
30 feare₍ₐ₎] O6; ~ , O3–5

30 is,] ~ ₐ O3–6
38 beleeves,] ~ . O3–6
45 friends₍ₐ₎] ~ , O3–6
46 any.] O5; ~ , O3–4
47 together,] O4; ~ : O3
48 thether.] O4 (thither.) ; ~ ₐ| O3

III.v

0.1 amnem,] ~ ₐ O3–6
7 rushest,] O4; ~ . O3
34 prov'd?] ~ . O3–6
40 knowing,] O6; ~ . O3–5
53 Saying,] ~ ₐ O3–4
53 upon,] O4; ~ ₐ O3

79 coate₍ₐ₎] ~ , O3–6
84 undetected.] O4; ~ : O3
89–90 floud,. . .stood?] O6;   ~?. . .
    ~ , O3–5
92 certaine] O4; cerraine O3

III.vi

(O1–2 present)
0 O1–2 read Amorum lib.3. Elegia
  6.
0.1–2 receptus,. . .potuit,] O3; ~ ₐ. . .
    ~ ₐ O1–2
2 had.] O3; ~ , O1–2
4 not.] O3; ~ , O1; ~ ₐ O2
8 et seq. Scithean] O3 (Sythian);
  Scithean O1–2. All names in O1–2
  are in roman
12 stirre.] O3; ~ , O1–2
16 shade] O3; shad O1–2
16 I,] ~ ? O1–2; ~ ₐ O3–6
16 say?] O3; ~ , O1–2

17 do,] ~ ? O1–6
18 done?] ~ , O1–2; ~ . O3–6
20 rustie.] O3; ~ , O1–2
26 light.] O3; ~ , O1–2
27 What] O2; what O1
27 What,] ~ ₐ O1–6
31 poynts?] O3; ~ , O1–2
34 al.] O2; ~ ₐ O1
36 haunted?] ~ , O1; ~ . O2–6
41 Pilius] O3 (Pylius); pilius O1–2
42 require.] O3; ~ , O1–2
44 againe?] O3; ~ , O1; ~ ₐ O2
46 This] O2; this O1
48 To] O2; to O1

48 me.] O2; ~ , O1
49 king‸...it?] O3; ~ ?...~ , O1–2
50 it?] O2; ~ , O1
52 touch.] O3; ~ , O1–2
58 loved,] O4; ~ ‸ O1–3
59 men,] O3; ~ ‸ O1–2
60 then.] O3; ~ , O1–2
62 *Thamiras*] Thamaris O1–2; *Tham-iris* O3–6
62 things?] O6; ~ , O1–2; ~ . O3–5

63–4 same?...came.] O3; ~ ,...~ ?
    O1; ~ ,...~ . O2
65 Yet] O2; yet O1
68 fight.] O2; ~ , O1
72 infamie.] O2; ~ , O1
76 downe,] O3; ~ ‸ O1–2
79 th'art] O2 (tha'rt); thart O1
81 on,] O3; ~ ‸ O1–2
81 her,] O3; ~ ‸ O1–2

III.vii

2 stand?] O6; ~ . O3–5
9 inferr'd,] O4; ~ ‸ O3
10 knighted] O4; kinghted O3
23 *Phœbus*] O6; *Phæbus* O3–5

26 sterne,] ~ . O3–6
32 brasse,] O5; ~ ‸ O3–4
35 possest,] O4; ~ ‸ O3

III.viii

2 assaile,] O6; ~ . O3–5
3 *Elegia*] O5; *Eeliga* O3–4
7 quite,] O4; ~ ‸ O3
22 wood?] ~ . O3–6
23 *Phœbus*] O5; *Phæbus* O3–4

30 fals-hood] fal-shood O3–5;
    falsehood O6
47 Ile] O6; I*le* O3; *Ile* O4–5
55 departing,] ~ ‸ O3–6
55 lov'd,] ~ ‸ O3–6

III.ix

14 broake.] O4; ~ ‸ O3
17 fields,] O4; ~ ‸ O3

44 forbeare] O4; fotbeare O3

III.x

28 endure.] O4; ~ , O3

III.xi

36 breede?] ~ , O3–6

III.xii

7 clouded,] O4; ~ ‸| O3
16 Piggs,] ~ ‸ O3–6
17 back.] O4; ~ ‸| O3

20 forsooke.] O4; ~ , O3
21 darts,] O4; ~ . O3

III.xiii

(O1–2 *present*)
0 O1–2 *read* Amorum lib. 3. Elegia 13.
4 paste.] O2; O1 *point uncertain*

6 it.] O2; ~ , O1
8 bewray?] O3; ~ , O1–2
10 too.] O2; ~ , O1

11 Will] O2; will O1
12 same?] O6; ~ : O1; ~ . O2–5
14 chaste,] O3; ~ ‸ O1–2
14 can.] O2; ~ , O1
18 feete.] O2; ~ , O1
28 grace.] O2; ~ , O1
30 slight.] O2; ~ , O1

34 raste?] ~ , O1 (*point uncertain*);
    ~ . O2–6
38 thorough] O3; through O1–2
40 remaine.] O3; ~ , O1–2
42 accusde.] O2; ~ , O1
46 eies.] O2; ~ , O1

III.xiv

2 set,] ~ . O3–5; ~ : O6
3 framde,] ~ . O3–6

11 *Sulmoes*] O4; *Snlmoes* O3
18 great] O4; grear O3

HISTORICAL COLLATION

[NOTE: The following editions are herein collated: O1 (*Certaine of Ovids Elegies*, n.d.); O2 (*Certaine of Ovids Elegies*, n.d.); O3 (*All Ovids Elegies*, n.d.); O4 (*Ovids Elegies*, n.d.); O5 (*All Ovids Elegies*, n.d.); O6 (*All Ovids Elegies*, n.d.); R (*Works* (reprint of O4 only) ed. Robinson, 1826), D¹ (*Works*, ed. Dyce, 1850); D² (*Works*, ed. Dyce, 1858); C (*Works*, ed. Cunningham, 1870); B (*Works*, ed. Bullen, 1885); TB (*Works*, ed. Tucker Brooke, 1910); M (*Poems*, ed. Martin, 1931); Rv (*Poems*, ed. MacLure, 1968). Reference is also made to Mal MS (Malone's queries in Bodleian Mal 133, a MS transcript of O2); and to Br (Broughton's notes in BM copy of Robinson).]

0 *P. Ovidii . . . Primus*] omit O1–2

I.i

(O1–2 *present*)
4 thy] the O2, R, C
5 upreard] prepar'd O3–6, R+
5 meant] meane O1–2
8 tooke] take O1–2
9 thee] the O5
11 What] That O1–2
15 sunne] sonne O1–2, R

19 *Tempe*] *Temple* O3–6
21 workes] worke O1–2
22 Love] I O1–2, R
22 numbers] number O1–2, R, C
28 Saying] Saving O5–6
34 praise] sprays D+
34.1 *omit*] C. Marlowe. O1–2

I.ii

(O1–2 *present*)
1 soft] so soft O2, R
3 tho,] tho‚ O1; tho. O5–6, B (~ ;); through R; tho'‚ C
7 so,] ~ ‚ O1–2, R, C
7 slender] tĕder O2; tender O6, R
9 striving] strugling O3–6, R+ (−B)
12 shakt] slackt O3–6; slak'd R
14 which] that O5–6
21 needes] need'st O2–6, R+
26 thy] *omit* O2
28 triumph] triumphs O1–2, R

31 meaning,] ~ ‚ O1–6, R
34 triumphing] *Triumphe* TB
36 hath] have O2–6, R+
38, 45 thy] thine O3–6, R+
41 wings,] ~ ‚ O5–6, D
44 woundes] wordes O2
45 thy] thine O3–6
48 Thee] The O4
51 kinsmans] kinsman R, D, C, B
52 the] thee O1–6, R, C
52 conquering] conquerings O5

I.iii

(O1–2 *present*)
1 hir] he O3–5; him O6
2 never] *omit* O2
3 aske] crave O2, D, B
4 Love] *Jove* O3–6, R, D, C, B
6 love] love thee O2, R
7 make me thine] cause me to be thine O2

9 lands] land O3–6, D+
13 gives] give O1–2, O4, R
18 or] ere O3–6, R+
18 shalt] shall O3, 5
21 horned] honored O5–6
22 Swanne] Bull O1–2; bird Mal MS
22 *Jove*] love O2
26.1 *omit*] C. Marlow. O1–2

I.iv

5 Wilt] With O4
12 warnings] warning O5–6
16 foote] feete O4, R
18 receive] return D, C, B
21 in] to O4, R, C
22 thombe] tombe O5–6
34 Gobbets] Goblets O3–6, R, TB

36 leane] leave O3–4, R
45 am] are O5–6
59 warne] warme O5–6
61 thee] *omit* O4; and R
62 will] *omit* O3–6, TB, Rv
66 be] in O5–6

I.v

(O1–2 *present*)
7 shamefaste] shamefac'd O6, R, D, C, B
9 a] her M
10 tresses] trells O2
12 lovers] wooers O3–6, R+ (−D)

12 sped] spread O1–2, R
23 likt] pleasde O2
24 naked] faire white O2; fair naked R
24 tyrde] tride O3–6
26.1 *omit*] C. Marlow. O1–2

I.vi

5 makes] make O3–6
9 vaine] vaines O4
14 Nor] Not O6
17 denne] dende O3–6; door R; den t' TB (*qy*)
34 were] we O6
50 abound] rebound B (*qy*)
53 beares] beare O6
54 Come] Some O4

58 these] the O5–6
60 Night‸ shamelesse, wine‸] ~ , ~ ‸ ~ , O3–6, R+
61 have I] I have O6
62 dores] gates O6
66 soules] *omit* O6
69 thee] the O5–6
72 distaind] disdaind O5–6

I.vii

4 hand] arme O6
9 sire] ire R, C, B, M
10 sharpe] *omit* B (*qy*)
12 ruffled] comely O6
13 *Atalanta*] *Atlante* O6
18 thy] the O6
20 tyed] died O6
36 hayres] haire O6
42 wantons] wanton O4–6, R

46 threatings] threatnings O5–6, R, D, C, B
51 lookes] locks O6
52 *Parian*] *Harian* O6
56 waters] water O5; water-tops O6
62 repell] expell O5–6
63 not] art O5–6
67 crime] crimes O6
68 thy] the R, C

I.viii

0 8] 5 O3–6
0.1 *meretricia*] *meritricio* O6; *meretricis* R, D, C, B
1 There...ere] Is there whoe'er Br MS

7 wrong] wrung D, C, B
13 nights] night O6, M
28 rich] but rich Br MS
28 state] estate D (*qy*)
31 fortune] fortunes O6

65 lines] lives O 3–6, R
77 thy] the O 5–6
78 heare] here O 6; hear; R
86 mockt] mocke O 6
90 tittle] little O 4, R
93 When causes fale] What were it for
O 4, R

97 bed mens] beds men O 3–6, R
108 grave] graves M
111 her] let her O 4
111 thin] thine O 3–6; *omit* R; her Br
MS
112 a] in O 6

I.ix

3 fits] sits TB
4 eld] old O 5–6
8 dores] door C, B
12 deserts] desert R, C, B
12 do] to O 3–6

14 fit] full O 4, R
25 Sooth] Such O 5–6
27 hands] armes O 6
41 faint, to] to faint O 3(u)

I.x

11 Ask'st] Ask't O 5–6
19 to] at R, D, C, B
29 spoiles] spoyle O 4, R
41 bed] bad O 5–6

56 May] Many O 3–6, R
56 lome] M; love O 3–6, R, D, C, B
59 verse] verses O 6
60 mine] my O 5–6

I.xi

1 skilfull] skilfuld O 3, 5
4 signes] sighes O 4; signs unto Br MS
4 to thee] omit O 4, R

17 in] and B
23 neede] needs B
23 tyre] try O 3–6, R

I.xii

5 more] most O 4, R
23 they] thy O 3–6

27 name] names O 6

I.xiii

(o 1–2 *present*)
1 on] ore O 3–6, R+
1 love] Love O 3–6
4 for] from O 3–6, R, C
12 courses] course O 2; counsell O 6
14 And…fight,] *omit* O 2
21 client] client both do O 1–2

24 setst] seest O 2
25 All] This O 1–2
29 thy] the O 6
39 heldst] hadst O 1–2
41 Punish ye] Doest punish O 3–6, R+
43 with] and O 2
47 chid] chide O 2–6, R

I.xiv

0.1 *nimia*] *mimia* O 3, 5
4 lockes] lackes O 3–4
10 neither] either O 3–6
13 Ad] And O 4–6, R, C, M, Rv
18 drave] drive O 3–6, R, D, C, B, TB

24 Thy] They O 3–6; The R, C
26 tramells] trannels O 3–6, D, B, TB
29 be] by O 5–6
37 see] see thy O 6
47 Which] With R, C, M

I.xv

(O 1–2 *present*)
2 tearmes] termst O 3–6, R+
2 my] our O 1–2
2 works] woks O 2; worke O 6
3 sprong] come O 1–6, R
4 dustie] rustie O 3–6
5 Nor] Or Br MS (*in* O 2 *reprint*)
6 sale] sail B
8 may] might O 1–2, R
8 my] thy O 4
10 into] to the O 1–2, R, C, B
10 doth] shall O 1–2, B
11 while] whiles O 6

13–14 The...weake.] *omit* O 1–2
17 be hard] hoord O 1–6, R (hoard);
   hard TB
22 *Argos*] Argo D, C, B
26 conquered] conquering O 1–2, R
32 nere] *omit* O 2
33 Let...verse] To verse let Kings
   give place O 3–6, R+
34 And] The O 1–2, B
37 be] the O 5–6
41 rackes] rocks O 2, D; rakes O 3–5,
   R+ (–D, B); takes O 6

I.xv

(*By* B. J.)
8 through] though O 6
9 whil'st] while O 6
14 in Arte] Arte in O 5

15 losse] less C
28 neate] neare O 6
37 The frost-drad] The frost-dead O 6;
   Frost-fearing *Jonson 1616 Folio*

II.i

1 my] thy O 3–6
17 *Joves*] loves O 4
19 weapons] weapon O 6
23 deduce] reduce O 3–6, R+

24 backe] blacke O 3–6
32 jades did] horses R, C
35 *Heroes* of] *Heroes*, O O 3–6, TB, Rv

II.ii

1 thy] my O 5–6
4 fact] pack C (*qy*)
5 me, soone‸] ~ ‸ ~ , O 3–6, R+
8 thy care] they care O 3–4
11 what] that O 4
12 un-protected] un-protested O 3–6
13 follow] followes O 5–6, D, B
14 thinke] thinkes O 3, O 5–6, D, C,

B
29 the] thy O 4
46 deifide] defide O 6
47 legges] leg O 6
52 heare] hears R, D, C, B
53 eares] yeares O 6
55 easily] easy R, C, B

II.iv

(O 1–2 *present*)
8 Am] And O 1–2, R, C
10 makes] make O 3–6, R+
12 burne] blushe O 1–6, R, C; And
   blush, I Mal MS
12 glance] glasse O 1–2
14 should] would O 3–6, D+

14 nimble...shees] quick...she is O 2,
   R
22 lie] be O 2
24 would] will O 4
28 hands] nimble handes O 2
29 she] her O 3–6, R+
31 with all] withall O 1–2, R

35 speake] say O 3–6, R+ (−B)
37–42 I thinke...faire.] omit O 1–2
37 what] that R
37 drest;] ~ ‸ O 3–5; ~ . O 6

41 blacke] browne O 4, R, C, M
43 Amber] Yellow O 1–2
46 that] and that O 4
48 ranging] raging O 6

II.v

1 No...so] No, love is not so Br MS
3 thy] my O 4
9 dares] dare O 5–6
11 griefe] grieve O 5
13 wretch] wench O 3–6, R, C
14 Not] Nor O 5–6
14 in] on O 3–6, R+

14 spilt] split O 6
16 your] her O 6
16 a] her O 6
25 her] the O 5–6
27 not] to O 5–6
40 staynes] staine so O 6
50 indue] endure O 6

II.vi

3 goodly] godly D+ (−TB)
3 breasts] breast B
4 your] her O 6
8 out] not O 3–6; now R, D, C, B
10 *Itis* is] It is as O 3–6; It is a R; Itys
    a D, C, B
22 saffrons] Saffron O 6
25 warres] waters O 6
30 did] didst O 6

35 Crowes] crow R+
35 survive] survives O 3–6, R+
38 worlds] words O 3–6
48 *Corinna...thy*] *Corinda...the* O 6
53 There] The O 6
53 abroad] about O 6
58 goodly] godly D+ (−TB)
59 great] small R, C, M

II.vii

0 7] 5 O 6
8 fault] heart O 6

9 thou doest] I doe O 6

II.viii

16 thy] my O 3–6, R
16 thee] the O 5–6, R
20 false] selfe O 3–6, R, D, C, B

20 *Carpathian*] *Carpathion* O 5–6
20 to] do O 5–6
26 fault] faults C, B

II.ix

4 thy] my O 5–6
13 hooked] crooked O 6
20 though] through O 6; to R
23 quiet] quit O 6

32 haven] heaven O 3–4, R
46 me...her] her...me O 3–6, R, TB,
    Rv
52 my] they O 5–6

416

II.x

(O 1–2 *present*)
5 rich in] in rich O 4, R
8 And this] This O 1–2
13 woods] wood | O 3
14 vast deep] deep vast O 1–2, B
29 who] whom R, C

29 slayes] layes O 3–6
31–2 souldiour...his...his]   souldiours...their...their O 3–6, R +
33 and] *omit* O 1–6, R, D, Rv
34 Being] And being O 1–6, R, D
36 set] let O 2

II.xi

2 wondring] wandring O 6
6 *Argos*] Argo D, C, B
7 known] know O 3–6
19 rockes] rocke O 3–6, R, TB

19 *Cerannia*] *Ceraunia* R, D, C, B
23 anchors] anchor O 4, R, C
42 the] thy O 3–6, B, TB, M

II.xii

2 bosome] bosomes O 5
12 his] this O 6
26 give.] *A couplet appears to be omitted*

here. Br MS
27 yet me] yet O 5–6; me D, C, B

II.xiii

3 with] from C, B
9 slipping] skipping C, B, Rv
10 skipping] slipping O 3–6, R, C, B; dipping TB

23 In white, with incense] In wives, with incest O 4; In wines, with incense R

II.xiv

1 Woman] women D, C, M
1 free] freed O 5–6
11 Or] On O 3–6, R
16 did] bid O 5

22 no] to O 3–6, R
29 At] And O 5–6
30 they] thee O 3–6, D (*but qy* they)
31 causes] caused O 6

II.xv

4 incircling] in circling O 5–6
7 Blest ring] Bestring O 4
7 thou] *omit* O 4, R; that Br MS
7 hand shalt] armes shall O 4, R; hand

shall C, B
22 be] by O 3–6
23 thy] my O 5–6

II.xvi

5 with] which O 3–4, R
12 My heate] My heart O 6
23 Dogs] dog O 6
34 in field O 5–6; the fields R, D, C, B

43 swearest] swear'd'st R, D, C, B
49 with] *omit* O 5–6
51 you] your O 3–6, R

II.xvii

4 the] *omit* D, C, B

19 smiths] some smiths O6

II.xviii

17 fro] from O4, R
18 buskind] busking O4, R; buskin O6
22 *Demophoon*] *Domoophon* O3, 5
35 thee] the O5–6

38 dead] deare O6, R
39 thou] I O6
40 wilt] will O5–6

II.xix

2 for] from O4, R, C, B
10 knowes] knew D (*qy*)
11 hale] haole O3–6; whole R
12 be] by O4–6, R
17 ha's] has O6

18 gave] ga' D, B
20 oft being] of being O5–6
46 effect] affect R+
48 she] he O6
60 pleasure] please O5–6

III.i

2 god-head] good head O3–6
10 she] we O5–6
12 cloake] looke O3–6, R
14 in] *omit* O3–6
14 paces] places O3–6
15 she] he O3–6; she Br MS
23 grave] great B

32 times] time O3–4
41 me] thee O4
42 thing] things O4, R, C
52 setting] sitting O3–6; sliding R
55 keeper] keepes O3–4; keepers O5–6
60 which] when O6
67 tittle] title O4–6, R

III.ii

11 their] her O4, R
15 *Pelops*] *Pelpos* O4
27 garments] garment C
28 gowne] gown's R, C, B
39 is] if O4; is't R
41 speake] spake O6

54 pleace] place O5–6; please R+
54 love] loves O3–6, R+
64 A] Or O3–6, R
68 thy...they] they...they O3, 5–6; they...thy O4
79 least] last O4, R, TB

III.iii

0 iii] 13 O4; 5 O5
10 to] by O3–6

16 others] other O6
45 did sweare] did sheare O4

III.iv

6 least] less D, C, B
29 that's...whore] that keepes away her love O4; that keeps away therefore R

38 customes] custome O4, R, C, B
40 *Remus*] *Romus* O4
46 so shall] thou shalt O4, R; so shalt C

III.v

1 reede-] redde- O3–6, R
7 now] how O6
7 rushest] gushest D, C, B, M
8 thicke] now O5–6
8 gushest] rushest O3–6, D, B, M; pushest R
14 Adders] Arrowes O3–6, R
15 seedes] fields O3–6, R, D, C, B
18 shall] e'er shall D, C, B

32 *Phthias*] *Phithias* O4
39 vast] west O4
44 his streame] his shame O3–6
46 fome] some O4
63 hundreth] hundred O6, R, C, B
85 While] Whilst O6
101 flouds] floude O5–6
104 *Nile*] *Ile* O3–6

III.vi

(O1–2 *present*)
2 wisht] wish O4
3 lovde] lovde her O1–2
8 That...is] her armes farre whiter, then O3–6, R+ (O4: wither)
11 sir] sire O3–5, R
16 I] Io O1–2
18 Seeing] When O3–6, R+ (−B)
19 that] and O1–2
20 neither] nor D (*qy*), C
26 had we] we had O3–6, R+ (−B)
27 *Thesalian*] *Thesalia* O2
28 May] Nay O5–6
28 droughs] drugges O3–6, R+
30 And] Had O2
30 needle] needles O3, O5–6, R+ (−B); needlesse O4
31 makes] make O2–6, R+
37 ad] and O2
38 vigor] rigor O2
40 wore] more O3
46 This] The O3–6, R+ (−B)

47 received] restored O2
47 in I get] and in I got O1–2
48 kisse] kiss'd R, D, C
49 to refuse] and refusde O1–2
51 a spring] aspiring O2
52 fruits] fruite O5–6
56 nor] and O3–6, R+
58 cause] caus'd D, C, B, M
58 loved] moned O3–4; moved O5–6
60 nor] ne O2
61 eares] yeares O1–2; eare O3–6, R, TB, Rv
65 it] I O4, R
66 then] like O4, R
70 now] *omit* O3–6, R+
71 cousenst] cousendst O1–2
72 sore losse] great hurt O2
74 her] *omit* O4
76 droupt] dropt O2
79 blood] bould O3, O5–6
81 that] *omit* O4, R
84 in] on O3, O5–6, D+ (−B)

III.vii

11 thy] *omit* O6
13 this] his O5–6
17 lie] lies R, D, C, B, TB
18 thy] they O3
18 fled] sled O3
24 in verse sing] sing verse in C
25 Not] Now O6
25 knowe] knewe O3–6
27 dart] darts O5–6

33 adulterer] adulteres O4
37 irons‸] ~ , O6
43 seas] Sea O6
46 thine owne] thy one O5–6
49 th'] *omit* O6
57 All, they] All, thee O4, R
62 her] she O3–6, R
63 keeper] keepe it O6

III.viii

2 goddesses] goodesses O 3
3 *Elegia*] *Elegy* D, C, B
11 necke] necks O 6
14 *Iulus*] *Iulius* O 4
16 *Adons*] *Adonus* O 4; *Adonis* O 5-6, R
17 and] the O 5-6
20 on] one O 4-5
24 unequald] uequall O 4, unequal R
29 lasts] last O 6

34 alone] above O 5-6
41 Thee] The O 5-6
52 unkeembd] unkeembe O 3-4
61 Their] Your M, Rv
62 comes] come M, Rv
62 and] to R
62 greete] greets D[1]
64 car'dst] carst O 3-6, Rv
65 thy] my O 6

III.ix

5 Thee] The C
10 their meate] there meate O 3
19-20 doth...feigne...maintaine]
  hath...feign'd...maintained Br

MS
22 teate-] tea- R; tear- Br MS
25 saw *Iasion*] *Iasion* saw C
46 with] *omit* O 5-6

III.x

1 me] we O 5-6
3 Now] Nor O 5-6

20 mens] men O 5-6

III.xi

0.1 *innotuisse*] *innocuisse* O 6; *inno-
  tuissam* R
1 was] war O 5
3 starres] starre O 3-4
7 bookes] lookes O 3-6, R
10 forth] out O 6

12 hands] hand O 6
14 they were] there was O 6
19 heare] here O 6
22 mad] made O 6
39 Sunne] Sea O 6

III.xii

5 my] may O 5-6
16 Hog-sties] hogsties' R, D, C, B, Rv;
  hogsty's M
22 give] given D, C, B, Rv

24 there] their O 5
27 white] their white O 5-6
35 th'] the O 6

III.xiii

(O 1-2 *present*)
2 know] wit O 2
5 trode] tred O 3-4
7 night] nights O 3-6, R, M, Rv
7 prankes] sports O 2
8 And] Or O 1-2

16 folke] people O 2
18 tricks] toyes O 2
22 yours ever mine] mine ever yours
  O 1-2
32 This] And this O 5-6
40 dying] dead O 3-6, R+

43 deede] deedes O 2
45 yeeld not] deny O 3–6, R+
46 mine] my O 6

47 garland] palme O 3–6, R+
50 I that] that I O 5–6

III.xiv

9 Whom] Who O 5–6
11 *Sulmoes*] *Snlmoes* O 3; *Salmoes* O 5–
6

12 ground] grounds R, C
14 so ere] to erre O 5–6
16 plucke] pluckt O 3–6, R

HERO AND LEANDER

TEXTUAL INTRODUCTION

The earliest known mention of *Hero and Leander* is the entry by John Wolf in the Stationers' Register on 28 September 1593 of 'a booke intituled Hero and Leander beinge an amorous poem devised by Christopher Marlow'.[1] Wolf does not seem to have brought out an edition; in 1598 when Edward Blount published what appears to be the first, his dedication to Sir Thomas Walsingham could scarcely have been written in such terms if an earlier edition had been marketed.[2] The book is a quarto-form octavo collating A–E⁴ (A1, E4 wanting, blank?), the title on sig. A2, the dedication on A3^{r-v}, the text starting on A4 and ending on E3^v. The imprint gives Adam Islip as the printer. The only copy known is that preserved in the Folger Shakespeare Library.

Publication of Blount's edition must have occurred early in 1598, or late in 1597, for on 2 March 1598 Blount transferred his copy to Paul Linley, who in the same year put out a quarto-form octavo 'Begun by *Christopher Marloe;* and | *finifhed by* George Chapman', the printer being Felix Kingston. This contains the second edition of Marlowe's part, set up in sigs A2–E3^r from Blount's edition, followed by the first printing of Chapman's continuation, his dedication to Lady Walsingham beginning on sig. E3^v and ending on E4^v, the text starting on sig. F1 with the *Finis* on N4^v. In Blount's quarto[3] Marlowe's part of the poem had been undivided,

[1] The most authoritative account of the printing history of *Hero and Leander* will be found in W. W. Greg, 'The Copyright of *Hero and Leander*', *The Library*, 4th series, XXIV (1944), 165–74.

[2] The history of *Hero and Leander* is in some part bound up with that of Marlowe's *Lucan*, since Wolf's entry for *Lucan* appears in the Register immediately above that for *Hero and Leander*. It is significant, then, that no edition of *Lucan* is known to have been published by Wolf, either. Whether there was a dispute between Wolf and Blount or some private transaction, Blount appears to have secured the copy for *Hero and Leander* without recorded transfer, and, it would seem, the copy for *Lucan* was also included in the arrangement.

[3] For convenience the various quarto-form octavo editions of this book will be called quartos, representing, in fact, the method of printing from the two halves of the cut full double sheets which produced what is technically an octavo, although distinguished as 4°-form 8°.

425

but Chapman imposed on it his own sestiad arrangement and wrote the rubrics for the first two sestiads that comprised Marlowe's share under his arrangement. This edition is preserved in the British Museum (C.40.e.68[1]) and in the Henry E. Huntington Library. Collation discloses that the Chapman first-edition text is invariant, although seven variants in the accidentals appear in the outer forme of sheet D in the reprint of Marlowe's text (II.10, 15, 90, 92, 122, 192, 202), the Huntington copy exhibiting the corrected and the British Museum the uncorrected state. These two 1598 editions – the Blount for the Marlowe and the Linley for the Chapman – represent the only authoritative texts. All succeeding editions are reprints wanting authority, with a history of mounting corruption.

On 26 June 1600 Linley transferred his rights both to *Hero and Leander* and to *Lucan* to John Flasket who in the same year reprinted the entire poem from Linley's text. Oddly, he advertised on the title 'Begunne by Christopher Marlowe: Whereunto is added the first booke of Lucan translated...translated by the same Author' although he printed the Chapman continuation and omitted *Lucan*.[1] This edition was reprinted in 1606 for Flasket, in 1609 for Edward Blount and W. Barret, in 1613 for the same two, in 1617 and 1622 for Blount, in 1629 for R. Hawkins, and in 1637 for W. Leake. No further edition appeared before 1815.

That Wolf secured the manuscript only four months after Marlowe's death suggests the possibility that he bought Marlowe's own papers, and this possibility is strengthened by the parallel history of *Lucan*, which he seems to have acquired at the same time and which gives some indication of having been set from holograph when it was eventually published in 1600 by Thomas Thorpe (see Textual Introduction). It is true that no external evidence associates Wolf's manuscript of *Hero and Leander* with that used as printer's copy in 1598 by Blount, but the probability that the *Lucan* also passed through Blount's hands assists in the conjecture that Blount's

---

[1] It is generally assumed that Flasket had first intended to print only the Marlowe part of *Hero and Leander* and thus to expand his book by adding *Lucan* but when the Chapman continuation became available to him he substituted that. This hypothesis is not without its difficulties; and it may seem as plausible to speculate that Marlowe's authorship being the chief attraction, Flacket merely omitted mention of Chapman although he proposed from the start to print the complete poem.

source was Wolf and thus that it was Wolf's copy that was used by Islip in 1598.[1] A disruption in the text at II.279–300 must be explained by the disordered nature of the printer's copy, appropriate for an authorial manuscript, since no evidence is present that it originated in any mechanical operation associated with the process of the composition and printing itself.[2] Tucker Brooke (1910) who first rearranged the lines correctly to mend not only the original misplacement but the attempted correction of the order by Singer (1821) that prevailed to Bullen (1885), conjectured that 'Owing probably to the displacement of a leaf in Marlowe's lost MS. these lines are given in wrong sequence', and subsequent editors have been content to follow this reconstruction. But the block of ten lines (291–300) that wrongly intervenes on sigs E2ᵛ–E3 between lines 278 and 279 is too short to suppose that it comprised a foul page of manuscript. Thus instead of the conjecture that a page in wrong order was set by the printer it is more probable to the evidence to suggest that lines 279–90 were in fact written on a separate slip as an addition to the manuscript that had originally contained lines 291–300 following 278, with lines 301ff. written immediately after 300. If the marking for the insertion of this revisory slip had been misunderstood by the compositor, he could have placed lines 279–90 after 300 instead of after 278. The text runs along smoothly enough without 279–90 in narrating the course of Leander's conquest although Marlowe's second thoughts much improve the description. Of course, such an error in placement could have occurred in the production of a scribal transcript as readily as in the

[1] Thorpe's dedication of *Lucan* to Blount strongly suggests some connection of Blount with its manuscript. Although *Lucan* was not specifically mentioned in Blount's 2 March 1598 transfer of *Hero and Leander* to Linley (they may well have been thought of as one manuscript, as evidenced by the Flasket 1600 titlepage?), yet Linley in transferring his rights to *Hero and Leander* to Flasket specifically included *Lucan*.

[2] The wrong arrangement of the lines starts four lines from the foot of sig. E2ᵛ with line 291 (in the present edition) succeeding line 278. Lines 295–300 then start sig. E3ʳ with the correct catchword 'Seeming' on E2ᵛ for the following word of line 295 on E3. Then after the sixth line on sig. E3 come lines 279–300, followed by 301ff. on the same page. No evidence is preserved on these two pages to suggest the possibility that for some unknown cause the printer himself made the transfer of the two blocks in error. If the type had pied and been reset in wrong order, it is most unlikely that the foot of one page and the head of the other parallel page in the forme would have been affected by such a pie.

compositor's typesetting, but the total body of evidence suggests the happy probability that Marlowe's part, like that of Chapman, was set from holograph. If so, the marked difference between the correctness of the text of *Hero and Leander* as against the errors in *Lucan* to be attributed to difficulty in the copy suggests, further, that the manuscript of *Lucan* was in something of a state that we may call 'foul papers' whereas the companion *Hero and Leander* manuscript was an authorial fair copy.[1]

As remarked above, only the Blount 1598 first edition of Marlowe's part (Q1) and the Linley 1598 edition (Q2) for Chapman's continuation have authority, and these become the respective copytexts, Q1 in the unique Folger Shakespeare Library copy and Q2 by collation for Chapman's part of the Henry E. Huntington and British Museum copies.[2] A fresh collation has been made of all the remaining editions to 1637 since the inaccessibility of some copies has prevented such a full record previously. Q3 (1600) was collated in the Bodleian copy and its unique variants in the inner formes of sheet D and E confirmed from the Huntington Library copy of Q3.[3] Q4 (1606) was consulted in British Museum C.71.6.32. For

---

[1] The hypothesis that *Lucan* was an authorial manuscript may be taken to aid the hypothesis that *Hero and Leander* was also holograph, given the connection that seems to have existed between the two documents beginning with their acquisition by Wolf. The fairness of the copy, then, may be attributed more readily to the author than to a scribal transcript.

[2] Chapman's work has become so identified with this poem as to make an edition of the complete work desirable here. It has not been thought necessary to reprint Henry Petowe's *Second Part of Hero and Leander* (1598). Incidentally, no basis exists for the belief of early nineteenth-century editors that the early part of Chapman's third sestiad is a Marlovian fragment and that Chapman's composition begins at III.183. The Chapman invention is quite obvious from the start of the third sestiad.

[3] Unique Q3 variants are found in II.68, 94 (D1ᵛ), II.191 (D3ᵛ), II.280 (E1ᵛ), II.304, 306, 308 (E2). Since some are not apparent misprints, Q4 (set paginally from Q3) should ordinarily have followed various of these readings. The easiest explanation would be that the Q3 copy used by Q4 was in a press-corrected variant state and so the Q3 errors were not passed on. As an alternative, if Q4 had been simultaneously set from divided copy, sheets D–E in Q4 could have been set from Q2. However, there are complications to either theory. That Q4 was set from a press-corrected copy of Q3 is agreeable to the evidence that in sheets D and E the unique variants of Q3 are confined to the inner formes. Against the hypothesis is the evidence that the two recorded copies of Q3 agree in these readings, something of an anomaly (although not an impossibility) if these were the uncorrected states of the formes. Moreover, another oddity exists. In the outer forme of sheet D, Q2–3 agree in plausible readings at

xeroxes of the unique perfect copy of Q5 (1609) the editor is indebted to the owner, Mr Allerton C. Hickmott.[1] Q6 (1613) was collated in British Museum copy C.57.i.45, Q7 (1617) in the Huntington copy, Q8 (1622) from Folger, Q9 (1629) from British Museum C.57.i.44, and Q10 (1637) from British Museum C.57.i.43. Each seems to have been set from its immediate predecessor.

Although not present, of course, in Q1, the Chapman division of Marlowe's text into two sestiads has been observed, and Chapman's introduction to each sestiad has been inserted.

The Historical Collation contains, in addition, the variant substantive readings from Sir Egerton Brydges' reprint in his *Restituta* (1815), II, 112–29, 161–71, 307–47, 458–67; S. W. Singer, *Select English Poets*, no. VIII (Chiswick, 1821); *Works*, ed. Robinson (1826); *Works*, ed. Dyce (1850 and 1858), *Works*, ed. Cunningham (1870), *Works*, ed. Bullen (1885), *Works*, ed. Tucker Brooke (1910), *Poems*, ed. L. C. Martin (Methuen, 1931), *Poems of George Chapman*, ed. Phyllis Bartlett (1941), and *Poems*, ed. Millar MacLure (Revels, 1968).

No evidence is known for the date of writing, but critics have generally favored 1593.

II.113 (D2^v) and II.246 (D4^v), and in sheet E in II.316 of E2 in the inner forme and II.334 of E2^v in the outer forme. In all of these cases Q4 ignores the Q2–3 variants from Q1. The case of II.334 is especially significant since here Q4 restores the Q1 reading *Dang'd* which in Q2–3 was *Hurl'd*. Since we cannot conjecture that this outer forme of Q3 by press-correction restored Q1 readings not in its Q2 copy, the whole hypothesis that Q4 was set from press-corrected formes of Q3 in sheets D and E collapses, and the only alternative is to take it that these two Q4 sheets (beginning with II.31) were set by a compositor who used Q1 as his copy. No contrary evidence opposes this hypothesis, although elsewhere Q3 was definitely copy for Q4.

[1] The Folger Shakespeare Library owns an imperfect copy of the 1609 edition, in which sheets B, C, D, and leaves L3, 4 have been supplied from Q8 of 1622.

To the Right Worshipfull, Sir Thomas
Walsingham, Knight

Sir, wee thinke not our selves discharged of the dutie wee owe to our friend, when wee have brought the breathlesse bodie to the earth: for albeit the eye there taketh his ever farwell of that beloved object, yet the impression of the man, that hath beene deare unto us, living an after life in our memory, there putteth us in mind of farther obsequies due unto the deceased. And namely of the performance of whatsoever we may judge shal make to his living credit, and to the effecting of his determinations prevented by the stroke of death. By these meditations (as by an intellectuall will) I suppose my selfe executor to the unhappily deceased author of this Poem, upon whom knowing that in his life time 10 *you bestowed many kind favours, entertaining the parts of reckoning and woorth which you found in him, with good countenance and liberall affection: I cannot but see so far into the will of him dead, but whatsoever issue of his brain should chance to come abroad, that the first breath it should take might be the gentle aire of your liking: for since his selfe had ben accustomed therunto, it would proove more agreeable and thriving to his right children, than any other foster countenance whatsoever. At this time seeing that this unfinished Tragedy happens under my hands to be imprinted; of a double duty, the one to your selfe, the other to the deceased, I present the same to your most* 20 *favourable allowance, offring my utmost selfe now and ever to bee readie, At your Worships disposing:*

Edward Blunt.

Hero and Leander

THE ARGUMENT OF THE FIRST SESTYAD

Heros description and her Loves,
The Phane of Venus*; where he moves*
His worthie Love-suite, and attaines;
Whose blisse the wrath of Fates restraines,
For Cupids *grace to* Mercurie,
Which tale the Author doth implie.

On *Hellespont* guiltie of True-loves blood,
In view and opposit two citties stood,
Seaborderers, disjoin'd by *Neptunes* might:
The one *Abydos*, the other *Sestos* hight.
At *Sestos*, *Hero* dwelt; *Hero* the faire,
Whom young *Apollo* courted for her haire,
And offred as a dower his burning throne,
Where she should sit for men to gaze upon.
The outside of her garments were of lawne,
The lining, purple silke, with guilt starres drawne,   10
Her wide sleeves greene, and bordered with a grove,
Where *Venus* in her naked glory strove,
To please the carelesse and disdainfull eies,
Of proud *Adonis* that before her lies.
Her kirtle blew, whereon was many a staine,
Made with the blood of wretched Lovers slaine.
Upon her head she ware a myrtle wreath,
From whence her vaile reacht to the ground beneath.
Her vaile was artificiall flowers and leaves,
Whose workmanship both man and beast deceaves.   20
Many would praise the sweet smell as she past,
When t'was the odour which her breath foorth cast.
And there for honie, bees have sought in vaine,
And beat from thence, have lighted there againe.
About her necke hung chaines of peble stone,

0–0.6 Chapman *in* Q2; *omitted* Q1   3 Seaborderers] Q9; Seaborders Q1–8

Which lightned by her necke, like Diamonds shone.
She ware no gloves, for neither sunne nor wind
Would burne or parch her hands, but to her mind,
Or warme or coole them: for they tooke delite
To play upon those hands, they were so white.   30
Buskins of shels all silvered, used she,
And brancht with blushing corall to the knee;
Where sparrowes pearcht, of hollow pearle and gold,
Such as the world would woonder to behold:
Those with sweet water oft her handmaid fils,
Which as shee went would cherupe through the bils.
Some say, for her the fairest *Cupid* pyn'd,
And looking in her face, was strooken blind.
But this is true, so like was one the other,
As he imagyn'd *Hero* was his mother.   40
And oftentimes into her bosome flew,
About her naked necke his bare armes threw.
And laid his childish head upon her brest,
And with still panting rockt, there tooke his rest.
So lovely faire was *Hero*, *Venus* Nun,
As nature wept, thinking she was undone;
Because she tooke more from her than she left,
And of such wondrous beautie her bereft:
Therefore in signe her treasure suffred wracke,
Since *Heroes* time, hath halfe the world beene blacke. 50
Amorous *Leander*, beautifull and yoong,
(Whose tragedie divine *Musæus* soong)
Dwelt at *Abidus*; since him, dwelt there none,
For whom succeeding times make greater mone.
His dangling tresses that were never shorne,
Had they beene cut, and unto *Colchos* borne,
Would have allur'd the vent'rous youth of *Greece*,
To hazard more, than for the golden Fleece.
Faire *Cinthia* wisht, his armes might be her spheare,
Greefe makes her pale, because she mooves not there.   60
His bodie was as straight as *Circes* wand,
Jove might have sipt out *Nectar* from his hand.

432

Even as delicious meat is to the tast,
So was his necke in touching, and surpast
The white of *Pelops* shoulder. I could tell ye,
How smooth his brest was, and how white his bellie,
And whose immortall fingars did imprint,
That heavenly path, with many a curious dint,
That runs along his backe, but my rude pen,
Can hardly blazon foorth the loves of men,   70
Much lesse of powerfull gods. Let it suffise,
That my slacke muse, sings of *Leanders* eies,
Those orient cheekes and lippes, exceeding his
That leapt into the water for a kis
Of his owne shadow, and despising many,
Died ere he could enjoy the love of any.
Had wilde *Hippolitus*, *Leander* seene,
Enamoured of his beautie had he beene,
His presence made the rudest paisant melt,
That in the vast uplandish countrie dwelt,   80
The barbarous *Thratian* soldier moov'd with nought,
Was moov'd with him, and for his favour sought.
Some swore he was a maid in mans attire,
For in his lookes were all that men desire,
A pleasant smiling cheeke, a speaking eye,
A brow for Love to banquet roiallye,
And such as knew he was a man would say,
Leander, thou art made for amorous play:
Why art thou not in love, and lov'd of all?
Though thou be faire, yet be not thine owne thrall.   90

    The men of wealthie *Sestos*, everie yeare,
(For his sake whom their goddesse held so deare,
Rose-cheekt *Adonis*) kept a solemne feast.
Thither resorted many a wandring guest,
To meet their loves; such as had none at all,
Came lovers home, from this great festivall.
For everie street like to a Firmament
Glistered with breathing stars, who where they went,
Frighted the melancholie earth, which deem'd,

Eternall heaven to burne, for so it seem'd,   100
As if another *Phaeton* had got
The guidance of the sunnes rich chariot.
But far above the loveliest, *Hero* shin'd,
And stole away th'inchaunted gazers mind,
For like Sea-nimphs inveigling harmony,
So was her beautie to the standers by.
Nor that night-wandring pale and watrie starre,
(When yawning dragons draw her thirling carre,
From *Latmus* mount up to the glomie skie,
Where crown'd with blazing light and majestie,   110
She proudly sits) more over-rules the flood,
Than she the hearts of those that neere her stood.
Even as, when gawdie Nymphs pursue the chace,
Wretched *Ixions* shaggie footed race,
Incenst with savage heat, gallop amaine,
From steepe Pine-bearing mountains to the plaine:
So ran the people foorth to gaze upon her,
And all that view'd her, were enamour'd on her.
And as in furie of a dreadfull fight,
Their fellowes being slaine or put to flight,   120
Poore soldiers stand with fear of death dead strooken,
So at her presence all surpris'd and tooken,
Await the sentence of her scornefull eies:
He whom she favours lives, the other dies.
There might you see one sigh, another rage,
And some (their violent passions to asswage)
Compile sharpe satyrs, but alas too late,
For faithfull love will never turne to hate.
And many seeing great princes were denied,
Pyn'd as they went, and thinking on her died.   130
On this feast day, O cursed day and hower,
Went *Hero* thorow *Sestos*, from her tower
To *Venus* temple, where unhappilye,
As after chaunc'd, they did each other spye.

103 above₍] Q2; ~ , Q1   133 where] Q2; were Q1
103 loveliest,] Brydges; ~ ₍ Q1-10

434

So faire a church as this, had *Venus* none,
The wals were of discoloured *Jasper* stone,
Wherein was *Proteus* carved, and o'rehead,
A livelie vine of greene sea agget spread;
Where by one hand, light headed *Bacchus* hoong,
And with the other, wine from grapes out wroong.   140
Of Christall shining faire, the pavement was,
The towne of *Sestos* cal'd it *Venus* glasse.
There might you see the gods in sundrie shapes,
Committing headdie ryots, incest, rapes:
For know, that underneath this radiant floure,
Was *Danaes* statue in a brazen tower,
Jove, slylie stealing from his sisters bed,
To dallie with *Idalian Ganimed*:
And for his love *Europa*, bellowing loud,
And tumbling with the Rainbow in a cloud: 150
Blood-quaffing *Mars*, heaving the yron net,
Which limping *Vulcan* and his *Cyclops* set:
Love kindling fire, to burne such townes as *Troy*,
Sylvanus weeping for the lovely boy
That now is turn'd into a *Cypres* tree,
Under whose shade the Wood-gods love to bee.
And in the midst a silver altar stood,
There *Hero* sacrificing turtles blood,
Vaild to the ground, vailing her eie-lids close,
And modestly they opened as she rose: 160
Thence flew Loves arrow with the golden head,
And thus *Leander* was enamoured.
Stone still he stood, and evermore he gazed,
Till with the fire that from his count'nance blazed,
Relenting *Heroes* gentle heart was strooke,
Such force and vertue hath an amorous looke.
    It lies not in our power to love, or hate,
For will in us is over-rul'd by fate.
When two are stript, long ere the course begin,
We wish that one should loose, the other win.   170

145 floure] *i.e.,* floor *as in* Singer's *query*   159 Vaild] *i.e., bowed or bent in reverence*

And one especiallie doe we affect,
Of two gold Ingots like in each respect.
The reason no man knowes, let it suffise,
What we behold is censur'd by our eies.
Where both deliberat, the love is slight,
Who ever lov'd, that lov'd not at first sight?
    He kneel'd, but unto her devoutly praid;
Chast *Hero* to her selfe thus softly said:
Were I the saint hee worships, I would heare him,
And as shee spake those words, came somewhat nere him.   180
He started up, she blusht as one asham'd;
Wherewith *Leander* much more was inflam'd.
He toucht her hand, in touching it she trembled,
Love deepely grounded, hardly is dissembled.
These lovers parled by the touch of hands,
True love is mute, and oft amazed stands.
Thus while dum signs their yeelding harts entangled,
The aire with sparkes of living fire was spangled,
A periphrasis And night deepe drencht in mystie *Acheron*,
of night. Heav'd up her head, and halfe the world upon,   190
Breath'd darkenesse forth (darke night is *Cupids* day.)
And now begins *Leander* to display
Loves holy fire, with words, with sighs and teares,
Which like sweet musicke entred *Heroes* eares,
And yet at everie word shee turn'd aside,
And alwaies cut him off as he replide.
At last, like to a bold sharpe Sophister,
With chearefull hope thus he accosted her.
    Faire creature, let me speake without offence,
I would my rude words had the influence,   200
To lead thy thoughts, as thy faire lookes doe mine,
Then shouldst thou bee his prisoner who is thine.
Be not unkind and faire, mishapen stuffe
Are of behaviour boisterous and ruffe.
O shun me not, but heare me ere you goe,
God knowes I cannot force love, as you doe.
My words shall be as spotlesse as my youth,

436

Full of simplicitie and naked truth.
This sacrifice (whose sweet perfume descending,
From *Venus* altar to your footsteps bending)   210
Doth testifie that you exceed her farre,
To whom you offer, and whose Nunne you are.
Why should you worship her? her you surpasse,
As much as sparkling Diamonds flaring glasse.
A Diamond set in lead his worth retaines,
A heavenly Nimph, belov'd of humane swaines,
Receives no blemish, but oft-times more grace,
Which makes me hope, although I am but base,
Base in respect of thee, divine and pure,
Dutifull service may thy love procure,   220
And I in dutie will excell all other,
As thou in beautie doest exceed Loves mother.
Nor heaven, nor thou, were made to gaze upon,
As heaven preserves all things, so save thou one.
A stately builded ship, well rig'd and tall,
The Ocean maketh more majesticall:
Why vowest thou then to live in *Sestos* here,
Who on Loves seas more glorious wouldst appeare?
Like untun'd golden strings all women are,
Which long time lie untoucht, will harshly jarre.   230
Vessels of Brasse oft handled, brightly shine,
What difference betwixt the richest mine
And basest mold, but use? for both not us'de,
Are of like worth. Then treasure is abus'de,
When misers keepe it; being put to lone,
In time it will returne us two for one.
Rich robes, themselves and others do adorne,
Neither themselves nor others, if not worne.
Who builds a pallace and rams up the gate,
Shall see it ruinous and desolate.   240
Ah simple *Hero*, learne thy selfe to cherish,
Lone women like to emptie houses perish.
Lesse sinnes the poore rich man that starves himselfe,
In heaping up a masse of drossie pelfe,

Than such as you: his golden earth remains,
Which after his disceasse, some other gains.
But this faire jem, sweet in the losse alone,
When you fleet hence, can be bequeath'd to none.
Or if it could, downe from th'enameld skie,
All heaven would come to claime this legacie, 250
And with intestine broiles the world destroy,
And quite confound natures sweet harmony.
Well therefore by the gods decreed it is,
We humane creatures should enjoy that blisse.
One is no number, mayds are nothing then,
Without the sweet societie of men.
Wilt thou live single still? one shalt thou bee,
Though never-singling *Hymen* couple thee.
Wild savages, that drinke of running springs,
Thinke water farre excels all earthly things: 260
But they that dayly tast neat wine, despise it.
Virginitie, albeit some highly prise it,
Compar'd with marriage, had you tried them both,
Differs as much, as wine and water doth.
Base boullion for the stampes sake we allow,
Even so for mens impression do we you.
By which alone, our reverend fathers say,
Women receave perfection everie way.
This idoll which you terme *Virginitie*,
Is neither essence subject to the eie, 270
No, nor to any one exterior sence,
Nor hath it any place of residence,
Nor is't of earth or mold celestiall,
Or capable of any forme at all.
Of that which hath no being, doe not boast,
Things that are not at all, are never lost.
Men foolishly doe call it vertuous,
What vertue is it that is borne with us?
Much lesse can honour bee ascrib'd thereto,
Honour is purchac'd by the deedes wee do. 280
Beleeve me *Hero*, honour is not wone,

Untill some honourable deed be done.
Seeke you for chastitie, immortall fame,
And know that some have wrong'd *Dianas* name?
Whose name is it, if she be false or not,
So she be faire, but some vile toongs will blot?
But you are faire (aye me) so wondrous faire,
So yoong, so gentle, and so debonaire,
As *Greece* will thinke, if thus you live alone,
Some one or other keepes you as his owne.   290
Then *Hero* hate me not, nor from me flie,
To follow swiftly blasting infamie.
Perhaps, thy sacred Priesthood makes thee loath,
Tell me, to whom mad'st thou that heedlesse oath?

    To *Venus*, answered shee, and as shee spake,
Foorth from those two tralucent cesternes brake,
A streame of liquid pearle, which downe her face
Made milk-white paths, wheron the gods might trace
To *Joves* high court. Hee thus replide: The rites
In which Loves beauteous Empresse most delites,   300
Are banquets, Dorick musicke, midnight-revell,
Plaies, maskes, and all that stern age counteth evill.
Thee as a holy Idiot doth she scorne,
For thou in vowing chastitie, hast sworne
To rob her name and honour, and thereby
Commit'st a sinne far worse than perjurie.
Even sacrilege against her Deitie,
Through regular and formall puritie.
To expiat which sinne, kisse and shake hands,
Such sacrifice as this, *Venus* demands.   310

    Thereat she smild, and did denie him so,
As put thereby, yet might he hope for mo.
Which makes him quickly re-enforce his speech,
And her in humble manner thus beseech.

    Though neither gods nor men may thee deserve,
Yet for her sake whom you have vow'd to serve,
Abandon fruitlesse cold Virginitie,
The gentle queene of Loves sole enemie.

Then shall you most resemble *Venus* Nun,
When *Venus* sweet rites are perform'd and done.   320
Flint-brested *Pallas* joies in single life,
But *Pallas* and your mistresse are at strife.
Love *Hero* then, and be not tirannous,
But heale the heart, that thou hast wounded thus,
Nor staine thy youthfull years with avarice,
Faire fooles delight to be accounted nice.
The richest corne dies, if it be not reapt,
Beautie alone is lost, too warily kept.
These arguments he us'de, and many more,
Wherewith she yeelded, that was woon before.   330
Heroes lookes yeelded, but her words made warre,
Women are woon when they begin to jarre.
Thus having swallow'd *Cupids* golden hooke,
The more she striv'd, the deeper was she strooke.
Yet evilly faining anger, strove she still,
And would be thought to graunt against her will.
So having paus'd a while, at last shee said:
Who taught thee Rhethoricke to deceive a maid?
Aye me, such words as these should I abhor,
And yet I like them for the Orator.   340
   With that *Leander* stoopt, to have imbrac'd her,
But from his spreading armes away she cast her,
And thus bespake him: Gentle youth forbeare
To touch the sacred garments which I weare.
   Upon a rocke, and underneath a hill,
Far from the towne (where all is whist and still,
Save that the sea playing on yellow sand,
Sends foorth a ratling murmure to the land,
Whose sound allures the golden *Morpheus*,
In silence of the night to visite us,)   350
My turret stands, and there God knowes I play
With *Venus* swannes and sparrowes all the day.
A dwarfish beldame beares me companie,
That hops about the chamber where I lie,

326 delight₍ₐ₎] Q2; ~ , Q1

440

And spends the night (that might be better spent)
In vaine discourse, and apish merriment.
Come thither; As she spake this, her toong tript,
For unawares (*Come thither*) from her slipt,
And sodainly her former colour chang'd,
And here and there her eies through anger rang'd.   360
And like a planet, mooving severall waies,
At one selfe instant, she poore soule assaies,
Loving, not to love at all, and everie part
Strove to resist the motions of her hart.
And hands so pure, so innocent, nay such,
As might have made heaven stoope to have a touch,
Did she uphold to *Venus*, and againe,
Vow'd spotlesse chastitie, but all in vaine.
Cupid beats downe her praiers with his wings,
Her vowes above the emptie aire he flings: 370
All deepe enrag'd, his sinowie bow he bent,
And shot a shaft that burning from him went,
Wherewith she strooken, look'd so dolefully,
As made Love sigh, to see his tirannie.
And as she wept, her teares to pearle he turn'd,
And wound them on his arme, and for her mourn'd.
Then towards the pallace of the Destinies,
Laden with languishment and griefe he flies.
And to those sterne nymphs humblie made request,
Both might enjoy ech other, and be blest.   380
But with a ghastly dreadfull countenaunce,
Threatning a thousand deaths at everie glaunce,
They answered Love, nor would vouchsafe so much
As one poore word, their hate to him was such.
Harken a while, and I will tell you why:
Heavens winged herrald, *Jove-borne Mercury*,
The self-same day that he asleepe had layd
Inchaunted *Argus*, spied a countrie mayd,
Whose carelesse haire, in stead of pearle t'adorne it,
Glist'red with deaw, as one that seem'd to skorne it: 390
Her breath as fragrant as the morning rose,

441

Her mind pure, and her toong untaught to glose.
Yet prowd she was, (for loftie pride that dwels
In tow'red courts, is oft in sheapheards cels.)
And too too well the faire vermilion knew,
And silver tincture of her cheekes, that drew
The love of everie swaine: On her, this god
Enamoured was, and with his snakie rod,
Did charme her nimble feet, and made her stay,
The while upon a hillocke downe he lay,   400
And sweetly on his pipe began to play,
And with smooth speech, her fancie to assay,
Till in his twining armes he lockt her fast,
And then he woo'd with kisses, and at last,
As sheap-heards do, her on the ground hee layd,
And tumbling in the grasse, he often strayd
Beyond the bounds of shame, in being bold
To eie those parts, which no eie should behold.
And like an insolent commaunding lover,
Boasting his parentage, would needs discover   410
The way to new *Elisium*: but she,
Whose only dower was her chastitie,
Having striv'ne in vaine, was now about to crie,
And crave the helpe of sheap-heards that were nie.
Herewith he stayd his furie, and began
To give her leave to rise: away she ran,
After went *Mercurie*, who us'd such cunning,
As she to heare his tale, left off her running.
Maids are not woon by brutish force and might,
But speeches full of pleasure and delight.   420
And knowing *Hermes* courted her, was glad
That she such lovelinesse and beautie had
As could provoke his liking, yet was mute,
And neither would denie, nor graunt his sute.
Still vowd he love, she wanting no excuse
To feed him with delaies, as women use:
Or thirsting after immortalitie,
All women are ambitious naturallie:

Impos'd upon her lover such a taske,
As he ought not performe, nor yet she aske.   430
A draught of flowing *Nectar*, she requested,
Wherewith the king of Gods and men is feasted.
He readie to accomplish what she wil'd,
Stole some from *Hebe* (*Hebe*, *Joves* cup fil'd,)
And gave it to his simple rustike love,
Which being knowne (as what is hid from *Jove?*)
He inly storm'd, and waxt more furious,
Than for the fire filcht by *Prometheus*;
And thrusts him down from heaven: he wandring here,
In mournfull tearmes, with sad and heavie cheare   440
Complaind to *Cupid*; *Cupid* for his sake,
To be reveng'd on *Jove*, did undertake,
And those on whom heaven, earth, and hell relies,
I mean the Adamantine Destinies,
He wounds with love, and forst them equallie,
To dote upon deceitfull *Mercurie*.
They offred him the deadly fatall knife,
That sheares the slender threads of humane life,
At his faire feathered feet, the engins layd,
Which th'earth from ougly *Chaos* den up-wayd: 450
These he regarded not, but did intreat,
That *Jove*, usurper of his fathers seat,
Might presently be banisht into hell,
And aged *Saturne* in *Olympus* dwell.
They granted what he crav'd, and once againe,
Saturne and *Ops*, began their golden raigne.
Murder, rape, warre, lust and trecherie,
Were with *Jove* clos'd in *Stigian* Emperie.
But long this blessed time continued not;
As soone as he his wished purpose got,   460
He recklesse of his promise, did despise
The love of th'everlasting Destinies.
They seeing it, both Love and him abhor'd,
And *Jupiter* unto his place restor'd.
And but that Learning, in despight of Fate,

Will mount aloft, and enter heaven gate,
And to the seat of *Jove* it selfe advaunce,
Hermes had slept in hell with ignoraunce.
Yet as a punishment they added this,
That he and *Povertie* should alwaies kis.   470
And to this day is everie scholler poore,
Grosse gold, from them runs headlong to the boore.
Likewise the angrie sisters thus deluded,
To venge themselves on *Hermes*, have concluded
That *Midas* brood shall sit in Honors chaire,
To which the *Muses* sonnes are only heire:
And fruitfull wits that in aspiring are,
Shall discontent run into regions farre;
And few great lords in vertuous deeds shall joy,
But be surpris'd with every garish toy.   480
And still inrich the loftie servile clowne,
Who with incroching guile, keepes learning downe.
Then muse not, *Cupids* sute no better sped,
Seeing in their loves, the Fates were injured.

The end of the first Sestyad.

THE ARGUMENT OF THE SECOND SESTYAD

Hero *of love takes deeper sence,*
And doth her love more recompence.
Their first nights meeting, where sweet kisses
Are th'only crownes of both their blisses.
*He swims t'*Abydus, *and returnes;*
Cold Neptune *with his beautie burnes,*
Whose suite he shuns, and doth aspire
Heros *faire towre, and his desire.*

By this, sad *Hero*, with love unacquainted,
Viewing *Leanders* face, fell downe and fainted.
He kist her, and breath'd life into her lips,
Wherewith as one displeas'd, away she trips.

*477 in aspiring] *stet* Q1–10   0–0.8 Chapman *in* Q2; *omitted* Q1
484.1 Q2; *omit* Q1

Yet as she went, full often look'd behind,
And many poore excuses did she find,
To linger by the way, and once she stayd,
And would have turn'd againe, but was afrayd,
In offring parlie, to be counted light.
So on she goes, and in her idle flight,   10
Her painted fanne of curled plumes let fall,
Thinking to traine *Leander* therewithall.
He being a novice, knew not what she meant,
But stayd, and after her a letter sent.
Which joyfull *Hero* answer'd in such sort,
As he had hope to scale the beauteous fort,
Wherein the liberall graces lock'd their wealth,
And therefore to her tower he got by stealth.
Wide open stood the doore, hee need not clime,
And she her selfe before the pointed time,   20
Had spread the boord, with roses strowed the roome,
And oft look't out, and mus'd he did not come.
At last he came, O who can tell the greeting,
These greedie lovers had, at their first meeting.
He askt, she gave, and nothing was denied,
Both to each other quickly were affied.
Looke how their hands, so were their hearts united,
And what he did, she willingly requited.
(Sweet are the kisses, the imbracements sweet,
When like desires and affections meet,   30
For from the earth to heaven, is *Cupid* rais'd,
Where fancie is in equall ballance pais'd.)
Yet she this rashnesse sodainly repented,
And turn'd aside, and to her selfe lamented.
As if her name and honour had beene wrong'd,
By being possest of him for whom she long'd:
I, and shee wisht, albeit not from her hart,
That he would leave her turret and depart.
The mirthfull God of amorous pleasure smil'd,
To see how he this captive Nymph beguil'd.   40
For hitherto hee did but fan the fire,

And kept it downe that it might mount the hier.
Now waxt she jealous, least his love abated,
Fearing her owne thoughts made her to be hated.
Therefore unto him hastily she goes,
And like light *Salmacis*, her body throes
Upon his bosome, where with yeelding eyes,
She offers up her selfe a sacrifice,
To slake his anger, if he were displeas'd,
O what god would not therewith be appeas'd?   50
Like *Æsops* cocke, this jewell he enjoyed,
And as a brother with his sister toyed,
Supposing nothing else was to be done,
Now he her favour and good will had wone.
But know you not that creatures wanting sence,
By nature have a mutuall appetence,
And wanting organs to advaunce a step,
Mov'd by Loves force, unto ech other lep?
Much more in subjects having intellect,
Some hidden influence breeds like effect.   60
Albeit *Leander* rude in love, and raw,
Long dallying with *Hero*, nothing saw
That might delight him more, yet he suspected
Some amorous rites or other were neglected.
Therefore unto his bodie, hirs he clung,
She, fearing on the rushes to be flung,
Striv'd with redoubled strength: the more she strived,
The more a gentle pleasing heat revived,
Which taught him all that elder lovers know,
And now the same gan so to scorch and glow,   70
As in plaine termes (yet cunningly) he crav'd it,
Love alwaies makes those eloquent that have it.
Shee, with a kind of graunting, put him by it,
And ever as he thought himselfe most nigh it,
Like to the tree of *Tantalus* she fled,
And seeming lavish, sav'de her maydenhead.
Ne're king more sought to keepe his diademe,
Than *Hero* this inestimable gemme.

446

Above our life we love a stedfast friend,
Yet when a token of great worth we send,   80
We often kisse it, often looke thereon,
And stay the messenger that would be gon:
No marvell then, though *Hero* would not yeeld
So soone to part from that she deerely held.
Jewels being lost are found againe, this never,
T'is lost but once, and once lost, lost for ever.
    Now had the morne espy'de her lovers steeds,
Whereat she starts, puts on her purple weeds,
And red for anger that he stayd so long,
All headlong throwes her selfe the clouds among   90
And now *Leander* fearing to be mist,
Imbrast her sodainly, tooke leave, and kist,
Long was he taking leave, and loath to go,
And kist againe, as lovers use to do.
Sad *Hero* wroong him by the hand, and wept,
Saying, let your vowes and promises be kept.
Then standing at the doore, she turnd about,
As loath to see *Leander* going out.
And now the sunne that through th'orizon peepes,
As pittying these lovers, downeward creepes.   100
So that in silence of the cloudie night,
Though it was morning, did he take his flight.
But what the secret trustie night conceal'd,
Leanders amorous habit soone reveal'd.
With *Cupids* myrtle was his bonet crownd,
About his armes the purple riband wound,
Wherewith she wreath'd her largely spreading heare,
Nor could the youth abstaine, but he must weare
The sacred ring wherewith she was endow'd,
When first religious chastitie she vow'd: 110
Which made his love through *Sestos* to bee knowne,
And thence unto *Abydus* sooner blowne,
Than he could saile, for incorporeal Fame,
Whose waight consists in nothing but her name,
Is swifter than the wind, whose tardie plumes,

447

Are reeking water, and dull earthlie fumes.
Home when he came, he seem'd not to be there,
But like exiled aire thrust from his sphere,
Set in a forren place, and straight from thence,
Alcides like, by mightie violence,   120
He would have chac'd away the swelling maine,
That him from her unjustly did detaine.
Like as the sunne in a Dyameter,
Fires and inflames objects remooved farre,
And heateth kindly, shining lat'rally;
So beautie, sweetly quickens when t'is ny,
But being separated and remooved,
Burnes where it cherisht, murders where it loved.
Therefore even as an Index to a booke,
So to his mind was yoong *Leanders* looke.   130
O none but gods have power their love to hide,
Affection by the count'nance is describe.
The light of hidden fire it selfe discovers,
And love that is conceal'd, betraies poore lovers.
His secret flame apparantly was seene,
Leanders Father knew where hee had beene,
And for the same mildly rebuk't his sonne,
Thinking to quench the sparckles new begonne.
But love resisted once, growes passionate,
And nothing more than counsaile, lovers hate.   140
For as a hote prowd horse highly disdaines,
To have his head control'd, but breakes the raines,
Spits foorth the ringled bit, and with his hoves,
Checkes the submissive ground: so hee that loves,
The more he is restrain'd, the woorse he fares,
What is it now, but mad *Leander* dares?
O *Hero, Hero,* thus he cry'de full oft,
And then he got him to a rocke aloft.
Where having spy'de her tower, long star'd he on't,
And pray'd the narrow toyling *Hellespont,*   150
To part in twaine, that hee might come and go,
But still the rising billowes answered no.

448

With that hee stript him to the yv'rie skin,
And crying, Love I come, leapt lively in.
Whereat the saphir visag'd god grew prowd,
And made his capring *Triton* sound alowd,
Imagining, that *Ganimed* displeas'd,
Had left the heavens, therefore on him hee seaz'd.
Leander striv'd, the waves about him wound,
And puld him to the bottome, where the ground   160
Was strewd with pearle, and in low corrall groves,
Sweet singing Meremaids, sported with their loves
On heapes of heavie gold, and tooke great pleasure,
To spurne in carelesse sort, the shipwracke treasure.
For here the stately azure pallace stood,
Where kingly *Neptune* and his traine abode.
The lustie god imbrast him, cald him love,
And swore he never should returne to *Jove*.
But when he knew it was not *Ganimed*,
For under water he was almost dead,   170
He heav'd him up, and looking on his face,
Beat downe the bold waves with his triple mace,
Which mounted up, intending to have kist him,
And fell in drops like teares, because they mist him.
Leander being up, began to swim,
And looking backe, saw *Neptune* follow him.
Whereat agast, the poore soule gan to crie,
O let mee visite *Hero* ere I die.
The god put *Helles* bracelet on his arme,
And swore the sea should never doe him harme.   180
He clapt his plumpe cheekes, with his tresses playd,
And smiling wantonly, his love bewrayd.
He watcht his armes, and as they opend wide,
At every stroke, betwixt them would he slide,
And steale a kisse, and then run out and daunce,
And as he turnd, cast many a lustfull glaunce,
And throw him gawdie toies to please his eie,
And dive into the water, and there prie

*187 throw] Dyce; threw Q 1–10

Upon his brest, his thighs, and everie lim,
And up againe, and close beside him swim,   190
And talke of love: *Leander* made replie,
You are deceav'd, I am no woman I.
Thereat smilde *Neptune*, and then told a tale,
How that a sheapheard sitting in a vale,
Playd with a boy so faire and so kind,
As for his love, both earth and heaven pyn'd;
That of the cooling river durst not drinke,
Least water-nymphs should pull him from the brinke.
And when hee sported in the fragrant lawnes,
Gote-footed Satyrs, and up-staring Fawnes,   200
Would steale him thence. Ere halfe this tale was done,
Aye me, *Leander* cryde, th'enamoured sunne,
That now should shine on *Thetis* glassie bower,
Descends upon my radiant *Heroes* tower.
O that these tardie armes of mine were wings,
And as he spake, upon the waves he springs.
Neptune was angrie that hee gave no eare,
And in his heart revenging malice bare:
He flung at him his mace, but as it went,
He cald it in, for love made him repent.   210
The mace returning backe, his owne hand hit,
As meaning to be veng'd for darting it.
When this fresh bleeding wound *Leander* viewd,
His colour went and came, as if he rewd
The greefe which *Neptune* felt. In gentle brests,
Relenting thoughts, remorse and pittie rests.
And who have hard hearts, and obdurat minds,
But vicious, harebraind, and illit'rat hinds?
The god seeing him with pittie to be moved,
Thereon concluded that he was beloved.   220
(Love is too full of faith, too credulous,
With follie and false hope deluding us.)
Wherefore *Leanders* fancie to surprize,
To the rich *Ocean* for gifts he flies.

*195 so kind] Brydges; kind Q1–10   *200 up-staring] *stet* Q1–10

'Tis wisedome to give much, a gift prevailes,
When deepe perswading Oratorie failes.
By this *Leander* being nere the land,
Cast downe his wearie feet, and felt the sand.
Breathlesse albeit he were, he rested not,
Till to the solitarie tower he got.   230
And knockt and cald, at which celestiall noise,
The longing heart of *Hero* much more joies
Then nymphs and sheapheards, when the timbrell rings,
Or crooked Dolphin when the sailer sings;
She stayd not for her robes, but straight arose,
And drunke with gladnesse, to the dore she goes.
Where seeing a naked man, she scriecht for feare,
Such sights as this, to tender maids are rare.
And ran into the darke her selfe to hide,
Rich jewels in the darke are soonest spide.   240
Unto her was he led, or rather drawne,
By those white limmes, which sparckled through the lawne.
The neerer that he came, the more she fled,
And seeking refuge, slipt into her bed.
Whereon *Leander* sitting, thus began,
Through numming cold, all feeble, faint and wan:
    If not for love, yet love for pittie sake,
Me in thy bed and maiden bosome take,
At least vouchsafe these armes some little roome,
Who hoping to imbrace thee, cherely swome.   250
This head was beat with manie a churlish billow,
And therefore let it rest upon thy pillow.
Herewith afrighted *Hero* shrunke away,
And in her luke-warme place *Leander* lay.
Whose lively heat like fire from heaven fet,
Would animate grosse clay, and higher set
The drooping thoughts of base declining soules,
Then drerie *Mars*, carowsing *Nectar* boules.
His hands he cast upon her like a snare,
She overcome with shame and sallow feare,   260
Like chast *Diana*, when *Acteon* spyde her,

Being sodainly betraide, dyv'd downe to hide her.
And as her silver body downeward went,
With both her hands she made the bed a tent,
And in her owne mind thought her selfe secure,
O'recast with dim and darksome coverture.
And now she lets him whisper in her eare,
Flatter, intreat, promise, protest and sweare,
Yet ever as he greedily assayd
To touch those dainties, she the *Harpey* playd,   270
And every lim did as a soldier stout,
Defend the fort, and keep the foe-man out.
For though the rising yv'rie mount he scal'd,
Which is with azure circling lines empal'd,
Much like a globe, (a globe may I tearme this,
By which love sailes to regions full of blis,)
Yet there with *Sysiphus* he toyld in vaine,
Till gentle parlie did the truce obtaine.
Wherein *Leander* on her quivering brest,
Breathlesse spoke some thing, and sigh'd out the rest;   280
Which so prevail'd, as he with small ado,
Inclos'd her in his armes and kist her to.
And everie kisse to her was as a charme,
And to *Leander* as a fresh alarme.
So that the truce was broke, and she alas,
(Poore sillie maiden) at his mercie was.
Love is not ful of pittie (as men say)
But deaffe and cruell, where he meanes to pray.
Even as a bird, which in our hands we wring,
Foorth plungeth, and oft flutters with her wing,   290
She trembling strove, this strife of hers (like that
Which made the world) another world begat,
Of unknowne joy. Treason was in her thought,
And cunningly to yeeld her selfe she sought.
Seeming not woon, yet woon she was at length,
In such warres women use but halfe their strength.

279–300 Wherein...tree:] TB; Q1–   288 pray] *i.e.,* prey
10 *order is* 291–300, 279–90

Leander now like Theban *Hercules*,
Entred the orchard of *Th'esperides*,
Whose fruit none rightly can describe, but hee
That puls or shakes it from the golden tree: 300
And now she wisht this night were never done,
And sigh'd to thinke upon th'approching sunne,
For much it greev'd her that the bright day-light,
Should know the pleasure of this blessed night,
And them like *Mars* and *Ericine* displayd,
Both in each others armes chaind as they layd.
Againe she knew not how to frame her looke,
Or speake to him who in a moment tooke,
That which so long so charily she kept,
And faine by stealth away she would have crept,   310
And to some corner secretly have gone,
Leaving *Leander* in the bed alone.
But as her naked feet were whipping out,
He on the suddaine cling'd her so about,
That Meremaid-like unto the floore she slid,
One halfe appear'd, the other halfe was hid.
Thus neere the bed she blushing stood upright,
And from her countenance behold ye might,
A kind of twilight breake, which through the heare,
As from an orient cloud, glymse here and there.   320
And round about the chamber this false morne,
Brought foorth the day before the day was borne.
So *Heroes* ruddie cheeke, *Hero* betrayd,
And her all naked to his sight displayd.
Whence his admiring eyes more pleasure tooke,
Than *Dis*, on heapes of gold fixing his looke.
By this *Apollos* golden harpe began,
To sound foorth musicke to the *Ocean*,
Which watchfull *Hesperus* no sooner heard,
But he the days bright-bearing Car prepar'd.   330

305 them] Broughton MS, Dyce; then   319 heare] *i.e.*, hair
     Q 1–10   *320 glymse] *stet* Q 1–10
                                            *330 days] Broughton MS, Rv; day Q 1–10

And ran before, as Harbenger of light,
And with his flaring beames mockt ougly night,
Till she o'recome with anguish, shame, and rage,
Dang'd downe to hell her loathsome carriage.

Desunt nonnulla.

TO MY BEST ESTEEMED
AND WORTHELY HONORED
LADY, THE LADY Walsingham,
one of the Ladies of her Majesties
Bed-chamber.

I present your Ladiship with the last affections of the first two Lovers that ever Muse *shrinde in the Temple of* Memorie*; being drawne by strange instigation to employ some of my serious time in so trifeling a subject, which yet made the first Author, divine* Musæus*, eternall. And were it not that wee must subject our accounts of these common received conceits to servile custome; it goes much against my hand to signe that for a trifling subject, on which more worthines of soule hath been shewed, and weight of divine wit, than can vouchsafe residence in the leaden gravitie of any* Mony-Monger*; in whose profession all serious subjects are concluded. But he that shuns trifles must shun the* 10 *world; out of whose reverend heapes of substance and austeritie, I can, and will, ere long, single, or tumble out as brainles and passionate fooleries, as ever panted in the bosome of the most ridiculous* Lover. *Accept it therfore (good* Madam*) though as a trifle, yet as a serious argument of my affection: for to bee thought thankefull for all free and honourable favours, is a great summe of that riches my whole thrift intendeth.*

Such uncourtly and sillie dispositions as mine, whose contentment hath other objects than profit or glorie; are as glad, simply for the naked merit of vertue, to honour such as advance her, as others that 20 *are hired to commend with deepeliest politique bountie.*

It hath therefore adjoynde much contentment to my desire of your true honour to heare men of desert in Court, adde to mine owne know-ledge of your noble disposition, how gladly you doe your best to preferre their desires; and have as absolute respect to their meere good parts, as if they came perfumed and charmed with golden incitements. And this most sweet inclination, that flowes from the truth and eternitie of Nobles*; assure your Ladiship doth more suite your other Ornaments, and makes more to the advancement of your Name, and happines of your proceedings, then if (like others) you displaied Ensignes of state* 30 *and sowrenes in your forehead; made smooth with nothing but sensualitie and presents.*

This poore Dedication (in figure of the other unitie betwixt Sir Thomas *and your selfe) hath rejoynd you with him, my honoured best friend, whose continuance of ancient kindnes to my still-obscured estate, though it cannot encrease my love to him, which hath ever been entirely circulare; yet shall it encourage my deserts to their utmost requitall, and make my hartie gratitude speake; to which the unhappines of my life hath hetherto been uncomfortable and painfull dumbnes.*   40

By your Ladiships vowd in
most wished service:
George Chapman.

THE ARGUMENT OF THE THIRD SESTYAD

> Leander *to the envious light*
> *Resignes his night-sports with the night,*
> *And swims the* Hellespont *againe;*
> Thesme *the Deitie soveraigne*
> *Of Customes and religious rites*
> *Appeares, improving his delites*
> *Since Nuptiall honors he neglected;*
> *Which straight he vowes shall be effected.*
> *Faire* Hero *left Devirginate*
> *Waies, and with furie wailes her state:*   10
> *But with her love and womans wit*
> *She argues, and approveth it.*

New light gives new directions, Fortunes new
To fashion our indevours that ensue,
More harsh (at lest more hard) more grave and hie
Our subject runs, and our sterne *Muse* must flie.
Loves edge is taken off, and that light flame,
Those thoughts, joyes, longings, that before became
High unexperienst blood, and maids sharpe plights,
Must now grow staid, and censure the delights,
That being enjoyd aske judgement; now we praise,
As having parted: Evenings crowne the daies.   10
    And now ye wanton loves, and yong desires,
Pied vanitie, the mint of strange Attires;
Ye lisping Flatteries, and obsequious Glances,
Relentfull Musicks, and attractive Dances,
And you detested Charmes constraining love,
Shun loves stolne sports by that these Lovers prove.
    By this the Soveraigne of Heavens golden fires,
And yong *Leander*, Lord of his desires,
Together from their lovers armes arose:
Leander into *Hellespontus* throwes   20
His *Hero*-handled bodie, whose delight

*0.6 improving] stet Q2–10

457

Made him disdaine each other Epethite.
And as amidst the enamourd waves he swims,

He cals Phœbus The God of gold of purpose guilt his lims,
the God of Gold, That this word guilt, including double sence,
since the vertue The double guilt of his *Incontinence,*
of his beams Might be exprest, that had no stay t'employ
creates it. The treasure which the Love-god let him joy
In his deare *Hero,* with such sacred thrift,
As had beseemd so sanctified a gift: 30
But like a greedie vulgar Prodigall
Would on the stock dispend, and rudely fall
Before his time, to that unblessed blessing,
Which for lusts plague doth perish with possessing.
Joy graven in sence, like snow in water wasts;
Without preserve of vertue, nothing lasts.
What man is he that with a welthie eie,
Enjoyes a beautie richer than the skie,
Through whose white skin, softer then soundest sleep,
With damaske eyes, the rubie blood doth peep,   40
And runs in branches through her azure vaines,
Whose mixture and first fire, his love attaines;
Whose both hands limit both Loves deities,
And sweeten humane thoughts like Paradise;
Whose disposition silken is and kinde,
Directed with an earth-exempted minde;
Who thinks not heaven with such a love is given?
And who like earth would spend that dower of heaven,
With ranke desire to joy it all at first?
What simply kils our hunger, quencheth thirst,   50
Clothes but our nakednes, and makes us live,
Praise doth not any of her favours give:
But what doth plentifully minister
Beautious apparell and delicious cheere,
So orderd that it still excites desire,
And still gives pleasure freenes to aspire,
The palme of *Bountie,* ever moyst preserving:
To loves sweet life this is the courtly carving.

Thus *Time*, and all-states-ordering *Ceremonie*
Had banisht all offence: *Times* golden *Thie*   60
Upholds the flowrie bodie of the earth
In sacred harmonie, and every birth
Of men, and actions makes legitimate,
Being usde aright; *The use of time is Fate.*
    Yet did the gentle flood transfer once more,
This prize of Love home to his fathers shore;
Where he unlades himselfe of that false welth
That makes few rich; treasures composde by stelth;
And to his sister kinde *Hermione*,
(Who on the shore kneeld, praying to the sea   70
For his returne) he all Loves goods did show
In *Hero* seasde for him, in him for *Hero*.
    His most kinde sister all his secrets knew,
And to her singing like a shower he flew,
Sprinkling the earth, that to their tombs tooke in
Streames dead for love to leave his ivorie skin,
Which yet a snowie fome did leave above,
As soule to the dead water that did love;
And from thence did the first white Roses spring,
(For love is sweet and faire in every thing)   80
And all the sweetned shore as he did goe,
Was crownd with odrous roses white as snow.
Love-blest *Leander* was with love so filled,
That love to all that toucht him he instilled.
And as the colours of all things we see,
To our sights powers communicated bee:
So to all objects that in compasse came
Of any sence he had, his sences flame
Flowd from his parts, with force so virtuall,
It fir'd with sence things meere insensuall.   90
    Now (with warme baths and odours comforted)
When he lay downe he kindly kist his bed,
As consecrating it to *Heros* right,
And vowd thereafter that what ever sight
Put him in minde of *Hero*, or her blisse,

Should be her Altar to prefer a kisse.
   Then laid he forth his late inriched armes,
In whose white circle Love writ all his charmes,
And made his characters sweet *Heros* lims,
When on his breasts warme sea she sideling swims.   100
And as those armes (held up in circle) met,
He said; see sister, *Heros* Carquenet,
Which she had rather weare about her neck,
Then all the jewels that doth *Juno* deck.
   But as he shooke with passionate desire,
To put in flame his other secret fire,
A musick so divine did pierce his eare,
As never yet his ravisht sence did heare:
When suddenly a light of twentie hews
Brake through the roofe, and like the Rainbow views   110
Amazd *Leander*; in whose beames came downe
The Goddesse *Ceremonie*, with a Crowne
Of all the stars, and heaven with her descended.
Her flaming haire to her bright feete extended,
By which hung all the bench of Deities;
And in a chaine, compact of eares and eies,
She led Religion; all her bodie was
Cleere and transparent as the purest glasse:
For she was all presented to the sence;
Devotion, Order, State, and Reverence,   120
Her shadowes were; Societie, Memorie;
All which her sight made live, her absence die.
A rich disparent Pentackle she weares,
Drawne full of circles and strange characters:
Her face was changeable to everie eie;
One way lookt ill, another graciouslie;
Which while men viewd, they cheerfull were and holy:
But looking off, vicious, and melancholy:
The snakie paths to each observed law,
Did *Policie* in her broad bosome draw: 130
One hand a Mathematique Christall swayes,
Which gathering in one line a thousand rayes

From her bright eyes, *Confusion* burnes to death,
And all estates of men distinguisheth.
By it *Morallitie* and *Comelinesse*,
Themselves in all their sightly figures dresse.
Her other hand a lawrell rod applies,
To beate back *Barbarisme*, and *Avarice*,
That followd eating earth, and excrement
And humane lims; and would make proud ascent   140
To seates of Gods, were *Ceremonie* slaine;
The *Howrs* and *Graces* bore her glorious traine,
And all the sweetes of our societie
Were Spherde, and treasurde in her bountious eie.
Thus she appeard, and sharply did reprove
Leanders bluntnes in his violent love;
Tolde him how poore was substance without rites,
Like bils unsignd; desires without delites;
Like meates unseasond; like ranke corne that growes
On Cottages, that none or reapes or sowes: 150
Not being with civill forms confirm'd and bounded,
For humane dignities and comforts founded:
But loose and secret all their glories hide,
Feare fils the chamber, darknes decks the Bride.
    She vanisht, leaving pierst *Leanders* hart
With sence of his unceremonious part,
In which with plaine neglect of Nuptiall rites,
He close and flatly fell to his delites:
And instantly he vowd to celebrate
All rites pertaining to his maried state.   160
So up he gets and to his father goes,
To whose glad eares he doth his vowes disclose:
The Nuptials are resolv'd with utmost powre,
And he at night would swim to *Heros* towre.
From whence he ment to *Sestus* forked Bay
To bring her covertly, where ships must stay,
Sent by his father throughly rigd and mand,
To waft her safely to *Abydus* Strand.

*167 his] Broughton MS, Dyce; her Q2–10

461

There leave we him, and with fresh wing pursue
Astonisht *Hero*, whose most wished view   170
I thus long have forborne, because I left her
So out of countnance, and her spirits bereft her.
To looke of one abasht is impudence,
When of sleight faults he hath too deepe a sence.
Her blushing het her chamber: she lookt out,
And all the ayre she purpled round about,
And after it a foule black day befell,
Which ever since a red morne doth foretell,
And still renewes our woes for *Heros* wo:
And foule it prov'd, because it figur'd so   180
The next nights horror, which prepare to heare;
I faile if it prophane your daintiest eare.
    Then thou most strangely-intellectuall fire,
That proper to my soule hast power t'inspire
Her burning faculties, and with the wings
Of thy unspheared flame visitst the springs
Of spirits immortall; Now (as swift as Time
Doth follow Motion) finde th'eternall Clime
Of his free soule, whose living subject stood
Up to the chin in the *Pyerean* flood,   190
And drunke to me halfe this *Musean* storie,
Inscribing it to deathles Memorie:
Confer with it, and make my pledge as deepe,
That neithers draught be consecrate to sleepe.
Tell it how much his late desires I tender,
(If yet it know not) and to light surrender
My soules darke ofspring, willing it should die
To loves, to passions, and societie.
    Sweet *Hero* left upon her bed alone,
Her maidenhead, her vowes, *Leander* gone,   200
And nothing with her but a violent crew
Of new come thoughts that yet she never knew,
Even to her selfe a stranger; was much like
Th'*Iberian* citie that wars hand did strike

---

*173 *of*] stet Q2–7   183 thou] Tucker Brooke; how Q2–10

By English force in princely *Essex* guide,
When peace assur'd her towres had fortifide;
And golden-fingred *India* had bestowd
Such wealth on her, that strength and Empire flowd
Into her Turrets; and her virgin waste
The wealthie girdle of the Sea embraste: 210
Till our *Leander* that made *Mars* his *Cupid*,
For soft love-sutes, with iron thunders chid:
Swum to her Towers, dissolv'd her virgin zone;
Lead in his power, and made Confusion
Run through her streets amazd, that she supposde
She had not been in her owne walls inclosde:
But rapt by wonder to some forraine state,
Seeing all her issue so disconsolate:
And all her peacefull mansions possest
With wars just spoyle, and many a forraine guest   220
From every corner driving an enjoyer,
Supplying it with power of a destroyer.
So far'd fayre *Hero* in th'expugned fort
Of her chast bosome, and of every sort
Strange thoughts possest her, ransacking her brest
For that that was not there, her wonted rest.
She was a mother straight and bore with paine,
Thoughts that spake straight and wisht their mother slaine;
She hates their lives, and they their own and hers:
Such strife still growes where sin the race prefers.   230
Love is a golden bubble full of dreames,
That waking breakes, and fils us with extreames.
She mus'd how she could looke upon her Sire,
And not shew that without, that was intire.
For as a glasse is an inanimate eie,
And outward formes imbraceth inwardlie:
So is the eye an animate glasse that showes
In-formes without us. And as *Phœbus* throwes
His beames abroad, though he in clowdes be closde,
Still glancing by them till he finde opposde,   240
A loose and rorid vapour that is fit

T'event his searching beames, and useth it
To forme a tender twentie-coloured eie,
Cast in a circle round about the skie.
So when our firie soule, our bodies starre,
(That ever is in motion circulare)
Conceives a forme; in seeking to display it,
Through all our clowdie parts, it doth convey it
Forth at the eye, as the most pregnant place,
And that reflects it round about the face.   250
And this event uncourtly *Hero* thought,
Her inward guilt would in her lookes have wrought:
For yet the worlds stale cunning she resisted
To beare foule thoughts, yet forge what lookes she listed,
And held it for a very sillie sleight,
To make a perfect mettall counterfeit:
Glad to disclaime her selfe; proud of an Art,
That makes the face a Pandar to the hart.
Those be the painted Moones, whose lights prophane
Beauties true Heaven, at full still in their wane.   260
Those be the Lapwing faces that still crie,
Here tis, when that they vow is nothing nie.
Base fooles, when every moorish fowle can teach
That which men thinke the height of humane reach.
But custome that the Apoplexie is
Of beddred nature and lives led amis,
And takes away all feeling of offence,
Yet brazde not *Heros* brow with impudence;
And this she thought most hard to bring to pas,
To seeme in countnance other then she was.   270
As if she had two soules; one for the face,
One for the hart; and that they shifted place
As either list to utter, or conceale
What they conceiv'd: or as one soule did deale
With both affayres at once, keeps and ejects
Both at an instant contrarie effects:
Retention and ejection in her powrs

*257 her selfe;] *stet* Q2–10

Being acts alike: for this one vice of ours,
That forms the thought, and swaies the countenance,
Rules both our motion and our utterance. 280
    These and more grave conceits toyld *Heros* spirits:
For though the light of her discoursive wits
Perhaps might finde some little hole to pas
Through all these worldly cinctures; yet (alas)
There was a heavenly flame incompast her;
Her Goddesse, in whose Phane she did prefer
Her virgin vowes; from whose impulsive sight
She knew the black shield of the darkest night
Could not defend her, nor wits subtilst art:
This was the point pierst *Hero* to the hart. 290
Who heavie to the death, with a deep sigh
And hand that languisht, tooke a robe was nigh,
Exceeding large, and of black Cypres made,
In which she sate, hid from the day in shade,
Even over head and face downe to her feete;
Her left hand made it at her bosome meete;
Her right hand leand on her hart-bowing knee,
Wrapt in unshapefull foulds twas death to see:
Her knee stayd that, and that her falling face,
Each limme helpt other to put on disgrace. 300
No forme was seene, where forme held all her sight:
But like an Embrion that saw never light:
Or like a scorched statue made a cole
With three-wingd lightning: or a wretched soule
Muffled with endles darknes, she did sit:
The night had never such a heavie spirit.
Yet might an imitating eye well see,
How fast her cleere teares melted on her knee
Through her black vaile, and turnd as black as it,
Mourning to be her teares: then wrought her wit 310
With her broke vow, her Goddesse wrath, her fame,
All tooles that enginous despayre could frame:

298 foulds_∧...see:] Broughton MS,   Q2–10±
    Dyce (~ ,...~;);   ~:...~ ∧

Which made her strow the floore with her torne haire,
And spread her mantle peece-meale in the aire.
Like *Joves* sons club, strong passion strooke her downe,
And with a piteous shrieke inforst her swoune:
Her shrieke, made with another shrieke ascend
The frighted Matron that on her did tend:
And as with her owne crie her sence was slaine,
So with the other it was calde againe.   320
She rose and to her bed made forced way,
And layd her downe even where *Leander* lay:
And all this while the red sea of her blood
Ebd with *Leander*: but now turnd the flood,
And all her fleete of sprites came swelling in
With childe of saile, and did hot fight begin
With those severe conceits, she too much markt,
And here *Leanders* beauties were imbarkt.
He came in swimming painted all with joyes,
Such as might sweeten hell: his thought destroyes   330
All her destroying thoughts: she thought she felt
His heart in hers, with her contentions melt:
And chid her soule that it could so much erre,
To check the true joyes he deserv'd in her.
Her fresh heat blood cast figures in her eyes,
And she supposde she saw in *Neptunes* skyes
How her star wandred, washt in smarting brine
For her loves sake, that with immortall wine
Should be embath'd, and swim in more hearts ease,
Than there was water in the *Sestian* seas.   340
Then said her *Cupid* prompted spirit; shall I
Sing mones to such delightsome harmony?
Shall slick-tongde fame patcht up with voyces rude,
The drunken bastard of the multitude,
(Begot when father Judgement is away,
And gossip-like, sayes because others say,
Takes newes as if it were too hot to eate,
And spits it slavering forth for dog-fees meate)
Make me for forging a phantastique vow,

Presume to beare what makes grave matrons bow? 350
Good vowes are never broken with good deedes,
For then good deedes were bad: vowes are but seedes,
And good deeds fruits; even those good deedes that grow
From other stocks than from th'observed vow.
That is a good deede that prevents a bad:
Had I not yeelded, slaine my selfe I had.
Hero Leander is, *Leander Hero*:
Such vertue love hath to make one of two.
If then *Leander* did my maydenhead git,
Leander being my selfe I still retaine it. 360
We breake chast vowes when we live loosely ever:
But bound as we are, we live loosely never.
Two constant lovers being joynd in one,
Yeelding to one another, yeeld to none.
We know not how to vow, till love unblinde us,
And vowes made ignorantly never binde us.
Too true it is that when t'is gone men hate
The joyes as vaine they tooke in loves estate:
But that's, since they have lost the heavenly light
Should shew them way to judge of all things right. 370
When life is gone death must implant his terror,
As death is foe to life, so love to error.
Before we love how range we through this sphere,
Searching the sundrie fancies hunted here:
Now with desire of wealth transported quite
Beyond our free humanities delight:
Now with ambition climing falling towrs,
Whose hope to scale our feare to fall devours:
Now rapt with pastimes, pomp, all joyes impure;
In things without us no delight is sure. 380
But love with all joyes crownd, within doth sit;
O Goddesse pitie love and pardon it.
This spake she weeping: but her Goddesse eare
Burnd with too sterne a heat, and would not heare.
Aie me, hath heavens straight fingers no more graces

383 she] Singer; he Q 2–10   385 straight] *i.e.*, strait

For such as *Hero*, then for homeliest faces?
Yet she hopte well, and in her sweet conceit
Waying her arguments, she thought them weight:
And that the logick of *Leanders* beautie,
And them together would bring proofes of dutie.   390
And if her soule, that was a skilfull glance
Of Heavens great essence, found such imperance
In her loves beauties; she had confidence
Jove lov'd him too, and pardond her offence.
Beautie in heaven and earth this grace doth win,
It supples rigor, and it lessens sin.
Thus, her sharpe wit, her love, her secrecie,
Trouping together, made her wonder why
She should not leave her bed, and to the Temple?
Her health sayd she must live; her sex, dissemble.   400
She viewd *Leanders* place, and wisht he were
Turnd to his place, so his place were *Leander*.
Aye me (sayd she) that loves sweet life and sence
Should doe it harme! my love had not gone hence,
Had he been like his place. O blessed place,
Image of Constancie. Thus my loves grace
Parts no where but it leaves some thing behinde
Worth observation: he renowmes his kinde.
His motion is like heavens Orbiculer:
For where he once is, he is ever there.   410
This place was mine: *Leander* now t'is thine;
Thou being my selfe, then it is double mine:
Mine, and *Leanders* mine, *Leanders* mine.
O see what wealth it yeelds me, nay yeelds him:
For I am in it, he for me doth swim.
Rich, fruitfull love, that doubling selfe estates
Elixer-like contracts, though separates.
Deare place I kisse thee, and doe welcome thee,
As from *Leander* ever sent to mee.

                    The end of the third Sestyad.

THE ARGUMENT OF THE FOURTH SESTYAD

Hero, *in sacred habit deckt,*
Doth private sacrifice effect.
Her Skarfs description wrought by fate,
Ostents, *that threaten her estate.*
The strange, yet Phisicall events,
Leanders *counterfeit presents.*
In thunder, Ciprides *descends,*
Presaging both the lovers ends.
Ecte *the Goddesse of remorce,*
With vocall and articulate force   10
Inspires Leucote, Venus *swan,*
T'excuse the beautious Sestian.
Venus, *to wreake her rites abuses,*
Creates the monster Eronusis;
Enflaming Heros *Sacrifice,*
With lightning darted from her eyes:
And thereof springs the painted beast,
That ever since taints every breast.

Eronusis,
or Dissi-
mulation

Now from *Leanders* place she rose, and found
Her haire and rent robe scattred on the ground:
Which taking up, she every peece did lay
Upon an Altar; where in youth of day
She usde t'exhibite private Sacrifice:
Those would she offer to the Deities
Of her faire Goddesse, and her powerfull son,
As relicks of her late-felt passion:
And in that holy sort she vowd to end them,
In hope her violent fancies that did rend them,   10
Would as quite fade in her loves holy fire,
As they should in the flames she ment t'inspire.
Then put she on all her religious weedes,
That deckt her in her secret sacred deedes:
A crowne of Isickles, that sunne nor fire

*0.14 s.n. *or*] stet Q2?

Could ever melt, and figur'd chast desire.
A golden star shinde in her naked breast,
In honour of the Queene-light of the East.
In her right hand she held a silver wand,
On whose bright top *Peristera* did stand,   20
Who was a Nymph, but now transformd a Dove,
And in her life was deare in *Venus* love:
And for her sake she ever since that time,
Chusde Doves to draw her Coach through heavens blew clime.
Her plentious haire in curled billowes swims
On her bright shoulder: her harmonious lims
Sustainde no more but a most subtile vaile
That hung on them, as it durst not assaile
Their different concord: for the weakest ayre
Could raise it swelling from her bewties fayre: 30
Nor did it cover, but adumbrate onelie ⎫
Her most heart-piercing parts, that a blest eie ⎬
Might see (as it did shadow) fearfullie, ⎭
All that all-love-deserving Paradise:
It was as blew as the most freezing skies,
Neere the Seas hew, for thence her Goddesse came:
On it a skarfe she wore of wondrous frame;
In midst whereof she wrought a virgins face,
From whose each cheeke a firie blush did chace
Two crimson flames, that did two waies extend,   40
Spreading the ample skarfe to either end,
Which figur'd the division of her minde,
Whiles yet she rested bashfully inclinde,
And stood not resolute to wed *Leander*.
This serv'd her white neck for a purple sphere,
And cast it selfe at full breadth downe her back.
There (since the first breath that begun the wrack
Of her free quiet from *Leanders* lips)
She wrought a Sea in one flame full of ships:
But that one ship where all her wealth did passe   50
(Like simple marchants goods) *Leander* was:
For in that Sea she naked figured him;

470

Her diving needle taught him how to swim,
And to each thred did such resemblance give,
For joy to be so like him, it did live.
Things senceles live by art, and rationall die,
By rude contempt of art and industrie.
Scarce could she work, but in her strength of thought
She feard she prickt *Leander* as she wrought:
And oft would shrieke so, that her Guardian frighted,   60
Would staring haste, as with some mischiefe cited.
They double life that dead things griefs sustayne:
They kill that feele not their friends living payne.
Sometimes she feard he sought her infamie,
And then as she was working of his eie,
She thought to pricke it out to quench her ill:
But as she prickt, it grew more perfect still.
Trifling attempts no serious acts advance;
The fire of love is blowne by dalliance.
In working his fayre neck she did so grace it,   70
She still was working her owne armes t'imbrace it:
That, and his shoulders, and his hands were seene
Above the streame, and with a pure Sea greene
She did so queintly shadow every lim,
All might be seene beneath the waves to swim.
     In this conceited skarfe she wrought beside
A Moone in change, and shooting stars did glide
In number after her with bloodie beames,
Which figur'd her affects in their extreames,
Pursiung Nature in her *Cynthian* bodie,   80
And did her thoughts running on change implie:
For maids take more delights when they prepare
And thinke of wives states, than when wives they are.
Beneath all these she wrought a Fisherman,
Drawing his nets from forth that Ocean;
Who drew so hard ye might discover well,
The toughned sinewes in his neck did swell:
His inward straines drave out his blood-shot eyes,
And springs of sweat did in his forehead rise:

Yet was of nought but of a Serpent sped,   90
That in his bosome flew and stung him dead.
And this by fate into her minde was sent,
Not wrought by meere instinct of her intent.
At the skarfs other end her hand did frame,
Neere the forkt point of the devided flame,
A countrie virgin keeping of a Vine,
Who did of hollow bulrushes combine
Snares for the stubble-loving Grashopper,
And by her lay her skrip that nourisht her.
Within a myrtle shade she sate and sung,   100
And tufts of waving reedes about her sprung:
Where lurkt two Foxes, that while she applide
Her trifling snares, their theeveries did devide:
One to the vine, another to her skrip,
That she did negligently overslip:
By which her fruitfull vine and holesome fare,
She suffred spoyld to make a childish snare.
These omenous fancies did her soule expresse,
And every finger made a Prophetesse,
To shew what death was hid in loves disguise,   110
And make her judgement conquer destinies.
O what sweet formes fayre Ladies soules doe shrowd,
Were they made seene and forced through their blood,
If through their beauties like rich work through lawn,
They would set forth their minds with vertues drawn,
In letting graces from their fingers flie,
To still their yas thoughts with industrie:
That their plied wits in numbred silks might sing
Passions huge conquest, and their needels leading
Affection prisoner through their own-built citties,   120
Pinniond with stories and *Arachnean* ditties.

   Proceed we now with *Heros* sacrifice;
She odours burnd, and from their smoke did rise
Unsavorie fumes, that ayre with plagues inspired,
And then the consecrated sticks she fired.

117 yas] *i.e.*, eyas

On whose pale flame an angrie spirit flew,
And beate it downe still as it upward grew.
The virgin Tapers that on th'altar stood,
When she inflam'd them burnd as red as blood:
All sad ostents of that too neere successe,   130
That made such moving beauties motionlesse.
Then *Hero* wept; but her affrighted eyes
She quickly wrested from the sacrifice:
Shut them, and inwards for *Leander* lookt,
Searcht her soft bosome, and from thence she pluckt
His lovely picture: which when she had viewd,
Her beauties were with all loves joyes renewd.
The odors sweetned, and the fires burnd cleere,
Leanders forme left no ill object there.
Such was his beautie that the force of light,   140
Whose knowledge teacheth wonders infinite,
The strength of number and proportion,
Nature had plaste in it to make it knowne
Art was her daughter, and what humane wits
For studie lost, intombd in drossie spirits.
After this accident (which for her glorie
Hero could not but make a historie)
Th'inhabitants of *Sestus*, and *Abydus*,
Did every yeare with feasts propitious,
To faire *Leanders* picture sacrifice,   150
And they were persons of especiall prize
That were allowd it, as an ornament
T'inrich their houses; for the continent
Of the strange vertues all approv'd it held:
For even the very looke of it repeld
All blastings, witchcrafts, and the strifes of nature
In those diseases that no hearbs could cure.
The woolfie sting of Avarice it would pull,
And make the rankest miser bountifull.
It kild the feare of thunder and of death;   160
The discords that conceits ingendereth
Twixt man and wife, it for the time would cease:

The flames of love it quencht, and would increase:
Held in a princes hand it would put out
The dreadfulst Comet: it would ease all doubt
Of threatned mischiefes: it would bring asleepe
Such as were mad: it would enforce to weepe
Most barbarous eyes: and many more effects
This picture wrought, and sprung *Leandrian* sects,
Of which was *Hero* first: For he whose forme   170
(Held in her hand) cleerd such a fatall storme,
From hell she thought his person would defend her,
Which night and *Hellespont* would quickly send her.
With this confirmd, she vowd to banish quite
All thought of any check to her delite:
And in contempt of sillie bashfulnes,
She would the faith of her desires professe:
Where her Religion should be Policie,
To follow love with zeale her pietie:
Her chamber her Cathedrall Church should be,   180
And her *Leander* her chiefe Deitie.
For in her love these did the gods forego;
And though her knowledge did not teach her so,
Yet did it teach her this, that what her hart
Did greatest hold in her selfe greatest part,
That she did make her god; and t'was lesse nought
To leave gods in profession and in thought,
Than in her love and life: for therein lies
Most of her duties, and their dignities.
And raile the brain-bald world at what it will;   190
Thats the grand Atheisme that raignes in it still.
Yet singularitie she would use no more,
For she was singular too much before:
But she would please the world with fayre pretext;
Love would not leave her conscience perplext.
Great men that will have lesse doe for them, still
Must beare them out though th'acts be nere so ill.
Meannes must Pandar be to Excellence,

196 them, still_Λ] Dyce; ~ _Λ_ ~ , Q2–10   198 Excellence] Q7; Excellencie Q2–6

474

Pleasure attones Falshood and Conscience:
Dissembling was the worst (thought *Hero* then)　　　200
And that was best now she must live with men.
O vertuous love that taught her to doe best,
When she did worst, and when she thought it lest.
Thus would she still proceed in works divine,
And in her sacred state of priesthood shine,
Handling the holy rites with hands as bold,
As if therein she did *Joves* thunder hold;
And need not feare those menaces of error,
Which she at others threw with greatest terror.
O lovely *Hero*, nothing is thy sin,　　　210
Wayd with those foule faults other Priests are in;
That having neither faiths, nor works, nor bewties,
T'engender any scuse for slubberd duties;
With as much countnance fill their holie chayres,
And sweat denouncements gainst prophane affayres,
As if their lives were cut out by their places,
And they the only fathers of the Graces.
　　Now as with setled minde she did repaire,
Her thoughts to sacrifice her ravisht haire,
And her torne robe which on the altar lay,　　　220
And only for Religions fire did stay;
She heard a thunder by the Cyclops beaten,
In such a volley as the world did threaten,
Given *Venus* as she parted th'ayrie Sphere,
Discending now to chide with *Hero* here:
When suddenly the Goddesse waggoners,
The Swans and Turtles that in coupled pheres,
Through all worlds bosoms draw her influence,
Lighted in *Heros* window, and from thence
To her fayre shoulders flew the gentle Doves,　　　230
Gracefull *Ædone* that sweet pleasure loves,
And ruffoot *Chreste* with the tufted crowne,
Both which did kisse her, though their Goddes frowne.
The Swans did in the solid flood, her glasse,

233 frowne] Q3; frownd Q2

Proyne their fayre plumes; of which the fairest was
Jove-lov'd *Leucote*, that pure brightnes is;
The other bountie-loving *Dapsilis*.
All were in heaven, now they with *Hero* were:
But *Venus* lookes brought wrath, and urged feare.
Her robe was skarlet, black her heads attire,   240
And through her naked breast shinde streames of fire,
As when the rarefied ayre is driven
In flashing streames, and opes the darkned heaven.
In her white hand a wreath of yew she bore,
And breaking th'icie wreath sweet *Hero* wore,
She forst about her browes her wreath of yew,
And sayd; now minion to thy fate be trew,
Though not to me, indure what this portends;
Begin where lightnes will, in shame it ends.
Love makes thee cunning; thou art currant now,   250
By being counterfeit: thy broken vow,
Deceit with her pide garters must rejoyne,
And with her stampe thou countnances must coyne,
Coynes, and pure deceits for purities:
And still a mayd wilt seeme in cosoned eies,
And have an antike face to laugh within,
While thy smooth lookes make men digest thy sin.
But since thy lips (lest thought forsworne) forswore,
Be never virgins vow worth trusting more.
    When Beauties dearest did her Goddesse heare   260
Breathe such rebukes gainst that she could not cleare;
Dumbe sorrow spake alowd in teares, and blood
That from her griefe-burst vaines in piteous flood,
From the sweet conduits of her favor fell:
The gentle Turtles did with moanes make swell
Their shining gorges: the white black-eyde Swans
Did sing as wofull Epicedians,
As they would straightwaies dye: when pities Queene
The Goddesse *Ecte*, that had ever beene
Hid in a watrie clowde neere *Heros* cries,   270

254 Coynes] *i.e.*, coyness   264 favor] Q9; savor Q2–8

Since the first instant of her broken eies,
Gave bright *Leucote* voyce, and made her speake,
To ease her anguish, whose swolne breast did breake
With anger at her Goddesse, that did touch
Hero so neere for that she usde so much.
And thrusting her white neck at *Venus*, sayd;
Why may not amorous *Hero* seeme a mayd,
Though she be none, as well as you suppresse
In modest cheekes your inward wantonnesse?
How often have wee drawne you from above,   280
T'exchange with mortals, rites for rites in love?
Why in your preist then call you that offence
That shines in you, and is your influence?
With this the furies stopt *Leucotes* lips,
Enjoynd by *Venus*; who with Rosie whips
Beate the kind Bird. Fierce lightning from her eyes
Did set on fire faire *Heros* sacrifice,
Which was her torne robe, and inforced hayre;
And the bright flame became a mayd most faire
For her aspect: her tresses were of wire,   *Description and* 290
Knit like a net, where harts all set on fire,   *Creation of*
Strugled in pants and could not get release: *Dissimulation.*
Her armes were all with golden pincers drest,
And twentie fashiond knots, pullies, and brakes,
And all her bodie girdled with painted Snakes.
Her doune parts in a Scorpions taile combinde,
Freckled with twentie colours; pyed wings shinde
Out of her shoulders; Cloth had never die, ⎫
Nor sweeter colours never viewed eie,   ⎬
In scorching *Turkie, Cares, Tartarie,*   ⎭   300
Than shinde about this spirit notorious;
Nor was *Arachnes* web so glorious.
Of lightning and of shreds she was begot;
More hold in base dissemblers is there not.
Her name was *Eronusis. Venus* flew
From *Heros* sight, and at her Chariot drew
This wondrous creature to so steepe a height,

477

That all the world she might command with sleight
Of her gay wings: and then she bad her hast,
Since *Hero* had dissembled, and disgrast   310
Her rites so much, and every breast infect
With her deceits; she made her Architect
Of all dissimulation, and since then
Never was any trust in maides nor men.
    O it spighted,
Fayre *Venus* hart to see her most delighted,
And one she chusde for temper of her minde,
To be the only ruler of her kinde,
So soone to let her virgin race be ended:
Not simply for the fault a whit offended;   320
But that in strife for chastnes with the Moone,
Spitefull *Diana* bad her shew but one,
That was her servant vowd, and liv'd a mayd,
And now she thought to answer that upbrayd,
Hero had lost her answer; who knowes not
Venus would seeme as farre from any spot
Of light demeanour, as the very skin
Twixt *Cynthias* browes; Sin is asham'd of Sin.
Up *Venus* flew, and scarce durst up for feare
Of *Phœbes* laughter, when she past her Sphere: 330
And so most ugly clowded was the light,
That day was hid in day; night came ere night,
And *Venus* could not through the thick ayre pierce,
Till the daies king, god of undanted verse,
Because she was so plentifull a theame,
To such as wore his Lawrell *Anademe*:
Like to a firie bullet made descent,
And from her passage those fat vapours rent,
That being not throughly rarefide to raine,
Melted like pitch as blew as any vaine,   340
And scalding tempests made the earth to shrinke
Under their fervor, and the world did thinke
In every drop a torturing Spirit flew,
It pierst so deeply, and it burnd so blew.

Betwixt all this and *Hero, Hero* held
Leanders picture as a *Persean* shield:
And she was free from feare of worst successe;
The more ill threats us, we suspect the lesse:
As we grow haples, violence subtle growes,
Dumb, deafe, and blind, and comes when no man knowes.　　　350

      The end of the fourth Sestyad.

THE ARGUMENT OF THE FIFT SESTYAD.

Day doubles her accustomd date,
As loth the night, incenst by fate,
Should wrack our lovers; Heros *plight,*
Longs for Leander, *and the night:*
Which, ere her thirstie wish recovers,
She sends for two betrothed lovers,
And marries them, that (with their crew,
Their sports and ceremonies due)
She covertly might celebrate,
With secret joy her owne estate.　　　10
She makes a feast, at which appeares
The wilde Nymph Teras, *that still beares*
An Ivory Lute, tels Omenous tales,
And sings at solemne festivales.

Now was bright *Hero* weary of the day,
Thought an Olympiad in *Leanders* stay.
Sol, and the soft-foote *Howrs* hung on his armes,
And would not let him swim, foreseeing his harmes:
That day *Aurora* double grace obtainde
Of her love *Phœbus*; she his Horses rainde,
Set on his golden knee, and as she list
She puld him back; and as she puld, she kist
To have him turne to bed; he lov'd her more,
To see the love *Leander Hero* bore.　　　10
Examples profit much: ten times in one,

346 *Persean*] Methuen (i.e. of *Perseus*); Persian Q2–10

479

In persons full of note, good deedes are done.
    Day was so long, men walking fell asleepe,
The heavie humors that their eyes did steepe,
Made them feare mischiefs. The hard streets were beds
For covetous churles, and for ambitious heads,
That spight of Nature would their busines plie.
All thought they had the falling *Epilepsie*,
Men groveld so upon the smotherd ground,
And pittie did the hart of heaven confound.   20
The Gods, the Graces, and the Muses came
Downe to the Destinies, to stay the frame
Of the true lovers deaths, and all worlds teares:
But death before had stopt their cruell eares.
All the Celestials parted mourning then,
Pierst with our humane miseries more then men.
Ah, nothing doth the world with mischiefe fill,
But want of feeling one anothers ill.
    With their descent the day grew something fayre,
And cast a brighter robe upon the ayre.   30
Hero to shorten time with merriment,
For yong *Alcmane*, and bright *Mya* sent,
Two lovers that had long crav'd mariage dues
At *Heros* hands: but she did still refuse,
For lovely *Mya* was her consort vowd
In her maids state, and therefore not allowd
To amorous Nuptials: yet faire *Hero* now
Intended to dispence with her cold vow,
Since hers was broken, and to marrie her:
The rites would pleasing matter minister   40
To her conceits, and shorten tedious day.
They came; sweet Musick usherd th'odorous way,
And wanton Ayre in twentie sweet forms danst
After her fingers; Beautie and Love advanst
Their ensignes in the downles rosie faces
Of youths and maids, led after by the Graces.
For all these, *Hero* made a friendly feast,
Welcomd them kindly, did much love protest,

Winning their harts with all the meanes she might,
That when her fault should chance t'abide the light,   50
Their loves might cover or extenuate it,
And high in her worst fate make pittie sit.
     She married them, and in the banquet came
Borne by the virgins: *Hero* striv'd to frame
Her thoughts to mirth. Aye me, but hard it is
To imitate a false and forced blis.
Ill may a sad minde forge a merrie face,
Nor hath constrained laughter any grace.
Then layd she wine on cares to make them sinke;
Who feares the threats of fortune, let him drinke.   60
     To these quick Nuptials entred suddenly
Admired *Teras* with the Ebon Thye,
A Nymph that haunted the greene *Sestyan* groves,
And would consort soft virgins in their loves,
At gaysome Triumphs, and on solemne dayes,
Singing prophetike Elegies and Layes:
And fingring of a silver Lute she tide,
With black and purple skarfs by her left side.
Apollo gave it, and her skill withall,
And she was term'd his Dwarfe she was so small.   70
Yet great in vertue, for his beames enclosde
His vertues in her: never was proposde
Riddle to her, or Augurie, strange or new,
But she resolv'd it: never sleight tale flew
From her charmd lips, without important sence,
Shewne in some grave succeeding consequence.
     This little Silvane with her songs and tales,
Gave such estate to feasts and Nuptiales,
That though oft times she forewent Tragedies,
Yet for her strangenes still she pleasde their eyes,   80
And for her smalnes they admir'd her so,
They thought her perfect borne and could not grow.
     All eyes were on her: *Hero* did command
An Altar deckt with sacred state should stand,
At the Feasts upper end close by the Bride,

On which the pretie Nymph might sit espide.
Then all were silent; every one so heares,
As all their sences climbd into their eares:
And first this amorous tale that fitted well
Fayre *Hero* and the Nuptials she did tell: 90

The tale of Teras.

Hymen that now is god of Nuptiall rites,
And crownes with honor Love and his delights,
Of *Athens* was, a youth so sweet of face,
That many thought him of the femall race:
Such quickning brightnes did his cleere eyes dart,
Warme went their beames to his beholders hart.
In such pure leagues his beauties were combinde,
That there your Nuptiall contracts first were signde.
For as proportion, white and crimsine, meet
In Beauties mixture, all right cleere, and sweet; 100
The eye responsible, the golden haire,
And none is held without the other, faire:
All spring together, all together fade;
Such intermixt affections should invade
Two perfect lovers: which being yet unseene,
Their vertues and their comforts copied beene,
In Beauties concord, subject to the eie;
And that, in *Hymen*, pleasde so matchleslie,
That lovers were esteemde in their full grace,
Like forme and colour mixt in *Hymens* face; 110
And such sweete concord was thought worthie then
Of torches, musick, feasts, and greatest men:
So *Hymen* lookt, that even the chastest minde
He mov'd to joyne in joyes of sacred kinde:
For onely now his chins first doune consorted
His heads rich fleece, in golden curles contorted;
And as he was so lov'd, he lov'd so too,
So should best bewties, bound by Nuptialls doo.
Bright *Eucharis*, who was by all men saide
The noblest, fayrest, and the richest maide, 120

482

Of all th'*Athenian* damzels, *Hymen* lov'd,
With such transmission, that his heart remov'd
From his white brest to hers; but her estate
In passing his, was so interminate
For wealth and honor, that his love durst feede
On nought but sight and hearing, nor could breede
Hope of requittall, the grand prise of love;
Nor could he heare or see but he must prove
How his rare bewties musick would agree
With maids in consort: therefore robbed he   130
His chin of those same few first fruits it bore,
And clad in such attire, as Virgins wore,
He kept them companie, and might right well,
For he did all but *Eucharis* excell
In all the fayre of Beautie: yet he wanted
Vertue to make his owne desires implanted
In his deare *Eucharis*; for women never
Love beautie in their sex, but envie ever.
His judgement yet (that durst not suite addresse,
Nor past due meanes presume of due successe)   140
Reason gat fortune in the end to speede
To his best prayers: but strange it seemd indeede,
That fortune should a chast affection blesse,
Preferment seldome graceth bashfulnesse.
Nor grast it *Hymen* yet; but many a dart
And many an amorous thought enthrald his hart,
Ere he obtaind her; and he sick became,
Forst to abstaine her sight, and then the flame
Rag'd in his bosome. O what griefe did fill him:
Sight made him sick, and want of sight did kill him.   150
The virgins wondred where *Diætia* stayd,
For so did *Hymen* terme himselfe a mayd.
At length with sickly lookes he greeted them:
Tis strange to see gainst what an extreame streame
A lover strives; poore *Hymen* lookt so ill,
That as in merit he increased still,

142 prayers] Brydges; prayes Q2–6; preies Q7–9; pryes Q10

By suffring much, so he in grace decreast.
Women are most wonne when men merit least:
If merit looke not well, love bids stand by,
Loves speciall lesson is to please the eye.   160
And *Hymen* soone recovering all he lost,
Deceiving still these maids, but himselfe most,
His love and he with many virgin dames,
Noble by birth, noble by beauties flames,
Leaving the towne with songs and hallowed lights,
To doe great *Ceres Eleusina* rites
Of zealous Sacrifice; were made a pray
To barbarous Rovers that in ambush lay,
And with rude hands enforst their shining spoyle,
Farre from the darkned Citie, tir'd with toyle.   170
And when the yellow issue of the skie
Came trouping forth, jelous of crueltie
To their bright fellowes of this under heaven,
Into a double night they saw them driven,
A horride Cave, the theeves black mansion,
Where wearie of the journey they had gon,
Their last nights watch, and drunke with their sweete gains,
Dull *Morpheus* entred, laden with silken chains,
Stronger then iron, and bound the swelling vaines
And tyred sences of these lawles Swaines.   180
But when the virgin lights thus dimly burnd;
O what a hell was heaven in! how they mournd
And wrung their hands, and wound their gentle forms
Into the shapes of sorrow! Golden storms
Fell from their eyes: As when the Sunne appeares,
And yet it raines, so shewd their eyes their teares.
And as when funerall dames watch a dead corse,
Weeping about it, telling with remorse
What paines he felt, how long in paine he lay,
How little food he eate, what he would say;   190
And then mixe mournfull tales of others deaths,
Smothering themselves in clowds of their owne breaths;
At length, one cheering other, call for wine,

484

The golden boale drinks teares out of their eine,
As they drinke wine from it; and round it goes,
Each helping other to relieve their woes:
So cast these virgins beauties mutuall raies,
One lights another, face the face displaies;
Lips by reflexion kist, and hands hands shooke,
Even by the whitenes each of other tooke.   200
   But *Hymen* now usde friendly *Morpheus* aide,
Slew every theefe, and rescude every maide.
And now did his enamourd passion take
Hart from his hartie deede, whose worth did make
His hope of bounteous *Eucharis* more strong;
And now came Love with *Proteus*, who had long
Inggl'd the little god with prayers and gifts,
Ran through all shapes, and varied all his shifts,
To win Loves stay with him, and make him love him:
And when he saw no strength of sleight could move him   210
To make him love, or stay, he nimbly turnd
Into Loves selfe, he so extreamely burnd.
And thus came Love with *Proteus* and his powre,
T'encounter *Eucharis*: first like the flowre
That *Junos* milke did spring, the silver Lillie,
He fell on *Hymens* hand, who straight did spie
The bounteous Godhead, and with wondrous joy
Offred it *Eucharis*. She wondrous coy
Drew back her hand: the subtle flowre did woo it,
And drawing it neere, mixt so you could not know it.   220
As two cleere Tapers mixe in one their light,
So did the Lillie and the hand their white:
She viewd it, and her view the forme bestowes
Amongst her spirits: for as colour flowes
From superficies of each thing we see,
Even so with colours formes emitted bee:
And where Loves forme is, Love is, Love is forme;
He entred at the eye, his sacred storme
Rose from the hand, Loves sweetest instrument:

*207 Inggl'd] *stet* Q2

It stird her bloods sea so, that high it went,   230
And beate in bashfull waves gainst the white shore
Of her divided cheekes; it rag'd the more,
Because the tide went gainst the haughtie winde
Of her estate and birth: And as we finde
In fainting ebs, the flowrie Zephire hurles
The greene-hayrd *Hellespont*, broke in silver curles,
Gainst *Heros* towre: but in his blasts retreate,
The waves obeying him, they after beate,
Leaving the chalkie shore a great way pale,
Then moyst it freshly with another gale: 240
So ebd and flowde the blood in *Eucharis* face,
Coynesse and Love striv'd which had greatest grace.
Virginitie did fight on Coynesse side;
Feare of her parents frownes, and femall pride,
Lothing the lower place, more then it loves
The high contents, desert and vertue moves.
With Love fought *Hymens* beautie and his valure,
Which scarce could so much favour yet allure
To come to strike, but fameles idle stood,
Action is firie valours soveraigne good.   250
But Love once entred, wisht no greater ayde
Then he could find within; thought, thought betrayd.
The bribde, but incorrupted Garrison,
Sung *Io Hymen*; there those songs begun,
And Love was growne so rich with such a gaine,
And wanton with the ease of his free raigne,
That he would turne into her roughest frownes
To turne them out; and thus he *Hymen* crownes
King of his thoughts, mans greatest Emperie:
This was his first brave step to deitie.   260
    Home to the mourning cittie they repayre,
With newes as holesome as the morning ayre,
To the sad parents of each saved maid:
But *Hymen* and his *Eucharis* had laid
This plat, to make the flame of their delight
Round as the Moone at full, and full as bright.

Because the parents of chast *Eucharis*
Exceeding *Hymens* so, might crosse their blis;
And as the world rewards deserts, that law
Cannot assist with force: so when they saw   270
Their daughter safe, take vantage of their owne,
Praise *Hymens* valour much, nothing bestowne:
Hymen must leave the virgins in a Grove
Farre off from *Athens*, and go first to prove
If to restore them all with fame and life,
He should enjoy his dearest as his wife.
This told to all the maids; the most agree:
The riper sort knowing what t'is to bee
The first mouth of a newes so farre deriv'd,
And that to heare and beare newes brave folks liv'd,   280
As being a carriage speciall hard to beare
Occurrents, these occurrents being so deare,
They did with grace protest, they were content
T'accost their friends with all their complement,
For *Hymens* good: but to incurre their harme,
There he must pardon them. This wit went warme
To *Adolesches* braine, a Nymph borne hie,
Made all of voyce and fire, that upwards flie:
Her hart and all her forces nether traine
Climbd to her tongue, and thither fell her braine,   290
Since it could goe no higher, and it must go:
All powers she had, even her tongue, did so.
In spirit and quicknes she much joy did take,
And lov'd her tongue, only for quicknes sake,
And she would hast and tell. The rest all stay,
Hymen goes one, the Nymph another way:
And what became of her Ile tell at last:
Yet take her visage now: moyst lipt, long fa'st,
Thin like an iron wedge, so sharpe and tart,
As twere of purpose made to cleave Loves hart.   300
Well were this lovely Beautie rid of her,

289 nether] Q10; neither Q1–9   298 fa'st] *i.e.*, fac'd
296 one] Singer; on Q2–10

487

And *Hymen* did at *Athens* now prefer
His welcome suite, which he with joy aspirde:
A hundred princely youths with him retirde
To fetch the Nymphs: Chariots and Musick went,
And home they came: heaven with applauses rent.
The Nuptials straight proceed, whiles all the towne,
Fresh in their joyes might doe them most renowne.
First gold-lockt *Hymen* did to Church repaire,
Like a quick offring burnd in flames of haire.   310
And after, with a virgin firmament,
The Godhead-proving Bride, attended went
Before them all; she lookt in her command,
As if forme-giving *Cyprias* silver hand
Gripte all their beauties, and crusht out one flame;
She blusht to see how beautie overcame
The thoughts of all men. Next before her went
Five lovely children deckt with ornament
Of her sweet colours, bearing Torches by,
For light was held a happie Augurie   320
Of generation, whose efficient right
Is nothing else but to produce to light.
The od disparent number they did chuse,
To shew the union married loves should use,
Since in two equall parts it will not sever,
But the midst holds one to rejoyne it ever,
As common to both parts: men therfore deeme,
That equall number Gods does not esteeme,
Being authors of sweet peace and unitie,
But pleasing to th'infernall Emperie,   330
Under whose ensignes Wars and Discords fight,
Since an even number you may disunite
In two parts equall, nought in middle left,
To reunite each part from other reft:
And five they hold in most especiall prise,
Since t'is the first od number that doth rise
From the two formost numbers unitie
That od and even are; which are two, and three,

For one no number is: but thence doth flow
The powerfull race of number. Next did go   340
A noble Matron that did spinning beare
A huswifes rock and spindle, and did weare
A Weathers skin, with all the snowy fleece,
To intimate that even the daintiest peece,
And noblest borne dame should industrious bee:
That which does good disgraceth no degree.
   And now to *Junos* Temple they are come,
Where her grave Priest stood in the mariage rome.
On his right arme did hang a skarlet vaile,
And from his shoulders to the ground did traile,   350
On either side, Ribands of white and blew;
With the red vaile he hid the bashfull hew
Of the chast Bride, to shew the modest shame,
In coupling with a man should grace a dame.
Then tooke he the disparent Silks, and tide
The Lovers by the wasts, and side to side,
In token that thereafter they must binde
In one selfe sacred knot each others minde.
Before them on an Altar he presented
Both fire and water: which was first invented,   360
Since to ingenerate every humane creature,
And every other birth produ'st by Nature,
Moysture and heate must mixe: so man and wife
For humane race must joyne in Nuptiall life.
Then one of *Junos* Birds, the painted Jay,
He sacrifisde, and tooke the gall away.
All which he did behinde the Altar throw,
In signe no bitternes of hate should grow
Twixt maried loves, nor any least disdaine.
Nothing they spake, for twas esteemd too plaine   370
For the most silken mildnes of a maid,
To let a publique audience heare it said
She boldly tooke the man: and so respected
Was bashfulnes in *Athens*: it erected

*353 the modest shame] *stet* Q 2–10

489

To chast *Agneia*, which is Shamefastnesse,
A sacred Temple, holding her a Goddesse.
And now to Feasts, Masks, and triumphant showes,
The shining troupes returnd, even till earths throwes
Brought forth with joy the thickest part of night,
When the sweet Nuptiall song that usde to cite   380
All to their rest, was by *Phemonœ* sung:
First *Delphian* Prophetesse, whose graces sprung
Out of the *Muses* well, she sung before
The Bride into her chamber: at which dore
A Matron and a Torch-bearer did stand;
A painted box of Confits in her hand
The Matron held, and so did other some
That compast round the honourd Nuptiall rome.
The custome was that every maid did weare,
During her maidenhead, a silken Sphere   390
About her waste, above her inmost weede,
Knit with *Minervas* knot, and that was freede
By the faire Bridegrome on the mariage night,
With many ceremonies of delight:
And yet eternisde *Hymens* tender Bride,
To suffer it dissolv'd so sweetly cride,
The maids that heard, so lov'd, and did adore her,
They wisht with all their hearts to suffer for her.
So had the Matrons, that with Confits stood
About the chamber, such affectionate blood,   400
And so true feeling of her harmeles paines,
That every one a showre of Confits raines.
For which the Brideyouths scrambling on the ground,
In noyse of that sweet haile her cryes were drownd.
And thus blest *Hymen* joyde his gracious Bride,
And for his joy was after deifide.
    The Saffron mirror by which *Phœbus* love,
 Greene *Tellus* decks her, now he held above
The clowdy mountaines: and the noble maide,

Sharp-visag'd *Adolesche*, that was straide　　　　　　410
Out of her way, in hasting with her newes,
Not till this houre th'*Athenian* turrets viewes:
And now brought home by guides, she heard by all
That her long kept occurrents would be stale,
And how faire *Hymens* honors did excell
For those rare newes, which she came short to tell.
To heare her deare tongue robd of such a joy,
Made the well-spoken Nymph take such a toy,
That downe she sunke: when lightning from above,
Shrunk her leane body, and for meere free love,　　　　420
Turnd her into the pied-plum'd *Psittacus*,
That now the Parrat is surnam'd by us,
Who still with counterfeit confusion prates,
Nought but newes common to the commonst mates.
This tolde, strange *Teras* toucht her Lute and sung
This dittie, that the Torchie evening sprung.

Epithalamion Teratos.

Come come deare night, Loves Mart of kisses,
Sweet close of his ambitious line,
The fruitfull summer of his blisses,
Loves glorie doth in darknes shine.　　　　　　430
O come soft rest of Cares, come night,
Come naked vertues only tire,
The reaped harvest of the light,
Bound up in sheaves of sacred fire.
　　Love cals to warre,
　　Sighs his Alarmes,
　　Lips his swords are,
　　The field his Armes.
Come Night and lay thy velvet hand
On glorious Dayes outfacing face;　　　　　　440
And all thy crouned flames command,
For Torches to our Nuptiall grace.
　　Love cals to warre,
　　Sighs his Alarmes,

Lips his swords are,
The field his Armes.
No neede have we of factious Day,
To cast in envie of thy peace,
Her bals of Discord in thy way:
Here beauties day doth never cease,   450
Day is abstracted here,
And varied in a triple sphere.
Hero, Alcmane, Mya, so outshine thee,
Ere thou come here let *Thetis* thrice refine thee.

   Love cals to warre,
   Sighs his Alarmes,
   Lips his swords are,
   The field his Armes.
The Evening starre I see:
Rise youths, the Evening starre   460
Helps Love to summon warre,
Both now imbracing bee.
Rise youths, Loves right claims more then banquets, rise.
Now the bright Marygolds that deck the skies,
Phœbus celestiall flowrs, that (contrarie
To his flowers here) ope when he shuts his eie,
And shut when he doth open, crowne your sports:
Now love in night, and night in love exhorts
Courtship and Dances: All your parts employ,
And suite nights rich expansure with your joy,   470
Love paints his longings in sweet virgins eyes:
Rise youths, Loves right claims more then banquets, rise.
Rise virgins, let fayre Nuptiall loves enfolde
Your fruitles breasts: the maidenheads ye holde
Are not your owne alone, but parted are;
Part in disposing them your Parents share,
And that a third part is: so must ye save
Your loves a third, and you your thirds must have.
Love paints his longings in sweet virgins eyes:

463 right] *i.e.*, rite   Q2-10
467 shut] Broughton MS, Dyce; shuts

Rise youths, Loves right claims more then banquets, rise.   480

Herewith the amorous spirit that was so kinde
To *Teras* haire, and combd it downe with winde,
Still as it Comet-like brake from her braine,
Would needes have *Teras* gone, and did refraine
To blow it downe: which staring up, dismaid
The timorous feast, and she no longer staid:
But bowing to the Bridegrome and the Bride,
Did like a shooting exhalation glide
Out of their sights: the turning of her back
Made them all shrieke, it lookt so ghastly black.   490
O haples *Hero*, that most haples clowde,
Thy soone-succeeding Tragedie foreshowde.
Thus all the Nuptiall crew to joyes depart,
But much-wrongd *Hero* stood Hels blackest dart:
Whose wound because I grieve so to display,
I use digressions thus t'encrease the day.

The end of the fift Sestyad.

THE ARGUMENT OF THE SIXT SESTYAD.

Leucote *flyes to all the windes,*
And from the fates their outrage bindes,
That Hero *and her love may meete.*
Leander (*with* Loves *compleate Fleete*
Mand in himselfe) puts forth to Seas,
When straight the ruthles Destinies,
With Ate *stirre the windes to warre*
Upon the Hellespont: *Their jarre*
Drownes poore Leander. Heros *eyes*
Wet witnesses of his surprise,   10
Her Torch blowne out: Griefe casts her downe
Upon her love, and both doth drowne.
In whose just ruth the God of Seas
*Transformes them to th'*Acanthides.

485 staring up] *i.e.*, starting up (*see* II.200)

No longer could the day nor Destinies
Delay the night, who now did frowning rise
Into her Throne; and at her humorous brests,
Visions and Dreames lay sucking: all mens rests
Fell like the mists of death upon their eyes,
Dayes too long darts so kild their faculties.
The windes yet, like the flowrs to cease began:
For bright *Leucote, Venus* whitest Swan,
That held sweet *Hero* deare, spread her fayre wings,
Like to a field of snow, and message brings   10
From *Venus* to the Fates, t'entreate them lay
Their charge upon the windes their rage to stay,
That the sterne battaile of the Seas might cease,
And guard *Leander* to his love in peace.
The Fates consent, (aye me dissembling Fates)
They shewd their favours to conceale their hates,
And draw *Leander* on, least Seas too hie
Should stay his too obsequious destinie:
Who like a fleering slavish Parasite,
In warping profit or a traiterous sleight,   20
Hoopes round his rotten bodie with devotes,
And pricks his descant face full of false notes,
Praysing with open throte (and othes as fowle
As his false heart) the beautie of an Owle,
Kissing his skipping hand with charmed skips,
That cannot leave, but leapes upon his lips
Like a cock-sparrow, or a shameles queane
Sharpe at a red-lipt youth, and nought doth meane
Of all his antick shewes, but doth repayre
More tender fawnes, and takes a scattred hayre   30
From his tame subjects shoulder; whips, and cals
For every thing he lacks; creepes gainst the wals
With backward humblesse, to give needles way:
Thus his false fate did with *Leander* play.
First to black *Eurus* flies the white *Leucote*,
Borne mongst the *Negros* in the *Levant* Sea,

On whose curld head the glowing Sun doth rise,⎱
And shewes the soveraigne will of Destinies, ⎬
To have him cease his blasts, and downe he lies.⎰
Next, to the fennie *Notus*, course she holds,   40
And found him leaning with his armes in folds
Upon a rock, his white hayre full of showres,
And him she chargeth by the fatall powres,
To hold in his wet cheekes his clowdie voyce.
To *Zephire* then that doth in flowres rejoyce.
To snake-foote *Boreas* next she did remove,
And found him tossing of his ravisht love,
To heate his frostie bosome hid in snow,
Who with *Leucotes* sight did cease to blow.
Thus all were still to *Heros* harts desire,   50
Who with all speede did consecrate a fire
Of flaming Gummes, and comfortable Spice,
To light her Torch, which in such curious price
She held, being object to *Leanders* sight,
That nought but fires perfum'd must give it light.
She lov'd it so, she griev'd to see it burne,
Since it would waste and soone to ashes turne:
Yet if it burnd not, twere not worth her eyes,
What made it nothing, gave it all the prize.
Sweet Torch, true Glasse of our societie;   60
What man does good, but he consumes thereby?
But thou wert lov'd for good, held high, given show:
Poore vertue loth'd for good, obscur'd, held low.
Doe good, be pinde; be deedles good, disgrast:
Unles we feede on men, we let them fast.
Yet *Hero* with these thoughts her Torch did spend.
When Bees makes waxe, Nature doth not intend
It shall be made a Torch: but we that know
The proper vertue of it make it so,
And when t'is made we light it: nor did Nature   70
Propose one life to maids, but each such creature
Makes by her soule the best of her free state,
Which without love is rude, disconsolate,

And wants Loves fire to make it milde and bright,
Till when, maids are but Torches wanting light.
Thus gainst our griefe, not cause of griefe we fight,
The right of nought is gleande, but the delight.
Up went she, but to tell how she descended,
Would God she were not dead, or my verse ended.
She was the rule of wishes, summe and end   80
For all the parts that did on love depend:
Yet cast the Torch his brightnes further forth;
But what shines neerest best, holds truest worth.
Leander did not through such tempests swim
To kisse the Torch, although it lighted him:
But all his powres in her desires awaked,
Her love and vertues cloth'd him richly naked.
Men kisse but fire that only shewes pursue,
Her Torch and *Hero*, figure shew, and vertue.

Now at opposde *Abydus* nought was heard,   90
But bleating flocks, and many a bellowing herd,
Slaine for the Nuptials, cracks of falling woods,
Blowes of broad axes, powrings out of floods.
The guiltie *Hellespont* was mixt and stainde
With bloodie Torrents, that the shambles raind;
Not arguments of feast, but shewes that bled,
Foretelling that red night that followed.
More blood was spilt, more honors were addrest,
Then could have graced any happie feast.
Rich banquets, triumphs, every pomp employes ⎫   100
His sumptuous hand: no misers nuptiall joyes. ⎬
Ayre felt continuall thunder with the noyse, ⎭
Made in the generall mariage violence:
And no man knew the cause of this expence,
But the two haples Lords, *Leanders* Sire,
And poore *Leander*, poorest where the fire
Of credulous love made him most rich surmisde.
As short was he of that himselfe he prisde,
As is an emptie Gallant full of forme,
That thinks each looke an act, each drop a storme,   110

That fals from his brave breathings; most brought up
In our *Metropolis*, and hath his cup
Brought after him to feasts; and much Palme beares,
For his rare judgement in th'attire he weares;
Hath seene the hot Low Countries, not their heat,
Observes their rampires and their buildings yet.
And for your sweet discourse with mouthes is heard
Giving instructions with his very beard.
Hath gone with an Ambassadour, and been
A great mans mate in travailing, even to *Rhene*,   120
And then puts all his worth in such a face,
As he saw brave men make, and strives for grace
To get his newes forth; as when you descrie
A ship with all her sayle contends to flie
Out of the narrow *Thames* with windes unapt,
Now crosseth here, then there, then this way rapt,
And then hath one point reacht; then alters all,
And to another crooked reach doth fall
Of halfe a burdbolts shoote; keeping more coyle,
Then if she danst upon the Oceans toyle: 130
So serious is his trifling companie,
In all his swelling ship of vacantrie.
And so short of himselfe in his high thought,
Was our *Leander* in his fortunes brought,
And in his fort of love that he thought won.
But otherwise he skornes comparison.
    O sweet *Leander*, thy large worth I hide
In a short grave; ill favour stormes must chide
Thy sacred favour; I, in floods of inck
Must drowne thy graces, which white papers drink,   140
Even as thy beauties did the foule black Seas:
I must describe the hell of thy disease,
That heaven did merit: yet I needes must see
Our painted fooles and cockhorse Pessantrie
Still still usurp, with long lives, loves, and lust,
The seates of vertue, cutting short as dust

142 disease] *i.e.*, dis-ease, *or* absence of ease

Her deare bought issue; ill, to worse converts,
And tramples in the blood of all deserts.
   Night close and silent now goes fast before
The Captaines and their souldiers to the shore,   150
On whom attended the appointed Fleete
At *Sestus* Bay, that should *Leander* meete.
Who fainde he in another ship would passe:
Which must not be, for no one meane there was
To get his love home, but the course he tooke.
Forth did his beautie for his beautie looke,
And saw her through her Torch, as you beholde
Sometimes within the Sunne, a face of golde,
Form'd in strong thoughts, by that traditions force,
That saies a God sits there and guides his course.   160
His sister was with him, to whom he shewd
His guide by Sea: and sayd; Oft have you viewd
In one heaven many starres, but never yet
In one starre many heavens till now were met.
See lovely sister, see, now *Hero* shines
No heaven but her appeares: each star repines,
And all are clad in clowdes, as if they mournd,
To be by influence of Earth out-burnd.
Yet doth she shine, and teacheth vertues traine,
Still to be constant in Hels blackest raigne: 170
Though even the gods themselves do so entreat them
As they did hate, and Earth as she would eate them.
   Off went his silken robe, and in he leapt;
Whom the kinde waves so licorously cleapt,
Thickning for haste one in another so,
To kisse his skin, that he might almost go
To *Heros* Towre, had that kind minuit lasted.
But now the cruell fates with *Ate* hasted
To all the windes, and made them battaile fight
Upon the *Hellespont*, for eithers right   180
Pretended to the windie monarchie.
And forth they brake, the Seas mixt with the skie,
And tost distrest *Leander*, being in hell,

As high as heaven; Blisse not in height doth dwell.
The Destinies sate dancing on the waves,
To see the glorious windes with mutuall braves
Consume each other: O true glasse to see,
How ruinous ambitious Statists bee
To their owne glories! Poore *Leander* cried
For help to Sea-borne *Venus*; she denied: 190
To *Boreas*, that for his *Atthæas* sake,
He would some pittie on his *Hero* take,
And for his owne loves sake, on his desires:
But Glorie never blowes cold Pitties fires.
Then calde he *Neptune*, who through all the noise,
Knew with affright his wrackt *Leanders* voice:
And up he rose, for haste his forehead hit
Gainst heavens hard Christall; his proud waves he smit
With his forkt scepter, that could not obay,
Much greater powers then *Neptunes* gave them sway.   200
They lov'd *Leander* so, in groanes they brake
When they came neere him; and such space did take
Twixt one another, loth to issue on,
That in their shallow furrowes earth was shone,
And the poore lover tooke a little breath:
But the curst Fates sate spinning of his death
On every wave, and with the servile windes
Tumbled them on him: And now *Hero* findes
By that she felt, her deare *Leanders* state.
She wept and prayed for him to every fate,   210
And every winde that whipt her with her haire
About the face, she kist and spake it faire,
Kneeld to it, gave it drinke out of her eyes
To quench his thirst: but still their cruelties
Even her poore Torch envied, and rudely beate
The bating flame from that deare foode it eate:
Deare, for it nourisht her *Leanders* life,
Which with her robe she rescude from their strife:
But silke too soft was, such hard hearts to breake,

204 shone] *i.e.*, shown

And she deare soule, even as her silke, faint, weake,   220
Could not preserve it: out, O out it went.
Leander still cald *Neptune*, that now rent
His brackish curles, and tore his wrinckled face ⎫
Where teares in billowes did each other chace, ⎬
And (burst with ruth) he hurld his marble Mace ⎭
At the sterne Fates: it wounded *Lachesis*
That drew *Leanders* thread, and could not misse
The thread it selfe, as it her hand did hit,
But smote it full and quite did sunder it.
The more kinde *Neptune* rag'd, the more he raste   230
His loves lives fort, and kild as he embraste.
Anger doth still his owne mishap encrease;
If any comfort live, it is in peace.
O theevish Fates, to let Blood, Flesh, and Sence ⎫
Build two fayre Temples for their Excellence,   ⎬
To rob it with a poysoned influence.   ⎭
Though soules gifts starve, the bodies are held dear
In ugliest things; Sence-sport preserves a Beare.
But here nought serves our turnes; O heaven and earth,
How most most wretched is our humane birth?   240
And now did all the tyrannous crew depart,   ⎫
Knowing there was a storme in *Heros* hart, · ⎬
Greater then they could make, and skornd their smart.⎭
She bowd her selfe so low out of her Towre,
That wonder twas she fell not ere her howre,
With searching the lamenting waves for him;
Like a poore Snayle, her gentle supple lim
Hung on her Turrets top so most downe right,
As she would dive beneath the darknes quite,
To finde her Jewell; Jewell, her *Leander*,   250
A name of all earths Jewels pleasde not her,
Like his deare name: *Leander*, still my choice,
Come nought but my *Leander*; O my voice
Turne to *Leander*: hence-forth be all sounds,
Accents, and phrases that shew all griefes wounds,
Analisde in *Leander*. O black change!
Trumpets doe you with thunder of your clange,

Drive out this changes horror, my voyce faints:
Where all joy was, now shrieke out all complaints.
Thus cryed she, for her mixed soule could tell　　　　　260
Her love was dead: And when the morning fell
Prostrate upon the weeping earth for woe,
Blushes that bled out of her cheekes did show,
Leander brought by *Neptune*, brusde and torne
With Citties ruines he to Rocks had worne,
To filthie usering Rocks that would have blood,
Though they could get of him no other good.
She saw him, and the sight was much much more,
Then might have serv'd to kill her; should her store
Of giant sorrowes speake? Burst, dye, bleede,　　　　　270
And leave poore plaints to us that shall succeede.
She fell on her loves bosome, hugg'd it fast,
And with *Leanders* name she breath'd her last.

　Neptune for pittie in his armes did take them,
Flung them into the ayre, and did awake them
Like two sweet birds surnam'd th'*Acanthides*,
Which we call Thistle-warps, that neere no Seas
Dare ever come, but still in couples flie,
And feede on Thistle tops, to testifie
The hardnes of their first life in their last:　　　　　280
The first in thornes of love, and sorrowes past.
And so most beautifull their colours show,
As none (so little) like them: her sad brow
A sable velvet feather covers quite,
Even like the forehead cloths that in the night,
Or when they sorrow, Ladies use to weare:
Their wings blew, red and yellow mixt appeare,
Colours, that as we construe colours paint
Their states to life; the yellow shewes their saint,
The devill *Venus*, left them; blew their truth,　　　　　290
The red and black, ensignes of death and ruth.
And this true honor from their love-deaths sprung,
They were the first that ever Poet sung.

FINIS.

265 he] *i.e.,* Nepture　　　　　*290 devill] *stet* Q2

TEXTUAL NOTES

I

477 in aspiring]   With the exception of Tucker Brooke and Bartlett, both of whom treat the text conservatively, editors have followed Singer's emendation of Q 2–10 'in aspiring' to 'inaspiring'. In the Methuen edition Martin (in a note approved by the Revels editor) states that '"Inaspiring" means unambitious as to gold, or other material things, or "Honour".' There is difficulty in accepting this interpretation, particularly its latter part. 'Honours chaire' of line 475 is highly desirable in the context since it is where the poets should sit, not '*Midas* brood'. Secondly, 'aspire' is or ought to be a good word, suitable for poets, if these are the fruitful wits, or for intelligent and learned men (if the reference to poets has been concluded). Because of its association with *upward* desire, it would be an odd word to limit solely to ambitions to make money, as Martin proposes, with the further difficulty that no noun is present which 'inaspiring' can modify grammatically or to which it can relate. Martin accepts 'Honors chaire' as the noun, apparently, but this would seem to be impossible. The final difficulty, although not an insuperable one, is that *O.E.D.* lists no occurrence of a word 'inaspiring' and, more significantly 'un-aspiring' does not appear before 1729. The interaction of these difficulties may lead to a re-examination of the case for the original reading 'in 'aspiring. *O.E.D.* lists as a meaning for *aspiration* that of a 'steadfast, upward desire, longing'. If we take the syntax to unravel to *wits that are fruitful in aspiring*, the proper connotations of the word are preserved, the original reading is vindicated, and we will not foist as an emendation a new word on the *O.E.D.* The strain is, in fact, less than trying to find a grammatical object other than 'Honors chaire' for the wits' inaspiration. See Chapman's III.155–6 for something of the same rhetorical device.

II

187 throw]   Q 2–10 'threw' seems to be a compositorial *e:o* confusion or else a sophistication to bring the word into a false parallel structure with the verb 'turnd' of the preceding line. The parallel structure, actually goes back to 'would he slide' of line 184, with the would' thereupon understood before 'steale', 'run out', 'daunce', 'cast', 'throw', 'dive', 'prie', and 'swim'. Dyce's emendation is a sound one.

195 so kind]   The line is deficient and something has dropped out, else this would be the only tetrameter in the Marlowe section. Tucker Brooke, Bartlett and MacLure decline to emend, but all other editors have taken the path of least resistance and have accepted the Q 9 alteration of 'lovely fair' (some prefer Q 10 'lovely, fair'). Martin notes 'lovely faire' in I.45 and quotes the same phrase from *Salmacis and Hermaphroditus* (1602). The Q 9 emendation can have no authority, of course, and may well have been drawn from I.45; in turn the *Salmacis and Hermaphroditus* phrase may come from the same source even though it is applied, as in line 195, to a

boy. If one starts from scratch, the simplest emendation, and the most natural, is to suppose that by memorial failure the compositor did not repeat 'so' before 'kind', an emendation made by the first editor Brydges but overlooked subsequently.

200 up-staring]   The Q5 modernization 'upstarting' has had some attraction for editors. The *O.E.D.* lists *upstaring* as a form of *upstarting* but only for hair standing on end, and in that sense 'staring up' is used by Chapman in V.485. This must be the meaning here, and the old form should be retained.

320 glymse]   This is not an error for *glimps'd* but as Brydges originally saw when he modernized to 'gleams', or as MacLure by normalizing to 'glims', it is an old form of *gleams*. To *glimpse* twilight through an orient cloud makes nonsense.

330 days]   A natural reluctance to tinker with what might be obscure Elizabethan grammar has led all editors but Broughton (in his notes on Robinson) and MacLure to retain Q2–10 'day'; but the grammar is indeed too obscure to credit. The omission of a final *s* through misreading or memorial failure is an easy compositorial error. It should be the day's car, then, that bears the brightness of the sun.

III

0.6 *improving*]   Martin points out the error in emending to *reprove* Chapman's Latinism, meaning *censuring, blaming*, from 'improbare', to disapprove, condemn.

167 his]   That Hero had a living father is shown by the only reference to him, in III.233, 'She mus'd how she could looke upon her Sire'; and from VI.104–6 it is clear that this father was not aware of the stratagem to transport Hero, or indeed that his daughter was in love with Leander. Dyce's emendation of 'his' for Q2–10 'her' (first proposed by Broughton) is required.

173 *of*]   The emendation to '*on*', first made in Q8 but adopted by most editors, is a sophistication according to *O.E.D.* which lists *look of* as a confusion of *look on*.

257 her selfe;]   The MacLure (Revels) silent emendation removing any punctuation after 'selfe' is tempting but nevertheless seems to represent a sophistication of the syntax. A comma in Q2 after 'selfe' might be taken for a formal caesural pause, but a semicolon is another matter, regardless of whether such a point might or might not have been in the manuscript. 'Glad to disclaime her selfe' requires some subject, which is not present if lines 257 and 258 are only one unit. If, on the other hand, the subject is 'she' in lines 253 and 254, then 'Glad to disclaime herself' (*O.E.D.*: 'refuse to acknowledge oneself to be') is in parallel structure with 'proud of an Art' and both depend upon 'To make a perfect mettall counterfeit', with *to be* (understood) parallel with 'To' of 'To make'. Martin's paraphrase remains the best interpretation: 'It would be a silly device also to take pleasure in concealing her own feelings, in disclaiming her true state, or to take pride in an art that makes the face give a lying account of the heart's condition.'

IV

0.14 s.n. *or*] In the only two preserved copies of Q2, the side note is partly trimmed off. In the Huntington copy, where slightly more is preserved than in BM, only a dot remains of the '*E*' of '*Erunosis*', marking the tip of the serif of its upper cross-bar, and only a portion of the second upright of the '*m*' in the divided '*Dissi-|mula-tion*' can be seen. This means that the '*D*' of '*Dissi-*' is indented to come under the '*u*' of '*Eronusis*'. But in every other side note on the verso of a page, as here, the types are set flush to the left margin; and it is significant that in the Huntington copy a dot of inked type at the right height for the tip of an '*r*' can be seen. A precise analogy is afforded in the Huntington copy in the side note to IV.290, on a verso, where '*of Dissi-*' is the line but only part of the stroke of the '*f*' is preserved from the trimming. Since the type would be set in the side note at 0.14 to the flush left margin, something must be present before '*Dissi-*', as indicated by the dot of ink, and it is presumably a missing '*or*'.

V

207 Inggl'd] Only the conservative Tucker Brooke and Bartlett have reproduced here correct Q2 'Inggl'd', all other editors following the unauthoritative Q3 'Iuggl'd', or *Juggl'd*. But Q2 does not have a turned 'u', and 'Juggl'd' makes little or no sense. Proteus has long *wheedled* or *coaxed* Cupid with gifts 'To win Loves stay with him', as in the *O.E.D.* definition of *to ingle*.

353 the modest shame] Although no editor has suggested it, some small temptation exists to speculate that 'the' should be 'that' to be in parallel structure with the next detail of the silks tied about the lovers' waists 'In token that thereafter they must binde' *etc.* The confusion of 'yᵗ' and 'yᵉ' in manuscript is an easy one. However, emendation is not necessary to straighten out the text, for one may readily supply 'that' or 'which' in the next line before 'should grace' in order to secure desirable syntax.

396 cride,] All editors have followed the Q2–10 full stop after 'cride' although Dyce, Cunningham, Bullen and Martin, conscious of something being wrong, altered the syntax by adding a comma after 'so' in 'so sweetly cride' to give 'so' the sense of 'thus' associated with 'dissolv'd' instead of modifying 'sweetly'. This expedient does violence to the natural meaning and in an uncharacteristic manner forces the caesura to follow a weak-accented monosyllable, very difficult to read. In addition this emendation destroys the natural parallelism between 'so sweetly cride' and 'so lov'd'. These are too great penalties to avoid the simple change of the full stop after 'cride' to a comma, a necessity amply illustrated elsewhere in the poem in the Emendations in the Accidentals appendix. If the Q2–10 lack of punctuation is respected, but the full stop after 'cride' is retained, an uncharacteristic intensive or exclamatory 'so' is forced on Chapman, to his discredit.

VI

290 devill] Q3's alteration of Q2 'devill' to 'dainty' has no authority and has been followed by no editor after Bullen except Martin, for it obscures the saint who turned out to be a devil.

EMENDATIONS OF ACCIDENTALS

First Sestiad

29 them:] Q8; ~ , Q1–7
53 *Abidus*;] ~ , Q1–10
57 allur'd] Q3; allu'rd Q1–2
65 shoulder.] ~ , Q1–4, 6–7; ~ : Q5, 8–10
70–1 men,...gods. Let] ~ ....~ , let Q1–10
72 eies,] ~ . Q1–10
86 Love] Q6; love Q1–5
93 feast.] ~ , Q1–10
134 spye.] ~ , Q1–10
142 glasse.] ~ , Q1–6; ~ : Q7–8; ~ ; Q9–10
150 cloud:] Q7; ~ , Q1–5; ~ ∧ Q6
169 stript,] ~ ∧ Q1–10
172 respect.] ~ , Q1–7; ~ ; Q9–10
184 *dissembled*.] Q4; ~ , Q1–3
186 stands.] Q5; ~ , Q1–4
191 day.)] Q8; ~ ∧) Q1–5; ~ ,) Q6–7
196 replide.] Q5; ~ , Q1–4
212 are.] Q5; ~ , Q1–4
213 her?] Q7; ~ , Q1–6

222 Loves] Q8; loves Q1–7
247 sweet∧] Q8; ~ , Q1–7
320 done.] Q8; ~ , Q1–7
329 arguments] Q2; argumsnts Q1
330 before.] ~ , Q1–10
336 thought] Q2; rhought Q1
343 him:] Q5; ~ . Q1–4
350 us,)] ~ .) Q1–10
352 day.] Q2; ~ , Q1
363 part∧] Q5; ~ , Q1–4
368 vaine.] ~ , Q1–10
377 Destinies] Q3; destinies Q1–2
416 rise:] Q8; ~ , Q1–7
428 naturallie:] ~ , Q1–10
436 *Jove*?] Q7; ~ ∧ Q1–6
439 heaven:] ~ , Q1–10
441 Cupid;] ~ , Q1–10
442, 452 *Jove*] Q2; Jove Q1
458 Emperie] Q2; Emprie Q1
459–60 not;...got,] ~ ,...~ ; Q1–3; ~ ,...~ , Q4–10

Second Sestiad

32 pais'd.)] ~ ∧) Q1–10
67 strength:] ~ , Q1–10
90 among.] Q2; ~ , Q1
94 do.] ~ , Q1–10
104 reveal'd.] ~ , Q1–10
168 *Jove*] Q3; Jove Q1–2

190 swim,] ~ . Q1–6; ~ : Q7–10
192 I.] Q5; ~ , Q1–4
290 wing,] ~ . Q1–10
298 Th'*esperides*,] ~ . Q1–10
316 appear'd,] Q6; ~ ∧ Q1–5

Chapman's Dedication

16 *honourable*] Q3; *honourble* Q2

Third Sestiad

4 flie.] ~ , Q2–10
6 became∧] Q7; ~ , Q1–6
35–6, 173–4, 231–2 *Indented in* Q2–10
43 limit∧] ~ , Q2–10

56 aspire,] ~ ∧ Q2–10
68 stelth;] *point uncertain*
113 descended.] ~ , Q2–10
178 foretell,] Q6; ~ : Q2–5

505

179 wo:] ~ , Q2–10
247 it,] Q6; ~ ∧ Q1–5
267 offence,] Q6; ~ : Q2–5
299 face,] ~ ∧ Q2–10
332 hers,...melt:] ~ :...~ , Q2–5;

~ ,...~ , Q6–10
340 *Sestian*] Sestian Q2–10
357 is] Q5; *is* Q2–4
295–6 *Indented in* Q2–10
400 sex,] ~ ∧ Q2–10

Fourth Sestiad

31–3 *brace wanting* Q2–10
35 skies,] Q6; ~ ∧ Q2–5
56–7, 62–3, 68–9 *Indented in* Q2–10
58 work,...thought∧] ~ ∧...~ , Q2–
4; ~ ,...~ , Q5–10
80 *Cynthian*] Cynthian Q2–10
121 *Arachnean*] Arachnean Q2–10
141 infinite,] Q7; ~ . Q2–6
143 knowne∧] ~ . Q2–10
189 dignities.] ~ , Q2–10
219 sacrifice∧...haire,] ~ ,...~ ∧ Q2–

10
230 Doves,] Q6; ~ . Q1–5
234 flood,] ~ ∧ Q2–10
247 sayd;] ~ , Q2–10
253 coyne,] Q6; ~ : Q2–5
254 purities:] ~ , Q2–10
300 *Cares*,] Q5; ~ ∧ Q2–4
312 deceits;] ~ , Q2–10
316 delighted,] Q6; ~ . Q2–5
319–20 ended:...offended;] ~ ;...~ :
Q2–5; ~ ,...~ , Q6–10

Fifth Sestiad

0.7 *crew*,] ~ ∧ Q2–10
11 much:] ~ ∧ Q2–7; ~ , Q8–10
90.1 Teras] Q7; *Teras* Q2–6
92 Love] Q8; love Q2–7
93 was,] ~ ∧ Q2–10
121 lov'd,] Q6; ~ ; Q2–5
123 hers;] ~ , Q2–10
162 most,] ~ . Q2–10
172 crueltie∧] ~ , Q2–10
192 breaths;] ~ . Q2–4; ~ , Q5–6; ~ :
Q7–10
206, 209, 212, 213, 247, 300 Love] *Love*
Q2–10
215 spring,] ~ ∧ Q2–10
227 ²·³Love] love Q2–10
229 Loves] loves Q2–10
242 grace.] ~ , Q2–10

252 betrayd.] ~ , Q2–5; ~ ∧ Q6–10
272 bestowne:] ~ . Q2–3; ~ , Q4–10
287 *Adolesches*] Adoleshes Q2–10
291 higher,] Q7; ~ : Q2–6
291 go:] ~ , Q2–10
292 tongue,] ~ ∧ Q2–10
300 Loves] Q7; *Loves* Q2–6
315 flame] ~ , Q2–4; ~ : Q8–10
345 bee:] ~ , Q2–6; ~ . Q7–10
412–13 viewes:...guides,] ~ ,...~ :
Q2–5; ~ ,...~ , Q6; ~ ;...,
Q7–10
459 see:] ~ , Q2–10
460 youths,...starre∧] Q8; ~ ∧...~ ,
Q2–7
463, 472, 480 Loves] loves Q2–10

Sixth Sestiad

0.10 *surprise*,] ~ ∧ Q2–10
0.14 Acanthides] *Acanthides* Q2–5;
Acantides Q6–10
44 voyce.] ~ , Q2–10
74 Loves] loves Q2–10
89 figure∧] ~ , Q2–10

107 surmisde.] ~ , Q2–10
114 weares;] ~ , Q2–10
117 heard∧] ~ , Q2–10
125 *Thames*] Thames Q2–10
134–5 brought,...won.] ~ ....~ ,
Q2–7; ~ ,...~ , Q8–10

162 sayd; Q7; ~ , Q2–6

190 denied:] ~ ₐ Q2–6, 8–10; ~ , Q7

200 sway.] ~ , Q2–10

209 felt,] ~ ₐ Q2–10

209 state.] ~ , Q2–6; ~ ; Q7–10

226 Fates:] ~ , Q2–10

264 torneₐ] Q6; ~ , Q2–5

275 themₐ] ~ . Q2–10

281 past.] ~ , Q2–10

291 ruth.] Q3; ~ , Q2

HISTORICAL COLLATION

[The following editions are herein collated. Q1 (Blount, 1598; Marlowe alone); Q2 (Linley, 1598, with Chapman); Q3 (1600); Q4 (1606); Q5 (1609); Q6 (1613); Q7 (1617); Q8 (1622); Q9 (1629); Q10 (1637); Bs (*Restituta*, ed. Sir Egerton Brydges, vol. II, 1815); S (*Select English Poets*, ed. Singer, no. VIII, 1821); R (*Works*, ed. Robinson, 1826); D¹ (*Works*, ed. Dyce, 1858); D² (*Works*, ed. Dyce, 1858); C (*Works*, ed. Cunningham, 1878); B (*Works*, ed. Bullen, 1885); TB (*Works*, ed. Tucker Brooke, 1910;) M (*Poems*, ed. Martin, Methuen, 1931); Bt (*Poems of Chapman*, ed. Bartlett, 1941); Rv (*Poems*, ed. MacLure, Revels, 1968). Reference is made to EP (passages quoted in *Englands Parnassus*, 1600), and to Bv (passages in Bodenham's *Belvedere*, 1600); to Mal MS (Malone's notes in Bodleian Q3; to Br MS (Broughton's notes and queries in the BM copy of Robinson); and Coll MS (Collier's notes and queries in the BM copy of Dyce¹).]

Dedication

0–24 *Omit* R
1 *not*] *omit* Q7–10
3 *ever*] *omit* Q10
5 *farther*] *other* Q9–10
7 *effecting*] *affecting* Q3–4, Bs, S
9 *an*] *omit* C
9 *unhappily*] *unhappy* Q4–10, Bs, S
10 *that*] *omit* Q8–10

10 *his*] *his that* Q8
13 *dead, but*] *dead, that* Q3–10, Bs–B
16 *thereunto*] *thereto* Q6–10
19 *hands*] *hand* Q10
19 *a*] *omit* Q10
21–2 *offring...and ever*] *omit* Bs
24 Edward Blunt.] E. B. Q2–10, Bs, S

First Sestiad

0–0.6 *Omit* Q1
0.1 *Loves*] *Love* Q6–10, D–B
3 Seaborderers] Seaborders Q1–8, Bs
4 the other] th'other Q8–10, Bs
4 hight] height Q10
9 were] was S, W, R
10 lining] linnen Q10
11 bordered] borderered Q6
17 ware] wore Q10, Bs
23 there] these Bs
31 Buskins] Buskets Bs
38 strooken] stricken Bs–R
40 his] her Q6–7
44 rockt] rocke Q3–10, Bs–B (C, B *qy* rockt)
54 make] may Q3–9, Bs–R
55 dangling] dandling Q7–10; daughter's Bs

72 sings] must sing Q6–10
73 Those] These Q6–10
94 wandring] wandred Q4–10, Bs–R
103 above₍ₐ₎] ~ , Q1
103 loveliest,] ~ ₍ₐ₎ Q1–10, Bt, Rv
107 Nor] Not EP, Bs
108 draw] drew Q10
108 thirling] thirsting EP, whirling Bs–R
119 And] Like EP
119 furie] a furie Q4–5
119 of a] of Q4–6
133 where] were Q1
137 carved...o'rehead] carv'd...overhead Q2–10, EP, Bs–D; carved...overhead C, B; carv'd...o'rehead Rv
139 Where by] Whereby Q8

144 incest] incests EP, BS, B

145 know, that] *omit* EP

145 floure] flowre *or* flower Q3–10, EP, Bs, S (*qy* floor), R; (flour D, C, B (*noting* floor)

151 heaving] having EP

152 Which] With EP

153 townes] fiers EP

159 Vaild] Taild Q2–10, Bs; Kneel'd S–R, Coll MS

159 vailing] veiling Bs–B

174 our] the EP

179 heare] beare Q10

180 those] these Q10

180 somewhat] something Q9–10

182 more] more wore Q3

184 *grounded*] *ground* Q10

187 while...signs] whiles...sights EP

189 *Omit* Q3–10, Bs–B

190 and] *omit* EP

204 behaviour] behaviours Q6–8

227 to] no Q4

230 harshly] quickly EP, Bs–R

232 betwixt] betweene EP, Q10

233 mold] earth EP

234 like] little EP

242 Lone] Loue Q2–3

243 sinnes] since Q2–4, Bs

246 disceasse] disease Q10

258 never-singling] never-singing R

259–60 drinke...Thinke] drinkes... Thinkes EP

260 farre excels...earthly] faire, exceeds ...other EP

261 neat] sweet Q10

261 wine] meate nere EP; wines Bs–R

262 albeit] al be EP

265 stampes] stampe EP

266 impression] impressions Q10

287 aye] ah Bs–R

294 mad'st thou] thou mad'st Q10

296 tralucent] translucent Bs–R

301 -revell] revelling EP

304 hast] hath Q5

305 and] of Coll MS

312 put] but Bs–R

312 thereby] then by C (*qy*)

326 delight,ₐ] ~ , Q1

326 nice] wise EP

327 richest] ripest EP

328 warily] early EP

329 many] may Q3

335 evilly] idly Bs

339 Aye] Ah Bs–R, C

347 on] upon Q10

353 beares] keepes Q10

358 *thither*] *hither* Q9–10

370 above] about D¹ (*qy*), D²

371 he] be B

373 strooken] stricken S–R

377 towards] toward Q9

389 pearle] pearles Q10

400 a hillocke] the hillocke Q3–10, Bs–R

404–11 *omit* Bs

406 in] on Q9–10, S–R

418 left] let B

420 pleasure] pleasures Q2–6, C, B

439 thrusts] thrust R

447 deadly fatall] fatall deadly Q10

448 threads] thread Bs–R

449 his] this Q5

456 began] begun Bs–R

457 lust] and lust Bs–B

461 recklesse] rechlesse Q5–10

465 but that] that but Q9–10

477 in aspiring] inaspiring S–C, M, Rv; high-aspiring B (*qy*)

479 lords] Lord Q7

484.1 *The...Sestyad.*] *omit* Q1

Second Sestiad

0–0.8 *Omit* Q1

3 life] *omit* R

17 lock'd] locke Q9–10

20 the pointed] th'appointed Bs–R

30 affections] like affections Q9–10, Bs–B

51 Like] Liks Q5

55 you] ye Q6–7

68 pleasing] pleasant Q3

71 he crav'd] he'd crave Bs–R; he crave D², C, B

73–6 *Omit* Bs

84 that] what Bs–R
85 being] been Q6–10
86 T'is] This Q10
86 for] *omit* Bs
87 steeds] steede EP
94 use] usde Q3
100 downeward] downewards Q9–10
103 what] when Q10
113 incorporeal] incorporall Q2–3
115 wind] windes Q10
118 aire] heir M
126 sweetly] quickly Q10
126 t'is] it's Q5–10
128 it cherisht] it's cherisht EP
131 but gods have power] have power
    but gods Q6–10
143 the] his Bs–R
161 groves] growes Q6–7
162 sported] spotted Q6–7
164 shipwracke] shipwrackt Q9–10, Bs,
    C
176 backe] up Bs
181 clapt] claps Q9–10
181 plumpe] plumpt Q8–9; plumpts
    Q10
182 bewrayd] betray'd Bs–R
184 would he] he would Bs–R
187 throw] threw Q1–10, Bs–R, Bt, Rv
191 talke] talkt Q3
195 faire] lovely fair Qx, D, C, B, M;
    lovely, faire Q10, S, R
195 so kind] kind Q1–10, S–Rv
200 up-staring] upstarting Q5–10, S, R,
    M
201 thence. Ere...done,] thence, ere...
    done. Q8–10
201 this] his Q7–10, Bs–R
204 radiant] raiant Q2–3
215 which] that Bs–R
215 brests] thoughts EP
225 Tis] It's Bv

242 those] whose Q10
246 Through] Though Q2–3
247 pittie] pitty's Bs–R
257 drooping] dropping Q8–10
260 sallow] shallow Q9–10
267 now] *omit* Q10
269 ever] ever after Q6–8
270 dainties] daintie Q6–7
272 foe-man] foe-men Q5–10
274 lines] lives Q2–3
277 *Sysiphus*] *Lysiphus* Q9
279–300 Q1–10, Bs *order is lines* 291–
    300, 279–90; S–B *order is lines* 289–
    300, 279–88
280 thing] things Q2–3
281 he] *omit* Q10
287 pittie] mercy EP
301 she] we Q10
304 this] the Q3
305 them] then Q1–10, Bs–R
305–6 displayd...layd] display...lay
    S–B
306 others] other Q3
308 who] whom Q3
309 charily] chearily Q10
314 cling'd] clung Bs–R
316 One] And Q2–3
318 behold] be bold Q10
319 heare] haire Q8–10; air Mal MS,
    Bs–B
320 glymse] gleames Bs; glimps'd S–B,
    M; glims Rv
330 days] day Q1–10, Bs–R, TB, Bt,
    M; bright Day-bearing D, C, B
332 flaring] flaming EP, Bs
334 Dang'd] Hurld Q2–3; Ding'd Br
    MS
334.1 *Desunt nonnulla.*] *The end of the
    second Sestyad.* Q2–10, Bs–R; *omit*
    D, C, B

(Q1 *not present for the rest of the poem*)

Dedication

1–43 *Omit* Q3–10, BsC
0.2 *night-sports*] ~ , ~ Q5
0.5 *religious rites*] religiourites Q6

0.6 *improving*] reproving S–B, TB
0.11 *womans*] womens Q10; woman
    Bs–R

Third Sestiad

7 maids] made Q6–9; make Q10
15 constraining] costraining Q5
24 s.n. *Omit* Q3–10, Bs–C
24 of purpose] apurpose Q10
30 so sanctified] to sanctifie Q10
32 on] of Bt
37 that] who Q10
39 soundest] the soundest Q6, 8–10
48 dower] power Q6–10
58 life] feast Br MS
63 and actions] audacious EP, R
64 *time*] times EP
68 composde] compass'd Br MS
71 goods] good Q7–10
79 thence] hence B
85 colours] colour Q9–10
90 meere] weere TB
96 her] the Q9–10
103 she] we Q9
104 doth] doe Q8–10, S–B
105 he] she Q5–10
106 in flame] inflame Q6
108 did] hid Q6
109 When] All EP
110 the Rainbow] rainebow EP
119 she] as she Q9–10
119 all] *omit* Q9–10
123 Pentackle] pinnacle EP
134 distinguisheth] extinguisheth Q10
140 ascent] assent Q3–7, Bs
141 seates] feates EP
141 were] where Q10
144 eie] eyes EP
165 forked] forged Q10
167 his] her Q2–10, Bs–R, TB
173 *of*] *on* Q8–10, S–Rv (−D, TB)
183 thou] how Q2–10; now Bs–R, C; ho D, B
183 strangely-intellectual] ~ , ~ Q6–10
189 stood] flood Q4–6
190 flood] stood Q4–6
196 it] I Q9–10
196 light] delight Q6–10
203 stranger; was] ~ , ~ Q6, D, C, B,

M, Rv; ~ ∧ ~ , Q7–10; ~ ∧ ~; S–R
206 When] Whence Q4–5, Bs
210 embraste] imblaste Q10
213 Towers] townes Q3–10, Bs–R; town D, C, M
213 virgin] virgins Q6, 8–10
224 and] *omit* Bs
226 that that] that which Q9–10, S–R
235 For] Like EP
236 inwardlie] outwardly EP
238 In-formes] In formes EP, Q7–8, Bs; Informes Q9–10
240 he] she EP
243 tender] *omit* EP
249 Forth] For Q10
257 her selfe;] ~ ∧ Rv
259 the] his Q5–10
263 fowle] foole Q3–10, Bs–B; boorish fool Br MS
265 But] Round headed EP
265 that] *omit* EP
265 the] *omit* Q10
276 effects] affects Q9–10
278 Being] Beings Q7
278 ours,] ~ . Q7–10
294 hid] had Q3–6, 8–10
295 over head] overhead Bs
298 foulds∧...see:] ~ :...~ ∧ Q2–10±, Bs–R
298 twas] was Q6–10
307 an imitating] a penetrating S–B
312 enginous] ingenious Bs
319 her sence] the sense Q9–10
325 sprites] spirits Q3–10, Bs–M (−TB)
326 childe] crowd Bs–R
328 imbarkt] imbakt Q5
333 chid] chide Q9–10, S–B
334 the] that Q10
334 he] she Q9–10
342 delightsome] delightfull Q10
343 slick-tongde] slick't tongue Q10
346 others] other Q10
347 Takes] Take Q6–10
348 meate] meet M (*qy*)

368 joyes] joy D (*qy*), C, B
380 *things*] thing Q9–10
382 pitie_∧] ~ , Q5–10
383 This] Thus Q9–10, S–B
383 she] he Q2–10, Bs
385 Aie] Ah C
385 straight] straight Q2–10, Bs–C
386 as] *omit* Q4–7; a Q8–10, Bs–R
387 she] he Q9–10

395 *in*] *omit* EP
400 health_∧...she_∧] ~ ,...~ _∧ Q6;
  ~ ,...~ , Q7–10, S–R
403 Aye] Ah C
403 life] love Q5–10
404 had] hath Q6–8
411 t'is] it is Q10
418.1 *third*] *second* Q9–10

Fourth Sestiad

0 FOURTH] third Q9–10
0.6 *presents*] *present* Q5
0.14 Eronusis] Eronosus Q6–10
0.14 s.n. *Omit* Q3–10, Bs–B
0.14 s.n. or] *omit* TB+
1 rose] arose Q3–5, Bs
4 an] the Bs–R
15 nor] not Q6
16 chast] strange Q9–10
17 in] on D¹, C
27 most] more Q10
30 bewties] beautious Q6–10
36 for] from Q6–10
38 she] she'd S–R
38 wrought] wore Bs
61 starting] startling B
62 *They*] Thy Q6–10
62 *griefs*] *griefe* EP, Q6–10, S–C
68 *no*] *to* Br MS
69 *blowne*] *drawne* Q10
82 delights] delight Q9–10, D, C, B, M
85 that] the Q9–10, D², B
86 ye] yet Q7–10
88 drave] drue Q9–10
91 stung] flung Q6
94 At] All Bs–R
95 forkt] forke Q6–10
101 waving] wavering Q6–10
101 about] above B
117 yas] yeasty Bt
118 might] must Q8–10
119 needels] needlesse Q7–10
123 burnd] burne Q4–7; burns Bs
129 burnd] then they burnd Q8–10
129 as red] *omit* Q4–10, Bs–R
130 successe] surcease Br MS

137 loves] love Q10
141 wonders] numbers Bs–R
161 conceits] conceit Q7–10, D, C, B, M
165 ease] end Q9–10
169 *Leandrian*] *Leanders* Q9–10
172 his] her Q10
175 check] cheeke Q9–10
179 her] and Br MS
180 should] shall Q10
191 in it] in't Q7–10
196 them, still] ~ _∧ ~ , Q2–10, S–R; ~ _∧ ~ _∧ Bs
198 Excellence] Excellencie Q2–6
201 now she] she now Q10
207 thunder] thunders Bs–R
212 nor bewties] not bewties Q9
213 any] an C
213 scuse] sense Q6–10, Bs; excuse C
215 denouncements] denouncement Q9–10
218 she] they Q10
223 volley] valley Q6–10
227 pheres] pairs Bs
232 ruffoot] rough-foot Bs
232 the] a Q10
233 frowne] frownd Q2
235 Proyne] Proine up Q9–10
235 fayre] *omit* Q5–10
239 lookes] looke Q9–10
248 portends] protends Q4
252 garters] ignorance Br MS
254 Coynes] Coyne Q7–10
254 pure] impure Q9–10
255 wilt] will Q9–10, Bs–R
256 antike] antique Bs
257 make] maks Q6; makes Q7–10

259 vow worth] vow with Q3–6, Bs; now with Q7–10
264 favor] savor Q2–8, Bs, Bt
265 moanes] moane Q10
270 a] the Q9–10
270 cries] eyes Br MS
271 eies] cries Br MS
279 your] yon Q10
283 is] in Q7–10
290 s.n. *Omit* Q3–10, Bs–B
291 all set] set all Q10, S–B
295 girdled] girt Q9–10, S–B
295 painted] printed EP

296 doune] downe EP, Q5; downy Bs
298 had] did EP
299 never] ever EP
301 shinde] shone Bs
305 *Eronusis*] *Eronusius* Q10; *Eronusus* S–R
314 nor] or Q9–10, D, C, B
317 temper] tempter Q9–10
321 in] for Q10
330 *Phœbes*] *Phœbus* Q10
337 Like] Likd Q10
346 *Persean*] Persian Q2–10, Bs–B

Fifth Sestiad

0.1 *her*] *his* B
0.3 *lovers*] *loves* R
6 love] lovd Q10
7 Set] Sat Bs–R
27 Ah, nothing...with] Nothing... so full of EP; Nothing the world with greater harme doth fill Bv
28 ill] will EP
31 with] for Q10
36 maids] maide Q4–10, Bs–B
54 striv'd] strove Bs–R
56 forced] forged EP
80 their] her Q5–10
86 might] may Q10
90 she did] did she D², C, B
98 first were] were first Q9–10
101 eye] eyes Q10
104 affections] affection Q7–10, S–R
129 would] will Q10
142 prayers] prayes Q2–6; preies Q7–9; pryes Q10
146 an amorous] enamorous Q10
146 enthrald] enthrilled D, C
149 his] her Q8–10
158 when] as when EP
158 men] *omit* Q5
162 Deceiving] Deceived S (*qy*), Br MS
169 hands] hand Bs–R
173 this] the Q10
178 silken] silke Q9–10
179 the] their Q9–10
192 breaths] breath Q10
194 drinks] drinke Q6, 10
197 virgins] virgin Bs

197 mutuall] mortall Q9–10
205 bounteous] beautious Br MS
207 Inggl'd] Juggled Q3–10, Bs–Rv (−TB, Bt)
215 That] From Br MS
216 hand] hands S–B
218 it] in Q7, 9–10
220 you] she Q10
233 the tide] their tide Q7–10
241 flowde] flood Q3–6
241 the blood] *omit* Q3–10, Bs–C
241 *Eucharis*] Eucharis's Bs–C
247 valure] valour M
248 favour] valure Q7–10
265 plat] plot Q5–10, Bs–R, C
277 the most] thy most Q10
278 sort] *omit* Q10
280 folks] folke Q6–10
289 nether] neither Q2–9, Bs
296 one] on Q2–10, Bs
299 Thin] Then Bs
313 all] *omit* Q7–10
322 light.] ~ ∧ Q9–10
328 does] doe Q3–10, Bs–B
338 are two] two Q9–10
344 intimate] imitate R
345 And] The EP
346 does] doth EP
357 thereafter] hereafter Q9–10
358 others] other Q3–5, Bs–R
365 Then] The Q6–10
365 painted] pained Q4–6
368 bitternes of hate] hate of bitterness Q6–10

378 earths] earth Q3–10, Bs, D, C, B
381 *Phemonœ*] *Phemonor* Q2–10, Bs
383 *Muses*ᴧ] ~ , Q5–10, Bs; ~ : — S–R
383 well,] ~ ᴧ Q3–10, Bs–R
390 maidenhead] maidenhood M
391 above] about Q7–10
396 soᴧ] ~ , D, C, B, M
396 cride,] ~ . Q2–10, Bs–Rv
403 scrambling] scräbling Q6–8; scrab-
    ling Q9–10
404 her] their Q2–10, Bs
411 her newes] the newes Q10
412 this] his Q3–10, Bs
414 would] should Q10
416 For] Far Bs–R
421 her] *omitted* Q3–6, Bs
426 that] whilst Br MS
426.1 *Epithalamion*] *Epithalmion* Q6–
    10
428 his] this Q9–10

433 The reaped] The reapest Q6–7;
    That reapest Q8–10
440 thy] the Bs
449 Her bals] Herbals Q9–10
449 thy] the Q10
450 Here] Her Q4–10
451 abstracted] obstracte Q9–10
453 *Alcmane*] *Alemane* Q6–7; *Almaine*
    Q8–10
454 here] heare Q9
464 deck] deckt Q3–5, Bs
467 shut] shuts Q2–10, Bs–R, B, TB
471 sweet] fair Bv
474 ye] you Q9–10
476 share] are Q9–10
477 ye] you Bs–R
485 staring] starting Q9–10
494 much-wrongd] much-rongd Q3;
    much-rong Q4–7; much wrung
    Bs–C, M

Sixth Sestiad

0.2 *bindes*] *blindes* Q3–10, Bs–B
0.3 *love*] *Loves* Bs
0.7 Ate] Arte Q4–5; *Art* Q6–10;
    Arté Bs
0.7 *stirre*] doe stirre Q9–10
0.7 *warre*] wars Q10
0.8 *jarre*] jarres Q6–10
0.9 *Drownes*] *Drowne* Q7–10
0.14 Acanthides] *Acantides* Q6–10
19 fleering] fleeting Q5–10
27 or a] or Q10
32 gainst] against Q5–10
33 humblesse] humblenesse Q6–10
36 mongst] amongst Q3–10
37 head] heads D¹ (*qy*), D², B
40 she] he Bs
42 rock] rocky Q6
64 pinde] *omit but with blank space* Bs
67 makes] make Q6–10, Bs–B
68 It] I Q9–10
68 shall] should Q5–10, D, C, B
71 one] on Q4, Bs
72 Makes] Make Q10
72 free] true Q3–10, Bs–C
92 cracks] crakes Q9–10
93 powrings] powring Q10

95 Torrents] torrent Q3–10, Bs–D, C
    (*qy* torrents)
104 this] his Q9–10
108 he prisde] he surprisde Q5–7; sur-
    pris'd Q8–10; so priz'd S–B
109 is] in Q5–10
117 for] as for Q6–7
124 sayle] sailes Q10
126 here, then] here, now C
128 another] a Bs
140 drink] drin | Q3–4
141 beauties] beauty Q10
142 disease] decease S–B
147 bought] brought Q7–9
150 their] *omit* Q3–7, Bs; the Q8–10,
    S–B
151 attended] attend Q10
166 her] hers Q8–10
173 silken] silke Q7–10
190 denied:] ~ ᴧ Q3–6, 8–10, Bs; ~ ,
    Q7
192 *Hero*] hero Bs
194 fires] fire Q7
196 wrackt] rack'd Bs
200 powers] power Q10
216 bating] baiting D², B

514

221 it: out] ~ _∧ ~ , Q6–7; ~ _∧ ~ :
  Q8–10
228 hit] knit Bs
238 Sence-] hence_∧ Bs
240 most most] most Q10
248 most] much C
250 Jewell; Jewell] jewel's jewel Br MS
251 earths] earth Bs
260 mixed] vexed Br MS
270 Burst] Oh, burst D¹ (qy), Bt; No:
  burst D² (qy), C

271 plaints] plants Q3–10
275 into] in Q6–10
281 and] that Q3–10, Bs–B
282 most] much M
285 cloths] cloath Q3–10, Bs–B
286 use] us'd Q3–10, Bs–R
290 devill] dainty Q3–10, Bs–B
290 them; blew_∧] ~ _∧ ~ , Q3–10, Bs
291 The] Their Q6–10
292 this] thus Q5–10
292 -deaths] -death Q3–10, Bs–B

MISCELLANEOUS PIECES

TEXTUAL INTRODUCTION

THE PASSIONATE SHEPHERD
TO HIS LOVE

Two basic traditions of this famous lyric have come down to us. The first is a four-stanza version as printed in *The Passionate Pilgrim* (PP) of 1599 and also found in the Bodleian MS Rawl. Poet. 148, fol. 96 (Rw MS), written about 1600, in Bodleian MS Ashmole 1486, fol. 6ᵛ (A MS), and in the Rosenbach manuscript described by S. A. Tannenbaum[1] (Rs MS). In this tradition the first three stanzas that appear in every form of the poem are present in the same order, but the poem concludes with the fourth, beginning 'A belt of straw....' Enough examples of this four-stanza form exist, not obviously related to each other, to indicate that it was something of a standard version.

At the opposite pole is a seven-stanza form.[2] The three added stanzas are (*a*) 'A gowne made of the finest wooll', (*b*) 'Thy silver dishes fill'd with meat', and (*c*) a new conclusion repeating the invitation, 'The shepherds swains shall dance and sing'. Of these three the easiest to dispose of is (*b*), which first appears in the popular ballad 'The Lover's Promises to his Beloved' entered in 1603, reproduced in the *Roxburghe Ballads*, edited by William Chappell, II (1872), 1–6 (Rx) and also edited from an almost identical text of about 1620 by Charles Hindley (Rx²) in the *Roxburghe Ballads*, II (1874), 282–3. This ballad offers a six-stanza version that substitutes 'Thy silver dishes' for the stanza 'A belt of straw' (the invitation-ending of the four-stanza poem) and then concludes with (*c*) 'The shepherds swains' and thus has only one invitation. In the second

[1] 'Unfamiliar Versions of Some Elizabethan Poems', *PMLA*, XLV (1930), 814–17.
[2] One should note, of course, that no seven-stanza version seems to have existed except by accident. The 'dishes' stanza in its earliest known appearance, in the 1603 Roxburghe ballad, substituted for the 'belt of straw' verses in a six-stanza version. Walton merely lifted the 'dishes' lines from the ballad and inserted it after the fourth stanza of the six-stanza *Helicon* version, where it is intrusive but performs some slight function of separating the two invitation stanzas. The Thornborough manuscript seems to be a conglomerate.

edition of *The Compleat Angler* in 1655 (W²), Izaak Walton, probably from this same ballad, took over the new 'dishes' stanza and inserted it in the penultimate position to create seven stanzas from the six-stanza version he had printed in 1653 largely based on *Englands Helicon*. The stanza is also found in the same position in a seven-stanza version copied into the *Thornborough Commonplace Book* (T MS), the material in which dates between 1580 and 1630.[1] This latter was either derived from another manuscript or written from memory, for the third line of the 'dishes' stanza 'Shall one and everye table bee' for 'Shall on an ivory table be' exhibits handwriting misreading or acute memorial sound confusion. With fair confidence this intrusive stanza can be pronounced non-Marlovian. Its apparent source in the ballad is suspicious and the fact that Walton took it over is of no significance for its authority. As will be suggested below, its position in the *Thornborough* T MS may indicate an accretion.

One would expect expansion, such as this seventh stanza, in a popular lyric and song, especially perhaps in ballad form. The same question also arises in connection with the six-stanza form known only in *Englands Helicon* of 1600 (EH), though apparently reprinted with improvements by Walton in 1653. Another six-stanza text, that in the 1603 Roxburghe ballad, has a different selection of stanzas although it apparently has some close relationship to the *Helicon* version. The *Helicon* six-stanza form expands the four-stanza one by adding 'A gown made of the finest wool' and concluding with a second invitation, 'The shepherds swains'. An intermediate state is represented by a unique five-stanza version printed by Sir Egerton Brydges in his edition of *The Poems of Sir Walter Raleigh* (1813), which Robinson reprinted in his collected edition of Marlowe. In the Brydges edition (Bd), the 'shepherds swains' stanza is omitted, 'the gown of wool' is inserted before the last stanza, and the poem ends with the same stanza of invitation as in the four-stanza version, the 'belt of straw'.

The authority of the six-stanza *Helicon* form, but specifically of its 'shepherds swains' stanza of invitation, is not materially aided

[1] This manuscript is provided in facsimile in A. D. Wraight and V. Stern (eds), *In Search of Christopher Marlowe* (1965), p. 130.

by its appearance in the Roxburghe ballad. On the other hand, the stanza does conclude the *Thornborough* T MS seven-stanza version; but whether this manuscript is more than a compilation is an open question. In 1925 R. S. Forsythe conjectured that the original Marlowe poem was of five stanzas and that the *Helicon* editor printed both versions of a variant ending as his stanzas five and six.[1] This hypothesis has a certain attractiveness although it does not solve the problem of whether the progenitor of the well-established four-stanza texts dropped by accident the 'gown of wool' stanza. The fact that the popular reply is usually in five stanzas might be thought helpful but actually it is of no aid to a five-stanza hypothesis. Whether or not the *Helicon* editor copied a six-stanza manuscript or himself conflated two versions to provide the double ending is not to be determined. What is clear, however, is that the 'shepherds swain' stanza as it appears in the *Helicon* has some difficulties.

> The Sheepheards Swaines shall daunce and sing,
> For thy delight each May-morning,
> If these delights thy minde may move;
> Then live with mee, and be my love.

The repetition of 'delight' – 'delights' in lines 2 and 3 is clumsy but is found in all texts, whether because these ultimately derive from the *Helicon*, as the present editor believes, or whether they are independent. Some grounds might exist for the conjecture that the manuscript that was the *Helicon* copy may have partly switched the last lines of the two invitation stanzas and thereby created the repetition; but more difficulty may rest in such a hypothesis than in the original problem. One point seems evident: traditionally the last line of the poem started with 'Then', no matter in which stanza it appeared – 'Then live with me and be my love'.[2] In the four-stanza form no unanimity prevails about the penultimate line. *The Passionate Pilgrim* (PP) reads in a paraphrase of the second line of the first stanza 'And if these pleasures may thee move', which is the form (except for the variant 'can') in Brydges and in the fifth stanza

---

[1] '*The Passionate Shepherd*; and English Poetry', *PMLA*, XL (1925), 693, fn. 2*a*.
[2] An exception is the ballad and Brydges which agree in 'To' although the ballad ends with 'shepherd swains' and Brydges with 'belt of straw'. But this 'To' is a contamination from the 'Reply'.

of the *Helicon* and thus in Walton.[1] On the other hand, the four-stanza versions except for PP all agree on 'thy mind may move', which is metrically impossible for 'pleasures'. Perhaps the most authoritative form is 'And if these things thy mind may move', the reading of A MS, Rs MS, and originally of Rw MS. The latter case is interesting. The copyist first wrote 'And if these thinges thy minde may move' but then (perhaps at a later time) deleted 'And', altered 'if' to 'If', and interlined 'delights' above deleted 'thinges'. It would seem that a version with 'If these delights' came to the attention of the writer, J. Lilliat. If the alterations in the first stanza were made at the same time, it could not have been the *Helicon*, but was some unknown text. If this had been a longer text than the Rw MS four stanzas, no space was available to expand the poem.

The use of 'things' means that the line must start with 'And', whereas with 'delights' it must start with 'If'. Thus a split tradition results in the third line of the invitational 'belt of straw' stanza, whether or not it concludes the poem. Two major texts, PP and EH, joined by Bd, read 'these pleasures may thee move', but the other versions read 'these things [or 'delights'] thy mind may move'. It is easy to believe that if 'things' were the original, 'delights' was derived from the influence of 'pleasures', although perhaps drawn, instead, from the 'Reply'.

It is also not difficult to take it that one of two things may have happened if the 'shepherds swains' stanza were an unauthoritative addition like that of 'dishes'. The position of this stanza is troublesome. Since it is invariably last, it repeats the invitation without any very effective reason and with the last two lines in substantially the same terms as the preceding stanza. Since it cannot be placed anywhere else, it must have been designed from its inception either as an alternative to the 'belt of straw' stanza, or as a re-enforcement by expansion of the 'belt of straw' stanza. It would seem probable that the writer of the second invitation started with the 'belt of straw' stanza in the form of PP and EH, 'pleasures may thee move', but that he also knew of the variant 'these things thy mind may move' which provided the opportunity to avoid an exact repetition

---

[1] The evidence of Folger MS V.a.169, of about 1670, is of no value, for it is an exact copy of Walton's 1653 *Angler*.

of phrase 'may thee move'. But to take over this line verbatim from the 'belts of straw' stanza and transfer it to the 'shepherds swains' created a difficulty, for the dance does not sort itself with the gifts as 'things'. It may have been, thus, that the writer modified the line by paraphrasing 'pleasures' as 'delights' to substitute for 'things', an expedient – very likely drawn from the 'Reply' – that also avoided the repetition of 'And if' in the two stanzas. The repetition of 'delight' in the second and third lines was the penalty that was paid.[1]

If there is anything to the conjecture that the sixth *Helicon* stanza was added to a form of the poem with a final stanza identical with that in the *Passionate Pilgrim*, the case is still not demonstrable whether this was the Marlovian reading of the 'belt of straw' stanza or whether the alternative reading 'things thy minde may move' was original, probably sophisticated to 'delights' in T MS and in the altered text of Rw MS. To this problem no immediate answer is available. Two early printed versions in 1599 and 1600 read 'And if these pleasures may thee move'; one manuscript to be dated about 1600, and another less certain in date, read 'And if these things thy mind may move', three of these four being four-stanza versions. The case would appear for the moment to be a standoff.

The problem of the missing, or added, 'gown of wool' stanza, wanting in all four-stanza texts, must be faced. The evidence is insufficient for any firm decision. The stanza is certainly not unworthy of the rest of the poem, in contrast to the 'silver dishes' lines. If it were an addition, it must be earlier in its tradition than the conjectured addition of the 'shepherds swain' stanza and would represent the poem in a form such as that found in the Brydges text of unknown date and origin. The evidence of the seven-stanza *Thornborough Commonplace Book* is ambiguous. This text transposes the natural order of the fourth and fifth stanzas to place the 'gown of wool' after the 'belt of straw'. The result of this placement is that the first four stanzas of the poem have been copied in the normal order of the four-stanza tradition, with the three suspicious stanzas

---

[1] It is difficult to envisage the writer working with a version that in the 'belt of straw' stanza read 'things', not 'pleasures', for in such a case 'things' might well have been left as it was. Except for the repetition of 'And if' in the two successive stanzas, 'pleasures' in the 'swains' stanza for 'delights' would have removed the weak repetition, if 'things' had been satisfactory in the fifth stanza.

appended, first the 'gown of wool', then 'silver dishes', and finally 'shepherds swains'. The order is manifestly impossible, for the fifth stanza interrupts the narrative continuity. It is tempting to conjecture that the copyist wrote down the four-stanza poem and then added to it the extra stanzas, in arbitrary order for the fifth and sixth, from other copies that he had. The alternative would be to suppose that he had as his basic copy a five-stanza version in the form known through Brydges but arbitrarily reversed the order of its fourth and fifth stanzas to separate the two invitations as widely as possible.

We do not know the date of 'The Nimphs reply to the Sheepheard', as it is entitled in the *Helicon*. It is clear, however, that the Reply essays a point by point, and stanza by stanza, refutation, and that it was modified in turn as 'The Passionate Shepherd' itself developed. That is, in the ballad the fifth stanza of the Reply reads

What should you talke of dainties then?
Of better meate than serveth men?
All that is vaine; this onely good
Which God doth blesse and send for food.

This can refer only to the 'silver dishes' stanza that may have been an invention of the ballad-maker as a substitute for the first invitation stanza, and correspondingly it replaces the fifth stanza found in the *Helicon* Reply that matches:

Thy belt of straw and Ivie buddes,
Thy Corall claspes and Amber studdes,
All these in mee no meanes can move,
To come to thee, and be thy love.

It is, then, of some import that in the four-stanza A MS and Rs MS versions the five-stanza reply omits all reference to gowns and shoes as found in the fourth *Helicon* or third Bd stanza

Thy gownes, thy shooes, thy beds of Roses,
Thy cap, thy kirtle, and thy poesies,
Soon breake, soone wither, soone forgotten:
In follie ripe, in reason rotten.

and starts '⟨Thy belt o⟩f strawe thy beds of Roses' before continuing with the second line of the *Helicon* fourth stanza, 'Thy cap...' the *Helicon* fifth stanza being omitted.

The Reply formula consists of an equal number of stanzas with the invitation (whether four or five) in which specific mention is made of details from the invitation stanzas: pleasures in one; flowers and fields in two, still referring to stanza one; flocks, fields, rocks, and rivers in three, referring to two;[1] then in the *Helicon* form gowns, shoes, beds of roses and posies in four, referring to *Helicon* stanzas three and four; belt of straw, buds, clasps, and studs in five, referring to stanza five; and in all a concluding stanza of summary rejection with no reference to any details. In the *Helicon*:

> But could youth last, and love still breede,
> Had joyes no date, nor age no neede,
> Then these delights my minde might move,
> To live with thee, and be thy love.[2]

In short, the texts of the various Replies make it clear that the basic structure is an equal number of stanzas to whatever form of the Marlowe poem is being used – four or five stanzas – plus an appended stanza of rejection that ends

> Then these delights my mind might move
> To live with thee and be thy love.

When the four-stanza Marlowe lyric is the basis for the reply, the Reply omits, with Marlowe, references to gowns and shoes. When the six-stanza Marlowe poem is the basis, the Reply never mentions the 'shepherds swains' and their dance on a May morning but it does give glancing reference, in the Roxburghe ballad and in the Thornborough T MS, to gowns and shoes by substituting these in the same stanza for the opening words of A MS and Rs MS, 'Thy belt[s] of straw'. The *Helicon* reply is unique in its stanza five, which rather literally answers the corresponding Marlowe stanza. Since the Roxburghe ballad and the *Thornborough* T MS contain the probably spurious 'silver dishes' stanza, their Replies correspond

---

[1] The *Helicon* version transposes stanzas two and three in the Reply, an unauthoritative variation according to the other texts.

[2] This is the general text of A MS, of Rs MS, of Bd, and of the Roxburghe ballad also. It would seem that the T MS final couplet 'Theise prettie pleasures myght me move | To lyve with thee and bee thy love' has unauthoritatively been influenced to repeat the third and fourth lines of the opening stanza of the Reply and can be ignored.

in a stanza that replaces the *Helicon* fifth stanza beginning 'A belt of straw', just as the 'silver dishes' stanza in the Marlowe poem in Rx, but not in T MS, substituted for the 'belt of straw' Marlowe stanza. The conclusion is inescapable that a four-stanza Marlowe lyric was well established that gave rise to a four-stanza-plus-one Reply. At some stage the addition of the fifth, or 'gown of wool' stanza, created a variant in the fourth stanza of the Reply by which gowns and shoes substituted in its first line for 'belt of straw'. In turn, it is possible to conjecture, the ensuing absence of a reference to the details in the 'belt of straw' stanza gave rise to the feeble sixth stanza of the *Helicon* (but not the Bd) Reply, just as the addition of the 'silver dishes' promoted a corresponding stanza in its Replies in Rx and T MS. The application of the evidence of the different forms of the Reply, thus, confirms the interpretation of the evidence previously suggested. The original Marlowe lyric consisted of four stanzas and circulated in this form with a corresponding five-stanza Reply, presumably the original. At a subsequent time the 'gown of wool' stanza was added and the Replies at first merely took cognizanace of it by altering their fourth stanza but later by adding a special stanza to follow the altered fourth. The unauthoritative addition of the 'silver dishes' stanza also affected its Replies in a roughly similar fashion.

This reconstruction does not point to the authorship. The 'silver dishes' on critical grounds is unlikely to be Marlowe's; the 'gowns of wool' could be if one is prepared to accept the hypothesis that after writing a four-stanza lyric that got into circulation Marlowe then revised the poem himself by adding the fifth stanza. One must consider that the Brydges text is the only five-stanza version extant, one that omits the 'shepherd swains' stanza that in all other texts is associated with the addition of the 'gowns of wool' verses. The evidence is insufficient to argue one way or another: whether the addition of three stanzas to the basic lyric was in three or in two stages. If in two, and if the 'shepherd swains' stanza were to be associated in a single revision with 'gowns of wool', then serious doubts might be cast not alone on the authenticity of 'shepherd swains' but on any stanza associated with it. The fact is interesting that no Reply takes account of the 'shepherds swains' stanza unless by a semi-repetition of its last two lines in the invariable final couplet of the Reply

> Then these delights my mind might move,
> To live with thee and be thy love.

The present editor suggests, however, that this Reply couplet cannot be an echo of the 'shepherds swains' stanza since it appears in every Reply regardless of its form, including the four-stanza lyric and its five-stanza answer. In short, the final couplet of the Reply antedates the tradition of the 'shepherds swains' stanza. If this hypothesis be accepted, it would seem clear that an answer is provided to one of the more puzzling features of the 'swains' stanza, which is its weak repetition of 'delight' – 'delights' in lines two and three. It now seems evident that the form of the 'belt of straw' stanza in the four-stanza version that substitutes 'delights' for 'things' as in the alteration in Rw MS or in the longer T MS has no possible authority and was under the influence of the Reply that followed. Correspondingly, it is possible to argue that when the 'shepherds swains' stanza was formulated as the new conclusion, the writer took over the language of the final couplet of the traditional Reply to piece it out. Since it seems almost impossible, according to the growth of the poem, for the 'swains' stanza to have influenced the earliest form of the Reply, the inference follows that the influence was in the other direction, in which case the 'shepherds swains' stanza is not Marlowe's.

One may remark another example of the effect of the Reply on the text of the original: the substitution of 'To' for the first word of the final line in both Rx and Bd must certainly have come from the influence of the invariable Reply conclusion, 'To live with thee and be thy love'.

If in these cases of the poem's development from the four-stanza beginning the form of the Reply, while conforming to the form of the lyric, has exercised in some details a reverse influence on the original, it is proper to enquire whether such a reverse influence will explain the problem of 'pleasures may thee move' as the penultimate line of the four-stanza *Passionate Pilgrim* version and of the five-stanza Brydges text (and the invariable form when the 'belt of straw' becomes only the first of two invitations), whereas 'these things thy mind may move' seems to be firmly established in the other four-stanza versions. That is, is it possible to conjecture that PP represents the original ending but that under the influence of the Reply the phrase 'thy mind may move' got itself transferred back to the original lyric? No certain answer can be provided. It seems to be a powerful argument that the *Passionate Pilgrim* and Brydges final stanza of invitation in this important detail remains the same after a second invitation has been added in other versions. On the other hand, the force of the agreement in 'these things' in the original form of Rw MS, in A MS, and in Rs MS is not to be ignored, and 'these things' requires 'thy mind may move'. The case is far from demonstrable. It is the present editor's opinion, however, that it is more difficult to conceive of 'these pleasures' being altered to 'these things' in corrupt transmission than that original 'these things' would be altered to 'these pleasures' in order to repeat 'pleasures', from the first stanza, in the conclusion.[1] If this is so, then 'delights' was the Reply word for 'things' in the original lyric, and 'pleasures' got itself substituted first as an artificial repetition of the key word in the first stanza and then as a necessary variant in the six-stanza form when, indeed, the added 'shepherds swain' stanza did take over the Reply formula of 'these delights thy mind may move'.

Difficult and problematic as is the question of the original form and stanzaic growth of the poem, it pales in comparison with the problem of recovering with any precision the exact form of the Marlowe text from the incomplete and imperfect evidence available. One or two observations may be made. The variants have some tendency to cluster in the early half of the poem. It is not entirely true that what we may take as the added stanzas are without problems, but these do show less variation than the manifestly original stanzas. Secondly, despite the fact that its six-stanza form includes at least one and perhaps two stanzas that may not be original, the *Englands Helicon* text for the four basic stanzas may be closer to

---

[1] Just so, in the Thornborough Reply the penultimate line forsakes the 'delights thy mind may move' formula in order to repeat 'Theise prettie pleasures myght thee move' from the second line of the first stanza.

Marlowe's than any other document. Thirdly, no family tree can be drawn for the known versions. There are many signs that the Rox-burghe ballad is an adaptation of the *Helicon* text although not un-affected by at least one other version. The same may be said of Walton. In some obscure way the *Passionate Pilgrim* seems to have some connection with the ballad, or *vice versa*, through its omission of the initial word 'Come', according to the ballad advertisement 'To a sweet new tune called Live with me, and be my Love'. It would be idle speculation that the tune may initially have been the setting for the *Pilgrim* stanzas in 1599 and then the ballad expanded the text under the influence of the *Helicon* in 1600, even though such a theory is not impossible. In many respects the *Thornborough Commonplace Book* seems a compilation based on a four-stanza version; but against this view is its use of the fully expanded reply more consistent with its seven-stanza lyric, although this may come, as do some T MS lines, from the ballad. At least in the final stanza of the lyric the T MS Marlowe version shows unmistakable influence from the ballad. The extraordinary variants in the Rosenbach manu-script and in the unknown manuscript used by Brydges probably indicate late debased versions, even though of the early stage of the poem in four and five stanzas.

Here and there a few assumptions can be made. For instance, the general authority of EH in the third and fourth lines of the first stanza can probably be established. Regardless of their order, the four items – valleys, groves, hills, and fields – are found in EH, Rw MS, A MS, Rx, Bd, and W. These items are paired in contrast: hills with valleys and groves with fields. The PP substitution of 'dales' for 'groves', thus, destroys the principle of contrast and weakly repeats 'valleys'. Similarly, the T MS substitution of 'woods' (from the next line) for 'hills' removes the pairing with 'valleys' and repeats 'groves'. From these variant elements Rs MS fashions a more logical but seemingly corrupt version that contrasts hills with dales, and woods with fields.

The exact language of the statement about the four details is less easy to establish, however. The EH line 'That Vallies, groves, hills, and fields' is the only seven-syllable line in the poem, made so by the caesural pause substituting for a weak syllable, again a unique device.[1] In addition to A MS the ballad is the only text to follow EH, although the value of this testimony is negative since the musical notes adjusted to the regular iambs would need to be altered for this line. On the other hand, some evidence accumulates that EH and A MS do indeed represent the original. The easiest smoothing is performed by adding a syllable after the caesura, as in 'the hills' of Rw MS in the original inscription, or 'or hills' of Walton, or 'and woods' of T MS. The diversity of alteration does not encourage the belief that any of these choices is authoritative. More to the point, however, is to notice that the reason for a change of the order in some texts seems to be to smooth the line by putting the two-syllable 'valleys' at the caesura so that its second syllable takes the metrical place of a connective between the pairs. PP and the revised Rw MS adopt this expedient with 'hills and valleys, dales and fields' in PP or 'hills and valleys, groves and fields' in Rw MS (c), and so in Bd with 'grove or valley, hill or field'.[2] It may be suggested that the variants that alter the order to place 'valleys' at the caesural pause are motivated not only by the fancied need to regularize the metre but also by a conventional parallelism that yokes the elements of each pair with a conjunction. The hypothesis that smoothing by sophistication of the EH text has occurred here is materially aided by the similar but more clearly unauthoritative regularization of the tenth line, for which see note 1 below.

In the fourth line two problems arise. All versions but EH have the plural 'mountains'. Here one cannot demonstrate the case whether the EH singular is uniquely under the influence of the singular verb 'yields', or whether the rest have sophisticated the singular to plural in the natural desire to join a plural mountains to plural hills, fields, and valleys. It might be thought that such unanimity of sophistication would be more difficult to credit than

[1] The tenth line in EH and some versions is also a syllable short, although here the variation is of eight syllables in a nine-syllable-line stanza with feminine endings. The syllable has been removed by the conventional device of truncating the first iamb in 'And a thousand fragrant posies'. It is interesting to see that even this small irregularity provoked alteration to restore regularity; the different forms this tinkering took no doubt indicate its lack of authority: 'Drest with' A MS, 'And make' Rs MS, 'And twine' Bd, 'And then' W.

[2] Interestingly, Rs MS makes the change to start the series with 'hills' by substituting 'dales' for 'valleys' and thus reproduces the same caesural pause as in EH.

the unique sophistication of EH; but if the Rx plural here is an example (when Rx follows EH so faithfully in every other crux in the first two stanzas), the pull towards conformity was stronger than the weak grammatical disturbance. Moreover, 'mountains yields' though more euphonious than 'birds sings', is not the most musical phrase possible. There is nothing wrong with a singular mountain from which plural valleys, groves, hills, and fields are being viewed; indeed, England customarily has individual mountains not mountain ranges. With some caution, then, the EH singular may be accepted. Any misgiving is caused by the contrast between 'mountain yields' and 'birds sings' in EH, whereas one of the simpler explanations for 'birds sings' is contamination from 'mountains yields'. Yet as will be suggested below, the variant 'Where' in the second stanza may be influenced by an original singular 'mountain'. As for the second, Marlowe's characteristic 'steepy' seems to have caused some trouble. Rw MS makes it 'steepest', but a tradition developed of substituting 'craggy', as in PP, A MS, and T MS. The direction of change seems obvious here.

Except for the question of the EH and T MS singular 'sings' in the fourth line of the second stanza versus the normal plural in the rest,[1] the problem of this stanza centers on the first two lines and their related variants. Only Rx follows EH in 'And we will sit', parallel with the first line of the third stanza. The rest favor 'Where we will sit', with PP reading 'There' and Rs MS 'Then'. But the two lines must be treated as one variant, for EH and Rx 'And we... | Seeing' is contrasted with invariable 'Where... | And see'. An argument can be advanced in favor of either version. The strong trochaic thrust of 'Seeing' in EH is attractive and not uncharacteristic of the metre of this poem; but it would be particularly susceptible of smoothing to a more regular rhythm. At first sight, moreover, the 'Where' of the alternative may seem suspiciously clumsy with the plural 'mountains' as a referent. But if the plural is a sophistication and the EH singular the original, then the 'Where' is appro-

---

[1] Here there is certainly some possibility that 'sings'—although by no means impossible Elizabethan grammar – has been contaminated by 'yields' from the preceding stanza. The singular 'birds sings' is almost impossible to pronounce without an especially strong caesural pause. Almost certainly, the conventional plural is right.

priate if the reading may be taken as antedating the change from singular to plural 'mountains'. The case is a most difficult one. If a reviser objected to 'Seeing', and substituted 'And see', clearly the first line beginning 'And we' must go, in which case an artificial connection could be established between the stanzas by inventing 'Where' to point to the site. The artificiality is perhaps compounded by the continuing influence in most of these versions on the third stanza, where for EH, Rx, and W 'And I' PP, A MS, and Rs MS read 'There', Rw MS and T MS 'Where', and Bd 'Pleas'd', perhaps to avoid the repetition of 'And' in the first and second lines and also to maintain a parallelism of sorts with the second stanza. Either 'There' or 'Where' is truly clumsy and otiose in the third stanza, and its appearance there as a related variant must inevitably affect one's view of its authority in the second stanza. Hence it may not be entirely a matter of opinion to take it that the connection with the first stanza established by the variant 'Where' is superfluous,[1] that the parallelism in the EH second and third stanzas is not necessarily due to contamination, and that if EH has been shown to be right in the first stanza it may also be right in the second. The present editor believes that the EH second stanza in its entirety is the original and that the others are early sophistications.

The third stanza presents no serious problem once the first line is established as 'And I will make'. The EH unique 'poesies' rhyming with 'roses' is repeated in the EH Reply and is probably compositorial or scribal; at any rate, 'poesies' is an acceptable form of 'posies'. Possibly the compositor or scribe misunderstood the sense that the bed was to be made of fragrant posies as well as of roses and thought that the lover was making 'poesies' or poetical mottoes. (This is certainly the misconception in Rs MS.) Whether the form was 'poesies', 'posies', or 'poses' in Marlowe is scarcely to be determined, although it might be thought more difficult for the 'posies' form to derive from original 'poses' than *vice versa*. All are acceptable words for the same thing.

[1] One may point out that even in the second stanza the sitting on the rocks establishes the place as the mountain without the signpost 'Where'. But since roses and straw are notably absent from mountains, it is better to imagine a change in locale, or probably a shift to a series of future promises, both of which are negated in this third stanza by the 'There' or 'Where' that emphasizes superfluously the mountain setting.

The chief problem in the fourth stanza is whether it is or is not Marlowe's, a matter discussed above. For the rest, the only witnesses vary in the third line. The word 'slippers' is found in EH, Rx, and W, but is 'shoes' in Bd; on the other hand, W and Bd agree against EH and Rx in lining the slippers or shoes 'choicely'. The patterns of influence here being so obscure, no certainty can hold about the earliest form of the line. The *Helicon* has as good a chance as any of reproducing it.

With the fifth stanza the only real problem is the form of its third and fourth lines, which generally varies according as the stanza is or is not the concluding invitation. The discussion above has suggested that the original conclusion must have started with 'Then' and very likely was preceded in the third line by 'if these things thy mind may move'. The *Helicon* form, it was suggested, despite the evidence of the *Passionate Pilgrim*, has been adjusted to a change in position away from the original conclusion.

In the sixth stanza something of a question arises whether the dancers are the 'shepherds swains' (presumably *shepherds*') or the 'shepherd swains' of Rx[1] and T MS; but one may guess that they are the young servants of the shepherds, as in EH. It is a little disturbing to notice the agreement of T MS and Rx in 'faire' for EH 'May', but the ballad has had an influence elsewhere on the manuscript.

According to the attempted reconstruction in this introduction, the text of the lyric is first given in what is conjectured to be its original four-stanza Marlowe form, the copy-text for convenience being *Englands Helicon* which, even though it prints a later, expanded form, seems to go back most purely for these four stanzas to the Marlovian original. Then, because the case is only conjectural, the more conventional six-stanza version is printed, the copy-text being *Englands Helicon*. To this fuller version is attached the extensive Historical Collation of variants, including what is taken to be a spurious seventh stanza 'The silver dishes'.

ILLUSTRISSIMÆ HEROINÆ...MARIÆ
PENBROKIÆ COMITISSÆ

This Latin dedicatory epistle to Mary, Countess of Pembroke, signed C. M., was prefixed to *Amintæ Gaudia Authore Thoma Watsono* (1592). Watson died in September 1592 and the book was entered in the Stationers' Register by its publisher Ponsonby on 10 November, 1592. On evidence of the close association of Thomas Watson and Marlowe, supported by the allusion (*littorea sunt Myrtus Veneris*) to *Amores*, I.i, Professor Mark Eccles has identified C. M. as Christopher Marlowe,[1] an attribution now generally accepted.

The copy-text is the Huntington Library copy. The translation is by Professor Eccles.

IN OBITUM HONORATISSIMI ROGERI
MANWOOD

Marlowe's epitaph on the Kentishman Sir Roger Manwood who died in December 1592 was first discovered by J. P. Collier written on the verso of the titlepage of a copy of the 1629 edition of *Hero and Leander* followed by various statements about Marlowe's life and reputation, and was reprinted in Collier's 'History of the English Stage' prefixed to his *Works of William Shakespeare* (1844), I, xliv. Although for some time under suspicion as a Collier forgery, the transcript has been fully authenticated by Professor Mark Eccles as genuine and the history of the copy traced up to the Sotheby sale of 15 February 1914, after which it disappeared.[2]

Preserved in the Folger Shakespeare Library as MS 750.1 is the commonplace book of the Kentish poet Henry Oxinden, born in

[1] *Christopher Marlowe in London* (1934), p. 164.

[2] 'Marlowe in Kentish Tradition', *Notes and Queries*, CLXIX (13, 20, 27 July, 24 August 1935) 20–3, 39–41, 58–61, 134–5. Professor Eccles prints complete information on the source and authority of the data about Marlowe that stemmed from the Canterbury vicar Simon Aldrich and discusses the Oxinden manuscript versions of the epitaph which he discovered in the Folger Shakespeare Library following the description of the Oxinden commonplace book by Dr Giles E. Dawson in *TLS*, 1 June 1933. Dr Eccles also provides a full account of Oxinden and this book.

Canterbury on 18 January 1609. On the flyleaf among some miscellaneous transcripts he wrote the first version of the epitaph (MS *a*), glossed a few of the Latin terms, and signed it 'C. Marlo. Auth: Hero & Lean.' On fol. 42 (MS *b*) Oxinden retranscribed the poem with some punctuation variants but getting 'secum' right, which in the first had been interlined above deleted 'scelerum' (line 6), but in error writing 'virtus' in line 9. At a later time he went over both transcripts and altered original 'cinerem' in line 9 to 'cineres'. The error 'exanguis' in line 11 for 'exsanguis' (which was also present in the 1629 *Hero and Leander*) was left untouched. The correction was made by Dyce. To this second transcript Oxinden appended: 'These verses above written were made by [Mar *deleted*] Christopher Marlo, who was a Shomakers son of Canterbury; it was this Marlo, who made the 2 first bookes of Hero & Leander, witnes Mr Alderich.'

The relationship of Oxinden's MS *a* to the transcript in *Hero and Leander* cannot be demonstrated but probability would dictate that Oxinden used it as his copy.

Dyce in 1850 was the first to reprint the epitaph, and took his text from Collier, followed by Cunningham and Bullen who reprinted Dyce. Tucker Brooke omitted it as a forgery as did Martin in the 1931 Methuen edition of Marlowe's *Poems*. More recently, it has been accepted and printed by MacLure in the 1968 Revels *Poems*. The present edition uses MS *a* from the flyleaf as copy-text. The apparatus lists the variants in MS *b* on fol. 42 from the MS *a* (not the edited) text, and also from Collier. The prose translation is appended through the courtesy of Professor Arthur F. Stocker of the University of Virginia.

THE PASSIONATE SHEPHERD
TO HIS LOVE

[Reconstruction of the original four-stanza lyric]

Come live with mee, and be my love,
And we will all the pleasures prove,
That Vallies, groves, hills and fieldes,
Woods, or steepie mountaine yeeldes.

And wee will sit upon the Rocks,   5
Seeing the Sheepheards feede theyr flocks,
By shallow Rivers, to whose falls,
Melodious byrds sing Madrigalls.

And I will make thee beds of Roses,
And a thousand fragrant posies,   10
A cap of flowers, and a kirtle,
Imbroydred all with leaves of Mirtle.

A belt of straw, and Ivie buds,
With Corall clasps and Amber studs,
And if these things thy minde may move,   15
Then live with mee, and be my love.

8 sing] PP + (−T MS); sings EH   may thee move, EH, PP
10 posies] W, Bd; poesies EH   16 Then] PP, A MS, T MS, Rs MS;
15 these things...move,] W, Rw MS   Come EH, Rw MS
    (u), A MS, Rs MS; these pleasures

THE PASSIONATE SHEPHERD
TO HIS LOVE

[Six-stanza version from *Englands Helicon*]

Come live with mee, and be my love,
And we will all the pleasures prove,
That Vallies, groves, hills and fieldes,
Woods, or steepie mountaine yeeldes.

And wee will sit upon the Rocks,   5
Seeing the Sheepheards feede theyr flocks,
By shallow Rivers, to whose falls,
Melodious byrds sing Madrigalls.

And I will make thee beds of Roses,
And a thousand fragrant posies,   10
A cap of flowers, and a kirtle,
Imbroydred all with leaves of Mirtle.

A gowne made of the finest wooll,
Which from our pretty Lambes we pull,
Fayre lined slippers for the cold: 15
With buckles of the purest gold.

A belt of straw, and Ivie buds,
With Corall clasps and Amber studs,
And if these pleasures may thee move,
Come live with mee, and be my love.

The Sheepheards Swaines shall daunce and sing,   20
For thy delight each May-morning.
If these delights thy minde may move;
Then live with mee, and be my love.   *Chr. Marlow.*

8 sing] PP+ (−T MS); sings EH   10 posies] W, Bd; poesies EH

ILLUSTRISSIMÆ HEROINÆ OMNIBUS ET ANIMI ET CORPORIS DOTIBUS ORNATISSIMÆ, MARIÆ PENBROKIÆ COMITISSÆ

Laurigera stirpe prognata Delia; Sydnæi vatis Apollinei genuina soror; Alma literatum parens, ad cuius immaculates amplexus, confugit virtus, barbarici et ignorantiæ impetu violata, ut olim a Threicio Tyranno Philomela; Poetarum nostri temporis, ingeniorumque omnium fœlicissime pullulantium, Musa; Dia proles, quæ iam rudi calamo, spiritus infundis elati furoris, quibus ipse misellus, plus mihi videor præstare posse, quam cruda nostra indoles proferre solet: Dignare Posthumo huic Amyntæ, ut tuo adoptivo filio patrocinari: Eoque magis quod moribundus pater, illius tutelam humillime tibi legaverat. Et licet illustre nomen tuum non solum 10 apud nos, sed exteras etiam nationes, latius propagatum est, quam aut unquam possit æruginosa Temporis vetustate aboleri, aut mortalium encomiis augeri, (quomodo enim quicquam possit esse infinito plus?) multorum tamen camænis, quasi siderum diademate redimita *Ariadne*, noli hunc purum Phœbi sacerdotem, stellam alteram coronæ tuæ largientem, aspernari: sed animi candore, quem sator hominum, atque deorum, Iupiter, prænobili familæ tuæ quasi hæreditarium alligavit, accipe, et tuere. Sic nos, quorum opes tenuissimæ, littorea sunt Myrtus Veneris, Nymphæque Peneiæ semper virens coma, prima quaque poematis pagina, Te Musarum dominam, 20 in auxilium invocabimus: tua denique virtus, quæ virtutem ipsam, ipsam quoque æternitatem superabit.

Honoris tui studiosissimus, C. M.

1 Delia;] ~ , AG
2 genuina] genuuia AG
2 literatum] literarũ AG

2 immaculates] immaculatos AG
3 barbarici] barbariei AG
5 pullulantium] pullutantium AG

TO THE MOST ILLUSTRIOUS NOBLE LADY, ADORNED WITH ALL GIFTS BOTH OF MIND AND BODY, MARY COUNTESS OF PEMBROKE

Delia born of a laurel-crowned race, true sister of Sidney the bard of Apollo, fostering parent of letters, to whose immaculate embrace virtue, outraged by the assault of barbarism and ignorance, flieth for refuge, as once Philomela from the Thracian tyrant; Muse of the Poets of our time, and of all most happily burgeoning wits; descendant of the gods, who impartest now to my rude pen breathings of a lofty rage, whereby my poor self hath, methinks, power to surpass what my unripe talent is wont to bring forth: Deign to be patron to this posthumous Amyntas, as to thine adoptive son: the rather that his dying father had most humbly bequeathed to thee his keeping. 10 And though thy glorious name is spread abroad not only among us but even among foreign nations, too far ever to be destroyed by the rusty antiquity of Time, or added to by the praise of mortals (for how can anything be greater than what is infinite?), yet, crowned as thou art by the songs of many as by a starry diadem Ariadne, scorn not this pure priest of Phoebus bestowing another star upon thy crown: but with that sincerity of mind which Jove the father of men and of gods hath linked as hereditary to thy noble family, receive and watch over him. So shall I, whose slender wealth is but the sea-shore myrtle of Venus, and Daphne's evergreen laurel, on the fore- 20 most page of every poem invoke thee as Mistress of the Muses to my aid: to sum up all, thy virtue, which shall overcome virtue herself, shall likewise overcome even eternity.

Most desirous to do thee honor, C.M.

Translation by Mark Eccles

IN OBITUM HONORATISSIMI VIRI ROGERI MANWOOD MILITIS, QUÆSTORII REGINALIS CAPITALIS BARONIS

Noctivagi terror, ganeonis triste flagellum,
Et Jovis Alcides, rigido vulturque latroni,
Urna subtegitur. Scelerum gaudete Nepotes.
Insons luctifica sparsis cervice capillis
Plange, fori lumen, venerandæ gloria legis   5
Occidit. Heu secum effœtas Acherontis ad oras
Multa abiit virtus. Pro tot virtutibus uni
Livor parce viro: non audacissimus esto
Illius in cineres, cuius tot milia vultus
Mortalium attonuit; sic cum te nuncia Ditis   10
Vulneret exsanguis, fœliciter ossa quiescant
Famaque marmorei superet monumenta sepulchri.

ON THE DEATH OF A MOST DISTINGUISHED MAN, SIR ROGER MANWOOD, LORD CHIEF BARON OF THE EXCHEQUER

The terror of him who prowls by night, the stern scourge of one who is profligate, both a Hercules, son of Jove, and a bird of prey upon the rough brigand, is encased in an urn. Rejoice, ye sons of wickedness; mourn, unoffending one, with hair in disorder over your pitiable neck. The light of officialdom, the glory of the worshipful law, lies dead. Alas, much virtue has passed with him to the barren shores of Acheron. In view of his so numerous virtues, spare, O Envy, this one man; be not overly presumptuous toward the ashes of one whose glance has held thunderstruck so many thousands of mortals. On these terms, when Death's pale messenger wounds you, may your bones rest happily, and may your fame survive the memorials of your marble tomb.

Translation by Arthur F. Stocker

0.1 Militis] 'M' *slightly doubtful as a majuscule* MS *a*
2 latroni,] ~ ∧ MS *a–b*
6 secum] *interlined above deleted* 'scelerum' MS *a*
9 cineres] *altered from* 'cinerem' MS *a–b*
9 milia] millia MS *a–b*
11 exsanguis] exanguis MS *a–b*

The Passionate Shepherd to his Love

[NOTE: The copy-text is EH: *Englands Helicon* (1600). Other texts collated are PP: *Passionate Pilgrim* (1599); Rx: 'Live with me and be my love' (*c.* 1603), *Roxburghe Ballads*; Rw MS: MS Rawl. Poet. 148, fol. 96 (*c.* 1600); A MS: MS Ashmole 1486, fol. 6ᵛ; T MS: Thornborough Commonplace Book; W¹: Walton's *Compleat Angler* (1653); W²: Walton's *Compleat Angler*, 1655; Rs MS: Rosenbach MS; Bd: *Poems of Sir Walter Raleigh*, ed. Sir Egerton Brydges (1813); F MS: Folger MS V.a.169 (*c.* 1670).]

1 Come] *omit* PP, Rx

1 Come live with mee] If thou wilt live Rs MS

2 And] Then Rs MS

2 all the pleasures] every pleasure Rs MS

3 Vallies, groves, hills and fieldes] hilles and vallies, dales and fields PP; valleis, groves, the hills and filds Rw MS (u); hills and valleis, groves, and filds Rw MS (c); vallyes groves and woods or feildes T MS; vallies, Groves, or hils, or fields W, F MS; hill or dales woodds or feildes Rs MS; grove or valley, hill or field Bd

4 Woods, or steepie mountaine yeeldes] And all the craggy mountaines yeeld PP; Woods, or steepy Mountaines yeelds Rx; Woods and steepest mountaynes yeelds Rw MS; Woods or craggi mountaines yeildes A MS; And craggie rockes or mountaines yeildes T MS; Or woods and steepie mountains yeelds W, F MS; Rivers or steepy mountaines yeildes Rs MS; Or wood and steepy mountain yield Bd

5 And] There PP; Where Rw MS, A MS, T MS, W, F MS, Bd; Then Rs MS

5 wee will] will we PP, Rs MS

5 sit] sett Rs MS

5 upon the] on rising Bd

6 Seeing] PP+ (−Rx)

6 theyr] our W, F MS

7 to] by PP

8 sing] sings EH, T MS

9 And] There PP, A MS, Rs MS; Where Rw MS, T MS; Pleas'd Bd

9 I will] will I PP, A MS, Bd; T wee will T MS

9 make] lye on Rs MS

9 thee] *omit* T MS

9 beds] a bedd PP, T MS

10 And] With PP; Drest with A MS; And then W, F MS; And make Rs MS; And twine Bd

10 a thousand] thowsande other T MS

10 fragrant] flagrant Rs MS

10 posies] poesies EH; poses PP, Rx, Rw MS, A MS, T MS, Rs MS

11 a kirtle] rural kirtle Bd

13–16 A gowne...gold.] *omit* PP, Rw MS, A MS, Rs MS; T MS *exchanges with lines 17–20*

13 A gowne made of] A jaunty gown of Bd

14 our pretty] the little T MS

15 Fayre lined slippers] Slippers lin'd choicely W, F MS; And shoes lin'd choicely Bd

17–20 A belt...love.] *omit* Rx

17 and] with T MS

18 Corall] amber T MS (u)

19 And if] If these, Bd

19 And if these pleasures may thee
move] And if these things thy mind
may move Rw MS (u), A MS, Rs
MS; If these delights thy minde may
move Rw MS (c), T MS

19 may] can Bd

20 Come] Then PP, A MS, T MS, Rs
MS; To Bd

20.1–4 *omit*] Thy silver dishes fil'd with
meate, | As precious as the Gods do
eate, | Shall on an Ivory Table be |
Prepar'd each day for thee and me.

Rx; Thy silver dishes for thy meat,
etc. (*as in* Rx) W²; Thy dyshes
shalbe filde with meate | Suche as
the gods doe use to eate | Shall one
and everye table bee | Preparde
eache daye for thee and mee T MS

21–4 The...love.] *omit* PP, Rw MS,
A MS, Rs MS, Bd

21 Sheepheards] shepparde Rx¹, T MS

22 May-] faire Rx, T MS

23 may] might Rx

24 Then] To Rx; Come T MS

In obitum Rogeri Manwood

Variants from MS *a* in MS *b* and in Collier

0.1 Militis] militis MS *b*

1 flagellum,] ~ ˄ MS *b*

3 subtegitur.] ~ , MS *b*; ~ : Coll.

5 lumen,] ~ ˄ MS *b*

6 Heu] heu MS *b*, Coll.

9 cineres] *altered from* 'cinerem' MS *b*
as also altered in MS *a*

9 vultus] virtus MS *b*

10 attonuit;] ~ : MS *b*

12 Famaque] Famaeque Coll.